Praise for *The Coming of the Third Reich*

"Will long remain the definitive English-language account . . . both gripping and precise . . . An always reliable, often magisterial synthesis of a vast body of scholarship, and a frequently deft blend of narrative and interpretation, Evans's book is an impressive achievement." —Benjamin Schwarz, *The Atlantic Monthly*

"Brilliant." —Richard Cohen, *The Washington Post*

"Richard Evans's *The Coming of the Third Reich* gives the clearest and most gripping account I've read of German life before and during the rise of the Nazis." —A. S. Byatt, *The Times Literary Supplement*

"Richard J. Evans's *Coming of the Third Reich* is an enormous work of synthesis— knowledgeable and reliable . . . vivid . . . Evans shows how the ingredients for Nazi triumph were assembled and what was needed to make them jell: add war and depression, cook in a turbulent political atmosphere for several years and serve hot." —Mark Mazower, *The New York Times Book Review*

"Why, Mr. Evans asks, did Germany deliver itself over to the Third Reich? Mr. Evans's answer is a brilliant and sweeping work of history. . . . He has mastered the vast scholarship on the politics, economics, ideology, and culture of Weimar Germany . . . more important, he has synthesized all this knowledge into a lucid, absorbing dramatic and accessible book." —Adam Kirsch, *The New York Sun*

"A masterly and most illuminating interpretation of its subject, which makes one look forward eagerly to the volumes to come." —Roger Morgan, *The Times Literary Supplement*

"The generalist reader, it should be emphasized, is well served. . . . The book reads briskly, covers all important areas—social and cultural—and succeeds in its aim of giving voice to the people who lived through the years with which it deals." —Roger K. Miller, *The Denver Post*

"Gripping . . . Evans broadens the historic perspective to demythologize how morbidly fertile the years before World War II were as an incubator for Hitler." —*Publishers Weekly* (starred review)

"A brilliant synthesis of German history, enumerating and elucidating the social, political, and cultural trends that made the rise of Nazism possible. . . . A peerless work . . . Of immense importance to general readers—and even some specialists— seeking to understand the origins of the Nazi regime." —*Kirkus Reviews* (starred review)

"Evans provides an erudite, fascinating, and sometimes painfully moving account of one society's slow collapse into nightmare and evil." —Timothy Giannuzzi, *Calgary Herald*

"One finally puts down this magnificent volume thirsty, on the one hand, for the next installment in the Nazi saga yet still haunted by the questions Evans poses and so masterfully grapples with." —Abraham Brumberg, *The Nation*

ABOUT THE AUTHOR

Richard J. Evans was educated at Oxford, has taught at Columbia and the University of London, and is currently Professor of Modern History at Cambridge. His books include *Death in Hamburg* (winner of the Wolfson Literary Award for History), *In Hitler's Shadow, Rituals of Retribution* (winner of the Fraenkel Prize in Contemporary History), *In Defense of History,* and *Lying About Hitler.*

RICHARD J. EVANS

The Coming of the Third Reich

PENGUIN BOOKS

PENGUIN BOOKS

Published by the Penguin Group

Penguin Group (USA) Inc., 375 Hudson Street, New York, New York 10014, U.S.A.

Penguin Group (Canada), 10 Alcorn Avenue, Toronto,
  Ontario, Canada M4V 3B2 (a division of Pearson Penguin Canada Inc.)

Penguin Books Ltd, 80 Strand, London WC2R 0RL, England

Penguin Ireland, 25 St Stephen's Green, Dublin 2, Ireland (a division of Penguin Books Ltd)

Penguin Group (Australia), 250 Camberwell Road, Camberwell,
  Victoria 3124, Australia (a division of Pearson Australia Group Pty Ltd)

Penguin Books India Pvt Ltd, 11 Community Centre, Panchsheel Park,
  New Delhi – 110 017, India

Penguin Books (NZ), cnr Airborne and Rosedale Roads, Albany,
  Auckland 1310, New Zealand (a division of Pearson New Zealand Ltd)

Penguin Books (South Africa) (Pty) Ltd, 24 Sturdee Avenue, Rosebank,
  Johannesburg 2196, South Africa

Penguin Books Ltd, Registered Offices:
80 Strand, London WC2R 0RL, England

First published in the United States of America by The Penguin Press,
a member of Penguin Group (USA) Inc. 2004
Published in Penguin Books 2005

10 9 8 7

THE LIBRARY OF CONGRESS HAS CATALOGED THE HARDCOVER EDITION AS FOLLOWS:
Evans, Richard J.
The coming of the Third Reich : a history / Richard J. Evans.
p. cm.
Includes bibliographical references and index.
ISBN 1-59420-004-1 (hc.)
ISBN 0 14 30.3469 3 (pbk.)
1. Germany—History—1871–1918. 2. Germany—History—1918–1933. 3. National
socialism—History. I. Title.
DD221.E94 2004
943.08—dc22   2003063205

Printed in the United States of America
Designed by Stephanie Huntwork

For Matthew and Nicholas

Contents

List of Illustrations

Photographic acknowledgements are given in parentheses.

1. The Bismarck memorial in Hamburg (copyright © Ullstein Bilderdienst, Berlin).
2. Antisemitic postcard from 'the only Jew-free hotel in Frankfurt', 1887.
3. German troops advancing across Belgium in 1914 (copyright © Imperial War Museum, Q 53446).
4. German prisoners of war taken by the Allies at the Battle of Amiens, August 1918 (copyright © Imperial War Museum, Q 9271).
5. German warplanes scrapped in fulfilment of the 1919 Treaty of Versailles (copyright © Simon Taylor).
6. Street battle in Berlin during the 'Spartacist uprising' of January 1919 (copyright © Hulton Getty).
7. Free Corps with a 'Red Guardist' they are about to execute during the suppression of the Munich Soviet, May 1919 (copyright © Mary Evans Picture Library).
8. Cartoon highlighting offences supposedly committed by French colonial troops during the Ruhr occupation of 1923 (copyright © Bildarchiv Preussischer Kulturbesitz).
9. The hyperinflation of 1923: 'So many thousand-mark notes for just one dollar!' (copyright © Bettmann/Corbis).
10. Cover of a German satirical periodical highlighting economic hardships imposed by the Treaty of Versailles (copyright © Bildarchiv Preussischer Kulturbesitz).
11. Otto Dix, *The Metropolis*, 1927–8 (photograph the Bridgeman Art Library and copyright © DACS, 2003).

Every effort has been made to trace copyright holders but this has not been possible in all cases. If notified, the publishers will be pleased to rectify any omissions at the earliest opportunity.

List of Maps and Diagrams

Preface

I

This book is the first of three on the history of the Third Reich. It tells the story of the origins of the Third Reich in the nineteenth-century Bismarckian Empire, the First World War and the bitter postwar years of the Weimar Republic. It goes on to recount the Nazis' rise to power through a combination of electoral success and massive political violence in the years of the great economic Depression from 1929 to 1933. Its central theme is how the Nazis managed to establish a one-party dictatorship in Germany within a very short space of time, and with seemingly little real resistance from the German people. A second book will deal with the development of the Third Reich from 1933 to 1939. It will analyse its central institutions, describe how it worked and what it was like to live in it, and recount its drive to prepare people for a war that would reinstate Germany's position as the leading power in Europe. The war itself is the subject of a third and final book that will deal with the rapid radicalization of the Third Reich's policies of military conquest, social and cultural mobilization and repression, and racial extermination, until it ended in total collapse and destruction in 1945. A concluding chapter will examine the aftermath of the twelve short years of the Reich's history and its legacy for the present and the future.

These three books are addressed in the first place to people who know nothing about the subject, or who know a little and would like to know more. I hope that specialists will find something of interest in them, but they are not the primary readership for which the books are intended. The legacy of the Third Reich has been widely discussed in the media in recent years. It continues to attract widespread attention. Restitution and compensation, guilt and apology have become sensitive political and moral issues. Images of the Third Reich, and museums and memorials calling attention to the impact of Nazi Germany between 1933 and 1945, are all around us. Yet the background to all this in the history of the Third Reich itself is often missing. That is what these three books aim to provide.

Anyone embarking on a project such as this must inevitably begin by asking whether it is really necessary to write yet another history of Nazi Germany. Surely we have had enough? Surely so much has already been written that there is little more to add? Undoubtedly, few historical topics have been the subject of such intensive research. The latest edition of the standard bibliography on Nazism, published by the indefatigable Michael Ruck in 2000, lists over 37,000 items; the first edition, which appeared in 1995, listed a mere 25,000. This startling increase in the number of titles is eloquent testimony to the continuing, never-ending outpouring of publications on the subject.[1] No historian can hope to master even a major portion of such an overwhelming literature. And indeed, some have found the sheer volume of information that is available so daunting, so seemingly impossible to pull together, that they have given up in despair. As a result, there have, in fact, been surprisingly few attempts to write the history of the Third Reich on a large scale. True, recent years have seen the publication of some excellent brief, synoptic surveys, notably by Norbert Frei and Ludolf Herbst,[2] some stimulating analytical treatments, particularly Detlev Peukert's *Inside Nazi Germany*,[3] and some useful collections of documents, of which the four-volume English-language anthology edited with extensive commentaries by Jeremy Noakes is outstanding.[4]

But the number of broad, general, large-scale histories of Nazi Germany that have been written for a general audience can be counted on the fingers of one hand. The first of these, and by far the most successful, was William L. Shirer's *The Rise and Fall of the Third Reich*, published in 1960. Shirer's book has probably sold millions of copies in the four decades or more since its appearance. It has never gone out of print and remains the first port of call for many people who want a readable general history of Nazi Germany. There are good reasons for the book's success. Shirer was an American journalist who reported from Nazi Germany until the United States entered the war in December, 1941, and he had a journalist's eye for the telling detail and the illuminating incident. His book is full of human interest, with many arresting quotations from the actors in the drama, and it is written with all the flair and style of a seasoned reporter's despatches from the front. Yet it was universally panned by professional historians. The emigré German scholar Klaus Epstein spoke for many when he pointed out that Shirer's book presented an 'unbelievably crude' account of German history, making it all seem to lead up inevitably to the Nazi seizure of power. It had 'glaring gaps' in its coverage. It concentrated far too much on high politics, foreign policy and military events, and even in 1960 it was 'in no way abreast of current scholarship dealing with the Nazi period'. Getting on for half a century later, this comment is even more justified than it was in Epstein's day. For all its virtues, therefore, Shirer's book cannot really deliver a history of Nazi Germany that meets the demands of the early twenty-first-century reader.[5]

An entirely different kind of survey was provided by the German political scientist Karl Dietrich Bracher's *The German Dictatorship*, published in 1969. This was the summation of Bracher's pioneering and still valuable studies of the fall of the Weimar Republic and the Nazi seizure of power, and it was strongest on the origins and growth of Nazism and its relation to German history, precisely those areas where Shirer was at his weakest. Nearly half the book was devoted to these subjects; the rest contained somewhat less extensive coverage of the political structure of the Third Reich, foreign policy, economy and society, culture and the arts, the wartime regime, and the breakdown of the Nazi system. Despite this unevenness, its coverage is masterly and authoritative, and it remains a classic. The great virtue of Bracher's treatment is its analytical clarity, and its determination to explain, account and interpret everything it covers. It is a book that one can return to again and again with profit. However, it is not only uneven in its treatment of the subject, it is also avowedly academic in its approach; it is often hard going for the reader; and it has inevitably been overtaken by research in many areas during the past three and a half decades.[6]

If Shirer represented the popular and Bracher the academic side of writing about Nazi Germany, then, recently, one author has successfully bridged the gap between the two. The British historian Ian Kershaw's two-volume *Hitler* successfully embeds Hitler's life in modern German history, and shows how his rise and fall were linked to wider historical factors. But Kershaw's *Hitler* is not a history of Nazi Germany. Indeed, following Hitler's own increasing isolation during the war, its focus inevitably becomes progressively narrower as it goes on. It concentrates on the areas to which Hitler devoted most attention, namely foreign policy, war and race. It cannot by definition adopt the perspectives of ordinary people or deal very much with the many areas with which Hitler was not directly concerned.[7] One of the principal aims of the present book and its two succeeding volumes, therefore, is to cover a wide range of major aspects of the history of the Third Reich: not only politics, diplomacy and military affairs but also society, the economy, racial policy, police and justice, literature, culture and the arts, with a breadth that for various reasons is missing in earlier approaches, to bring these together and to show how they were related.

The success of Kershaw's biography demonstrated that research into Nazi Germany is an international business. The most recent large-scale general account to appear of the subject has also been by a British historian: Michael Burleigh's *The Third Reich: A New History*. It brings home to readers right from the start the violence at the heart of the Nazi regime, to an extent and degree that no other book manages to do. Too often, as Burleigh rightly complains, academic authors paint a somewhat bloodless, almost abstract picture of the Nazis, as if the theories and debates about them were more important than the people themselves. His book dramatically redresses the balance. Burleigh's major purpose was to deliver a moral history of the Third Reich. *The Third Reich: A New History* concentrates mainly on mass murder, resistance and collaboration, political violence and coercion, crimes and atrocities. In doing so, it powerfully reasserts a vision of Nazi Germany as a totalitarian dictatorship that has been too often underplayed in recent years. But it omits any detailed consideration of foreign policy, military strategy, the economy, social change, culture and the arts, propaganda, women and the family, and many other aspects of Nazi Germany that have been the subject of recent research. Moreover, in prioritizing moral judgment, it has a tendency to downplay explanation and analysis. Nazi ideology, for example, is dismissed as 'guff', 'pretentious nonsense' and so on, to highlight the immorality of Germans abandoning their moral duty to think. But there is something to be said for a different approach that, like Bracher's, takes these ideas seriously, however repulsive or ridiculous they may seem to a modern reader, and explains how and why so many people in Germany came to believe them.[8]

This history tries to combine the virtues of previous accounts such as these. It is, in the first place, like Shirer's book, a narrative account. It aims to tell the story of the Third Reich in chronological order, and to show how one thing led to another. Narrative history fell out of fashion for many years in the 1970s and 1980s, as historians everywhere focused on analytical approaches derived mainly from the social sciences. But a variety of recent, large-scale narrative histories have shown that it can be done without sacrificing analytical rigour or explanatory power.[9] Like Shirer, too, this book attempts to give voice to the people who lived through the years with which it deals. The partisan distortion of German historical scholarship under the Nazis, the cult of personality, and the veneration of leadership by history-writers in the Third Reich, caused German historians after the Second World War to react by editing individual personalities out of history altogether. In the 1970s and 1980s, under the influence of modern social history, they were interested above all in broader structures and processes.[10] The work this generated immeasurably advanced our understanding of Nazi Germany. But real human beings almost disappeared from view in the quest for intellectual understanding. So one of the purposes of the present work has been to put individuals back into the picture; and all the way through I have tried to quote as much as possible from the writings and speeches of contemporaries, and to juxtapose the broader narrative and analytical sweep of the book with the stories of the real men and women, from the top of the regime down to the ordinary citizen, who were caught up in the drama of events.[11]

Recounting the experience of individuals brings home, as nothing else can, the sheer complexity of the choices they had to make, and the difficult and often opaque nature of the situations they confronted. Contemporaries could not see things as clearly as we can, with the gift of hindsight: they could not know in 1930 what was to come in 1933, they could not know in 1933 what was to come in 1939 or 1942 or 1945. If they had known, doubtless the choices they made would have been different. One of the greatest problems in writing history is to imagine oneself back in the world of the past, with all the doubts and uncertainties people faced in dealing with a future that for the historian has also become the past.

Developments that seem inevitable in retrospect were by no means so at the time, and in writing this book I have tried to remind the reader repeatedly that things could easily have turned out very differently to the way they did at a number of points in the history of Germany in the second half of the nineteenth century and the first half of the twentieth. People make their own history, as Karl Marx once memorably observed, but not under conditions of their own choosing. Those conditions included not only the historical context in which they lived, but also the way in which they thought, the assumptions they acted upon, and the principles and beliefs that informed their behaviour.[12] A central aim of this book is to re-create all these things for a modern readership, and to remind readers that, to quote another well-known aphorism about history, 'the past is a foreign country: they do things differently there'.[13]

For all these reasons, it seems to me inappropriate for a work of history to indulge in the luxury of moral judgment. For one thing, it is unhistorical; for another, it is arrogant and presumptuous. I cannot know how I would have behaved if I had lived under the Third Reich, if only because, if I had lived then, I would have been a different person from the one I am now. Since the early 1990s, the historical study of Nazi Germany, and increasingly that of other subjects too, has been invaded by concepts and approaches derived from morality, religion and the law. These might be appropriate for reaching a judgment on whether or not some individual or group should be awarded compensation for sufferings endured under the Nazis, or on the other hand forced to make restitution in some form or other for sufferings inflicted on others, and in these contexts it is not only legitimate but also important to apply them. But they do not belong in a work of history.[14] As Ian Kershaw has remarked: 'for an outsider, a non-German who never experienced Nazism, it is perhaps too easy to criticise, to expect standards of behaviour which it was well-nigh impossible to attain in the circumstances.'[15] At this distance of time, the same principle holds good for the great majority of Germans, too. So I have tried as far as possible to avoid using language that carries a moral, religious or ethical baggage with it. The purpose of this book is to understand: it is up to the reader to judge.

Understanding how and why the Nazis came to power is as important today as it ever was, perhaps, as memory fades, even more so. We need to get into the minds of the Nazis themselves. We need to discover why their opponents failed to stop them. We need to grasp the nature and operation of the Nazi dictatorship once it was established. We need to figure out the processes through which the Third Reich plunged Europe and the world into a war of unparalleled ferocity that ended in its own cataclysmic collapse. There were other catastrophes in the first half of the twentieth century, most notably, perhaps, the reign of terror unleashed by Stalin in Russia during the 1930s. But none has had such a profound or lasting effect. From its enthronement of racial discrimination and hatred at the centre of its ideology to its launching of a ruthless and destructive war of conquest, the Third Reich has burned itself onto the modern world's consciousness as no other regime, perhaps fortunately, has ever managed to do. The story of how Germany, a stable and modern country, in less than a single lifetime led Europe into moral, physical and cultural ruin and despair is a story that has sobering lessons for us all; lessons, again, which it is for the reader to take from this book, not for the writer to give.

I I

Explaining how this happened has occupied historians and commentators of many kinds since the very beginning. Dissident and émigré intellectuals such as Konrad Heiden, Ernst Fraenkel and Franz Neumann published analyses of the Nazi Party and the Third Reich during the 1930s and 1940s that are still worth reading today, and had a lasting effect in guiding the direction of research.[16] But the first real attempt to put the Third Reich in its historical context after the event was written by the leading German historian of the day, Friedrich Meinecke, immediately after the end of the Second World War. Meinecke blamed the rise of the Third Reich above all on Germany's growing obsession with world power from the late nineteenth century onwards, beginning with Bismarck and getting more intense in the age of Kaiser Wilhelm II and the First World War. A militaristic spirit had spread through Germany, he thought, giving the army a balefully decisive influence over the political situation. Germany had acquired impressive industrial might; but this had been achieved by an over-concentration on a narrowly technical education at the expense of broader moral and cultural instruction. 'We were searching for what was "positive" in Hitler's work,' wrote Meinecke of the educated upper-middle-class elite to which he belonged; and he was honest enough to add that they had found something they thought met the needs of the day. But it had all turned out to be an illusion. Looking back over a life long enough for him to remember the unification of Germany under Bismarck in 1871 and everything that happened between then and the fall of the Third Reich, Meinecke concluded tentatively that there was something flawed in the German nation-state from the very moment of its foundation in 1871.

Meinecke's reflections, published in 1946, were as important for their limitations as for their brave attempt to rethink the political beliefs and aspirations of a lifetime. The old historian had stayed in Germany throughout the Third Reich, but, unlike many others, he had never joined the Nazi Party, nor had he written or worked on its behalf. But he was still limited by the perspectives of the liberal nationalism in which he had grown up. The catastrophe, for him, was, as the title of his 1946 reflections put it, a *German* catastrophe, not a Jewish catastrophe, a European catastrophe or a world catastrophe. At the same time, he gave primacy, as German historians had long done, to diplomacy and international relations in bringing about the catastrophe, rather than in social, cultural or economic factors. The problem for Meinecke lay essentially not in what he referred to in passing as the 'racial madness' that had gripped Germany under the Nazis, but in the Third Reich's Machiavellian power politics, and its launching of a bid for world domination that had eventually led to its own destruction.[17]

For all its inadequacies, Meinecke's attempt to understand raised a series of key questions which, as he predicted, have continued to occupy people ever since. How was it that an advanced and highly cultured nation such as Germany could give in to the brutal force of National Socialism so quickly and so easily? Why was there such little serious resistance to the Nazi takeover? How could an insignificant party of the radical right rise to power with such dramatic suddenness? Why did so many Germans fail to perceive the potentially disastrous consequences of ignoring the violent, racist and murderous nature of the Nazi movement?[18] Answers to these questions have varied widely over time, between historians and commentators of different nationalities, and from one political position to another.[19] Nazism was only one of a number of violent and ruthless dictatorships established in Europe in the first half of the twentieth century, a trend so widespread that one historian has referred to the Europe of this era as a 'Dark Continent'.[20] This raises in turn the questions of how far Nazism was rooted in German history, and how far, on the other hand, it was the product of wider European developments, and the extent to which it shared central characteristics of its origins and rule with other European regimes of the time.

Such comparative considerations suggest that it is questionable to assume that it was somehow less likely for an economically advanced and culturally sophisticated society to fall into an abyss of violence and destruction than it was for one that was less so. The fact that Germany had produced a Beethoven, Russia a Tolstoy, Italy a Verdi, or Spain a Cervantes, was wholly irrelevant to the fact that all these countries experienced brutal dictatorships in the twentieth century. High cultural achievements across the centuries did not render a descent into political barbarism more inexplicable than their absence would have done; culture and politics simply do not impinge on each other in so simple and direct a manner. If the experience of the Third Reich teaches us anything, it is that a love of great music, great art and great literature does not provide people with any kind of moral or political immunization against violence, atrocity, or subservience to dictatorship. Indeed, many commentators on the left from the 1930s onwards argued that the advanced nature of German culture and society was itself the major cause of Nazism's triumph. The German economy was the most powerful in Europe, German society the most highly developed. Capitalist enterprise had reached an unprecedented scale and degree of organization in Germany. Marxists argued that this meant that class conflict between the owners of capital and those they exploited had been ratcheted up until it reached breaking point. Desperate to preserve their power and their profits, big businessmen and their hangers-on used all their influence and all the propagandistic means at their disposal to call into being a mass movement that was dedicated to serving their interests – the Nazi Party – and then to lever it into power and benefit from it once it was there.[21]

This view, elaborated with considerable sophistication by a whole variety of Marxist scholars from the 1920s to the 1980s, should not be dismissed out of hand as mere propaganda; it has inspired a wide range of substantial scholarly work over the years, on both sides of the Iron

Curtain that divided Europe during the Cold War between 1945 and 1990. But as a broad, general explanation it begs many questions. It more or less ignored the racial doctrines of Nazism, and altogether failed to explain the fact that the Nazis directed such venomous hatred towards the Jews not only in rhetoric but also in reality. Given the considerable resources devoted by the Third Reich to persecuting and destroying millions of people, including many who were impeccably middle-class, productive, well-off and in no small number of cases capitalists themselves, it is hard to see how the phenomenon of Nazism could be reduced to the product of a class struggle against the proletariat or an attempt to preserve the capitalist system that so many Jews in Germany contributed to sustaining. Moreover, if Nazism was the inevitable outcome of the arrival of imperialistic monopoly capitalism, then how could one account for the fact that it only emerged in Germany, and not in other, similarly advanced capitalist economies like Britain, Belgium, or the United States?[22]

Just such a question was what many non-Germans asked during the Second World War, and at least some Germans posed to themselves immediately afterwards. Above all in the countries that had already experienced one war against the Germans, in 1914–18, many commentators argued that the rise and triumph of Nazism were the inevitable end-products of centuries of German history. In this view, which was put forward by writers as varied as the American journalist William L. Shirer, the British historian A. J. P. Taylor and the French scholar Edmond Vermeil, the Germans had always rejected democracy and human rights, abased themselves before strong leaders, rejected the concept of the active citizen, and indulged in vague but dangerous dreams of world domination.[23] In a curious way, this echoed the Nazis' own version of German history, in which the Germans had also held by some kind of basic racial instinct to these fundamental traits, but had been alienated from them by foreign influences such as the French Revolution.[24] But as many critics have pointed out, this simplistic view immediately raises the question of why the Germans did not succumb to a Nazi-style dictatorship long before 1933. It ignores the fact that there were strong liberal and democratic traditions in German history, traditions which found their expression in political upheavals such as the 1848 Revolution, when authoritarian regimes were overthrown all over Germany. And it makes it harder, rather than easier, to explain how and why the Nazis came to power, because it ignores the very widespread opposition to Nazism which existed in Germany even in 1933, and so prevents us from asking the crucial question of why that opposition was overcome. Without recognizing the existence of such opposition to Nazism within Germany itself, the dramatic story of Nazism's rise to dominance ceases to be a drama at all: it becomes merely the realization of the inevitable.

It has been all too easy for historians to look back at the course of German history from the vantage-point of 1933 and interpret almost anything that happened in it as contributing to the rise and triumph of Nazism. This has led to all kinds of distortions, with some historians picking choice quotations from German thinkers such as Herder, the late eighteenth-century apostle of nationalism, or Martin Luther, the sixteenth-century founder of Protestantism, to illustrate what they argue are ingrained German traits of contempt for other nationalities and blind obedience to authority within their own borders.[25] Yet when we look more closely at the work of thinkers such as these, we discover that Herder preached tolerance and sympathy for other nationalities, while Luther famously insisted on the right of the individual conscience to rebel against spiritual and intellectual authority.[26] Moreover, while ideas do have a power of their own, that power is always conditioned, however indirectly, by social and political circumstances, a fact that historians who generalized about the 'German character' or 'the German mind' all too often forgot.[27]

A different current of thought, sometimes put forward by the same writers, has emphasized not the importance of ideology and belief in German history, but their unimportance. Germans, it has sometimes been said, had no real interest in politics and never got used to the give-and-take of democratic political debate. Yet of all the myths of German history that have been mobilized to account for the coming of the Third Reich in 1933, none is less convincing than that of the 'unpolitical German'. Largely the creation of the novelist Thomas Mann during the First World War, this concept subsequently became an alibi for the educated middle class in Germany, which could absolve itself from blame for supporting Nazism by accepting criticism for the far less serious offence of failing to oppose it. Historians of many varieties have claimed that the German middle class had withdrawn from political activity after the debacle of

1848, and taken refuge in money-making or literature, culture and the arts instead. Educated Germans put efficiency and success above morality and ideology.[28] Yet there is plenty of evidence to the contrary, as we shall see in the course of this book. Whatever Germany suffered from in the 1920s, it was not a lack of political commitment and belief, rather, if anything, the opposite.

German historians, not surprisingly, found such broad and hostile generalizations about the German character highly objectionable. In the aftermath of the Second World War, they tried their best to deflect criticism by pointing to the wider European roots of Nazi ideology. They drew attention to the fact that Hitler himself was not German but Austrian. And they adduced parallels with other European dictatorships of the age, from Mussolini's Italy to Stalin's Russia. Surely, they argued, in the light of the general collapse of European democracy in the years from 1917 to 1933, the coming of the Nazis should be seen, not as the culmination of a long and uniquely German set of historical developments, but rather as the collapse of the established order in Germany as elsewhere under the cataclysmic impact of the First World War.[29] In this view, the rise of industrial society brought the masses onto the political stage for the first time. The war destroyed social hierarchy, moral values and economic stability right across Europe. The Habsburg, the German, the Tsarist and the Ottoman Empires all collapsed, and the new democratic states that emerged in their wake quickly fell victim to the demagogy of unscrupulous agitators who seduced the masses into voting for their own enslavement. The twentieth century became an age of totalitarianism, culminating in the attempt of Hitler and Stalin to establish a new kind of political order based on total police control, terror, and the ruthless suppression and murder of real or imagined opponents in their millions on the one hand, and continual mass mobilization and enthusiasm whipped up by sophisticated propaganda methods on the other.[30]

Although it is easy enough to see how such arguments served the interests of Western exponents of the Cold War in the 1950s and 1960s by implicitly or explicitly equating Stalin's Russia with Hitler's Germany, the concept of both as varieties of a single phenomenon has recently undergone something of a revival.[31] And certainly there is nothing illegitimate about comparing the two regimes.[32] The idea of totalitarianism as a general political phenomenon went back as far as the early 1920s. It was used in a positive sense by Mussolini, who along with Hitler and Stalin made the claim to a total control of society that involved the effective re-creation of human nature in the form of a 'new' type of human being. But whatever the similarities between these various regimes, the differences between the forces that lay behind the origins, rise and eventual triumph of Nazism and Stalinism are too strikingly different for the concept of totalitarianism to explain very much in this area. In the end, it is more useful as a description than as an explanation, and it is probably better at helping us to understand how twentieth-century dictatorships behaved once they had achieved power than in accounting for how they got there.

To be sure, there were some similarities between Russia and Germany before the First World War. Both nations were ruled by authoritarian monarchies, backed by a powerful bureaucracy and a strong military elite, confronting rapid social change brought about by industrialization. Both these political systems were destroyed by the profound crisis of defeat in the First World War, and both were succeeded by a brief period of conflict-ridden democracy before the conflicts were resolved by the advent of dictatorships. But there were also many crucial differences, principal among them the fact that the Bolsheviks completely failed to win the level of mass public support in free elections which provided the essential basis for the Nazis' coming to power. Russia was backward, overwhelmingly peasant, lacking in the basic functions of a civil society and a representative political tradition. It was a dramatically different country from the advanced and highly educated industrial Germany, with its long-nurtured traditions of representative institutions, the rule of law and a politically active citizenry. It is certainly true that the First World War destroyed the old order all over Europe. But the old order differed substantially from one country to another, and it was destroyed in differing ways, with differing consequences. If we are looking for another country with comparable developments, then, as we shall see, Italy, nineteenth-century Europe's other newly unified nation alongside Germany, is a much better place to start than Russia.

Searching for an explanation of the origins and rise of Nazism in German history undeniably runs the risk of making the whole process seem inevitable. At almost every turn, however, things might have been different. The triumph of Nazism was far from a foregone conclusion right up to the early months of 1933. Yet it was no historical accident, either.[33] Those who argued that Nazism came to power as part of an essentially Europe-wide set of developments are right to have done so up to a point. But they have paid far too little attention to the fact that Nazism, while far from being the unavoidable outcome of the course of German history, certainly did draw for its success on political and ideological traditions and developments that were specifically German in their nature. These traditions may not have gone back as far as Martin Luther, but they could certainly be traced back to the way German history developed in the course of the nineteenth century, and above all to the process by which the country was turned into a unified state under Bismarck in 1871. It makes sense to start at this point, therefore, as Friedrich Meinecke did in his reflections of 1946, when searching for the reasons why the Nazis came to power little over six decades later and wrought such havoc on Germany, Europe and the world with so little opposition from the majority of Germans. As we shall see in the course of this book and the two succeeding volumes, there are many different answers to these questions, ranging from the nature of the crisis that overtook Germany in the early 1930s, to the way in which the Nazis established and consolidated their rule once they had achieved power, and weighing them all up against each other is no easy task. Yet the burden of German history undeniably played a role, and it is with German history that this book, therefore, has to begin.

III

The early twenty-first century is a particularly good moment for undertaking a project of this kind. Historical research on the Third Reich has gone through three major phases since 1945. In the first, from the end of the war to the middle of the 1960s, there was a heavy concentration on answering the questions addressed primarily in the present volume. Political scientists and historians such as Karl Dietrich Bracher produced major works on the collapse of the Weimar Republic and the Nazi seizure of power.[34] In the 1970s and 1980s the focus shifted to the history of the years 1933 to 1939 (the subject of the second volume of this study), aided by the return of vast quantities of captured documents from Allied custody to the German archives. In particular, Martin Broszat and Hans Mommsen produced a series of path-breaking studies of the internal structures of the Third Reich, arguing against the prevailing view that it was a totalitarian system in which decisions made at the top, by Hitler, were implemented all the way down, and examining the complex of competing power centres whose rivalry, they argued, drove the regime on to adopt steadily more radical policies. Their work was complemented by a mass of new research into the history of everyday life under the Nazis, concentrating in particular on the years up to the outbreak of the Second World War.[35] Since the 1990s research has entered a third phase, in which there has been a particular focus on the years 1939–45 (the subject of the third volume of this study). The discovery of new documents in the archives of the former Soviet bloc, the increasing public prominence given to the persecution and extermination of the Jews and others, from homosexuals to 'asocials', from slave labourers to the handicapped, by the Nazis, have all generated a large quantity of important new knowledge.[36] The time seems right, therefore, to attempt a synthesis that brings the results of these three phases of research together, and to take advantage of the great quantity of new material, from the diaries of Joseph Goebbels and Victor Klemperer to the records of the meetings of the German cabinet and the appointments book of Heinrich Himmler, that has become available recently.

For any historian, a task such as this is a bold, if not rash or even foolhardy undertaking: doubly so for a historian who is not German. However, I have been thinking about the historical questions dealt with in this book for many years. My interest in German history was first seriously awakened by Fritz Fischer, whose visit to Oxford during my time there as an undergraduate was a moment of major intellectual significance. Later, in Hamburg researching for my doctorate, I was able to share a little of the extraordinary excitement generated by Fischer and his team, whose opening up of the question of continuity in modern German history created a real sense of ferment, even crusade, among the younger German historians whom he gathered around him. At that time, in the early 1970s, I was interested mainly in the origins of the Third Reich in the Weimar Republic and the Wilhelmine Empire; only later did I come to write about the ways in which Nazi Germany aroused heated controversy amongst modern German historians, and to do some archival research on the period 1933–45 myself, as part of a larger project on the death penalty in modern German history.[37] Over these years I was lucky enough to be helped in many ways by a whole range of German friends and colleagues, notably Jürgen Kocka, Wolfgang Mommsen, Volker Ullrich and Hans-Ulrich Wehler. Numerous, often lengthy stays in Germany generously funded by institutions such as the Alexander von Humboldt Foundation and the German Academic Exchange Service helped educate me, I hope, into a better understanding of German history and culture than I set out with at the beginning of the 1970s. Few countries could have been more generous or more open to outsiders wishing to study their problematic and uncomfortable past. And the community of specialists on German history in Britain has been a constant support throughout; early on, during my time at Oxford, Tim Mason was a particular source of inspiration, and Anthony Nicholls guided my researches with a sure hand. Of course, none of this in the end can ever compensate for the fact that I am not a native German; but perhaps the distance that is inevitably the result of being a foreigner can also lend a certain detachment, or at least a difference of perspective, that may go some way to balancing out this obvious disadvantage.

Although I had written about the origins, consequences and historiography of the Third Reich, researched part of its history in the archives, and taught a slowly evolving, document-based course on it to undergraduates over a period of more than twenty years, it was not until the 1990s that I was prompted to devote my attention to it full-time. I shall always be grateful, therefore, to Anthony Julius for asking me to act as an expert witness in the libel case brought by David Irving against Deborah Lipstadt and her publishers, and to the whole defence team, and most especially leading counsel Richard Rampton QC and my research assistants Nik Wachsmann and Thomas Skelton-Robinson, for many hours of fruitful and provocative discussion on many aspects of the history of the Third Reich that surfaced during the case.[38] It was a privilege to be involved in a case whose importance turned out to be greater than any of us expected. Apart from this, one of the major surprises of the work we did on the case was the discovery that many aspects of the subjects we were dealing with were still surprisingly ill-documented.[39] Another, just as important, was that there was no really wide-ranging, detailed overall account of the broader historical context of Nazi policies towards the Jews in the general history of the Third Reich itself, despite the existence of many excellent accounts of those policies in a narrower framework. This sense of the growing fragmentation of knowledge on Nazi Germany was strengthened when I was asked soon afterwards to sit on the British government's Spoliation Advisory Panel, considering claims for the restitution of cultural objects alienated unjustly from their original owners in the years from 1933 to 1945. Here was another area where answering specialized questions sometimes depended on historical knowledge of the wider context, yet there was no general history of Nazi Germany to which I could direct the other members of the panel to help them in this regard. At the same time, my direct confrontation with these important legal and moral dimensions of the Nazi experience through working in these two very different contexts convinced me more than ever of the need for a history of the Third Reich that did not take moral or legal judgment as its frame of reference.

These, then, are some of the reasons why I have written this book. They may help to explain some of its distinctive features. To begin with, in a history such as this, directed to a wide readership, it is important to avoid technical terms. Since this is a book for English-language readers, I have translated German terms into the English equivalent in almost every instance. Retaining the German is a form of mystification, even romanticization, which ought to be avoided. There are only three exceptions. The first is *Reich*, which, as Chapter 1 explains, had particular, untranslateable resonances in German far beyond its English equivalent of 'empire', with its associated term *Reichstag*, referring to the German national parliament. This is a word which ought to be familiar to every English-speaking reader, and it would be artificial to speak, for example, of the 'Third Empire' instead of the 'Third Reich' or the 'Parliament fire' instead of the 'Reichstag fire'. The title *Kaiser* has also been retained in preference to the rough English equivalent of 'Emperor' because it, too, awakened specific and powerful historical memories. Some other German words or terms associated with the Third Reich have also gained currency in English, but in so doing they have become divorced from their original meaning: *Gauleiter* for instance just means a Nazi tyrant, so to give it a more precise meaning I have translated it everywhere as 'Regional Leader'. Similarly, Hitler is referred to throughout not as *Führer* but as the English equivalent of the term, 'Leader'. And although everyone is familiar with the title of Hitler's book *Mein Kampf*, few probably know that it means *My Struggle* unless they know German.

One of the purposes of translation is to allow English-speaking readers to gain a feeling for what these things actually meant; they were not mere titles or words, but carried a heavy ideological baggage with them. Some German words have no exact English equivalent, and I have chosen to be inconsistent in my translation, rendering *national* variously as 'national' or 'nationalist' (it has the flavour of both) and a similarly complex term, *Volk*, as 'people' or 'race', according to the context. The translations are not always mine, but where I have taken them from existing English-language versions I have always checked them against the originals and in some cases altered them accordingly. Specialist readers who know German will probably find all this rather irritating; they are advised to read the German edition of this book, which is published simultaneously under the title *Das Dritte Reich*, I: *Aufstieg*, by the Deutsche Verlags-Anstalt.

In a similar way, bearing in mind that this is not a specialist academic monograph, I have tried to limit the endnotes as far as possible. They are designed mainly to enable readers to check the statements made in the text; they are not intended to provide full bibliographical references to the topics under consideration, nor do they, with very few exceptions, include discussion of detailed subjects of secondary interest. I have tried, however, to point the interested reader to relevant further reading where he or she would like to pursue a topic in greater depth than has been possible in this book. Where there is an English translation of a German book, I have tried to cite it in this edition in preference to the German original. To keep the notes within bounds, only information necessary to locating the source has been provided, namely, author, title and subtitle, place and date of publication. Modern publishing is a global business, with the major players based in a number of different countries, so only the principal place of publication has been given.

One of the most difficult problems in writing about Nazi Germany is posed by the permeation of the language of the time by Nazi terminology, as Victor Klemperer long ago noted in his classic study of what he called *Lingua tertii Imperii*, the language of the Third Reich.[40] Some historians

distance themselves from it by putting all Nazi terms into inverted com-
mas, or adding some disapproving epithet: thus the 'Third Reich' or even
the 'so-called "Third Reich"'. In a book such as this, however, to adopt
either of these procedures would seriously compromise readability.
Although it should not be necessary to say this, it is as well that I note at
this point that Nazi terminology employed in this book simply reflects its
use at the time: it should not be construed as an acceptance, still less
approval, of the term in question as a valid way of denoting what it refers
to. Where the Nazi Party is concerned I have used the capital initial letter
for Party, where other parties are referred to, I have not; similarly, the
Church is the formal organization of Christians, a church is a building;
Fascism denotes the Italian movement led by Mussolini, fascism the
generic political phenomenon.

If all of this makes what follows clearer and more readable, it will have
served its purpose. And if the book itself is, as I hope, easy to follow,
then much of the credit must go to the friends and colleagues who kindly
agreed to read the first draft at short notice, expunged many infelicities
and rooted out errors, in particular, Chris Clark, Christine L. Corton,
Bernhard Fulda, Sir Ian Kershaw, Kristin Semmens, Adam Tooze, Nik
Wachsmann, Simon Winder and Emma Winter. Bernhard Fulda, Christian Goeschel and Max Horster checked through the notes and located
original documents; Caitlin Murdock did the same for the stormtrooper
autobiographies stored in the Hoover Institution. Bernhard Fulda, Liz
Harvey and David Welch kindly supplied some key documents. I am
greatly indebted to all of them for their help. Andrew Wylie has been a
superb agent whose persuasive powers have ensured that this book has
the best possible publishers; Simon Winder at Penguin has been a tower
of strength in London, and it has been a pleasure to work closely with
him on the book. In New York, Scott Moyers has buoyed me up with
his enthusiasm and helped greatly with his shrewd comments on the
typescript, and in Germany, Michael Neher has performed a miracle of
organization in getting the German edition out so quickly. It was a
pleasure to work once again with the translators themselves, Holger
Fliessbach and Udo Rennert, and also with András Bereznáy, who drew
the maps. I am also grateful to Chloe Campbell at Penguin who has
put so much effort into helping with the picture research, obtaining
permissions and tracking down originals for the illustrations, to Simon

Taylor for his generous help in providing some of the pictures, to Elizabeth Stratford for her meticulous copy-editing of the final text, and to the production and design teams at both publishers for putting the book together.

Finally, my biggest debt, as always, is to my family, to Christine L. Corton for her practical support and her publishing expertise, and to her and to our sons Matthew and Nicholas, to whom these volumes are dedicated, for sustaining me during a project that deals with difficult and often terrible events of a kind that we have all been fortunate not to have experienced in our own lives.

Cambridge, July 2003

I

THE LEGACY OF
THE PAST

GERMAN PECULIARITIES

I

Is it wrong to begin with Bismarck? On several levels, he was a key figure in the coming of the Third Reich. For one thing, the cult of his memory in the years after his death encouraged many Germans to long for the return of the strong leadership his name represented. For another, his actions and policies in the mid-to-late nineteenth century helped create an ominous legacy for the German future. Yet in many ways he was a complex and contradictory figure, as much European as German, as much modern as traditional. Here, too, his example pointed forwards to the tangled mixture of the new and the old that was so characteristic of the Third Reich. It is worth calling to mind that a mere fifty years separated Bismarck's foundation of the German Empire in 1871 from the electoral triumphs of the Nazis in 1930–32. That there was a connection between the two seems impossible to deny. It was here, rather than in the remote religious cultures and hierarchical polities of the Reformation or the 'Enlightened Absolutism' of the eighteenth century, that we find the first real moment in German history which it is possible to relate directly to the coming of the Third Reich in 1933.[1]

Born in 1815, Otto von Bismarck made his reputation as the wild man of German conservatism, given to brutal statements and violent actions, never afraid to state with forceful clarity what more cautious spirits were afraid to say out loud. Coming from a traditional, aristocratic background, rooted both in the Junker landowning class and the civil service nobility, he seemed to many to represent Prussianism in an extreme form, with all its virtues and vices. His domination over German politics in the second half of the nineteenth century was brutal, arrogant, complete. He could not conceal his contempt for liberalism, socialism, parliamentarism, egalitarianism and many other aspects of the modern world. Yet this seemed to do no harm to the almost mythical reputation he acquired after his death as the creator of the German Empire. On the centenary of his birth, in 1915, when Germany was in the midst of fighting the First World War, a humane liberal such as the historian Friedrich Meinecke could take comfort, even inspiration, from the image of the 'Iron Chancellor' as a man of force and power: 'It is the spirit of Bismarck', he wrote, 'which forbids us to sacrifice our vital interests and has forced us to the heroic decision to take up the prodigious struggle against East and West, to speak with Bismarck: "like a strong fellow, who has two good fists at his disposal, one for each opponent".'[2] Here was the great and decisive leader whose lack many Germans felt acutely at this crucial juncture in their country's fortunes. They were to feel the absence of such a leader even more acutely in the years after the war ended.

Yet in reality Bismarck was a far more complex character than this crude image, fostered by his acolytes after his death. He was not the reckless, risk-taking gambler of later legend. Too few Germans subsequently remembered that it was Bismarck who was responsible for defining politics as 'the art of the possible.'[3] He always insisted that his technique was to calculate the way events were going, then take advantage of them for his own purposes. He himself put it more poetically: 'A statesman cannot create anything himself. He must wait and listen until he hears the steps of God sounding through events; then leap up and grasp the hem of his garment'.[4] Bismarck knew that he could not force events into any pattern that he wanted. If, then – to adopt another of his favourite metaphors – the art of politics consisted in navigating the ship of state along the stream of time, in what direction was that stream flowing in nineteenth-century Germany? For more than a millennium before the century began, Central Europe had been splintered into myriad autonomous states, some of them powerful and well organized, like Saxony and Bavaria, others small or medium-sized 'Free Cities', or tiny principalities and knighthoods which consisted of little more than a castle and a modestly sized estate. These were all gathered together in the so-called Holy Roman Reich of the German Nation, founded by Charlemagne in 800 and dissolved by Napoleon in 1806. This was the famous 'thousand-year Reich' which it ultimately became the Nazis' ambition to emulate. By the time it collapsed under the weight of Napoleon's invasions, the Reich was in a parlous condition; attempts to establish a meaningful degree of central authority had failed, and powerful and ambitious member states such as Austria and Prussia had tended increasingly to throw their weight around as if the Reich did not exist.

When the dust settled after Napoleon's defeat at Waterloo in 1815, the European states set up a successor organization to the Reich in the form of the German Confederation, whose borders were roughly the same and included, as before, the German and Czech-speaking parts of Austria. For a while, the police system established across Central Europe by the Austrian Chancellor Prince Metternich successfully kept the lid on the boiling cauldron of liberal and revolutionary activity stirred up amongst an active minority of educated people before 1815 by the French. Yet by the middle of the 1840s, a new generation of intellectuals, lawyers, students and local politicians had grown dissatisfied with the situation. They came to believe that the quickest way to rid Germany of its many great and petty tyrannies was to sweep away the individual member states of the Confederation and replace them with a single German polity founded on representative institutions and guaranteeing the elementary rights and freedoms – freedom of speech, freedom of the press and so on – which were still denied in so many parts of Germany. Popular discontent generated by the poverty and starvation of the 'Hungry Forties' gave them their chance. In 1848, revolution broke out in Paris and flashed across Europe. Existing German governments were swept away and the liberals came to power.[5]

The revolutionaries quickly organized elections in the Confederation, including Austria, and a national parliament duly assembled at Frankfurt. After much deliberation the deputies voted through a list of fundamental rights and established a German constitution along classic liberal lines. But they were unable to gain control over the armies of the two leading states, Austria and Prussia. This proved decisive. By the autumn of 1848, the monarchs and generals of the two states had recovered their nerve. They refused to accept the new constitution, and, after a wave of radical-democratic revolutionary activity swept across Germany the following spring, they forcibly dissolved the Frankfurt Parliament and sent its deputies home. The revolution was over. The Confederation was re-established, and the leading revolutionaries were arrested, imprisoned or forced into exile. The following decade has been widely seen by historians as a period of deep reaction, when liberal values and civic freedoms were crushed under the iron heel of German authoritarianism.

Many historians have regarded the defeat of the 1848 Revolution as a crucial event in modern German history – the moment, in the historian A.J.P. Taylor's famous phrase, when 'German history reached its turning-point and failed to turn'.[6] Yet Germany did not embark upon a straight or undeviating 'special path' towards aggressive nationalism and political dictatorship after 1848.[7] There were to be many avoidable twists and turns along the way. To begin with, the fortunes of the liberals had undergone a dramatic transformation once more by the beginning of the 1860s. Far from being a complete return to the old order, the post-revolutionary settlement had sought to appease many of the liberals' demands while stopping short of granting either national unification or parliamentary sovereignty. Trial by jury in open court, equality before the law, freedom of business enterprise, abolition of the most objection-able forms of state censorship of literature and the press, the right of assembly and association, and much more, were in place almost every-where in Germany by the end of the 1860s. And, crucially, many states had instituted representative assemblies in which elected deputies had freedom of debate and enjoyed at least some rights over legislation and the raising of state revenues.

It was precisely the last right that the resurgent liberals used in Prussia in 1862 to block the raising of taxes until the army was brought under the control of the legislature, as it had, fatally, not been in 1848. This posed a serious threat to the funding of the Prussian military machine. In order to deal with the crisis, the Prussian King appointed the man who was to become the dominant figure in German politics for the next thirty years – Otto von Bismarck. By this time, the liberals had correctly decided that there was no chance of Germany uniting, as in 1848, in a nation-state that included German-speaking Austria. That would have meant the break-up of the Habsburg monarchy, which included huge swathes of territory, from Hungary to Northern Italy, that lay outside the boundaries of the German Confederation, and included many millions of people who spoke languages other than German. But the liberals also considered that following the unification of Italy in 1859–60, their time had come. If the

Italians had managed to create their own nation-state, then surely the Germans would be able to do so as well.

Bismarck belonged to a generation of European politicians, like Benjamin Disraeli in Britain, Napoleon III in France or Camillo Cavour in Italy, who were prepared to use radical, even revolutionary means to achieve fundamentally conservative ends. He recognized that the forces of nationalism were not to be gainsaid. But he also saw that after the frustrations of 1848, many liberals would be prepared to sacrifice at least some of their liberal principles on the altar of national unity to get what they wanted. In a series of swift and ruthless moves, Bismarck allied with the Austrians to seize the disputed duchies of Schleswig-Holstein from the Kingdom of Denmark, then engineered a war over their administration between Prussia and Austria which ended in complete victory for the Prussian forces. The German Confederation collapsed, to be followed by the creation of a successor institution without the Austrians or their south German allies, named by Bismarck for want of a more imaginative term the North German Confederation. Immediately, the majority of the Prussian liberals, sensing that the establishment of a nation-state was just around the corner, forgave Bismarck for his policy (pursued with sublime disdain for parliamentary rights over the previous four years) of collecting taxes and funding the army without parliamentary approval. They cheered him on as he engineered another war, with the French, who rightly feared that the creation of a united Germany would spell the end of the predominance in European power-politics which they had enjoyed over the past decade and a half.[8]

The crushing of the French armies at Sedan and elsewhere was followed by the proclamation of a new German Empire, in the Hall of Mirrors at the former French royal palace of Versailles. Built by Louis XIV, the 'Sun King', at the height of his power nearly two hundred years before, the palace was now turned into a humiliating symbol of French impotence and defeat. This was a key moment in modern German and indeed European history. To liberals, it seemed the fulfilment of their dreams. But there was a heavy price for them to pay. Several features of Bismarck's creation had ominous consequences for the future. First of all, the decision to call the new state 'the German Reich' inevitably conjured up memories of its thousand-year predecessor, the dominant power in Europe for so many centuries. Some, indeed, referred to Bismarck's creation as the

'Second Reich'. The use of the word implied, too, that where the First Reich had failed, in the face of French aggression, the Second had succeeded. Among the many aspects of his creation that survived the fall of Bismarck's German Reich in 1918, the continued use of the term 'German Empire', *Deutsches Reich*, by the Weimar Republic and all its institutions was far from being the least significant. The word 'Reich' conjured up an image among educated Germans that resonated far beyond the institutional structures Bismarck created: the successor to the Roman Empire; the vision of God's Empire here on earth; the universality of its claim to suzerainty; in a more prosaic but no less powerful sense, the concept of a German state that would include all German speakers in Central Europe – 'one People, one Reich, one Leader', as the Nazi slogan was to put it.[9] There always remained those in Germany who thought Bismarck's creation only a partial realization of the idea of a true German Reich. Initially, their voices were drowned by the euphoria of victory. But with time, their number was to grow.[10]

The constitution which Bismarck devised for the new German Reich in 1871 in many ways fell far short of the ideals dreamed of by the liberals in 1848. Alone of all modern German constitutions, it lacked any declaration of principle about human rights and civic freedoms. Formally speaking, the new Reich was a loose confederation of independent states, much like its predecessor had been. Its titular head was the Emperor or Kaiser, the title taken over from the old head of the Holy Roman Reich and ultimately deriving from the Latin name 'Caesar'. He had wide-ranging powers including the declaration of war and peace. The Reich's institutions were stronger than those of the old, with a nationally elected parliament, the Reichstag – the name, deriving from the Holy Roman Reich, was another survival across the revolutionary divide of 1918 – and a number of central administrative institutions, most notably the Foreign Office, to which more were added as time went on. But the constitution did not accord to the national parliament the power to elect or dismiss governments and their ministers, and key aspects of political decision-making, above all on matters of war and peace, and on the administration of the army, were reserved to the monarch and his immediate entourage. Government ministers, including the head of the civilian administration, the Reich Chancellor – an office created by Bismarck and held by him for some twenty years – were civil servants, not party politicians, and they were beholden to the Kaiser, and not to the people or to their parliamentary representatives. With time, the influence of the Reichstag grew, though not by very much. With only mild exaggeration, the great revolutionary thinker Karl Marx described the Bismarckian Reich, in a convoluted phrase that captured many of its internal contradictions, as a 'bureaucratically constructed military despotism, dressed up with parliamentary forms, mixed in with an element of feudalism yet at the same time already influenced by the bourgeoisie'.[11]

II

The power of the military and in particular of the Prussian officer corps was not simply the product of times of war. It derived from a long historical tradition. In the seventeenth and eighteenth centuries, the expanding Prussian state had organized itself along largely military lines, with the neo-feudal system of landowners – the famous Junkers – and serfs, intermeshing neatly with the military recruiting system for officers and men.[12] This system was dismantled with the ending of serfdom, and the traditional prestige of the army was badly dented by a series of crushing defeats in the Napoleonic wars. In 1848 and again in 1862 Prussian liberals came close to bringing the military under parliamentary control. It was above all in order to protect the autonomy of the Prussian officer corps from liberal interference that Bismarck was appointed in 1862. He immediately announced that 'the great questions of the day are not decided by speeches and majority resolutions – that was the great mistake of 1848 and 1849 – but by iron and blood'.[13] He was as good as his word. The war of 1866 destroyed the Kingdom of Hanover, incorporating it into Prussia, and expelled Austria and Bohemia from Germany after centuries in which they had played a major part in shaping its destinies, while the war of 1870–71 took away Alsace-Lorraine from France and placed it under the direct suzerainty of the German Empire. It is with some justification that Bismarck has been described as a 'white revolutionary'.[14] Military force and military action created the Reich; and in so doing they swept aside legitimate institutions, redrew state boundaries and overthrew long-established traditions, with a radicalism and a ruthlessness that cast a long shadow over the subsequent development of Germany. They also thereby legitimized the use of force for political ends to a degree well beyond what was common in most other countries except when they contemplated imperial conquests in other parts of the world. Militarism in state and society was to play an important part in undermining German democracy in the 1920s and in the coming of the Third Reich.

Bismarck saw to it that the army was virtually a state within a state, with its own immediate access to the Kaiser and its own system of self-government. The Reichstag only had the right to approve its budget every seven years, and the Minister of War was responsible to the army rather than to the legislature. Officers enjoyed many social and other privileges and expected the deference of civilians when they met on the street. Not surprisingly, it was the ambition of many a bourgeois professional to be admitted as an officer in the army reserve; while, for the masses, compulsory military service produced familiarity with military codes of conduct and military ideals and values.[15] In times of emergency, the army was entitled to establish martial law and suspend civil liberties, a move considered so frequently during the Wilhelmine period that some historians have with pardonable exaggeration described the politicians and legislators of the time as living under the permanent threat of a *coup d'état* from above.[16]

The army impacted on society in a variety of ways, most intensively of all in Prussia, then after 1871 more indirectly, through the Prussian example, in other German states as well. Its prestige, gained in the stunning victories of the wars of unification, was enormous. Non-commissioned officers, that is, those men who stayed on after their term of compulsory military service was over and served in the army for a number of years, had an automatic right to a job in state employment when they finally left the army. This meant that the vast majority of policemen, postmen, railwaymen and other lower servants of the state were ex-soldiers, who had been socialized in the army and behaved in the military fashion to which they had become accustomed. The rule-book of an institution like the police force concentrated on enforcing military models of behaviour, insisted that the public be kept at arm's length and ensured that, in street marches and mass demonstrations, the crowd would be more likely to be treated like an enemy force than an assembly of citizens.[17] Military concepts of honour were pervasive enough

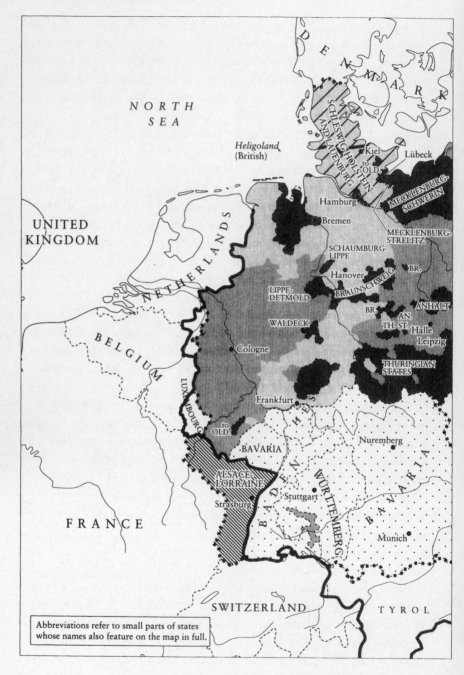

NORTH
SEA

DENMARK

Heligoland
(British)

SCHLESWIG-HOLSTEIN
AND LAUENBURG

Kiel
to OLD.

Lübeck

MECKLENBURG-SCHWERIN

UNITED
KINGDOM

Hamburg

Bremen

MECKLENBURG-STRELITZ

NETHERLANDS

SCHAUMBURG-LIPPE

Hanover

BR.

LIPPE-DETMOLD

BRAUNSCHWEIG

ANHALT

BELGIUM

WALDECK

BR.

AN.
ST.

Halle

Leipzig

TH.

Cologne

THURINGIAN
STATES

LUXEMBOURG

Frankfurt

to
OLD.

BAVARIA

HESSE

Nuremberg

ALSACE-LORRAINE

BADEN

WÜRTTEMBERG

BAVARIA

Strasburg

Stuttgart

FRANCE

Munich

SWITZERLAND

TYROL

Abbreviations refer to small parts of states
whose names also feature on the map in full.

Map 1. The Unification of Germany, 1864–1871

to ensure the continued vitality of duelling among civilian men, even amongst the middle classes, though it was also common in Russia and France as well.[18]

Over time, the identification of the officer corps with the Prussian aristocracy weakened, and aristocratic military codes were augmented by new forms of popular militarism, including in the early 1900s the Navy League and the veterans' clubs.[19] By the time of the First World War, most of the key positions in the officer corps were held by professionals, and the aristocracy was dominant mainly in traditional areas of social prestige and snobbery such as the cavalry and the guards, much as it was in other countries. But the professionalization of the officer corps, hastened by the advent of new military technology from the machine gun and barbed wire to the aeroplane and the tank, did not make it any more democratic. On the contrary, military arrogance was strengthened by the colonial experience, when German armed forces ruthlessly put down rebellions of indigenous peoples such as the Hereros in German South-West Africa (now Namibia).[20] In 1904–7, in an act of deliberate genocide, the German army massacred thousands of Herero men, women and children and drove many more of them into the desert, where they starved. From a population of some 80,000 before the war, the Hereros declined to a mere 15,000 by 1911 as a result of these actions.[21] In an occupied part of the German Empire such as Alsace-Lorraine, annexed from France in 1871, the army frequently behaved like conquerors facing a hostile and refractory population. Some of the most flagrant examples of such behaviour had given rise in 1913 to a heated debate in the Reichstag, in which the deputies passed a vote of no-confidence in the government. This did not of course force the government to resign, but it illustrated none the less the growing polarization of opinion over the role of the army in German society.[22]

The extent to which Bismarck managed to control the army's wilder impulses and restrain its desire for massive territorial annexations in the wake of its military victories was not realized by many at the time. Indeed, particularly after his enforced resignation in 1890, the myth emerged – encouraged not least by the disgruntled ex-Chancellor and his followers – of Bismarck himself as a charismatic leader who had ruthlessly cut the Gordian knots of politics and solved the great questions of the day by force. It was Bismarck's revolutionary wars in the 1860s that remained in the German public memory, not the two subsequent decades in which he tried to maintain the peace in Europe in order to allow the German Reich to find its feet. As the diplomat Ulrich von Hassell, a leader of the conservative resistance to Hitler in 1944, confided to his diary during a visit to Bismarck's old residence at Friedrichsruh:

It is regrettable how false is the picture which we ourselves have created of him in the world, as the jackbooted politician of violence, in childish pleasure at the fact that someone finally brought Germany to a position of influence again. In truth, his great gift was for the highest diplomacy and moderation. He understood uniquely how to win the world's trust, the exact opposite of today.[23]

The myth of the dictatorial leader was not the expression of an ancient, ingrained aspect of the German character; it was a much more recent creation.

It was fuelled in the early twentieth century by the public memory of Bismarck's tough stance against those whom he regarded as the internal enemies of the Reich. In the 1870s, reacting against the Pope's attempts to strengthen his hold over the Catholic community through the Syllabus of Errors (1864) and the Declaration of Papal Infallibility (1871), Bismarck inaugurated what liberals dubbed the 'struggle for culture', a series of laws and police measures which aimed to bring the Catholic Church under the control of the Prussian state. The Catholic clergy refused to co-operate with laws requiring them to undergo training at state institutions and submit clerical appointments to state approval. Before long, those who contravened the new laws were being hounded by the police, arrested and sent to gaol. By the mid-1870s, 989 parishes were without incumbents, 225 priests were in gaol, all Catholic religious orders apart from those involved in nursing had been suppressed, two archbishops and three bishops had been removed from office and the Bishop of Trier had died shortly after his release from nine months in prison.[24] What was even more disturbing was that this massive assault on the civil liberties of some 40 per cent of the population of the Reich was cheered on by Germany's liberals, who regarded Catholicism as so serious a threat to civilization that it justified extreme measures such as these.

The struggle eventually died down, leaving the Catholic community an embittered enemy of liberalism and modernity and determined to prove its loyalty to the state, not least through the political party it had formed in order, initially, to defend itself against persecution, the so-called Centre Party. But before this process was even complete, Bismarck struck another blow against civil liberties with the Anti-Socialist Law, passed by the Reichstag after two assassination attempts on the aged Kaiser Wilhelm I in 1878. In fact, Germany's fledgling socialist movement had nothing to do with the would-be assassins and was a law-abiding organization, putting its trust in the parliamentary route to power. Once more, however, the liberals were persuaded to abandon their liberal principles in what was presented to them as the national interest. Socialist meetings were banned, socialist newspapers and magazines suppressed, the socialist party outlawed. Capital punishment, previously in abeyance in Prussia and every other major German state, was reintroduced. Mass arrests and the widespread imprisonment of socialists followed.[25]

The consequences of the Anti-Socialist Law were, if anything, even more far-reaching than those of the struggle with the Catholic Church. It, too, completely failed in its immediate aim of suppressing supposed 'enemies of the Reich'. The socialists could not legally be banned from standing in parliamentary elections as individuals, and as Germany's industrialization gathered pace and the industrial working class increased ever more rapidly in numbers, so socialist candidates won an ever-growing share of the vote. After the law was allowed to lapse in 1890, the socialists reorganized themselves in the Social Democratic Party of Germany. By the eve of the First World War the party had over a million members, the largest political organization anywhere in the world. In the 1912 elections, despite an inbuilt bias of the electoral system in favour of conservative rural constituencies, it overtook the Centre Party as the largest single party in the Reichstag. The repression of the Anti-Socialist Law had driven it to the left, and from the beginning of the 1890s onwards it adhered to a rigid Marxist creed according to which the existing institutions of Church, state and society, from the monarchy and the army officer corps to big business and the stock market, would be overthrown in a proletarian revolution that would bring a socialist republic into being. The liberals' support for the Anti-Socialist Law caused the Social Democrats to distrust all 'bourgeois' political parties and to reject any idea of co-operating with the political supporters of capitalism or the exponents of what they regarded as a merely palliative reform of the existing political system.[26] Vast, highly disciplined, tolerating no dissent, and seemingly unstoppable in its forward march towards electoral dominance, the Social Democratic movement struck terror into the hearts of the respectable middle and upper classes. A deep gulf opened up between the Social Democrats on the one hand and all the 'bourgeois' parties on the other. This unbridgeable political divide was to endure well into the 1920s and play a vital role in the crisis that eventually brought the Nazis to power.

At the same time, however, the party was determined to do everything it could to remain within the law and not to provide any excuse for the oft-threatened reintroduction of a banning order. Lenin was once said to have remarked, in a rare flash of humour, that the German Social Democrats would never launch a successful revolution in Germany because when they came to storm the railway stations they would line up in an orderly queue to buy platform tickets first. The party acquired the habit of waiting for things to happen, rather than acting to bring them about. Its massively elaborate institutional structure, with its cultural organizations, its newspapers and magazines, its pubs, its bars, its sporting clubs and its educational apparatus, came in time to provide a whole way of life for its members and to constitute a set of vested interests that few in the party were prepared to jeopardize. As a law-abiding institution, the party put its faith in the courts to prevent persecution. Yet remaining within the law was not easy, even after 1890. Petty chicanery by the police was backed up by conservative judges and prosecutors, and by courts that continued to regard the Social Democrats as dangerous revolutionaries. There were few Social Democratic speakers or party newspaper editors who had not by 1914 spent several terms of imprisonment after being convicted of *lèse-majesté* or insulting state officials; criticizing the monarch or the police or even the civil servants who ran the country could still count as an offence under the law. Combating the Social Democrats became the business of a whole generation of judges, state prosecutors, police chiefs and government officials before 1914. These men, and the majority of their middle- and upper-class supporters, never accepted the Social Democrats as a legitimate political movement. In their eyes, the law's purpose was to uphold the existing institutions of state and society, not to act as a neutral referee between opposing political groups.[27]

The liberals were certainly of no help in remedying this situation. They themselves lost heavily in terms of votes and seats in the Reichstag in the course of the 1880s and 1890s, though they managed to retain a good deal of support in Germany's towns and cities. Not the least of their problems was the fact that they had repeatedly split in the course of the late nineteenth century, and, even after the more left-oriented groups had joined forces again in 1910, this still left two mainstream liberal parties, the National Liberals and the Progressives, whose differences went back to the refusal of the latter to forgive Bismarck for collecting taxes in Prussia without parliamentary authorization in the 1860s. Things were just as divided on the right of the political spectrum, however, where there was not one Conservative Party but two, since those who had supported Bismarck's merging of Prussian particularism into the institutions of the Reich in 1871 – anathema to the die-hard Prussian nobility, the Junkers – maintained a separate identity as the so-called 'Free Conservatives'. Moreover, these two largely Protestant, north German parties had to contend with an even larger political party of the right, the Centre, whose antimodernism and support for the Reich were tempered by its advocacy of social welfare and its critical attitude towards German colonial rule in Africa. Thus Germany before 1914 had not two mainstream political parties but six – the Social Democrats, the two liberal parties, the two groups of Conservatives, and the Centre Party, reflecting among other things the multiple divisions of German society, by region, religion and social class.[28] In a situation where there was a strong executive not directly responsible to the legislature, this weakened the prospect of party-politics being able to play a determining role in the state.

III

Far from causing a general disillusion with politics, the competition of all these rival political parties helped heat up the political atmosphere until it reached positively feverish dimensions by 1914. Universal manhood suffrage in Reichstag elections, backed by a more or less secret ballot and strict rules of electoral propriety, gave voters confidence in the electoral system. Voter participation reached the astonishing figure of 85 per cent of those eligible to cast their ballot in the Reichstag election of 1912.[29]

All the evidence goes to show that voters took their duty seriously, and thought carefully about how to reconcile their ideological position with the broader political scenario when it came, as it often did, to voting a second time in run-off ballots under the system of proportional representation adopted by the German constitution for elections to the Reichstag. The electoral system, guaranteed by legal provisions and safeguards, opened up a space for democratic debate and convinced millions of Germans of many political hues that politics belonged to the people.[30] Moreover, the daily press in Imperial Germany was almost entirely political, with each newspaper explicitly tied to one or other of the various parties and putting its point of view in almost everything it published.[31] Politics were not just the staple diet of conversation amongst the elites and the middle classes, but formed a central focus of discussion in working-class pubs and bars and even governed people's choice of leisure activities.[32]

Political discussion and debate turned increasingly after the beginning of the twentieth century to the topic of Germany's place in Europe and the world. Germans were increasingly aware of the fact that Bismarck's creation of the Reich was incomplete in a number of different ways. To begin with, it included substantial ethnic and cultural minorities, the legacy of previous centuries of state aggrandisement and ethnic conflict. There were Danes in the north, French-speakers in Alsace-Lorraine and a small Slavic group called the Sorbs in central Germany; but above all there were millions of Poles, inhabiting parts of the former Kingdom of Poland annexed by Prussia in the eighteenth century. Already under Bismarck the state increasingly tried to Germanize these minorities, attacking the use of their languages in the schools and actively encouraging settlement by ethnic Germans. By the eve of the First World War, the use of German was mandatory in public meetings throughout the Reich, and land laws were being reformed in such a way as to deprive the Poles of their fundamental economic rights.[33] The notion that ethnic minorities were entitled to be treated with the same respect as the majority population was a view held only by a tiny and diminishing minority of Germans. Even the Social Democrats thought of Russia and the Slavic East as lands of backwardness and barbarism by 1914, and had little or no sympathy for the efforts of Polish-speaking workers in Germany to organize in defence of their rights.[34]

Looking beyond Germany and Europe to the wider world, the Reich Chancellors who came into office after Bismarck saw their country as a second-class nation when compared with Britain and France, both of which had major overseas empires that spanned the globe. A latecomer on the scene, Germany had only been able to pick up the scraps and crumbs left over by European colonial powers that had enjoyed a head start on them. Tanganyika, Namibia, Togoland, Cameroon, New Guinea, assorted Pacific islands and the Chinese treaty port of Jiaozhou were virtually all the territories that made up Germany's overseas empire on the eve of the First World War. Bismarck had thought them of little importance and lent his assent to their acquisition with great reluctance. But his successors came to take a different view. Germany's prestige and standing in the world demanded, as Bernhard von Bülow, Foreign Secretary in the late 1890s, then Reich Chancellor until 1909, put it, a 'place in the sun'. A start was made on the construction of a massive battle fleet, whose long-term aim was to win colonial concessions from the British, lords of the world's largest overseas empire, by threatening, or even carrying out, the crippling or destruction of the main force of the British Navy in a titanic confrontation in the North Sea.[35]

These increasingly ambitious dreams of world power were articulated above all by Kaiser Wilhelm II himself, a bombastic, self-important and extremely loquacious man who lost few opportunities to express his contempt for democracy and civil rights, his disdain for the opinions of others and his belief in Germany's greatness. The Kaiser, like many of those who admired him, had grown up after Germany had been united. He had little awareness of the precarious and adventurous route by which Bismarck had achieved unification in 1871. Following the Prussian historians of his day, he thought of the whole process as historically preordained. He knew none of the nervous apprehension about Germany's future that had led Bismarck to adopt such a cautious foreign policy in the 1870s and 1880s. Admittedly, the Kaiser's character was too erratic, his personality too mercurial, for him to have any really consistent effect on the conduct of state affairs, and all too often his ministers found themselves working to counter his influence rather than implement his wishes. His constant declarations that he was the great leader that Germany needed merely served to draw attention to his deficiencies in this respect, and played their part, too, in fostering the nostalgic myth of Bismarckian decisiveness and guile. Many Germans came to contrast the ruthlessness of Bismarck's amoral statesmanship, in which the end justified the means and statesmen could say one thing while doing, or preparing to do, another, with Wilhelm's impulsive bombast and ill-considered tactlessness.[36]

Personalities aside, all of these features of the Germany that Bismarck created could be observed to a greater or lesser degree in other countries as well. In Italy the charismatic example of Garibaldi, leader of the popular forces that helped unite the nation in 1859, provided a model for the later dictator Mussolini. In Spain, the army was no less free of political control than it was in Germany, and in Italy, as in Germany, it reported to the sovereign rather than to the legislature. In Austria-Hungary, the civil service was just as strong and parliamentary institutions even more limited in their power. In France, a Church–state conflict raged that was not far behind that of the German 'struggle for culture' in its ideological ferocity. In Russia, a concept equivalent to that of the Reich was also applied to domestic politics and Russia's relations with its nearest neighbours.[37] The Tsarist regime in Russia repressed the socialists even more severely than did its German counterpart and did not yield an inch to the German authorities in its drive to assimilate the Poles, millions of whom were also under its sway. Liberalism, however defined, was weak in all the major states of Eastern and Central Europe by 1914, not just in the German Reich. The political scene was still more fragmented in Italy than it was in Germany, and the belief that war was justified to achieve political aims, in particular the creation of a land empire, was common to many European powers, as the outbreak of the First World War was to show with such terrible clarity in August 1914. All over the Continent, the growing forces of democracy threatened the hegemony of conservative elites. The late nineteenth and early twentieth centuries were the age of nationalism not just in Germany, but everywhere in Europe, and the 'nationalization of the masses' was taking place in many other countries as well.[38]

Yet in no nation in Europe other than Germany were all these conditions present at the same time and to the same extent. Moreover, Germany was not just any European country. Much has been written by historians about various aspects of Germany's supposed backwardness at this time, its alleged deficit of civic values, its arguably antiquated social structure, its seemingly craven middle class and its apparently neo-feudal aristocracy. This was not how most contemporaries saw it at the time. Well before the outbreak of the First World War, Germany was the Continent's wealthiest, most powerful and most advanced economy. In the last years of peace, Germany was producing two-thirds of continental Europe's output of steel, half its output of coal and lignite and twenty per cent more electrical energy than Britain, France and Italy combined.[39] By 1914, with a population of around 67 million, the German Empire commanded far greater resources of manpower than any other continental European power with the exception of Russia. By comparison, the United Kingdom, France and Austria-Hungary each had a population of between 40 and 50 million at this time. Germany was the world leader in the most modern industries, such as chemicals, pharmaceuticals and electricity. In agriculture, the massive use of artificial fertilizers and farm machinery had transformed the efficiency of the landed estates of the north and east by 1914, by which time Germany was, for example, producing a third of the world's output of potatoes. Living standards had improved by leaps and bounds since the turn of the century if not before. The products of Germany's great industrial firms, such as Krupps and Thyssen, Siemens and AEG, Hoechst and BASF, were famous for their quality the world over.[40]

Viewed nostalgically from the perspective of the early interwar years, Germany before 1914 seemed to many to have been a haven of peace, prosperity and social harmony. Yet beneath its prosperous and self-confident surface, it was nervous, uncertain and racked by internal tensions.[41] For many, the sheer pace of economic and social change was frightening and bewildering. Old values seemed to be disappearing in a welter of materialism and unbridled ambition. Modernist culture, from abstract painting to atonal music, added to the sense of disorientation in some areas of society.[42] The old-established hegemony of the Prussian landed aristocracy, which Bismarck had tried so hard to preserve, was undermined by the headlong rush of German society into the modern age. Bourgeois values, habits and modes of behaviour had triumphed in the upper and middle reaches of society by 1914; yet simultaneously they were themselves being challenged by the growing self-assertion of the industrial working class, organized in the massive Social Democratic labour movement. Germany, unlike any other European country, had become a nation-state not before the industrial revolution, but at its height; and on the basis, not of a single state, but of a federation of many different states whose German citizens were bound together principally by a common language, culture and ethnicity. Stresses and strains created by rapid industrialization interlocked with conflicting ideas about the nature of the German state and nation and their place in the larger context of Europe and the world. German society did not enter nationhood in 1871 in a wholly stable condition. It was riven by rapidly deepening internal conflicts which were increasingly exported into the unresolved tensions of the political system that Bismarck had created.[43] These tensions found release in an increasingly vociferous nationalism, mixed in with alarmingly strident doses of racism and antisemitism, which were to leave a baleful legacy for the future.

GOSPELS OF HATE

I

Towards the end of 1889, a Berlin primary school headmaster, Hermann Ahlwardt, was facing the prospect of financial ruin. Born in 1846 into an impoverished family in Pomerania, he found the income he earned in his lowly position in the Prussian educational hierarchy too little to cover his considerable daily living expenses. In desperation, he committed a crime that seemed almost deliberately calculated to shock the sensibilities of his superiors: he stole money from the funds collected to pay for the children's Christmas party at his school. Soon enough, his misdemeanour was discovered and he was dismissed from his post. This deprived him of his last remaining source of income. Many people would have been crushed by these disasters and overwhelmed by feelings of guilt and remorse. But not Hermann Ahlwardt. 'The headmaster', as he soon came to be known by the general public, decided to go onto the offensive. Looking around for someone to blame for his misfortunes, his attention quickly focused on the Jews.[44]

Germany's Jewish community at this time was a highly acculturated, successful group distinguished from other Germans mainly by its religion.[45] In the course of the nineteenth century, civil disabilities attaching to non-Christians in the German states had gradually been removed, much as formal religious discrimination in other countries had been abolished – for example, in Britain through Catholic Emancipation in 1829. The last remaining legal impediments to full and equal legal rights were swept away with German unification in 1871. Now that civil marriage had been introduced in place of religious ceremonies all over Germany, the number of intermarriages between Jews and Christians began to grow rapidly. In Breslau, for instance, there were 35 Jewish-Christian marriages for every 100 purely Jewish marriages by 1915, compared with only 9 in the late 1870s. Very few of the Christian partners in such marriages came from the families of converted Jews themselves, and the marriages were scattered right across the social scale. In 1904, 19 per cent of Jewish men in Berlin and 13 per cent of Jewish women married Christian partners. In Düsseldorf, a quarter of all Jews who married had Christian partners in the mid-1900s, rising to a third by 1914. By the eve of the First World War, there were 38 intermarriages for every 100 purely Jewish marriages; in Hamburg the figure was as high as 73. Jews also began to convert to Christianity in growing numbers; 11,000 converted in the first seventy years of the nineteenth century and 11,500 in the remaining three decades. Between 1880 and 1919, some 20,000 German Jews were baptized. Success was slowly dissolving the identity of the Jewish community as an enclosed religious group.[46]

The 600,000 or so practising Jews who lived in the German Empire were a tiny religious minority in an overwhelmingly Christian society, constituting around 1 per cent of the population as a whole. Excluded for centuries from traditional sources of wealth such as landowning, they remained outside the ranks of the Reich's establishment as informal social discrimination continued to deny them a place in key institutions such as the army, the universities and the top ranks of the civil service; indeed, their access to such institutions actually declined in the 1890s and 1900s.[47] Converted Jews suffered sufficiently from everyday anti-semitism for many of them to change their names to something more Christian-sounding.[48] As many as 100,000 German Jews reacted to discrimination in the nineteenth century by emigrating, notably to the United States; but most stayed, particularly as the economy began to boom towards the end of the century. Those who remained were concentrated in the larger towns and cities, with a quarter of Germany's Jews living in Berlin by 1910, and nearly a third by 1933. Within these cities they clustered into particular districts; nearly half of Hamburg's Jews lived in the two middle-class precincts of Harvestehude and Rotherbaum in 1885, nearly two-thirds of Frankfurt's Jews in four of the city's fourteen precincts in 1900; 70 per cent of Berlin's Jews lived in five central and western districts, most of them overwhelmingly middle class, by 1925. Even in the cities with the largest Jewish populations – Berlin, Breslau and Frankfurt – they constituted a very tiny minority, making up no more than 4.3 per cent, 6.4 per cent and 7.1 per cent of the population respectively in 1871.[49]

Many Jews found a place in business and the professions. Alongside the great banking family of the Rothschilds there emerged many other important Jewish-owned finance houses, such as the banking firm of Bleichröder, to whom Bismarck entrusted his personal finances.[50] New types of retailing such as the department stores, of which there were about 200 in Germany before the First World War, often had Jewish owners such as the Tietz family or the Wertheim brothers.[51] Jewish men were particularly well represented in medicine, the law, science and research, university teaching, journalism and the arts.[52] The Jewish community was turning slowly from an ostracized religious minority into one ethnic group among many in an increasingly multi-cultural society, alongside other minorities like Poles, Danes, Alsatians, Sorbs and the rest. Like the other groups, it had its own increasingly secular representative institutions, notably the Central Association of German Citizens of the Jewish Faith, founded in 1893. Unlike most of the other groups, however, it was generally economically successful, and, rather than having their own political party, its members tended to join, and sometimes take leading positions in, mainstream political parties, particularly on the left and in the centre of the political spectrum. Most Jews identified strongly with German nationalism, and if the liberal parties were particularly attractive to them, this was not least because of their unequivocal support for the creation of a German nation-state.[53] By and large, then, the Jewish story in the late nineteenth century was a success story, and Jews were associated above all with the most modern and progressive developments in society, culture and the economy.[54]

It was developments such as these that made the Jews the target for disgruntled and unscrupulous agitators like Hermann Ahlwardt. For the disaffected and the unsuccessful, those who felt pushed aside by the Juggernaut of industrialization and yearned for a simpler, more ordered, more secure, more hierarchical society such as they imagined had existed in the not-too-distant past, the Jews symbolized cultural, financial and social modernity. Nowhere was this more the case than in Ahlwardt's adopted city of Berlin. In 1873, the city's economy was dealt a hammer-blow when the frantic round of spending and investing that had accompanied the euphoria of the Reich's foundation came to an abrupt end. A worldwide economic depression, sparked by the failure of railway investments in the United States, brought widespread bankruptcies and business failures in Germany. Small businesses and workshops were particularly badly hit. In their incomprehension of the wider forces that were destroying their livelihood, those most severely affected found it easy to believe the claims of Catholic and conservative journalists that Jewish financiers were to blame.

As the depression went on, the journalists were joined by the court preacher Adolf Stöcker. A man of humble origin who embarked on a crusade to win back the working classes from the influence of Social Democracy, Stöcker founded a Christian Social Party that fought elections in the 1880s on an explicitly antisemitic platform. The new cause was aided by Max Libermann von Sonnenberg, who helped organize a national petition for the removal of Jews from public positions in 1880. Particularly extreme was Ernst Henrici, whose rhetoric was so vehement that it caused riots in the Pomeranian town of Neustettin, culminating in the burning of the local synagogue. It was towards this movement that Hermann Ahlwardt gravitated in the late 1880s, avenging his disgrace with a book blaming his financial misfortunes on the machinations of Jewish money-lenders and suggesting that Jews were all-powerful in German society. Unfortunately for him, the evidence he provided for his claims, in the shape of documents showing the German government to be in the pay of the Jewish banker Gerson von Bleichröder, turned out to have been written by Ahlwardt himself, and he was sentenced to four months in prison. No sooner was he released than he produced another set of sensational and equally unfounded claims, this time declaring that a Jewish arms manufacturer had supplied the army with rifles that were deliberately faulty, in order to further a Franco-Jewish conspiracy to undermine German military effectiveness. Predictably enough, these claims earned Ahlwardt another prison sentence, this time of five months.[55]

But he never served it. For in the meantime he had succeeded in persuading the peasant farmers of a deeply rural constituency in Brandenburg to elect him to the Reichstag. Travelling round their farms, he told them that their misfortunes, brought on them in fact by a world depression in agricultural prices, had been caused by the Jews, a distant and to them obscure religious minority who lived far away in the big towns and financial centres of Europe and the Reich. A seat in the Reichstag gave Ahlwardt parliamentary immunity. His success testified to the appeal of such demagogy to rural voters, and indeed other antisemites such as the Hessian librarian Otto Böckel succeeded in getting elected as well, not least by offering the peasants concrete measures such as co-operative organizations in order to get over their economic difficulties. By the early 1890s the threat of such antisemites to the electoral hegemony of the German Conservative Party in rural districts was perceived to be so serious that the party itself, alarmed by a government policy that seemed likely to damage farming interests still further, voted onto its programme a demand for the combating of the 'widely obtruding and decomposing Jewish influence on our popular life' at its Tivoli conference in 1893.[56]

This proved in the end to be a turning-point in the fortunes of Germany's motley collection of political antisemites. Although a serious attempt was made by another antisemitic agitator, Theodor Fritsch, to bring the various strands of political antisemitism together and direct the movement's appeal towards the economically discontented urban lower middle class, the egotism of figures like Böckel prevented any real union from taking place, and the antisemites were riven by internecine disputes. Fritsch's influence was to be exerted in another way. He continued to publish innumerable popular antisemitic tracts which were widely read, right up to and beyond his death in September 1933, by which time he was sitting in the Reichstag as a representative of the Nazi Party. Throughout the prewar years, however, he remained a marginal political figure. By the early 1900s, the antisemites had been undermined by the effective coalition of the Berlin Christian Social movement with the Conservative Party, and stymied in Catholic areas by the willingness of the Centre Party to engage in a similar kind of antisemitic rhetoric. Mavericks such as Böckel and Ahlwardt lost their seats, and their parties, together with the urban-based organizations of antisemites such as Fritzsch, faded away into nothingness. Ahlwardt himself alienated even other antisemites with the violence of his language. He left for the United States for a while, and on his return devoted himself to combating the evils of Freemasonry. In 1909 he was in prison again, this time for blackmail; evidently his continuing financial difficulties had driven him to attempt even more directly criminal solutions than before. He finally died, somewhat anticlimactically, in a traffic accident, in 1914.[57]

I I

Ahlwardt was an extreme but in some ways not untypical representative of a new kind of antisemitism that was emerging in Germany and else-where in Europe towards the end of the nineteenth century. Traditional antisemitism focused on the non-Christian religion of the Jews, and derived its political power from biblical sanction. The New Testament blamed the Jews for Christ's death, condemning them to perpetual oblo-quy by declaring that they had willingly agreed to let Christ's blood be upon them and their descendants. As a non-Christian minority in a society governed by Christian beliefs and Christian institutions, the Jews were obvious and easy targets for popular hatred in times of crisis such as the Black Death in the mid-fourteenth century, when rampaging mobs all over Europe blamed the Jews for the mortality that afflicted so many of the population, and took their revenge in countless acts of violence and destruction. It was no accident that the history of modern antisemitism in Germany began with the court preacher Adolf Stöcker. Christian hostility to the Jews provided a crucial launch-pad for modern antisemit-ism, not least because it often harboured a strong element of racial prejudice itself and was subsumed into racial antisemitism in a variety of ways. But by the late nineteenth century it was becoming increasingly out of date, at least in its purest, most traditional form, particularly as the Jews were ceasing to be an easily identifiable religious minority and were beginning to convert and marry into Christian society at an increasing pace. Searching for a scapegoat for their economic difficulties in the 1870s, lower-middle-class demagogues and scribblers turned to the Jews, not as a religious but a racial minority, and began to advocate not the total assimilation of Jews into German society, but their total exclusion from it.[58]

The credit for this turn, if credit is the right word, is generally given to the obscure writer Wilhelm Marr, whose pamphlet *The Victory of Jew-dom over Germandom Viewed from a Non-confessional Standpoint*, published in 1873, was the first to insist that, as he put it in a later work:

'There must be no question here of parading religious prejudices when it is a question of race and when the difference lies in the "blood". '[59] Borrowing from the fashionable theories of the French racist Count Joseph Arthur de Gobineau, Marr contrasted Jews not with Christians but with Germans, insisting that the two were distinct races. The Jews, he declared, had gained the upper hand in the racial struggle, and were virtually running the country; no wonder, then, that honest German artisans and small businessmen were suffering. Marr went on to invent the word 'antisemitism' and, in 1879, to found the League of Antisemites, the world's first organization with this word in its title. It was dedicated, as he said, to reducing the Jewish influence on German life. His writing struck an apocalyptically pessimistic note. In his 'Testament' he proclaimed that: 'The Jewish question is the axis around which the wheel of world history revolves,' going on to record gloomily his view that: 'All our social, commercial, and industrial developments are built on a Jewish world view.'[60]

The roots of Marr's despair were personal as much as anything else. Constantly in financial difficulties, he was badly hit by the financial troubles of the 1870s. His second wife, who was Jewish, supported him financially until her death in 1874; his third wife, whom he divorced after a brief and disastrous relationship, was half-Jewish, and he blamed her in part for his lack of money, since he had to pay her substantial sums to bring up their child. Marr concluded from this – boldly elevating his personal experience into a general rule of world history – that racial purity was admirable, racial mixing a recipe for calamity. Given these very personal roots of his antisemitism, it is not surprising that Marr did not become closely involved in active politics; the League of Antisemites was a failure, and he refused to support the antisemitic parties because he considered them too conservative.[61] But he was quickly joined as a propagandist of the new racial antisemitism by a range of other writers. The revolutionary Eugen Dühring, for example, equated capitalism with the Jews and argued that socialism had to be aimed chiefly at removing the Jews from financial and political influence. The nationalist historian Heinrich von Treitschke argued that the Jews were undermining German culture, and popularized the phrase 'the Jews are our misfortune', words that would become a slogan for many antisemites in the following years, including the Nazis. Writers such as these were far from marginal figures of the sort represented by Hermann Ahlwardt. Eugen Dühring, for example, exerted a sufficiently powerful attraction over the socialist movement for Friedrich Engels to pen his famous tract the *Anti-Dühring* in a successful attempt to combat its influence within the socialist labour movement in 1878. Heinrich von Treitschke's history was one of the most widely read of all German histories in the nineteenth century, and his diatribes against what he saw as Jewish materialism and dishonesty aroused a massive reaction amongst his fellow-professors in Berlin, including the classicist Theodor Mommsen, the pathologist Rudolf Virchow and the historian Gustav von Droysen, who joined with many other German academics in condemning their colleague's 'racial hatred and fanaticism' in unequivocal terms.[62]

Such reactions were a reminder that for all the rapidly growing influence of antisemitic writers, the vast majority of respectable opinion in Germany, left and right, middle class and working class, remained opposed to racism of this kind. Attempts to get the German people to swallow antisemitic ideas whole met with little success. The German working class in particular, and its main political representative, the Social Democratic Party (the largest political organization in Germany, with more seats in the Reichstag than any other party after 1912, and the highest number of votes in national elections long before that), was resolutely opposed to antisemitism, which it regarded as backward and undemocratic. Even ordinary rank-and-file party members rejected its slogans of hatred. As one worker was heard to remark by a police agent listening out for political talk in the pubs and bars of Hamburg in 1898:

National feeling must not degenerate into one nation setting itself above another. Worse still, if one regards the Jews as a subordinate race, and thus fights the race. Can the Jews help it if they descend from another lineage? They have always been an oppressed people, hence their scattering (over the world). For the Social Democrat it's self-evident that he wants the equality of everyone with a human spirit. The Jew's not the worst by a long way.[63]

Other workers on other occasions were heard to pour scorn on the antisemites, condemn antisemitic violence and support the Jewish desire for civil equality. Such views were entirely typical of workers in the labour movement milieu before 1914.[64]

The worst the Social Democrats could be accused of was not taking seriously enough the threat posed by antisemitism, and of allowing a few antisemitic stereotypes to creep into a small number of cartoons printed in their entertainment magazines.[65] In some areas, the Social Democrats and antisemites supported each other in electoral run-offs, but this did not imply approval of each other's principles, merely a desire to make temporary common cause as parties of protest against established elites.[66] In a few backward small towns and villages, mainly in the deeply rural east, medieval accusations of ritual murder were occasionally brought against local Jews and won some popular support, even arousing protest demonstrations on occasion. Not one of them was ever proved by the courts. Small businessmen, shopkeepers, artisans and peasant farmers were more inclined to overt antisemitism than most, continuing a tradition of organized popular antisemitism that can be traced back at least as far as the 1848 Revolution in some areas, though not in its modern, racist form.[67] But among the educated middle classes, non-Jewish businessmen and professionals for the most part worked quite happily with Jewish colleagues, whose representation in the liberal political parties was sufficiently strong to prevent these from taking on board any of the central arguments or attitudes of the antisemites. The antisemitic parties remained a fringe, protest phenomenon and largely disappeared shortly after the turn of the century.

Nevertheless, their decline and fall was to some extent deceptive. One of the reasons for their disappearance lay in the adoption of antisemitic ideas by the mainstream parties whose constituents included the economically imperilled lower-middle-class groups to which the antisemites had originally appealed – the Conservatives and the Centre Party. The Conservatives built on the antisemitic policies contained in their 1893 Tivoli programme and continued to demand the reduction of what they thought of as the subversive influence of Jews in public life. Their antisemitic prejudices appealed to significant groups in Protestant rural society in north Germany and to the artisans, shopkeepers and small businessmen represented in the party's Christian-social wing. For the much larger, though under the Reich arguably less influential, Centre Party, the Jews, or rather a distorted and polemical image of them, symbolized liberalism, socialism, modernity – all the things the Church rejected. Such a view appealed to large numbers of peasants and artisans in the party, and was spread by autonomous protest groups amongst the Catholic peasantry whose ideas were not dissimilar to those of Otto Böckel; it was also shared by much of the Church hierarchy, for much the same reason. In the Vatican, religious and racial antisemitism merged in some of the anti-Jewish diatribes published by clerical writers in a few of the more hardline Ultramontane newspapers and magazines.[68]

Moreover, antisemitic prejudice was powerful enough in the higher reaches of society, the court, the civil service, the army and the universities to constitute a permanent reminder to Jews that they were less than equal members of the German nation.[69] The antisemites succeeded in placing 'the Jewish question' on the political agenda, so that at no time was Jewish participation in key social institutions not a matter for discussion and debate. Yet this was all relatively low-level, even by the standards of the time. A historian once speculated on what would happen if a time-traveller from 1945 arrived back in Europe just before the First World War, and told an intelligent and well-informed contemporary that within thirty years a European nation would make a systematic attempt to kill all the Jews of Europe and exterminate nearly six million in the process. If the time-traveller invited the contemporary to guess which nation it would be, the chances were that he would have pointed to France, where the Dreyfus affair had recently led to a massive outbreak of virulent popular antisemitism. Or it might be Russia, where the Tsarist 'Black Hundreds' had been massacring large numbers of Jews in the wake of the failed Revolution of 1905.[70] That Germany, with its highly acculturated Jewish community and its comparative lack of overt or violent political antisemitism, would be the nation to launch this exterminatory campaign would hardly have occurred to him. Antisemitic politics were still very much on the fringe. But some of the antisemites' propaganda claims were beginning to gain a hearing in the political mainstream – for example, the idea that something called the 'Jewish spirit' was somehow 'subversive', or that Jews had supposedly 'excessive' influence in areas of society such as journalism and the law. Moreover, the antisemitic parties had introduced a new, rabble-rousing, demagogic style of politics that had freed itself from the customary restraints of political decorum. This, too, remained on the fringes, but, here again, it had now become possible to utter in parliamentary sessions and electoral meetings hatreds and prejudices that in the mid-nineteenth century would have been deemed utterly inappropriate in public discourse.[71]

What the 1880s and early 1890s were essentially witnessing, in addition to this domestication of antisemitism, was the assembling, on the fringes of political and intellectual life, of many of the ingredients that would later go into the potent and eclectic ideological brew of National Socialism. A key role in this process was played by antisemitic writers like the popular novelist Julius Langbehn, whose book *Rembrandt as Educator* (published in 1890) declared the Dutch artist Rembrandt to be a classic north German racial type, and pleaded for German art to return to its racial roots, a cultural imperative that would later be taken up with great enthusiasm by the Nazis. These authors developed a new language of vehemence and violence in their diatribes against the Jews. The Jews, for Langbehn, were a 'poison for us and will have to be treated as such'; 'the Jews are only a passing plague and a cholera', as he put it in 1892. Langbehn's book went through forty reprints in little over a year and continued to be a best-seller long after, combining scurrilous attacks on what its author called 'Jews and idiots, Jews and scoundrels, Jews and whores, Jews and professors, Jews and Berliners' with a call for the restoration of a hierarchical society led by a 'secret Kaiser' who would one day emerge from the shadows to restore Germany to its former glory.[72]

Such ideas were taken up and elaborated by the circle that gathered around the widow of the composer Richard Wagner at Bayreuth. Wagner had made his home in this north Bavarian town until his death in 1883 and his epic music-dramas were played every year in the opera house he had had constructed specially for the purpose. They were designed not least to propagate pseudo-Germanic national myths, in which heroic figures from Nordic legend were to serve as model leaders for the German future. Wagner himself had already been a cultural antisemite in the early 1850s, arguing in his notorious book *Judaism in Music* that the 'Jewish spirit' was inimical to musical profundity. His remedy was for the complete assimilation of Jews into German culture, and the replacement of the Jewish religion, indeed all religion, by secular aesthetic impulses of the sort he poured into his own music-dramas. But towards the end of his life his views took on an increasingly racist tone under the influence of his second wife, Cosima, daughter of the composer Franz Liszt. By the end of the 1870s she was recording in her diaries that Wagner, whose outlook on civilization was distinctly pessimistic by this time, had read

Wilhelm Marr's antisemitic tract of 1873 and broadly agreed with it. As a consequence of this shift in his position, Wagner no longer desired the assimilation of the Jews into German society, but their exclusion from it. In 1881, discussing Lessing's classic play *Nathan the Wise* and a disastrous fire in the Vienna Ring Theatre, in which more than four hundred people, many of them Jewish, had died, Cosima noted that her husband said 'in a vehement quip that all Jews should burn in a performance of "Nathan"'.[73]

After Wagner's death, his widow turned Bayreuth into a kind of shrine, at which a band of dedicated followers would cultivate the dead Master's sacred memory. The views of the circle she gathered round her at Bayreuth were rabidly antisemitic. The Wagner circle did its best to interpret the composer's operas as pitting Nordic heroes against Jewish villains, although his music was of course capable of being interpreted in many other ways as well. Among its leading figures were Ludwig Schemann, a private scholar who translated Gobineau's treatise on racial inequality into German in 1898, and the Englishman Houston Stewart Chamberlain, born in 1855, who married one of Wagner's daughters and in due course published an admiring biography of the great man. While Cosima and her friends propagated their ideas through the periodical publication the *Bayreuth Papers*, Schemann went round the country addressing antisemitic meetings and founding a variety of radical racist organizations, most notably the Gobineau Society in 1894. None of them was particularly successful. But Schemann's championing of the French racial theorist still did a great deal to bring Gobineau's term 'Aryan' into vogue amongst German racists. Originally used to denote the common ancestors of the speakers of Germanic languages such as English and German, the term soon acquired a contemporary usage, as Gobineau put forward his argument that racial survival could only be guaranteed by racial purity, such as was supposedly preserved in the German or 'Aryan' peasantry, and that racial intermingling spelled cultural and political decline.[74]

It was Chamberlain who had the greatest impact, however, with his book *The Foundations of the Nineteenth Century*, published in 1900. In this vaporous and mystical work Chamberlain portrayed history in terms of a struggle for supremacy between the Germanic and Jewish races, the only two racial groups that retained their original purity in a world of miscegenation. Against the heroic and cultured Germans were pitted the ruthless and mechanistic Jews, whom Chamberlain thus elevated into a cosmic threat to human society rather than simply dismissing them as a marginal or inferior group. Linked to the racial struggle was a religious one, and Chamberlain devoted a good deal of effort to trying to prove that Christianity was essentially Germanic and that Jesus, despite all the evidence, had not been Jewish at all. Chamberlain's work impressed many of his readers with its appeal to science in support of its arguments; his most important contribution in this respect was to fuse antisemitism and racism with Social Darwinism. The English scientist Charles Darwin had maintained that the animal and plant kingdoms were subject to a law of natural selection in which the fittest survived and the weakest or least well adapted went to the wall, thus guaranteeing the improvement of the species. Social Darwinists applied this model to the human race as well.[75] Here were assembled already, therefore, some of the key ideas that were later to be taken up by the Nazis.

III

Chamberlain was not alone in putting forward such views. A variety of authors, scientists and others contributed to the emergence in the 1890s of a new, tough, selectionist variant of Social Darwinism, one that emphasized not peaceful evolution but the struggle for survival. A characteristic representative of this school of thought was the anthropologist Ludwig Woltmann, who argued in 1900 that the Aryan or German race represented the height of human evolution and was thus superior to all others. Therefore, he claimed, the 'Germanic race has been selected to dominate the earth'.[76] But other races, he claimed, were preventing this from happening. The Germans, in the view of some, needed more 'living-space' – the German word was *Lebensraum* – and it would have to be acquired at the expense of others, most likely the Slavs. This was not because the country was literally overcrowded – there was no evidence for that – but because those who advanced such views were taking the idea of territoriality from the animal kingdom and applying it to human society. Alarmed by the growth of Germany's burgeoning cities, they sought the restoration of a rural ideal in which German settlers would lord it over 'inferior' Slav peasants, just as they had done, so historians were beginning to tell them, in East Central Europe in the Middle Ages.[77] Such visions of international politics as an arena of struggle between different races for supremacy or survival had become common currency in Germany's political elite by the time of the First World War. Men such as War Minister Erich von Falkenhayn, Naval Secretary Alfred von Tirpitz, Reich Chancellor Bethmann Hollweg's adviser Kurt Riezler, and Chief of the Imperial Naval Cabinet Georg Alexander von Müller, all saw war as a means of preserving or asserting the German race against the Latins and the Slavs. War, as General Friedrich von Bernhardi famously put it in a book published in 1912, was a 'biological necessity': 'Without war, inferior or decaying races would easily choke the growth of healthy budding elements, and a universal decadence would follow.' Foreign policy was no longer to be conducted between states, but between races. Here was one beginning of the downgrading of the importance of the state that was to play such an important role in Nazi foreign policy.[78]

Success in war, an increasing preoccupation among Germany's leaders and politicians from the centre to the right after the turn of the century, also (for some) demanded the undertaking of positive steps to bring about the improvement of the race. One aspect of the selectionist turn in Social Darwinism during the 1890s was to put greater emphasis than before on 'negative selection'. It was all very well improving the race by better housing, health care nutrition, hygiene and sanitation and similar policies, some argued. But this would do little to counteract the influence of society's abandonment of the principle of the struggle for survival by caring for the weak, the unhealthy and the inadequate. Such a policy, argued some medical scientists, whose views were reinforced by the emergence of the fledgling science of genetics, was bringing about the increasing degeneracy of the human race. It had to be counteracted by a scientific approach to breeding that would reduce or eliminate the weak and improve and multiply the strong. Among those who argued along these lines was Wilhelm Schallmayer, whose essay advocating a eugenic approach to social policy won first prize in a national competition organized by the industrialist Alfred Krupp in 1900. Alfred Ploetz was yet another medical man who thought that the height of human evolution so far had been reached by the Germans. He suggested that inferior specimens should be sent to the front if a war came, so that the unfit would be eliminated first. Most widely read of all was Ernst Haeckel, whose popularization of Darwinian ideas, *The Riddle of the World*, became a runaway best-seller when it was published in 1899.[79]

It would be a mistake to see such views as forming a coherent or unified ideology, however, still less one that pointed forward in a straight line to Nazism. Schallmayer, for instance, was not antisemitic, and he vehemently rejected any idea of the superiority of the 'Aryan' race. Nor was Woltmann hostile towards Jews, and his fundamentally positive attitude towards the French Revolution (whose leaders, he somewhat implausibly claimed, were racially Germanic, like all great historical figures) was far from congenial to the Nazis. For his part, Haeckel certainly argued that capital punishment should be used on a large scale to eliminate criminals from the chain of heredity. He also advocated the killing of the mentally ill through the use of chemical injections and electrocution. Haeckel was a racist, too, and pronounced the verdict that no woolly-haired race had ever achieved anything of historical importance. But on the other hand he thought that war would be a eugenic catastrophe because it would kill off the best and bravest young men in the country. As a consequence, Haeckel's disciples, organized in the self-styled 'Monist League', became pacifists, rejecting the idea of war altogether – not a doctrine that would endear them to the Nazis. Many of them would suffer dearly for their principles when war finally came in 1914.[80]

The nearest any of this came to prefiguring Nazi ideology was in the writings of Ploetz, who spiced his theories with a strong dose of antisemitism and collaborated with Nordic supremacist groups. Still, before the First World War there seems little evidence that Ploetz himself considered the 'Aryan' race superior to others, although one of his closest collaborators, Fritz Lenz, certainly did. Ploetz took a ruthlessly meritocratic line on eugenic planning, arguing, for example, that a panel of doctors should attend all births and determine whether the baby was fit to survive or should be killed as weak and inadequate. The Darwinist Alexander Tille openly advocated the killing of the mentally and physically unfit, and agreed with Ploetz and Schallmayer that children's illnesses should be left untreated so that the weak could be eliminated from the chain of heredity. In 1905 Ploetz and his sometime brother-in-law, the like-minded Ernst Rüdin, founded the Racial Hygiene Society to propagate their views. It rapidly gained influence in the medical and welfare professions. Gobineau had been in many ways a conservative, and thought that the eugenic ideal was embodied in the aristocracy. These German thinkers took a far tougher and potentially more revolutionary line, often regarding hereditary traits as largely independent of social class.[81]

By the eve of the First World War, their ideas had spread in one form or another to areas such as medicine, social work, criminology and the law. Social deviants such as prostitutes, alcoholics, petty thieves, vagrants and the like were increasingly regarded as hereditarily tainted, and calls amongst experts for such people to be forcibly sterilized had become too loud to escape attention. Such was the influence of these ideas on the welfare establishment that even the Social Democrats could take seriously the proposal of Alfred Grotjahn to link housing and welfare improvements with the compulsory sterilization of the insane, the 'workshy' and the alcoholic.[82] Developments such as these reflected the growing influence of the medical profession over rapidly growing specialisms such as criminology and social work. The triumphs of German medical science in discovering the bacilli that caused diseases such as cholera and tuberculosis in the nineteenth century had given it unparalleled intellectual prestige as well as inadvertently furnishing antisemites with a whole new language in which to express their hatred and fear of the Jews. As a result, it had brought about a widespread medicalization of society, in which ordinary people, including an increasing proportion of the working class, had begun to adopt hygienic practices such as washing regularly, disinfecting bathrooms, boiling drinking water and so on. The concept of hygiene began to spread from medicine to other areas of life, including not only 'social hygiene' but also, crucially, 'racial hygiene'.

To be sure, for all the discussion and debate over these issues, the effect that such ideas had on government policies and their implementation before 1914 was not very great. Beyond the scientific establishment, propagandists for the breeding of a blond, Aryan super-race such as the self-styled Lanz von Liebenfels, editor of *Ostara: Newspaper for Blond People*, appealed only to an underworld of extremist politics and tiny, eccentric political sects.[83] Nevertheless, despite all these qualifications, the emergence of these ideas, together with the increasing role they played in public debate, was a significant element in the origins of Nazi ideology. Several fundamental principles united virtually everyone in this motley crowd of scientists, doctors and propagandists for racial hygiene. The first was that heredity played a significant role in determining human character and behaviour. The second, which followed on from this, was that society, led by the state, should manage the population in order to increase national efficiency. The 'fit' had to be persuaded, or forced, to breed more, the 'unfit' to breed less. Thirdly, however these terms were understood, the racial hygiene movement introduced an ominously rational and scientific categorization of people into those who were 'valuable' to the nation and those who were not. 'Low quality' – the German term was *minderwertig*, literally, 'worth-less' – became a stock term used by social workers and medical men for many kinds of social deviant before the First World War. By labelling people in this way, the race hygienists opened the way towards the control, the abuse and finally the extermination of the 'valueless' by the state, through measures such as forcible sterilization and even execution, which some of them at least were already advocating before 1914. Finally, such a technocratically rationalistic approach to population management presupposed an entirely secular, instrumental approach to morality. Christian precepts such as the sanctity of marriage and parenthood, or the equal value of every being endowed with an immortal soul, were thrown out of the window. Whatever else such ideas were, they were not traditional or backward-looking. Indeed, some of their proponents, such as Woltmann and Schallmayer, thought of themselves as being on the left rather than the right of the political spectrum, although their ideas were shared by very few of the Social Democrats. Fundamentally, racial hygiene was born of a new drive for society to be governed by scientific principles irrespective of all other considerations. It represented a new variant of German nationalism, one which was never likely to be shared by conservatives or reactionaries, or endorsed by the Christian Churches or indeed by any form of organized or established religion.[84]

Both antisemitism and racial hygiene were to be key components of Nazi ideology. They were both part of a general secularization of thought in the late nineteenth century, aspects of a far wider rebellion against what increasing numbers of writers and thinkers were coming to see as the stolid and stultifying complacency of the liberal, bourgeois attitudes that had dominated Germany in the middle part of the century. The self-satisfaction of so many educated and middle-class Germans at the achievement of nationhood in the 1870s was giving way to a variety of dissatisfactions born of a feeling that Germany's spiritual and political development had come to a halt and needed pushing forward again. These were expressed forcefully by the sociologist Max Weber's inaugural lecture, in which he dubbed the unification of 1871 a 'youthful prank' of the German nation.[85] The most influential prophet of such views was the philosopher Friedrich Nietzsche, who railed in powerful, punchy prose against the ethical conservatism of his day. In many ways he was a comparable figure to Wagner, whom he hugely admired for much of his life. Like Wagner, he was a complex figure whose work was capable of being interpreted in a wide variety of senses. His writings argued for the individual to be freed from the conventional moral restrictions of the time. They were commonly interpreted before 1914 as a call for personal emancipation. They had a strong influence on a variety of liberal and radical groups, including, for example, the feminist movement, where one of the most imaginative figures, Helene Stöcker, penned numerous essays in sub-Nietzschean prose, declaring the master's message to be that women should be free to develop their own sexuality outside marriage, with the aid of mechanical contraceptives and equal rights for illegitimate children.[86]

Yet others took a different lesson altogether from the writings of the great philosopher. Nietzsche was a vigorous opponent of antisemitism, he was deeply critical of the vulgar worship of power and success which had resulted (in his view) from the unification of Germany by military force in 1871, and his most famous concepts, such as the 'will to power' and the 'superman' were intended by him to apply only to the sphere of thought and ideas, not to politics or action. But the power of his prose allowed such phrases to be reduced all too easily to slogans, ripped from their philosophical context and applied in ways of which he would have greatly disapproved. His concept of an ideal human being, freed from moral constraints and triumphing through will-power over the weak, could be appropriated without too much difficulty by those who believed, as he did not, in the breeding of the human race according to racial and eugenic criteria. Central to such interpretations was the influence of his sister Elisabeth Förster, who vulgarized and popularized his ideas, emphasizing their brutal, elitist aspects, and made them palatable to extreme right-wing nationalists. Writers such as Ernst Bertram, Alfred Bäumler and Hans Günther reduced Nietzsche to a prophet of power, and his concept of the superman to a plea for the coming of a great German leader unfettered by moral constraints or Christian theology.[87]

Others, drawing on German anthropological studies of indigenous societies in New Guinea and other parts of the German colonial empire, took Nietzsche's spiritual elitism a step further and called for the creation of a new society ruled by a band of brothers, an elite of vigorous young men who would rule the state rather like a medieval knightly brother-hood. In this deeply misogynistic view of the world, women would have no role to play except to breed the elite of the future, a belief shared in less radical ways by many of the eugenicists and racial hygienists. Academic writers like Heinrich Schurtz propagated the ideology of the band of brothers through a variety of publications, but it had its greatest effect in areas such as the youth movement, in which young, mostly middle-class men devoted themselves to hiking, communing with nature, singing nationalist songs around camp fires and pouring scorn on the staid politics, hypocritical morality and social artificiality of the adult world. Writers such as Hans Blüher, strongly influenced by the youth movement, went to even greater extremes in their plea for the state to be reorganized along anti-democratic lines and led by a close-knit group of heroic men united by homoerotic ties of love and affection. Advocates of such ideas already began to found pseudo-monastic, conspiratorial organizations before the First World War, notably the Germanic Order, established in 1912. In the world of such tiny secular sects, 'Aryan' symbolism and ritual played a central role, as their members reclaimed runes and sun-worship as essential signs of Germanness, and adopted the Indian symbol of the swastika as an 'Aryan' device, under the influence of the Munich poet Alfred Schuler and the race theorist Lanz von Liebenfels, who flew a swastika flag from his castle in Austria in 1907. Strange though ideas like these were, their influence on many young middle-class men who passed through the youth movement organizations before the First World War should not be underestimated. If nothing else, they contributed to a widespread revolt against bourgeois convention in the generation born in the 1890s and 1900s.[88]

What such currents of thought emphasized was in sharp contrast to the bourgeois virtues of sobriety and self-restraint, and diametrically opposite to the principles on which liberal nationalism rested, such as freedom of thought, representative government, tolerance for the opinions of others and the fundamental rights of the individual. The great majority of Germans still most probably believed in these things at the turn of the century. Certainly Germany's most popular political party, the Social Democrats, regarded itself as the guardian of the principles which the German liberals, in their view, had so signally failed to defend. The liberals themselves were still very much a force to be reckoned with, and there were even signs of a modest liberal revival in the last years of peace before 1914.[89] But already by this time, serious attempts had begun to weld together some of the ideas of extreme nationalism, antisemitism and the revolt against convention into a new synthesis, and to give it organizational shape. The political maelstrom of radical ideologies out of which Nazism would eventually emerge was already swirling powerfully well before the First World War.[90]

THE SPIRIT OF 1914

I

Across the border, in German-speaking Austria, another version of radical antisemitism was provided by Georg Ritter von Schönerer, the son of a railway engineer who had been given a title of nobility by the Habsburg Emperor as a reward for his services to the state. The year after its defeat by Prussia in 1866, the Habsburg monarchy had restructured itself into two equal halves, Austria and Hungary, bound together by the person of the Emperor, Franz Josef, and his central administration in Vienna. That administration was staffed overwhelmingly by German-speakers, and the six million or so Austrian Germans reconciled themselves to their expulsion from the German Confederation by identifying strongly with the Habsburgs and regarding themselves as the Empire's ruling group. But Schönerer was not satisfied with this. 'If only we belonged to the German Empire!' he exclaimed in the Austrian Parliament in 1878. A radical, improving landlord, Schönerer was a proponent of universal manhood suffrage, the complete secularization of education, the nationalization of the railways – a reflection, perhaps, of his father's occupation – and state support for small farmers and artisans. He regarded the Hungarians and the other nationalities in the Habsburg monarchy as brakes on the progress of the Germans, who would, he thought, do far better economically and socially in a union with the German Reich.[91]

As time went on, Schönerer's belief in German racial superiority became allied to an increasingly intense form of antisemitism. He augmented his eleven-point German-nationalist Linz Programme of 1879 with a twelfth point in 1885, demanding 'the removal of Jewish influence from all sections of public life' as a precondition for the reforms he wanted to achieve. Schönerer's presence in the Austrian Parliament allowed him to campaign against the influence of Jews in, for example, railway companies, and gave him immunity from prosecution when he used extravagant language to condemn them. He founded a series of organizations to propagate his views, and one of them, the Pan-German Association, succeeded in getting twenty-one deputies elected to the Parliament in 1901. It soon broke up amid bitter personal quarrels among the leadership. But its example spawned other antisemitic organizations as well. Its constant harping upon the supposedly evil influence of the Jews made it easier for a cynical communal politician such as the Christian-Social conservative Karl Lueger to use antisemitic demagogy to win enough support to install him as Mayor of Vienna on behalf of the rising right-wing Christian Social Party in 1897. Lueger held this post for the next decade, stamping his influence indelibly on the city through a mixture of rabble-rousing populism and imaginative, socially progressive municipal reform.[92]

Schönerer never enjoyed this kind of popular support. But where Lueger's antisemitism, though influential, was essentially opportunistic – 'I decide who's a Yid', he once famously said, when criticized for dining with influential Jews in Vienna – Schönerer's was visceral and unyielding. He proclaimed antisemitism, indeed, 'the greatest achievement of the century'.[93] As time went on, his ideas became even more extreme. Describing himself as a pagan, Schönerer spearheaded an anti-Catholic movement under the slogan 'away from Rome', and coined the pseudo-medieval greeting 'hail!' – *Heil!* – using it in Parliament, to the general outrage of the deputies, in 1902, when he ended a speech by declaring his allegiance to the German rather than the Austrian royal family – 'Up with and hail to the Hohenzollerns!' Schönerer's followers called him 'the Leader' (*Führer*), another term which his movement probably introduced into the political vocabulary of the far right. He proposed to rename annual festivals and the months of the year by Germanic titles such as 'Yulefest' (Christmas) and 'Haymoon' (June). Even more eccentric was his proposal for a new calendar dating from the defeat of a Roman army by the Germanic Cimbri at the battle of Noreia in 118 BC. Schönerer actually held a (not very successful) festival to inaugurate the new millennium with the year 2001 n.N. (the initials standing for *nach Noreia*, 'after Noreia').[94]

Schönerer was an uncompromising racial antisemite. 'Religion's all the same, it's race that is to blame', was one of his typically catchy slogans. His extremism got him into trouble with the authorities on more than one occasion, notably in 1888, when a false newspaper report of the death of Kaiser Wilhelm I caused him to storm into the guilty newspaper's offices and physically attack members of its staff. After he had publicly toasted Wilhelm as 'our glorious Emperor', the outraged Habsburg Emperor, Franz Josef, deprived him of his noble title, while the Parliament waived his immunity so that he could serve a four-month term in gaol. This did not prevent him from declaring after his release that 'he longed for the day when a German army would march into Austria and destroy it'. Such extremism meant that Schönerer never really left the fringes of politics. In 1907, indeed, he failed to secure re-election to the Austrian Parliament and the number of deputies who followed his line dwindled to three. Schönerer was perhaps more interested in spreading ideas than in winning power. But in this guise, he was to have a considerable influence on Nazism later on.[95]

Antisemitism in Austria was far from being a separate phenomenon from its German counterpart. The common language and common culture with Germany, and the fact that Austria had been part of the 'Holy Roman Reich of the German Nation' for over a thousand years, and then of the German Confederation until its rude expulsion by Bismarck in 1866, meant that intellectual and political influences crossed the border without too much difficulty. Schönerer, for example, was a self-confessed disciple of the German antisemite Eugen Dühring. Citizens of the German Reich, particularly in the Catholic south, who looked to Vienna for inspiration, could not help but notice Lueger's combination of social reform, Catholic allegiance and antisemitic rhetoric. Schönerer's racial definition of the Jews, his cult of the 'Aryan' myth, his avowed paganism and distaste for Christianity, his belief in the superiority of the Germans and his contempt for other races, especially the Slavs, were in part shared by the more extreme antisemites within the German Empire. None of his ideas could be seen as alien; they were essentially part of the same extremist current of thought. Schönerer's Pan-Germanism doomed him to failure while the Habsburg monarchy continued to exist. But if it should ever fall, then its German-speaking minorities would be confronted in an acute form with the question of whether they wanted to join the

German Reich or form a separate state on their own. In this eventuality, Pan-Germanism would come into its own.

II

In the German Reich itself, the accession of Kaiser Wilhelm II in 1888 quickly led to a serious weakening of Bismarck's position as Reich Chancellor. When the two differed over the renewal or the lapsing of the Anti-Socialist Law, with its manifold restrictions on civil liberties, Bismarck was forced to resign. The lapsing of the law gave rise to a whole range of new social and political movements in all parts of the political spectrum. New, colourful figures appeared on the political scene, contrasting with the drabness of Bismarck's immediate successors as Chancellor, Caprivi and Hohenlohe. Among them was one at least who attracted admiration as precisely the kind of hero the German nationalists were looking for. Carl Peters was a classic colonial adventurer of the late nineteenth century, whose exploits quickly became the stuff of legend. When Bismarck reluctantly acquired nominal German colonies in 1884, Peters set out to turn his paper conquests into real ones. On reaching the East African coast, he organized an expedition and departed for the interior, where he concluded a number of treaties with indigenous rulers. Characteristically, he had neglected to consult the German government about this, and Bismarck repudiated the treaties when he heard about them. Peters got into further trouble when it was revealed that he had not only been maltreating his bearers but had also had sexual relations with African women. Reports of his misdemeanours shocked bourgeois opinion. But this did not deter Peters from pursuing his quest to found a great German Empire in Africa.[96]

Peters's fertile imagination and restless spirit led him to found a variety of organizations, including a Society for German Colonization in 1884, which merged with a like-minded group in 1887 to form the German Colonial Society. Such was Peters's prominence, combined with the influence of his supporters, that Bismarck felt obliged to recognize his East African venture and declare a German protectorate over the areas he had explored, the first step in the creation of the German colony of Tanganyika. In 1890, however, Bismarck's successor Leo von Caprivi agreed to surrender some of the territory Peters had claimed, most notably the island of Zanzibar, to the British in return for their cession to Germany of the North Sea island of Heligoland. Outraged, Peters chaired a meeting organized early in 1891 by a group of nationalists including the young civil servant Alfred Hugenberg, who was later to play a fateful role in the rise and triumph of Nazism. They founded a General German League, renamed the Pan-German League in 1894. The aim of the new organization was to push vigorously for German expansion abroad and the Germanization of national minorities at home. In this it was joined in 1894 by the Society for the Eastern Marches; this group, which had relatively close ties with government compared to those enjoyed by the Pan-Germans, devoted itself to the destruction of Polish identity in Germany's eastern provinces. Another, not dissimilar organization, founded in 1881 in response to struggles over official languages in the Habsburg monarchy, was the German School Association, which sought to preserve the German language in areas of German settlement outside the boundaries of the Reich; it was later renamed the Association for Germandom Abroad, in recognition of a substantial broadening of its remit to cover all aspects of German culture in the rest of the world.[97]

More nationalist associations were to follow. The most significant, perhaps, was the Navy League, founded in 1898 with money from the arms manufacturer Krupp, who had an obvious interest in the construction of a big German navy being approved by the Reichstag at the time. Within a decade it was dwarfing the other nationalist groups, with a membership totalling well over 300,000 if affiliated organizations were counted as well. By contrast, the other nationalist pressure-groups were seldom able to exceed a membership of around 50,000, and the Pan-Germans seemed to be permanently stuck below the 20,000 mark.[98] Most of these pressure-groups were run by professional agitators like August Keim, an army officer whose journalistic activities had caused him promotion problems. Such men were prominent in a number of nationalist associations and often provided their radical driving force; Keim, for example, was a leading figure in both the Navy League and the Defence League and founded other, less well known associations such as the German League for the Prevention of the Emancipation of Women (1912), which aimed to send women back to the home to bear more children for the Reich.[99]

Alongside such marginal men were ranged disgruntled notables seeking a new outlet for their political drive in an increasingly democratic world, where the deference to the propertied and the educated that had sustained the electoral fortunes of the National Liberals and other parties further to the right from the 1860s to the 1880s no longer functioned effectively. Many of these agitators had achieved their status by working hard to get a university degree then moving up slowly through the ranks of the less fashionable parts of the civil service. Here, too, a degree of social anxiety was an important driving force. Identification, perhaps over-identification, with the German nation gave all the leading figures in the nationalist associations, whatever their background, a sense of pride and belonging, and an object for commitment and mobilization.[100] The membership of these various organizations also frequently overlapped, and it was far from unusual for two or more of them to make common cause in a particular political fight despite their frequent personal and political rivalries.

Alongside the specific aims that each organization followed, and irrespective of the frequent internal rows which plagued them, the nationalist associations generally agreed that Bismarck's work of building the German nation was woefully incomplete and urgently needed to be pushed to its conclusion. Increasingly, too, they began to think that the Reich leadership was failing to do its duty in this respect. The nationalists' beliefs were laid bare in a particularly dramatic way in 1912, when the Chairman of the Pan-German League, the lawyer Heinrich Class, writing under a pseudonym, published a manifesto with the arresting title: *If I Were the Kaiser*. He was not modest in his aims. If he had the power wielded by Wilhelm II, Class let it be known, he would deal first of all with the internal enemies of the Reich, the Social Democrats and the Jews. The Social Democratic victory in the Reichstag elections earlier in the year was, he thundered, the result of a Jewish conspiracy to undermine the nation. The Jews were subverting German art, destroying German creativity, corrupting the German masses. If he were Kaiser, Class wrote, they would immediately lose their civil rights and be classified as aliens. The Social Democrats would be banned and their leading officials, parliamentary deputies, newspaper editors and union secretaries would be expelled from Germany. The Reichstag suffrage would be restructured so as to give more voting power to the educated and the propertied, and only the best men would be allowed to bear office. National rallies and patriotic festivals would rally the mass of the people to the national cause.[101]

Internal pacification, the nationalists argued, would include the suppression of minority cultures such as that of the Poles in the eastern provinces of Prussia, driving them from their landholdings, banning the use of their language, and using force if necessary to bring the supposedly inferior and uncivilized 'Slavs' to heel. Led by Class, the Pan-Germans and their allies advocated a massive arms build-up, greater even than that already launched by the Navy Laws from 1898 onwards. This would be followed by a war in which Germany would conquer Europe and annex German-speaking areas such as Switzerland, the Netherlands, Belgium, Luxemburg and Austria. They brushed aside any consideration for the other nationalities who inhabited these areas, and passed over the linguistic and cultural differences that made it unlikely that even Flemish separatists in Belgium, let alone other kinds of political dissident, would support them. They added on Romania for strategic reasons. And they noted that the Belgian and Dutch overseas possessions, including, for example, the Congo, would provide the basis for a massive new colonial empire that would far outweigh its British counterpart. Borrowing eclectically from Nietzsche, Langbehn, Darwin, Treitschke and other writers, and frequently vulgarizing their ideas in the process, wrenching them out of context, or simplifying them to the point of unrecognizability, the Pan-Germans and their nationalist allies founded their ideology on a world-view that had struggle, conflict, 'Aryan' ethnic superiority, anti-semitism and the will to power as its core beliefs.[102]

However, at the same time as they harboured these almost limitless ambitions for German world domination, the Pan-German League and the other nationalist associations also sounded a strong note of alarm, even despondency, about Germany's current state and future prospects. The German people, they believed, were surrounded by enemies, from the 'Slavs' and 'Latins' encircling Germany from without, to the Jews, Jesuits, socialists and sundry subversive agitators and conspirators undermining it from within. Pan-German racism was expressed in the linguistic usage through which they reduced every nation to a simple, uniformly acting racial entity – 'Germandom', 'Slavdom', 'Anglo-Saxondom' or 'Jewdom'. Other races were outbreeding the Germans and threatening to 'flood' them; or, like the French, they were declining and therefore exerting a corrupting influence through their decadence. The extreme nationalists portrayed themselves as voices in the wilderness; unless they were heard, it would be too late. Desperate peril demanded desperate remedies. Only by a return to the racial roots of the German nation in the peasantry, the self-employed artisan and small businessman, and the traditional nuclear family, could the situation be rescued. The big cities were sinks of un-German immorality and disorder. Strong measures were needed to restore order, decency and a properly German concept of culture. A new Bismarck was needed, tough, ruthless, unafraid to pursue aggressive policies at home and abroad, if the nation was to be saved.[103]

As time went on, the nationalist associations became more vocal in their criticism of the German government for what they regarded as its weakness at home and abroad. Jolted into radical action by the Social Democratic election victory of 1912, following on what they regarded as the humiliating outcome for Germany of an international crisis over Morocco the previous year, the usually quarrelsome nationalist associations joined forces in support for the newly founded Defence League, which aimed to do for the army what the Navy League had done for the fleet. The new organization was far more independent from the government than the Navy League was; it shared in full the views of the Pan-Germans, and it achieved a membership of 90,000 within two years of its foundation in 1912, giving the Pan-Germans the kind of mass base they had always failed to create for themselves. Meanwhile, the Pan-Germans launched a joint campaign with the Colonial Society to persuade the government to stop recognizing the legal validity of marriages between German settlers and black Africans in the colonies. Prominent members of the Conservative Party began to work with the Pan-Germans. In August 1913 the Agrarian League, a huge pressure-group of large and small landowners with very close ties to the Conservatives, joined with the Central Association of German Industrialists and the national organization of artisans and handicraftsmen to form the 'Cartel of Productive Estates'. Not only did the Cartel have a membership running into the millions, it also incorporated many of the central aims and beliefs of the Pan-Germans, including the sidelining or elimination of the Reichstag, the suppression of the Social Democrats and the pursuit of an aggressive foreign policy up to and including the launching of a major war of conquest.[104]

These extreme nationalist pressure-groups were not the product of any kind of manipulative strategy by Wilhelmine elites; they were a genuinely populist movement of political mobilization from below. But they had no constituency at all in the working class; the furthest their reservoir of support went down the social scale was to white-collar workers and clerks, one of whose trade unions, the virulently antisemitic German-National Commercial Employees' Union, railed against the Jewish business interests which they supposed were keeping their members' wages down, and attacked the intrusion of women into secretarial and administrative positions as the product of Jewish attempts to destroy the German family.[105] Yet the new prominence of the nationalist associations from 1912 onwards put huge pressure on the German government. It became even greater as the Pan-Germans won new friends in the right-wing press. One of the Pan-Germans' supporters, the retired general Konstantin von Gebsattel, impressed by *If I Were the Kaiser*, composed a lengthy memorandum calling for a fight against 'Jewish machinations and rabble-rousing by Social Democratic leaders', a Reich that was 'not parliamentarian', a Kaiser who really ruled instead of being just a figurehead and conducted an aggressive foreign policy with an 'armoured fist', and a franchise which restricted the influence of the masses to a minimum.

In the proposals put forward in the memorandum, Jews were to be treated as aliens, barred from acquiring land and deprived of their property if they emigrated. They were to be excluded from state-run professions such as the civil service, the law, the universities and the army. Baptism, of course, made no difference to the fact that someone was a Jew in Gebsattel's eyes; anyone with more than a quarter of 'Jewish blood' in his or her veins was to be treated as a Jew and not a German. The 'Jewish press' was to be closed down. All this was necessary because, he said, the whole life of Germany was dominated by 'the Jewish spirit', which was superficial, negative, destructively critical and materialistic. It was time for the true German spirit to re-emerge – deep, positive and idealistic. All this was to be brought about by an effective *coup d'état* from above, secured by the declaration of a military state of siege and the introduction of martial law. Gebsattel and his friend the Pan-German leader Heinrich Class regarded the memorandum as moderate in tone.

The alleged moderation had a reason; the idea was to send it to Crown Prince Friedrich Wilhelm, the heir to the throne, who was known for his sympathies with the nationalist cause. He in turn forwarded it with enthusiasm to his father and to the man currently holding the office of state once occupied by Bismarck, Reich Chancellor Theobald von Bethmann Hollweg.[106]

Bethmann and the Kaiser courteously but firmly rejected Gebsattel's ideas, regarding them as impractical and indeed dangerous to the stability of the monarchy. The Reich Chancellor admitted that the 'Jewish Question' was an area in which there were 'great dangers for Germany's further development'. But, he went on, Gebsattel's draconian solutions could not be taken seriously. The Kaiser poured more cold water on the proposals by warning his son that Gebsattel was a 'weird enthusiast' whose ideas were often 'downright childish'. Still, he too conceded that even if it was economically inadvisable to expel the Jews from Germany, it was important to 'exclude the Jewish influence from the army and the administration and as far as possible to limit it in all the activities of art and literature'. In the press, too, he considered, 'Jewdom has found its most dangerous happy-hunting-ground', though a general restriction of press freedom as advocated by Gebsattel would, he thought, be counter-productive. Antisemitic stereotypes had thus penetrated to the highest levels of the state, reinforced in the Kaiser's case by his own reading of Houston Stewart Chamberlain's *The Foundations of the Nineteenth Century*, which he praised as a wake-up call to the German nation. Moreover, as the Pan-Germans, undeterred, stepped up their criticism of the Chancellor both in public and behind the scenes, Bethmann felt increasingly constrained to adopt a tough line in his foreign policy, with fateful results in the crisis that led to the outbreak of the First World War in August 1914.[107]

III

Like other European nations, Germany went into the First World War in an optimistic mood, fully expecting to win, most probably in a relatively short space of time. Military men like the War Minister, Erich von Falkenhayn, expected a longer conflict and even feared that Germany

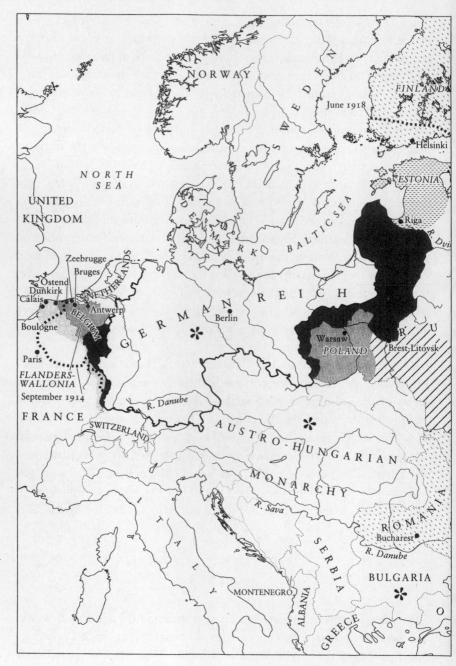

Map 2. German Expansion in the First World War

might eventually be defeated. But their expert view did not communicate itself to the masses or, indeed, to many of the politicians in whose hands Germany's destiny lay.[108] The mood of invincibility was buoyed up by the massive growth of the German economy over the previous decades, and fired on by the stunning victories of the German army in 1914–15 on the Eastern Front. An early Russian invasion of East Prussia led the Chief of the German General Staff to appoint a retired general, Paul von Hindenburg, born in 1847 and a veteran of the war of 1870–71, to take over the campaign with the aid of his Chief of Staff, Erich Ludendorff, a technical expert and military engineer of non-noble origins who had won a reputation for himself with the attack on Liège at the beginning of the war. The two generals enticed the invading Russian armies into a trap and annihilated them, following this with a string of further victories. By the end of September 1915 the Germans had conquered Poland, inflicted huge losses on the Russian armies and driven them back over 250 miles from the positions they had occupied the previous year.

These achievements made the reputation of Hindenburg as a virtually invincible general. A cult of the hero quickly developed around him, and his massive, stolid presence seemed to provide an element of stability amid the changing fortunes of war. But he was in fact a man of limited political vision and ability. He acted in many ways as a front for his energetic subordinate Ludendorff, whose ideas about the conduct of the war were far more radical and ruthless than his own. The pair's triumphs in the East contrasted sharply with the stalemate in the West, where within a few months of the outbreak of war, some eight million troops were facing each other along 450 miles of trenches from the North Sea to the Swiss border, unable to penetrate to a meaningful degree into the enemy lines. The soft ground allowed them to construct line after line of deep defensive trenches. Barbed-wire entanglements impeded the enemy's advance. And machine-gun emplacements all along the line mowed down any troops from the other side that succeeded in getting close enough to be shot at. Both sides threw increasing resources into this futile struggle. By 1916 the strain was beginning to tell.

In all the major combatant nations, there was a change of leadership in the middle years of the war, reflecting a perceived need for greater energy and ruthlessness in mobilizing the nation and its resources. In France, Clemenceau came to power, in Britain Lloyd George. In Germany, characteristically, it was not a radical civilian politician, but the two most successful generals, Hindenburg and Ludendorff, who took over the reins of power in 1916. The 'Hindenburg Programme' attempted to galvanize and reorganize the German economy to bend it to the overriding purpose of winning the war. Run by another middle-class general, Wilhelm Groener, the War Office co-opted the trade unions and civilian politicians in the task of mobilization. But this was anathema to the industrialists and the other generals. Groener was soon dispensed with. Pushing the civilian politicians aside, Hindenburg and Ludendorff established a 'silent dictatorship' in Germany, with military rule behind the scenes, severe curbs on civil liberties, central control of the economy and the generals calling the shots in the formulation of war aims and foreign policy. All of these developments were to provide significant precedents for the more drastic fate that overtook German democracy and civil freedom less than two decades later.[109]

The turn to a more ruthless prosecution of the war was counter-productive in more than one sense. Ludendorff ordered a systematic economic exploitation of the areas of France, Belgium and East-Central Europe occupied by German troops. The occupied countries' memory of this was to cost the Germans dearly at the end of the war. The generals' inflexible and ambitious war aims alienated many Germans in the liberal centre and on the left. And the decision at the beginning of 1917 to undertake unrestricted submarine warfare in the Atlantic in order to cut off British supplies from the United States only provoked the Americans to enter the war on the Allied side. From 1917, the mobilization of the world's richest economy began to weigh heavily on the Allied side, and by the end of the year American troops were coming onto the Western Front in ever increasing numbers. The only really bright spot from the German point of view was the continuing string of military successes in the East.

But these, too, had a price. The relentless military pressure of the German armies and their allies in the East bore fruit early in 1917 in the collapse of the inefficient and unpopular administration of the Russian Tsar Nicholas II and its replacement with a Provisional Government in the hands of Russian liberals. These proved no more capable than the Tsar, however, of mobilizing Russia's huge resources for a successful war. With near-famine conditions at home, chaos in the administration and growing defeat and despair at the front, the mood in Moscow and St Petersburg turned increasingly against the war, and the already precarious legitimacy of the Provisional Government began to disappear into thin air. The chief beneficiary of this situation was the only political grouping in Russia that had offered consistent opposition to the war from the very beginning: the Bolshevik Party, an extremist, tightly organized, ruthlessly single-minded Marxist group whose leader, Vladimir Ilyich Lenin, had argued all along that defeat in war was the quickest way to bring about a revolution. Seizing his chance, he organized a swift coup in the autumn of 1917 that met with little immediate resistance.

The 'October Revolution' soon degenerated into bloody chaos. When opponents of the Bolsheviks attempted a counter-coup, the new regime responded with a violent 'red terror'. All other parties were suppressed. A centralized dictatorship under Lenin's leadership was established. A newly formed Red Army led by Leon Trotsky fought a bitter Civil War against the 'Whites', who aimed to re-establish the Tsarist regime. Their efforts could not help the Tsar himself, whom the Bolsheviks quickly put to death, along with his family. The Bolsheviks' political police organization, the Cheka, ruthlessly suppressed the regime's opponents from every part of the political spectrum, from the moderate socialist Mensheviks, the anarchists and the peasant Social Revolutionaries on the left to liberals, conservatives and Tsarists on the right. Thousands were tortured, killed or brutally imprisoned in the first camps in what was to become a vast system of confinement by the 1930s.[110]

Lenin's regime eventually triumphed, seeing off the 'Whites' and their supporters, and establishing its control over much of the former Tsarist Empire. The Bolshevik leader and his successors moved to construct their version of a communist state and society, with the socialization of the economy representing, in theory at least, common ownership of property, the abolition of religion guaranteeing a secular, socialist consciousness, the confiscation of private wealth creating a classless society, and the establishment of 'democratic centralism' and a planned economy giving unprecedented, dictatorial powers to the central administration in Moscow. All this, however, was happening in a state and society that Lenin knew to be economically backward and lacking in modern resources. More advanced economies, like that of Germany, had in his view more developed social systems, in which revolution was even more likely to break out than had been the case in Russia. Indeed, Lenin believed that the Russian Revolution could scarcely survive unless successful revolutions of the same type took place elsewhere as well.[111]

So the Bolsheviks formed a Communist International ('Comintern') to propagate their version of revolution in the rest of the world. In doing so they could take advantage of the fact that socialist movements in many countries had split over the issues raised by the war. In Germany in particular, the once-monolithic Social Democratic Party, which began by supporting the war as a mainly defensive operation against the threat from the East, had been beset by increasing doubts as the scale of the annexations demanded by the government began to become clear. In 1916 the party split into pro-war and anti-war factions. The majority continued, with reservations, to support the war and to propagate moderate reforms rather than wholesale revolution. Amongst the minority of 'Independent Social Democrats', a few, led by Karl Liebknecht and Rosa Luxemburg, founded the German Communist Party in December 1918. They were eventually joined by the mass of the minority's supporters in the early 1920s.[112]

It would be difficult to exaggerate the fear and terror that these events spread amongst many parts of the population in Western and Central Europe. The middle and upper classes were alarmed by the radical rhetoric of the Communists and saw their counterparts in Russia lose their property and disappear into the torture chambers and prison camps of the Cheka. Social Democrats were terrified that if the Communists came to power in their own country they would meet the fate suffered by the moderate socialist Mensheviks and the peasant-oriented Social Revolutionaries in Moscow and St Petersburg. Democrats everywhere were conscious from the outset that Communism was intent on suppressing human rights, dismantling representative institutions and abolishing civil freedoms. Terror led them to believe that Communism in their own countries should be stopped at any cost, even by violent means and through the abrogation of the very civil liberties they were pledged to defend. In the eyes of the right, Communism and Social Democracy amounted to two sides of the same coin, and the one seemed no less a threat than the other. In Hungary, a short-lived Communist regime under Béla Kun took power in 1918, tried to abolish the Church, and was swiftly overthrown by the monarchists led by Admiral Miklós Horthy.

The counter-revolutionary regime proceeded to institute a 'White terror' in which thousands of Bolsheviks and socialists were arrested, brutally maltreated, imprisoned and killed. Events in Hungary gave Central Europeans for the first time a taste of the new levels of political violence and conflict that were to emerge from the tensions created by the war.[113]

In Germany itself, the threat of Communism still seemed relatively remote at the beginning of 1918. Lenin and the Bolsheviks quickly negotiated a much-needed peace settlement to give themselves the breathing-space they required to consolidate their newly won power. The Germans drove a hard bargain, annexing huge swathes of territory from the Russians at the Treaty of Brest-Litovsk early in 1918. As large numbers of German troops were transferred from the now-redundant Eastern Front to reinforce a new spring offensive in the West, final victory seemed just around the corner. In his annual proclamation to the German people in August 1918, the Kaiser assured everybody that the worst of the war was over. This was true enough, but not in the sense he intended.[114] For the huge blood-letting that Ludendorff's spring offensive had caused in the German army opened the way for the Allies, reinforced by massive numbers of fresh American troops and supplies, to breach German lines and advance rapidly along the Western Front. Morale in the German army started to collapse, and ever-larger numbers of troops began to desert or surrender to the Allies. The final blows came as Germany's ally Bulgaria sued for peace and the Habsburg armies in the South began to melt away in the face of renewed Italian attacks.[115] Hindenburg and Ludendorff were obliged to inform the Kaiser at the end of September that defeat was inevitable. A massive tightening of censorship ensured that newspapers continued to hold out the prospect of final victory for some time afterwards when in reality it had long since disappeared. The shock waves sent out by the news of Germany's defeat were therefore all the greater.[116] They were to prove too strong for what remained of the political system of the empire that Bismarck had created in 1871.

It was in this cauldron of war and revolution that Nazism was forged. A mere fifteen years separated the defeat of Germany in 1918 from the advent of the Third Reich in 1933. Yet there were to be many twists and turns along the way. The triumph of Hitler was by no means inevitable in 1918, any more than it had been pre-programmed by the previous course of German history. The creation of the German Reich and its rise to economic might and Great Power status had created expectations in many people, expectations that, it was clear by this time, the Reich and its institutions were unable to fulfil. The example of Bismarck as a supposedly ruthless, tough leader who was not afraid to use violence and deception to gain his ends, was present in the minds of many, and the determination with which he had acted to curb the democratizing threat of political Catholicism and the socialist labour movement was widely admired in the Protestant middle classes. The 'silent dictatorship' of Hindenburg and Ludendorff had put the precepts of ruthless, authoritarian rule into practice at a moment of supreme national crisis in 1916 and created an ominous precedent for the future.

The legacy of the German past was a burdensome one in many respects. But it did not make the rise and triumph of Nazism inevitable. The shadows cast by Bismarck might eventually have been dispelled. By the time the First World War came to an end, however, they had deepened almost immeasurably. The problems bequeathed to the German political system by Bismarck and his successors were made infinitely worse by the effects of the war; and to these problems were added others that boded even more trouble for the future. Without the war, Nazism would not have emerged as a serious political force, nor would so many Germans have sought so desperately for an authoritarian alternative to the civilian politics that seemed so signally to have failed Germany in its hour of need. So high were the stakes for which everybody was playing in 1914–18, that both right and left were prepared to take measures of an extremism only dreamed of by figures on the margins of politics before the war. Massive recriminations about where the responsibility for Germany's defeat should lie only deepened political conflict. Sacrifice, privation, death, on a huge scale, left Germans of all political hues bitterly searching for the reason why. The almost unimaginable financial expense of the war created a vast economic burden on the world economy which it was unable to shake off for another thirty years, and it fell most heavily upon Germany. The orgies of national hatred in which all combatant nations had indulged during the war left a terrible legacy of bitterness for the future. Yet as the German armies drifted home, and the Kaiser's regime prepared reluctantly to hand over to a democratic successor, there still seemed everything to play for.

DESCENT INTO CHAOS

I

In November 1918 most Germans expected that, since the war was being brought to an end before the Allies had set foot on German soil, the terms on which the peace would be based would be relatively equitable. During the previous four years, debate had raged over the extent of territory Germany should seek to annex after the achievement of victory. Even the official war aims of the government had included the assignment to the Reich of a substantial amount of territory in Western and Eastern Europe, and the establishment of complete German hegemony over the Continent. Pressure-groups on the right went much further.[117] Given the extent of what Germans had expected to gain in the event of victory, it might have been expected that they would have realized what they stood to lose in the event of defeat. But no one was prepared for the peace terms to which Germany was forced to agree in the Armistice of 11 November 1918. All German troops were forced to withdraw east of the Rhine, the German fleet was to be surrendered to the Allies, vast amounts of military equipment had to be handed over, the Treaty of Brest-Litovsk had to be repudiated and the German High Seas Fleet had to be surrendered to the Allies along with all the German submarines. In the meantime, to ensure compliance, the Allies maintained their economic blockade of Germany, worsening an already dire food-supply situation. They did not abandon it until July the following year.[118]

These provisions were almost universally felt in Germany as an unjustified national humiliation. Resentment was hugely increased by the actions taken, above all by the French, to enforce them. The harshness of the Armistice terms was thrown into sharp relief by the fact that many

Germans refused to believe that their armed forces had actually been defeated. Very quickly, aided and abetted by senior army officers themselves, a fateful myth gained currency among large sections of public opinion in the centre and on the right of the political spectrum. Picking up their cue from Richard Wagner's music-drama *The Twilight of the Gods*, many people began to believe that the army had only been defeated because, like Wagner's fearless hero Siegfried, it had been stabbed in the back by its enemies at home. Germany's military leaders Hindenburg and Ludendorff claimed shortly after the war that the army had been the victim of a 'secret, planned, demagogic campaign' which had doomed all its heroic efforts to failure in the end. 'An English general said correctly: the German army was stabbed in the back.'[119] Kaiser Wilhelm II repeated the phrase in his memoirs, written in the 1920s: 'For thirty years the army was my pride. For it I lived, upon it I laboured, and now, after four and a half brilliant years of war with unprecedented victories, it was forced to collapse by the stab-in-the-back from the dagger of the revolutionist, at the very moment when peace was within reach!'[120] Even the Social Democrats contributed to this comforting legend. As the returning troops streamed into Berlin on 10 December 1918, the party leader Friedrich Ebert told them: 'No enemy has overcome you!'[121]

Defeat in war brought about an immediate collapse of the political system created by Bismarck nearly half a century before. After the Russian Revolution of February 1917 had hastened Tsarist despotism to its end, Woodrow Wilson and the Western Allies had begun to proclaim that the war's principal aim was to make the world safe for democracy. Once Ludendorff and the Reich leadership concluded that the war was irremediably lost, they therefore advocated a democratization of the Imperial German political system in order to improve the likelihood of reasonable, even favourable peace terms being agreed by the Allies. As a far from incidental by-product, Ludendorff also reckoned that if the terms were not so acceptable to the German people, the burden of agreeing to them would thereby be placed on Germany's democratic politicians rather than on the Kaiser or the army leadership. A new government was formed under the liberal Prince Max of Baden, but it proved unable to control the navy, whose officers attempted to put to sea in a bid to salvage their honour by going down fighting in a last hopeless battle against the British fleet. Not surprisingly, the sailors mutinied; within a few days the uprisings had spread to the civilian population, and the Kaiser and all the princes, from the King of Bavaria to the grand Duke of Baden, were forced to abdicate. The army simply melted away as the Armistice of 11 November was concluded, and the democratic parties were left, as Ludendorff had intended, to negotiate, if negotiate was the word, the terms of the Treaty of Versailles.[122]

As a result of the Treaty, Germany lost a tenth of its population and 13 per cent of its territory, including Alsace-Lorraine, ceded back to France after nearly half a century under German rule, along with the border territories of Eupen, Malmédy and Moresnet. The Saarland was lopped off from Germany under a mandate with the promise that its people would eventually be able to decide whether they wanted to become part of France; it was clearly expected that in the end they would, at least if the French had anything to do with it. In order to ensure that German armed forces did not enter the Rhineland, British, French and, more briefly, American troops were stationed there in considerable numbers for much of the 1920s. Northern Schleswig went to Denmark, and, in 1920, Memel to Lithuania. The creation of a new Polish state, reversing the partitions of the eighteenth century in which Poland had been gobbled up by Austria, Prussia and Russia, meant the loss to Germany of Posen, much of West Prussia, and Upper Silesia. Danzig became a 'Free City' under the nominal control of the newly founded League of Nations, the forerunner of the United Nations organization established after the Second World War. In order to give the new Poland access to the sea, the peace settlement carved out a 'corridor' of land separating East Prussia from the rest of Germany. Germany's overseas colonies were seized and redistributed under mandates from the League of Nations.[123]

Just as significant, and just as much of a shock, was the refusal of the victorious powers to allow the union of Germany and German-speaking Austria, which would have meant the fulfilment of the radical dreams of 1848. As the constituent nations of the Habsburg Empire broke away at the very end of the war to form the nation-states of Hungary, Czecho-slovakia and Yugoslavia, or to join new or old neighbouring nation-states such as Poland and Romania, the six million or so German-speakers left in Austria proper, sandwiched along and beside the Alps between Germany and Italy, overwhelmingly considered that the best course of action was to join the German Reich. Almost nobody considered rump

Austria to be either politically or economically viable. For decades the vast majority of its population had thought of themselves as the leading ethnic group in the multi-national Habsburg monarchy, and those who, like Schönerer, had advocated the solution of 1848 – splitting away from the rest and joining the German Reich – had been confined to the lunatic fringe. Now, however, Austria was suddenly cut off from the hinterlands, above all in Hungary, on which it had formerly been so dependent economically. It was saddled with a capital city, Vienna, whose population, swollen by suddenly redundant Habsburg bureaucrats and military administrators, constituted over a third of the total living in the new state. What had previously been political eccentricity now seemed to make political sense. Even the Austrian socialists thought that joining the more advanced German Reich would bring socialism nearer to fulfilment than trying to go it alone.[124]

Moreover, the American President Woodrow Wilson had declared, in his celebrated 'Fourteen Points' which he wished the Allied powers to be working for, that every nation should be able to determine its own future, free from interference by others.[125] If this applied to the Poles, the Czechs and the Yugoslavs, then surely it should apply to the Germans as well? But it did not. What, the Allies asked themselves, had they been fighting for, if the German Reich ended the war bigger by six million people and a considerable amount of additional territory, including one of Europe's greatest cities? So the union was vetoed. Of all the territorial provisions of the Treaty, this seemed the most unjust. Proponents and critics of the Allied position could argue over the merits of the other provisions and dispute the fairness or otherwise of the plebiscites that decided the territorial issue in places like Upper Silesia; but on the Austrian issue there was no room for argument at all. The Austrians wanted union; the Germans were prepared to accept union; the principle of national self-determination demanded union. The fact that the Allies forbade union remained a constant source of bitterness in Germany and condemned the new 'Republic of German-Austria', as it was known, to two decades of conflict-ridden, crisis-racked existence in which few of its citizens ever came to believe in its legitimacy.[126]

Many Germans realized that the Allies justified their ban on a German-Austrian union, as so much else in the Treaty of Versailles, by Article 231, which obliged Germany to accept the 'sole guilt' for the outbreak

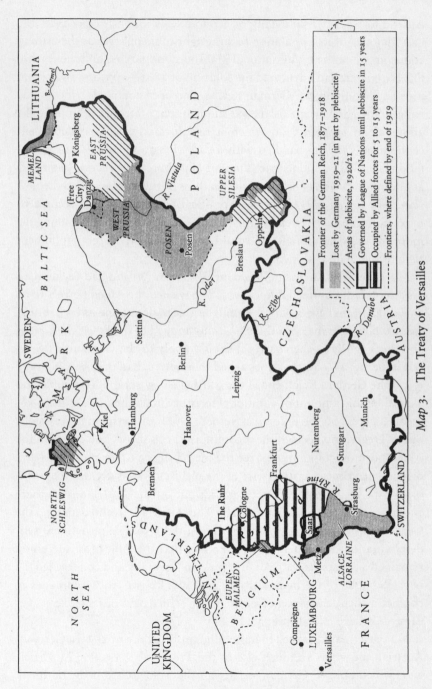

Map 3. The Treaty of Versailles

of the war in 1914. Other articles, equally offensive to Germans, ordained the trial of the Kaiser and many others for war crimes. Significant atrocities had indeed been committed by German troops during the invasions of Belgium and northern France in 1914. But the few trials that did take place, in Leipzig, before a German court, almost uniformly failed because the German judiciary did not accept the legitimacy of most of the charges. Out of 900 alleged war criminals initially singled out for trial, only seven were eventually found guilty, while ten were acquitted and the rest never underwent a full trial. The idea took root in Germany that the whole concept of war crimes, indeed the whole notion of laws of war, was a polemical invention of the victorious Allies based on mendacious propaganda about imaginary atrocities. This left a fateful legacy for the attitudes and conduct of German armed forces during the Second World War.[127]

The real purpose of Article 231, however, was to legitimize the imposition by the Allies of punitive financial reparations on Germany in order to compensate the French and the Belgians, in particular, for the damage caused by four and a quarter years of German occupation They seized over two million tons of merchant ships, five thousand railway engines and 136,000 coaches, 24 million tons of coal and much more. Financial reparations were to be paid in gold over a number of years stretching far into the future.[128] Just in case this did not prevent Germany from financing a reconstruction of its armed might, the Treaty also obliged the army to be restricted to a maximum strength of 100,000, and banned the use of tanks, heavy artillery and conscription. Six million German rifles, over 15,000 aeroplanes, more than 130,000 machine guns and a great deal of other military equipment had to be destroyed. The German navy was effectively dismantled and barred from building any large new ships, and Germany was not allowed to have an air force at all. Such were the terms with which the Germans were presented as the condition of peace by the Western Allies in 1918–19.[129]

II

All of this was greeted with incredulous horror by the majority of Germans.[130] The sense of outrage and disbelief that swept through the German upper and middle classes like a shock wave was almost universal, and had a massive impact on many working-class supporters of the moderate Social Democrats as well. Germany's international strength and prestige had been on an upward course since unification in 1871, so most Germans felt, and now, suddenly, Germany had been brutally expelled from the ranks of the Great Powers and covered in what they considered to be undeserved shame. Versailles was condemned as a dictated peace, unilaterally imposed without the possibility of negotiation. The enthusiasm which so many middle-class Germans had demonstrated for war in 1914 flipped over into burning resentment at the terms of peace four years later.

In fact, the peace settlement created new opportunities for German foreign policy in East-Central Europe, where the once-mighty Habsburg and Romanov empires had been replaced by a squabbling congeries of small and unstable states such as Austria, Czechoslovakia, Hungary, Poland, Romania and Yugoslavia. The Treaty's territorial provisions were mild compared with what Germany would have imposed on the rest of Europe in the event of victory, as the programme drawn up by the German Chancellor Bethmann Hollweg in September 1914 had clearly indicated in principle, and the Treaty of Brest-Litovsk, concluded with the defeated Russians in the spring of 1918, had graphically demonstrated in practice. A German victory would have led to a huge reparations bill being served on the defeated Allies, too, no doubt many times larger than that which Bismarck had sent to the French after the war of 1870–71. The reparations bills that Germany actually did have to pay from 1919 onwards were not beyond the country's resources to meet and not unreasonable given the wanton destruction visited upon Belgium and France by the occupying German armies. In many ways, the peace settlement of 1918–19 was a brave attempt at marrying principle and pragmatism in a dramatically altered world. In other circumstances it might have stood a chance of success. But not in the circumstances of 1919, when almost any peace terms would have been condemned by German nationalists who felt they had been unjustly cheated of victory.[131] The lengthy Allied military occupation of parts of western Germany, along the Rhine valley, from the end of the war until almost the end of the 1920s, also aroused widespread resentment and intensified German nationalism in the areas affected. One Social Democrat, born in 1888, and previously a pacifist, reported later: 'I came to feel the rifle butt of the French and became patriotic again.'[132] Although the British and the Americans stationed troops in a large area of the Rhineland, it was the French, both there and in the Saar, who aroused the most resentment. Particular outrage was caused by their banning of German patriotic songs and festivals, their encouragement of separatist movements in the area, and their outlawing of radical nationalist groups. A miner in the Saarland alleged that the state mines' new French owners expressed their Germano-phobia in their harsh treatment of the workers.[133] Passive resistance, particularly amongst patriotic minor state officials such as railway clerks, who refused to work for the new French authorities, encouraged a hatred of the politicians in Berlin who had accepted this state of affairs, and a rejection of German democracy for failing to do anything about it.[134]

But if the peace settlement outraged the majority of ordinary Germans, that was nothing to the effect it had on the apostles of extreme national-ism, notably the Pan-Germans. The Pan-Germans had greeted the out-break of war in 1914 with unbounded enthusiasm, verging on ecstasy. For men like Heinrich Class, it was the fulfilment of a lifetime's dream. Things seemed at last to be going their way. The hugely ambitious plans for territorial annexation and European hegemony drawn up by the Pan-German League before the war now seemed to have a chance of becoming reality, as the government, led by Bethmann Hollweg, drew up a set of war aims that came very close to them in their sweep and scope. Pressure-groups such as the industrialists, and parties such as the Conservatives, all clamoured for extensive new territories to be added to the German Reich after victory.[135] But victory did not come and oppo-sition to annexationism grew. In these circumstances, Class and the Pan-Germans began to realize that they needed to make another serious attempt to broaden the basis of their support in order to put pressure on the government again. But as they tried out various schemes of alliance with other groups to this end, they were suddenly outflanked by a new movement, launched by Wolfgang Kapp, a former civil servant, estate

owner and associate of the business magnate and founder-member of the
Pan-Germans, Alfred Hugenberg. For Kapp, no nationalist movement
would succeed without a mass base; and in September 1917, he launched
the German Fatherland Party, whose programme centred on annexationist war aims, authoritarian constitutional changes, and other planks
of the Pan-German platform. Backed by Class, by industrialists, by the
former Naval Secretary Alfred von Tirpitz, and indeed by all the annexationist groups including the Conservative Party, the new organization
presented itself as being above the party-political fray, committed only
to the German nation, not to any abstract ideology. Teachers, Protestant
pastors, army officers and many others jumped on the bandwagon.
Within a year, the Fatherland Party was claiming a membership of no
less than one and a quarter million.[136]

But all was not quite as it seemed. For a start, the membership figures
were inflated by a lot of double-counting of people who were enrolled
both as individuals and as members of constituent organizations, so that
the true number of people who belonged was no more than 445,000,
according to an internal memorandum of September 1918. And then,
Class and the Pan-Germans were quickly pushed aside because the leadership thought their association would deter potential supporters from less
extreme parts of the political spectrum. The Fatherland Party ran into a
great deal of opposition from liberals, and encountered massive suspicion
from the government, who banned officers and troops from joining and
told civil servants they were not to help it in any way. The party's ambition
to recruit the working class was frustrated both by the Social Democrats,
who levelled withering criticism at its divisive ideology, and from the war
wounded, whose attendance (by invitation) at a Fatherland Party meeting
in Berlin in January 1918 led to angry exchanges with the speakers and
resulted in the super-patriots in the audience throwing them out of the
meeting and the police being called in to break up the fighting. All of this
pointed to the fact that the Fatherland Party was in effect another version
of previous ultra-nationalist movements, even more dominated than they
were by middle-class notables. It did nothing new to win working-class
support, it did not have any working-class speakers, and for all its
demagogy, it entirely lacked the common touch. It stayed firmly within
the boundaries of respectable politics, eschewed violence, and revealed,
more than anything else, the bankruptcy of conventional Pan-German

political ambitions; a bankruptcy confirmed when the Pan-German League proved unable to cope with the new political world of postwar Germany and fell into sectarian obscurity after 1918.[137]

III

What transformed the extreme nationalist scene was not the war itself, but the experience of defeat, revolution and armed conflict at the war's end. A powerful role was played here by the myth of the 'front generation' of 1914–18, soldiers bound together in a spirit of comradeship and self-sacrifice in a heroic cause which overcame all political, regional, social and religious differences. Writers such as Ernst Jünger, whose book *Storm of Steel* became a best-seller, celebrated the experience of the fighting man and cultivated the rapid growth of nostalgia for the unity of the wartime years.[138] This myth exercised a powerful appeal in particular over the middle classes, for whom hardships shared, both in reality and in spirit, with workers and peasants in the trenches during the war, provided material for nostalgic literary celebration in the postwar years.[139] Many soldiers bitterly resented the outbreak of revolution in 1918. Units returning from the front sometimes disarmed and arrested workers' and soldiers' councils in the localities through which they passed.[140] Some combatants were converted to radical nationalism as revolutionaries offered them insults rather than plaudits on their return, forcing them to tear off their epaulettes and abandon their allegiance to the black-white-red Imperial flag. As one such veteran later recalled:

On 15 November 1918 I was on the way from the hospital at Bad Nauheim to my garrison at Brandenburg. As I was limping along with the aid of my cane at the Potsdam station in Berlin, a band of uniformed men, sporting red armbands, stopped me, and demanded that I surrender my epaulettes and insignia. I raised my stick in reply; but my rebellion was soon overcome. I was thrown (down?), and only the intervention of a railroad official saved me from my humiliating position. Hate flamed in me against the November criminals from that moment. As soon as my health improved somewhat, I joined forces with the groups devoted to the overthrow of the rebellion.[141]

Other soldiers experienced an 'ignominious' and 'humiliating' home-coming in a Germany that had overthrown the institutions for which they had been fighting. 'Was it for this', one of them later asked, 'that the fresh youth of Germany was mowed down in hundreds of battles?'[142] Another veteran, who had lost his leg in combat and was in a military hospital on 9 November 1918, reported:

I shall never forget the scene when a comrade without an arm came into the room and threw himself on his bed crying. The red rabble, which had never heard a bullet whistle, had assaulted him and torn off all his insignia and medals. We screamed with rage. For this kind of Germany we had sacrificed our blood and our health, and braved all the torments of hell and a world of enemies for years.[143]

'Who had betrayed us?', another asked, and the answer was not long in coming: 'bandits who wanted to reduce Germany to a shambles . . . fiendish aliens.'[144]

Such feelings were not universal among the troops, and the experience of defeat did not turn all the veterans into political cannon-fodder for the extreme right. Large numbers of troops had deserted at the end of the war, faced with the overwhelming force of their Allied opponents, and showed no desire to continue fighting.[145] Millions of working-class soldiers went back to their previous political milieu, among the Social Democrats, or gravitated towards the Communists.[146] Some of the veterans' pressure-groups were adamant that they never wanted themselves or anyone else to go through again the kind of experiences to which they had been subjected in 1914–18. Yet, in the end, ex-soldiers and their resentments did play a crucial part in fostering a climate of violence and discontent after the war was over, and the shock of adjusting to peacetime conditions pushed many towards the far right. Those who were already politically socialized into conservative and nationalist traditions found their views radicalized in the new political context of the 1920s. On the left, too, a new willingness to use violence was conditioned by the experience, real or vicarious, of the war.[147] As distance grew from the war, so the myth of the 'front generation' generated a widespread feeling that the veterans who had sacrificed so much for the nation during the war deserved far better treatment than they actually got, a feeling naturally shared by many veterans themselves.[148]

The most important of the veterans' associations fully shared these resentments and campaigned vigorously for a return to the old Imperial system under which they had fought. Known as the 'Steel Helmets: League of Front-Soldiers', it was founded on 13 November 1918 by Franz Seldte, the owner of a small soda-water factory in Magdeburg. Born in 1882, Seldte had been an active member of a student duelling corps before he fought on the Western Front, where he was decorated for bravery. At an early public meeting, when members of the audience doubted his commitment to the nationalist cause, Seldte demonstratively waved at them the stump of his left arm, which he had lost at the Battle of the Somme. Instinctively cautious and conservative, he preferred to emphasize the Steel Helmets' primary function as a source of financial support for old soldiers fallen on hard times. He easily fell under the influence of stronger characters, particularly those whose principles were firmer than his own. One such figure was his fellow-leader of the Steel Helmets, Theodor Duesterberg, another ex-army officer who had fought on the Western Front before taking on a series of staff jobs, particularly liaising with allied powers such as Turkey and Hungary. Duesterberg, born in 1875, had been educated in an army cadet school and was a Prussian officer in the classic mould, obsessed with discipline and order, inflexible and unbending in his political views and, like Seldte, completely incapable of adjusting to a world without the Kaiser. Both men therefore believed that the Steel Helmets should be 'above politics'. But this meant in practice that they wanted to overcome party divisions and restore the patriotic spirit of 1914. The organization's 1927 Berlin manifesto declared: 'The Steel Helmets proclaim the battle against all softness and cowardice, which seek to weaken and destroy the consciousness of honour of the German people through renunciation of the right of defence and will to defence.' It denounced the Treaty of Versailles and demanded its abrogation, it wanted the restoration of the black-white-red national flag of the Bismarckian Reich, and it ascribed the economic problems of Germany to 'the deficiency in living-space and the territory in which to work'. In order to implement this programme, strong leadership was necessary. The spirit of comradeship born in the war had to provide the basis for a national unity that would overcome present party differences. By the mid-1920s the Steel Helmets boasted some 300,000 members. They were a formidable and decidedly militaristic presence on the streets when they held their marches and rallies; in 1927, indeed, no fewer than 132,000 members in military uniforms took part in a march-past in Berlin as a demonstration of their loyalty to the old order.[149]

For most Germans, as for the Steel Helmets, the trauma of the First World War, and above all the shock of the unexpected defeat, refused to be healed. When Germans referred to 'peacetime' after 1918, it was not to the era in which they were actually living, but to the period before the Great War had begun. Germany failed to make the transition from wartime back to peacetime after 1918. Instead, it remained on a continued war footing; at war with itself, and at war with the rest of the world, as the shock of the Treaty of Versailles united virtually every part of the political spectrum in a grim determination to overthrow its central provisions, restore the lost territories, end the payment of reparations and re-establish Germany as the dominant power in Central Europe once more.[150] Military models of conduct had been widespread in German society and culture before 1914; but after the war they became all-pervasive; the language of politics was permeated by metaphors of warfare, the other party was an enemy to be smashed, and struggle, terror and violence became widely accepted as legitimate weapons in the political struggle. Uniforms were everywhere. Politics, to reverse a famous dictum of the early nineteenth-century military theorist Carl von Clausewitz, became war pursued by other means.[151]

The First World War legitimized violence to a degree that not even Bismarck's wars of unification in 1864–70 had been able to do. Before the war, Germans even of widely differing and bitterly opposed political beliefs had been able to discuss their differences without resorting to violence.[152] After 1918, however, things were entirely different. The changed climate could already be observed in parliamentary proceedings. These had remained relatively decorous under the Empire, but after 1918 they degenerated all too often into unseemly shouting matches, with each side showing open contempt for the other, and the chair unable to keep order. Far worse, however, was the situation on the streets, where all sides organized armed squads of thugs, fights and brawls became commonplace, and beatings-up and assassinations were widely used. Those who carried out these acts of violence were not only former soldiers, but also included men in their late teens and twenties who had been too young to fight in the war themselves and for whom civil violence became a way of legitimizing themselves in the face of the powerful myth of the older generation of front-soldiers.[153] Not untypical was the experience of the young Raimund Pretzel, child of a well-to-do senior civil servant, who remembered later that he and his schoolfriends played war games all the time from 1914 to 1918, followed battle reports with avid interest, and with his entire generation 'experienced war as a great, thrilling, enthralling game between nations, which provided far more excitement and emotional satisfaction than anything peace could offer; and that', he added in the 1930s, 'has now become the underlying vision of Nazism.'[154] War, armed conflict, violence and death were often for them abstract concepts, killing something they had read about and had processed in their adolescent minds under the influence of a propaganda that presented it as a heroic, necessary, patriotic act.[155]

Before long, political parties associated themselves with armed and uniformed squads, paramilitary troops whose task it was to provide guards at meetings, impress the public by marching in military order through the streets, and to intimidate, beat up and on occasion kill members of the paramilitary units associated with other political parties. The relationship between the politicians and the paramilitaries was often fraught with tension, and paramilitary organizations always maintained a greater or lesser degree of autonomy; still, their political colouring was usually clear enough. The Steel Helmets, ostensibly just a veterans' association, left no doubt about their paramilitary functions when they paraded through the streets or engaged in brawls with rival groups. Their affinities with the hard right became closer from the middle of the 1920s, when they took a more radical stance, banning Jews from membership despite the fact that the organization was intended to provide for all ex-front-soldiers, and there were plenty of Jewish veterans who needed its support as much as anyone else did. The Nationalists also founded their own 'Fighting Leagues' which they had a better chance of bending to their purpose than they did with the confused and divided Steel Helmets. In 1924 the Social Democrats took a leading part in founding the Reichsbanner Black-Red-Gold, signifying their allegiance to the Republic by incorporating the colours of its flag into their title, though in alliance with the far more ambivalent concept of the Reich; and the Communists set up the Red Front-Fighters' League, where the term 'Red Front' itself was a telling incorporation of a military metaphor into the political struggle.[156] On the far right there were other, smaller 'Combat Leagues', shading off into illegal, conspiratorial groups such as the 'Organization Escherich', closely associated with the Steel Helmets, and the 'Organization Consul', which belonged to a murky world of political assassination and revenge killings. Bands of uniformed men marching through the streets and clashing with each other in brutally physical encounters became a commonplace sight in the Weimar Republic, adding to the general atmosphere of violence and aggression in political life.[157]

The German Revolution of 1918–19 did not resolve the conflicts that had been boiling up in the country in the final phase of the war. Few were entirely satisfied with the Revolution's results. On the extreme left, revolutionaries led by Karl Liebknecht and Rosa Luxemburg saw in the events of November 1918 the opportunity to create a socialist state run by the workers' and soldiers' councils that had sprung up all over the country as the old Imperial system disintegrated. With the model of Lenin's Bolshevik Revolution in Russia before their eyes, they pressed on with plans for a second revolution to complete their work. For their part, the mainstream Social Democrats feared that the revolutionaries might institute the kind of 'red terror' that was now taking place in Russia. Afraid for their lives, and conscious of the need to prevent the country from falling into complete anarchy, they sanctioned the recruitment of heavily armed paramilitary bands consisting of a mixture of war veterans and younger men, and known as the Free Corps, to put down any further revolutionary uprisings.

In the early months of 1919, when the extreme left staged a poorly organized uprising in Berlin, the Free Corps, egged on by the mainstream Social Democrats, reacted with unprecedented violence and brutality. Liebknecht and Luxemburg were murdered, and revolutionaries were mown down or summarily executed in a number of German cities where they had taken control or appeared to be a threat. These events left a permanent legacy of bitterness and hatred on the political left, made worse by another major outbreak of political violence in the spring of 1920. A Red Army of workers, initially formed by left-wing Social Democrats and Communists to defend civil liberties in the industrial region of the Ruhr in the face of an attempted right-wing coup in Berlin, began to advance more radical political demands. Once the attempted coup had been defeated by a general strike, the Red Army was put down by Free Corps units, backed by the mainstream Social Democrats and supported by the regular army, in what amounted in effect to a regional civil war. Well over a thousand members of the Red Army were slaughtered, most of them prisoners 'shot while trying to escape'.[158]

These events doomed any kind of co-operation between Social Democrats and Communists to failure from the outset. Mutual fear, mutual recriminations and mutual hatred between the two parties far outweighed any potential purpose they might have had in common. The legacy of the 1918 Revolution was scarcely less ominous on the right. Extreme violence against the left had been legitimized, if not encouraged, by the moderate Social Democrats; but this in no way exempted them from being a target themselves, as the Free Corps now turned on their masters. Many of the Free Corps leaders were former army officers whose belief in the 'stab-in-the-back' myth was unshakeable. The depth of the Free Corps' hatred of the Revolution and its supporters was almost without limit. The language of their propaganda, their memoirs, their fictional representations of the military actions they took part in, breathed a rabid spirit of aggression and revenge, often bordering on the pathological. The 'reds', they believed, were an inhuman mass, like a pack of rats, a poisonous flood pouring over Germany, requiring measures of extreme violence if it was to be held in check.[159]

Their feelings were shared to a greater or lesser extent by large numbers of regular officers, and by the vast majority of right-wing politicians. Scores of young students and others who had missed the war now flocked to their banner. For these people, socialists and democrats of any hue were no better than traitors – the 'November criminals' or 'November traitors' as they were soon dubbed, the men who had first stabbed the army in the back, then in November 1918 committed the double crime of overthrowing the Kaiser and signing the Armistice. For some democratic politicians, indeed, signing the Treaty of Versailles was tantamount to signing their own death warrant, as Free Corps members formed secret assassination squads to root out and kill those they regarded as traitors to the nation, including the democratic politician Walther Rathenau, the leading socialist Hugo Haase, and the prominent Centre Party deputy Matthias Erzberger.[160] Political violence reached fresh heights in 1923, a year marked not only by the bloody suppression of an abortive Communist uprising in Hamburg but also by gun battles between rival political groups in Munich and armed clashes involving French-backed separatists in the Rhineland. In the early 1920s, extreme leftists such as Karl Plättner and Max Hölz carried out campaigns of armed robbery and 'expropriation' that ended only when they were arrested and sentenced to lengthy terms of imprisonment.[161]

It was in this atmosphere of national trauma, political extremism, violent conflict and revolutionary upheaval that Nazism was born. Most of the elements that went into its eclectic ideology were already current in Germany before 1914 and had become even more familiar to the public during the war. The dramatic collapse of Germany into political chaos towards the end of 1918, a chaos that endured for several years after the war, provided the spur to translate extreme ideas into violent action. The heady mixture of hatred, fear and ambition that had intoxicated a small number of Pan-German extremists suddenly gained a crucial extra element: the willingness, determination even, to use physical force. National humiliation, the collapse of the Bismarckian Empire, the triumph of Social Democracy, the threat of Communism, all this seemed to some to justify the use of violence and murder to implement the measures which Pan-Germans, antisemites, eugenicists and ultra-nationalists had been advocating since before the turn of the century, if the German nation was ever to recover.

Yet such ideas still remained those of a minority even after 1918, and the use of physical force to put them into effect was still confined to a tiny, extremist fringe. German society and politics were polarized into extremes by the collapse of 1918–19, not converted to a general enthusiasm for extreme nationalism. And, crucially, the centre ground of politics was still occupied by people and parties committed to the creation of a stable, functioning parliamentary democracy, to social reform, to cultural freedom and to economic opportunity for all. The collapse of the Wilhelmine Reich was their chance too, and they seized it willingly. Before ultra-nationalism could break out into the political mainstream, it had to smash the barriers created by Germany's first democracy, the Weimar Republic.

2

THE FAILURE OF
DEMOCRACY

THE WEAKNESSES OF WEIMAR

I

Fear and hatred ruled the day in Germany at the end of the First World War. Gun battles, assassinations, riots, massacres and civil unrest denied Germans the stability in which a new democratic order could flourish. Yet somebody had to take over the reins of government after the Kaiser's abdication and the collapse of the Reich created by Bismarck. The Social Democrats stepped into the breach. A group of leading figures in the labour movement emerged in the confusion of early November 1918 to form a revolutionary Council of People's Delegates. Uniting, for a brief period at least, the two wings of the Social Democratic movement (the Majority, who had supported the war, and the Independents, who had opposed it), the Council was led by Friedrich Ebert, a long-time Social Democratic Party functionary. Born in 1871, the son of a tailor, he became a saddler and entered politics through his trade union activities. He worked on the editorial staff of the Social Democratic newspaper in Bremen, then in 1893 opened a pub in the city, which like so many such institutions functioned as a centre for local labour organizations. By 1900 he was active in Bremen's municipal politics, and as leader of the local Social Democrats he did much to improve the party's effectiveness. In 1905 he was elected secretary to the national party's central committee in Berlin, and in 1912 he entered the Reichstag.

Ebert won the respect of his party not as a great orator or charismatic leader, but as a calm, patient and subtle negotiator who always seemed to bring the different factions of the labour movement together. He was a typical pragmatist of the second generation of Social Democratic leaders, accepting the party's Marxist ideology but concentrating his

THE FAILURE OF DEMOCRACY 79

efforts on the day-to-day improvement of working-class life through his expertise in areas such as labour law and social insurance. It was his hard work that was mainly responsible for the remodelling and improved efficiency of the party's administration and electoral machine before the war, and he took a great deal of the credit for the party's famous victory in the Reichstag elections of 1912. On the death of the party's long-term leader August Bebel in 1913, Ebert was elected joint leader of the party alongside the more radical Hugo Haase. Like many Social Democratic organizers, Ebert put loyalty to the party above almost everything else, and his outrage at the refusal of Haase and other opponents of the war to follow majority decisions in the party was a major factor in persuading him to bring about their expulsion. Led by Haase, the dissidents formed the Independent Social Democrats in 1917 and worked from a variety of points of view to bring about an end to the war. Ebert believed in discipline and order, compromise and reform, and worked hard to bring about a co-operation with the Centre Party and the left-liberals during the war, in order to push the Kaiser's administration towards an acceptance of parliamentarism. His main aim in 1918–19 was formulated by the characteristic concern of the sober administrator: to keep essential services going, to stop the economy from collapsing and to restore law and order. He was converted to the view that the Kaiser should abdicate only by the realization that a social revolution would break out if he did not, and, he added in conversation with the Kaiser's last Chancellor, Prince Max of Baden, 'I don't want that, indeed I hate it like sin.'[1]

Instead of revolution, Ebert wanted parliamentary democracy. In collaboration with the Centre Party and the left-wing liberals, now renamed the Democrats, Ebert and his associates in the Council of People's Delegates organized nationwide elections to a Constituent Assembly early in 1919, against the opposition of more radical elements who looked to the workers' and soldiers' councils to form the basis of some kind of Soviet-style administration. Many ordinary electors in Germany, whatever their private political views, saw voting for the three democratic parties as the best way to prevent the creation of a German Soviet and ward off the threat of a Bolshevik revolution. Not surprisingly, therefore, the Social Democrats, the left-liberal Democrats and the Centre Party gained an overall majority in the elections to the Constituent Assembly. This met early in 1919 in the central German town of Weimar, long associated with the life and work of the eighteenth- and early nineteenth-century German poet, novelist and dramatist Johann Wolfgang von Goethe.[2] The constitution which it approved on 31 July 1919 was essentially a modified version of the constitution established by Bismarck for his new Reich nearly half a century before.[3] In place of the Kaiser there was a Reich President who was to be elected, like the President of the United States, by popular vote. Not only did this give him independent legitimacy in his dealings with the legislature, it also encouraged his use of the extensive emergency powers which he was granted under the constitution's Article 48. In times of trouble, he could rule by decree and use the army to restore law and order in any federated state if he thought they were under threat.

The power to rule by decree was only intended for exceptional emergencies. But Ebert, as the Republic's first President, made very extensive use of this power, employing it on no fewer than 136 separate occasions. He deposed legitimately elected governments in Saxony and Thuringia when they threatened, in his view, to foment disorder. Even more dangerously, during the 1920 civil war in the Ruhr he issued a backdated decree applying the death penalty to public-order offences and retrospectively legitimizing many of the summary executions that had already been carried out on members of the Red Army by units of the Free Corps and the regular army.[4] It was significant that on both occasions these powers were used to suppress perceived threats to the Republic from the left, whereas they went virtually unused against what many saw as the far greater threat to it posed by the right. There were virtually no effective safeguards against an abuse of Article 48, since the President could threaten to use the power given him by Article 25 to dissolve the Reichstag should it reject a Presidential decree. Moreover, decrees could in any case be used to create a *fait accompli* or to bring about a situation in which the Reichstag had little option but to approve them (for example, though this was never intended, they could be used to intimidate and suppress opposition to the government in power). In some circumstances, no doubt, there was probably little alternative to some kind of rule by decree. But Article 48 included no proper provisions for the ultimate reassertion of power by the legislature in such an eventuality; and Ebert used it not just for emergencies but also in non-emergency situations where steering legislation through the Reichstag would have been too difficult. In the end, Ebert's excessive use, and occasional misuse, of the Article widened its application to a point where it became a potential threat to democratic institutions.[5]

Ebert's achievement in steering the Weimar Republic into being was undeniable. Yet he made many hasty compromises that were to return to haunt the Republic in different ways later on. His concern for a smooth transition from war to peace led him to collaborate closely with the army without demanding any changes in its fiercely monarchist and ultra-conservative officer corps, which he was certainly in a position to do in 1918–19. Yet Ebert's willingness to compromise with the old order did not do anything to endear him to those who regretted its passing. Throughout the years of his Presidency, he was subjected to a remorseless campaign of vilification in the right-wing press. For those who thought that the head of state should possess a remote, Olympian dignity far from the ordinariness of everyday life, a widely publicized newspaper photograph of the squat, podgy figure of the Reich President on a seaside holiday with a couple of friends, dressed only in bathing-trunks, exposed him to ridicule and contempt. Other opponents in the muck-raking right-wing press attempted to smear him through associating him with financial scandals. Ebert, perhaps foolishly, responded by firing off no fewer than 173 libel suits at those responsible, without ever once gaining satisfaction.[6] In a criminal trial held in 1924, in which the accused was charged with calling Ebert a traitor to his country, the court fined the man the token sum of 10 marks because, as it concluded, Ebert had indeed shown himself to be a traitor by maintaining contacts with striking munitions workers in Berlin in the last year of the war (although he had in fact done so in order to bring the strike to a rapid, negotiated end).[7] The unending wave of hatred poured over Ebert by the extreme right had its effect, not merely in undermining his position but also in wearing him down personally, both mentally and physically. Obsessed with trying to clear his name from all these smears, Ebert neglected a ruptured appendix that could have been dealt with quite easily by the medical science of the time, and he died, aged 54, on 28 February 1925.[8]

The elections to the post of President that followed were a disaster for the democratic prospects of the Weimar Republic. The baleful influence of Weimar's political fragmentation and lack of legitimacy made itself felt here, since in the first round, none of the candidates looked like winning, so the right drafted in the reluctant figure of Field Marshal Paul von Hindenburg as a rallying-point for their divided supporters. In the subsequent run-off, if either the Communists or the autonomous Bavarian wing of the Centre Party had voted for Hindenburg's best-supported opponent, the Catholic politician Wilhelm Marx, the Field Marshal might have been defeated. But, thanks to the egotism above all of the Bavarians, he was elected by a clear majority. A symbol par excellence of the old military and Imperial order, Hindenburg was a bulky, physically imposing man whose statuesque appearance, military uniform, war service medals and legendary reputation – mostly undeserved – for winning the great Battle of Tannenberg and for guiding Germany's military destiny thereafter, made him into a much-revered figurehead, above all for the right. Hindenburg's election was greeted by the forces of the right as a symbol of restoration. 'On 12/5,' reported the conservative academic Victor Klemperer (an alarmed and unsympathetic observer) in his diary, 'as *Hindenburg* was sworn in, there were black-white-red flags everywhere. The Reich flag only on official buildings.' Eight out of ten Imperial flags Klemperer observed on this occasion were, he said, the small ones of the kind used by children.[9] For many, Hindenburg's election was a big step away from Weimar democracy in the direction of a restoration of the old monarchical order. A rumour duly did the rounds that Hindenburg had felt it necessary to ask the ex-Kaiser Wilhelm, now in exile in Holland, for permission before he took up the post of President. It was untrue, but it said a great deal for Hindenburg's reputation that it gained currency.[10]

Once in office, and influenced by his strong sense of duty, Hindenburg, to the surprise of many, stuck to the letter of the constitution; but, as his seven-year term of office wore on, and he moved into his eighties, he became ever more impatient with the complexities of political events and ever more susceptible to the influence of his inner circle of advisers, all of whom shared his instinctive belief that the monarchy was the only legitimate sovereign power in the German Reich. Persuaded of the correctness of the use of Presidential emergency powers by the example of his predecessor, Hindenburg began to feel that a conservative dictatorship exercised in his name was the only way out of the crisis into which the Republic fell at the beginning of the 1930s. Whatever influence Hindenburg's election might therefore have had in reconciling opponents of the Republic to its existence in the short run, in the long run it was an unmitigated disaster for Weimar democracy. By 1930 at the latest, it had become clear that the Presidential power was in the hands of a man who had no faith in democratic institutions and no intention of defending them from their enemies.[11]

II

Besides the office of Reich President, Weimar's constitution provided for a national legislature, named, as before, the Reichstag, but now elected by all adult women as well as all adult men, and by a more direct form of proportional representation than had been used before 1918. In effect, the electors voted for the party of their choice, and each party was allotted a number of seats in the Reichstag precisely corresponding to the proportion of votes it received in the election. Thus, a party that received 30 per cent of the vote would be allotted 30 per cent of the seats, and, more worryingly, a party that received 1 per cent of the vote would be allotted 1 per cent of the seats. It has often been said that such a system favoured small parties and fringe groups, and this was no doubt true. Yet the fringe parties never achieved a combined vote of more than 15 per cent, so it was in practice seldom necessary for the larger parties to take them into account when forming a government. Where proportional representation did have an effect, it was in evening out the chances of the larger parties in the competition for votes, so that, if a first-past-the-post electoral system had been in operation, the bigger parties would have done better, and more stable coalition governments with a smaller number of coalition partners might have been possible, thus perhaps persuading a greater number of people of the virtues of parliamentarism.[12]

As it was, changes of government in the Weimar Republic were very frequent. Between 13 February 1919 and 30 January 1933 there were no fewer than twenty different cabinets, each lasting on average 239 days, or somewhat less than eight months. Coalition government, it was sometimes said, made for unstable government, as the different parties were constantly squabbling over personalities and policies. It also made for weak government, since all they could settle on was the lowest common denominator and the line of least resistance. However, coalition government in Weimar was not just the product of proportional representation. It also arose out of long-standing and deep fissures within the German political system. The parties that had dominated the Imperial scene all survived into the Weimar Republic. The Nationalists were formed by the amalgamation of the old Conservative Party with other, smaller groups. The liberals failed to overcome their differences and remained divided into left (Democrats) and right (People's Party). The Centre Party remained more or less unchanged, though its Bavarian wing split off to form the Bavarian People's Party. On the left, the Social Democrats had to face a new rival in the form of the Communist Party. But none of this was solely or even principally the product of proportional representation. The political milieux out of which these various parties emerged had been in existence since the early days of the Bismarckian Empire.[13]

These milieux, with their party newspapers, clubs and societies, were unusually rigid and homogeneous. Already before 1914 this had resulted in a politicization of whole areas of life that in other societies were much freer from ideological identifications. Thus, if an ordinary German wanted to join a male voice choir, for instance, he had to choose in some areas between a Catholic and a Protestant choir, in others between a socialist and a nationalist choir; the same went for gymnastics clubs, cycling clubs, football clubs and the rest. A member of the Social Democratic Party before the war could have virtually his entire life encompassed by the party and its organizations: he could read a Social Democratic newspaper, go to a Social Democratic pub or bar, belong to a Social Democratic trade union, borrow books from the Social Democratic library, go to Social Democratic festivals and plays, marry a woman who belonged to the Social Democratic women's organization, enrol his children in the Social Democratic youth movement and be buried with the aid of a Social Democratic burial fund.[14] Similar things could be said of the Centre Party (which could rely on the mass organization of supporters in the People's Association for a Catholic Germany, the Catholic Trade Union movement, and Catholic leisure clubs and societies of all kinds) but also to a certain extent of other parties too.[15] These sharply defined political-cultural milieux did not disappear with the advent of the Weimar Republic.[16] But the emergence of commercialized mass leisure, the 'boulevard press', based on sensation and scandal, the cinema, cheap novels, dance-halls and leisure activities of all kinds began in the 1920s to provide alternative sources of identification for the young, who were thus less tightly bound to political parties than their elders were.[17] The older generation of political activists were too closely tied to their particular political ideology to find compromise and co-operation with other politicians and their parties very easy. In contrast to the situation after 1945, there was no merger of major political parties into larger and more effective units.[18] As in a number of other respects, therefore, the political instability of the 1920s and early 1930s owed more to structural continuities with the politics of the Bismarckian and Wilhelmine eras than to the novel provisions of the Weimar constitution.[19]

Proportional representation did not, as some have claimed, encourage political anarchy and thereby facilitate the rise of the extreme right. An electoral system based on a first-past-the-post system, where the candidate who won the most votes in each constituency automatically won the seat, might well have given the Nazi Party even more seats than it eventually obtained in the last elections of the Weimar Republic, though since the parties' electoral tactics would have been different under such a system, and its arguably beneficial effects in the earlier phases of the Republic's existence might have reduced the overall Nazi vote later on, it is impossible to tell for sure.[20] Similarly, the destabilizing effect of the constitution's provision for referendums or plebiscites has often been exaggerated; other political systems have existed perfectly happily with such a provision, and in any case the actual number of plebiscites that actually took place was very small. The campaigning they involved certainly helped keep the overheated political atmosphere of the Republic at boiling point. But national plebiscites had little direct political effect, despite the fact that one provincial plebiscite did succeed in overthrowing a democratic government in Oldenburg in 1932.[21]

In any case, the governmental instability of Weimar has itself often been overdrawn, for the frequent changes of government concealed long-term continuities in particular ministries. Some posts, notably the Ministry of Justice, were used as bargaining counters in inter-party coalition negotiations and so saw a succession of many different ministers, no doubt putting more power than usual into the hands of the senior civil servants, who stayed there all through, though their freedom of action was curtailed by the devolution of many functions of judicial

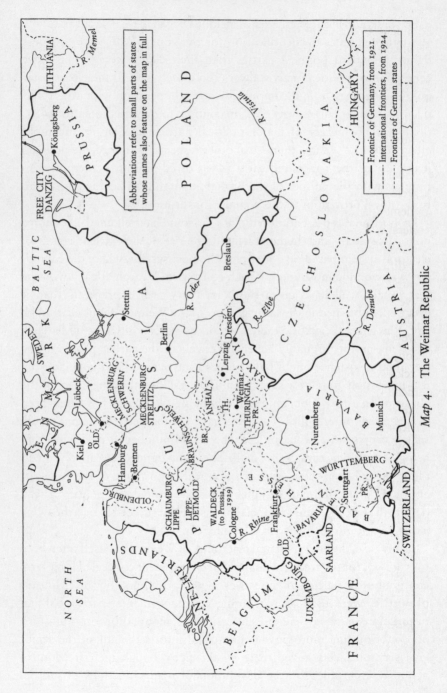

Map 4. The Weimar Republic

administration to the federated states. But others became the virtual perquisite of a particular politician through all the vagaries of coalition-building, thus making it easier to formulate and implement strong and decisive policies. Gustav Stresemann, the leading figure in the People's Party, for instance, was Foreign Minister in nine successive administrations and remained in office for an unbroken period of over six years. Heinrich Brauns, a Centre Party deputy, was Minister of Labour in twelve successive cabinets, from June 1920 up to June 1928. Otto Gessler, a Democrat, was Army Minister in thirteen successive governments, from March 1920 to January 1928. Such ministers were able to develop and implement long-term policies irrespective of the frequent turnover of leadership experienced by the governments they served in. Other ministries were also occupied by the same politicians through two, three or four different governments.[22] Not by chance, it was in such areas that the Republic was able to develop its strongest and most consistent policies, above all in the fields of foreign affairs, labour and welfare.

The ability of the Reich government to act firmly and decisively, however, was always compromised by another provision of the constitution, namely its decision to continue the federal structure which Bismarck had imposed on the Reich in 1871 in an effort to sugar the pill of unification for German princes such as the King of Bavaria and the Grand Duke of Baden. The princes had been unceremoniously thrown out in the Revolution of 1918, but their states remained. They were equipped now with democratic, parliamentary institutions, but still retained a good deal of autonomy in key areas of domestic policy. The fact that some of the states, like Bavaria, had a history and an identity going back many centuries, encouraged them to obstruct the policies of the Reich government if they did not like them. On the other hand, direct taxation was now in the hands of the Reich government, and many of the smaller states were dependent on handouts from Berlin when they got into financial difficulties. Attempts at secession from the Reich might seem threatening, especially in the Republic's troubled early years, but in reality they were never strong enough to be taken seriously.[23] Worse problems could be caused by tensions between Prussia and the Reich, since the Prussian state was bigger than all the rest combined; but through the 1920s and early 1930s Prussia was led by moderate, pro-republican governments which constituted an important counterweight to the extremism and instability of states such as Bavaria. When all these factors are taken into account, therefore, it does not seem that the federal system, for all its unresolved tensions between the Reich and the states, was a major factor in undermining the stability and legitimacy of the Weimar Republic.[24]

III

All in all, Weimar Germany's constitution was no worse than the constitutions of most other countries in the 1920s, and a good deal more democratic than many. Its more problematical provisions might not have mattered so much had circumstances been different. But the fatal lack of legitimacy from which the Republic suffered magnified the constitution's faults many times over. Three political parties were identified with the new political system – the Social Democrats, the liberal German Democratic Party, and the Centre Party. After gaining a clear majority of 76.2 per cent of the vote in January 1919, these three parties combined won just 48 per cent of the vote in June 1920, 43 per cent of the vote in May 1924, 49.6 per cent in December 1924, 49.9 per cent in 1928 and 43 per cent in September 1930. From 1920 onwards they were thus in a permanent minority in the Reichstag, outnumbered by deputies whose allegiance lay with the Republic's enemies to the right and to the left. And the support of these parties of the 'Weimar coalition' for the Republic was, at best, often more rhetorical than practical, and, at worst, equivocal, compromised or of no political use at all.[25]

The Social Democrats were considered by many to be the party that had created the Republic, and often said so themselves. Yet they were never very happy as a party of government, took part in only eight out of the twenty Weimar cabinets and only filled the office of Reich Chancellor in four of them.[26] They remained locked in the Marxist ideological mould of the prewar years, still expecting capitalism to be overthrown and the bourgeoisie to be replaced as the ruling class by the proletariat. Whatever else it was, Germany in the 1920s was undeniably a capitalist society, and playing a leading role in government seemed to many Social Democrats to sit rather uneasily alongside the verbal radicalism of their ideology. Unused to the experience of government, excluded from political participation for two generations before the war, they found the experience of collaborating with 'bourgeois' politicians a painful one. They could not rid themselves of their Marxist ideology without losing a large part of their electoral support in the working class; yet on the other hand a more radical policy, for example of forming a Red Army militia from workers instead of relying on the Free Corps, would surely have made their participation in bourgeois coalition governments impossible and called down upon their heads the wrath of the army.

The main strength of the Social Democrats lay in Prussia, the state that covered over half the territory of the Weimar Republic and contained 57 per cent of its population. Here, in a mainly Protestant area with great cities such as Berlin and industrial areas like the Ruhr, they dominated the government. Their policy was to make Prussia a bastion of Weimar democracy, and, although they did not pursue reforms with any great vigour or consistency, removing them from power in Germany's biggest state became a major objective of Weimar democracy's enemies by the early 1930s.[27] In the Reich, however, their position was far less dominant. Their strength at the beginning of the Republic owed a good deal to the support of middle-class voters who considered that a strong Social Democratic Party would offer the best defence against Bolshevism by effecting a quick transition to parliamentary democracy. As the threat receded, so their representation in the Reichstag went down, from 163 seats in 1919 to 102 in 1920. Despite a substantial recovery later on – 153 seats in 1928, and 143 in 1930 – the Social Democrats permanently lost nearly two and a half million votes, and, after receiving 38 per cent of the votes in 1919, they hovered around 25 per cent for the rest of the 1920s and early 1930s. Nevertheless, they remained an enormously powerful and well-organized political movement that claimed the allegiance and devotion of millions of industrial workers across the land. If any one party deserved to be called the bulwark of democracy in the Weimar Republic, it was the Social Democrats.

The second arm of the 'Weimar coalition', the German Democratic Party, was a somewhat more enthusiastic participant in government, serving in virtually all the cabinets of the 1920s. It had, after all, been a Democrat, Hugo Preuss, who had been the principal author of the much-maligned Weimar constitution. But although they won 75 seats in the election of January 1919, they lost 36 of them in the next election, in

June 1920, and were down to 28 seats in the election of May 1924. Victims of the rightward drift of middle-class voters, they never recovered.[28] Their response to their losses after the elections of 1928 was disastrous. Led by Erich Koch-Weser, leading figures in the party joined in July 1930 with a paramilitary offshoot of the youth movement known as the Young German Order and some individual politicians from other middle-class parties, to transform the Democrats into the State Party. The idea was to create a strong centrist bloc that would stem the flow of bourgeois voters to the Nazis. But the merger had been precipitate, and closed off the possibility of joining together with other, larger political groups in the middle. Some, mostly left-wing Democrats, objected to the move and resigned. On the right, the Young German Order's move lost it support among many of its own members. The electoral fortunes of the new party did not improve, and only 14 deputies represented it in the Reichstag after the elections of September 1930. In practice the merger meant a sharp shift to the right. The Young German Order shared the scepticism of much of the youth movement about the parliamentary system, and its ideology was more than tinged with antisemitism. The new State Party continued to keep the Social Democratic coalition in Prussia afloat until the state elections of April 1932, but its aim, announced by the historian Friedrich Meinecke, was now to achieve a shift in the balance of political power away from the Reichstag and the states and towards a strong, unitary Reich government. Here too, therefore, a steady erosion of support pushed the party to the right; but the only effect of this was to wipe out whatever distinguished it from other, more effective political organizations that were arguing for the same kind of thing. The State Party's convoluted constitutional schemes not only signalled its lack of political realism, but also its weakening commitment to Weimar democracy.[29]

Of the three parties of the 'Weimar coalition', only the Centre Party maintained its support throughout, at around 5 million votes, or 85 to 90 seats in the Reichstag, including those of the Bavarian People's Party. The Centre Party was also a key part of every coalition government from June 1919 to the very end, and with its strong interest in social legislation probably had as strong a claim to have been the driving force behind the creation of Weimar's welfare state as the Social Democrats did. Socially conservative, it devoted much of its time to fighting pornography, contraception and other evils of the modern world, and to defending Catholic interests in the schools system. Its Achilles heel was the influence inevitably wielded over it by the Papacy in Rome. As head of the Catholic Church, Pope Pius XI was increasingly worried by the advance of atheistic communists and socialists during the 1920s. Together with his Nuncio in Germany, Eugenio Pacelli, who subsequently became Pope Pius XII, he profoundly distrusted the political liberalism of many Catholic politicians and saw a turn to a more authoritarian form of politics as the safest way to preserve the Church's interests from the looming threat of the godless left. This led to his conclusion of a Concordat with Mussolini's Fascist regime in Italy in 1929 and later on to the Church's support for the 'clerico-fascist' dictatorship of Engelbert Dollfuss in the Austrian civil war of 1934, and the Nationalists under General Franco in the Spanish Civil War that began in 1936.[30]

With such signals emanating from the Vatican even in the 1920s, the prospects for political Catholicism in Germany were not good. They became markedly worse in December 1928, when a close associate of Papal Nuncio Pacelli, Prelate Ludwig Kaas, a priest who was also a deputy in the German Reichstag, succeeded in being elected leader of the Centre Party as a compromise candidate during a struggle between factions of the right and left over the succession to the retiring chairman, Wilhelm Marx. Under Pacelli's influence, however, Kaas veered increasingly towards the right, pulling many Catholic politicians with him. As increasing disorder and instability began to grip the Reich in 1930 and 1931, Kaas, now a frequent visitor to the Vatican, began to work together with Pacelli for a Concordat, along the lines of the agreement recently concluded with Mussolini. Securing the future existence of the Church was paramount in such a situation. Like many other leading Catholic politicians, Kaas considered that this was only really possible in an authoritarian state where police repression stamped out the threat from the left. 'Never', declared Kaas in 1929, 'has the call for leadership on the grand scale echoed more vividly and impatiently through the soul of the German people as in the days when the Fatherland and its culture have been in such peril that the soul of all of us has been oppressed.'[31] Kaas demanded among other things much greater independence for the executive from the legislature in Germany. Another leading Centre Party politician, Eugen Bolz, Minister-President of Württemberg, put it more

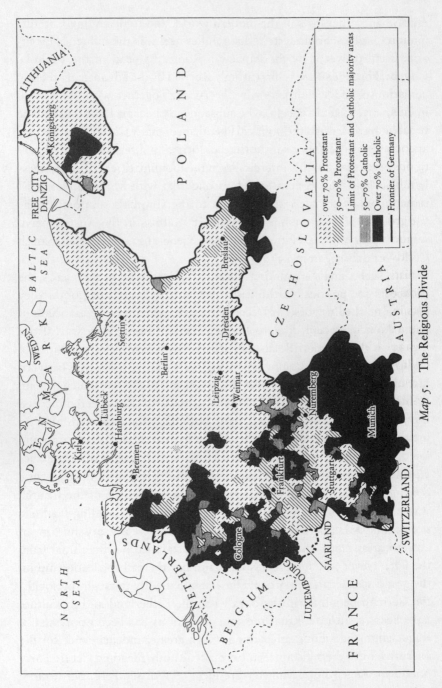

Map 5.   The Religious Divide

bluntly when he told his wife early in 1930: 'I have long been of the opinion that the Parliament cannot solve severe domestic political problems. If a dictator for ten years were a possibility – I would want it.'[32] Long before 30 January 1933, the Centre Party had ceased to be the bulwark of Weimar democracy that it had once been.[33]

Thus, even the major political props of democracy in the Weimar Republic were crumbling by the end of the 1920s. Beyond them, the democratic landscape was even more desolate. No other parties offered serious support to the Republic and its institutions. On the left, the Republic was confronted with the mass phenomenon of the Communists. In the revolutionary period from 1918 to 1921 they were a tightly knit, elite group with little electoral support, but when the Independent Social Democrats, deprived of the unifying factor of opposition to the First World War, fell apart in 1922, a large number of them joined the Communists, who thus became a mass party. Already in 1920 the combined forces of the Independent Social Democrats and the Communists won 88 seats in the Reichstag. In May 1924 the Communists won 62 seats, and, after a small drop later in the year, they were back to 54 in 1928 and 77 in 1930. Three and a quarter million people cast their votes for the party in May 1924 and over four and a half million in September 1930. These were all votes for the destruction of the Weimar Republic.

Through all the twists and turns of its policies during the 1920s, the Communist Party of Germany never deviated from its belief that the Republic was a bourgeois state whose primary purposes were the protection of the capitalist economic order and the exploitation of the working class. Capitalism, they hoped, would inevitably collapse and the 'bourgeois' republic would be replaced by a Soviet state along Russian lines. It was the duty of the Communist Party to bring this about as soon as possible. In the early years of the Republic this meant preparing for an 'October revolution' in Germany by means of an armed revolt. But, after the failure of the January uprising in 1919 and the even more catastrophic collapse of plans for an uprising in 1923, this idea was put on hold. Steered increasingly from Moscow, where the Soviet regime, under the growing influence of Stalin, tightened its financial and ideological grip on Communist parties everywhere in the second half of the 1920s, the German Communist Party had little option but to swing to a more moderate course in the mid-1920s, only to return to a radical, 'leftist'

position at the end of the decade. This meant not only refusing to join
with the Social Democrats in the defence of the Republic, but even actively
collaborating with the Republic's enemies in order to bring it down.[34]
Indeed, the party's hostility to the Republic and its institutions even
caused it to oppose reforms that might lead the Republic to become more
popular among the working class.[35]

This implacable opposition to the Republic from the left was more
than balanced by rabid animosity from the right. The largest and most
significant right-wing challenge to Weimar was mounted by the Nationalists, who gained 44 Reichstag seats in January 1919, 71 in June 1920, 95
in May 1924 and 103 in December 1924. This made them larger than
any other party with the exception of the Social Democrats. In both
elections of 1924 they won around 20 per cent of the vote. One in five
people who cast their ballot in these elections thus did so for a party that
made it clear from the outset that it regarded the Weimar Republic as
utterly illegitimate and called for a restoration of the Bismarckian Reich
and the return of the Kaiser. This was expressed in many different ways,
from the Nationalists' championing of the old Imperial flag, black, white
and red, in place of the new Republican colours of black, red and gold,
to their tacit and sometimes explicit condoning of the assassination of
key Republican politicians by armed conspiratorial groups allied to the
Free Corps. The propaganda and policies of the Nationalists did much
to spread radical right-wing ideas across the electorate in the 1920s and
prepare the way for Nazism.

During the 1920s, the Nationalists were a partner in two coalition
governments, but the experience was not a happy one. They resigned
from one government after ten months, and when they came into another
cabinet half-way through its term of office, they were forced to make
compromises that left many party members deeply dissatisfied. Severe
losses in the elections of October 1928, when the Nationalists' representation in the Reichstag fell from 103 seats to 73, convinced the right
wing of the party that it was time for a more uncompromising line. The
traditionalist party chairman Count Westarp was ousted and replaced by
the press baron, industrialist and radical nationalist Alfred Hugenberg,
who had been a leading light of the Pan-German movement since its
inception in the 1890s. The Nationalist Party programme of 1931,
drafted under Hugenberg's influence, was distinctly more right wing than

its predecessors. It demanded among other things the restoration of the Hohenzollern monarchy, compulsory military service, a strong foreign policy directed at the revision of the Treaty of Versailles, the return of the lost overseas colonies and the strengthening of ties with Germans living in other parts of Europe, especially Austria. The Reichstag was to retain only a supervisory role and a 'critical voice' in legislation, and to be joined by 'a representational body structured according to professional rankings in the economic and cultural spheres' along the lines of the corporate state being created at the time in Fascist Italy. And, the programme went on, 'we resist the subversive, un-German spirit in all forms, whether it stems from Jewish or other circles. We are emphatically opposed to the prevalence of Jewdom in the government and in public life, a prevalence that has emerged ever more continuously since the revolution.'[36]

Under Hugenberg, the Nationalists also moved away from internal party democracy and closer to the 'leadership principle'. The party's new leader made strenuous efforts to make party policy on his own and direct the party's Reichstag delegation in its votes. A number of Reichstag deputies opposed this, and a dozen of them split off from the party in December 1929 and more in June 1930, joining fringe groups of the right in protest. Hugenberg allied the party with the extreme right, in an attempt to get a popular referendum to vote against the Young Plan, an internationally agreed scheme, brokered by the Americans, for the rescheduling of reparations payments, in 1929. The failure of the bitterly fought campaign only convinced Hugenberg of the need for even more extreme opposition to Weimar and its replacement by an authoritarian, nationalist state harking back to the glorious days of the Bismarckian Empire. None of this worked. The Nationalists' snobbery and elitism prevented them from winning a real mass following and rendered their supporters vulnerable to the blandishments of the truly populist demagoguery practised by the Nazis.[37]

Less extreme, but only marginally less vehemently opposed to the Republic, was the smaller People's Party, the heir of the old pro-Bismarckian National Liberals. It won 65 seats in the 1920 election and stayed around 45 to 50 for the rest of the decade, attracting about 2.7 to 3 million votes. The party's hostility to the Republic was partly masked by the decision of its leading figure, Gustav Stresemann, to recognize political realities for the moment and accept the legitimacy of the Republic, more out of necessity than conviction. Although he was never fully trusted by his party, Stresemann's powers of persuasion were considerable. Not least thanks to his consummate negotiating skills, the People's Party took part in most of the Republic's cabinets, unlike the Nationalists, who stayed in opposition for the greater part of the 1920s. Yet this meant that the majority of governments formed after the initial phase of the Republic's existence contained at least some ministers who were dubious, to say the least, about its right to exist. Moreover, Stresemann, already in difficulties with his party, fell ill and died in October 1929, thus removing the principal moderating influence from the party's leadership.[38] From this point on it, too, gravitated rapidly towards the far right.

Even in the mid-1920s, therefore, the political system was looking extremely fragile. In other circumstances it might have survived. In retrospect, indeed, the period 1924–8 has been described by many as 'Weimar's Golden Years'. But the idea that democracy was on the way to establishing itself in Germany at this time is an illusion created by hindsight. There was in reality no sign that it was becoming more secure; on the contrary, the fact that the two major bourgeois parties, the Centre Party and the Nationalists, soon fell into the hands of avowed enemies of democracy boded ill for the future, even without the shocks to come. That the allegiance of the People's Party to the Republic, such as it was, owed everything to the persistence and intelligent leadership of one man, Gustav Stresemann, was another sign of fragility. Not even in the relatively favourable circumstances of 1928 had the parties of the 'Weimar Coalition' succeeded in gaining a majority in the Reichstag. The widespread feeling after 1923 that the threat of a Bolshevik revolution had receded meant that the bourgeois parties were no longer so willing to compromise with the Social Democrats in the interests of preserving the Republic as a bulwark against Communism.[39] And more ominously still, paramilitary organizations such as the Steel Helmets were beginning to extend their struggle from the streets to the hustings in an attempt to win more influence for their anti-Republican views. Meanwhile, political violence, though it fell short of the open civil war that characterized much of the Republic's opening phase, still continued at an alarmingly high level throughout the mid-1920s.[40] The brutal fact was that, even in 1928, the Republic was as far away from achieving stability and legitimacy as ever.

IV

The Weimar Republic was also weakened by its failure to win the whole-hearted support of the army and the civil service, both of which found it extremely difficult to adjust to the transition from the authoritarian Reich to the democratic Republic in 1918. For the army leadership in particular, defeat in 1918 posed an alarming threat. Led by one of its most intelligent and perceptive officers, General Wilhelm Groener, the General Staff agreed with the Majority Social Democrats under Friedrich Ebert that the threat of the revolutionary workers' and soldiers' council would best be warded off if they worked in tandem to secure a stable parliamentary democracy. From Groener's point of view this was an act of expediency, not of faith. It secured the preservation of the old officer corps in the reduced circumstances of the German army after the Treaty of Versailles. The army's numbers were restricted to 100,000, it was banned from using modern technology such as tanks, and a mass conscript military force had to give way to a small professional one. Groener ran into fierce opposition from army diehards for compromising with the Social Democrats, just as his opposite number, the Social Democrats' military specialist Gustav Noske, ran into fierce criticism from his party comrades for allowing the officer corps to remain intact instead of replacing it with a more democratic structure and personnel.[41] But in the desperate circumstances of 1918–19, their line won through in the end.

Within a short space of time, however, the workers' and soldiers' councils had faded from the political scene, and the need for compromise with the forces of democracy seemed to many leading officers to have lost its urgency. This became dramatically clear in March 1920, when Free Corps units, protesting against their impending redundancy, marched on Berlin and overthrew the elected government in a bid to restore an authoritarian regime on the lines of the old monarchy. Led by the Pan-German former civil servant and leading light of the old Fatherland Party, Wolfgang Kapp, the insurrectionists were also supported by elements within the armed forces in a number of areas. When the chief of the army command, General Walther Reinhardt, tried to ensure the forces' loyalty to the government, he was ousted in favour of the more right-wing General Hans von Seeckt. Seeckt promptly banned all army units from opposing the plotters and turned a blind eye to those which backed them. Subsequently, he ordered the army to co-operate in the bloody suppression of the workers' armed uprising against the putsch in the Ruhr. Seeckt had indeed been hostile to the Republic from the beginning. Aloof, authoritarian and unapproachable, his upper-class credentials advertised by the monocle he wore over his left eye, he epitomized the traditions of the Prussian officer class. But he was also a political realist who saw that the possibilities of overthrowing the Republic by force were limited. He aimed therefore to keep the army united and free from parliamentary control waiting for better times. In this he had the full support of his fellow-officers.[42]

Under Seeckt's leadership, the army retained in its 'war flag' the old Imperial colours of black, white and red. Seeckt distinguished sharply between the German state, which incorporated the abstract ideal of the Reich, and the Republic, which he regarded as a temporary aberration. General Wilhelm Groener, Seeckt's mentor, described the army in 1928 as the 'only power' and an 'element of power within the state that no one can disregard'.[43] Under Seeckt's leadership, the army was far from being a neutral organization, standing aloof from the party-political fray, whatever Seeckt might have claimed.[44] Seeckt did not hesitate to intervene against the elected government when he believed that it went against the Reich's interests. He even considered taking over the Chancellorship himself on one occasion, with a programme that envisaged the centralization of the Reich and the curbing of Prussian autonomy, the abolition of the trade unions and their replacement by 'occupational chambers' (rather like those later created by Mussolini in Italy), and in general the 'suppression of all tendencies directed against the existence of the Reich and against the legitimate authority of the Reich and the state, through the use of the means of power of the Reich'.[45] In the end, he succeeded in toppling the government, but did not manage to become Chancellor himself; that was to be left to one of his successors, General Kurt von Schleicher, who belonged to Seeckt's close group of advisers in the years when he ran the army command.

A law unto itself for most of the time, the army did its best during the 1920s to circumvent the restrictions placed upon it by the Treaty of Versailles. Making common cause behind the scenes with another diminished and resentful Great Power, the Soviet Union, the army leadership arranged for clandestine training sessions in Russia for officers anxious to learn how to use tanks and aeroplanes, and willing to engage in experiments with poison gas.[46] Secret arrangements were made to train auxiliary troops, in an attempt to get round the limit of 100,000 imposed by the Treaty on the army's strength, and the army was constantly eyeing the paramilitaries as a potential military reserve.[47] These subterfuges and others, including training with make-believe tanks, made clear that the army had no intention of abiding by the terms of the 1919 Peace Settlement and would break free from it as soon as circumstances allowed. Far from being led exclusively by dyed-in-the-wool Prussian conservatives, these clandestine circumventions of the Treaty were organized above all by modern-minded technicians, impatient with the constraints of democratic politics and international agreements.[48] The disloyalty of the army, and the repeated intrigues of its leading officers against civilian governments, boded ill for the Republic's continued viability in a real crisis.[49]

If Germany's first democracy could not expect much support from its military servants, then neither could it hope for much support from its civil servants, whom it likewise inherited from the old German Reich. The civil service was of huge importance because it covered a very wide area of society and included not just officials working in the central administration of the Reich but also all those state employees who had secured the tenure, status and emoluments originally designed for senior administrators. They included officials working for the federated states, for state enterprises like the railways and the postal service, and for state institutions such as universities and schools, so that university professors and high-school teachers fell into this category as well. The numbers of civil servants in this broad sense were enormous. Below this relatively exalted level there were millions more state servants living off salaries or wages paid by state institutions. The German state railway was by far the largest single employer in the Weimar Republic, for instance, with 700,000 people working for it at the end of the 1920s; it was followed by the postal service with 380,000. If family members, dependants and pensioners are added on, about 3 million people relied for their support on the railways alone.[50] Altogether, by the end of the 1920s there were 1.6 million civil servants in Germany, about half of whom worked for the state proper, the other half for public utilities such as the railways.

With such a large number of state employees, it was clear that the state employment sector was politically extremely diverse, with hundreds of thousands of employees belonging to socialist trade unions, liberal political parties or pressure-groups of widely varying political orientation. A million civil servants belonged to the liberal German Civil Servants' League in 1919, though 60,000 split off to form a more right-wing group in 1921 and another 350,000 seceded to form a trade union the following year. Civil servants were in no sense, therefore, uniformly hostile to the Republic at the outset, despite their training and socialization in the years of the Wilhelmine Reich.[51]

As the leading figure in the transitional revolutionary administration, Friedrich Ebert appealed on 9 November 1918 for all civil servants and state employees to continue working in order to avoid anarchy.[52] The overwhelming majority stayed on. Civil servants' career structure and duties were unchanged. The Weimar constitution made them irremovable. However it might have appeared in theory, in practice this step made it virtually impossible to dismiss civil servants, given the extreme difficulty of proving in law that they had violated their oath of allegiance.[53] As an institution that derived from the authoritarian and bureaucratic states of the late eighteenth and early nineteenth centuries, long before the advent of parliaments and political parties, the higher civil service in particular had long been accustomed to regard itself as the true ruling caste, above all in Prussia. Up to 1918, for instance, all government ministers had been civil servants, appointed by the monarch, not by the Reichstag or the legislative assemblies of the federated states. In some Reich ministries, where there was a rapid turnover of ministers under the Republic, the top civil servant could wield enormous power, as with Curt Joël in the Ministry of Justice, who served virtually throughout the Republic, while no fewer than seventeen Justice Ministers came and went, before he finally became Minister himself in 1930. For such men, administrative continuity was the supreme dictate of duty, overriding all political considerations. Whatever they might have thought privately of the Kapp putschists in March 1920, senior civil servants in Berlin, including financial officials, thus carried on with their work in defiance of the putschists' orders for them to stand down.[54]

The neutrality of civil servants on this occasion owed a good deal to their characteristically punctilious insistence on the duties imposed by their oath of allegiance. Later on, in 1922, the government introduced a new law designed to bind civil servants even more closely to the Republic and impose disciplinary sanctions on those who consorted with its enemies. But this measure was relatively toothless. Only in Prussia was there a serious effort, led by Carl Severing and Albert Grzesinski, successive Social Democratic Ministers of the Interior, to replace old Imperial administrators, above all in the provinces, with Social Democrats and others loyal to the Republic.[55] Nevertheless, even the Prussian efforts at creating a civil service loyal to the principles of democracy as well as imbued with a sense of duty in serving the government of the day proved insufficient in the end. Because Severing and Grzesinski thought that the parties should be represented in the higher civil service roughly in proportion to their place in the Prussian coalition cabinets, this meant that a good number of important posts were held by men from parties such as the Centre Party, the People's Party and to a degree the State Party, whose allegiance to the Republic was rapidly becoming more tenuous from the end of the 1920s onwards. In the rest of Germany, including the level of the Reich civil service, even this degree of reform was barely even attempted, let alone achieved, and the civil service was far more conservative, even in parts downright hostile to the Republic.[56]

The problem, however, was not so much that the higher civil service was actively helping to undermine Weimar; rather, it was that the Republic did too little to ensure that civil servants at whatever level were actively committed to the democratic political order and would resist any attempt to overthrow it. And those civil servants who were actively hostile to the Republic – probably a minority, considered overall – were able to survive with relative impunity. Thus, for instance, one senior Prussian civil servant, born in 1885, and a member of the Nationalist Party after 1918, founded a variety of fringe groups for civil servants and others, aiming explicitly to combat 'the Reichstag, the red headquarters', to frustrate the policies of the 'treasonous and godless Social Democrats', to oppose the 'imperialist world power' of the Catholic Church and finally to fight against 'all Jews'. His antisemitism, fairly latent before 1918, became explicit after the Revolution. Thereafter, he later recalled, 'whenever a Jew was carrying on impertinently on the elevated [railway] or on the train and would not accept my scolding without further impertinence, I threatened to throw him off the moving train . . . if he did not shut up immediately'. On one occasion he threatened 'Marxist' workers with a gun. His was an obviously extreme example of a civil servant opposed to the Republic. Yet he was not dismissed, only disciplined twice and denied promotion, despite being tried on one occasion for disturbing the peace. 'I always', he wrote, 'took it to be a weakness of my political enemies in the civil service that they let me get off so easily every time.' The worst that happened to him under the Republic was a blockage of his career prospects.[57]

There can be little doubt that, even in the Republican bastion of Prussia, the vast majority of civil servants had little genuine loyalty to the constitution to which they had sworn their allegiance. Should the Republic be threatened with destruction, very few of them indeed would even think of coming to its aid. Devotion to duty kept them working when the state was challenged, as in the Kapp putsch of 1920, but it would also keep them working when the state was overthrown. Here was another central institution whose loyalty was to an abstract concept of the Reich rather than to the concrete principles of democracy. In this as in other respects, Weimar was weak in political legitimacy from the start.[58] It was beset by insurmountable problems of political violence, assassination and irreconcilable conflicts about its right to exist. It was unloved and undefended by its servants in the army and bureaucracy. It was blamed by many for the national humiliation of the Treaty of Versailles. And it also had to face enormous economic problems, beginning with the massive monetary inflation that made life so difficult for so many in the years when it was trying to establish itself.

THE GREAT INFLATION

I

Even the most diehard reactionary might eventually have learned to tolerate the Republic if it had provided a reasonable level of economic stability and a decent, solid income for its citizens. But from the start it was beset by economic failures of a dimension unprecedented in German history. As soon as the First World War had begun, the Reich government had started to borrow money to pay for it. From 1916 onwards, expenditure had far exceeded the revenue that the government had been able to raise from loans or indeed from any other source. Naturally enough, it had expected to recoup its losses by annexing rich industrial areas to the west and east, by forcing the defeated nations to pay large financial reparations, and by imposing a new German-dominated economic order on a conquered Europe.[59] But these expectations were dashed. In the event, it was Germany that was the defeated nation and Germany that had to foot the bill. This made things far worse than before. The government had been printing money without the economic resources to back it. Before the war, the dollar had been worth just over 4 paper marks on the exchange in Berlin. By December 1918 it took nearly twice as many marks to buy a US dollar. The rate continued to decline to just over 12 marks to the dollar in April 1919 and 47 by the end of the year.[60]

Successive governments of the Weimar Republic were caught in a political trap that was at least partly of their own making. The need to export government revenue to other countries in the form of reparations payments meant an additional drain on resources at a time when wartime debts still had to be paid and Germany's economic resources and domestic market had shrunk. Heavily populated industrial areas in Lorraine and

Silesia had been removed under the terms of the Treaty. Industrial production was only 42 per cent in 1919 of what it had been in 1913, and
the country was producing less than half the grain it had produced before
the war. Massive expenditure was required to fund the adjustment to a
peacetime economy, and to provide welfare measures for ex-soldiers
seeking jobs, or unable to find them because of war disability. Yet if any
government sought to bridge the gap by raising taxes by any more than
a small amount, it would immediately be accused by its enemies on the
nationalist right of imposing taxes in order to meet Allied reparations
bills. It seemed politically more astute to most governments to tell foreign
powers instead that Germany's currency problems would only be solved
by the abolition of reparations, or at least by rescheduling them to what
would be a more acceptable level. The energy and aggressiveness with
which various German governments pursued this dangerous policy
varied, and during 1920 and 1921 the slide of the mark against the dollar
was arrested more than once. Still, by November 1921 Germans who
wanted to buy a US dollar had to pay 263 marks for it, and by July 1922
the cost had almost doubled again, to 493 marks.[61]

Inflation on this scale had different effects on different players in
the economic game. The ability to borrow money to purchase goods,
equipment, industrial plant and the like, and pay it back when it was
worth a fraction of its original value, helped stimulate industrial recovery
after the war. In the period up to the middle of 1922, economic growth
rates in Germany were high, and unemployment low. Without this background of virtually full employment, a general strike, such as the one
which frustrated the Kapp putsch in March 1920, would have been far
more difficult to mount. Real taxation rates were also low enough to
stimulate demand. The German economy managed the transition to a
peacetime basis more effectively than some European economies where
inflation was less marked.[62]

But the recovery was built on sand. For, despite a few temporary
respites in the process, the inflation proved to be unstoppable. It took
over 1,000 marks to buy a US dollar in August 1922, 3,000 in October,
and 7,000 in December. The process of monetary depreciation was taking
on a life of its own. The political consequences were catastrophic. The
German government could not make the required reparations payments
any longer, since they had to be tendered in gold, whose price on the

international market it could no longer afford to meet. Moreover, by the end of 1922 it had fallen seriously behind in its deliveries of coal to the French, another part of the reparations programme. So French and Belgian troops occupied Germany's leading industrial district, the Ruhr, in January 1923 in order to seize the missing coal and force the Germans to fulfil their obligations under the Treaty. The government in Berlin almost immediately proclaimed a policy of passive resistance and non-cooperation with the French in order to deny the occupiers facilities to garner the fruits of Ruhr industrial production for themselves. The struggle was only called off towards the end of September. Passive resistance made the economic situation worse. Anyone who wanted to buy a dollar in January 1923 had to pay over 17,000 marks for it; in April 24,000; in July 353,000. This was hyperinflation on a truly staggering scale, and the dollar rate in marks for the rest of the year is best expressed in numbers that soon became longer than anything found even in a telephone directory: 4,621,000 in August; 98,860,000 in September; 25,260,000,000 in October; 2,193,600,000,000 in November; 4,200,000,000,000 in December.[63] Newspapers soon began informing their readers about the nomenclature of big numbers, which varied confusingly from one country to another. The French, one columnist noted, called a million million a trillion, while 'for us on the other hand, a trillion is equal to a million billion (1,000,000,000,000,000,000,000), and we must only hope to God that we don't get into these or even higher numerical values with our everyday currency, merely because of the overcrowding of the lunatic asylums that it would cause.'[64]

At its height, the hyperinflation seemed terrifying. Money lost its meaning almost completely. Printing presses were unable to keep up with the need to produce banknotes of ever more astronomical denominations, and municipalities began to print their own emergency money, using one side of the paper only. Employees collected their wages in shopping baskets or wheelbarrows, so numerous were the banknotes needed to make up their pay packets; and immediately rushed to the shops to buy supplies before the continuing plunge in the value of money put them out of reach. The school student Raimund Pretzel later remembered how at the end of every month his father, a senior civil servant, would collect his salary, rush off to buy a season ticket for the railway so that he could get to work for the next month, send off cheques for regular outgoings, take the entire family for a haircut, then hand over what was left to his wife, who would go with the children to the local wholesale market and buy heaps of non-perishable foodstuffs off which they had to live until the next pay-packet came in. For the rest of the month the family had no money at all. Letters had to be mailed with the latest denomination banknotes stapled to the envelope, since postage stamps of the right value could not be printed fast enough to keep pace with the price rise. The German correspondent of the British *Daily Mail* reported on 29 July 1923: 'In the shops the prices are typewritten and posted hourly. For instance, a gramophone at 10 a.m. was 5,000,000 marks but at 3 p.m. it was 12,000,000 marks. A copy of the *Daily Mail* purchased on the street yesterday cost 35,000 marks but today it cost 60,000 marks.'[65]

The most dramatic and serious effects were on the price of food. A woman sitting down in a café might order a cup of coffee for 5,000 marks and be asked to give the waiter 8,000 for it when she got up to pay an hour later. A kilo of rye bread, that staple of the German daily diet, cost 163 marks on 3 January 1923, more than ten times that amount in July, 9 million marks on 1 October, 78 billion marks on 5 November and 233 billion marks a fortnight later, on 19 November.[66] At the height of the hyperinflation, over 90 per cent of the expenditure of an average family went on food.[67] Families on fixed incomes started selling their possessions so that they could have something to eat. Shops began hoarding food in anticipation of immediate price rises.[68] Unable to afford the most basic necessities, crowds began to riot and to loot food shops. Gunfights broke out between gangs of miners, who sallied forth into the countryside to strip the fields bare, and the farmers who were trying to protect their crops and were at the same time unwilling to sell them for worthless banknotes. The collapse of the mark made it difficult if not impossible to import supplies from abroad. The threat of starvation, particularly in the area occupied by the French, where passive resistance was crippling the transport networks, was very real.[69] Malnutrition caused an immediate rise in deaths from tuberculosis.[70]

Not untypical was the experience of the academic Victor Klemperer, whose diaries offer a personal insight into the larger sweep of German history in this period. Living very much from hand to mouth on temporary teaching contracts, Klemperer, a war veteran, was pleased to receive a small additional war gratuity in February 1920, but, as he complained, 'what was earlier a small income is now just a tip'.[71] Over the following months, Klemperer's diary was increasingly filled with financial calculations as inflation gathered pace. Already in March 1920 he was encountering 'foragers, little people with rucksacks' on the train outside Munich.[72] As time went on, Klemperer paid increasingly fantastic bills 'with a kind of dull fatalism'.[73] In 1920 he at last gained a permanent appointment at Dresden Technical University. But it did not bring financial security. Each month he received an increasingly astronomical salary with back payments to make up for inflation since the last payment. Despite receiving nearly a million marks' salary at the end of May 1923, he was still unable to pay his gas and tax bills. Everyone he knew was working out how to make money speculating on the Stock Exchange. Even Klemperer had a try, but his first gain, 230,000 marks, paled into insignificance in comparison with that of his colleague Professor Förster, 'one of the worst antisemites, Teutonic agitators and patriots in the university', who was said to be making half a million marks a day playing the markets.[74]

An habitué of cafés, Klemperer paid 12,000 marks for a coffee and cake on 24 July; on 3 August he noted that a coffee and three cakes cost him 104,000 marks.[75] On Monday, 28 August Klemperer reported that a few weeks previously he had obtained ten tickets for the cinema, one of his main pleasures in life, for 100,000 marks. 'Immediately after that, the price increased immeasurably, and most recently our 10,000-mark seat has already cost 200,000. Yesterday afternoon,' he went on, 'I wanted to buy a new stock. The middle rows of the stalls already cost 300,000 marks', and these were the second cheapest seats in the house; a further price increase had already been announced for the following Thursday, three days later.[76] By 9 October he was reporting: 'Our visit to the cinema yesterday cost 104 million, including the money for the fare.'[77] The situation brought him, like many others, to the brink of despair:

Germany is collapsing in an eerie, step-by-step manner . . . The dollar stands at over 800 million, it stands every day at 300 million more than the previous day. All that's not just what you read in the paper, but has an immediate impact on one's own life. How long will we still have something to eat? Where will we next have to tighten our belts?[78]

Klemperer spent more and more of his time scrambling about for money, writing on 2 November:

Yesterday I waited for money in the university cashier's office the whole morning up to almost 2 o'clock and in the end I didn't get a penny, not even what was left from the October payment, since the dollar rose yesterday from 65 to 130 billion, so today I will have to pay my gas bill and other things at twice yesterday's price. In the case of gas that is likely to make a difference of a good 150 billion.[79]

Food riots were breaking out in Dresden, he reported, some of them with an antisemitic tinge, and Klemperer began to fear that his house would be broken into in the frantic search for supplies. Work was impossible. 'Money matters take up a very great deal of time and frazzle one's nerves.'[80]

Germany was grinding to a halt. Businesses and municipalities could no longer afford to pay their workers or buy supplies for public utilities. By 7 September sixty out of the ninety tram routes in Berlin had stopped running.[81] The situation clearly could not continue any longer. The country was brought back from the brink by a combination of astute political moves and clever financial reforms. Beginning his long period of service as Foreign Minister in August 1923, Gustav Stresemann, who combined the office with the Reich Chancellorship for the first few months, initiated a policy of 'fulfilment', negotiating the withdrawal of the French from the Ruhr in September in return for a guarantee that Germany would meet its reparations payments, come what might. As a result, the international community agreed to look again at the reparations system, and a plan drawn up by a committee under the chairmanship of the American financial expert Charles Dawes was negotiated and accepted the following year.

The Dawes Plan did not hold out any prospect of an end to the payments, but at least it put in place a series of arrangements to ensure that paying them was a practical proposition, and for the next five years they were indeed paid without too many problems.[82] Stresemann's policy did not earn him any plaudits from the nationalist right, who resisted any concession to the principle of reparations. But the extent of the hyper-inflation by this time convinced most people that this was the only realistic policy, a view they would most probably not have taken a year or so earlier.[83] On the financial front, the Stresemann government appointed

Hjalmar Schacht, an astute financier with strong political connections, to head the central state bank, the Reichsbank, on 22 December 1923. A new currency had already been issued on 15 November, the Rentenmark, whose value was tied to the price of gold.[84] Schacht put a number of measures in place to defend the Rentenmark from speculation, and as the new currency, soon renamed the Reichsmark, became more widely available, it replaced the old one and achieved general acceptance.[85] The hyperinflation was over.

Other countries were affected by postwar inflation, but none so badly as Germany. At the height of the hyperinflation, which varied from country to country, prices stood at 14,000 times their prewar level in Austria, 23,000 times in Hungary, 2,500,000 times in Poland and 4,000 million times in Russia, although the inflation here was not strictly comparable to its counterparts elsewhere since the Bolsheviks had largely withdrawn the Soviet economy from the world market. These rates were bad enough. But in Germany, prices had reached a billion times their prewar level, a decline that has entered the annals of economic history as the greatest hyperinflation ever. It was noticeable that all these countries had not fought on the winning side in the war. Each country eventually stabilized its currency, but without much reference to the others. No viable new international financial system emerged in the 1920s to compare with the elaborate set of institutions and agreements that was to govern international finance after the Second World War.[86]

II

The consequences both of the hyperinflation and of the way it came to an end were momentous. Yet its long-term effects on the economic situation of Germany's population are hard to measure. It used to be thought that it destroyed the economic prosperity of the middle class. But the middle class was a very diverse group in economic and financial terms. Anyone who had invested money in war bonds or other loans to the state lost it, but anyone who had borrowed a large sum of money as a mortgage for a house or flat was likely to end up acquiring the property for virtually nothing. Often these two situations were united to one degree or another in the same person. But for those who depended on a fixed income, the results were ruinous. Creditors were embittered. The economic and social cohesion of the middle class was shattered, as winners and losers confronted one another across new social divides. The result was a growing fragmentation of the middle-class political parties in the second half of the 1920s, rendering them helpless in the face of demagogic assaults from the far right. And, crucially, as the deflationary effects of the stabilization began to bite, all social groups felt the pinch. Popular memory conflated the effects of the inflation, the hyperinflation and the stabilization into a single economic catastrophe in which virtually every group in German society was a loser.[87] Victor Klemperer was a typical figure in this process. When the stabilization came, the 'fear of sudden monetary devaluation, the mad rush of having to shop' were over, but 'destitution' came in their place, for in the new currency Klemperer had virtually nothing of any value and hardly any money at all. After all his speculation, he concluded gloomily, 'my shares have a value of scarcely 100 marks, my cash reserves at home about the same, and that's all – my life insurance is utterly and completely lost. 150 paper millions are = 0.015 pfennigs.'[88]

As money lost its value, goods became the only thing worth having, and a huge crime wave swept the country. Convictions for theft, which had numbered 115,000 in 1913, peaked at 365,000 in 1923. Seven times more offenders were convicted of handling stolen goods in 1923 than in 1913. So desperate were the poor even in 1921 that a Social Democratic newspaper reported that out of 100 men sent to Berlin's Plötzensee prison, 80 had no socks on, 60 were without shoes and 50 did not even have a shirt on their back.[89] Pilfering in the Hamburg docks, where workers had traditionally helped themselves to a portion of the cargoes they were paid to load and unload, reached unprecedented levels. Workers were said to be refusing to load some goods on the grounds that they could not use any of them. Trade unions reported that many workers only went to the quayside in order to steal, and that anyone who tried to stop them was beaten up. Coffee, flour, bacon and sugar were favoured booty. In effect, workers were increasingly enforcing payment in kind as money wages declined in value. So widespread did the phenomenon become that some foreign shipping firms began unloading goods elsewhere in 1922–3.[90] A similar economy of theft and barter began to replace money transactions in other trades and other centres as well.

Violence, or the threat of violence, sometimes made itself evident in spectacular ways. Gangs of up to two hundred heavily armed youths were seen storming barns in the countryside and carrying off the produce. Yet, despite this atmosphere of barely controllable criminality, convictions for wounding fell from 113,000 in 1913 to a mere 35,000 in 1923, and there was a comparable fall in other categories of crime not directly related to theft. Almost everybody seemed to be concentrating on stealing small amounts of food and supplies in order to stay alive. There were reports of girls selling themselves for packets of butter. Bitterness and resentment at this situation were increased by the feeling that some people were making huge profits from it, through illicit currency dealing, cross-border smuggling, profiteering and the illegal moving of goods. The black marketeer and the profiteer had become objects of denunciation by populist demagogues even before galloping inflation became hyperinflation. Now they became popular hate-figures. There was a widespread feeling that profiteers were partying the night away while honest shopkeepers and artisans were having to sell their household furniture to buy a loaf of bread. Traditional moral values appeared to many to be in decline along with traditional monetary values.[91] The descent into chaos – economic, social, political, moral – seemed to be total.[92]

Money, income, financial solidity, economic order, regularity and predictability had been at the heart of bourgeois values and bourgeois existence before the war. Now all this seemed to have been swept away along with the equally solid-seeming political system of the Wilhelmine Reich. A widespread cynicism began to make itself apparent in Weimar culture, from films like Dr Mabuse the Gambler to Thomas Mann's The Confessions of the Swindler Felix Krull (written in 1922 though put aside and not completed until more than thirty years later). It was not least as a consequence of the inflation that Weimar culture developed its fascination with criminals, embezzlers, gamblers, manipulators, thieves and crooks of all kinds. Life seemed to be a game of chance, survival a matter of the arbitrary impact of incomprehensible economic forces. In such an atmosphere, conspiracy theories began to abound. Gambling, whether at the card table or on the Stock Exchange, became a metaphor for life. Much of the cynicism that gave Weimar culture its edge in the mid-1920s and made many people eventually long for the return of idealism, self-sacrifice and patriotic dedication, derived from the disorienting effects of the hyperinflation.[93] Hyperinflation became a trauma whose influence affected the behaviour of Germans of all classes long afterwards. It added to the feeling in the more conservative sections of the population of a world turned upside down, first by defeat, then by revolution, and now by economics. It destroyed faith in the neutrality of the law as a social regulator, between debtors and creditors, rich and poor, and undermined notions of the fairness and equity that the law was supposed to maintain. It debased the language of politics, already driven to hyperbolic over-emphasis by the events of 1918–19. It lent new power to stock fantasy-images of evil, not just the criminal and the gambler, but also the speculator and, fatefully, the financially manipulative Jew.[94]

III

Among the groups widely regarded as winners in the economic upheavals of the early 1920s were the big industrialists and financiers, a fact that caused widespread resentment against 'capitalists' and 'profiteers' in many quarters of German society. But German businessmen were not so sure they had gained so much. Many of them looked back to the Wilhelmine Reich with nostalgia, a time when the state, the police and the courts had kept the labour movement at bay and business itself had bent the ear of government in key matters of economic and social policy. Misconceived though this rose-tinted retrovision might have been, the fact remained that big business had indeed held a privileged position before the war despite occasional irritations with state interference in the economy.[95] The rapidity and scale of Germany's industrialization had not only made the country into mainland Europe's major economic power by 1914, it had also created a business sector that was remarkable for the scale of its enterprises and the public prominence of its managers and entrepreneurs. Men like the arms manufacturer Krupp, the iron and steel magnates Stumm and Thyssen, the shipowner Ballin, the electricity company bosses Rathenau and Siemens, and many more, were household names, rich, powerful and politically influential.

Such men tended, with varying emphases, to resist unionization and reject the idea of collective bargaining. During the war, however, they had softened their antagonism under the impact of growing state interference in labour relations, and on 15 November 1918 business and the unions, represented respectively by Hugo Stinnes and Carl Legien, signed a pact establishing a new framework of collective bargaining, including recognition of the eight-hour day. Both sides had an interest in warding off the threat of sweeping socialization from the extreme left, and the agreement preserved the existing structure of big business while giving the unions equal representation on a nationwide network of joint bargaining committees. Like other elements of the Wilhelmine establishment, big business accepted the Republic because it seemed the most likely way of warding off something worse.[96]

Things did not, then, seem too bad for business during the early years of the Republic. Once they had cottoned on to the fact that the inflation was going to continue, many industrialists purchased large quantities of machinery with borrowed money that had lost its value by the time they came to pay it back. But this did not mean, as some have claimed, that they drove on the inflation because they saw its advantages for themselves. On the contrary, many of them were confused about what to do, above all during the hyperinflation of 1923, and the gains they made from the whole process were not as spectacular as has often been alleged.[97] Moreover, the sharp deflation that was the inevitable outcome of currency stabilization brought serious problems for industry, which had in many cases invested in more plant than it needed. Bankruptcies multiplied, the huge industrial and financial empire of Hugo Stinnes collapsed, and major companies sought refuge in a wave of mergers and cartels, most notably the United Steelworks, formed in 1924 from a number of heavy industrial companies, and the massive I.G. Farben, the German Dye Trust, created the same year from the chemical firms of Agfa, BASF, Bayer, Griesheim, Hoechst and Weiler-ter-Meer, to form the largest corporation in Europe and the fourth largest in the world after General Motors, United States Steel and Standard Oil.[98]

Mergers and cartels were designed not only to achieve market dominance but also to cut costs and increase efficiency. The new enterprises set great store by rationalizing their production along the lines of the super-efficient Ford Motor Company in the United States. 'Fordism', as it was known, automated and mechanized production wherever possible in the interests of efficiency. It was accompanied by a drive to reorganize work in accordance with new American time-and-motion studies, known as 'Taylorism', much debated in Germany during the second half of the 1920s.[99] Changes along these lines were achieved to a spectacular degree in the coal-mining industry in the Ruhr, where 98 per cent of coal was extracted by manual labour before the war, but only 13 per cent by 1929. The use of pneumatic drills to dig out the coal, and of mechanized conveyor belts to take it to the loading point, combined with a reorganization of working practices to bring about an increase of the annual output of coal per miner from 255 tons in 1925 to 386 tons by 1932. Such efficiency gains enabled the mining companies to reduce the size of their labour force very quickly, from 545,000 in 1922 to 409,000 in 1925 and 353,000 in 1929. Similar processes of rationalization and mechanization happened in other areas of the economy, notably in the rapidly growing automobile industry.[100] Yet in other areas, such as iron and steel production, efficiency gains were achieved not so much by mechanization and modernization as by mergers and monopolies. For all the discussions and debates about 'Fordism', 'Taylorism' and the like, much of German industry still had a very traditional look to it at the end of the 1920s.[101]

Adjusting to the new economic situation after stabilization in any case meant retrenchment, cost-cutting and job losses. The situation was made worse by the fact that the relatively large birth-cohorts born in the prewar years were now coming onto the job market, more than replacing those killed in the war or by the devastating influenza epidemic that swept the world immediately afterwards. The labour census of 1925 revealed that there were five million more people in the available workforce than in 1907; the next census, held in 1931, showed an additional million or more. By the end of 1925, under the twin impacts of rationalization and generational population growth, unemployment had reached a million; in March 1926, it topped three million.[102] In the new circumstances, business lost its willingness to compromise with the labour unions. Stabilization meant that employers were no longer able to pass on the costs of wage raises by raising their prices. The organized structure of collective bargaining that had been agreed between employers and unions during the First World War fell apart. It was replaced by increasingly acrimonious relations between business and labour, in which labour's room for manoeuvre became ever more restricted. Yet employers continued to feel frustrated in their drive to cut costs and improve productivity by the strength of the unions and the legal and institutional obstacles placed in their way by the state. The system of arbitration put in place by the Weimar Republic loaded the dice in favour of the unions during labour disputes, or so the employers felt. When a bitter dispute over wages in the iron and steel industry in the Ruhr was settled by compulsory arbitration in 1928, the employers refused to pay the small wage increase that had been awarded, and locked over 200,000 metalworkers out of their plants for four weeks. The workers were not only backed by the Reich government, led by the Social Democrats in a Grand Coalition formed earlier in the year, but also got paid relief by the state. To the employers it began to seem as if the whole structure of the Weimar Republic was ranged against them.[103]

Things were made worse from their point of view by the financial obligations that the state placed on them. In order to try and alleviate the worst consequences of the stabilization for workers, and to prevent the recurrence of the near-collapse of welfare provision that had occurred during the hyperinflation, the government introduced an elaborate scheme of unemployment insurance in stages in the years 1926 and 1927. Designed to cushion some 17 million workers against the effects of job losses, the most substantial of these laws, passed in 1927, required the same contributions from employers as employees, and set up a state fund to cope with major crises when the number of unemployed exceeded the figure with which it was designed to cope. Since this was only 800,000, it was obvious that the scheme would get into serious trouble should numbers go any higher. In fact, they had exceeded the limit even before the scheme came into effect.[104] Not surprisingly, this welfare system represented a growing state intervention in the economy which business disliked. It piled on extra costs by enforcing employers' contributions to workers' benefit schemes, and it imposed an increasing tax burden on business enterprise and indeed on well-off businessmen themselves. Most hostile of all were the heavy industrialists of the Ruhr. Legal restrictions on hours of work prevented them in many cases from utilizing their plant round the clock. Contributions to the unemployment benefit scheme launched in 1927 were seen as crippling. In 1929 the industrialists' national organization announced its view that the country could no longer afford this kind of thing and called for swingeing cuts in state expenditure accompanied by the formal ending of the bargain with labour that had preserved big business at the time of the 1918 Revolution. Claims that it was the welfare system rather than the state of the international economy that was causing their problems were exaggerated, to say the least; but the new mood of hostility towards the unions and the Social Democrats among many employers in the second half of the 1920s was unmistakeable none the less.[105]

Big business was thus already disillusioned with the Weimar Republic by the late 1920s. The influence it had enjoyed before 1914, still more during the war and the postwar era of inflation, now seemed to be drastically diminished. Moreover, its public standing, once so high, had suffered badly as a result of financial and other scandals that had surfaced during the inflation. People who lost their fortunes in dubious investments searched for someone to blame. Such scapegoating focused in 1924–5 on the figure of Julius Barmat, a Russian-Jewish entrepreneur who had collaborated with leading Social Democrats in importing food supplies immediately after the war, then invested the credits he obtained from the Prussian State Bank and the Post Office in financial speculation during the inflation. When his business collapsed towards the end of 1924, leaving 10 million Reichsmarks of debts, the far right took the opportunity to run a scurrilous press campaign accusing leading Social Democrats such as the former Chancellor Gustav Bauer of taking bribes. Financial scandals of this kind were exploited more generally by the far right to back up claims that Jewish corruption was exerting undue influence on the Weimar state and causing financial ruin to many ordinary middle-class Germans.[106]

What could business do to remedy this situation? Its room for political manoeuvre was limited. From the beginning of the Republic, business sought both to insulate industry from political interference, and to secure political influence, or at least good will, through financial donations to the 'bourgeois' parties, notably the Nationalists and the People's Party. Large concerns often had a financial hold on major newspapers through their investments, but this seldom translated into a direct political input. Where the owner did intervene frequently in editorial policy, as in the case of Alfred Hugenberg (whose press and media empire expanded rapidly during the Weimar Republic), this often had little to do with the specific interests of business itself. By the early 1930s, indeed, leading businessmen were so irritated by Hugenberg's right-wing radicalism that they were plotting to oust him from the leadership of the Nationalist

Party. Far from speaking with one voice on the issues that affected it, business was split from top to bottom not only by politics, as the example of Hugenberg suggests, but by economic interest, too. Thus, while the Ruhr iron, steel and mining companies were furiously opposed to the Weimar welfare state and the Weimar system of collective bargaining, companies like Siemens or I.G. Farben, the giants of the more modern sectors of the economy, were more willing to compromise. Some conflict of interest also existed between export-oriented industries, which did relatively well during the years of stabilization and retrenchment, and industries producing mainly for the home market, which included, once again, the Ruhr iron and steel magnates. Even among the latter, however, there were serious differences of opinion, with Krupp actually opposing the hard-line stance taken by the employers in the 1928 lock-out.[107] By the end of the 1920s, business was divided in its politics and hemmed in by the restrictions placed on it by the Weimar state. It had lost much of the political influence it had enjoyed during the inflation. Its frustration with the Republic was soon to erupt into open hostility on the part of some of its most influential representatives.

CULTURE WARS

I

The conflicts that rent Weimar were more than merely political or economic. Their visceral quality derived much from the fact that they were not just fought out in parliaments and elections, but permeated every aspect of life. Indifference to politics was hardly a characteristic of the German population in the years leading up to the Third Reich. People arguably suffered from an excess of political engagement and political commitment. One indication of this could be found in the extremely high turnout rates at elections – no less than 80 per cent of the electorate in most contests.[108] Elections met with none of the indifference that is allegedly the sign of a mature democracy. On the contrary, during election campaigns in many parts of Germany every spare inch of outside walls and advertising columns seemed to be covered with posters, every window hung with banners, every building festooned with the colours of one political party or another. This went far beyond the sense of duty that was said by some to have driven voters to the polls in prewar years. There seemed to be no area of society or politics that was immune from politicization.

Nowhere was this more obvious than in the press. No fewer than 4,700 newspapers appeared in Germany in the year 1932, 70 per cent of them on a daily basis. Many of them were local, with a small circulation, but some of them, like the liberal *Frankfurt Newspaper* (*Frankfurter Zeitung*), were major broadsheets with an international reputation. Such organs formed only a small part of the politically oriented press, which together made up about a quarter of all newspapers. Nearly three-quarters of the politically oriented papers owed their allegiance to the

Centre Party or its equivalent in the south, the Bavarian People's Party, or to the Social Democrats.[109] The political parties set great store by their daily papers. *Forwards* (*Vorwärts*) for the Social Democrats, and the *Red Flag* (*Rote Fahne*) for the Communists were key parts of their respective parties' propaganda apparatus, and headed up an elaborate structure of weekly magazines, local newspapers, glossy illustrated periodicals and specialist publications. A newspaper propaganda organizer like the Communist press chief Willi Münzenberg could win an almost mythical reputation as a creator and manipulator of the media.[110] At the opposite end of the political spectrum, an equally legendary status was occupied by Alfred Hugenberg, who as chairman of the board of the arms manufacturer Krupps had purchased the Scherl newspaper firm in 1916. Two years later, he also acquired a major news agency through which he supplied large sections of the press with stories and leading articles during the Weimar years. By the late 1920s Hugenberg had in addition become owner of the mammoth film production company, the UFA. Hugenberg used his media empire to propagate his own, virulently German nationalist ideas across the land, and to spread the message that it was time for a restoration of the monarchy. Such was his reputation that by the end of the 1920s he was being referred to as the 'uncrowned king' of Germany and 'one of the most powerful men' in the land.[111]

Yet, whatever people thought, media power of this kind did not translate directly into political power. Hugenberg's domination of the media had absolutely no effect in stopping the relentless decline of the Nationalists after 1924. Political papers in general had small circulations: in 1929, for instance, the *Red Flag* sold 28,000 copies a day, *Forwards* 74,000 a day, and Hugenberg's *The Day* (*Der Tag*) just over 70,000. These were not impressive figures by any stretch of the imagination. Moreover, sales of the *Red Flag* dropped to 15,000 just as the Communist vote was beginning to increase in the early 1930s. Overall, the circulation of the overtly political press fell by nearly a third between 1925 and 1932. The up-market liberal quality dailies also lost circulation.[112] The *Frankfurt Newspaper*, probably the most prestigious of the liberal quality dailies, slipped from 100,000 in 1915 to 71,000 in 1928. As newspaper editors realized only too well, many readers of the pro-Weimar liberal press voted for parties that were opposed to Weimar. The political power of editors and proprietors seemed limited here, too.[113]

What was undermining the political press in the 1920s was, above all, the rise of the so-called 'boulevard papers', cheap, sensational tabloids that were sold on the streets, particularly in the afternoons and evenings, rather than depending on regular subscribers. Heavily illustrated, with massive coverage of sport, cinema, local news, crime, scandal and sensation, these papers placed the emphasis on entertainment rather than information. Yet they, too, could have a political orientation, like Hugenberg's *Night Edition* (*Nachtausgabe*), whose circulation grew from 38,000 in 1925 to 202,000 in 1930, or Münzenberg's *World in the Evening* (*Welt am Abend*), which boosted its sales from 12,000 in 1925 to 220,000 in 1930. By and large, the pro-Weimar press found it hard to keep up with such competition, though the liberal-oriented Ullstein press empire did produce the successful *Tempo* (145,000 in 1930) and *BZ at Midday* (*BZ am Mittag*, 175,000 in the same year). The Social Democrats were unable to compete in this market.[114] It was at this level that the politics of the press had a real impact. Scandal-sheets undermined the Republic with their sensational exposure of real or imagined financial wrongdoings on the part of pro-Republic politicians; illustrations could convey the contrast with Imperial days. The massive publicity the popular press gave to murder trials and police investigations created the impression of a society drowning in a wave of violent crime. Out in the provinces, ostensibly unpolitical local papers, often fed by right-wing press agencies, had a similar, if more muted effect. Hugenberg's press empire might not have saved the Nationalists from decline; but its constant harping on the iniquities of the Republic was another factor in weakening Weimar's legitimacy and convincing people that something else was needed in its stead. In the end, therefore, the press did have some effect in swaying the minds of voters, above all in influencing them in a general way against Weimar democracy.[115]

The emergence of the sensationalist popular press was only one among many new and, for some people, disquieting developments on the media and cultural scene in the 1920s and early 1930s. Experimental literature, the 'concrete poetry' of the Dadaists, the modernist novels of Alfred Döblin, the social-critical plays of Bertolt Brecht, the biting polemical journalism of Kurt Tucholsky and Carl von Ossietzky, all divided readers between a minority who rose to the challenge of the new, and the majority who regarded such work as 'cultural Bolshevism'. Alongside the vibrant radical literary culture of Berlin there was another literary world, appealing to the conservative nationalist part of the middle classes, rooted in nostalgia for the lost Bismarckian past and prophesying its return with the longed-for collapse of the Weimar Republic. Particularly popular was Oswald Spengler's *The Fall of the West*, which divided human history into natural cycles of spring, summer, autumn and winter, and located early twentieth-century Germany in the winter phase, characterized by 'tendencies of an irreligious and unmetaphysical urban cosmopolitanism', in which art had suffered a 'preponderance of foreign art-forms'.

In politics, according to Spengler, winter was recognizable by the rule of the inorganic, cosmopolitan masses and the collapse of established state forms. Spengler won many adherents with his claim that this heralded the beginning of an imminent transition to a new spring, that would be 'agricultural-intuitive' and ruled by an 'organic structure of political existence', leading to the 'mighty creations of an awakening, dream-laden soul'.[116] Other writers gave the coming period of revival a new name that was soon to be taken up with enthusiasm by the radical right: the Third Reich. This concept was popularized by the neo-conservative writer Arthur Moeller van den Bruck, whose book of this title was published in 1923. The ideal of the Reich had arisen, he proclaimed, with Charlemagne and been resurrected under Bismarck: it was the opposite of the government by party that characterized the Weimar Republic. At present, he wrote, the Third Reich was a dream: it would require a nationalist revolution to make it reality. The political parties that divided Germany would then be swept away. When the Third Reich finally came, it would encompass all political and social groupings in a national revival. It would restore the continuity of German history, recreating its medieval glory; it would be the 'final Reich' of all.[117] Other writers, such as the jurist Edgar Jung, took up this concept and advocated a 'conservative revolution' that would bring about 'the Third Reich' in the near future.[118]

Below this level of somewhat rarified abstraction were many other writers who in one way or another glorified the alleged virtues that, in their view, the Weimar Republic negated. The ex-army officer Ernst Jünger propagated the myth of 1914, and in his popular book *Storm of Steel* exalted the image of the front-line troops who had found their true being only in the exercise of violence and the suffering, and inflicting, of pain.[119] The Free Corps spawned a whole canon of novels celebrating the veterans' hatred of revolutionaries, often expressed in blood-curdling terms, portraying murder and mayhem as the ultimate expression of a resentful masculinity in search of revenge for the collapse of 1918 and the coming of revolution and democracy.[120] In place of the feeble compromises of parliamentary democracy, authors such as these, and many others, proclaimed the need for strong leadership, ruthless, uncompromising, hard, willing to strike down the enemies of the nation without compunction.[121] Others looked back to an idyllic rural world in which the complexities and 'decadence' of modern urban life were wholly absent, as in Adolf Bartels's novel *The Dithmarshers*, which had sold over 200,000 copies by 1928.[122]

All of this expressed a widespread sense of cultural crisis, and not just among conservative elites. Of course, many aspects of modernist culture and the media had already been in evidence before the war. Avant-garde art had impinged on the public consciousness with the work of Expressionists such as Ernst Ludwig Kirchner, August Macke or Emil Nolde, and abstract painters such as the Russian-born but Munich-based Wassily Kandinsky. Atonal and expressionist music was emanating from the Second Viennese school of Schoenberg, Webern, Berg and Zemlinsky, while sexually explicit drama in the form of plays such as *Spring's Awakening* by Frank Wedekind had already caused a major furore. There had been constant disputes under the Wilhelmine Reich about the limits of propriety in literature and the threat posed by allegedly unpatriotic and subversive, or pornographic and immoral books, many of which were subject to bans imposed by the police.[123]

The sense of cultural crisis which the emergence of modernist art and culture generated amongst the middle classes after the turn of the century was held in check under the Wilhelmine regime, and in its more extreme forms remained confined to a small minority. After 1918, however, it became far more widespread. The ending, or at least the scaling-down, of the censorship that had been so harsh during the war and always active during the Wilhelmine period, encouraged the media to venture into areas that had previously been taboo. The theatre became the vehicle for radical experimentation and left-wing agitprop.[124] Cheaper reproduction and printing techniques made it easier to publish inexpensive illustrated papers and magazines for the mass market. Controversy swirled in particular around Weimar's Bauhaus, created by the architect Walter Gropius in a merger of the Weimar Art Academy and the Weimar School of Arts and Crafts. An educational centre that sought to join high art with practical design, its staff included Wassily Kandinsky, Oskar Schlemmer, Paul Klee, Theo van Doesberg, and László Moholy-Nagy. Its bohemian students, both male and female, were unpopular with the townspeople, and its radically simple, clean and ultra-modern designs were condemned by local politicians as owing more to the art-forms of primitive races than to anything German. State funding was withdrawn in 1924 and the Bauhaus moved to Dessau, but it continued to be dogged by controversy, especially under its new director, Hannes Meyer, whose Communist sympathies led in 1930 to his replacement by the architect Mies van der Rohe. Mies expelled the Communist students and replaced the Bauhaus's earlier communitarian ethos with a more structured, even authoritarian regime. But the Nazi majority elected to the town council in November 1931 closed it down following an official inspection by Paul Schulze-Naumburg, the ultra-conservative author of a book on *Art and Race*. It then moved to a factory site in Berlin, but from this time on was no more than a shadow of its former self. The fate of the Bauhaus illustrated how difficult it was for avant-garde culture to receive official acceptance even in the culturally relaxed atmosphere of the Weimar Republic.[125]

New means of communication added to the sense of old cultural values under threat. Radio first began to make a real mark as a popular cultural institution during this period: a million listeners had registered by 1926, and another 3 million by 1932, and the airwaves were open to a wide variety of opinion, including the left. Cinemas had already opened in the larger towns before 1914, and by the late 1920s films were attracting mass audiences which increased still further with the coming of the talkies at the end of the decade. A sense of aesthetic disorientation was prompted amongst many cultural conservatives by Expressionist films such as *The Cabinet of Dr Caligari*, with its famously odd-angled sets, and by erotically charged movies like *Pandora's Box*, starring the American actress Louise Brooks. A sharp satire on bourgeois convention such as *The Blue Angel*, based on a book by Heinrich Mann and starring Emil Jannings and Marlene Dietrich, ran into trouble with its production company, Hugenberg's UFA, not least for its portrayal of the cynical and manipulative eroticism of its central female character.[126] The film of Erich Maria Remarque's novel *All Quiet on the Western Front* aroused a furious campaign on the part of ultra-nationalists who thought its pacifist message unpatriotic.[127]

Bourgeois culture had held up bland ideals of beauty, spiritual elevation and artistic purity that seemed mocked by the manifestations of Dada, while the 'New Objectivity' (*Neue Sachlichkeit*, literally 'new matter-of-factness') placed everyday events and objects at the centre in an attempt to aestheticize modern urban life. This was not to everyone's taste. Instead of losing themselves in portentous thoughts inspired by the mythical world of Wagner's *Ring* cycle or the ritual religious music-drama of *Parsifal*, dress-suited bourgeois opera-goers were now confronted with the Kroll Opera's production of Paul Hindemith's *News of the Day*, in which a naked diva sang an aria sitting in a bathtub. Alongside the mellifluous Late Romanticism of Germany's leading establishment composer, Richard Strauss, formerly an *enfant terrible* but now the composer of slight and emotionally undemanding operas such as *Intermezzo* and *The Egyptian Helena*, audiences were now treated to Alban Berg's Expressionist masterpiece *Wozzeck*, set among the poor and down-trodden of the early nineteenth century and incorporating atonal music and everyday speech patterns. The conservative composer Hans Pfitzner struck a chord when he denounced such tendencies as symptoms of national degeneracy, and ascribed them to Jewish influences and cultural Bolshevism. The German musical tradition, he thundered, had to be protected from such threats, which were made more acute by the Prussian government's appointment in 1925 of the Austrian-Jewish atonalist Arnold Schoenberg to teach composition at the state music academy in Berlin. Musical life was central to bourgeois identity in Germany, more, probably, than in any other European country: such developments struck at its very core.[128]

An even greater threat, in this view, was posed by the American influence of jazz, which found its way into works such as *The Threepenny Opera*, with music by Kurt Weill and lyrics by Bertolt Brecht. A caustic denunciation of exploitation set in a world of thieves and criminals, it sent shock waves through the cultural world on its first performance in 1928; a similar effect was produced by Ernst Krenek's *Jonny Strikes Up*, which was premiered in February 1927 and featured a black musician as its protagonist. Many modernist composers found jazz a stimulus to renewing their art. It was, of course, principally a popular art form, played in various styles at myriad night-clubs and bars, above all in Berlin, shading off into dance-halls, revue theatres and hotels. Visiting big bands and chorus lines such as the Tiller Girls enlivened the Berlin scene, while the more daring could spend an evening at a club such as the Eldorado, 'a supermarket of eroticism', as the popular composer Friedrich Hollaender called it, and watch Anita Berber perform pornographic dances with names such as 'Cocaine' and 'Morphium' to an audience liberally sprinkled with transvestites and homosexuals, until her early death in 1928 from drug abuse. Cabaret shows added to all this an element of biting, anti-authoritarian political satire and aroused pompous conservatives to anger with their jokes about the 'nationalist and religious sentiments and practices of Christians and Germans', as one of them angrily complained. The wrath of conventional moralists was aroused by dances such as the tango, the foxtrot and the charleston, while racist rhetoric was directed against black musicians (though there were very few of them and most were employed mainly as drummers or dancers, to lend a flavour of the exotic to the performance).

The leading music critic Alfred Einstein called jazz 'the most disgusting treason against all occidental civilized music', while Hans Pfitzner, in a vitriolic attack on the Frankfurt Conservatory for including jazz on its curriculum, railed against its supposed primitivism as a product of what he called 'nigger blood', the 'musical expression of Americanism'.[129] Jazz and swing seemed to be the crest of a wave of cultural Americanization, in which such widely differing phenomena as Charlie Chaplin films and the modern industrial methods of 'Fordism' and 'Taylorism' were viewed by some as a threat to Germany's supposedly historic identity. Mass production held out the prospect of mass consumption, with the great department stores offering an astonishing variety of international goods, while foreign-owned chain-stores such as Woolworth's put at least some of them within the grasp of the ordinary working-class family. Mass housing schemes and designs for modern living challenged the conservative ideal of folk-based style and aroused fierce debate. For cultural critics on the right, the influence of America, symbol par excellence of modernity, signified a pressing need to resurrect the German way of living, German traditions, German ties to blood and soil.[130]

Older Germans in particular felt alienated, not least by the new atmosphere of cultural and sexual freedom that followed the end of official censorship and police controls in 1918 and was epitomized for many by the nightclubs of Berlin. One army officer, born in 1878, later recalled:

Returning home, we no longer found an honest German people, but a mob stirred up by its lowest instincts. Whatever virtues were once found among the Germans seemed to have sunk once and for all into the muddy flood . . . Promiscuity, shamelessness and corruption ruled supreme. German women seemed to have forgotten their German ways. German men seemed to have forgotten their sense of honour and honesty. Jewish writers and the Jewish press could 'go to town' with impunity, dragging everything into the dirt.[131]

The feeling that order and discipline had been swept away by the Revolution, and that moral and sexual degeneracy were taking over society, was to be found on the left as well as on the right. Social Democrats and Communists often took a rather puritanical view of personal relationships, putting political commitment and self-sacrifice above personal fulfilment, and many were shocked by the openly hedonistic culture of many young people in Berlin and elsewhere during the 'Roaring Twenties'. The commercialization of leisure, in the cinema, the tabloid press, the dance-hall and the radio, was alienating many young people from the sterner, more traditional values of labour movement culture.[132]

The sexual freedom evidently enjoyed by the young in the big cities was a particular source of disapproval in the older generation. Here, too, there had been harbingers before the war. The rise of a large and vociferous feminist movement had accustomed the public and the press to women speaking out on all kinds of issues, occupying at least some positions of responsibility, and making their own way in the world. On 'International Proletarian Women's Day', 8 March, the bigger cities saw annual demonstrations in the streets for women's suffrage from 1910 onwards, with even middle-class feminists staging a procession, albeit in carriages, in 1912. Alongside the eventually successful campaign for female suffrage came, if only from a minority of feminists, demands for sexual fulfilment, equal rights for unmarried mothers and the provision of free contraceptive advice. The ideas of Freud, with their tendency to ascribe sexual motives to human actions and desires, were already being discussed before the war.[133] Berlin in particular, as it grew rapidly to the size and status of a cosmopolitan metropolis, had already become the centre for a variety of social and sexual subcultures, including a thriving gay and lesbian scene.[134]

Critics linked these trends to what they saw as the looming decline of the family, caused principally by the growing economic independence of women. The rapid emergence of a service sector in the economy, with its new employment possibilities for women, from sales positions in the great department stores to secretarial work in the booming office world (driven by the powerful feminizing influence of the typewriter), created new forms of exploitation but also gave increasing numbers of young, unmarried women a financial and social independence they had not enjoyed before. This became even more marked after 1918, when there were 11.5 million women at work, making up 36 per cent of the working population. Although this was by no means a dramatic change from the situation before the war, many of them were now in publicly conspicuous jobs such as tram-conducting, serving in department stores, or, even if it was only a handful, in the legal, university and medical professions.[135] Increased female competition for male jobs, and a more general fear among nationalists that Germany's strength was being sapped by the birth rate decline that set in around the turn of the century, merged with wider cultural anxieties to produce a backlash that was already becoming evident before 1914.[136] There was a discernible crisis of masculinity in Germany before the war, as nationalists and Pan-Germans began to clamour for women's return to home and family in order to fulfil their destiny of producing and educating more children for the nation. The sharpness of the reaction to the feminist challenge meant that the feminists were forced onto the defensive, began to marginalize their more radical supporters and increasingly stressed their impeccably nationalist credentials and their desire not to go too far with their demands for change.[137]

After 1918, women were enfranchised and able to vote and stand for election at every level from local councils up to the Reichstag. They were formally given the right to enter the major professions, and the part they played in public life was far more prominent than it had been before the war. Correspondingly, the hostility of those male supremacists who believed that women's place was in the home now won a much wider hearing. Their disapproval was reinforced by the far more open display of sexuality than before the war in the liberated atmosphere of the big cities. Even more shocking to conservatives was the public campaigning for gay rights by individuals such as Magnus Hirschfeld, founder of the harmless-sounding Scientific-Humanitarian Committee, in 1897. In fact, Hirschfeld was openly homosexual, and in numerous publications propagated the controversial idea that homosexuals were a 'third sex' whose orientation was the product of congenital rather than environmental factors. His Committee was dedicated to the abolition of Paragraph 175 of the Reich Criminal Code, which outlawed 'indecent activity' between adult males. What aroused the wrath of conservatives was the fact that in 1919 the Social Democratic state government of Prussia gave Hirschfeld a large grant to convert his informal Committee into a state-funded Institute for Sexual Science, with its premises in the grand Tiergarten district in the centre of the capital city. The Institute offered sex counselling, held popular question-and-answer sessions on topics like 'what is the best way to have sex without making a baby?' and campaigned for the reform of all the laws regulating sexual behaviour. Hirschfeld quickly built up a wide range of international contacts, organized in the World League for Sexual Reform, of which his Institute was the effective headquarters in the 1920s. He was the driving force behind the spread of public and private birth control and sex counselling clinics in the Weimar Republic. Not surprisingly, he was repeatedly vilified by the Nationalists and the Nazis, whose attempt to tighten up the law still further, with the support of the Centre Party, was narrowly defeated by the votes of the Communists, Social Democrats and Democrats on the Criminal Law Reform Committee of the Reichstag in 1929.[138]

Nationalist hostility was driven by more than crude moral conservatism. Germany had lost 2 million men in the war, and yet the birth rate was still in rapid decline. Between 1900 and 1925, live births per thousand married women under the age of 45 fell very sharply indeed, from 280 to 146. Laws restricting the sale of condoms were eased in 1927, and by the early 1930s there were more than 1,600 vending machines in public places, with one Berlin firm alone producing 25 million condoms a year. Sex counselling centres were opened, offering contraceptive advice, and many of these, like Hirschfeld's Institute, were funded or in some cases actually operated by the Prussian and other regional governments, to the outrage of moral conservatives. Abortion was far more controversial, not least because of the serious medical risks it entailed, but here, too, the law was relaxed, and the offence reduced in 1927 from a felony to a misdemeanour. The thundering denunciation of birth control by the Papal Encyclical *Casti Connubii* in December 1930 added fuel to the flames of debate, and in 1931 some 1,500 rallies and demonstrations were held in a massive Communist campaign against the evils of backstreet abortions.[139]

To many people, such campaigns seemed part of a deliberate plot to destroy the fertility and fecundity of the German race. Was it not, conservatives and radical nationalists asked, all the consequence of female emancipation and the morally subversive advocacy of sexuality untrammelled by any desire to procreate? To nationalists, the feminists seemed to be little better than national traitors for encouraging women to work outside the home. Yet the feminists themselves were scarcely less alarmed by the new atmosphere of sexual liberation. Most of them had castigated the double standard of sexual morality – freedom for men, purity for women – before the war, and advocated instead a single standard of sexual restraint for both sexes. Their puritanism, expressed in campaigns against pornographic books and sexually explicit films and paintings, and in denunciations of young women who preferred dance-halls to reading-groups, seemed ridiculous to many women amongst the younger generation, and by the late 1920s the traditional feminist organizations, already deprived of their principal cause by the achievement of female suffrage, were complaining of an ageing membership and a failing appeal to the young.[140] Feminism was on the defensive, and the middle-class women who were the mainstay of its support were deserting their traditional liberal milieu for parties of the right. The feminist movement felt the need to defend itself against charges of undermining the German race by insisting on its support for nationalist revision of the Treaty of Versailles, for rearmament, for family values and for sexual self-restraint. As time was to show, the appeal of right-wing extremism to women proved no less potent than it was to men.[141]

II

Young people, and especially adolescent boys, were already developing a distinctive cultural style of their own before the First World War. A key role in this was played by the 'youth movement', a disparate but rapidly growing collection of informal clubs and societies that focused on activities such as hiking, communing with nature and singing folk songs and patriotic verses while sitting around camp fires. Of course, all the political parties attempted to recruit young people, particularly after 1918, by providing them with their own organizations – the Bismarck Youth for the Nationalists, for example – or the Windthorst League for the Centre Party – but what was striking about the youth movement in general was its independence from formal political institutions, often combined with a contempt for what its leading figures saw as the moral compromises and dishonesties of adult political life. The movement fostered a distrust of modern culture, city life and formal political institutions. Many if not most youth groups wore paramilitary uniforms along the lines of the Boy Scouts, and were more than tinged with antisemitism, often refusing to admit Jews to their ranks. Some underlined the need for moral purity, and rejected smoking, drinking or liaisons with girls. Others, as we have seen, were male supremacist. Even if the responsibility of the youth movement for paving the way for Nazism has been exaggerated by historians, the overwhelming majority of the independent youth organizations were still hostile to the Republic and its politicians, nationalist in outlook and militaristic in character and aspirations.[142]

The influence of the youth movement, which was at its strongest in the Protestant middle class, was scarcely countered by the impact of the educational system on young Germans. 'The whole lot of high school pupils are nationalistic,' reported Victor Klemperer in 1925. 'They learn it thus from the teachers.'[143] But the situation was perhaps a little more complicated than he imagined. Under the Wilhelmine Reich, the Kaiser's personal influence was exercised in favour of displacing liberal traditions of German education, based on classical models, with patriotic lessons focusing on German history and the German language. By 1914 many teachers were nationalist, conservative and monarchist in outlook, while textbooks and lessons pursued very much the same kind of political line.

But a sizeable minority also held to a variety of opinions on the liberal centre and left. In the 1920s, moreover, states dominated by the Social Democrats, notably Prussia, made strenuous efforts to persuade the schools to educate their pupils as model citizens loyal to the new Republic's democratic institutions, and the atmosphere in the school system changed accordingly. Millions of young people emerged from their schooling as convinced Communists or Social Democrats, or gave their allegiance to the Centre Party, besides the other millions who adhered to conservative views or the politics of the radical right. In the end, neither those teachers who were liberal or Social Democratic nor those who were conservative and monarchist seem to have exercised much influence on the political views of their pupils, and many of their political ideas were dismissed by their charges as lacking in any relevance to what they perceived as the daily realities of life under the Weimar Republic. For young men who subsequently became Nazis, the beginnings of political commitment often lay more in political rebellion against the rigidities of the school system than in the inspiration of Nazi or proto-Nazi teachers. One nationalist school student, born in 1908, remembered that he was always clashing with his teachers 'because from childhood I have hated slavish submissiveness'; he admitted being politicized by a nationalist teacher, but commented at the same time that his idol's teaching 'formed a strong contrast to everything else that was taught in school'; another nursed a long-term grudge against his former school, which had repeatedly punished him for insulting Jewish fellow-students.[144]

Where the political allegiance of the young to the far right was at its most obvious was in Germany's universities, many of them famous centres of learning with traditions going back to the Middle Ages. Some leftish professors did manage to secure appointments under the Weimar Republic, but they were few in number. Universities were still elite institutions after the war, and drew almost all their students from the middle classes. Particularly powerful were the student duelling corps, conservative, monarchist and nationalist to a man. Some of them played an active role in the violence that attended the suppression of the revolutionary outbreaks that took place in 1919–21. To neutralize their influence, students in all universities established democratic representative institutions of a sort appropriate to the new Republic early in 1919, the General Student Unions. All students had to belong to these, and were entitled to vote for representatives on their governing bodies.[145]

The Student Unions formed a national association and began to have some influence in areas such as student welfare and university reform. But they too fell under the influence of the far right. Under the impact of political events, from the final acceptance of the Treaty of Versailles in 1919 to the French invasion of the Ruhr in 1923, fresh generations of students streamed into nationalist associations, and flocked to the colours of the traditional student corps. Soon, right-wing slates of candidates were being elected to all the Student Unions, while students' disillusion with Germany's new democracy grew as inflation rendered their incomes worthless and overcrowding made conditions in the universities ever more unbearable. Student numbers grew rapidly, from 60,000 in 1914 to 104,000 in 1931, not least under the impact of demographic change. Governments poured money into widening access, and universities became a significant route to upward social mobility for the sons of lower civil servants, small businessmen and even to some extent manual labourers. The financial problems of the Republic forced many students to work their way through university, creating further resentment. Already in 1924, however, the chances of the swelling numbers of graduates finding a place in the job market began to decline; from 1930 they were almost non-existent.[146]

The vast majority of professors, as their collective public declarations of support for German war aims in 1914–18 had shown, were also strongly nationalist. Many contributed to the right-wing intellectual atmosphere with their lectures denouncing the Peace Settlement of 1919. They added to this with administrative resolutions and decisions attacking what they saw as the threat of 'racially alien' Jewish students coming to the university from the east. Many wrote in alarmist terms about the looming prospect (which existed largely in their own imaginations) of whole subject areas in the universities being dominated by Jewish professors, and framed their hiring policy accordingly. In 1923 a massive wave of nationalist outrage swept through German universities when the French occupied the Ruhr, and student groups took an active part in stirring up resistance. Well before the end of the 1920s, the universities had become political hotbeds of the extreme right. A generation of graduates was being created that thought of itself as an elite, as graduates still did in a society where only a very small proportion of the population ever managed to get into university; but an elite that in the wake of the First World War put action above thought, and national pride above abstract learning; an elite to which racism, antisemitism and ideas of German superiority were almost second nature; an elite that was determined to combat the feeble compromises of an over-tolerant liberal democracy with the same toughness that their elders had shown in the First World War.[147] For such young men, violence seemed a rational response to the disasters that had overtaken Germany. To the most intelligent and highly educated, the older generation of ex-soldiers seemed too emotionally scarred, too disorderly: what was needed was sobriety, planning and utter ruthlessness in the cause of national regeneration.[148]

All these influences were in the end secondary as far as the majority of these students' contemporaries were concerned. Far more important to them was the overriding experience of political dislocation, economic privation, war, destruction, civil strife, inflation, national defeat and partial occupation by foreign powers, an experience shared by young people born in the decade or so leading up to the First World War. A young clerk, born in 1911, later wrote:

We were not spared anything. We knew and felt the worries in the house. The shadow of necessity never left our table and made us silent. *We were rudely pushed out of our childhood and not shown the right path.* The struggle for life got to us early. Misery, shame, hatred, lies, and civil war imprinted themselves on our souls and made us mature early.[149]

The generation born between the turn of the century and the outbreak of the First World War was indeed a generation of the unconditional, ready for anything; in more than one respect, it was to play a fateful role in the Third Reich.

III

Weimar's radically modernist culture was obsessed, to what many middle-class people must have felt was an unhealthy degree, by deviance, murder, atrocity and crime. The graphic drawings of an artist like George Grosz were full of violent scenes of rape and serial sex killers, a theme found in the work of other artists of the day as well. Murderers were central figures in films such as Fritz Lang's *M*, plays like Bertolt Brecht's *The Threepenny Opera* and novels such as Alfred Döblin's modernist masterpiece, *Berlin Alexanderplatz*. The trials of real serial killers like Fritz Haarmann or Peter Kürten, 'the Düsseldorf vampire', were nationwide media sensations, with graphic reporting in the press catering to a mass readership that followed every twist and turn of events. Corruption became a central theme even of novels about Berlin written by foreign visitors, as in Christopher Isherwood's *Mr Norris Changes Trains*. The criminal became an object of fascination as well as fear, fuelling respectable anxieties about social order and adding to middle-class distaste at the inversion of values that seemed to be at the centre of modernist culture. The huge publicity given to serial killers convinced many, not only that the death penalty had to be rigorously enforced against such 'bestial' individuals, but also that censorship needed to be reintroduced to stop their celebration in popular culture and the daily boulevard press.[150] Meanwhile the inflation and disorder of the postwar years had seen the emergence of organized crime on a scale almost rivalling that of contemporary Chicago, particularly in Berlin, where the 'ring associations' of the burgeoning criminal underworld were celebrated in films like *M*.[151]

The feeling that crime was out of control was widely shared among those whose job it was to maintain the law and order that so many people thought was now under threat. The entire judicial system of the Wilhelmine period was transported unchanged to the Weimar era; the Civil and Criminal Law Codes were almost entirely unamended, and attempts to liberalize them, for example by abolishing the death penalty, ran into the sands.[152] As before, the judiciary was a body of men trained for the judge's role from the beginning, not (as in England for example) appointed to the judiciary after a relatively long career at the bar. Many judges in office during the 1920s had thus been members of the judiciary for decades, and had imbibed their fundamental values and attitudes in the age of Kaiser Wilhelm II. Their position was strengthened under the Republic, since it was a basic political principle of the new democracy, like others, that the judiciary should be independent of political control, a principle quickly and uncontroversially anchored in Articles 102 and 104 of the constitution. Rather like the army, therefore, the judiciary was able to operate for long stretches of time without any real political interference.[153]

The judges were all the more independent because the vast majority of them regarded laws promulgated by legislative assemblies rather than by a divinely ordained monarch as no longer neutral but, as the chairman of the German Judges' Confederation (which represented eight out of the roughly ten thousand German judges) put it, 'party, class and bastard law . . . a law of lies'. 'Where several parties exercise rule,' he complained, 'the result is compromise laws. These constitute mishmash laws, they express the cross-purposes of the ruling parties, they make bastard law. All majesty is fallen. The majesty of the law, too.'[154] There was some justification, perhaps, in the complaint that the political parties were exploiting the judicial system for their own purposes and creating new laws with a specific political bias. The extreme right- and left-wing parties maintained specific departments devoted to the cynical business of making political capital out of trials, and kept a staff of political lawyers who developed a battery of highly sophisticated and utterly unscrupulous techniques for turning court proceedings into political sensations.[155] No doubt this further contributed to discrediting Weimar justice in the eyes of many. Yet the judges themselves, in the altered context of the advent of a parliamentary democracy, could be regarded as exploiting trials for their own political purposes, too. After years, indeed decades, of treating Social Democratic and left-liberal critics of the Kaiser's government as criminals, judges were unwilling to readjust their attitudes when the political situation changed. Their loyalty was given, not to the new Republic, but to the same abstract ideal of the Reich which their counterparts in the officer corps continued to serve; an ideal built largely on memories of the authoritarian system of the Bismarckian Reich.[156] Inevitably, perhaps, in the numerous political trials which arose from the deep political conflicts of the Weimar years, they sided over-whelmingly with those right-wing offenders who claimed also to be acting in the name of this ideal, and cheered on the prosecution of those on the left who did not.

In the mid-1920s the left-wing statistician Emil Julius Gumbel pub-lished figures showing that the 22 political murders committed by left-wing offenders from late 1919 to mid-1922 led to 38 convictions, including 10 executions and prison sentences averaging 15 years apiece. By contrast, the 354 political murders which Gumbel reckoned to have been committed by right-wing offenders in the same period led to 24 convictions, no executions at all, and prison sentences averaging a mere 4 months apiece; 23 right-wing murderers who confessed to their crimes were actually acquitted by the courts.[157] Of course, these statistics may not have been entirely accurate. And there were frequent amnesties of 'political prisoners' agreed on by the extreme parties in the Reichstag with enough support from other political groupings to get them through, so that many political offenders were released only after serving a relatively short time in gaol. But what mattered about the behaviour of the judges was the message it sent to the public, a message bolstered by numerous prosecutions of pacifists, Communists and other people on the left for treason throughout the Weimar years. According to Gumbel, while only 32 people had been condemned for treason in the last three peacetime decades of the Bismarckian Reich, over 10,000 warrants were issued for treason in the four – also relatively peaceful – years from the beginning of 1924 to the end of 1927, resulting in 1,071 convictions.[158]

A substantial number of court cases dealt with people brave enough to expose the secret armaments and manoeuvres of the army in the press. Perhaps the most famous instance was that of the pacifist and left-wing editor Carl von Ossietzky, who was condemned in 1931 to eighteen months' imprisonment for publishing in his magazine The World Stage (Die Weltbühne) an article revealing that the German army was training with combat aircraft in Soviet Russia, an act that was illegal according to the terms of the Treaty of Versailles.[159] Another, equally celebrated case involved the left-wing journalist Felix Fechenbach. His offence, committed in 1919, was to have published Bavarian files from 1914 relating to the outbreak of the First World War, because this had – in the opinion of the court – damaged the interests of Germany in the peace negotiations by suggesting an element of German responsibility. Fechenbach was sentenced to eleven years' imprisonment in Munich by a so-called People's Court, an emergency body set up to dispense summary justice on looters and murderers during the Bavarian Revolution of 1918.[160] These had been adapted to deal with 'treason' cases during the counter-revolution of the following year. They were not wound up until 1924 despite their outlawing by the Weimar constitution five years previously. The creation of these courts, with their bypassing of the normal legal system, including the absence of any right of appeal against their verdicts, and their implicit ascription of justice to 'the people' rather than to the law, set an ominous precedent for the future, and was to be taken up again by the Nazis in 1933.[161]

In order to try and counter these influences, the Social Democrats managed to push through a Law for the Protection of the Republic in 1922; the resulting State Court was intended to remove the trial of right-wing political offenders from an all-too-sympathetic judiciary and place it in the hands of appointees of the Reich President. The judiciary soon managed to neutralize it, and it had little effect on the overall pattern of verdicts.[162] Friedrich Ebert and the Social Democrats, although supposedly committed to opposing the death penalty as a matter of political principle, inserted it into the Law for the Protection of the Republic and gave retrospective approval to summary executions carried out in the civil disorders of the immediate postwar period. In doing so, they made it easier for a future government to introduce similarly draconian laws for the protection of the state, and to confound a central principle of justice – that no punishments should be applied retrospectively to offences which did not carry them at the time they were committed.[163] This, too, was a dangerous precedent for the future.

The regular courts had little time for the principles enunciated in the Law for the Protection of the Republic. Judges almost invariably showed leniency towards an accused man if he claimed to have been acting out of patriotic motives, whatever his crime.[164] The Kapp putsch of 1920, for instance, led to the condemnation of only one of the participants in this armed attempt to overthrow the legitimately elected government, and even he was sentenced to no more than a brief period of confinement in a fortress because the judges counted his 'selfless patriotism' as a mitigating factor.[165] In 1923 four men won their appeal to the Reich Court, the old-established supreme judicial authority in the land, against a sentence of three months' imprisonment each for shouting at a meeting of the Young German Order, a right-wing youth group, in Gotha, the words: 'We don't need a Jew-republic, boo to the Jew-republic!' In its judgment the Reich Court declared somewhat unconvincingly that the meaning of these words was unclear:

They could mean the new legal and social order in Germany, in whose establishment the participation of German and foreign Jews was outstanding. They could also mean the excessive power and the excessive influence that a number of Jews that is small in relation to the total population exercises in reality in the view of large sections of the people . . . It has not even been explicitly established that the accused shouted abuse at the constitutionally anchored form of state of the Reich, only that they shouted abuse at the present form of state of the Reich. The possibility of a legal error is thereby not excluded.[166]

The distinction the Reich Court made between the two kinds of state, and the hint that the Weimar Republic was merely some kind of temporary aberration which was not 'constitutionally anchored', demonstrated only too clearly where the judges' real allegiance lay. Such verdicts could not fail to have an effect. Political and indeed other trials were major events in the Weimar Republic, attended by large numbers of people in the public galleries, reported at length and in parts verbatim in the press, and debated passionately in legislative assemblies, clubs and societies. Verdicts such as these could only give comfort to the far-right opponents of the Republic and help to undermine its legitimacy.

The right-wing and anti-Republican bias of the judiciary was shared by state prosecutors as well. In considering what charges to bring against right-wing offenders, in dealing with pleas, in examining witnesses, even in framing their opening and closing speeches, prosecutors routinely treated nationalist beliefs and intentions as mitigating factors. In these various ways, judges and prosecutors, police, prison governors and warders, legal administrators and law enforcement agents of all kinds undermined the legitimacy of the Republic through their bias in favour of its enemies. Even if they did not deliberately set out to sabotage the new democracy, even if they accepted it for the time being as an unavoidable necessity, the effect of their conduct was to spread the assumption that in some way it did not represent the true essence of the German Reich. Few of them seem to have been convinced democrats or committed to trying to make the Republic work. Where the law and its administrators were against it, what chance did it have?

THE FIT AND THE UNFIT

I

If there was one achievement through which the Weimar Republic could claim the loyalty and gratitude of the masses, it was the creation of a new welfare state. Of course, Germany did not lack welfare institutions before 1914, particularly since Bismarck had pioneered such things as health insurance, accident insurance and old age pensions in an attempt to wean the working classes away from Social Democracy. Bismarck's schemes, which were elaborated and extended in the years following his departure from office, were pioneering in their day, and cannot be dismissed simply as fig-leaves for governmental authoritarianism. Some of them, notably the health insurance system, covered millions of workers by 1914 and incorporated a substantial element of self-governance that gave many workers the chance of electoral participation. Yet none of these schemes reached anywhere near the bottom of the social scale, where police-administered poor relief, bringing with it the deprivation of civil rights including the right to vote, was the norm right to the end of the Wilhelmine period. Still, even here, the operation of the system had been reformed and standardized by 1914, and the new profession of social work that had emerged on the back of the Bismarckian reforms was busy assessing and regulating the poor, the unemployed and the destitute as well as the ordinary worker.[167]

On the basis of this modern version of Prussian bureaucratic paternalism, however, the Weimar Republic erected a far more elaborate and comprehensive structure, combining, not without tension, the twin influences of social Catholicism and Protestant philanthropy on the one hand, and Social Democratic egalitarianism on the other.[168] The Weimar constitution itself was full of far-reaching declarations of principle about the importance of family life and the need for the state to support it, the government's duty to protect young people from harm, the citizen's right to work, and the nation's obligation to provide everybody with a decent home.[169] On the basis of such principles, a whole raft of legislation was steered through the Reichstag, from laws dealing with youth welfare (1922) and juvenile courts (1923) to regulations providing relief and job training for the war disabled (1920), decrees replacing poor relief with public welfare (1924) and above all, as we have seen, the statutory provision of unemployment benefits in 1927. Existing schemes of health insurance, pensions and the like were further elaborated and extended to all. Massive housing schemes, many of them socially innovative, were initiated, with over 300,000 new or renovated homes being provided between 1927 and 1930 alone. The number of hospital beds increased by 50 per cent from prewar days, and the medical profession also expanded accordingly to keep pace. Infectious diseases declined sharply, and a network of clinics and social welfare institutions now supported socially vulnerable individuals, from single mothers to youths who got into trouble with the police.[170]

The creation of a free and comprehensive welfare system as the entitlement of all its citizens was one of the major achievements of the Weimar Republic, perhaps in retrospect its most important. But for all its elaboration, it failed in the end to live up to the grandiose promises made in the 1919 constitution; and the gap between promise and delivery ended by having a major effect on the legitimacy of the Republic in the eyes of many of its citizens. First, the economic difficulties that the Republic experienced almost from the outset placed a burden on its welfare system that it was simply unable to sustain. There were very large numbers of people who required support as a result of the war. Some 13 million German men served in the armed forces between 1914 and 1918. Over two million of them were killed. According to one estimate, this was the equivalent of one death for every 35 inhabitants of the Reich. This was nearly twice the proportion of war deaths in the United Kingdom, where one soldier died for every 66 inhabitants, and almost three times that of Russia, where there was one war death for every 111 inhabitants. By the end of the war, over half a million German women were left as war widows and a million German children were without fathers. About 2.7 million men came back from the war with wounds, amputations and disabilities, to form a permanent source of discontent as the politicians' promised rewards for their service to the nation failed to materialize to anyone's satisfaction.

The government increased taxes on the better-off to try and cope, until the real tax burden virtually doubled as a percentage of real national income, from 9 per cent in 1913 to 17 per cent in 1925, according to one admittedly biased estimate.[171] Yet this was in no way enough to cover expenditure, and governments dared not go any further for fear of being accused of raising tax revenues to pay reparations and alienating even further those who paid the most taxes. Not only did the economy have to bear the burden of unemployment insurance after 1927, it was in 1926 still paying pensions to nearly 800,000 disabled former soldiers and 360,000 war widows, and supporting over 900,000 fatherless children and orphans, and all this on top of an existing system of state support for the elderly. The payment of pensions took up a higher proportion of state expenditure than anything apart from reparations.[172] Finally, the welfare system boosted an already swollen bureaucracy in the Reich and the federated states, which increased in size by 40 per cent between 1914 and 1923, almost doubling the cost of public administration per head of the German population in the process.[173] Such massive expenditure might have been feasible in a booming economy, but in the crisis-racked economic situation of the Weimar Republic it was simply not possible without printing money and fuelling inflation, as happened between 1919 and 1923, or, from 1924, by cutting back on payments, reducing the staffing levels of state welfare institutions and imposing ever more stringent means-testing on claimants.

Many claimants thus quickly realized that the welfare system was not paying them as much as they needed. Local administrators were particularly stingy, since local authorities bore a sizeable proportion of the financial burden of welfare payments. They frequently demanded that claimants should hand over their savings or their property as a condition of receiving support. Welfare snoopers reported on hidden sources of income and encouraged neighbours to send in denunciations of those who refused to reveal them. Moreover, welfare agencies, lacking the staff necessary to process a large number of claims rapidly, caused endless delays in responding to applications for support as they corresponded with other agencies to see if claimants had received benefits previously, or tried to shift the burden of supporting them elsewhere. Thus, the Weimar welfare administration quickly became an instrument of discrimination and control, as officials made it clear to claimants that they would only receive the minimum due to them, and enquired intrusively into their personal circumstances to ensure that this was the case.

None of this endeared the Republic to those whom it was intended to help. Complaints, rows, fisticuffs, even demonstrations were far from uncommon inside and outside welfare offices. A sharp insight into the kind of problems which the welfare system was confronting, and the way it went about dealing with them, is provided by the example of a saddler and upholsterer, Adolf G.[174] Born in 1892, Adolf had fought in the 1914–18 war and sustained a serious injury – not in a heroic battle against the enemy, however, but from a kick in his stomach by a horse. It required no fewer than six intestinal operations in the early 1920s. An old industrial accident and a family with six children put him into further categories of welfare entitlement apart from war injury. Unable to find a job after the war, he devoted himself to campaigning for state support instead. But the local authorities in Stuttgart demanded as a condition of continuing his accident benefits after 1921 that he surrender his radio receiver and aerial, since these were banned from the municipal housing in which he lived. When he refused to do this, he was evicted with his family, a move to which he responded with a vigorous campaign of letter-writing to the authorities, including the Labour Ministry in Berlin. He acquired a typewriter to make his letters more legible and tried to acquire other kinds of benefits reflecting his situation as a war invalid and a father of a large family. The conflict escalated. In 1924 he was imprisoned for a month and a half for assisting an attempted abortion, presumably because he and his wife thought that in the circumstances six children were enough; in 1927 he was fined for insulting behaviour; in 1930 his benefits were cut and restricted to certain purposes such as the purchase of clothes, while his housing allowance was paid direct to his landlord; he was charged in 1931 with welfare fraud because he had been trying to make a little money on the side as a rag-and-bone man, and again in 1933 for busking. He approached political organizations of the right and left in order to get help. An attempt to persuade the authorities that he needed three times more food than the average man because his stomach injury left him unable to digest most of what he ate was rebuffed with stony formality. In 1931, at the end of his tether, he wrote to the Labour Ministry in Berlin comparing the Stuttgart welfare officials to robber barons of the Middle Ages.[175]

What angered the somewhat obsessive Adolf G. was not just the poverty in which he and his family were condemned to live, but still more the insults done to his honour and standing even in the lower reaches of German society by a welfare apparatus that seemed determined to question his motives and his entitlements in seeking the support that he felt he deserved. The anonymous, rule-bound welfare bureaucracy insulted his individuality. Such feelings were far from uncommon among welfare claimants, particularly where their claim for support resulted from the sacrifices they had made during the war. The huge gulf between the Weimar Republic's very public promises of a genuinely universal welfare system based on need and entitlement, and the harsh reality of petty discrimination, intrusion and insult to which many claimants were exposed on the part of the welfare agencies, did nothing to strengthen the legitimacy of the constitution in which these promises were enshrined.[176]

More ominous by far, however, was the fact that health and welfare agencies, determined to create rational and scientifically informed ways of dealing with social deprivation, deviance and crime, with the ultimate aim of eliminating them from German society in generations to come, encouraged new policies that began to eat away at the civil liberties of the poor and the handicapped. As the social welfare administration mushroomed into a huge bureaucracy, so the doctrines of racial hygiene and social biology, already widespread among welfare professionals before the war, began to acquire more influence. The belief that heredity played some part in many kinds of social deviance, including not only mental deficiency and physical disability but also chronic alcoholism, persistent petty criminality and even 'moral idiocy' in groups such as prostitutes (many of whom were in fact forced into sex work by economic circumstances), hardened into a dogma. Medical scientists and social administrators began to compile elaborate card-indexes of the 'asocial', as such deviants were now commonly called. Liberal penal reformers argued that, while some inmates in state prisons could be reclaimed for society by the right sort of educational programmes, a great many of them were completely incorrigible, largely because of the inherited degeneracy of their character.[177] The police played their part, too, identifying a large number of 'professional criminals' and 'habitual offenders' to place under intensive surveillance. This frequently became a self-fulfilling prophecy, as surveillance and identification left released prisoners no chance of engaging in an honest trade. In Berlin alone, the police fingerprint collection numbered over half a million ten-finger cards by 1930.[178]

The spread of such ideas through the professional worlds of medicine, law enforcement, penal administration and social work had very real consequences. Psychologists asked to assess the mental health of convicted criminals began to use biological criteria, as in the case of an unemployed vagrant, Florian Huber, convicted of armed robbery and murder in Bavaria in 1922: 'Huber', concluded a psychological assessment of the young man, who had suffered severe injuries in war action, earning him the award of the Iron Cross,

although in other respects he cannot be proven to be hereditarily damaged, demonstrated some physical evidence of degeneracy: the structure of his physiognomy is asymmetrical to the extent that the right eye is situated markedly lower than the left, he has a tendency towards full-throatedness, his earlobes are elongated, and above all he has been a stutterer since youth.[179]

This was taken as evidence, not that he was unfit to stand trial, but that he was incorrigible and should therefore be executed, which indeed he was. Legal officials in many parts of Germany now made liberal use of terms such as 'vermin' or 'pest' to describe criminals, denoting a new, biological way of conceptualizing the social order as a kind of body, from which harmful parasites and alien micro-organisms had to be removed if it was to flourish. In the search for more precise and comprehensive ways of defining and applying such concepts, a medical expert, Theodor Viernstein, founded a 'Criminal-Biological Information Centre' in Bavaria in 1923, to gather information about all known criminal offenders, their families and their background, and thereby to identify hereditary chains of deviance. By the end of the decade Viernstein and his collaborators had collected a vast index of cases and were well on the way to realizing their dream. Soon, similar centres had been founded in Thuringia, Württemberg and Prussia as well. Many experts thought that once such dynasties of 'inferior' human beings had been mapped out, compulsory sterilization was the only way to prevent them reproducing themselves further.[180]

In 1920 two such experts, the lawyer Karl Binding and the forensic psychiatrist Alfred Hoche, went one crucial step beyond this and argued, in a short book in which they coined the phrase 'a life unworthy of life', that what they called 'ballast existences', people who were nothing but a burden on the community, should simply be killed. The incurably ill and the mentally retarded were costing millions of marks and taking up thousands of much-needed hospital beds, they argued. So doctors should be allowed to put them to death. This was an ominous new development in the debate over what to do with the mentally ill, the handicapped, the criminal and the deviant. In the Weimar Republic it still met with impassioned hostility on the part of most medical men. The Republic's fundamental insistence on the rights of the individual prevented even the doctrine of compulsory sterilization from gaining any kind of official approval, and many doctors and welfare officers still doubted the ethical legitimacy or social effectiveness of such a policy. The very considerable influence of the Catholic Church and its welfare agencies was also directed firmly against such policies. As long as economic circumstances made it possible to imagine that the Republic's social aspirations could one day be realized, the continuing debate on compulsory sterilization and involuntary 'euthanasia' remained unresolved.[181]

II

Middle-class Germans reacted to the 1918 Revolution and the Weimar Republic in a wide variety of ways. Perhaps the most detailed account we have of one man's response is from the diaries of Victor Klemperer, whose experience of the inflation we have already noted. Klemperer was in many ways typical of the educated middle-class German who just wanted to get on with his life, and relegated politics to a relatively small part of it, though he voted at elections and always took an interest in what was going on in the political world. His career was neither entirely conventional nor outstandingly successful. After making a living as a newspaper writer, Klemperer had turned to the university world, qualifying shortly before the war with the obligatory two theses, the first on German, the second on French literature. As a relative newcomer and outsider, he was obliged to start his academic career in a post at the University of Naples, from where he observed the deterioration of the international situation before 1914 with concern. He supported the German declaration of war in 1914 and considered the German cause a just one. He returned to Germany and joined up, served on the Western Front and was invalided out in 1916, working in the army censorship office up to the end of the war.

Like other middle-class Germans, Klemperer saw his hopes for a stable career dashed with the defeat of Germany. For such a man, only a return to orderly and political circumstances could provide the basis for a steady income and a permanent job in a German academic institution.[182] The events of the last two months of 1918 were upsetting to him in more than one respect. He wrote in his diary:

The newspaper now brings so much shame, disaster, collapse, things previously considered impossible, that I, filled to bursting with it, just dully accept it, hardly read any more ... After all I see and hear, I am of the opinion that the whole of Germany will go to the Devil if this Soldiers' and Workers' *Un-Council*, this dictatorship of senselessness and ignorance, is not swept out soon. My hopes are pinned on any general of the army that is returning from the field.[183]

Working temporarily in Munich, he was alarmed by the antics of the revolutionary government early in 1919 – 'they talk enthusiastically of freedom and their tyranny gets ever worse' – and recorded hours spent in libraries trying to do his academic work while the bullets of the invading Free Corps whizzed past outside.[184] Normality and stability were what Klemperer wanted; yet they were not to be had. In 1920, as we have seen, he managed to obtain a professorship at Dresden Technical University, where he taught French literature, researched and wrote, edited a journal and became increasingly frustrated as he saw younger men obtain senior positions at better institutions. In many ways he was a typical moderate conservative of his time, patriotic, bourgeois, German through and through in his cultural attitudes and identity, and a believer in the notion of national character, which he expressed at length in his historical work on eighteenth-century French literature.

Yet in one crucial respect he was different. For Victor Klemperer was

Jewish. The son of a preacher in the extremely liberal Reform Synagogue in Berlin, he had been baptized as a Protestant, one of a growing number of German Jews who acculturated in this way. This was more a social than a religious decision, since he does not seem to have had a very strong religious faith of any kind. In 1906 he provided further evidence of his acculturation by marrying a non-Jewish German woman, the pianist Eva Schlemmer, with whom he came to share many intellectual and cultural interests, above all, perhaps, an enthusiasm for the cinema. The couple remained childless. Yet, through all the vicissitudes of the 1920s, it was his marriage that gave stability to his life, despite the couple's increasingly frequent bouts of ill-health, exaggerated perhaps by growing hypochondria.[185] Throughout the 1920s he lived a stable, if less than completely contented life, disturbed early on by fears of civil war, although this never materialized and looked less likely after 1923.[186] He filled his diary with reports of his work, his holidays, his amusements, his relationships with his family, friends and colleagues, and other aspects of the daily routine. 'I often ask myself', he wrote on 10 September 1927, 'why I write such an extensive diary', a question to which he had no real answer: it was simply a compulsion – 'I can't leave it alone.'[187] Publication was dubious. So what was his purpose? 'Just collect life. Always collect. Impressions, knowledge, reading, events, everything. And don't ask why or what for.'[188]

Klemperer occasionally let slip that he felt his career blocked by the fact that he was Jewish. Despite his increasing output of scholarly works on French literary history, he was stuck in Dresden's Technical University with no prospect of moving to a post in a major university institution. 'There are reactionary and liberal universities,' he noted on 26 December 1926: 'The reactionaries don't take any Jews, the liberal ones always have two Jews already and don't take a third.'[189] The growth of antisemitism in the Weimar Republic also posed problems for Klemperer's political position. 'It's gradually becoming clear to me', he wrote in September 1919, 'how new and insurmountable a hindrance antisemitism means for me. And I volunteered for the war! Now I am sitting, baptized and nationalistic, between all stools.'[190] Klemperer was rather unusual amongst middle-class Jewish professionals in his conservative political views. The increasingly rabid antisemitism of the German Nationalists, with whose general political line he rather sympathized, made it impossible for him to support them, despite all his nostalgia for the prewar days of the Bismarckian and Wilhelmine Reich. Like many Germans, Klemperer found himself 'apathetic and indifferent' when he contemplated the violent party-political conflicts of the Weimar Republic.[191] Instinctively hostile to the left, Klemperer was none the less obliged to record in March 1920, as he heard the news of the Kapp putsch in Berlin:

My inclination to the right has suffered greatly . . . as a result of permanent antisemitism. I would dearly like to see the current putschists put up against a wall, I truly cannot work up any enthusiasm for the oath-breaking army, and really not at all for the immature and disorderly students – but neither can I for the 'legal' Ebert government either and less still for the radical left. I find them all off-putting.

'What an agonizing tragicomedy', he wrote, 'that 5,000–8,000 soldiers can overthrow the whole German Reich.'[192]

Surprisingly, perhaps, for a man who devoted his working life to the study of French literature, he was very much in favour of waging another war against the French – perhaps as a result of his experiences on the Western Front during the war, still more as a result of his evident outrage at the Treaty of Versailles. But this hardly seemed possible under the Weimar Republic. On 20 April 1921 he wrote:

The monarchy is my banner, I long for the old German power, I want all the time to strike once again against France. But what kind of disgusting company one keeps with the German racists! It will be even more disgusting if Austria joins us. And everything we now feel was felt with more or less justification by the French after 70. And I would not have become a professor under Wilhelm II, and yet . . .[193]

Already in 1925 he was regarding the election of Hindenburg as President as a potential disaster, comparable to the assassination of the Archduke Franz Ferdinand in 1914. 'Fascism everywhere. The terrors of the war have been forgotten, the Russian terror is driving Europe into reaction.'[194] As time went on, Klemperer grew weary of the constant political excitement. In August 1932, as the Weimar Republic entered its final turbulent phase, he wrote:

Moreover: I don't need to write the history of my times. And the information I provide is dull, I am half repelled, half full of a fear to which I don't want to surrender myself, completely without enthusiasm for any party. The whole thing is meaningless, undignified, miserable – nobody plays a part for himself, everyone's a puppet ... Hitler before the gates – or who else? And what will become of me, the Jewish professor?

He preferred instead to write about the small black kitten that had wandered into their house, and instantly became their pet.[195] Under the influence not only of the threatening political situation, but also of his wife's serious, clinical depression and frequent illnesses, Klemperer wrote less and less, and seemed by the end of 1932 on the verge of abandoning his diary altogether.

Klemperer's political pessimism owed a lot to the personal troubles he was experiencing. Yet his attitude was shared by many patriotic, liberal-conservative German Jews who felt ill at ease amidst the conflicts of the Weimar Republic. Beyond that, his distaste for the extremes of politics and his disquiet at the violence and fanaticism that surrounded him was surely characteristic of many middle-class Germans, whatever their background. His Jewish ethnicity not only caused him to suffer some adverse discrimination, but it also gave him a sharp and sardonic eye for political developments that were ominous for the future, as he rightly guessed. Yet he did not suffer unduly from antisemitism, he did not experience any violence, indeed, he did not record a single instance of a personal insult in his diary at this time. In formal terms, Jews such as Klemperer enjoyed far more freedom and equality under the Weimar Republic than they had ever done before. The Republic opened up new opportunities for Jews in the civil service, politics and the professions as well as in government: a Jewish Foreign Minister like Walther Rathenau would have been unthinkable under the Wilhelmine Reich, for instance. The Jewish-owned parts of the press, particularly the newspapers controlled by the two liberal Jewish firms of Mosse and Ullstein, which together produced over half the newspapers sold in Berlin in the 1920s, strongly supported the liberal institutions of the Republic. The arts' new-found freedom from censorship and official disapproval brought many Jewish writers, painters and musicians to prominence as apostles of modernist culture, where they mingled easily with non-Jewish figures like the composer Paul Hindemith, the poet and playwright Bertolt Brecht, or the artists Max Beckmann and George Grosz. Jews signalled their support for the Republic by voting particularly for the Democrats, and to a lesser extent for the parties of the left.[196]

On the other hand, partly in reaction to these developments, the 1920s also witnessed a broadening and deepening of the currents of antisemitism in German politics and society. Even before the war, the Pan-Germans and others on the right had pumped out propaganda accusing the Jews of undermining the German nation. This kind of racist conspiracy theory was more than shared by military leaders such as Ludendorff. It found notorious expression during the war in the so-called Jewish census of October 1916, ordered by senior army officers who hoped it would give them support in refusing Jews admission to the officer corps once the war was over. The aim was to reveal the cowardly and disloyal nature of the Jews by showing statistically that Jews were under-represented in the army, and that those who had joined up were over-represented in desk-jobs. In fact, it showed the reverse: many Jewish Germans, like Victor Klemperer, were nationalist to the core, and identified strongly with the Reich. German Jews were over- rather than under-represented in the armed forces and at the front. Confounding the expectations of anti-semitic officers to such a degree, the results of the census were suppressed. But the knowledge that it had been ordered caused a great deal of anger among German Jews, even if the attitudes it revealed were not shared by the majority of rank-and-file troops.[197]

After the war, the widespread belief on the right that the German army had been 'stabbed in the back' by revolutionaries in 1918 translated easily into antisemitic demagogy. It was, men like Ludendorff evidently believed, 'the Jews' who had done the stabbing, who led subversive institutions like the Communist Party, who agreed to the Treaty of Versailles, who set up the Weimar Republic. In fact, of course, the German army was defeated militarily in 1918. There was, as we have seen, no stab-in-the-back. Leading politicians who signed the Treaty, like Matthias Erzberger, were not Jewish at all. If Jews like Rosa Luxemburg were over-represented in the Communist Party leadership, or, like Eugen Leviné in the revolutionary upheavals in Munich early in 1919, they were not acting as Jews but as revolutionaries, alongside many non-Jews (such as Karl Liebknecht, whom many right-wingers thought instinctively must be Jewish because of his ultra-left political views). Most Jewish Germans supported the solid liberal parties of the centre, or to a lesser extent the Social Democrats, rather than the revolutionary left, whose violent activism shocked and appalled a respectable citizen like Klemperer. Nevertheless, the events of 1918–19 gave a boost to antisemitism on the right, convincing many waverers that racist conspiracy theories about the Jews were correct after all.[198]

Alongside extreme right-wing propaganda scapegoating Jews for the catastrophes of 1918–19, there also emerged a more popular form of antisemitism, directed particularly at war profiteers and the small number of financiers who managed to get rich quick in the throes of the inflation. Antisemitism had always surged at times of economic crisis, and the economic crises of the Weimar Republic dwarfed anything that Germany had witnessed before. A fresh source of conflict arose in the gathering pace of immigration on the part of impoverished Jewish refugees fleeing antisemitic violence and civil war in Russia. There were perhaps 80,000 'Eastern Jews' in Germany before the First World War, and their arrival, along with that of a much larger number of immigrant workers from Poland and elsewhere, had led the Reich government to introduce a virtually unique kind of citizenship law in 1913, allowing only those who could show German ancestry to claim German nationality.[199] After the war there was a renewed influx, as the Bolshevik Revolution swept across Russia, prompting antisemitic pogroms and murders on a huge scale by the Revolution's Tsarist opponents. Although the immigrants acculturated quickly, and were relatively few in number, they nevertheless formed an easy target for popular resentments. At the height of the hyperinflation, on 6 November 1923, a newspaper reporter observed serious disturbances in a district of Berlin with a high proportion of Jewish immigrants from the East:

Everywhere in the side-streets a howling mob. Looting takes place under cover of darkness. A shoe-shop at the corner of Dragoon Street is ransacked, the shards of the window-panes are lying around on the street. Suddenly a whistle sounds. In a long human chain, covering the entire width of the street, a police cordon advances. 'Clear the street!' an officer cries. 'Go into your houses!' The crowd slowly moves on. Everywhere with the same shouts: 'Beat the Jews to death!' Demagogues have manipulated the starving people for so long that they fall upon the wretched creatures who pursue a miserable goods trade in the Dragoon Street cellar . . . it is inflamed racial hatred, not hunger, that is driving them to loot.

Young lads immediately follow every passer-by with a Jewish appearance, in order to fall upon him when the moment is right.[200]

Such a public outburst of violence was symptomatic of the new preparedness of antisemites, like so many other groups on the fringes of German politics, to stir up or actively employ violence and terror to gain their ends, rather than remaining content, as they mostly had been before 1914, with mere words. A wave of still imperfectly documented incidents of personal violence against Jews and their property, attacks on synagogues, acts of desecration carried out in Jewish cemeteries, was the result.[201]

It was not just an unprecedented willingness to translate vehement prejudice into violent action that broadly distinguished post-1918 antisemitism from its prewar counterpart. While the overwhelming majority of Germans still rejected the use of physical force against Jews during the Weimar Republic, the language of antisemitism became embedded in mainstream political discourse as never before. The 'stab-in-the-back', the 'November traitors', the 'Jewish Republic', the 'Jewish-Bolshevik conspiracy' to undermine Germany – all these and many similar demagogic slogans could be regularly read in the papers, whether as expressions of editorial opinion or in reporting of political incidents, speeches and trials. They could be heard day after day in legislative assemblies, where the rhetoric of the Nationalists, the second largest party after the Social Democrats during the middle years of the Republic, was shot through with antisemitic phrases. These were more extreme and more frequently employed than they had been by the Conservatives before the war, and were amplified by splinter groups of the right that collectively enjoyed much more support than the antisemitic parties of Ahlwardt, Böckel and their ilk. Closely allied to many of these groups was the German Protestant Church, deeply conservative and nationalist by conviction and also prone to outbursts of antisemitism; but Catholic antisemitism also took on new vigour in the 1920s, animated by fear of the challenge of Bolshevism, which had already launched violent attacks on Christianity in Hungary and Russia at the end of the war. There were large swathes of the German electorate on the right and in the centre that fervently desired a rebirth of German national pride and glory after 1918. They were to a greater or lesser degree convinced as a result that this had to be achieved by overcoming the spirit of 'Jewish' subversion that had supposedly brought Germany to its knees at the end of the war.[202] The sensibility of many Germans was so blunted by this tide of antisemitic rhetoric that they failed to recognize that there was anything exceptional about a new political movement that emerged after the end of the war to put antisemitism at the very core of its fanatically held beliefs: the Nazi Party.

3

THE RISE OF NAZISM

BOHEMIAN REVOLUTIONARIES

I

When Kurt Eisner was released from Cell 70 in Munich's Stadelheim gaol under a general amnesty proclaimed in October 1918, there was little indication that he was soon to become one of Germany's leading revolutionaries. Best known as a theatre critic, he personified the bohemian lifestyle associated with Munich's Schwabing district, close to the city centre.[1] His appearance advertised his bohemianism. Small and heavily bearded, he went around wearing a black cloak and a huge, broad-brimmed black hat; a pair of little steel-rimmed spectacles was perched on his nose. Eisner was not a native Bavarian, but came from Berlin, where he was born into a middle-class Jewish family in 1867. He was identified with the right-wing fringe of the Social Democratic Party, losing his job with its local newspaper in the early 1900s because of his support for the 'revisionists' who wanted the Social Democrats to abandon their Marxism. Like many 'revisionists', however, Eisner was opposed to the war. He took a leading role in forming the anti-war Independent Social Democratic Party and subsequently organized a series of strikes in January 1918 to try to bring an end to the conflict.[2]

When things began to fall apart on 7 November 1918, it was Eisner who, thanks to his gift for rhetoric and his disdain for political convention, took the lead in Munich. As the Majority Social Democrats proposed a traditional political march through the Bavarian capital in an orderly demonstration for peace, led by a brass band and carrying banners, Eisner jumped onto the speakers' platform and told the crowd to occupy the army barracks and take control of the city. Accompanied by a group of followers, Eisner proceeded to do just that, meeting with no resistance from the soldiers. Obtaining authorization from the local revolutionary workers' and soldiers' council, Eisner proclaimed Bavaria a Republic and established a revolutionary government staffed by Majority and Independent Social Democrats, with himself at its head. But his government failed utterly in the basic tasks of maintaining food supplies, providing jobs, demobilizing the troops and keeping the transport system going. The conservative Bavarian peasantry, outraged at the events in Munich, were withholding foodstuffs, and the Allies had requisitioned most of the railway locomotives. Workers began to heckle Eisner and shout him down at meetings. In cabinet, Eisner was angrily told by one of its members: 'You are an anarchist . . . You are no statesman, you are a fool . . . We are being ruined by bad management.'[3] Not surprisingly, therefore, elections held on 12 January resulted in a crushing victory for the Majority Social Democrats and a humiliating defeat for Eisner's Independents.

Eisner was everything the radical right in Bavaria hated: a bohemian and a Berliner, a Jew, a journalist, a campaigner for peace during the war, and an agitator who had been arrested for his part in the January strikes of 1918. Indeed, with his secretary, the journalist Felix Fechenbach, he even published secret and incriminating documents on the outbreak of the war from the Bavarian archives. He was, in short, the ideal object onto which the 'stab-in-the-back' legend could be projected. On 21 February 1919, the far right's detestation found its ultimate expression as a young, aristocratic student, Count Anton von Arco-Valley, shot Eisner twice at point-blank range as he was walking through the street on his way to the Bavarian Parliament, killing him instantly.[4] The assassination unleashed a storm of violence in the Bavarian capital. Eisner's guards immediately shot and wounded Arco-Valley, who was surrounded by an angry crowd; only Fechenbach's prompt intervention saved him from being lynched on the spot. While the injured assassin was bundled off to the same cell in Stadelheim prison that Eisner had occupied only the year before, one of Eisner's socialist admirers walked into the Parliament shortly afterwards, drew a gun, and in full view of all the other deputies in the debating chamber, fired two shots at Eisner's severest critic, the Majority Social Democratic leader Erhard Auer, who barely survived his wounds. Meanwhile, ironically, a draft resignation document was discovered in Eisner's pocket. The assassination had been completely pointless.

Afraid of further violence, however, the Bavarian Parliament suspended its meetings, and, without a vote, the Majority Social Democrats declared themselves the legitimate government. A coalition cabinet headed by an otherwise obscure Majority Social Democrat, Johannes Hoffmann, was formed, but it was unable to restore order as massive street demonstrations followed Eisner's funeral. In the power vacuum that ensued, arms and ammunition were distributed to the workers' and soldiers' councils. News of the outbreak of a Communist Revolution in Hungary suddenly galvanized the far left into declaring a Council Republic in which Parliament would be replaced by a Soviet-style regime.[5] But the leader of the new Bavarian Council Republic was no Lenin. Once more, literary bohemianism had come to the fore, this time in the form of a dramatist rather than a critic. Only 25, Ernst Toller had made his name as a poet and playwright. More of an anarchist than a socialist, Toller enrolled like-minded men in his government, including another playwright, Erich Mühsam, and a well-known anarchist writer, Gustav Landauer. Faced with the outspoken support of the Munich workers' and soldiers' councils for what Schwabing's wits soon dubbed 'the regime of the coffee house anarchists', Hoffmann's Majority Social Democratic cabinet fled to Bamberg, in northern Bavaria. Meanwhile, Toller announced a comprehensive reform of the arts, while his government declared that Munich University was open to all applicants except those who wanted to study history, which was abolished as hostile to civilization. Another minister announced that the end of capitalism would be brought about by the issue of free money. Franz Lipp, the Commissar for Foreign Affairs, telegraphed Moscow to complain that 'the fugitive Hoffmann has taken with him the keys to my ministry toilet', and declared war on Württemberg and Switzerland 'because these dogs have not at once loaned me sixty locomotives. I am certain', he added, 'that we will be victorious.'[6]

An attempt by the Hoffmann government to overthrow the Council Republic with an improvised force of volunteers was easily put down by the 'Red Army' recruited from the armed members of the workers' and soldiers' councils. Twenty men died in the exchanges of fire, however, and the situation was now clearly becoming much more dangerous. On the same day as the fighting took place, organized Communists under the Russian Bolsheviks Max Levien and Eugen Leviné pushed the 'coffee house anarchists' brusquely aside. Without waiting for the approval of the German Communist Party, they established a Bolshevik regime in Munich and opened communications with Lenin, who asked politely whether they had managed to nationalize the banks yet. Levien, who had been accidentally caught in Germany at the outbreak of war in 1914 and drafted into the German army, followed Lenin's instructions, and began arresting members of the aristocracy and the upper middle class as hostages. While the main church in Munich was turned into a revolutionary temple presided over by the 'Goddess Reason', the Communists set about expanding and training a Red Army, which soon numbered 20,000 well-armed and well-paid men. A series of proclamations announced that Bavaria was going to spearhead the Bolshevization of Europe; workers had to receive military training, and all weapons in private possession had to be surrendered on pain of death.[7]

All this frightened the Hoffmann government far more than the week-long regime of the coffee house anarchists had done. The spectre loomed of an axis of Bolshevik revolutionary regimes in Budapest, Munich and possibly Vienna as well. The Majority Social Democrats in Bamberg clearly needed a serious fighting force at their disposal. Hoffmann signed up a force of 35,000 Free Corps soldiers under the leadership of the Bavarian colonel Franz Ritter von Epp, backed by regular military units including an armoured train. They were equipped with machine guns and other serious military hardware. Munich was already in chaos, with a general strike crippling production, and public services at a standstill. Looting and theft were spreading across the city, and now it was blockaded by the Free Corps as well. No quarter would be given, they announced; anyone in Munich found bearing arms would immediately be shot. Terrified, the Munich workers' and soldiers' councils passed a vote of no-confidence in the Communists, who had to resign, leaving the city without a government. In this situation, a panicky unit of the Red Army began to take reprisals against hostages imprisoned in a local school, the Luitpold Gymnasium. These included six members of the Thule Society, an antisemitic, Pan-German sect, founded towards the end of the war. Naming itself after the supposed location of ultimate 'Aryan' purity, Iceland ('Thule'), it used the 'Aryan' swastika symbol to denote its racial priorities. With its roots in the pre-war 'Germanic Order', another conspiratorial organization of the far right, it was led by the self-styled Baron von Sebottendorf, who was in reality a convicted forger known to the police as Adam Glauer. The Society included a number of people who were to be prominent in the Third Reich.[8] It was known that Arco-Valley, the assassin of Kurt Eisner, had been trying to become a member of the Thule Society. In an act of revenge and desperation, the Red Army soldiers lined up ten of the hostages, put them in front of a firing squad, and shot them dead. Those executed included the Prince of Thurn and Taxis, the young Countess von Westarp and two more aristocrats, as well as an elderly professor who had been arrested for making an uncomplimentary remark in public about a revolutionary poster. A handful of prisoners taken from the invading Free Corps made up the rest.

The news of these shootings enraged the soldiers beyond measure. As they marched into the city, virtually unopposed, their victory became a bloodbath. Leading revolutionaries like Eugen Leviné were arrested and summarily shot. The anarchist Gustav Landauer was taken to Stadelheim prison, where soldiers beat his face to a pulp with rifle butts, shot him twice, then kicked him to death in the prison courtyard, leaving the body to rot for two days before it was removed. Coming across a meeting of a Catholic craftsmen's society on 6 May, a drunken Free Corps unit, told by an informer that the assembled workmen were revolutionaries, arrested them, took them to a nearby cellar, beat them up and killed a total of 21 of the blameless men, after which they rifled the corpses for valuables. Numerous other people were 'shot trying to escape', killed after being reported as former Communists, mown down after being denounced for supposedly possessing arms, or hauled out of houses from which shots had allegedly been fired, and executed on the spot. All in all, even the official estimates gave a total of some 600 killed at the hands of the invaders; unofficial observers made the total anything up to twice as high.[9] After the bloodbath, moderates such as Hoffmann's Social Democrats, despite having commissioned the action, did not stand much of a chance in Munich. A 'White' counter-revolutionary government eventually took over, and proceeded to prosecute the remaining revolutionaries while letting off the Free Corps troops, a few of whom had been convicted for their murderous atrocities, with the lightest of sentences. Munich became a playground for extremist political sects, as virtually every social and political group in the city burned with resentment, fear and lust for revenge.[10] Public order had more or less vanished.

All this was deeply disturbing to the officers who were now faced with the task of reconstructing a regular army from the ruins of the old one. Not surprisingly, considering the fact that the workers' and soldiers' councils had enjoyed considerable influence amongst the troops, those who ran the new army were concerned to ensure that soldiers received the correct kind of political indoctrination, and that the many small political groups springing up in Munich posed no threat to the new, post-revolutionary political order. Among those who were sent to receive political indoctrination in June 1919 was a 30-year-old corporal who had been in the Bavarian army since the beginning of the war and had stayed in it through all the vicissitudes of Social Democracy, anarchy and Communism, taking part in demonstrations, wearing a red armband along with the rest of his comrades, and disappearing from the scene with most of them when they had been ordered to defend Munich against the invading forces in the preceding weeks. His name was Adolf Hitler.[11]

II

Hitler was the product of circumstances as much as anything else. Had things been different, he might never have come to political prominence. At the time of the Bavarian Revolution, he was an obscure rank-and-file soldier who had so far played no part in politics of any kind. Born on 20 April 1889, he was a living embodiment of the ethnic and cultural concept of national identity held by the Pan-Germans; for he was not German by birth or citizenship, but Austrian. Little is known about his childhood, youth and upbringing, and much if not most of what has been written about his early life is highly speculative, distorted or fantastical. We do know, however, that his father Alois changed his name from that of his mother, Maria Schicklgruber, to whom he had been born out of wedlock in 1837, to that of his stepfather, Johann Georg Hiedler or Hitler, in 1876. There is no evidence that any of Hitler's ancestors was Jewish. Johann Georg freely acknowledged his true paternity of Hitler's father. Alois was a customs inspector in Braunau on the Inn, a minor but

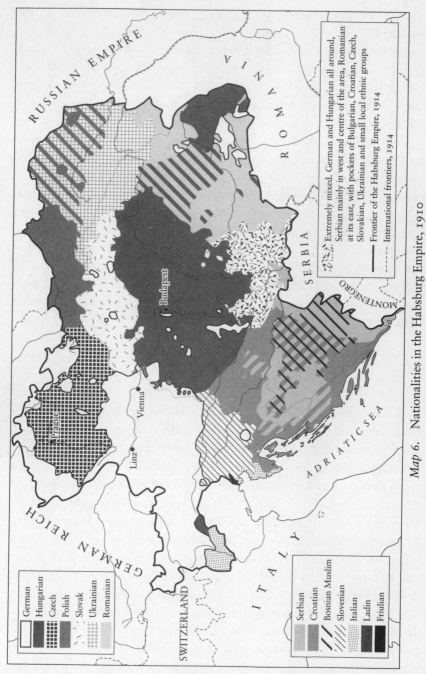

RUSSIAN EMPIRE

ROMANIA

SERBIA

MONTENEGRO

ADRIATIC SEA

ITALY

SWITZERLAND

GERMAN REICH

Budapest

Vienna

Linz

Prague

Extremely mixed. German and Hungarian all around, Serbian mainly in west and centre of the area, Romanian at its east, with pockets of Bulgarian, Croatian, Czech, Slovakian, Ukrainian and small local ethnic groups

——— Frontier of the Habsburg Empire, 1914

------- International frontiers, 1914

German
Hungarian
Czech
Polish
Slovak
Ukrainian
Romanian

Serbian
Croatian
Bosnian Muslim
Slovenian
Italian
Ladin
Friulian

Map 6. Nationalities in the Habsburg Empire, 1910

respectable official of the Austrian government. He married three times; Adolf was the only child of his third marriage to survive infancy apart from his younger sister Paula. 'Psychohistorians' have made much of Adolf's subsequent allusions to his cold, stern, disciplinarian and sometimes violent father and his warm, much-loved mother, but none of their conclusions can amount to any more than speculation.[12]

What is clear is that the Hitler family was often on the move, changing houses several times before settling in 1898 in a suburb of Linz, which Adolf ever after regarded as his home town. The young Hitler did poorly at school and disliked his teachers, but otherwise does not seem to have stood out amongst his fellow-pupils. He was clearly unfitted for the regular, routine life and hard work of the civil service, for which his father had intended him. After his father's death early in 1903, he lived in a flat in Linz, where he was looked after by his mother, his aunt and his younger sister, and dreamed of making a future career as an artist while spending his time drawing, talking with friends, going to the opera and reading. But in 1907 two events occurred which put an end to this idle life of fantasizing. His mother died of breast cancer, and his application to the Viennese Academy of Art was rejected on the grounds that his painting and drawing were not good enough; he would do better, he was told, as an architect. Certainly, his forte lay in drawing and painting buildings. He was particularly impressed by the heavy, oppressive, historicist architecture of the public buildings on Vienna's Ringstrasse, constructed as symbolic expressions of power and solidity at a time when the real political foundations of the Habsburg monarchy were beginning to crumble.[13] From the very beginning, buildings interested Hitler mainly as statements of power. He retained this interest throughout his life. But he lacked the application to become an architect. He tried again to join the Academy of Art, and was rejected a second time. Disappointed and emotionally bereft, he moved to Vienna. He took with him, in all probability, two political influences from Linz. The first was the Pan-Germanism of Georg Ritter von Schönerer, whose supporters in the town were particularly numerous, it seems, in the school that Hitler attended. And the second was an unquenchable enthusiasm for the music of Richard Wagner, whose operas he frequently attended in Linz; he was intoxicated by their romanticization of Germanic myth and legend, and by their depiction of heroes who knew no fear. Armed with these beliefs, and confident in his future destiny as a great artist, he spent the next five years in the Austrian capital.[14]

Hitler's subsequent account of this period lent a retrospective coherence to it that it does not seem to have possessed in reality. There is, again, little reliable independent evidence about what he did or thought. But a few things seem clear enough. First, unable to come to terms with his failure to get into the Academy, Hitler conceived a violent hatred for bourgeois convention, the establishment, rules and regulations. Rather than train or apply for a regular job, he lived an idle, chaotic, bohemian life, and spent his savings on going to Wagner operas. When the money ran out, he was forced to sleep rough, or find night-quarters in a doss-house. Things only looked up when he received some money from his aunt, and began to sell small paintings, mostly copies, providing himself with the means to live in a Men's Home, where he rented a cheap room and was able to use the library and the reading-room. Here he stayed for three years, living a life that belonged to the outermost fringes of bohemian culture.

The political views Hitler had imbibed in Linz were strengthened as he encountered in a more direct form the Pan-Germanism of Schönerer that had been so influential in Linz. Hitler undoubtedly loathed the Habsburg monarchy and its capital city, whose institutions had denied him the fulfilment of his artistic ambitions. He found Schönerer's demand that the German-speaking areas of Austria be absorbed into the German Empire irresistibly appealing as a result. The racial mixing of Vienna was repulsive to him; only a racially homogeneous nation could be a successful one. But Schönerer, he realized, was incapable of winning the support of the masses. This was the achievement of Vienna's Mayor Karl Lueger, whose antisemitic demagogy revealed, Hitler thought, a true understanding of men. Hitler could scarcely ignore the everyday antisemitism of the kind of newspapers that were available in the reading-room of the Men's Home, and the cheap antisemitic pamphlets he later described reading at this time. And his enthusiasm for Wagner, whose operas he went to hundreds of times in this period, can only have strengthened his political views. Virtually all the followers of Schönerer, Wagner and Lueger were antisemitic by this time, many of them rabidly so, and there is no reason why Hitler should have been an exception. The fact that he sold his pictures to Jewish traders and borrowed money from Jewish inmates of the Men's Home does not mean that he was not antisemitic. Nevertheless, it is likely that his antisemitism at this time had an abstract, almost theoretical quality to it; his hatred of Jews only became visceral, personal and extreme at the end of the First World War.[15]

Some of the most interesting pages of Hitler's later autobiographical work *My Struggle* (*Mein Kampf*) describe the feelings of excitement he experienced when watching Social Democratic mass demonstrations in Vienna. He found the Social Democrats' Marxism abhorrent, and thought their propaganda full of loathsome and vicious slanders and lies. Why did the masses believe in it, then, rather than in the doctrines of someone like Schönerer? His answer was that the Social Democrats were intolerant of other views, suppressed them within the working class as far as they could, projected themselves simply and strongly and won over the masses by force. 'The psyche of the great masses', he wrote, 'is not receptive to anything that is half-hearted and weak . . . The masses love a commander more than a petitioner.' He added: 'I achieved an equal understanding of the importance of physical terror towards the individual and the masses . . . Terror at the place of employment, in the factory, in the meeting hall, and on the occasion of mass demonstrations will always be successful unless opposed by equal terror.' The Social Democrats, he concluded, 'command weaklings in both mind and force. They know how to create the illusion that this is the only way of preserving the peace, and at the same time, stealthily but steadily, they conquer one position after another, sometimes by silent backmail, sometimes by actual theft . . .' All of this may have been to some extent retrospective rationalization, as Hitler projected his own feelings and purposes back onto the most successful mass movement of the Austria of his youth. But, certainly for anyone who lived in Vienna before 1914, there was no escaping the power of the Social Democrats over the masses, and it is reasonable to suppose that Hitler was impressed by it and learned from it even as he rejected the doctrines which the Social Democrats purveyed.[16]

Perhaps the most important political lesson he derived from his time in Vienna, however, was a deep contempt for the state and the law. There is no reason to disbelieve his later statement that as a follower of Schönerer he considered the Habsburg monarchy to be the oppressor of the Germanic race, forcing it to mix with others and denying it the chance of uniting with Germans in the Reich. 'If the species itself is in danger of being oppressed or utterly eliminated,' he wrote, 'the question of legality is reduced to a subordinate rule.' Racial self-preservation was a higher principle than legality, which could often be no more than a cloak for tyranny. Any means were justified in this struggle. Moreover, the 'rotten state' of the Habsburgs was completely dominated by parliamentarism, a political system for which Hitler acquired an abiding contempt by spending a great deal of time in the public gallery of the Austrian Parliament, where parties of rival nationalities shouted and screamed at each other, each in its own language, and prevented anything much being achieved. He conceived a special hatred for the Czechs, who were specially disruptive. It was Schönerer's mistake to try and reach his goal through Parliament, he thought. Hitler concluded that only a strong leader directly elected by the people could get anything done.[17]

There is no indication, however, that Hitler thought of himself as that leader before 1914, or indeed that he considered entering politics at all. On the contrary, he was still wedded to the idea of becoming an artist. The abject financial misery to which his failure to achieve this ambition had brought him was alleviated somewhat by the payment of a legacy from his father's estate, which he received at the age of 24, on 20 April 1913. Hitler quickly wound up his affairs in Vienna and departed for Germany, thus giving practical expression to the Pan-Germanism he had imbibed from Schönerer. He later described, with every appearance of authenticity, the happiness he felt when he moved to Munich, leaving behind him the colourful and, to him, repulsive racial cosmopolitanism of the Austrian capital and the sense of political confusion and decline that characterized the Habsburg political system. Such a system, he felt, was not worth fighting for, and not the least reason why he left was to avoid the military service for which he was shortly to become liable. Now he was in Germany, he felt at home.

He rented a room on the edge of Schwabing, and resumed the kind of life he had led in Vienna, copying postcards of famous Munich buildings in watercolour and selling enough of them to make a meagre living. Like other Schwabing bohemians, he whiled away much of his time in coffee houses and beer-cellars, but he was an outsider to the real bohemian world as well as the world of respectable society, for while men like Eisner, Toller, Landauer or Mühsam were heavily involved in the theatre, discussing anarchist utopias, or making a name for themselves as poets and writers, Hitler continued his previous, aimless existence, and made no attempt to acquire in Munich the artistic training he had been denied in Vienna. And while the official art establishment remained closed to him, the unofficial avant-garde that generated so much excitement in the more fashionable of Schwabing's coffee houses, with painters like Wassily Kandinsky, Paul Klee, Franz Marc, August Macke and the 'Blue Rider' group, broke with convention and moved into Expressionism and abstraction. The avant-garde aroused in Hitler only incomprehension and revulsion. His own practice of art was limited to painstaking, lifeless reproductions of buildings; his own taste in art never moved beyond the kind of conventional, classically inspired representations that were the stock-in-trade of the Academy that he had so wanted to join in Vienna.[18] What Hitler did share with the Schwabing bohemians, however, was an inner contempt for bourgeois convention and rules, and a belief that art could change the world.

Hitler was rescued from his existence as a bohemian on the margins of cultural life by the outbreak of the First World War. A photograph exists of him in the crowd that gathered in the centre of Munich on 2 August to celebrate the declaration of war, his face shining with excitement. Three days later, he volunteered to join the Bavarian army. In the chaos and confusion of the first days of the war, when vast numbers were volunteering, nobody seems to have thought of checking up on whether or not he was a German citizen. He was enlisted on 16 August, and was sent almost immediately to the Western Front. This was, he wrote later, a 'release from the painful feelings of my youth'. For the first time, he had a mission he could believe in and follow, and a close-knit group of comrades with whom he could identify. His heart 'overflowed with proud joy' at the fact that he was now fighting for Germany.[19] For the next four years he remained with his regiment, acting as a dispatch runner, gaining promotion to corporal, and winning two decorations for bravery, the second being the Iron Cross, First Class, on the recommendation, ironically, of a Jewish officer. Shortly afterwards he was caught in a poison-gas attack, a frequent occurrence on both sides in the later stages of the war. Temporarily blinded, he was sent to a military hospital at Pasewalk, in Pomerania in the German north-east, to recover. Here he learned in due course of the German defeat, the Armistice and the Revolution.[20]

In *My Struggle*, Hitler described this as 'the greatest villainy of the century', the negation of all his hopes, rendering all his sacrifices futile. As he was told the news, 'everything went black before my eyes', he tottered back to his dormitory and wept. There is no reason to doubt that it was a terrible trauma for him. The memory of 1918 was to play a central role in all his subsequent thought and action. How had the disaster happened? Searching for an explanation, Hitler seized eagerly on the rapidly spreading story of the 'stab-in-the-back'. The Jews, whom he already regarded with suspicion and distaste, must have been to blame, he thought. All the inchoate and confused ideas and prejudices he had so far garnered from Schönerer, Lueger, Wagner and the rest now suddenly fell into a coherent, neat and utterly paranoid pattern. Once more, he looked to propaganda as the prime political mover: enemy war propaganda, undermining Germany's will from without, Jewish, socialist propaganda spreading doubt and defeatism from within. Propaganda, he learned from contemplating the disaster, must always be directed at the masses:

All propaganda must be popular and its intellectual level must be adjusted to the most limited intelligence among those it is addressed to. Consequently the greater the mass it is intended to reach, the lower its purely intellectual level will have to be ... The receptivity of the great masses is very limited, their intelligence is small, but their power of forgetting is enormous. In consequence of these facts, all effective propaganda must be limited to a very few points and must harp on these in slogans until the last member of the public understands what you want him to understand by your slogan.

And it had to appeal to the emotions rather than to reason, because: 'The people in their overwhelming majority are so feminine by nature and attitude that sober reasoning determines their thoughts and actions far less than emotion and feeling.' Finally, propaganda had to be continuous and unvarying in its message. It should never admit a glimmer of doubt in its own claims, or concede the tiniest element of right in the claims of the other side.[21]

Armed with these thoughts – or perhaps earlier, more rudimentary versions of them – Hitler obeyed his superior officer's orders and went along to the political instruction courses in June 1919 that were to launch him on his political career. The moment was the right one. Munich was a world that in the view of many conservatives had been turned upside down, and it was time to put it the right way up again. Where Prussia had failed, Bavaria could show the way. The whole language of politics in Munich after the overthrow of the Communist regime was permeated by nationalist slogans, antisemitic phrases, reactionary keywords that almost invited the rabid expression of counter-revolutionary sentiment. Hitler was to prove adept as few others were at mastering its cadences and mobilizing the stereotypical images of the enemies of order into an emotionally violent language of extremism.[22]

III

The courses Hitler attended were designed to root out any lingering socialist sentiments from regular Bavarian troops and indoctrinate them with the beliefs of the far right. Among the lecturers were the conservative Munich history professor Karl Alexander von Müller, and the Pan-German economic theorist Gottfried Feder, who put an antisemitic gloss on economics by accusing the Jews of destroying the livelihood of hard-working 'Aryans' through using capital unproductively. So readily did Hitler imbibe the ideas of such men that he was picked out by his superiors and sent as an instructor on a similar course in August 1919. Here for the first time he discovered a talent for speaking to a large audience. Comments by those attending his lectures referred admiringly to his passion and commitment and his ability to communicate with simple, ordinary men. They also noted the vehemence of his antisemitism. In a letter written on 16 September, Hitler expounded his beliefs about the Jews. The Jews, he wrote, in a biological metaphor of the kind that was to recur in many subsequent speeches and writings, brought about 'the racial tuberculosis of peoples'. He rejected 'antisemitism from purely emotional grounds' which led to pogroms, in favour of an 'antisemitism of reason', which had to aim at 'the planned legislative combating and removal of the Jews' privileges'. 'Its final aim must unshakeably be the removal of the Jews altogether.'[23]

In the rabidly vengeful, ultra-nationalist atmosphere of the months following the Free Corps' violent suppression of the Munich Revolution, such sentiments were far from unusual. Hitler had by now become a trusted political agent of the army. In this capacity he was sent to report on one of a large range of political groups that sprang up in Munich in this period, to see whether it was dangerous or whether it could be enrolled in the cause of counter-revolution. This was the German Workers' Party, founded on 5 January 1919 by one Anton Drexler, a locksmith who had previously belonged to the Fatherland Party. Drexler insisted that he was a socialist and a worker, opposed to unearned capital, exploitation and profiteering. But this was socialism with a nationalistic twist. Drexler ascribed the evils he fought to the machinations of the Jews, who had also devised the pernicious ideology of Bolshevism. He directed his appeal not to industrial workers but to the 'productive estates', to all those who lived from honest labour.[24] In the short run, this meant the lower middle classes, but equally, in a tradition going back to Adolf Stöcker's Christian Social movement in the 1880s and echoing many similar nationalist initiatives in both Germany and Austria before and above all immediately after the war, Drexler's party sought in the longer term to win the working class over from Marxism and enlist it in the service of the Pan-German cause.

The fledgling party was in fact another creation of the hyperactive Thule Society. There was nothing unusual about Drexler or his tiny party in the far-right hothouse of Munich after the defeat of the Revolution. What was unusual was the attention Hitler aroused when he went to a meeting of the party on 12 September 1919 and spoke passionately from the floor against a previous speaker who had advocated Bavaria's separation from the Reich. Impressed, Drexler readily acquiesced when Hitler, again acting on the orders of his army superiors, applied to join. Although he later claimed to have been only the seventh person to join the party, he was in fact enrolled as member number 555. This was less impressive than it sounded; the German Workers' Party membership began, following a habit long established amongst fringe political groups, not with the number 1, but with the number 501, to suggest that it enjoyed a membership of hundreds rather than just a few score.[25]

Hitler, still encouraged by his superior officers in the army, rapidly became the party's star speaker. He built on his success to push the party into holding ever larger public meetings, mostly in beer-halls, advertised in advance by brash poster campaigns, and often accompanied by rowdy scenes. By the end of March 1920, now indispensable to the Party, he had clearly decided that this was where his future lay. Demagogy had restored to him the identity he had lost with the German defeat. He left the army and became a full-time political agitator. The appeal of radical antisemitism in counter-revolutionary Munich was obvious, and had already been tapped by a much larger organization with similar views, the German-Racial Defence and Defiance League. This was yet another far-right group that used the swastika as its main political symbol. With its headquarters in Hamburg, the League boasted some 200,000 members all over Germany, drawn from ex-members of the Fatherland Party, from disgruntled ex-soldiers and from nationalist-inclined students, teachers and white-collar workers. It ran a sophisticated propaganda machine, churning out millions of leaflets and putting on mass meetings where the public numbered thousands rather than the hundreds which Drexler's organization was able to attract.[26] The League was far from being the only far-right movement of this kind; another, much smaller one, the German-Socialist Party, led by the engineer Alfred Brunner, also had branches in a number of German cities, though its membership was only a tenth of the size of the League's. But neither had a speaker whose pulling power in any way compared to Hitler's.[27]

While conventional right-wing politicians delivered lectures, or spoke in a style that was orotund and pompous, flat and dull, or rough and brutish, Hitler followed the model of Social Democratic orators such as Eisner, or the left-wing agitators from whom he later claimed to have learned in Vienna. And he gained much of his oratorical success by telling his audiences what they wanted to hear. He used simple, straightforward language that ordinary people could understand, short sentences, power-ful, emotive slogans. Often beginning a speech quietly, to capture his audience's attention, he would gradually build to a climax, his deep, rather hoarse voice would rise in pitch, climbing in a crescendo to a ranting and screaming finale, accompanied by carefully rehearsed dra-matic gestures, his face glistening with sweat, his lank, dark hair falling forward over his face as he worked his audience into a frenzy of emotion. There were no qualifications in what he said; everything was absolute, uncompromising, irrevocable, undeviating, unalterable, final. He seemed, as many who listened to his early speeches testified, to speak straight from the heart, and to express their own deepest fears and desires. Increasingly, too, he exuded self-confidence, aggression, belief in the ultimate triumph of his party, even a sense of destiny. His speeches often began with an account of his own poverty-stricken early life, to which he drew an implicit parallel with the downcast, downtrodden and desperate state of Germany after the First World War, then, his voice rising, he would describe his own political awakening, and point to its counterpart in Germany's future recovery and return to glory. Without necessarily using overtly religious language, Hitler appealed to religious archetypes of suffering, humiliation, redemption and resurrection lodged deep within his listeners' psyche; and in the circumstances of postwar and post-revolutionary Bavaria, he found a ready response.[28]

Hitler's speeches reduced Germany's complex social, political and economic problems to a simple common denominator: the evil machinations of the Jews. In *My Struggle*, describing how, in his view, Jewish subversives had undermined the German war effort in 1918, he declared:

If at the beginning of the war and during the war twelve or fifteen thousand of these Hebrew corrupters of the people had been held under poison gas, as happened to hundreds of thousands of our very best German workers in the field, the sacrifice of millions at the front would not have been in vain. On the contrary: twelve thousand scoundrels eliminated in time might have saved the lives of a million real Germans, valuable for the future. But it just happened to be in the line of bourgeois 'statesmanship' to subject millions to a bloody end on the battlefield without batting an eyelid, but to regard ten or twelve thousand traitors, profiteers, usurers, and swindlers as a sacred national treasure and openly proclaim their inviolability.[29]

Such uncompromising radicalism lent Hitler's public meetings a revivalist fervour that was hard for less demagogic politicians to emulate. The publicity he won was enhanced by the tactic of advertising them with red posters, to attract the left, with the result that protests from socialist listeners often degenerated into fisticuffs and brawls.

In the climate of postwar counter-revolution, national brooding on the 'stab-in-the-back', and obsession with war profiteers and merchants of the rapidly mushrooming hyperinflation, Hitler concentrated especially on rabble-rousing attacks on 'Jewish' merchants who were supposedly pushing up the price of goods: they should all, he said, to shouts of approval from his audiences, be strung up.[30] Perhaps to emphasize this anti-capitalist focus, and to align itself with similar groups in Austria and

Czechoslovakia, the party changed its name in February 1920 to the National Socialist German Workers' Party; hostile commentators soon abbreviated this to the word 'Nazi', just as the enemies of the Social Democrats had abbreviated the name of that party earlier on to 'Sozi'. Despite the change of name, however, it would be wrong to see Nazism as a form of, or an outgrowth from, socialism. True, as some have pointed out, its rhetoric was frequently egalitarian, it stressed the need to put common needs above the needs of the individual, and it often declared itself opposed to big business and international finance capital. Famously, too, antisemitism was once declared to be 'the socialism of fools'. But from the very beginning, Hitler declared himself implacably opposed to Social Democracy and, initially to a much smaller extent, Communism: after all, the 'November traitors' who had signed the Armistice and later the Treaty of Versailles were not Communists at all, but the Social Democrats and their allies.[31]

The 'National Socialists' wanted to unite the two political camps of left and right into which, they argued, the Jews had manipulated the German nation. The basis for this was to be the idea of race. This was light years removed from the class-based ideology of socialism. Nazism was in some ways an extreme counter-ideology to socialism, borrowing much of its rhetoric in the process, from its self-image as a movement rather than a party, to its much-vaunted contempt for bourgeois convention and conservative timidity. The idea of a 'party' suggested allegiance to parliamentary democracy, working steadily within a settled democratic polity. In speeches and propaganda, however, Hitler and his followers preferred on the whole to talk of the 'National Socialist movement', just as the Social Democrats had talked of the 'workers' movement' or, come to that, the feminists of the 'women's movement' and the apostles of prewar teenage rebellion of the 'youth movement'. The term not only suggested dynamism and unceasing forward motion, it also more than hinted at an ultimate goal, an absolute object to work towards that was grander and more final than the endless compromises of conventional politics. By presenting itself as a 'movement', National Socialism, like the labour movement, advertised its opposition to conventional politics and its intention to subvert and ultimately overthrow the system within which it was initially forced to work.

By replacing class with race, and the dictatorship of the proletariat with the dictatorship of the leader, Nazism reversed the usual terms of socialist ideology. The synthesis of right and left was neatly symbolized in the Party's official flag, personally chosen by Hitler in mid-1920: the field was bright red, the colour of socialism, with the swastika, the emblem of racist nationalism, outlined in black in the middle of a white circle at the centre of the flag, so that the whole ensemble made a combination of black, white and red, the colours of the official flag of the Bismarckian Empire. In the wake of the 1918 Revolution these came to symbolize rejection of the Weimar Republic and all it stood for; but by changing the design and adding the swastika, a symbol already used by a variety of far-right racist movements and Free Corps units in the postwar period, the Nazis also announced that what they wanted to replace it with was a new, Pan-German, racial state, not the old Wilhelmine status quo.[32]

By the end of 1920, Hitler's early emphasis on attacking Jewish capitalism had been modified to bring in 'Marxism', or in other words Social Democracy, and Bolshevism as well. The cruelties of the civil war and 'red terror' in Lenin's Russia were making an impact, and Hitler could use them to lend emphasis to common far-right views of the supposedly Jewish inspiration behind the revolutionary upheavals of 1918–19 in Munich. Nazism would also have been possible, however, without the Communist threat; Hitler's anti-Bolshevism was the product of his antisemitism and not the other way round.[33] His principal political targets remained the Social Democrats and the vaguer spectre of 'Jewish capitalism'. Borrowing the stock arguments of antisemitism from before the war, Hitler declared in numerous speeches that the Jews were a race of parasites who could only live by subverting other peoples, above all the highest and best of all races, the Aryans. Thus they divided the Aryan race against itself, both organizing capitalist exploitation on the one hand and leading the struggle against it on the other.[34] The Jews, he said in a speech delivered on 6 April 1920, were 'to be exterminated'; on 7 August the same year he told his audience that they should not believe 'that you can fight a disease without killing the cause, without annihilating the bacillus, and do not think that you can fight racial tuberculosis without taking care that the people are free of the cause of racial tuberculosis'. Annihilation meant the violent removal of the Jews from Germany by any means. The 'solution of the Jewish question', he told his listeners in April 1921, could only be solved by 'brute force'. 'We know', he said in

January 1923, 'that if they come to power, our heads will roll in the sand; but we also know that when we get our hands on power: "Then God have mercy on you!" '[35]

THE BEER-HALL PUTSCH

I

At the end of the First World War, General Erich Ludendorff, Germany's military dictator for the last two years or so of the conflict, thought it prudent to remove himself from the political scene for a while. Dismissed from office on 25 October 1918 after a bitter row with the newly appointed last, liberal government of the Kaiser, he lingered on for a while in Berlin, then, donning dark glasses and false whiskers, he slipped across the Baltic to Sweden to sit out the Revolution. By February 1919 he evidently thought the worst was over and returned to Germany. Such was the prestige he had gained in the war that he quickly became the figurehead of the radical right. A Pan-German annexationist in 1914–18, and a rabid opponent of the Peace Settlement, he immediately began conspiring to overthrow the new Republican order. Gathering a group of his former aides around him, he lent his support to the short-lived putsch mounted against the government in Berlin by Wolfgang Kapp and the Free Corps in March 1920, and when this failed, left for the more congenial atmosphere of Munich. Here he soon came into contact with the ultra-nationalist circle that had by now gathered round the previously unknown figure of Adolf Hitler.[36]

By the time the two eventually met, Hitler had acquired the first members of the devoted band of enthusiasts who would play a key role in one capacity or another in the growth of the Nazi Party and the building of the Third Reich. Most devoted of all was the student Rudolf Hess, a pupil of the geopolitical theorist Karl Haushofer at Munich University. The son of an authoritarian businessman who had refused to allow him to study before the war, Hess seemed to be looking for a strong leader to whom he could bind himself unconditionally. Like a number of subsequently prominent Nazis, he came from outside the German Reich: Hess was born in Alexandria in 1894. Service in the war, which he ended as an Air Force lieutenant, gave him one kind of authority to obey, study with Haushofer another. Neither gave him what he really wanted, any more than did the Free Corps or the Thule Society, of which Hess was also a member. It was eventually provided by Hitler, whom he met in 1920. Antisemitism was a shared passion: Hess denounced the 'pack of Jews' who he thought had betrayed Germany in 1918, and even before he met Hitler he led expeditions to working-class districts of Munich to slip thousands of antisemitic leaflets under the front doors of workers' flats.[37] Henceforth, Hess directed all the force of his hero-worship towards Hitler. Naive, idealistic, without personal ambition or greed, and, according to Haushofer, not very bright, Hess had an inclination to believe in irrational and mystical doctrines such as astrology; his dog-like devotion to Hitler was almost religious in its fervour; he regarded Hitler as a kind of Messiah. From now on, he would be Hitler's silent, passive slave, drinking in his master's words at the regular coffee round in the Café Heck, and gradually taking much of the burden of the routine work Hitler so hated off his shoulders. In addition, he introduced Hitler to an elaborate version of the common Pan-German theory of 'living-space', Lebensraum, with which Haushofer justified German claims to conquer Eastern Europe, and which the novelist Hans Grimm popularized with his best-seller Race without Space (Volk ohne Raum) in 1926.[38]

Useful to Hitler in another way was the failed racist poet and dramatist Dietrich Eckart, a former medical student. Eckart was already active in far-right circles in December 1918, when he started publishing a political weekly, In Plain German (Auf gut deutsch), with backing from a number of Bavarian businessmen and also the political fund of the army. Eckart blamed his failure to get his plays performed on what he believed to be the Jewish domination of culture. He was in personal contact with other racists and 'Aryan' supremacists like Houston Stewart Chamberlain, whose work he did much to popularize. Like many antisemites, he defined as 'Jewish' anyone who was 'subversive' or 'materialistic', including, among others (in his view), Lenin and Kaiser Wilhelm II. Well connected and well off, Eckart, like Hess, was a member of the Thule Society and raised the funds from his friends, and from the army, for the Nazi Party to buy the Society's ailing newspaper, the *Racial Observer* (*Völkischer Beobachter*), in December 1920. He became editor himself, bringing much-needed journalistic experience to its twice-weekly editions and expanding it into a daily early in 1923. Eventually, however, his relative independence, and his rather patronizing attitude towards Hitler, led to a cooling of relations between the two men, and he was dismissed as editor of the paper in March 1923, dying later in the year.[39]

Two associates he brought into the Party from the Thule Society served Hitler more reliably, however, and a good deal longer. The first of these was the Baltic-German architect Alfred Rosenberg. Another leading Nazi from beyond the Reich, he was born in Reval, Estonia, in 1893. He fled the Russian Revolution, conceiving an intense hatred for Bolshevism, and at the end of the war arrived in Munich, where he became a contributor to Eckart's little magazine. He had already become an antisemite before 1914, as a result of reading Houston Stewart Chamberlain's work at the age of 16. An enthusiast for the Tsarist police forgery *The Protocols of the Elders of Zion*, which purported to provide evidence of an international Jewish plot to subvert civilization, Rosenberg also read Gobineau and Nietzsche, and after the war wrote polemical tracts attacking Jews and Freemasons. His main desire was to be taken seriously as an intellectual and a cultural theorist. In 1930 Rosenberg was to publish his *magnum opus*, named *The Myth of the Twentieth Century* in homage to the principal work of his idol, Houston Stewart Chamberlain. This was intended to provide the Nazi Party with a major work of theory. The book had sold over a million copies by 1945 and some of its ideas were not without influence. But Hitler himself claimed never to have read more than a small part of it and disliked what he saw as its pseudo-religious tone, and it is unlikely that more than a few of the most dedicated readers managed to plough their way through its acres of turgid prose to the end. Still, in their frequent conversations in Munich cafés, Rosenberg more than anyone probably turned Hitler's attention towards the threat of Communism and its supposed creation by a Jewish conspiracy, and alerted Hitler to what he considered the fragile nature of the Soviet Russian polity. Through Rosenberg, Russian antisemitism, with its extreme conspiracy theories and its exterminatory thrust, found its way into Nazi ideology in the early 1920s. 'Jewish-Bolshevism' now became a major target of Hitler's hate.[40]

The other man whom Eckart brought into the Nazi Party was Hans Frank. He was born in Karlsruhe in 1900, the son of a lawyer who initially followed in his father's footsteps. While still a law student, in 1919, he joined the Thule Society and served in the Epp Free Corps in the storming of Munich. Frank quickly fell under Hitler's spell, though he never became one of his inner circle. Hearing him speak in January 1920, Frank felt, like many others, that Hitler's words came directly from the heart: 'He uttered what was in the consciousness of all those present,' he said later. Throughout his life, he was fascinated by the pornography of violence: he admired brutal men of action, and frequently used the language of violence with a directness and aggression unmatched by almost any other leading Nazi, in an attempt to seem like them; but his legal training and background gave him a residual belief in the law that sometimes sat uneasily alongside his penchant for coarse language and his defence of murderous actions. He qualified as a lawyer, with a doctorate in 1924, and his legal expertise, however limited, was to prove extremely useful to the Party. Up to 1933 he represented it in over 2,400 cases brought against its members, usually for acts of violence of one kind or another. Soon after he defended some Nazi thugs in court for the first time, a senior lawyer who had been one of his teachers said: 'I beg you to leave these people alone! No good will come of it! Political movements that begin in the criminal courts will end in the criminal courts!'[41]

By the time these men and many more like them had become part of the Nazi Party, the fledgling movement had an official Programme, composed by Hitler and Drexler with a little help from the 'racial economist' Gottfried Feder, and approved on 24 February 1920. Its 25 points included the demand for 'the union of all Germans in a Greater Germany', the revocation of the 1919 Peace Treaties, 'land and territory (colonies) to feed our people', the prevention of 'non-German immigration', and the death penalty for 'common criminals, usurers, profiteers etc.' Jews were to be denied civil rights and registered as aliens, and they were to be banned from owning or writing for German newspapers. A pseudo-socialist note was sounded by the demand for the abolition of unearned incomes, the confiscation of war profits, the nationalization of business trusts and the introduction of profit-sharing. The Programme concluded with a demand for 'the creation of a strong central state power for the

Reich' and the effective replacement of the federated state parliaments by corporations based on estate and occupation'.[42] It was a typical far-right document of its time. In practice, it did not mean very much, and, like the Social Democrats' Erfurt Programme of 1891, was often bypassed or ignored in the everyday political struggle, although it was soon declared to be 'unalterable', so as to prevent it from becoming a focus for internal dissension.[43]

Dissension there was, however, with other causes, principally Drexler's efforts to merge the party with other far-right organizations in the Bavarian capital. Drexler had his eye in particular on the 'German-Socialist Party', a similar-sized group with virtually identical aims to those of the Nazis. Unlike the Nazi Party, it had a presence in north Germany. A merger would give more influence to those who, like Feder, disapproved of the vulgarity of Hitler's constant rabble-rousing speeches. Hitler, fearing he would be submerged in the new movement, scotched the negotiations in April 1921 by threatening to resign. Another crisis blew up when Hitler was with Eckart in Berlin on a fund-raising mission for the *Racial Observer*. Merger talks began again in his absence, this time also involving a third small antisemitic party, based in Augsburg and led by one Otto Dickel, whose abilities as a public speaker were rated by some almost as highly as Hitler's own. Unable to prevent the Nazi Party going along with Dickel's scheme to create a merged 'Western League' (named after his somewhat mystical racist tract *The Resurrection of the West*), Hitler threw a tantrum and resigned from the Party altogether. This brought matters to a head, as Drexler back-pedalled and asked Hitler to name the conditions on which he would rejoin. In the end, few were prepared to do without the man whose demagogy had been the sole reason for the Party's growth over the previous months. The merger plans were abandoned. Hitler's uncompromising conditions were accepted with acclaim at an extraordinary general meeting on 29 July: they culminated in the demand that he should be made Party chairman 'with dictatorial powers' and that the Party be purged of the 'foreign elements which have now penetrated it'.[44]

Having secured his complete mastery over the Nazi Party, Hitler now enjoyed its full support for the propaganda campaign he quickly unfolded. It soon descended from provocation to violence. On 14 September 1921 a group of young Nazis went with Hitler to a meeting of the Bavarian League, a separatist organization, and marched onto the platform with the intention of silencing the speaker, Otto Ballerstedt. Someone switched all the lights off, and when they came on again, chants of 'Hitler' prevented Ballerstedt from continuing. As the audience protested, Hitler's young thugs attacked the separatist leader, beat him up, and pushed him roughly off the platform onto the floor, where he lay bleeding profusely from a head wound. Soon the police appeared and closed the meeting down. Ballerstedt insisted on prosecuting Hitler, who duly served a month in Munich's Stadelheim gaol. The police warned him that if he continued in this way he would be sent back to Austria as an alien. The warning had little effect. In early November 1921, shortly after his release, Hitler was at the centre of another beer-cellar brawl, with beer-mugs flying across the room as Nazis and Social Democrats traded blows. Soon the Nazis were arming themselves with knuckle-dusters, rubber truncheons, pistols and even grenades. In the summer of 1922, a crowd of Nazis shouted, whistled and spat at Reich President Ebert as he was visiting Munich. An outing to a nationalist rally in Coburg in October 1922 culminated in a pitched battle with Social Democrats in which the Nazis eventually drove their opponents from the streets with their rubber truncheons.[45] Not surprisingly, the Nazi Party was soon banned in most German states, especially after the murder of Foreign Minister Rathenau in June 1922, when the Berlin government attempted a clampdown on far-right extremists whether or not they had been involved in the assassination. But not in right-wing Bavaria.[46]

The new note of physical violence in the Nazi campaign reflected not least the rapid growth of the Party's paramilitary wing, founded early in 1920 as a 'hall protection' group, soon renamed the 'Gymnastics and Sports Section'. With their brown shirts and breeches, jackboots and caps – a uniform that only found its final form in 1924[47] – its members soon became a familiar sight on Munich's streets, beating up their opponents on the streets and attacking anyone they thought looked like a Jew. What turned them from a small group of bully-boys into a major paramilitary movement was a series of events that had little to do with Hitler. The relative immunity from police interference which they enjoyed reflected in the first place the fact that the Bavarian government, led by Gustav Ritter von Kahr, had long been sympathetic to paramilitary movements of the far right, as part of the counter-revolutionary 'white terror' of

1919–20. In this atmosphere, Captain Hermann Ehrhardt, former commander of a Free Corps brigade, had established an elaborate network of assassination squads that had carried out political murders all over Germany, including the killing of several leading Republican politicians, and the murder of a number of their own members whom they suspected as double agents.[48] Kahr himself regarded the Republic as a Prussian creation, to be countered by the maintenance of Bavaria as a centre of anti-Republican 'order', and to this end he maintained a massive, so-called Denizens' Defence Force, set up immediately after the crushing of the Communist Council Republic in the spring of 1919. Heavily armed and militarily equipped, it clearly contravened the terms of the Treaty of Versailles and was compulsorily wound up early in 1921. Its dissolution was the signal for a reorganization of Bavaria's radical right and a sharp increase in the incidence of violence, as its members reformed into a huge variety of armed bands, many of them Bavarian separatist in orientation, all of them antisemitic.[49]

Ehrhardt brought his Free Corps veterans into the Nazis' 'Gymnastics and Sports Section' in August 1921; they were hardened graduates of violent confrontations with Poles and others in Silesia, where the Peace Settlement had created massive German resentment by lopping off territory held by Germany before the war to give to the newly founded Polish state. The deal with Ehrhardt was brokered by Ernst Röhm, another Free Corps veteran, who had participated in the assault on Munich in the early spring of 1919. Born in 1887, the son of a Bavarian railway official, Röhm had joined the army in 1906 and became an officer two years later. He served at the front in the war, but was invalided out – shrapnel had partially destroyed his nose and badly damaged his face, and he had been seriously wounded at Verdun. After this, Röhm worked for the War Ministry in Bavaria and was in charge of arranging the supply of weapons, first for Kahr's Denizens' Defence Force and then for its fragmented successor groups. Known to such people as the 'machine-gun king', Röhm boasted a huge range of contacts on the far right. Among other things, he was a staff officer and enjoyed a high reputation in the army, and acted as a liaison officer with the paramilitaries. He clearly had a talent for organization. But his interest did not really lie in politics. Ernst Röhm was the epitome of a front-line generation that had come to believe in its own myth.[50]

Röhm's penchant was for mindless violence, not political conspiracy. An analysis of his writings has shown that he used words like 'prudent', 'compromise', 'intellectual', 'bourgeois' or 'middle-class' almost invariably in a pejorative sense; his positive, admiring expressions included 'strapping', 'daredevil', 'ruthless' and 'faithful'. The first words of his autobiography, published in Munich in 1928, were: 'I am a soldier.' He described himself as 'contrary' and complained: 'The Germans have forgotten how to hate. Feminine complaining has taken the place of masculine hatred.'[51] 'Since I am an immature and wicked person,' he wrote with characteristic openness, 'war and unrest appeal to me more than well-behaved bourgeois order.'[52] He had no interest at all in ideas, and glorified the rough and brutal lifestyle of the soldier in his acts as well as his creed. He had nothing but contempt for civilians, and revelled in the lawlessness of wartime life. Drinking and carousing, fighting and brawling cemented the band of brothers among whom he found his place; women were treated with disdain, strangers to the military life had no place in his world.

Röhm saw in Hitler, whose own penchant for using physical violence to further his ends was already more than obvious, a natural vehicle for his desires, and took the lead in building up the Party's paramilitary wing movement, renamed the 'Storm Division' (*Sturmabteilung*, or SA) in October 1921. His connections in the army hierarchy, in the upper levels of Bavarian politics, and with the paramilitaries, were invaluable to the fledgling organization. At the same time, however, he always maintained a degree of independence from Hitler, never really fell under his personal spell, and sought to use his movement as a vehicle for his own cult of ceaseless violent activism rather than placing the stormtroopers unconditionally at the Party's disposal. The SA remained a formally separate organization, therefore, and Röhm's relations with the Nazi Party's leader always retained an uneasy undertone. With Röhm in the lead, the stormtroopers soon began to grow in numbers. Yet by August 1922 they still counted no more than 800 in their ranks, and other, long since forgotten paramilitary movements such as the Reich War Flag, or the Bavaria and Reich League, which had no fewer than 30,000 members, all of them armed, were far more prominent. It needed much more than the influence of Ehrhardt and Röhm and the demagogy of Hitler before the Nazis and their paramilitary movement could seize the initiative in Bavarian politics.[53]

II

In 1922 the Nazis' hopes were sharply raised when news came in of Benito Mussolini's 'March on Rome' on 28 October, which had immediately led to the Fascist leader's appointment as Prime Minister of Italy. Where the Italians had succeeded, surely their German counterparts could not be far behind? As so often with Mussolini, the image was more than the reality. Born in 1883 and in his early life a prominent socialist journalist, Mussolini had changed his politics dramatically during his campaign for Italy's entry into the war, and at the war's end he became the spokesman for Italian feelings of injured pride as the Peace Settlement failed to deliver the hoped-for gains. In 1919 he launched his Fascist movement, which used violent tactics, terror and intimidation against its left-wing opponents, who were alarming industrialists, employers and businessmen with policies such as occupying factories in pursuit of their demand for common ownership of the means of production. Rural unrest also drove landowners into the arms of the Fascist squads, and, as the situation deteriorated in the course of 1920 and 1921, Mussolini was carried along by the dynamism of his movement. His rise to prominence indicated that postwar conflict, civil strife, murder and war were not confined to Germany. They were widespread across Eastern, Central and Southern Europe. They included the Russo-Polish War, which only ended in 1921, armed irredentist conflicts in many of the successor states to the Habsburg Empire, and the creation of short-lived dictatorships in Spain and Greece.

Mussolini's example influenced the Nazi Party in a number of ways, notably in its adoption in late 1922 and early 1923 of the title of 'Leader' – *Duce* in Italian, *Führer* in German – to denote the unquestionable authority of the man at the movement's head. The growing cult of Hitler's personality in the Nazi Party, fuelled by the Italian precedent, also helped convince Hitler himself that it was he, and not some figure yet to come, who was destined to lead Germany into a future national rebirth, a conviction that was indelibly confirmed by the events of the autumn of 1923.[54] By this time, the Nazis had also begun to borrow from the Italian Fascists the rigid, outstretched right-arm salute with which they ritually greeted their leader in an imitation of the ceremonies of Imperial Rome; the leader responded by raising his own right hand, but crooked back at the elbow, palm opened upwards, in a gesture of acceptance. The Nazi Party's use of elaborate standards to carry its flags also derived from the practice of the Italian Fascists. Mussolini's main practical influence on Hitler at this period, however, was to convince him that the tactic of a march on the capital was the quickest way to power. As the Fascist squads began to seize control of major cities and towns in the Italian north, Mussolini, drawing on the famous example of the revolutionary Giuseppe Garibaldi during the unification of Italy more than sixty years before, declared that he would use them as a base for a 'march on Rome'. In order to avoid bloodshed, the Italian King and the leading politicians capitulated and appointed him Prime Minister, a position which he used with increasing ruthlessness to establish a dictatorial, one-party state by the end of the decade.[55]

Mussolini's Fascist movement shared many key characteristics not only with Nazism but also with other extremist movements of the right, for example in Hungary, where Gyula Gömbös was referring to himself as a 'National Socialist' as early as 1919. Italian Fascism was violent, ceaselessly active, it despised parliamentary institutions, it was militaristic, and it glorified conflict and war. It was bitterly opposed not only to Communism but also, even more importantly, to socialism and to liberalism. It favoured an organic view of society, in which class interests and popular representation would be replaced by appointed institutions cutting across the classes and uniting the nation. It was masculinist and anti-feminist, seeking a state in which men would rule and women would be reduced mainly to the functions of childbearing and childrearing. It elevated the leader to a position of unchallenged authority. It espoused a cult of youth, declaring its intention of sweeping away old institutions and traditions and creating a new form of human being, tough, anti-intellectual, modern, secular and above all fanatically devoted to the cause of his own nation and race.[56] In all these respects, it provided a model and a parallel for the emerging Nazi Party.

Early Nazism, therefore, like the myriad competing movements of the far right in the immediate postwar years, belonged firmly in this wider context of the rise of European fascism. For a long time, Hitler looked admiringly to Mussolini as an example to follow. The 'march on Rome' galvanized the nascent fascist movements of Europe much as Garibaldi's march on Rome and the subsequent unification of Italy had galvanized the nationalist movements of Europe sixty or so years earlier. The tide of history seemed to be moving in Hitler's direction; democracy's days were numbered. As the situation in Germany began to deteriorate with increasing rapidity in the course of 1922 and 1923, Hitler began to think that he could do the same in Germany as Mussolini had done in Italy. When the German government defaulted on reparations payments, and French troops occupied the Ruhr, nationalists in Germany exploded with rage and humiliation. The Republic's loss of legitimacy was incalculable; the government had to be seen to be doing something to oppose the occupation. A widespread campaign of civil disobedience, encouraged by the German government, led to further reprisals on the part of the French, with arrests, imprisonments and expulsions. Among many examples of French repression, nationalists remembered how one war veteran and railway worker was sacked and deported with his family for delivering a pro-German speech at a war memorial; another man, a schoolteacher, suffered the same fate after getting his pupils to turn their backs when French troops marched past.[57] Schoolboy gangs shaved the heads of women thought to be 'shamelessly consorting with the French', while others, less dramatically, demonstrated their patriotism by walking miles to school rather than travelling by the French-run railway. A few workers actively tried to sabotage the occupation; one of them, Albert Leo Schlageter, a former Free Corps soldier, was executed for his activities, and the nationalist right, led by the Nazis, quickly seized on the incident as an example of the brutality of the French and the weakness of the Berlin government, turning Schlageter into a much-publicized nationalist martyr in the process. Industry ground to a standstill, further exacerbating the country's already dire financial problems.[58]

Nationalists had a potent propaganda weapon in the presence of black French colonial troops amongst the occupying forces. Racism was endemic in all European societies in the interwar years, as it was indeed in the United States and other parts of the world too. It was generally assumed by Europeans that dark-skinned people were inferior human beings, savages whom it was the white man's mission to tame.[59] The use of colonial troops by the British and French during the First World War had excited a certain amount of unfavourable comment in Germany; but it was their presence on German territory itself, first of all in the occupied part of the Rhineland, then in 1923 during the brief French march into the Ruhr, that really opened the floodgates for lurid racist propaganda. Many Germans living in the Rhineland and the Saar felt humiliated that, as one of them later put it, 'Siamese, Senegalese and Arabs made themselves the masters of our homeland'.[60] Soon, cartoonists were arousing racist and nationalist emotions by penning crude, semi-pornographic sketches of bestial black soldiers carrying off innocent white German women to a fate worse than death. On the right, this became a potent symbol of Germany's national humiliation during the Weimar years, and the myth of the mass rape of German women by French colonial troops became so powerful that the few hundred mixed-race children to be found in Germany in the early 1930s were almost universally regarded as the offspring of such incidents. In fact, the overwhelming majority of them actually seem to have been the result of consensual unions, often between German colonists and indigenous Africans in the German colonies before or during the war.[61]

As the Nazis and many more who thought like them exploited these fears and resentments to the full, the government in Berlin seemed powerless to do anything about it. Plans and conspiracies began to multiply. Hitler was not the only person to contemplate a march on Berlin: the 'National-Bolshevist' Hans von Hentig, who was to become Germany's most distinguished criminologist after 1945, was also starting to gather arms and troops in a hare-brained scheme to use the Communist Party as an ally in a violent seizure of power with the aim of getting Germany to repudiate the Treaty of Versailles.[62] The idea was not very realistic, whoever tried to put it into action; both Germany's federal structure and its constitution made a repetition of what had happened in Italy extremely unlikely. Nevertheless, it quickly took root. Hitler embarked on a massive propaganda offensive, berating the 'November criminals' in Berlin for their weakness, and building up in a crescendo of public demonstrations against the French.

His prospects were greatly improved at this time by the accession of a further group of new and very useful supporters to the Nazi movement. Among them was Ernst 'Putzi' Hanfstaengl, a tall, part-American socialite from a wealthy background in the world of art dealing and publishing, whose snobbery always prevented him from falling wholly under Hitler's spell. But Hanfstaengl thought Hitler's petty-bourgeois simplicity – his appalling taste in art, his ignorance of wine, his clumsy table manners –

simply underlined his patent sincerity. His lack of polish was an essential precondition of his uncanny ability to connect with the masses. Like many other admirers of Hitler, Hanfstaengl first came into contact with him by attending one of his speeches; for his part, Hitler was overwhelmed by Hanfstaengl's drawing-room sophistication, and enjoyed listening to him playing Wagner on the piano, marching round the room and conducting with his arms as the strains of the master sounded out. More seriously, Hanfstaengl was able to introduce Hitler to influential people in Munich high society, including publishers, businessmen and army officers. Such circles found it amusing to patronize him, were entertained when he appeared at their elegant parties dressed in an army coat and carrying a dog-whip, and shared enough of his views to guarantee his loans – as the wife of the piano manufacturer Bechstein did – and to support him in various other ways. Only the most dedicated, however, like the businessman Kurt Lüdecke, gave Hitler money in any great quantity. Otherwise, the Nazi Party had to rely on its friends in high places, like the former diplomat Max Erwin von Scheubner-Richter, to steer a small portion of business funds meant for Ludendorff in their direction while it continued to draw most of its income from Party membership dues.[63]

A very different kind of backing was provided in October 1922 by the arrival in the Nazi Party, with his followers in Nuremberg, of Julius Streicher, another ex-soldier, sporting, like Hitler, the Iron Cross, and a founder-member of the German-Socialist Party after the war. Impressed by Hitler's progress, Streicher brought so many supporters into the Nazi Party that it virtually doubled in size overnight. Protestant Franconia was an ideal recruiting-ground for Nazism, with its resentful peasantry, its susceptibility to the appeal of antisemitism and the absence of any dominant established political party. Streicher's accession extended the Party's influence significantly further northwards. But in acquiring Streicher, the Party also acquired a vicious antisemite whose extreme hatred of the Jews matched even Hitler's, and a man of violence who carried a heavy whip in public and personally beat up his helpless opponents once he had achieved a position of power. In 1923 Streicher founded a sensational popular newspaper, *The Stormer (Der Stürmer)*, which rapidly established itself as the place where screaming headlines introduced the most rabid attacks on Jews, full of sexual innuendo, racist caricatures, made-up accusations of ritual murder and titillating, semi-pornographic stories of Jewish men seducing innocent German girls. So extreme was the paper, and so obviously obsessive was its brutish-looking, shaven-headed editor, that Streicher never acquired a great deal of influence within the movement, whose leaders regarded him with some distaste, and the paper was even banned for a period under the Third Reich.

Yet Streicher was not just a thug. A former schoolteacher, he was also a poet whose lyrics have been described as 'quite attractive', and, like Hitler, he painted watercolours, though in his case only as a hobby. Streicher, too, fancied himself as an artist; he was not without education, he was a professional journalist and was also, therefore, in a sense, a bohemian like Hitler. His ideas, though expressed in an extreme form, were not particularly unusual in the right-wing circles of the day, and owed a lot, as he himself acknowledged, to the influence of prewar German antisemitism, particularly Theodor Fritsch. And Streicher's antisemitism was in no sense on the outer fringe of the Nazi movement. Hitler, indeed, later commented that Streicher, in a way, '*idealised* the Jew. The Jew is baser, fiercer, more diabolical than Streicher depicted him.' He may not have been an effective administrator, Hitler conceded, and his sexual appetite led him into all kinds of trouble, but Hitler always remained loyal to him. At times, when it was important for Nazism to present a respectable face, *The Stormer* could be an embarrassment; but only as a matter of tactics, never as an issue of principle or belief.[64]

III

In 1923, Hitler and the Nazi Party felt no particular need to look respectable. Violence seemed the obvious way to power. The far-right Bavarian government of Gustav Ritter von Kahr, sympathetic to the paramilitaries, had fallen in September 1921. Since then, Kahr and his friends had been embroiled in intrigues against the government led by Eugen von Knilling and his Bavarian People's Party. As many moderate conservatives were to do later on, Knilling and his allies felt that the Nazis were a threat, and disliked their violence, but considered that their heart was in the right place and their idealism only needed to be used in a more productive and healthy way. So they, too, were relatively tolerant of the Nazis' activities. Moreover, on the one occasion on which they tried to crack down by banning a Nazi Party rally at the end of January 1923, fearing it would become violent, the army commander in Bavaria, General Hermann von Lossow, was contacted by Röhm and agreed to support Hitler's right to hold the rally providing he gave a guarantee that it would be peaceful. Kahr, at this time regional governor of Upper Bavaria, supported him, and the Bavarian government backed down.[65]

Events now moved rapidly towards a climax. Much of the time they were beyond Hitler's control. In particular, Ernst Röhm, quite independently from him, succeeded in getting the main paramilitary organizations in Bavaria together in a Working Community of Patriotic Fighting Leagues, which included some much larger groups than the Nazi brownshirts. These groups surrendered their weapons to the regular army, whose Bavarian units under General von Lossow were clearly readying themselves for the much-bruited march on Berlin and an armed confrontation with the French in the Ruhr, and they enrolled the paramilitaries as auxiliaries and started to train them. Into this witches' brew of paramilitary conspiracy there now came General Ludendorff. An attempt by Hitler to seize the initiative by demanding the return of the brownshirts' weapons from the army met with a cool rebuff. He was forced to yield to Ludendorff as the figurehead of the conspiracy when the paramilitaries staged a huge parade in Nuremberg at the beginning of September, with as many as 100,000 uniformed men taking part. Hitler was named political leader of the paramilitaries, but, far from being in control of the situation, he was being swept along by events.[66]

Röhm's role in the reorganized paramilitary movement was crucial, and he now resigned as head of the small Nazi stormtrooper organization in order to concentrate on it. He was succeeded by a man who was to play a key role in the subsequent development of the Nazi movement and the Third Reich: Hermann Göring. Born in 1893 in Rosenheim, Bavaria, Göring was another man of action, but of a very different stamp from Röhm. He came from an upper-middle-class Bavarian background; his father had played a key role in the German colonization of Namibia before the war and was a convinced German imperialist. From 1905 to 1911 Göring attended military college, latterly in Berlin, and ever afterwards regarded himself as a Prussian soldier rather than a Bavarian. During the war, he became a well-known flying ace, ending it in command of the fighter squadron founded by the 'Red Baron' von Richthofen. His exploits as a pilot had earned him Germany's highest military decoration, the *Pour le mérite*, and a popular reputation as a swashbuckling daredevil. Fighter pilots were widely regarded as a kind of modern knight in armour, whose derring-do contrasted dramatically with the dull, mechanized slaughter of the trenches, and Göring was lionized in aristocratic circles, strengthening his upper-crust social contacts by marrying in February 1922 a Swedish Baroness, Karin von Kantzow. Like many other wartime fighters, he continued to search for a life of action after the conflict was over, briefly belonging to a Free Corps, then becoming a show flier in Scandinavia, and finally, through the influence of his wife, finding his way into Hitler's movement towards the end of 1922. At this time, therefore, Göring was a dashing, handsome, romantic figure, whose exploits were celebrated in numerous adulatory popular books and magazine articles.

Göring's longing for action found its fulfilment in the Nazi movement. Ruthless, energetic and extremely egotistical, Göring nevertheless fell completely under Hitler's spell from the very start. Loyalty and faithfulness were for him the highest virtues. Like Röhm, Göring too regarded politics as warfare, a form of armed combat in which neither justice nor morality had a part to play; the strong won, the weak perished, the law was a mass of 'legalistic' rules that were there to be broken if the need arose. For Göring, the end always justified the means, and the end was always what he conceived of as the national interest of Germany, which he considered had been betrayed by Jews, democrats and revolutionaries in 1918. Göring's aristocratic connections, his chiselled good looks, his cosmopolitan mastery of French, Italian and Swedish, and his reputation as a chivalrous fighter-pilot persuaded many that he was a moderate, a diplomatist even; Hindenburg and many like him thought of Göring as the acceptable face of Nazism, an authoritarian conservative like themselves. The appearance was deceptive; he was as ruthless, as violent and as extreme as any of the leading Nazis. These varying qualities, allied to the rapidly growing abnegation of his will before Hitler's, made him the ideal choice as the new leader of the stormtroopers in place of Röhm early in 1923.[67]

With Göring in charge, the stormtroopers could now be expected to toe the Nazi line again. Preparations went ahead, in conjunction with the wider paramilitary movement, which Röhm steered as far as he was able, for a rising throughout the spring and early summer of 1923. The crisis finally came when the Reich government in Berlin was forced to resign on 13 August. Its successor, a broad coalition that included the Social Democrats, was led by Gustav Stresemann, a right-wing liberal nationalist who over the coming years was to prove himself the Republic's most skilled, most subtle and most realistic politician. Stresemann realized that the campaign of passive resistance to the French occupation of the Ruhr had to be ended, and the galloping hyperinflation brought under control. He instituted a policy of 'fulfilment', in which Germany would fulfil the terms of the Peace Settlement, including the payment of reparations, while lobbying behind the scenes for them to be changed. His policy met with notable success during the next six years, during which he held the position of Reich Foreign Minister. But to the extreme nationalists it was nothing more than national betrayal. Realizing that they were now likely to stage an uprising, the Bavarian government appointed Kahr as a General State Commissioner with full powers to maintain order. Backed by Lossow and the police chief, Hans Ritter von Seisser, Kahr banned a series of meetings planned by the Nazis for 27 September while they pursued their own plans for the overthrow of the government in Berlin. Pressure mounted on all sides for action; amongst the rank-and-file of the paramilitaries, as Hitler was repeatedly warned, it was becoming almost irresistible.[68]

In Berlin, the army leader General Hans von Seeckt refused to go along with the plans of Lossow, Seisser and Kahr. He preferred to remove Stresemann's government by backstairs intrigue, which indeed he eventually did, though it was succeeded by another coalition in which Stresemann remained Foreign Minister. Feverish negotiations in Munich failed to produce any unity between the Bavarian army under Lossow, the police under Seisser, and the paramilitaries, whose political representative was of course Hitler. Aware that he would lose the support of the paramilitaries if he dithered any longer, and worried that Kahr was himself considering action, Hitler, now backed by Ludendorff, decided on a putsch. The Bavarian government would be arrested, and Kahr and his allies would be forced to join with the paramilitaries in a march on Berlin. The date for the putsch was set, more under the pressure of events than by any search for a symbolic date, for 9 November, the anniversary of the outbreak of the Revolution of 1918 that had overthrown the Kaiser's regime. On the evening of 8 November, Hitler and a body of heavily armed stormtroopers broke into a meeting addressed by Kahr in the *Bürgerbräukeller*, a beer-cellar just outside the centre of Munich. Hitler ordered one of his men to fire a pistol-shot into the ceiling to silence the crowd, then announced that the hall was surrounded. The Bavarian government, he declared, was deposed. While Göring calmed the audience, Hitler took Kahr, Lossow and Seisser into an adjoining room and explained that he would march on Berlin, installing himself at the head of a new Reich government; Ludendorff would take over the national army. They would be rewarded for their support with important positions themselves. Returning to speak to the crowd, Hitler won them over with a dramatic plea for backing in what he called his action against 'the November criminals of 1918'. Kahr and his companions had no option but to return to the podium and, joined now by Ludendorff, declare their support.[69]

But translating histrionic demonstrations into political power was not so easy. The Nazis' plans for a putsch were half-baked. Röhm occupied the army headquarters in Munich, and Nazi units also took over the police headquarters, but other buildings including, crucially, the army barracks, remained in government hands, and while Hitler went into the city to try and sort things out, Ludendorff released Kahr and the other prisoners, who promptly backtracked on their enforced compliance with the plot and immediately got in touch with the army, the police and the media to repudiate Hitler's actions. Back in the beer-cellar, Hitler and Ludendorff decided to march on the city centre. They gathered about two thousand armed supporters, each of whom had been paid 2 billion marks (worth just over three dollars on this particular day) from a hoard of more than 14,000 billion marks 'confiscated' from two supposedly Jewish banknote printers in raids carried out by brownshirt squads on Hitler's orders. The column set off at midday on 9 November and, encouraged by the cheers of their supporters, they marched through the centre of the city in the direction of the Ministry of War. At the end of the street they were met by an armed cordon of police. According to the official report, they pressed pistols with their safety catches off against the policemen's chests, spat on them and pointed fixed bayonets in their direction. Then someone on one side or the other – there were conflicting claims – fired a shot. For half a minute the air was filled with whizzing bullets as both sides let fly. Göring fell, shot in the leg; Hitler dropped, or was pushed, to the ground, dislocating his shoulder. Scheubner-Richter, Hitler's diplomat friend and connection to patrons in high places, was killed outright. Altogether, fourteen marchers were shot dead, and four policemen. As the police moved in to arrest Ludendorff, Streicher, Röhm and many others, Göring managed to get away, fleeing first to Austria, then Italy, before settling in Sweden, becoming addicted in the process to the morphine he took to relieve the pain of his wound. Hitler was taken off, his arm in a sling, to Hanfstaengl's country house, where he was arrested on 11 November. The putsch had come to an ignominious end.[70]

REBUILDING THE MOVEMENT

I

It did not take Hitler long to recover his nerve after the events of 9 November 1923. He knew that he could implicate a whole range of prominent Bavarian politicians in the putsch attempt, and expose the army's involvement in training paramilitaries for a march on Berlin. Aware of this threat, which had emerged already during Hitler's interrogation, the Bavarian government managed to persuade the authorities in Berlin to hold the trial not in the Reich Court in Leipzig, but before a specially constituted 'People's Court' in Munich, where they had more control over events.[71] It seems likely that they offered Hitler leniency in return for his agreement to carry the can. As judge they picked Georg Neithardt, a well-known nationalist who had been appointed by Bavaria's reactionary Justice Minister Franz Gürtner in 1919 and had presided over Hitler's previous trial, early in 1922. When the trial began, on 26 February 1924, Hitler was allowed to appear in civilian dress, wearing his Iron Cross, and to address the court for hours on end without interruption. While Neithardt let him bully and insult prosecution witnesses, the state prosecutor failed to call a number of key figures whose testimony would have proved damaging to the defence case. The court suppressed evidence of Ludendorff's involvement, and rejected a plea for Hitler to be deported as an Austrian citizen, because he had served in the German army and shown himself to be a German patriot.[72] Hitler took the entire responsibility on himself, declaring that serving the interests of Germany could not be high treason. The 'eternal Court of History', he declared, 'will judge us . . . as Germans who wanted the best for their people and their fatherland.'[73]

Despite the fact that the participants in the putsch had shot dead four policemen and staged an armed and (in any reasonable legal terms) treasonable revolt against a legitimately constituted state government, both offences punishable by death, the court sentenced Hitler to a mere five years in prison for high treason, and the others were indicted to similar or even lighter terms. Ludendorff, as expected, was acquitted. The court grounded its leniency in the fact that, as it declared, the participants in the putsch 'were led in their action by a pure patriotic spirit and the most noble will'. The judgment was scandalous even by the biased standards of the Weimar judiciary. It was widely condemned, even on the right. Hitler was sent to an ancient fortress at Landsberg am Lech, west of Munich, where he took over the cell held up to that point by Count Arco-Valley, the assassin of Kurt Eisner. This was what was called 'fortress incarceration', a mild form of imprisonment for offenders thought to have acted from honourable motives, such as, before the war, gentlemen of honour who had killed their opponent in a duel. Hitler's cell was large, airy and comfortably furnished. Visitors had free access. Over five hundred of them came during the course of his stay. They brought him presents, flowers, letters and telegrams from well-wishers outside. He was able to read, indeed there was little else to do when he was not receiving visitors, and he ploughed his way through a variety of books by authors such as Friedrich Nietzsche and Houston Stewart Chamberlain, searching them in the main for confirmation of his own views. More importantly, at the suggestion of the Nazi publisher Max Amann, Hitler also sat down to dictate an account of his life and opinions up to this point to two of his fellow-prisoners, his chauffeur Emil Maurice and his factotum Rudolf Hess, an account published the following year under the title, probably proposed by Amann, of *My Struggle*.[74]

My Struggle has been seen by some historians as a kind of blueprint for Hitler's later actions, a dangerous and devilish book that was unfortunately ignored by those who should have known better. It was nothing of the kind. Heavily edited by Amann, Hanfstaengl and others in order to make it more literate and less incoherent than the rambling first draft, it was none the less turgid and tedious, and sold only modest numbers of copies before the Nazis achieved their electoral breakthrough in 1930. After that it became a best-seller, above all during the Third Reich, when not to own a copy was almost an act of treason. Those people who read it, probably a relatively small proportion of those who bought it, must have found it difficult to gain anything very coherent out of its confused *mélange* of autobiographical reminiscences and garbled political declamations. Hitler's talent for winning hearts and minds lay in his public oratory, not in his writing. Still, no one who read the book could have been left in any doubt about the fact that Hitler considered racial conflict to be the motor, the essence of history, and the Jews to be the sworn enemy of the German race, whose historic mission it was, under the guidance of the Nazi Party, to break their international power and annihilate them entirely. 'The nationalization of our masses', he declared, 'will succeed only when, aside from all the positive struggle for the soul of our people, their international poisoners are exterminated.'[75]

The Jews were now linked indissolubly in Hitler's mind with 'Bolshevism' and 'Marxism', which received far greater prominence in *My Struggle* than the finance capitalism that had so obsessed him during the period of monetary inflation. For Russia was where Germany's conquest of 'living-space' would be made at the same time as the elimination of the 'Jewish-Bolsheviks' who he supposed ruled the Soviet state. These ideas were laid out in more detail in the book's second volume, composed in 1925 and published the following year; they were central to Hitler's ideology from now on. 'The boundaries of the year 1914 mean nothing at all for the German future,' he declared. Drawing a comparison with the vast Eastern conquests of Alexander the Great, he announced that 'the end of Jewish rule in Russia will also be the end of Russia as a state'. The soil now occupied by 'Russia and her vassal border states' would in future be given over to 'the industrious work of the German plough'.[76]

Hitler's beliefs were clearly laid out in *My Struggle*, for all to see who wished to. No one familiar with the text could have emerged from reading it with the view that all Hitler wanted was the revision of the Treaty of Versailles, the restoration of the German borders of 1914 or the self-determination of German-speaking minorities in Central Europe. Nor could anyone have doubted the visceral, fanatical, indeed murderous quality of his antisemitism. But beliefs and intentions are not the same as blueprints and plans. When it came to working out how to implement these views, Hitler's text naturally reflected the politics of the particular period in which it was written. At this time, the French were the enemy, having only recently withdrawn from the Ruhr. The British, by contrast, looked like a possible ally in the struggle against Bolshevism, having lent their support to the 'White' forces in the Russian civil war only a few years before. A little later, when Hitler composed another, similar work, unpublished during his lifetime, the clash between Italy and Germany over the South Tyrol was on the international agenda, and so he concentrated on that.[77] What remained central through all these tactical twists and turns, however, was the long-term drive for 'living-space' in the East, and the fierce desire to annihilate the Jews. This, again, could not be done all at once, and Hitler obviously, at this stage, had no clear idea as to how it would be achieved, or when. Here, too, there would be tactical manoeuvres along the way, and a variety of interim solutions would present themselves. But none of this affected the genocidal quality of Hitler's hatred of the Jews, or his paranoid conviction that they were responsible for all of Germany's ills and that the only long-term solution was their complete annihilation as a biological entity; a conviction easily discernible not only from the language of *My Struggle*, but also from the words and phrases he used in his speeches, and the atmosphere of revivalist intolerance in which they were held.[78] The Jews were a 'pestilence', 'worse than the Black Death', a 'maggot in the decomposing body of Germany', and they would be driven from what he thought of as their positions of power, and then expelled from the country altogether, if necessary by force. What would happen to the Jews of Eastern Europe once Germany had acquired its living-space there, he could not say; but the murderous violence of his language left little doubt that their fate would not be a pleasant one.[79]

The composition of his book, the massive publicity he gained from the trial, the adulation that poured in from the nationalist right after the attempted putsch, all helped convince Hitler, if he had not been convinced before, that he was the man to turn these views into reality. The failed putsch also taught him that he would not even be able to take the first step – the acquisition of supreme power in Germany itself – by relying on paramilitary violence alone. A 'march on Rome' was out of the question in Germany. It was essential to win mass public support, by the propaganda and public-speaking campaigns which Hitler knew were his forte. The revolutionary conquest of power, still favoured by Röhm, would not work in any case if it was undertaken without the support of the army, so conspicuously lacking in November 1923. Hitler did not, as was sometimes later said, even by himself, embark on a path of 'legality' in the wake of the failed putsch. But he did realize that toppling the Weimar 'system' would require more than a few ill-directed gunshots, even in a year of supreme crisis such as 1923. Coming to power clearly required collaboration from key elements in the establishment, and although he had enjoyed some support in 1923, it had not proved sufficient. In the next crisis, which was to occur less than a decade later, he made sure he had the army and the key institutions of the state either neutralized, or actively working for him, unlike in 1923.[80]

Meanwhile, however, the situation of the Nazi Party seemed almost irretrievable in the wake of Hitler's arrest and imprisonment. The paramilitary groups broke up in disorder, and their arms were confiscated by the government. Kahr, Lossow and Seisser, badly compromised by the putsch, were pushed aside by a new cabinet under the Bavarian People's Party leader, Heinrich Held. Bavarian separatism and ultra-nationalist conspiracies gave way to more conventional regional politics. The situation calmed down as the hyperinflation came to an end and the policy of 'fulfilment' took hold in Berlin, bearing fruit almost immediately with the rescheduling of reparations under the Dawes Plan. Deprived of their leader, the Nazis split up into tiny squabbling factions again. Röhm continued to try and reunite the remaining fragments of the paramilitaries in allegiance to Ludendorff. Hitler put Alfred Rosenberg in charge of the Nazi Party as virtually the only leading figure left in the country who was still at large. But Rosenberg proved completely incapable of establishing any authority over the movement.[81]

Both the Nazi Party and the brownshirts were now illegal organizations. They were completely unprepared for a clandestine existence. Opinions differed widely on what tactics to use in future – paramilitary or parliamentary – and rivalries between figures like Streicher and Ludendorff, as well as the congeries of ultra-nationalist groups who emerged to try to claim the Nazi succession, were crippling attempts to resurrect the movement. Hitler more or less washed his hands of all these squabbles, announcing his withdrawal from politics to write his book. Matters were not much improved when Hitler was released on parole, by a decision of the Bavarian Supreme Court and against the advice of the state prosecutorial service, on 20 December 1924. He still had almost four years of his sentence to run, during which he had to be careful not to violate

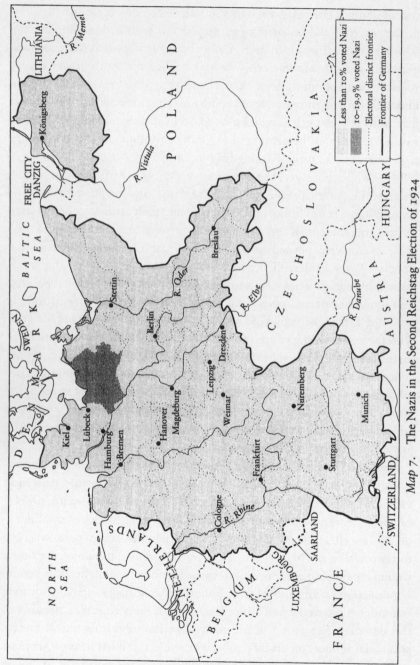

Map 7.   The Nazis in the Second Reichstag Election of 1924

the conditions of his parole. He was not allowed to speak in public in most parts of Germany until 1927; he was still banned in Prussia, which covered over half the Weimar Republic's land surface and contained the majority of its population, as late as 1928. The ultra-nationalist right was humiliated in the national elections of 1924. The only ray of sunshine in the gloom was provided by the Austrian government, which scotched official attempts to get Hitler repatriated by refusing to accept him.[82]

II

Nevertheless, Hitler still had a few friends in high places. One key figure was the Bavarian Justice Minister Franz Gürtner, who sympathized with his nationalist ideas. Gürtner agreed to lift the ban on the Nazi Party and its newspaper, the *Racial Observer*, when the Bavarian state of emergency was finally ended on 16 February 1925.[83] Armed with his newly won prestige and self-confidence as the nationalist hero of the putsch and the subsequent trial, Hitler promptly refounded the Nazi Party, calling on his former followers to join it and (a key new point) to submit themselves unconditionally to his leadership. Julius Streicher, Gottfried Feder, the Party journalist and propagandist Hermann Esser and others publicly buried their differences in a show of solidarity. Hitler moved to push his most serious rivals out onto the margins of politics. First, as it became legal to reconstitute the brownshirt organization, he insisted that it be subordinated to the Party, and cut its links with the other paramilitary groups; Ernst Röhm, who rejected this view, was ousted, left politics and was forced to become a salesman and then a factory hand before accepting an invitation to go to Bolivia to instruct the country's troops in the ways of European warfare.[84] And secondly, Hitler worked steadily to undermine the continuing prestige of Ludendorff, who was not only a serious rival but was also rapidly becoming more extreme in his views. Under the influence of Mathilde von Kemnitz, whom he married in 1926, Ludendorff founded the Tannenberg League, which published conspiracy-theory literature attacking not only Jews but also Jesuits and the Catholic Church – a certain recipe for electoral disaster in Bavaria and other pious parts of southern Germany. Ludendorff's fate was sealed when he stood as a candidate for the Presidency in the 1925 elections on behalf of the Nazi Party and received a derisory 1.1 per cent of the vote. There is some evidence that Hitler himself had persuaded him to stand in the knowledge that his reputation would be irreparably harmed by the attempt.[85] From now until his death in 1937, Ludendorff and his Tannenberg League remained on the fringes of politics, condemned to complete irrelevance and lacking in any kind of mass support. Nothing demonstrated more clearly than this the changed situation of extreme nationalism in Germany: the all-powerful military dictator of the First World War had been pushed out to the margins of politics by the upstart Nazi politician; the general had been displaced by the corporal.

With Ludendorff safely out of the way, Hitler had no serious rival on the extreme right any more. He could now concentrate on bringing the rest of the ultra-nationalist movement to heel. While disparate groups in the south gravitated into the orbit of the Nazi Party, the various branches of the Party in northern and western Germany were undergoing something of a revival. The person mainly responsible for this was another Bavarian, Gregor Strasser, a pharmacist from Landshut. Born in 1892, the son of a politically active lawyer, Strasser was well educated and well read, and his middle-class upbringing and manners made him an attractive figure in the eyes of many potential sympathizers of the Nazi movement. At the same time, like many bourgeois German men of his generation, he was stamped by the experience of 1914, the spirit of unity that he believed needed to be re-created among all Germans. After finishing his military service as a lieutenant, Strasser sought to re-create this experience and to right what he believed to be Germany's wrongs. He fought with the Free Corps in Munich at the end of the war and then built up his own paramilitary group, which brought him into contact with Hitler. For Strasser, it was the cause rather than the leader that mattered. On 9 November 1923 he led his brownshirt unit into Munich to seize a key bridge over the river, as arranged, and when the putsch backfired he took his unit back to Landshut again, where he was duly arrested.[86]

But in the end his rather peripheral participation in the putsch did not seem to the authorities to warrant particularly harsh treatment. Strasser therefore remained at large while the other Nazi leaders either fled or were landed in gaol. In April 1924 he was elected to the Bavarian Parliament. He proved to be a talented administrator, bringing together many of the fragments of the shattered ultra-right. Once the Nazi Party was legal again, Hitler, recognizing his ability, sent him to revive it in north Germany. By the end of 1925, Strasser's tireless recruitment drive had increased the number of branches nearly fourfold, using a pronounced emphasis on the 'socialist' aspects of Nazi ideology to try and win over the industrial working class in areas like the Ruhr. Strasser was contemptuous of the other ultra-right groups which thought 'the primitive solution of antisemitism to be adequate'. He told Oswald Spengler in July 1925 that Nazism was different because it sought 'a German revolution' through a German form of socialism.[87] His idea of socialism, however, while it involved the state taking a 51 per cent stake in major industries and 49 per cent in all other businesses, also included the return of the guilds and the payment of wages in kind rather than in money. 'Socialist' ideas of this kind were developed by Strasser in conjunction with a number of Nazi leaders in the new branches of the Party in various parts of North Germany. These Party branches owed little or nothing to the leadership of Hitler during this period; the Party, as it were, was largely reconstituting itself, independently of headquarters in Munich. Soon, perhaps inevitably, Strasser and his allies were voicing their suspicions of what they regarded as the corrupt and dictatorial clique under Hermann Esser that was running the Party's Munich office while Hitler was composing the second volume of My Struggle. Many of them had not even met Hitler in person, and so had not fallen under the spell of his growing personal charisma. They particularly disliked the existing Nazi Party Programme, and declared their intention of replacing it with one more in tune with their own ideas.[88]

Particularly prominent in these moves was another new recruit to the Party, the young ideologue Joseph Goebbels. Born in 1897 in the industrial town of Rheydt on the Lower Rhine, son of a clerk, Goebbels was given a grammar-school education and went on to study Ancient Philology, German, and History at Bonn University, gaining a Ph.D. in Romantic literature at Heidelberg University in 1921, which entitled him to be addressed, as he was ever after, as 'Dr Goebbels'. But despite his doctorate, Goebbels was not destined for the academic life. He too was a kind of bohemian, already occupying his spare time in his student days with writing plays and dreaming of an artistic future. Throughout the 1920s he wrote and rewrote the novel that was eventually published in

1929 as *Michael: A German Fate in the Pages of a Diary*. The novel was mainly a vehicle for Goebbels's own vague and confused conceptions of a national revival, based on fanatical faith and belief in the future, for which the novel's hero eventually sacrifices himself. By such means, Goebbels sought to give meaning to a life dominated by his own very obvious physical disability: a club foot, which made him walk with a limp. It exposed him to merciless teasing at school, and indeed throughout his life, and rendered him unfit for military service in the First World War. Perhaps in compensation, Goebbels came to believe that he was destined for great things; he kept a diary, he pursued women and love affairs with extraordinary vigour and a surprising degree of success, and he spurned any ordinary means of earning a living. Instead, he read avidly – Dostoevsky, Nietzsche, Spengler, and above all Houston Stewart Chamberlain, who convinced him that the rebirth of the West prophesied by Spengler could only be achieved by the removal of the Jews.[89]

Goebbels was different in some ways from the other leading Nazis. His intellect and temperament were often described as 'Latin', perhaps because he avoided vague philosophical and rhetorical declamation and instead spoke and wrote with a remarkable clarity and openness mixed on occasion with sarcastic humour.[90] Like many others, however, he had been profoundly shocked by Germany's defeat in the First World War. He spent the winter semester of 1919–20 in Munich – it was common for German students to change universities at least once during their studies – and so, as well as being exposed to the extreme right-wing atmosphere of student life, he now imbibed the rabidly nationalist atmosphere of the counter-revolution in the city in those months. Although he sympathized with men like Count Arco-Valley, whose imprisonment for the assassination of Kurt Eisner deeply dismayed him, Goebbels did not really discover his political commitment, or his political abilities, until 1924, when, after coming into contact with a number of ultra-nationalist groups, he was introduced to the Nazi Party by an old school friend.

As Goebbels made his way in the Nazi Party, he met Erich Koch, a Rhenish Nazi and former member of the violent wing of resistance against the French. He also encountered Julius Streicher, whom he described privately as a 'Berserker' and 'perhaps somewhat pathological'.[91] And he was impressed by Ludendorff, whom he already admired as the great general from the First World War. Soon, Goebbels had become a Party organizer in the Rhineland. He developed into an effective orator, perhaps the most effective of all the Nazi speakers apart from Hitler himself, lucid, popular, and quick-witted in response to hecklers. He began turning his literary talents to political use in articles for the Nazi press, giving a pseudo-socialist twist to the Nazi creed. Goebbels had finally found his *métier*. Within a few months he was one of the most popular Nazi orators in the Rhineland, attracting the attention of leading figures in the regional Party and starting to play a significant role in deciding its policy. It was Joseph Goebbels as much as Gregor Strasser who was behind the north German challenge to the Munich Party leadership in 1925. But he too soon began to fall under Hitler's spell, enthused by a reading of *My Struggle* ('who is this man,' he wrote: 'half plebeian, half God!').[92] Meeting him in person for only the second time, on 6 November 1925, Goebbels was impressed by his 'big blue eyes. Like stars.' Hitler was, he thought after hearing him speak, 'the born tribune of the people, the coming dictator'.[93]

Goebbels and Hitler failed to see eye to eye on many central issues. Alerted to the growing assertiveness of the north Germans, Hitler summoned them to a meeting on 14 February 1926 in Bamberg, Franconia, where Julius Streicher had built up a large following for him. The Nazi leader spoke for two hours, rejecting their views and reasserting his belief in the centrality of the conquest of 'living-space' in Eastern Europe for the future of German foreign policy. Whereas Strasser and Goebbels had urged the Nazis to join in the campaign to expropriate the German princes, who had retained their extensive properties in the country after their deposition in the Revolution of 1918, Hitler damned such a campaign as an attack on private property. 'Horrifying!' wrote Goebbels in his diary: 'Probably one of the greatest disappointments of my life. I no longer believe fully in Hitler.'[94] But, although Goebbels now wondered whether Hitler was a reactionary, he did not offer any overt opposition to Hitler at the meeting. Shocked at Hitler's tough stance, Strasser capitulated completely and dropped his proposals. In return, Hitler mollified the north Germans by removing Hermann Esser, whose corruption had so angered them, from his post in Munich.[95]

In April 1926 Hitler brought Goebbels to Munich to give a speech, providing him with a car and generally giving him the red-carpet treatment. At Nazi Party headquarters, Hitler confronted Goebbels and his two co-leaders of the Westphalian Region of the Party, Franz Pfeffer von Salomon, another leading north German Nazi, and, like so many leading Nazis, an ex-army man and Free Corps member, and Karl Kaufmann, who had made his name by organizing violent resistance to the French during their occupation of the Ruhr. Hitler berated these men for going their own way in ideological matters, lectured them on his views of the Party's policies, then offered to let bygones be bygones if they submitted unconditionally to his leadership. Goebbels was converted on the spot. Hitler, he confided to his diary, was 'brilliant'. 'Adolf Hitler,' he wrote, thinking of the 1923 putsch, 'I love you because you are both great and simple at the same time. What one calls a genius.'[96] From now on he was entirely under Hitler's spell; unlike some of the other Nazi leaders, he was to remain so right up to the end. Hitler rewarded him by putting him in charge of the tiny and internally divided Nazi Party in Berlin, as Regional Leader, or *Gauleiter*. Pfeffer von Salomon was made head of the brownshirt paramilitaries, and Gregor Strasser became Reich Propaganda Leader of the Party. Meanwhile, the annual Party meeting reaffirmed the 1920 Party Programme and underlined Hitler's total dominance over the movement, placing all the key appointments, and in particular those of the Regional Leaders, in his hands.[97]

This meeting was required by law; and following legal requirements it duly re-elected Hitler as Party Leader. The true nature of the Party's inner workings was demonstrated, however, by a Party rally, held in July 1926 and attended by up to 8,000 brownshirts and Party members. Its time was almost wholly taken up with rituals of obeisance to Hitler, the swearing of personal oaths of loyalty to him, and mass marches and displays, including the parading of the 'Blood Flag' that had been held above the ill-fated march on Munich in November 1923.[98] This set the tone in a modest way for the far more grandiose Party rallies of future years. But at this point, though now united and disciplined under Hitler's unquestioned leadership, the Nazi Party was still very small. The developments of the following three years, up to late 1929, were to lay the foundation for the Party's subsequent success. But more would be required than leadership and organization if the Nazis were to gain the popular backing that Hitler now sought.[99]

III

The years 1927–8 saw the creation of a new basic structure for the Nazi Party across the country. In 1928 the Party Regions were realigned to follow the boundaries of the Reichstag constituencies – only 35 of them, all very large, to conform to Weimar's system of proportional representation by party list – to signal the primacy of their electoral functions. Within a year or so of this, a new intermediate organizational layer of districts (*Kreise*) had been created between the Regions and the local branches. A new generation of younger Nazi activists played the most prominent role at these levels. They pushed aside the generation left over from prewar Pan-German and conspiratorial organizations, and outnumbered those who had taken an active part in the Free Corps, the Thule Society and similar groups. But it is important to remember that even the older generation of leading Nazis were themselves still young men, particularly when compared with the greying, middle-aged politicians who led the mainstream political parties. In 1929 Hitler was still only 40, Goebbels 32, Göring 36, Hess 35, Gregor Strasser 37. Their role remained crucial, especially in providing leadership and inspiration to the younger generation.

Goebbels, for example, made his reputation above all as Regional Leader of Berlin, where his fiery speeches, his incessant activity, his outrageous provocations of the Nazis' opponents, and his calculated staging of street-fights and meeting-hall brawls to gain the attention of the press won the Party a mass of new adherents. More publicity accrued from the Berlin Party's aggressive and extremely defamatory campaigns against figures such as the Berlin deputy police chief Bernhard Weiss, whose Jewish descent Goebbels drew attention to through calling him 'Isidor' – an entirely made-up name, commonly used by antisemites for Jews, and borrowed on this occasion, ironically, from the Communist press.[100] Goebbels's violence and extremism earned the Nazi Party in Berlin an eleven-month ban from the city's Social Democratic authorities in 1927–8; but they also won him the allegiance and admiration of younger activists such as the 19-year-old Horst Wessel, a pastor's son who had abandoned his university law studies for the world of the paramilitaries, most recently the brownshirts. 'What this man has shown in oratorical gifts and talent for organization', he wrote of 'our Goebbels' in 1929, 'is unique . . . The S.A. would have let itself be hacked to bits for him.'[101]

A great deal of in-fighting took place over key posts in the Party organization at a local and regional level. On the whole, however, as Max Amann told one local activist towards the end of 1925, Hitler

takes the view on principle that it is not the job of the Party leadership to 'install' branch leaders. Herr Hitler takes the view today more than ever that the most effective fighter in the National Socialist movement is the man who pushes his way through on the basis of his achievements as a leader. If you yourself write that you enjoy the trust of almost all the members in Hanover, why don't you then take over the leadership of the branch?[102]

In this way, Hitler thought, the most ruthless, the most dynamic and the most efficient would rise to positions of power within the movement. He was later to apply the same principle in running the Third Reich. It helped ensure that the Nazi Party at every level became ceaselessly active, constantly marching, fighting, demonstrating, mobilizing. Yet this did not bring immediate rewards. By the end of 1927 the Party still had only some 75,000 members and a mere seven deputies elected to the Reichstag. The hopes of men like Strasser and Goebbels that it would be able to win over the industrial working class had proved to be illusory.[103]

Recognizing the difficulties of breaking into the Social Democratic and Communist heartlands, the Nazis turned instead to rural society in Protestant north Germany, where rising peasant discontent was spilling over into demonstrations and campaigns of protest. The contradictory effects of inflation and stabilization on the farming community had merged into a general crisis of agriculture by the late 1920s. While large landowners and farmers had bought machinery on hire purchase and were thus able to modernize at very little real cost to themselves, peasants tended to hoard money and so lost it, or spent it on domestic goods and so gained no benefit for their businesses. After the inflation, government measures to ease credit restrictions on agriculture to help recovery only made things worse, as peasants borrowed heavily to make good their losses, expecting a fresh round of inflation, then found they were unable to pay the money back because prices were declining instead of rising. Bankruptcies and foreclosures were already rising in number towards the end of the 1920s, and small farmers were turning to the extreme right in their despair.[104] Larger farmers and big landowners were suffering from the downturn in agricultural prices, and were unable to pay what they regarded as excessively high taxes to support the Weimar welfare state.[105] Both the Prussian and the Reich governments had tried to alleviate the situation by tariffs, subsidies, import controls and the like, but all these proved wholly inadequate to the situation.[106] Farmers of all types had modernized, mechanized and rationalized in order to try and deal with the agricultural depression since the early 1920s, but it was not enough. Pressure for high import tariffs on foodstuffs grew more insistent as the farming community began to see this as the only way to protect their income. In this situation, the Nazis' promise of a self-sufficient, 'autarchic' Germany, with foreign food imports more or less banned, seemed increasingly attractive.[107]

Realizing that they were winning support in rural areas in the Protestant north without really trying, the Nazis accelerated the shift in their propaganda from the urban working class to other sectors of the population. Now the Party turned its attention to rural districts and began to mount serious recruiting drives in areas like Schleswig-Holstein and Oldenburg.[108] Hitler retreated still further from the 'socialist' orientation of the Party in north Germany, and even 'clarified', or in other words amended, Point 17 of the Party Programme, on 13 April 1928, in order to reassure small farmers that its commitment to 'the expropriation of land for communal purposes without compensation' referred only to 'Jewish companies which speculate in land'.[109] The Nazis lost 100,000 votes in the Reichstag elections of May 1928, and with a mere 2.6 per cent of the vote were only able to get 12 deputies into the legislature, among them Gottfried Feder, Joseph Goebbels, Hermann Göring and Gregor Strasser. None the less, in some rural areas of the Protestant north they did much better. While they could only manage 1.4 per cent in Berlin and 1.3 per cent in the Ruhr, for example, they scored no less than 18.1 and 17.7 per cent respectively in two counties in Schleswig-Holstein. A vote of 8.1 per cent in another area inhabited by discontented Protestant small farmers, namely Franconia, reinforced the feeling that, as the Party newspaper put it on 31 May, 'the election results from the rural areas in particular have proved that with a smaller expenditure of energy, money and time, better results can be achieved there than in the big cities'.[110] The Party soon revamped its propaganda appeal to the farming

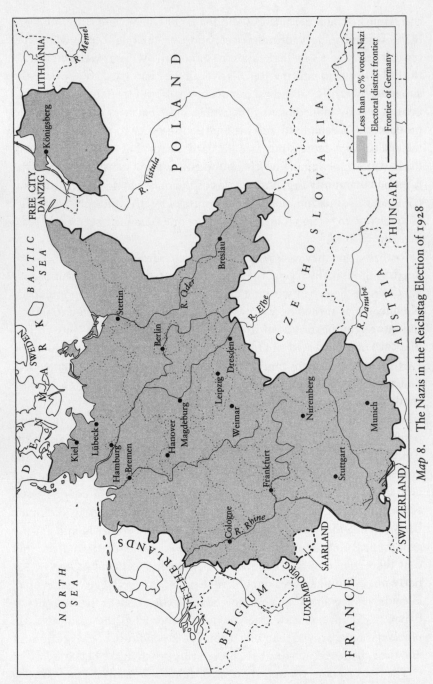

Map 8.   The Nazis in the Reichstag Election of 1928

community, telling them that it would create a special position for them in the Third Reich. Farmers of all kinds would be granted a 'corporation' of their own, in which they would work together in harmony and with the full backing of the state. Refractory farmhands, many of whom were active in the Social Democratic Party, would be brought to heel, and labour costs would at last come under tight control. After years of unsuccessful, sometimes violent protest, farmers in Schleswig-Holstein flocked to the support of the Nazi Party. It did no harm to its cause that the Party was led locally by members of the farming community, nor that it laid unmistakeable stress on an ideology of 'blood and soil' in which the peasant would be the core of the national identity. Even some of the larger landowners, traditionally identified with the Nationalists, were convinced. The Nazi Party's support amongst middling and small landowners skyrocketed. Soon, farmers' sons were providing the manpower for stormtrooper units being despatched to fight the Communists in the big cities.[111]

Thus, the new strategy soon began to bear fruit. The Party's membership grew from 100,000 in October 1928 to 150,000 a year later, while in local and state elections its vote now began to increase sharply, rising to 5 per cent in Saxony, 4 per cent in Mecklenburg and 7 per cent in Baden. In some rural areas of Protestant Saxony it nearly doubled its share of the vote, increasing, for example, from 5.9 per cent in the Schwarzenberg district in 1928 to 11.4 per cent in 1929.[112] In June 1929 the Nazi Party took over its first municipality, the Franconian town of Coburg. Here they won 13 out of the 25 seats on the council in the wake of a successful campaign for the removal of the previous council after it had sacked the local Nazi leader, a municipal employee, for making antisemitic speeches. The victory reflected in part the huge effort the Party put into the elections, with top speakers like Hermann Göring and even Hitler himself appearing at the hustings. But it also demonstrated that there was electoral capital to be won in local politics, where the Party now became much more active than before.[113]

And in the autumn of 1929 there was a further electoral bonus for the Party, in the shape of the campaign against the Young Plan (which involved the reduction and rescheduling of reparations payments, but not their abolition) organized by the Nationalists. Their leader, Alfred Hugenberg, enlisted the support of the Nazis and other ultra-right groups in his efforts to win acceptance for a referendum on his proposal for a law to reject the plan and prosecute any government ministers who signed it. Not only did the Nazis gain publicity from this campaign, they also won a degree of respectability on the mainstream right through the presence of Hitler on the organizing committee, along with such Pan-German stalwarts as Heinrich Class and the Steel Helmet leaders Franz Seldte and Theodor Duesterberg. The referendum itself was a failure, with only 5.8 million votes in favour. But the campaign had revealed to many supporters of the Nationalists how much more dynamic the brown-shirted and jackbooted Nazis were than the frock-coated and top-hatted leaders of their own party.[114]

Meanwhile, Hitler was soon whipping up popular enthusiasm again, his charisma now reinforced by the leadership cult that had grown up around him within the Party. An important symbolic expression of this was the use of the 'German greeting', 'Hail Hitler!' with outstretched right arm, whether or not Hitler was present. Made compulsory in the movement in 1926, it was also used increasingly as a sign-off in correspondence. These customs reinforced the movement's total dependence on Hitler, and were enthusiastically propagated by the second tier of leaders who had now gathered around him, whether, as with Gregor Strasser, for tactical reasons, to cement the Party's unity, or, as with Rudolf Hess, out of blind, religious faith in the person of the 'Leader', as he was now generally known.[115] At the Party rally, held in Nuremberg in August 1929, and the first such meeting since 1927, the Party's new-found confidence and coherence was demonstrated in a huge propaganda display, attended, so the police thought, by as many as 40,000 people, all united in their adulation for the Leader.[116]

By this time the Nazi Party had become a formidable organization, its regional, district and local levels staffed with loyal and energetic functionaries, many of them well educated and administratively competent, and its propaganda appeal channelled through a network of specialist institutions directed at particular constituents of the electorate.[117] Despite Hitler's repeated insistence that politics was a matter for men, there was now a Nazi women's organization, the self-styled German Women's Order, founded by Elsbeth Zander in 1923 and incorporated as a Nazi Party affiliate in 1928. Its membership was estimated by the police to have reached 4,000 by the end of the decade, nearly half the

Nazi Party's total female membership of 7,625. The German Women's Order was one of those paradoxical women's organizations that campaigned actively in public for the removal of women from public life: militantly anti-socialist, anti-feminist and antisemitic. Its practical activities included running soup kitchens for brownshirts, helping with propaganda campaigns, hiding weapons and equipment for the Nazi paramilitaries when they were being sought by the police, and providing nursing services for wounded activists through its sub-organization the 'Red Swastika', a Nazi version of the Red Cross.[118]

Zander was an effective speaker by all accounts, but she was not much of an organizer, and early in 1931 her German Women's Order collapsed amid a welter of accusations and counter-accusations, of which the charge of financial corruption was the most serious. The Order was so deeply in debt that Zander herself, as the responsible official, faced personal bankruptcy. In addition, there were scurrilous reports that Zander was having an affair with the Order's chauffeur, while brownshirts were appearing at some of its meetings dressed in women's clothes. Gregor Strasser, now the Party's Organizational Leader, responded by dissolving all the Nazi Party's female affiliates, politely but effectively removing Zander from a position of authority, and replacing them on 6 July 1931 with the National Socialist Women's Organization (NS-Frauenschaft), which was initially at least a decentralized body with its regional associations controlled by the Regional Leaders. Soon, however, it was successful enough to acquire a nationwide identity, with its own magazine for women and not only a greater degree of autonomy for its own regional leaders but also a greater degree of co-ordination between them.[119] The fundamental problem for Nazi women, however, lay in the Party's ineradicable male chauvinism, a conviction that women's role was not to take part in politics but to stay at home and bear children. For the time being, it had to compromise its position in the interests of winning over female voters, but in the long run, if the Nazis ever came to power, its anti-feminist women activists seemed doomed to argue themselves out of a role.

Alongside the organizations catering for women there was also one directed at youths aged between 14 and 18, founded in 1922. This initially had the rather cumbersome title of the Youth League of the National Socialist German Workers' Party; but in 1926 it was renamed the Hitler

Youth. Beginning as a recruiting agency for the brownshirts, it was revamped in 1929 under Kurt Gruber as a rival to the myriad informal youth groups that existed on the Weimar scene, most of them opposed to the Republic. It, too, met with little success to begin with; even in January 1932 it only had a thousand members in the whole of Berlin.[120] Backing it up was a National Socialist School Pupils' League, founded in 1929, and a League of German Maidens, established the following year.[121] All these organizations were soon dwarfed in size and significance by the National Socialist German Students' League, founded in 1926 by Wilhelm Tempel. The League, too, did relatively little until 1928, when it was taken over by Baldur von Schirach, who proved to be a durable and increasingly important figure in the Nazi movement. Born in 1907 in Berlin, he was the son of a traditionalist, ex-army theatre director in Weimar, who was married to a wealthy American woman. Schirach grew up in culturally conservative, antisemitic circles in Weimar. He was educated at a boarding school whose head emphasized character-building rather than academic education. The young Schirach was profoundly influenced by his elder brother's suicide in October 1919, announced in a letter to his family as a response to 'Germany's misfortune'. By the mid-1920s he was reading Houston Stewart Chamberlain, and when he discovered Hitler's *My Struggle* he was converted to Nazism, developing his commitment into real hero-worship when he heard Hitler speak in the town in 1925. Soon he had attracted the Leader's attention with a seemingly endless outpouring of poems glorifying the movement and its chief. They have been described as 'superior to the outpourings of other racist versifiers' and were published in a collected volume in 1929.[122]

During his studies in Munich (which he never completed) he joined the National Socialist German Students' League, quickly rising to the top of the branch based at Munich University, where he had been advised to study by Hitler. It was his success in this capacity that propelled him to the leadership of the national League in 1928, replacing Wilhelm Tempel. Schirach purged the League of its social-revolutionary elements and led it in extremely vigorous campaigning for seats on the student unions of individual universities. Pushing aside the traditional, rather stuffy duelling corps and fraternities, the League gained a reputation for provocative actions, and campaigned on issues such as the reduction of overcrowding in lectures (by imposing a limit on the number of Jewish students), the dismissal of pacifist professors, the creation of new chairs in subjects like Racial Studies and Military Science, and the harnessing of the universities to the national interest, away from the pursuit of knowledge as an end in itself. By the summer of 1932 they had already gained a much-trumpeted success in combination with right-wing professors and local politicians in hounding Emil Julius Gumbel, a particularly hated figure as a Jew, a socialist, a pacifist and a campaigner against right-wing judicial bias, from his chair in Heidelberg, prompting the declaration from a Frankfurt magazine that 'Heidelberg has thus opened the era of the Third Reich in the sphere of academia'.[123]

Carefully avoiding antagonizing the fraternities, Schirach rapidly increased the League's vote in student elections, and in July 1931 the League was able to take over the national organization of the General Students' Unions with the help of other, sympathetic right-wing groups. In 1932 the students voted the 'leadership principle' through the national Union, abolishing elections altogether. Even though total membership of the Nazi Students' League did not even reach 10 per cent of national fraternity membership, the Nazis had completely taken over student representation in Germany. Impressed by such successes, Hitler appointed Schirach to the leadership of the Hitler Youth on 3 October 1931.[124]

Not just women, young people, students, and school pupils, but also many other sectors of German society were catered for by specially designed Nazi organizations by the end of the 1920s. There were groups for civil servants, for the war-wounded, for farmers, and for many other constituencies, each addressing its particular, specifically targeted propaganda effort. There was even a kind of trade union movement, the clumsily named National Socialist Factory Cell Organization, which met with a conspicuous lack of success in trying to attract industrial workers, who were either already organized in socialist-oriented or Catholic or Communist trade unions, or out of a job and so not in need of a trade union.[125] Yet the Nazis still had a particular appeal to the lower middle classes at this time, to artisans, shopkeepers and the self-employed. Often they gathered up such people from other, similar movements. The German Nationalist Commercial Employees' Union, for example, played a significant role in politicizing many young men and turning them in the direction of Nazism.[126] Founded in the Wilhelmine period, it articulated the resentments of male clerks in a world where women were coming into secretarial and similar jobs in ever larger numbers, and big employers in the banks, finance corporations, insurance companies and so on were often perceived as Jewish by religion, ethnic origin or simply character. Well before the war, it had launched furious attacks on Jews as the architects of the proletarianization of their members.[127] One junior civil servant, born in 1886, joined the union in 1912 and later noted that he thought that the government was dominated by Jews even under the Kaiser. When he finally left the Nationalists for the Nazis in 1932 after attending a Party rally, he noted that 'this was what I had been looking for since 1912'.[128] With many older Nazis from such backgrounds it must have been the same.

Strasser encouraged the establishment of this extremely elaborate structure of subdivisions within the movement, even if many of the different branches, like the Hitler Youth or the Factory Cell Organization, had very few members and did not seem to be going anywhere very fast. For he had a long-term aim in mind. All of this was intended to form the basis for the creation of a society run by Nazified social institutions once Hitler came to power. Strasser expended a great deal of energy and diplomacy in the creation of this embryonic Nazi social order. In the shorter run, it helped the Party direct its electoral appeal towards virtually every constituency in German society, helping to politicize social institutions that had previously considered themselves more or less unpolitical in their nature. It meant that the Party would be able to expand with ease should it suddenly gain a rapid influx of new members. And the whole structure was held together by unconditional loyalty to a leader whose power was now absolute, and whose charisma was fed on a daily basis by the adulation of his immediate group of subordinates.[129]

THE ROOTS OF COMMITMENT

I

The Nazi movement as it had developed by the late 1920s was dependent on the energy and fanaticism of its active members. Without them, it would have been just another political party. The Third Reich was created not least by the ordinary, street-level members of the brownshirts and the Nazi Party. What was it, then, that bound young men to the Nazi movement with such a terrifyingly single-minded sense of commitment? Where did the wellsprings of brownshirt violence lie? Hitler's charisma obviously played a part; yet much of the Party, especially in north Germany, came into being virtually without him. The dynamism of the movement had deeper roots. The autobiographies and diaries of a variety of leading Nazis provide some clues. And there is an excellent contemporary source that allows us some unique insights into the mindset of the Nazi activist. In 1934 the sociologist Theodore Abel, a professor at New York's Columbia University, obtained the co-operation of the Nazi Party for an essay competition in which people who had joined the Party or the brownshirts before 1 March 1933 were asked to write brief testimonies. Several hundred were sent in, and although both the Party and the respondents saw this as an opportunity to impress Americans with the sincerity and commitment of their movement, Abel's insistence that the prize would go to the most honest and trustworthy account seems to have ensured a reasonable degree of accuracy, at least as far as the testimonies could be checked.[130]

For the grass-roots Party activist, the elaborate theories of men like Rosenberg, Chamberlain, Spengler and other intellectuals were a closed book. Even popular writers such as Lagarde and Langbehn appealed mainly to the educated middle classes. Far more important were durable popular antisemitic propagandists such as Theodor Fritsch, whose *Handbook on the Jewish Question*, published in 1888, reached its fortieth edition in 1933. Fritsch's publishing house, the Hammer Verlag, survived the First World War, and continued to produce a lot of popular pamphlets and tracts which were quite widely read amongst rank-and-file Nazis.[131] As one stormtrooper wrote in 1934:

After the war, I became very much interested in politics, and eagerly studied newspapers of all political shadings. In 1920 for the first time I read in a right-wing newspaper an advertisement for an antisemitic periodical and became a subscriber of the *Hammer* of Theodor Fritsch. With the help of this periodical, I got to know the devastating influence of the Jews on people, state and economy. I must still admit today that this periodical was for me really the bridge to the great movement of Adolf Hitler.[132]

More significant still, however, was the inspiration provided by the basic elements of Nazi propaganda – the speeches by Hitler and Goebbels, the marches, the banners, the parades. At this level, ideas were more likely to be acquired through organs such as the Nazi press, election pamphlets and wall-posters than through serious ideological tracts. Among ordinary Party activists in the 1920s and early 1930s, the most important aspect of Nazi ideology was its emphasis on social solidarity – the concept of the organic racial community of all Germans – followed at some distance by extreme nationalism and the cult of Hitler. Antisemitism, by contrast, was of significance only for a minority, and for a good proportion of these it was only incidental. The younger they were, the less important ideology was at all, and the more significant were features such as the emphasis on Germanic culture and the leadership role of Hitler. By contrast, ideological antisemitism was strongest amongst the older generation of Nazis, testifying to the latent influence of antisemitic groups active before the war, and the nationalistic families in which many of them had grown up.[133]

Men often came to the paramilitary wing of the Nazi Party after serving at the front in 1914–18, then becoming involved in far-right organizations such as the Thule Society or the Free Corps.[134] Young Rudolf Höss, for example, the future commandant of Auschwitz, came to the Party this way. Born in 1901 in Baden-Baden, he grew up in south-west Germany in a Catholic family. His father, a salesman, intended him for the priesthood, and, according to Höss, instilled in him a strong sense of duty and obedience; but he also intoxicated him with tales of his own past days as a soldier in Africa and the selflessness and heroism of the missionaries. Höss lost his faith as the result, he later wrote, of the betrayal of a secret he had confided in his confessor. When the war broke out, he enrolled in the Red Cross and then in his father's old regiment in 1916, serving in the Middle East. At the end of the war, his parents both dead, he enlisted in a Free Corps unit in the Baltic, where he experienced the brutality of civil war at first hand.

Back in Germany, Höss enrolled in a clandestine successor organization to his Free Corps, and in 1922 he joined in the brutal murder of a man he and his comrades believed was a Communist spy in their ranks, beating him into a bloody mess with clubs, slitting his throat with a knife, and finishing him off with a revolver. Höss was arrested and imprisoned in the Brandenburg penitentiary, where he learned, he later reported, the incorrigible nature of the criminal mind. He was shocked by the 'filthy, insolent language' of his fellow-prisoners, and appalled at the way in which the prison had become a school for criminals instead of a place to reform them. Clean, neat and tidy, and accustomed to discipline, Höss quickly became a model prisoner. The crude bullying and corruption of some of the warders suggested to him that a more honest and more humane approach towards the prisoners might have had a good effect. But quite a few of his fellow-inmates were, he concluded, absolutely beyond redemption.[135] A few months before his arrest, he had become a member of the Nazi Party. He was to spend most of the rest of the 1920s in gaol, though, like many such men, he was released well before completing his sentence as a result of an agreement between the far left and far right deputies in the Reichstag to vote through a general amnesty for political prisoners.[136] Clearly, however, when he was not in prison, the Nazi Party provided him with the discipline, order and commitment he so obviously needed in life.

One of Höss's associates in the murder was another member of the Rossbach Free Corps, Martin Bormann, born in 1900, son of a post office clerk and trained as a farm manager. During the war he enrolled in the army but was assigned to a garrison and saw no active service. However, like Höss, he found it impossible to fit into civilian life. He came into contact with the Free Corps through providing them with a base on the estate where he worked in Mecklenburg. As well as joining the Free Corps, he also enrolled in an 'Association Against the Arrogance of the Jews', another tiny and otherwise insignificant fringe group on the far right. Bormann was not as closely involved in the murder as Höss, and only had to serve a year in gaol. In February 1925 he was released, and by the end of 1926 he had become a full-time employee of the Nazi Party, carrying out myriad administrative tasks, first in Weimar, then in Munich. A hopelessly incompetent speaker and, unlike Höss, not constitutionally inclined to physical violence, Bormann became an expert on insurance for the Party and its members, organized financial and other kinds of relief for brownshirts in distress and slowly began to make himself indispensable to the movement. But the fact that he was above all an administrator cannot disguise the fanatical nature of his political commitment. Like Höss and so many others, he reacted to the defeat of Germany in the First World War by turning to the most extreme forms of resentful nationalism, rabid antisemitism and hatred of parliamentary democracy. Quickly coming into contact with Hitler, he fell totally under his spell, and soon began to impress the Nazi leader with his boundless, unconditional admiration and loyalty. To others in the Party hierarchy, especially lower down the ranks, he could show an entirely different side, revealing in the process a brutal ambition that was eventually to make him one of the key figures in the Third Reich, above all in its later stages during the war.[137]

With men such as these, even more with slightly older figures who had gained their military experience through active service in the central battlefields of the war, it was clear that the Free Corps were indeed, as has been said, the 'vanguard of Nazism', providing a good part of the leadership cadre of the Party in the mid-1920s.[138] Yet already by this time a younger generation was entering the Party, the postwar generation, eager to emulate the now legendary exploits of the front-line soldiers. A few drifted over from the Communists, attracted by political extremism, activism and violence irrespective of ideology. 'I quit the party in 1929', reported one, 'because I could no longer agree with the orders from the Soviet Union.' For this particular activist, however, violence was a way of life. He continued to attend Party rallies of all descriptions and to throw himself into street fighting alongside his old comrades until a local

Nazi leader offered him a position.[139] Violence was like a drug for such men, as it clearly was for Rudolf Höss, too. Often, they had only the haziest notion of what they were fighting for. One young Nazi reported that witnessing opponents trying to break up a Nazi meeting 'made me instinctively a National Socialist' even before he became acquainted with the Party's goals.[140] Another, joining the Nazi movement in 1923, lived a life of almost incessantly violent activism, suffering beatings, stabbings and arrests for the best part of a decade, as he recounted in detail in his autobiographical essay; these clashes, rather than the actual ideas of the movement, were what gave his life significance. For one young man, born in 1906 into a Social Democratic family, hostility to the Communists was at the core of his commitment. The times he experienced in the unit of the stormtroopers known as the 'murderers' storm' were, he later said, 'too wonderful and perhaps also too hard to write about'.[141]

A particularly graphic, though by no means untypical account of stormtrooper activities was provided by a schoolteacher, born in 1898, who had fought in the war and, after far-right activities in the early 1920s, joined the Nazis in 1929. He was called up one evening with his brownshirt group to defend a Nazi rally in a nearby town against the 'reds':

We all gathered at the entrance of the town and put on white armbands, and then you could hear the thundering marching of our column of about 250 men. Without weapons, without sticks, but with clenched fists, we marched in strict order and iron discipline into the catcalls and screaming of the crowds before the meeting-hall. They had sticks and fence-boards in their hands. It was 10 o'clock at night. With a few manoeuvres in the middle of the street, we pushed the crowd against the walls to clear the street. Just at that moment, a carpenter drove through with a small truck and a black coffin in it. As he went by, one of us said: 'Well, let's see whom we can put in there.' The screams, cries, whistles and howls grew ever more intense.

The two rows of our column stood still, charged up with energy. A signal, and we go marching into the hall, where a few hundred rioters are trying to shut up our speaker. We came just in time, marching in step along the walls until we had closed the ring around them, leaving an opening only at the entrance. A whistle sounds. We tighten the ring. Ten minutes later . . . we had put them out into the fresh air. The meeting goes on while outside all hell breaks loose. We then escorted the speaker back out, cutting once more through the swirling mob in closed formation.

For this stormtrooper, the 'Marxists' were the enemy, as they were for many ex-soldiers fighting in what he called 'the spirit of the frontline comradeship, risen from the smoke of the sacrificial vessels of the war, and finding its way into the hearts of the awakened German people'.[142]

I I

'Old fighters' such as these proudly listed the injuries and insults they had received at the hands of their opponents. The 'persecution, harassment, scorn and ridicule' they had to suffer only stiffened their resolve.[143] At one meeting, in Idar-Oberstein, according to a Party activist, born in 1905, four hundred stormtroopers turned up, including himself:

One after the other, our four speakers had their say, interrupted by furious howling and catcalls. But when, in the ensuing discussion, an interlocutor was reprimanded for saying, 'We don't want the brown plague in our beautiful town', tumult broke out. There followed a battle with beer steins, chairs, and the like, and in two minutes the hall was demolished and everyone cleared out. We had to take back seven heavily injured comrades that day and there were rocks thrown at us and occasional assaults in spite of the police protection.[144]

Yet the depth of hatred and resentment which Nazi stormtroopers felt against the Social Democrats as well as the Communists can only be understood in terms of their feeling that they were under constant attack not just from the Social Democrats' paramilitary affiliate, the Reichsbanner, but also in many areas from the police, who in Prussia at least were controlled by Social Democratic ministers such as Carl Severing and Albert Grzesinski. 'The terror of police and government against us', as one stormtrooper put it, was another source of resentment against the Republic.[145]

Such men were outraged that they should be arrested for beating up or killing people they considered to be Germany's enemies, and blamed the prison sentences they sometimes had to suffer on the 'Marxist judicial authorities' and the 'corruption' of the Weimar Republic.[146] Their hatred

1. The pseudo-medievalism of the Bismarck memorial in Hamburg, unveiled in 1906, promises a revival of past German glories under a new national leader.

2. Antisemitic postcard from 'the only Jew-free hotel in Frankfurt', 1887. Such attitudes were a new phenomenon in the 1880s.

Facing page

3. (*top*) The promise of victory: German troops advance confidently across Belgium in 1914.

4. (*middle*) The reality of defeat: German prisoners of war taken by the Allies at the Battle of Amiens, August 1918.

5. (bottom) The price to be paid: the skeletons of German warplanes scrapped in fulfilment of the 1919 Treaty of Versailles.

This page

6. (*top*) Descent into chaos: a street battle in Berlin during the 'Spartacist uprising' of January 1919.

7. (*right*) Revenge of the right: a Free Corps lieutenant in charge of a firing squad photographs his irregulars with the 'Red Guardist' they are about to execute during their bloody suppression of the Munich Soviet, May 1919.

8. A racist cartoon in a German satirical magazine highlights the murders, robberies and sex offences supposedly committed by French colonial troops during the Ruhr occupation of 1923.

9. The hyperinflation of 1923: 'So many thousand-mark notes for just one dollar!'

10. The balance-sheet of reparations, 1927: 14,000 suicides in Germany are the result, according to a satirical periodical, of economic hardship caused by the financial burden imposed on the country by the Treaty of Versailles.

11. The Roaring Twenties in Berlin: artist Otto Dix's bitter view of German society in 1927-28; war veterans are forced out to the margins, while women of easy virtue and their clients live it up at a jazz party.

12. The beer-hall putsch: armed Nazi stormtroopers wait outside Munich city hall, November 1923, for the takeover that never came.

13. Hitler relaxing, but not drinking, with his friends in a Munich beer-cellar in 1929. Gregor Strasser is on the far left.

14. Hitler leads a street march at an early Nazi Party rally in Weimar, 1926, while stormtroopers clear the way. A hatless Rudolf Hess can be seen to his left, with Heinrich Himmler directly behind.

15. The face of fanaticism: stormtroopers listen to a speech at an open-air rally, 1930.

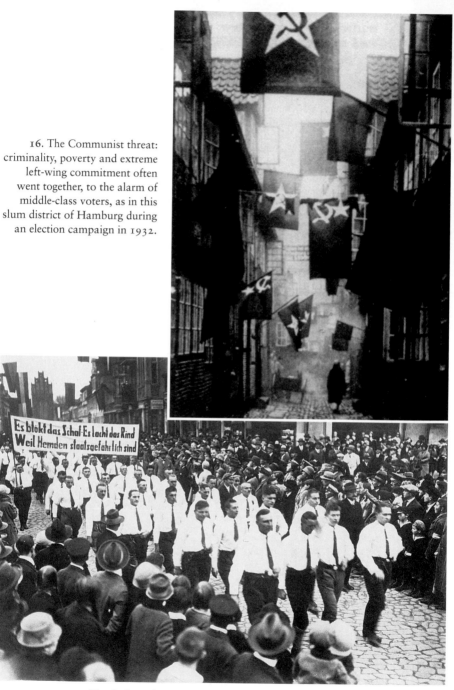

16. The Communist threat: criminality, poverty and extreme left-wing commitment often went together, to the alarm of middle-class voters, as in this slum district of Hamburg during an election campaign in 1932.

17. The futility of Brüning's ban on uniforms (December 1930): the brownshirts wear white shirts instead, and the effect is the same.

18. A pacifist poster warns in 1930 that 'anyone who votes for the
right votes for war', and Nazism can mean only death and destruction.
'German,' it asks rhetorically, 'shall he grab you again?'

19. The violence of the visual image: where the Nazis lead in 1928, other parties follow in later elections. (a) 'Smash the world-foe, International High Finance' – Nazi election poster, 1928. (b) 'An end to this system!' – Communist election poster, 1932. (c) 'Clear the way for List 1!' – the Social Democratic worker elbows aside the Nazi and the Communist, 1930. (d) 'Against civil war and inflation' – the People's Party knocks down its rivals to right and left, an example of wishful thinking from 1932.

20. The choice before the electorate in September 1930: the parties target women, benefit claimants, young people and other specific social groups.

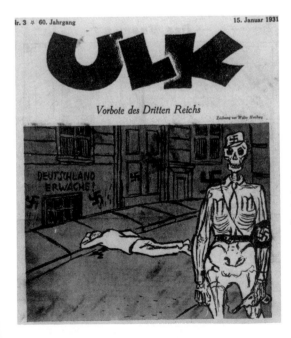

21. 'Harbinger of the Third Reich'. A Social Democratic poster warns against the violence of the Nazis, January 1931. After scrawling 'Germany, awake!' and daubing swastikas on the walls, the figure of Death, dressed in a brownshirt uniform and holding a pistol, kills an opponent and marches on.

22. (*top*) Drowning out the opposition: Nazis use loudhailers to shout 'Hail, Hitler!' during the election campaign of March 1933.

23. (*below*) The respectable face of Nazism: Hitler, in formal attire, meets leading businessmen shortly after his appointment as Reich Chancellor in January 1933.

24. The reality on the streets: Communists and Social Democrats arrested by stormtroopers acting as 'auxiliary police' await their fate in a torture cellar of the brownshirts in the spring of 1933.

25. The first concentration camps, 1933: Social Democrats are registered on their arrival at the Oranienburg camp.

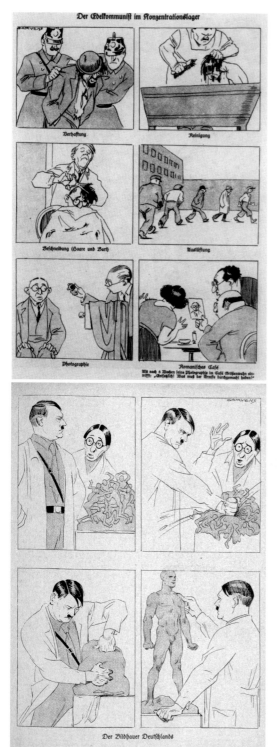

26. 'The noble Communist in the concentration camp'. Nazi propaganda gave wide publicity to the camps but tried to give them a positive image. According to this cartoon from 14 May 1933, 'arrest' was followed by a 'clean-up', a 'cut (hair and beard)' – the German word is the same as that for circumcision – an 'airing' and a 'photograph'. In Berlin's 'Romanesque Café' and the 'Café Megalomania', well-known haunts of modernist artists and radical writers, the supposedly Jewish regulars lament their friend's transformation six weeks later: 'What the poor man must have gone through!'

27. Hitler's cultural revolution: out of a mass of squabbling pygmies, 'Germany's sculptor' creates a new giant German ready to take on the world.

28. The exiles: the Nazi satirical journal *The Nettle* portrays the flight of Germany's most eminent writers and intellectuals as a triumph for the German nation: while Thomas Mann works the hurdy-gurdy, others, mostly Jewish, slink away from Germany to his tune. Among those caricatured are Albert Einstein, Lion Feuchtwanger and Karl Marx. 'What is gone, won't return.'

29. 'Against the un-German spirit': Nazi students burn Jewish and leftist books outside Berlin University on 10 May 1933.

30. 'Germans! Defend yourselves! Do not buy from Jews!' Stormtroopers paste stickers onto a Jewish shop window during the boycott of 1 April 1933, while shoppers look on.

31. Continuity in the National Socialist Revolution: a postcard from 1933 draws a direct line from Frederick the Great of Prussia through Bismarck to Hitler.

for the 'reds' was almost without measure. One young Nazi still inveighed in 1934 against 'the red flood . . . hordes of red mercenaries, lurking in the dark', or as another brownshirt put it, the 'red murder mob . . . the screaming, screeching hordes . . . hate-filled, furious faces worthy of study by a criminologist'.[147] Their hatred was fuelled by countless clashes, all the way up to terrifying incidents such as a notorious gun battle between Communists and brownshirts that broke out on a train in Berlin-Lichtenfels on 27 March 1927. The brownshirts contrasted Communist criminality with what they saw as their own selfless idealism. One storm-trooper reported with pride that the struggle of the late 1920s 'demanded financial as well as psychological sacrifices of every comrade. Night after night, leaflets for which we ourselves had to pay had to be distributed. Every month there was a rally . . . which always gave our little local branch of 5–10 members 60 marks of debts since no innkeeper would rent us a hall without advance payment.'[148] The oft-repeated claim that many brownshirts only joined the organization because it offered them free food, drink, clothing and accommodation, not to mention exciting and brutal kinds of entertainment, does scant justice to the fanaticism which motivated many of them. Only the oldest activists joined in the expectation of getting a job or receiving financial support. For the young, it did not matter so much.[149] Nazi student leaders often got themselves deeply into debt by paying personally for posters and pamphlets.[150] With many others it must have been the same.

Of course, testimonies such as these, addressed to an American soci-ologist, were bound to emphasize the self-sacrifice and dedication of their writers.[151] Nevertheless, it is difficult to grasp the full extent of the stormtroopers' fanaticism and hatred unless we accept that they often did feel they were making sacrifices for their cause. Hitler himself drew attention to this when he told an audience in January 1932 not to

forget that it is a sacrifice when today many hundreds of thousands of men of the National Socialist movement climb onto trucks every day, protect meetings, put on marches, sacrifice night after night and return only at daybreak – and then either back to the workshop and factory, or out to collect their pittance as unemployed; when they buy their uniforms, their shirts, their badges, and even pay their own transportation from what little they have – believe me, that is already a sign of the power of an ideal, a great ideal![152]

The Nazi Party depended on such commitment; much of its power and dynamism came from the fact that it was not dependent on big business or bureaucratic institutions such as trade unions for its financial support, as the 'bourgeois' parties and the Social Democrats to varying degrees were, still less on the secret subsidies of a foreign power, along the lines of the Moscow-financed Communists.[153]

Many people were won over to Nazism by Hitler's demagogy. Now presented in dramatically staged mass rallies and huge open-air meetings, Hitler's speeches at the end of the 1920s had a power greater than ever before. One young nationalist, born in 1908, had attended meetings addressed by such luminaries of the extreme right as Hugenberg and Ludendorff before he finally found inspiration when he

heard the Leader Adolf Hitler speak in person. After this, there was only one thing for me, either to win with Adolf Hitler or to die for him. The personality of the Leader had me totally in its spell. He who gets to know Adolf Hitler with a pure and true heart will love him with all his heart. He will love him not for the sake of materialism, but for Germany.[154]

There are many other such testimonies, from an antisemitic metalworker, born in 1903, who discovered at a Hitler meeting in 1927 that 'our Leader radiates a power which makes us all strong', to another storm-trooper, born in 1907, who declared that he fell under Hitler's spell in 1929 in Nuremberg: 'How his blue eyes sparkled when his stormtroopers marched past him in the light of the torches, an endless sea of flames rippling through the streets of the ancient Reich capital.'[155]

Much of the Nazis' appeal lay in their promise to end the political divisions that had plagued Germany throughout the Weimar Republic. One 18-year-old clerk, attending rallies at a regional election in 1929, was impressed by the Nazi speaker's

sincere commitment to the German people as a whole, whose greatest misfortune was being divided into so many parties and classes. Finally a practical proposal for the renewal of the people! Destroy the parties! Do away with classes! True national community! These were goals to which I could commit myself without reservation.[156]

Relatively few, in the end, were converted to active participation in the movement by reading political or ideological tracts. Word of mouth was what counted. Yet not everyone was mesmerized by Hitler's speaking. A serious and idealistic young middle-class Nazi like Melita Maschmann, for example, admired him as a 'man of the people' who had risen from obscurity, but even at the annual Party rally she was so busy, as she wrote later, that 'I could not permit myself the "debauchery" of ecstatic rapture'. Parades and shows she found boring and pointless. For her, Nazism was more a patriotic ideal than a cult of the individual leader.[157] For Nazism's middle-class supporters, especially perhaps women, street violence was often something to be grudgingly tolerated or studiously ignored.

Many such people came only hesitatingly to Nazism. Even joining the Party often denoted a level of commitment far lower than that of the young brownshirts interviewed by Theodore Abel. A substantial proportion of the Party's members left after only a relatively short time in its ranks. Nevertheless, by the early 1930s it was beginning to extend its appeal beyond the lower middle class that had provided its backbone since its foundation. Always anxious to claim working-class support, Party officials frequently classified members as workers when in reality they were something else. Detailed local investigations have shown that the standard accounts of Party membership, based on an internal Party census of 1935, have portrayed the working-class element as anything up to twice what it actually was, namely about 10 per cent in Germany's second city, Hamburg, ten years earlier, in 1925.[158] Wage-earners also seem to have been the social group most prone to leave the Party and therefore the least likely to show up in the 1935 figures on which most calculations are based. But Hamburg was a traditional centre of the labour movement, whose strength made it difficult for the Nazis to make any inroads. In parts of Saxony, where the labour movement was weaker, and traditional, small-scale industries gave the economy a very different shape to the modern, highly rationalized industrial centres such as Berlin or the Ruhr, manual wage labourers accounted for a higher proportion of Party members. Younger workers, who had not joined a union because they had never had a job, were particularly susceptible to the appeal of the Nazi Party in Saxony. As many as a third of Nazi Party members in the province may have belonged to the working class in a basic economic sense in the late 1920s. The lower middle class in town and country remained heavily over-represented in comparison to its numbers in the population as a whole. By the early 1930s, however, the proportion of middle- and upper-class Party members in the Saxon Nazi Party was increasing, as the Party became more respectable. Slowly, the Nazis were escaping their modest and humble roots and beginning to attract members of Germany's social elites.[159]

III

Among the new generation of leading Nazis who entered the movement in the mid-1920s, one man was to play a particularly prominent role in the Third Reich. At first sight, few would have considered that Heinrich Himmler, born in Munich on 7 October 1900, was destined to reach any kind of prominence at all. His father was a Catholic schoolteacher of sufficiently conservative views to have been considered fit to give private tuition to a young member of the Bavarian royal family for a time in the 1890s. Coming from a respectable background in the educated middle class, Heinrich, a sickly child with poor eyesight, went through several different schools, but received what appeared to be a solid academic education at grammar schools in Munich and Landshut. A school friend, Georg Hallgarten, who later became a well-known left-wing historian, testified to Himmler's intelligence and ability. School reports described Himmler as a conscientious, hard-working, ambitious, able and well-mannered student, a model pupil in every way. His patriotic father, however, made strenuous efforts to get him into the army, even declaring himself willing to cut short his son's education in order to do this. Young Heinrich's diaries and reading notes show how strongly he imbibed the mythology of 1914, the idea of war as the summit of human achievement and the concept of struggle as the moving force of human history and human existence. But he only got as far as training in the cadets, and never saw action on the front line. Here was a particularly clear example of a man of the post-front generation who bitterly regretted not having been able to fight in the war and spent much of his later life trying to make good this crucial absence in his early life.[160]

After passing the school-leaving examination with flying colours, Himmler, following his father's advice, went on to study agriculture at the Technical High School in Munich, and here, too, he excelled, graduating with a mark of 'very good' in 1922. He also joined a duelling fraternity, and after some trouble in finding a swordsman who took him seriously enough to accept a challenge, duly acquired the obligatory facial scars. In the meantime, however, he joined Kahr's Denizens' Defence Force, and then fell under the influence of Ernst Röhm, who impressed him with his military zeal. The far-right milieu into which he had now plunged directed him towards revolutionary antisemitism, and by 1924 he was inveighing 'against the hydra of the black and red International, of Jews and Ultramontanism, of freemasons and Jesuits, of the spirit of commerce and cowardly bourgeoisie'.[161] With his large head, his short-back-and-sides, his pudding-basin haircut, round glasses, receding chin and pencil moustache, Himmler looked very much like the schoolmaster his father had been, not at all like a fanatical nationalist streetfighter. A few months later, he brandished a standard rather than a pistol when he joined a unit of Röhm's Reich War Flag group that briefly occupied the Bavarian War Ministry in the first phase of the abortive Munich putsch on 8–9 November.[162]

Himmler got away from the putsch without being arrested, and so had his opportunity to rise in the movement at a time when Hitler was in prison or banned from speaking and the Nazi Party was in disarray. He hitched his wagon, wisely at this date, to Gregor Strasser's rising star, becoming first his secretary, then deputy Regional Leader in two different districts, and deputy Reich Propaganda Leader. But he was not Strasser's disciple. For by this time he had fallen under Hitler's spell, less through a reading of My Struggle, on which he recorded some critical notes ('the first chapters on his own youth contain many weak points') than through personal contact in his various official capacities, which included of course attending Hitler's speeches. To the young Himmler, still only in his mid-twenties, and hopelessly adrift in the choppy seas of post-putsch paramilitary politics, Hitler offered certainty, a leader to admire, a cause to follow. From 1925 onwards, when he joined the newly reconstituted Nazi Party, Himmler developed a boundless hero-worship of the Nazi leader; he kept a portrait of Hitler on his office wall and is even on occasion said to have engaged it in conversation.[163]

In 1926 he married, and his wife, seven years older than he was, influenced him strongly in the direction of occultism, herbalism, homeopathy and other unconventional beliefs, some of which he was later to try and force on his subordinates. Although Himmler's marriage did not prosper, these ideas did. Gradually abandoning the conventional Catholic piety of his youth, he became an enthusiast for 'blood and soil', joining the Artamans, a nationalist settlement group to which Rudolf Höss also belonged. Here Himmler came under the influence of Richard Walther Darré, an enthusiast for 'Nordic' racial ideas. Darré, born in Argentina in 1895 and educated, somewhat incongruously, in Wimbledon, England, had served in the German army during the war. Then he had become a specialist in selective animal breeding, which led him into the politics of 'blood and soil', though not immediately into the Nazi Party. Himmler imbibed from Darré a fixed belief in the destiny of the Nordic race, the superiority of its blood over that of the Slavs, the need to keep its blood pure, and the central role of a solid German peasantry in ensuring the future of the Germanic race. Driven by this obsession with the peasantry, Himmler for a while himself took up farming, but he did not do well, since he spent too much time in political campaigning, and the times were in any case bad for agricultural business.[164]

On 6 January 1929 Hitler appointed the faithful Himmler as head of his personal Protection Formation – *Schutzstaffel*, quickly known by its initials as the SS. This had its origins in a small unit formed early in 1923 to act as Hitler's bodyguard and protect the Party headquarters. It was refounded in 1925, when Hitler realized that the brownshirts under Röhm would never show him the unconditional loyalty which he required. Its initial commander was Julius Schreck, commander of the brownshirt 'Assault Squad' before Hitler's imprisonment, and from the first it was conceived as an elite formation, in contrast to the catch-all mass paramilitary movement of the brownshirts. In the intra-party intrigues of the mid-1920s the SS went through a number of leaders, all of whom failed to assert its independence from the growing power of the brownshirts, though they did manage to build it up as a closely disciplined, tightly knit corps of men. Himmler succeeded where they had failed.

Despising the rough elements who had formed its first group of recruits, he self-consciously set out to create it as a real elite, bringing in former army officers like the Pomeranian aristocrat Erich von dem Bach-Zelewski, and Free Corps veterans such as Friedrich Karl, Baron von Eberstein. Inheriting a formation of just 290 men, Himmler had increased the strength of the SS to a thousand by the end of 1929 and nearly three thousand a year later. Over the objections of the brownshirt leadership, he persuaded Hitler to make the SS fully independent in 1930, giving it a new uniform, black instead of brown, and a new, strictly hierarchical, quasi-military structure. As discontent and impatience rose within the brownshirt organization, and the threat of independent action grew, Hitler turned the SS into a kind of internal party police. It became more secretive, and began collecting confidential information not only on the Party's enemies but on leading members of the brownshirts as well.[165]

With the creation of the SS, the basic structure of the Nazi movement was complete. By the end of the 1920s Hitler had emerged, partly through circumstances, partly through his own speaking ability and his own ruthlessness, partly through the desperate need of the extreme right for a strong leader, as the unquestioned dictator of the movement, the object of a rapidly growing cult of personality. There were still tensions within the movement; these were to surface dramatically in the following few years up to 1934. There were still people in leading positions, such as Strasser and Röhm, who were prepared to criticize Hitler and take a different line from his if they thought it necessary. But Hitler had built up around him a crucial group of men whose devotion to him was wholly unconditional – men like Goebbels, Göring, Hess, Himmler, Rosenberg, Schirach and Streicher. Under their leadership, and thanks to Strasser's organizational talent, the Nazi movement by the middle of 1929 had become an elaborate, well-organized political body whose appeal was directed to virtually every sector of the population. Its propaganda was becoming rapidly more sophisticated. Its paramilitary wing was taking on the Communist Red Front-Fighters and Social Democratic Reichsbanner in the streets. Its internal police force, the SS, was poised to take action against the dissident and the disobedient in its own ranks. It had acquired, modified and elaborated a crude, largely unoriginal, but fanatically held ideology centred on extreme nationalism, hate-filled antisemitism and contempt for Weimar democracy. It was determined to gain power on the basis of popular support at the polls and rampaging violence on the streets, then tear up the Peace Treaties of 1919, rearm, reconquer the lost territories in East and West and create 'living-space' for ethnic German colonization of East-Central and Eastern Europe.

The cult of violence, derived not least from the Free Corps, was at the heart of the movement. By 1929 it could be seen in operation on a daily basis on the streets. The Nazi movement despised the law, and made no secret of its belief that might was right. It had also evolved a way of diverting legal responsibility from the Party leadership for acts of violence and lawlessness committed by brownshirts and other elements within the movement. For Hitler, Goebbels, the Regional Leaders and the rest only gave orders couched in rhetoric that, while violent, was also vague: their subordinates would understand clearly what was being hinted at and go into action straight away. This tactic helped persuade a growing number of middle- and even some upper-class Germans that Hitler and his immediate subordinates were not really responsible for the blood shed by the brownshirts on the streets, in bar-room brawls and in rowdy meetings, an impression strengthened by the repeated insistence of the brownshirt leaders that they were acting independently of the Nazi Party bosses. By 1929 Hitler had attracted the support, sympathy and to some extent even the financial backing of some well-connected people, especially in Bavaria. And his movement had extended its operations across the whole country, attracting significant electoral support, above all among crisis-racked small farmers in Protestant areas of north Germany and Franconia.

None of this could disguise the fact, however, that in the autumn of 1929, the Nazi Party was still very much on the fringes of politics. With only a handful of deputies in the Reichstag, it had to compete with a number of other fringe organizations of the right, some of which, for example the self-styled Economy Party, were larger and better supported than it was itself; and all of these still paled into insignificance in comparison to mainstream organizations of the right such as the Nationalist Party and the Steel Helmets. Moreover, although they did not command the support of a majority of the electorate any more, the three parties that were the mainstay of Weimar democracy, the Social Democrats, the Centre Party and the Democrats, were still in government, in a 'Grand Coalition' that also included the party of Germany's long-serving, moderate and highly successful Foreign Minister, Gustav Stresemann. The Republic seemed to have weathered the storms of the early 1920s – the inflation, the French occupation, the armed conflicts, the social dislocation – and to have entered calmer waters. It would need a catastrophe of major dimensions if an extremist party like the Nazis was to gain mass support. In 1929, with the sudden collapse of the economy in the wake of the Stock Exchange crash in New York, it came.

4

TOWARDS THE SEIZURE
OF POWER

THE GREAT DEPRESSION

I

'After long, planless wanderings from city to city,' an unemployed 21-year-old printer from Essen wrote in the autumn of 1932, 'my path took me to the port of Hamburg. But what a disappointment! Here was yet more misery, more unemployment than I had expected, and my hopes of getting work here were dashed. What should I do? Without relatives here, I had no desire to become a vagabond.' The young man was not in the end forced to join the ever-growing hordes of homeless men living on the streets and roads of Germany's towns and cities – anything between 200,000 and half a million of them, according to official estimates; he eventually found support in a voluntary labour scheme run by the Church.[1] But many more had no such luck. Unemployment destroyed people's self-respect and undermined their status, especially that of men, in a society where men's prestige, recognition, even identity itself derived above all from the job they did. Throughout the early 1930s, men could be seen on street corners, with placards round their necks: 'Looking for work of any kind'. Schoolchildren, when asked for their opinion on the matter by sociologists, often replied that the unemployed became socially degraded,

for the longer they are without work, the lazier they get, and they feel more and more humiliated, because they are always seeing other people who are decently dressed and they get annoyed because they want that too, and they become criminals . . . They still want to live! Older people often don't want that any more at all.[2]

Children were observed playing 'signing on' games, and when some of them were asked by an investigator in December 1932 to write short autobiographical essays, unemployment featured here too: 'My father has now been unemployed for over three years,' wrote one 14-year-old schoolgirl: 'We still used to believe earlier on that father would get a job again some time, but now even we children have abandoned all hope.'[3]

Prolonged unemployment varied in its impact on the individual. The young could be more optimistic about finding a job than the middle-aged. Despondency got worse the longer people went without a job. Interviews carried out in the summer of 1932 revealed far gloomier attitudes than surveys conducted eighteen months before. People put off marriage plans, married couples put off having children. Young men roamed the streets aimlessly, sat listlessly at home, spent the day playing cards, wandering through public parks, or riding endlessly round and round on the electric trains of Berlin's Circle Line.[4] In this situation, action often seemed better than inaction; boredom turned to frustration. Many unemployed men, even young boys and girls, tried to make a meagre living by hawking, busking, house-cleaning, street trading or any one of a number of traditional makeshifts of the economically marginal. Groups of children haunted Berlin's fashionable nightspots offering to 'look after' wealthy people's cars, a primitive form of protection racket practised in other, less innocuous forms by grown-ups, too. Informal hiking clubs and working-class youth groups easily became so-called 'wild cliques', gangs of young people who met in disused buildings, scavenged food, stole to make a living, fought with rival gangs, and frequently clashed with the police. Crime rates as such did not climb as spectacularly as they had done during the inflation, but there was a 24 per cent increase in arrests for theft in Berlin between 1929 and 1932 none the less. Prostitution, male and female, became more noticeable and more widespread, the product of Weimar's sexual tolerance as much as of its economic failure, shocking the respectable classes by its openness. At its lower end, hawking and street-selling shaded off into begging.[5] German society seemed to be descending into a morass of misery and criminality. In this situation, people began to grasp at political straws: anything, however extreme, seemed better than the hopeless mess they appeared to be in now.

How had this situation come about? Unemployment had already been high following the economic reforms that had brought the great inflation to an end in 1923. But by the early 1930s the situation had worsened immeasurably. The German economy's recovery after the inflation had been financed not least by heavy investment from the world's largest economy, the United States. German interest rates were high, and capital flowed in; but, crucially, reinvestment mainly took the form of short-term loans. German industry came to depend heavily on such funds in its drive to rationalize and mechanize. Firms such as Krupps and the United Steelworks borrowed very large sums of money. American enterprises invested directly in Germany, with Ford automobiles owning factories in Berlin and Cologne, and General Motors buying up the Opel car factory in Rüsselsheim, near Frankfurt, in 1929. German banks took out foreign loans to finance their own investments in German business.[6] This was an inherently precarious situation for German industry and banking, and at the end of the decade it turned to catastrophe.

In the course of 1928, all leading industrialized countries began to impose monetary restrictions in the face of a looming recession. The United States began cutting its foreign lending. Such measures were necessary to preserve gold reserves, the basis of financial stability in the era of the Gold Standard, when currency values everywhere were tied to the value of gold, as they had been in Germany since the stabilization had come into effect. As individual countries started drawing up the monetary drawbridges, industry began to suffer. There was virtually no growth in industrial production in Germany in 1928–9 and by the end of that winter unemployment had already reached nearly two and a half million. Investment slowed down sharply, possibly because companies were spending too much on wages and welfare payments, but more likely because there was simply a shortage of capital. The German government found it difficult to raise money by issuing bonds because investors knew what inflation had done to the bonds issued during the war. International markets had very little confidence in the German state to deal with the economic problems of the day. It soon became clear that their lack of faith was entirely justified.[7]

On 24 October 1929, 'Black Thursday', the unmistakeable signs of a business crisis in the United States caused a sudden outburst of panic selling on the New York Stock Exchange. Share prices, already overvalued in the eyes of some, began to plummet. Early the following week, on 29 October, 'Black Tuesday', panic selling set in again, worse by far than before; 16.4 million shares were sold, a record unsurpassed for the next four decades.[8] As frantic traders scrambled to sell before stocks fell even further in value, there were scenes of pandemonium on the floor of the New York Stock Exchange. But these dramatic days of disaster were only the most visible aspects of what turned out to be a prolonged and seemingly inexorable decline over the next three years. The *New York Times* index fell from a high of 452 points in September 1929 to 58 points by July 1932. On 29 October, ten billion dollars were wiped off the value of the major American companies, twice the amount of all money in circulation in the United States at the time and almost as much as America had spent on financing its part in the Great War. Company after company went bust. American demand for imports collapsed. Banks plunged into crisis as their investments disappeared. And as American banks saw their losses mount, they started calling in the short-term loans with which so much of German industry had been financing itself for the past five years.[9]

American banks began withdrawing their funds from Germany at the worst possible moment, precisely when the already flagging German economy needed a sharp stimulus to revive it. As they lost funds, German banks and businesses tried to redress the balance by taking out more short-term loans. The faster this happened, the less stable the economy began to look, and the more foreign and domestic asset-holders began to transfer capital outside the country.[10] Unable to finance production, firms began to cut back drastically. Industrial production, already stagnant, now began to fall with breathtaking speed. By 1932, it had dropped in value by 40 per cent of its 1929 level, a collapse matched only by Austria and Poland among European economies in its severity. Elsewhere, the fall was no more than a quarter; in Britain it was 11 per cent. With the withdrawal of funds and the collapse of businesses, banks began to get into difficulties. After a number of small banks failed in 1929–30, the two biggest Austrian banks went under and then, in July 1931, the big German banks began to come under pressure.[11] Business failures multiplied. An attempt to create a larger internal market by forging a customs union between Germany and Austria was squashed by international intervention, for the political motivation behind it – a step in the direction of the political union between the two countries that had been banned by the Treaty of Versailles – was obvious to everyone. Thrown back onto its own resources, the German economy plunged into deep depression. Unemployment rates now rose almost exponentially. With millions of people in the great cities unemployed, less money was available to spend on food, the already severe agricultural crisis deepened dramatically, and farmers were unable to escape foreclosure and bankruptcy as the banks called in the loans on which so many of them depended. Agricultural workers were thrown out of work as farms and estates went under, spreading unemployment to the countryside as well as the towns.[12]

By 1932, roughly one worker in three in Germany was registered as unemployed, with rates even higher in some heavy industrial areas such as Silesia or the Ruhr. This dwarfed all previous unemployment rates, even during the worst period of the stabilization cutbacks. Between 1928 and 1932, unemployment rose from 133,000 to 600,000 in Germany's biggest industrial centre, Berlin, from 32,000 to 135,000 in the trading city and seaport of Hamburg, and from 12,000 to 65,000 in the industrial town of Dortmund, in the Rhine-Ruhr area. Industry was obviously hardest hit; but white-collar workers lost their jobs, too, with over half a million out of work by 1932.[13] The rise was frighteningly swift. By the winter of 1930–31 there were already over five million unemployed, little more than a year after the onset of the Depression; the number rose to six million a year later. At the beginning of 1932, it was reported that the unemployed and their dependants made up about a fifth of the entire population of Germany, nearly thirteen million people, all told.[14] The true figure may have been even higher, since women who lost their jobs often failed to register themselves as unemployed.[15]

These terrifying figures told only part of the story. To begin with, many millions more workers only stayed in their jobs at a reduced rate, since employers cut hours and introduced short-time work in an attempt to adjust to the collapse in demand. Then many trained workers or apprentices had to accept menial and unskilled jobs because the jobs they were qualified for had disappeared. These were still the lucky ones. For what caused the real misery and desperation was the lengthy duration of the crisis, starting – at a time when unemployment was already fairly high – in October 1929 and showing no signs of abating for the next three years. Yet the benefits system, introduced a few years before, was designed only to cope with a far lower level of unemployment – a maximum of 800,000 compared to the six million who were without a job by 1932 – and provided relief only for a few months at most, not for three whole years and more. Things were made worse by the fact that the drastic fall in people's income caused a collapse in tax revenues. Many local authorities had also got into trouble because they had financed their own welfare and other schemes by taking out American loans themselves, and these were now being called in, too. Yet under the unemployment benefit system, the burden of supporting the long-term jobless after their period of insurance cover had run out shifted first to central government in the form of 'crisis benefits' then, after a further period of time, devolved onto local authorities in the form of 'welfare unemployment support'. Central government was unwilling to take the unpopular measures that would be required to bridge the gap. Employers felt that they could not increase contributions when their businesses were in trouble. Unions and workers did not want to see benefits cut. The problem seemed insoluble. And those who suffered were the unemployed, who saw their benefits repeatedly cut, or terminated altogether.[16]

II

As the Depression bit deeper, groups of men and gangs of boys could be seen haunting the streets, squares and parks of German towns and cities, lounging (so it seemed to the bourgeois man or woman unaccustomed to such a sight) threateningly about, a hint of potential violence and criminality always in the air. Even more menacing were the attempts, often successful, by the Communists to mobilize the unemployed for their own political ends. Communism was the party of the unemployed par excellence. Communist agitators recruited the young semi-criminals of the 'wild cliques'; they organized rent strikes in working-class districts where people were barely able to pay the rent anyway; they proclaimed 'red districts' like the Berlin proletarian quarter of Wedding, inspiring fear into non-Communists who dared to venture there, sometimes beating them up or threatening them with guns if they knew them to be associated with the brownshirts; they marked down certain pubs and bars as their own; they proselytized among children in working-class schools, politicized parents' associations and aroused the alarm of middle-class teachers, even those with left-wing convictions. For the Communists, the

class struggle passed from the workplace to the street and the neighbourhood as more and more people lost their jobs. Defending a proletarian
stronghold, by violent means if necessary, became a high priority of the
Communist paramilitary organization, the Red Front-Fighters' League.[17]

The Communists were frightening to the middle classes, not merely
because they made politically explicit the social threat posed by the
unemployed on the streets, but also because they grew rapidly in numbers
throughout the early 1930s. Their national membership shot up from
117,000 in 1929 to 360,000 in 1932 and their voting strength increased
from election to election. By 1932, in an area such as the north-west
German littoral, including Hamburg and its adjacent Prussian port of
Altona, fewer than 10 per cent of party members had a job. Roughly
three-quarters of the people who joined the party in October 1932 were
jobless.[18] Founding 'committees of the unemployed', the party staged
parades, demonstrations, 'hunger marches' and other street-based events
on an almost daily basis, often ending in prolonged clashes with the
police. No opportunity was lost to raise the political temperature in what
the party leaders increasingly thought was a terminal crisis of the capitalist
system.[19]

These developments drove an ever-deeper cleft between the Communists and the Social Democrats in the final years of the Republic. There
was already a legacy of bitterness and hatred bequeathed by the events
of 1918–19, when members of the Free Corps in the service of the Social
Democratic minister Gustav Noske had murdered prominent Communist
leaders, most notably Karl Liebknecht and Rosa Luxemburg. The murders were publicly recalled at every ceremony that the Communist Party
staged in their memory. To this was now added the divisive influence of
unemployment, as jobless Communists railed against Social Democrats
and trade unionists still in work, and Social Democrats grew increasingly
alarmed at the violent and disorderly elements who seemed to be flocking
to join the Communists. Further resentment was added by the habit of
Social Democratic union bosses of identifying Communists to employers
for redundancy, and the practice of employers sacking young, unmarried
workers before older, married ones, which again in many cases meant
members of the Communist Party losing their jobs. Rank-and-file Communists' ambivalence about the Social Democratic roots of the labour
movement led to a love–hate relationship with the party's 'older brother',

in which it was always desirable to make common cause, but only on the Communists' own terms.[20]

The roots of Communist extremism ran deep. Radical young workers, especially, felt betrayed by the Social Democrats, their hopes for a thoroughgoing revolution – stoked up by the older generation of Social Democratic activists – dashed just when they seemed on the point of being realized. The growing influence of the Russian model of a close-knit, conspiratorial organization helped cement a spirit of solidarity and cease-less activity amongst the most committed. A graphic account of the life of the committed Communist activist during the Weimar Republic was later provided by the memoirs of Richard Krebs, a sailor born in Bremen in 1904 into the family of a Social Democratic seafaring man. Krebs was present as an adolescent in the 1918–19 Revolution in his home town and witnessed the brutality of its suppression by the Free Corps. In Hamburg, Krebs fought in food riots and fell into the company of some Communists on the waterfront. Clashes with the police strengthened his hatred of them, and their bosses, the Social Democratic rulers of the city. Krebs later described how committed Communists would attend street demonstrations with pieces of lead piping in their belts and stones in their pockets, ready to pelt the police with. When mounted police charged, young activists in the Red Front-Fighters' League plunged their knives into the horses' legs, causing them to bolt. In this atmosphere of conflict and violence, a young tough like Krebs could feel himself at home, and he joined the Communist Party in May 1923, leafleting sailors on the waterfront during the day and attending basic political education courses in the evenings.[21]

His grasp of Marxist-Leninist theory was minimal, however:

I was class-conscious because class-consciousness had been a family tradition. I was proud to be a worker and I despised the bourgeois. My attitude to conven-tional respectability was a derisive one. I had a keen one-sided sense of justice which carried me away into an insane hatred of those I thought responsible for mass suffering and oppression. Policemen were enemies. God was a lie, invented by the rich to make the poor be content with their yoke, and only cowards resorted to prayer. Every employer was a hyena in human form, malevolent, eternally gluttonous, disloyal and pitiless. I believed that a man who fought alone could never win; men must stand together and fight together and make life better for all engaged in useful work. They must struggle with every means at their disposal, shying at no lawless deed as long as it would further the cause, giving no quarter until the revolution had triumphed.[22]

Imbued with this spirit of fiery commitment, Krebs led an armed detachment of Red Front-Fighters in the abortive Hamburg Revolution of October 1923, as Communists stormed a police station and erected barricades.[23] Not surprisingly, he felt it necessary to flee the scene after the failure of the uprising, and resumed his seafaring life. Escaping to Holland, then Belgium, he made contact with the local Communists. In no time his knowledge of English had led him to be commissioned by one of the Soviet secret agents who were present in many branches of the party – though probably not in so many as he later claimed – to spread Communist propaganda in California. Here he was ordered by the local party agents to kill a renegade who they believed had betrayed the party. Botching the attempt – deliberately, he claimed – Krebs was arrested and imprisoned in St Quentin. When he was released in the early 1930s, Krebs became a paid official of the seamen's section of the Comintern, the international organization of Communist parties across the world, directed from Moscow, and began acting as a courier for the party, taking money, leaflets and much else from one country to another, and then from one part of Germany to another.[24]

Richard Krebs's memoirs, which read like a thriller, portrayed a Communist Party bound together by iron ties of discipline and commitment, its every move dictated by the Soviet secret police agents from the GPU, successor to the Cheka, who ran every national organization from behind the scenes. The feeling that the Comintern was behind strikes, demonstrations and attempts at revolution in many parts of the world struck fear into many middle-class Germans, even though these activities were almost uniformly unsuccessful. The conspiratorial structure of the Comintern, and the undoubted presence of Soviet agents in the German party from the days of Karl Radek onwards, undoubtedly fuelled bourgeois anxieties. Yet Krebs painted too smooth a picture of the workings of the Comintern. In reality, strikes, labour unrest, even fights and riots often owed more to the temper of the 'Red Front-Fighters' on the ground than to any plans laid by Moscow and its agents. And men like Krebs were unusual. The turnover in Communist Party membership was more than

50 per cent in 1932 alone, meaning that hundreds of thousands of the unemployed had been close enough to the party to belong, at least for a while, but also that the party was often unable to hold the allegiance of most of its members for more than a few months at a time. Long-term members like Krebs constituted a hard and disciplined but relatively small core of activists, and the Red Front-Fighters' League became an increasingly professionalized force.[25] Words counted for a lot in such circumstances. Communist rhetoric had become a good deal more violent since the inauguration of the 'third period' by the Comintern leadership in Moscow in 1928. From this point onwards, the party directed its venom principally against the Social Democrats. Every German government in its eyes was 'fascist'; fascism was the political expression of capitalism; and the Social Democrats were 'social fascists' because they were the main supporters of capitalism, taking workers away from revolutionary commitment and reconciling them to Weimar's 'fascist' political system. Anyone in the leadership who tried to question this line was dismissed from his party post. Anything that would help overthrow the 'fascist' state and its Social Democratic supporters was welcome.[26]

The leader of the Communist Party of Germany at this time was the Hamburg trade union functionary Ernst Thälmann. There could be no doubt about his working-class credentials. Born in 1886, he had taken a variety of short-term jobs, including working in a fishmeal plant and driving wagons for a laundry, before being called up and serving on the Western Front in the First World War. A Social Democrat since 1903, Thälmann gravitated to the left wing of the party during the war and threw himself into political activity during the revolution of 1918, joining the 'revolutionary shop stewards' and becoming the leader of the Independent Social Democrats in Hamburg in 1919. Elected to the city parliament the same year, he joined the Communists when the Independents split up in 1922, and became a member of the national Central Committee. During this time he continued to work as a manual labourer, in tough trades such as ship-breaking. Uneducated, brawny, an instinctive revolutionary, Thälmann incorporated the Communist ideal of the revolutionary worker. He was anything but an intellectual; he won the sympathy of his proletarian audiences not least through his obvious struggles with complicated Marxist terminology; his speeches were passionate rather than carefully argued, but his audiences felt this showed his honesty and his sincerity. As a party leader and a professional politician in the mid- and late 1920s and early 1930s, Thälmann was often obliged to dress in collar and tie; but it became a set feature of his speeches that at some point he would take them off, to general and enthusiastic applause, and become a simple worker once more. His hatred of the generals and the bosses was palpable, his distrust of the Social Democrats obvious.

Like many rank-and-file Communists, Thälmann followed the party line laid down by the Comintern in Moscow as it changed this way and that, often in response to Stalin's tactical needs in his struggle to marginalize his intra-party rivals at home. Thälmann's faith in the revolution was absolute, and in consequence so too was his faith in the only revolutionary state in the world, the Soviet Union. Others in the party leadership may have been more subtle, more ruthless and more intelligent, like the Berlin party chief Walter Ulbricht; and the Politbureau and Central Committee, together with the Comintern in Moscow, may have been the arbiters of party policy and strategy; but Thälmann's personal standing and rhetorical gifts made him an indispensable asset to the party, which twice put him forward as its candidate in the elections for the post of Reich President, in 1925 and 1932. By the early 1930s, therefore, he was one of the best-known – and, to the middle and upper classes, one of the most feared – politicians in the land. He was more than a mere figurehead but less than a genuine leader, perhaps. But he remained the personal incorporation of German Communism in all its intransigence and ambition, driving the party towards the foundation of a 'Soviet Germany'.[27]

Led by a man such as Thälmann, the Communist Party thus seemed a looming threat of unparalleled dimensions to many middle-class Germans in the early 1930s. A Communist revolution seemed far from impossible. Even a sober and intelligent, conservative moderate like Victor Klemperer could ask himself in July 1931: 'Is the government going to fall? Is Hitler going to follow, or Communism?'[28] In many ways, however, Communist power was an illusion. The party's ideological animus against the Social Democrats doomed it to impotence. Its hostility to the Weimar Republic, based on its extremist condemnation of all its governments, even the 'Grand Coalition' led by Hermann Müller, as 'fascist', blinded it completely to the threat posed by Nazism to the Weimar political system. Its optimism about an imminent total and final collapse of capitalism had some plausibility in the dire economic circumstances of 1932. But in retrospect it was completely unfounded. Moreover, a party consisting largely of the unemployed was inevitably short of resources and weakened by the poverty and inconstancy of its members. So strapped for cash were Communist Party members that one Communist pub or bar after another had to close during the Depression, or passed into the hands of the Nazis. Between 1929 and 1933, per capita consumption of beer in Germany fell by 43 per cent, and in these circumstances the better-funded brownshirts moved in. What one historian has called a 'quasi-guerrilla warfare' was being conducted in the poorer quarters of Germany's big cities, and the Communists were slowly being beaten back into their heartlands in the slums and tenement districts by the continual brutal pressure of brownshirt violence. In this conflict, bourgeois sympathies were generally on the side of the Nazis, who, after all, were not threatening to destroy capitalism or create a 'Soviet Germany' if they came to power.[29]

III

Although unemployment was above all a working-class phenomenon, economic difficulties had been wearing down the morale of other social groups as well. Well before the onset of the Depression, for instance, the drive to reduce government expenditure in the retrenchment that had to underpin the currency stabilization after 1923 led to a wave of dismissals in the state sector. Between 1 October 1923 and 31 March 1924, 135,000 out of 826,000 civil servants, mostly in the state railway system, the post, telegraph and Reich printing services, had been sacked, along with 30,000 out of 61,000 white-collar workers and 232,000 out of 706,000 state-employed manual labourers.[30] A further wave of cuts came after 1929, with a cumulative reduction in civil service salaries of between 19 and 23 per cent between December 1930 and December 1932. Many civil servants at all levels were dismayed at the inability of their trade union representatives to stop the cuts. Their hostility to the government was obvious. Some drifted into the Nazi Party; many others were put off by the Nazis' open threat to purge the civil service if they came to power. Nevertheless, anxiety and disillusion with the Republic became widespread in the civil service as a result of the cuts.[31]

Many other middle-class occupations felt their economic and social position was under threat during the Weimar Republic. White-collar workers lost their jobs, or feared that they might, as banks and finance houses got into difficulties. Tourist agents, restaurants, retailing, mail-order firms, a huge variety of employers in the service sector ran into trouble as people's purchasing power declined. The Nazi Party, now equipped with its elaborate structure of specialist subdivisions, saw this, and began to direct its appeal to the professional and propertied middle classes. All of this was anathema to those Nazis who, like Otto Strasser, brother of the Party organizer Gregor, continued to emphasize the 'social-ist' aspect of National Socialism and felt that Hitler was betraying their ideals. Angered by the support given by Otto Strasser and his publishing house to left-wing causes such as strikes, Hitler summoned the leading men in the Party to a meeting in April 1930 and ranted against Strasser's views. As a way of trying to neutralize Otto Strasser's influence, he now appointed Goebbels Reich Propaganda Leader of the Party. But, to Goebbels's annoyance, Hitler repeatedly postponed decisive action, hoping that Otto Strasser's propaganda apparatus would still be of some use in the regional elections that took place in June 1930. Only after this, and Strasser's publication of an unflattering account of his row with Hitler earlier in the year, did he decide to purge the party of Otto Strasser and his supporters, who pre-empted this move by resigning on 4 July 1930. The split was a serious one. Observers held their breath to see if the Party would survive this exodus of its left wing. But things had changed markedly from the days when Goebbels and his friends had revived the Party in the Ruhr with socialist slogans. The dissidents' departure revealed that Strasser and his ideas had little support within the Party; even his brother Gregor disowned him. Otto Strasser vanished from serious politics, to spend the rest of his life in Germany, and, later, in exile, dreaming up small, sectarian organizations to propagate his views to tiny audiences of the like-minded.[32]

Having shed the last vestiges of 'socialism', Hitler now moved to build more bridges to the conservative right. In the autumn of 1931 he joined with the Nationalists in the so-called 'Harzburg Front', producing a joint declaration with Hugenberg at Bad Harzburg on 11 October stating their readiness to join together in ruling Prussia and the Reich. Though the Nazis emphasized their continued independence – Hitler, for example, refusing to review a march-past of the Steel Helmets – this marked a significant extension of the collaboration that had first taken place in the campaign against the Young Plan in 1929. At the same time, Hitler took serious steps to persuade industrialists that his Party posed no threat to them. His address to some 650 businessmen at the Industry Club in Düsseldorf in January 1932 appealed to his audience by denouncing Marxism as the source of Germany's ills – he did not refer to the Jews in the speech even once – and by emphasizing his belief in the importance of private property, hard work and proper rewards for the able and the enterprising. However, the solution to the economic woes of the moment, he said, was mainly political. Idealism, patriotism and national unity would create the basis for economic revival. These would be provided by the National Socialist movement, whose members sacrificed their time and money, and risked their lives day and night, in the struggle against the Communist threat.[33]

Delivered in a two-and-a-half-hour oration, these remarks were extremely general, and offered nothing concrete in the way of economic policies at all. They revealed Hitler's Social Darwinist view of the economy, in which struggle was the way to success. This cannot have impressed his knowledgeable audience very much. The senior industrialists were disappointed. The Nazis later declared that Hitler had won over big business at last. But there was little concrete evidence to show this was the case. Neither Hitler nor anyone else followed up the occasion with a fund-raising campaign amongst the captains of industry. Indeed, parts of the Nazi press continued to attack trusts and monopolies after the event, while other Nazis attempted to win votes in another quarter by championing workers' rights. When the Communist Party's newspapers portrayed the meeting in conspiratorial terms, as a demonstration of the fact that Nazism was the creature of big business, the Nazis went out of their way to deny this, printing sections of the speech as proof of Hitler's independence from capital.

The result of all this was that business proved not much more willing to finance the Nazi Party than it had been before. True, one or two individuals like Fritz Thyssen were enthusiastic, and provided funds to subsidize the extravagant tastes of leading Nazis such as Hermann Göring and Gregor Strasser. And, in broad terms, the speech was reassuring. When the time came, it made it that much easier for big business to come round to the support of the Nazi Party. But in January 1932 this still lay some way in the future. For the time being, the Nazi Party continued, as before, to finance its activities mainly through the voluntary contributions of its members, through entry fees to its meetings, through the income from its press and publications and through donations from small firms and businesses rather than large ones. The antisemitism which Hitler had so conspicuously forgotten to mention when talking to representatives of large industrial firms was far more likely to have an appeal in quarters such as these.[34] Nevertheless, Nazism now had a respectable face as well as a rough one, and was winning friends among the conservative and nationalist elites. As Germany plunged deeper into the Depression, growing numbers of middle-class citizens began to see in the youthful dynamism of the Nazi Party a possible way out of the situation. All would depend on whether the Weimar Republic's fragile democratic structures held up under the strain, and whether the Reich government could produce the right policies to stop them from collapsing altogether.

THE CRISIS OF DEMOCRACY

I

The Depression's first political victim was the Grand Coalition cabinet led by the Social Democrat Hermann Müller, one of the Republic's most stable and durable governments, in office since the elections of 1928. The Grand Coalition was a rare attempt to compromise between the ideological and social interests of the Social Democrats and the 'bourgeois' parties left of the Nationalists. It was held together mainly by its common effort to secure the Young Plan, an effort made in the teeth of bitter opposition from the Nationalists and the extreme right. Once the plan was agreed towards the end of 1929, there was little left to bind the parties to one another. Following the onset of the Depression in October 1929, the coalition's constituent parties failed to agree on how to tackle the rapidly worsening unemployment problem. Deprived of the moderating influence of its former leader Gustav Stresemann, who died in October 1929, the People's Party broke with the coalition over the Social Democrats' refusal to cut unemployment benefits, and the government was forced to tender its resignation on 27 March 1930.[35]

Although few realized it at the time, this marked the beginning of the end of Weimar democracy. From this point on, no government ruled with the support of a parliamentary majority in the Reichstag. Indeed, those who had President Hindenburg's ear saw the fall of the Grand Coalition as a chance to establish an authoritarian regime through the use of the Presidential power of rule by decree. Particularly influential in this respect was the German army, represented by the Minister of Defence, General Wilhelm Groener. His appointment in January 1928 to replace the Democrat politician Otto Gessler had signalled the liberation of the army from any kind of political control, and was cemented by the right of the army chief to report directly to the President instead of going through the cabinet. Despite the limitations placed by the Treaty of Versailles on its numbers and equipment, the army remained by a long way the most powerful, most disciplined and most heavily armed force in Germany. While civilian institutions of one kind and another, from the political parties to the legislature itself, crumbled, the army remained united. For most of the 1920s, since the debacle of the Kapp putsch, it had stayed quiet, focusing its attention on building up illegal equipment and manpower, but in the crisis of the early 1930s it saw its opportunity. Rearmament and the rebuilding of Germany as a great power could, in the view of men like Groener's political adviser, Colonel, later General Kurt von Schleicher, now be grasped by freeing the state from the shackles of parliamentary coalitions. And the more Germany descended into political chaos and extremist violence, the more pivotal the position of the army became. Already in the autumn of 1930 Groener was telling officers: 'Not a brick can be moved any more in the political process in Germany without the word of the army being thrown decisively onto the scales.'[36]

The army threw its weight into the political process initially in order to protect itself from budgetary cutbacks, which it successfully did. While all around it state institutions were having their budgets slashed, the army's stayed intact. But it still remained generally aloof from the Nazi Party. Older officers, schooled in the stern traditions of Prussian monarchism, were generally resistant to the populist appeal of radical nationalist politics. Even here, however, there were some who openly favoured the Nazis, like Colonel Ludwig Beck.[37] And younger officers were much more susceptible to Nazi propaganda. Already in 1929 a number of junior officers were engaging in discussions with the Nazis and debating the prospects for a 'national revolution'. The army leadership under Groener and Schleicher combated these tendencies vigorously, engaging in counter-propaganda and having the three ringleaders in the discussions arrested and put on trial in 1930 for preparing an act of high treason. The trial outraged other young officers, even those who were not inclined to collaborate with the Nazis. The army leadership, wrote one of them, had caved in to the 'Novemberists' and tried men whose only motivation was 'unselfish love of the fatherland'. Ninety per cent of the officers, he added, thought the same way.[38]

The trial was the occasion for a widely publicized speech delivered by Hitler from the witness box, where he was summoned by Hans Frank, the Nazi lawyer who was acting for one of the defendants. The Nazi Party, he declared, had no intention of committing high treason or subverting the army from within. Its intention was to come to power by legal means, and he had expelled those, like Otto Strasser, who had urged it to carry out a revolution. The Party would win a majority in an election and form a legitimately constituted government. At that point, he said, to cheers from the public benches, the real traitors, the 'November criminals' of 1918, would be put on trial, and 'heads will roll'. But until then, the Party would stay within the law. The court made Hitler swear to the veracity of his testimony on oath. 'Now we are strictly legal', Goebbels is reported to have said. Putzi Hanfstaengl, recently put in charge of Hitler's foreign press relations, made sure that the speech was reported around the world. He sold three articles by Hitler outlining the Nazi Party's aims and methods, in suitably bowdlerized form, to William Randolph Hearst, the American press baron, for 1,000 Reichsmarks each. The money enabled Hitler to use the Kaiserhof Hotel in the centre of Berlin as his headquarters whenever he stayed in the capital from then on. In Germany itself, Hitler's reassurances dispelled the fears of many middle-class Germans about the Nazi Party's intentions.[39]

The court was not impressed by Hitler, whom it reprimanded for abusing his position as a witness, and sentenced the young officers to eighteen months' imprisonment, cashiering two of them from the army.[40] The conservatism of the judiciary was almost bound to put the court on the side of the army. Still, the sentences did nothing to stop young army officers from continuing their flirtation with Nazism. Schleicher's attempts to counter such ideas, curb the radicalism of the younger officers and restore political discipline in the army, were less than effective, not least because he admitted openly to the officer corps that he sympathized with the 'national part' of the Nazis' programme, and particularly with 'the wave of indignation brought forth by the National Socialist movement against Bolshevism, treason, filth etc. Here', he said, 'the National Socialist campaign undoubtedly has extremely stirring effects.'[41] Sympathy with the Nazis meant co-operating with them, but such was the arrogance and self-importance of the army leaders that they still thought they could bend the Nazis to their will and enlist them as military and political auxiliaries, much as they had done with other paramilitary groups in the early 1920s. Time was to show how misguided this policy really was.

The newly prominent political position of the army found expression in the appointment by Hindenburg, acting above all on the advice of senior officers, including Schleicher, of Müller's successor as Chancellor. From the outset there was no attempt to appoint a government that would rest on the democratic support of the parties represented in the Reichstag. Instead, a 'cabinet of experts' would be put in place, with the intention of bypassing the Reichstag through the use of Hindenburg's power to rule by emergency decree. Of course, the scope of rule by decree was limited, and many measures, above all the budget, still had to be approved by the Reichstag. Steps were taken to ensure that this did not appear as the inauguration of an authoritarian regime. The new cabinet included such well-known Reichstag politicians as Josef Wirth, a former Reich Chancellor, for the Centre Party, Hermann Dietrich, for the Democrats (renamed the State Party in July 1930), Martin Schiele, for the Nationalists, Julius Curtius, for the People's Party, and Viktor Bredt, for the small Economy Party. But it did not include the Social Democrats, to whom Hindenburg and his advisers were unwilling to entrust the power of ruling by decree. Without the Social Democrats it had no parliamentary majority. But this did not seem to matter any more.

The new government was led by a man whose appointment as Reich Chancellor proved in retrospect to be a fatal choice. Superficially, the President's nomination of Heinrich Brüning, born in 1885, as Reich Chancellor was defensible in democratic terms. As floor leader of the Centre Party's deputies in the Reichstag, he represented the political force that more than any other had been the mainstay of parliamentary democracy in the Weimar Republic. But already by the time of his appointment the Centre, under the influence of its new leader Prelate Ludwig Kaas, was moving towards a more authoritarian position, more narrowly concerned with defending the interests of the Catholic Church. Moreover, Brüning himself was at best a fair-weather friend of Weimar democracy. A former army officer, he had been shocked by the November Revolution, and remained a staunch monarchist all his life. In his memoirs, indeed, he portrayed the restoration of the monarchy as his main purpose after becoming Chancellor. Yet in doing so he was probably lending retrospective coherence to a political career that was dominated, like that of so many politicians, by short-term imperatives.[42] Despite his inner conviction that a return to the Bismarckian system would be best for all, he had no detailed plan to restore the monarchy, let alone bring back the Kaiser. Nevertheless, his instincts were authoritarian at heart.[43] He planned to reform the constitution by reducing the power of the Reichstag and combining the offices of Reich Chancellor and Prussian Minister-President in his own person, thus removing the Social Democrats from their dominance of Germany's largest state. Brüning did not have sufficient backing from Hindenburg to put this idea into effect, but it remained on the table, ready for anyone to use who did. Brüning also began to restrict democratic rights and civil liberties.[44] In March 1931, for instance, he introduced sharp curbs on the freedom of the press, especially when it published criticisms of his own policies. By mid-July the liberal *Berlin Daily News-Sheet* (*Berliner Tageblatt*) was estimating that up to a hundred newspaper editions were being banned every month across the country. By 1932 the Communist newspaper *The Red Flag* was being banned on more than one day in three. Press freedom was seriously compromised long before the Nazis came to power.[45]

In effect, Brüning thus began the dismantling of democratic and civil freedoms that was to be pursued with such vigour under the Nazis. Some, indeed, have argued that his much-criticized economic policy during the crisis was in part designed to weaken the trade unions and the Social Democrats, two of the main forces that kept Weimar democracy afloat.[46] To be sure, Brüning was not a dictator and his appointment did not mark the end of Weimar democracy. Brüning had not reached his position in the Centre Party without becoming adept at political calculation and manoeuvre, or skilled in constructing political coalitions and alliances. He had won himself a considerable reputation as a specialist on finance and taxation, and a man who knew his way around in these often rather technical areas was clearly needed at the helm in 1930. But the room for manoeuvre was becoming rapidly narrower after 1930, not least because of his own catastrophic political miscalculations. And even his staunchest defenders have never maintained that he was a charismatic or inspiring leader. Austere in appearance, secretive, inscrutable, given to taking decisions without sufficient consultation, denied the gift of rhetoric, Brüning was not the man to win mass support from an electorate increasingly appalled at the economic chaos and political violence that were plunging the country into a crisis whose dimensions beggared even those of 1923.[47]

II

Brüning's major task was to deal with the rapidly deteriorating economic situation. He chose to do this by radically deflationary measures, above all by cutting government expenditure. Government revenues were sinking fast, and the possibilities of borrowing to meet the state's obligations were virtually non-existent. Moreover, while Germany's currency had been stabilized after the great inflation of 1923 by tying it to the value of gold, it was by no means clear that it had been stabilized at the right level. The values arrived at were regarded as sacrosanct, however, so that the only way of dealing with a currency that became overvalued, because its reserves were being drained by a balance of payments deficit, was to cut prices and wages and raise interest rates at home.[48] Finally, reparations still loomed over the German economic scene, even though they had been rescheduled and in effect substantially reduced by the Young Plan in the summer of 1930. Brüning hoped to cut German domestic prices by reducing demand, and so make exports more competitive on the international market, a policy by no means unwelcome to the export manufacturers who were among his strongest supporters.[49] This was not a very realistic policy at a time when world demand had slumped to an unprecedented degree.

Cuts in government expenditure came first. A series of measures, culminating in emergency decrees promulgated on 5 June and 6 October 1931, reduced unemployment benefits in a variety of ways, restricted the period for which they could be claimed, and imposed means-testing in an increasing number of cases. The long-term unemployed thus saw their standard of living being steadily reduced as they went from unemployment insurance pay onto state-financed crisis benefits, then local authority welfare support and finally no support at all. By late 1932 there were only 618,000 people left on unemployment insurance pay, 1,230,000 on crisis benefits, 2,500,000 on welfare support and over a million whose period of joblessness had run through the time-limits now set on all of these and so lacked any kind of regular income.[50] Whatever Brüning's wider aims might have been, growing poverty made the economic situation worse. People who were barely in a situation to supply themselves and their families with the basic necessities of life were hardly going to spend enough money to stimulate industry and the service sector into recovery. Moreover, fear of inflation was such that even without the international agreements (such as the Young Plan) that depended on maintaining the value of the Reichsmark, devaluation (the quickest way to boost exports) would have been politically extremely hazardous. In any case, Brüning refused to devalue, because he wanted to demonstrate to the international community that reparations were causing real misery and suffering in Germany.[51]

In the summer of 1931, however, the situation changed. A fresh crisis hit the economy as the flight of capital reached new heights, leading to the collapse of the Darmstadt and National (or Danat) Bank, heavily dependent on foreign loans, on 13 July, and threatening a collapse of credit more generally.[52] The impossibility of baling out the German government with foreign loans had become starkly clear in any case: one calculation estimated that the amount required to cover the budgetary deficit in Germany would be greater than the entire gold reserves of the United States. International financial co-operation had been made effectively impossible by the rigidities imposed by the Gold Standard. Brüning and his advisers saw no alternative but to put a stop on the convertibility of the Reichsmark, a step they had been so far reluctant to take because of their fear that it would cause inflation. From this point onwards, therefore, the Reichsmark could no longer be exchanged for foreign currency.[53]

This rendered the Gold Standard meaningless as far as Germany was concerned, allowing a more flexible approach to monetary policy, and permitting an expansion of the currency supply that could, theoretically at least, ease the government's financial situation and allow it to begin reflating the economy through job-creation schemes.[54] Fatally, however, Brüning refused to take such a step, because he was nervous that printing money that was not tied to the value of gold would cause inflation. Of all the long-term effects of the German inflation, this was probably the most disastrous. But it was not the only reason why Brüning persisted with his deflationary policies long after feasible alternatives had become available. For, crucially, he also hoped to use the continuing high unemployment rate to complete his dismantling of the Weimar welfare state, reduce the influence of labour and thus weaken the opposition to the plans he was now concocting to reform the constitution in an authoritarian, restorationist direction.[55]

The bank crisis put into Brüning's hands another card that he was unwilling to use. In view of the flight of foreign funds from the German economy in the spring and early summer of 1931, reparations payments, along with other international capital movements, were suspended by the Hoover Moratorium, issued on 20 June 1931. This removed another political constraint on the freedom of manoeuvre of the German government. Up to now, almost any economic policy it had undertaken – such as increasing taxes, or boosting government revenue in some other way – had run the risk of being accused by the far right of contributing to the hated reparations payments. This was now no longer the case. Yet for Brüning this was not enough. It was still possible, he thought, that once the crisis was over the Moratorium would be lifted and demands for reparations payments would resume.[56] So he did nothing, even though the means of escape were now there and voices were already being raised in public in favour of stimulating demand through government-funded job-creation schemes.[57]

Brüning's deflationary stance could not be shaken. The events of 1931 made the Depression even worse than before. And it showed no signs of ending. Brüning himself told people that he expected it to last until 1935. This was a prospect that many, and not just amongst the unemployed and the destitute, found too appalling to contemplate.[58] Soon Brüning, who issued another emergency decree on 8 December requiring wages to be reduced to their 1927 level and ordering a reduction of various prices, was being called 'the Hunger Chancellor'.[59] Satirists compared him to the mass-murderer of the early 1920s, Fritz Haarmann, whose habit of chopping up the bodies of his victims was the occasion of a nursery-rhyme used to frighten small children and still repeated in Germany today:

> Wait a while and just you'll see,
> And Brüning will come up to you
> With the ninth emergency decree
> And make mincemeat out of you.[60]

There never was a ninth emergency decree; but even after promulgating only four of them, Brüning found himself the most unpopular Chancellor there had yet been in the Weimar Republic.[61]

III

Like many traditional conservatives, Brüning wanted to curb or emasculate the rabid radicalism of the extreme right, and at times showed some courage in attempting to do so. Like them, however, he also underestimated its power and influence. His adherence to what he regarded as Prussian virtues of piety, objectivity, non-partisanship and selfless service to the state derived not least from the patriotic traditions of the Centre Party since Bismarck's attack on the supposed national disloyalty of the Catholics in the 1870s. It gave him a lasting distrust of party politics, and an instinctive faith in the political reliability of a Prussian political icon such as President Hindenburg – a faith that turned out in the end to be completely misplaced.[62] Moreover, this was not Brüning's only fateful miscalculation. From the outset, he used the threat of wielding Hindenburg's power under Article 25 of the constitution to call new Reichstag elections to bring the Social Democrats, the major oppositional force, into line. When they joined with the Nationalists and the Communists in refusing to approve a starkly deflationary budget, he had no hesitation in putting this threat into action and brought about a dissolution of the Reichstag. Ignoring the evidence of local and regional elections that had brought massive gains for the Nazis, the Social Democrats assumed that voters would continue to act along well-worn lines, and had every hope of a result that would provide sufficient support for their way of thinking. Like many Germans, Brüning and his political opponents on the left still found it impossible to take the Nazis' extremist rhetoric and bullying tactics on the street as anything other than evidence of their inevitable political marginality. They did not conform to the accepted rules of politics, so they could not expect to be successful.[63]

The election campaign was fought in an atmosphere of feverish, unprecedented excitement. Goebbels and the Nazi Party organization pulled out all the stops. In speech after speech, attended by crowds of up to 20,000 in the larger cities, Hitler ranted against the iniquities of the

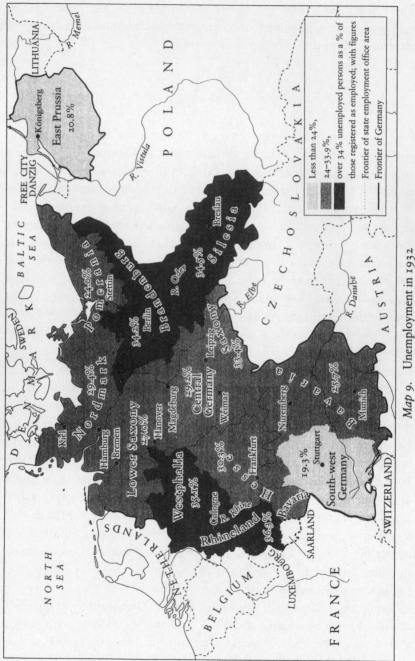

Map 9. Unemployment in 1932

Weimar Republic, its fatal internal divisions, its multiplicity of warring factions and self-interested parties, its economic failure, its delivery of national humiliation. In place of all this, he shouted, democracy would be overcome, the authority of the individual personality reasserted. The revolutionaries of 1918, the profiteers of 1923, the traitorous supporters of the Young Plan, the Social Democratic placemen in the civil service ('revolutionary parasites') would all be purged. Hitler and his Party offered a vague but powerful rhetorical vision of a Germany united and strong, a movement that transcended social boundaries and overcame social conflict, a racial community of all Germans working together, a new Reich that would rebuild Germany's economic strength and restore the nation to its rightful place in the world. This was a message that had a powerful appeal to many who looked nostalgically back to the Reich created by Bismarck, and dreamed of a new leader who would resurrect Germany's lost glory. It was a message that summed up everything that many people felt was wrong with the Republic, and gave them the opportunity to register the profundity of their disillusion with it by voting for a movement that was its opposite in every respect.

Below this very general level, the Nazi propaganda apparatus skilfully targeted specific groups in the German electorate, giving campaigners training in addressing different kinds of audience, advertising meetings extensively in advance, providing topics for particular venues and picking the speaker to suit the occasion. Sometimes local non-Nazis and prominent sympathizers from conservative backgrounds shared the platform with the main Nazi speaker. The elaborate organization of the Party's subdivisions recognized the growing divisions of German society into competing interest-groups in the course of the Depression and tailored their message to their particular constituency. Antisemitic slogans would be used when addressing groups to whom they might have an appeal; where they were clearly not working, they were abandoned. The Nazis adapted according to the response they received; they paid close attention to their audiences, producing a whole range of posters and leaflets designed to win over different parts of the electorate. They put on film shows, rallies, songs, brass bands, demonstrations and parades. The campaign was masterminded by the Reich Propaganda Leader, Joseph Goebbels. His propaganda headquarters in Munich sent out a constant stream of directives to local and regional Party sections, often providing

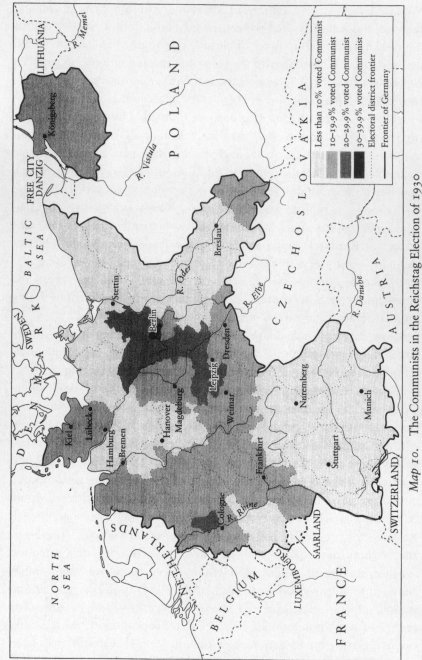

Map 10. The Communists in the Reichstag Election of 1930

fresh slogans and fresh material for the campaign. As the campaign reached its climax, the Nazis, driven by a degree of commitment that exceeded even that of the Communists, outdid all other parties in their constant, frenetic activism and the intensity of their propaganda effort.[64]

The results of the Reichstag elections of September 1930 came as a shock to almost everyone, and delivered a seismic and in many ways decisive blow to the political system of the Weimar Republic. True, the Centre Party, the major electoral force behind the Brüning government, could feel moderately pleased at boosting its vote from 3.7 million to 4.1 million, thereby increasing its seats in the Reichstag from 62 to 68. Brüning's main opponents, the Social Democrats, lost ten seats, declining from 153 to 143, but still remained the largest party in the legislature. To this extent the election gave a very mild fillip to Brüning. However, the centrist and right-wing parties on which Brüning might possibly hope to build his government suffered catastrophic losses, with the Nationalists declining from 73 seats to 41, the People's Party from 45 to 31, the Economy Party (a recently founded middle-class special-interest group) from 31 to 23, and the State Party from 25 to 20. The parties represented in Brüning's first cabinet thus lost 53 out of 236 seats, bringing their total down to 183. And not even all of these were solidly behind the Chancellor: the People's Party was deeply divided over whether to support him, and the Nationalist leader Alfred Hugenberg was bitterly critical of the Brüning government and forced out of his party the moderate Reichstag deputies who still wanted to give it a chance. After September 1930 Hugenberg was virtually unopposed amongst the Nationalists in his policy of trying to co-operate with the National Socialists in a drive to bring down the Republic and replace the Reich Chancellor with someone even further to the right.[65]

As this suggests, the political forces which could be expected to offer incessant and unremitting opposition to the Brüning government and all its works, in the belief that this would hasten the Republic's demise, received a substantial boost from the 1930 elections. The Communists, buoyed up by their popularity among the unemployed, increased their mandate from 54 seats to 77. But the biggest shock was the increase in the Nazi vote. Only 0.8 million people had supported the National Socialists in the Reichstag election of 1928, giving the party a mere 12 seats in the national legislature. Now, in September 1930, their votes

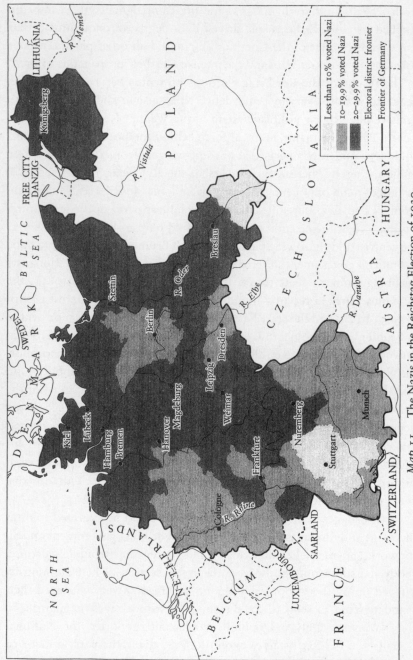

Map 11.   The Nazis in the Reichstag Election of 1930

increased to 6.4 million, and no fewer than 107 Nazi deputies took up their seats in the Reichstag. 'Fantastic,' gloated Joseph Goebbels in his diary on 15 September 1930, '. . . an unbelievable advance . . . I hadn't expected that.'[66] Sympathetic newspapers registered the result as a 'world sensation' that announced a new phase of Germany's history. Only the Communists dismissed it as a flash in the pan ('what's coming next can only be decline and fall').[67]

Yet the Nazis' gains reflected deep-seated anxieties in many parts of the electorate. In some rural constituencies in the north the Nazi vote amounted to a landslide: 68 per cent in Wiefelstede in the Weser-Ems constituency, 57 per cent in Brünen in the Düsseldorf West constituency, 62 per cent in Schwesing in Schleswig-Holstein.[68] To some extent, Brüning might have seen this coming, since elections for state legislatures and town councils all over Germany had been registering strong gains for the Nazis since 1928. His chances of getting what he wanted from the elections of 1930 were therefore very small even before the campaign started. Yet the triumph of the Nazis in the Reichstag election was much greater than anyone had anticipated. In many places, indeed, it far outran the impact of Nazi propaganda, and the Party scored votes of 25 to 28 per cent in remote rural areas of the Protestant north to which its organizational effort had barely penetrated.[69]

How can this dramatic success be explained? The Nazis were seen, particularly by Marxists of various hues, as the representatives of the lower middle classes, but in this election they had clearly burst the bounds of this particular constituency and succeeded in winning the support not only of white-collar workers, shopkeepers, small businessmen, farmers and the like, but also of many voters further up the social scale, in the professional, mercantile and industrial bourgeoisie.[70] It was above all the Nazis who profited from the increasingly overheated political atmosphere of the early 1930s, as more and more people who had not previously voted began to flock to the polls. Roughly a quarter of those who voted Nazi in 1930 had not voted before. Many of these were young, first-time voters, who belonged to the large birth-cohorts of the pre-1914 years. Yet these electors do not seem to have voted disproportionately for the Nazis; the Party's appeal, in fact, was particularly strong amongst the older generation, who evidently no longer considered the Nationalists vigorous enough to destroy the hated Republic. Roughly a third of the

Nationalist voters of 1928 voted for the Nazis in 1930, a quarter of the Democratic and People's Party voters, and even a tenth of Social Democratic voters.[71]

The Nazis did particularly well among women, whose previous tendency to stay away from the polls sharply diminished in 1930, an important change since there were many more female voters than male as a result both of military casualties in the First World War and of the growing tendency of women to live longer than men. In the city of Cologne, for instance, the percentage poll amongst women jumped from an average of 53 per cent in 1924 to 69 per cent in 1930; in the East Prussian commune of Ragnitz, from 62 per cent to 73 per cent. Their previous avoidance of radical parties such as the Nazis disappeared, though their over-proportional support for the Centre largely remained. For all the speculation of contemporaries, and some later historians, about the special reasons why women might have voted Nazi – ranging from their supposed greater susceptibility to the emotional appeal of the Party's propaganda to their alleged disillusion with the Republic for failing to bring them equality – the fact is that there is no indication that they cast their votes for any different reasons than those which led men to support the Party. But cast them they now did.[72]

Whether its voters were men or women, young or old, the Nazi Party did particularly well in Protestant north Germany, east of the Elbe, and much less well in the Catholic south and west. It attracted voters in the countryside but not to the same degree in urban-industrial areas. In some parts of Schleswig-Holstein and Oldenburg, deeply rural areas in the Protestant north, it won over 50 per cent of the vote. Yet, contrary to a widespread contemporary view, the Nazis did not do any better in small towns than in large ones overall; the effects of religious allegiance, which meant that a Protestant voter was twice as likely to support the Nazis as a Catholic one, were far more important in rural areas, perhaps because the influence of the clergy was greater in the countryside and secularization had made greater progress in the towns, whatever their size. Some Catholics did vote Nazi, but the great majority stayed loyal to the Centre Party in 1930, locked into its cultural milieu and insulated against the appeal of the radical right by its patent hostility by this time to democracy, the Jews and the modern world.[73]

The Social Democrats, too, as we have seen, together with the Communists, proved relatively resilient in the face of the Nazis' electoral challenge in 1930. But this does not mean that the Nazis completely failed to win any working-class votes. Wage-earning manual labourers and their spouses made up nearly half the electorate in Germany, one of the world's most advanced industrial societies, while the two working-class parties combined regularly secured just under a third of the vote in Weimar elections, so a significant number of workers and their spouses must have voted for other parties on a regular basis. In such a large and varied social group, these included many Catholic workers, workers in small, often paternalistically managed firms, manual labourers in the state sector (the railways, the postal service and so on) and employees who were not unionized (including especially female manual workers). Rural labourers in Protestant areas with a relatively small proportion of manual labourers proved particularly susceptible to the Nazi appeal, though workers on the great landed estates tended to stick with the Social Democrats. The Nazi propaganda effort, indeed, was directed in particular at workers, borrowing images and slogans from the Social Democrats, attacking 'reaction' as well as 'Marxism', and presenting the Party as heir to Germany's socialist tradition. It failed to make much more than a small dent in the Social Democratic and Communist vote, but still exerted a sufficiently strong appeal to previously non-committed workers to ensure that some 27 per cent of Nazi voters in September 1930 were manual labourers.[74]

Since, as we have seen, the working class constituted nearly half the electorate, and the Nazi Party obtained just over 18 per cent of the vote, this still meant that the Party was less attractive to workers than to members of other social classes, and left the great majority of working-class electors voting for other parties. Where the Social Democratic or Communist tradition was strong, unionization high, and labour-movement culture active and well supported, the cohesive power of the socialist milieu generally proved resistant to the Nazis' appeal.[75] The Nazis, in other words, reached parts of the working class that the traditional left-wing parties failed to reach.[76] Social and cultural factors accounted for their appeal, rather than economic ones; for the unemployed voted Communist, not Nazi. Workers who were still in jobs in September 1930 were fearful of the future, and if they were not insulated by a strong labour movement milieu, they frequently turned to the Nazis to defend themselves against the looming threat of the Communist Party.[77]

While the Nazis directed their propaganda particularly at workers, they were surprisingly neglectful of white-collar employees, who may well have resented Nazi attacks on many of the institutions for which they worked, from finance houses to department stores. Many female employees in low-paid jobs belonged to the working-class political milieu by origin or marriage and so voted Social Democrat, like a good proportion of male white-collar workers, and not just those who were employed by the unions and other labour movement institutions. White-collar workers in the private sector were also one of the groups least affected by the Depression. Despite a widespread contemporary belief to the contrary, therefore, white-collar workers, like manual labourers, were somewhat under-represented among the ranks of Nazi voters in 1930. By contrast, civil servants were over-represented, perhaps reflecting the fact that government cutbacks had put hundreds of thousands of them out of work and reduced the income of many more to the level of a skilled manual labourer or below. The Nazis' appeal to the self-employed, particularly in Protestant rural areas, was even greater; many of these, of course, were small farmers.[78]

The Nazi Party had established itself with startling suddenness in September 1930 as a catch-all party of social protest, appealing to a greater or lesser degree to virtually every social group in the land. Even more than the Centre Party, it succeeded in transcending social boundaries and uniting highly disparate social groups on the basis of a common ideology, above all but not exclusively within the Protestant majority community, as no other party in Germany had managed to do before. Already weakened in the aftermath of the inflation, the bourgeois parties, liberal and conservative, proved unable to retain their support in the face of the economic catastrophe that had broken over Germany towards the end of 1929. Middle-class voters, still repelled by the Nazis' violence and extremism, turned to splinter-groups of the right in even greater numbers than they had already done in 1924 and 1928, increasing their representation in the Reichstag from 20 seats to 55, but substantial numbers also flocked to the Nazi banner in September 1930, joining with members of other social groups, including farmers, various kinds of workers, civil servants, first-time voters (including many women) and voters from older age groups, to expand the Nazi vote massively in a powerful expression of their dissatisfaction, resentment and fear.[79]

In the increasingly desperate situation of 1930, the Nazis managed to project an image of strong, decisive action, dynamism, energy and youth that wholly eluded the propaganda efforts of the other political parties, with the partial exception of the Communists. The cult of leadership which they created around Hitler could not be matched by comparable efforts by other parties to project their leaders as the Bismarcks of the future. All this was achieved through powerful, simple slogans and images, frenetic, manic activity, marches, rallies, demonstrations, speeches, posters, placards and the like, which underlined the Nazis' claim to be far more than a political party: they were a *movement*, sweeping up the German people and carrying them unstoppably to a better future. What the Nazis did not offer, however, were concrete solutions to Germany's problems, least of all in the area where they were most needed, in economy and society. More strikingly still, the public disorder which loomed so large in the minds of the respectable middle classes in 1930, and which the Nazis promised to end through the creation of a tough, authoritarian state, was to a considerable extent of their own making. Many people evidently failed to realize this, blaming the Communists instead, and seeing in the violence of the brown-uniformed Nazi stormtroopers on the streets a justified, or at least understandable reaction to the violence and aggression of the Red Front-Fighters' League.

Voters were not really looking for anything very concrete from the Nazi Party in 1930. They were, instead, protesting against the failure of the Weimar Republic. Many of them, too, particularly in rural areas, small towns, small workshops, culturally conservative families, older age groups, or the middle-class nationalist political milieu, may have been registering their alienation from the cultural and political modernity for which the Republic stood, despite the modern image which the Nazis projected in many respects. The vagueness of the Nazi programme, its symbolic mixture of old and new, its eclectic, often inconsistent character, to a large extent allowed people to read into it what they wanted to and edit out anything they might have found disturbing. Many middle-class voters coped with Nazi violence and thuggery on the streets by writing it off as the product of excessive youthful ardour and energy. But it was far more than that, as they were soon to discover for themselves.[80]

THE VICTORY OF VIOLENCE

I

The young brownshirt activist Horst Wessel had made himself thoroughly hated by Berlin's Communist paramilitaries by 1930. Idealistic, intelligent and well educated, he had caught the attention of Joseph Goebbels, who had sent him to study the well-organized Nazi youth movement in Vienna in the first half of 1928. Back in Berlin, Wessel had quickly risen to a position of local prominence in the brownshirt organization in the Friedrichshain district, where he led a 'storm' or branch of the Nazi paramilitaries. He proceeded to unleash a particularly energetic and provocative campaign on the streets, including a brownshirt attack on the local Communist Party headquarters, in which four Communist workers were seriously injured. Heinz Neumann, known as the Goebbels of the Communist Party, and Berlin editor of the Communist daily, *The Red Flag*, responded with a new slogan issued to party cadres: 'Beat the fascists wherever you find them!'[81]

It was in this atmosphere that Wessel's landlady, the widow of a Communist, went to a tavern in the area on 14 January 1930 to ask for help in dealing with her tenant, who, she said, had not only refused to pay rent for his live-in girlfriend but had also responded to the landlady's demands by threatening her with violence. Whether or not this was true was another matter, for there was evidence that the real cause of the dispute was her attempt to raise Wessel's rent. The landlady was also afraid that, if the girlfriend did not move out, she would lose her legal right to the flat, which she did not own, but rented herself, not least because the girlfriend was a prostitute (whether or not she was still working subsequently became the subject of heated and somewhat prurient debate). The key factor here was the widow's connection to the Communist Party. Despite their disapproval of the landlady's insistence at the time of her husband's death on giving him a church funeral, the Communists decided to help her deal with her tenant. Only the previous day, they claimed, a local Communist had been shot in a fight with the brownshirts. The dispute offered an ideal opportunity to get even. Conscious of the likelihood that Wessel would be armed, they sent to a nearby tavern for a well-known local tough, Ali Höhler, who was known to possess a gun, to provide the muscle in a punitive expedition to Wessel's flat. Höhler was not only a member of the neighbouring branch of the Red Front-Fighters' League, but also had convictions for petty crimes, perjury and pimping. A member of one of Berlin's organized crime syndicates, he illustrated the connections between Communism and criminality that were likely to be forged at a time when the party based itself in the poor districts and 'criminal quarters' of Germany's big cities. Together with the Communist Erwin Rückert, Höhler climbed the stairs to Wessel's flat, while the others stood watch outside. As Wessel opened the door, Höhler opened fire. Wessel fell, badly wounded in the head, and lingered on in hospital for a few weeks before he finally died from his injury on 23 February.[82]

When the Communists mounted a hurried propaganda campaign to depict Wessel as a pimp and Höhler's deed as part of an underworld dispute unconnected with the Red Front-Fighters' League, Goebbels went into overdrive to present him as a political martyr. He interviewed Wessel's mother, and extracted from her a portrait of her son as an idealist who had rescued his girlfriend from a life of prostitution and sacrificed himself out of missionary zeal for the cause of the Fatherland. The Communists, by contrast, Goebbels trumpeted, had shown their true colours by enrolling a common criminal like Höhler in their ranks. Wessel was hardly cold in his grave before Goebbels began work on blowing his memory up into a full-scale cult. Innumerable articles in the Nazi press all over the country praised him as a 'martyr for the Third Reich'. A solemn funeral procession was staged – it would have been much bigger but for police restrictions on its size – and watched, so Goebbels claimed, by up to 30,000 people lining the streets on the way to the church. Chants, attacks and attempts at disruption by the Red Front-Fighters' League led to wild and violent scenes on the fringes of the ceremony. At the graveside, while Göring, Prince August Wilhelm of Prussia and various other dignitaries looked on, Goebbels praised Wessel in terms that deliberately recalled Christ's sacrifice for humankind – 'Through sacrifice to redemption'. 'Wherever Germany is,' he declared, 'you are there too, Horst Wessel!' Then a choir of stormtroopers sang some verses that Wessel himself had written a few months earlier:

> The flag's held high! The ranks are tightly closed!
> SA men march with firm courageous tread.
> Together with us, marching in our ranks in spirit, are those
> Comrades Red Front and Reaction shot dead!
>
> Clear the streets for the brown battalions,
> Clear the streets for the Storm Division man!
> The swastika's already gazed on full of hope by millions.
> The day for freedom and bread is at hand!
>
> The last time now there sounds the call to meet!
> For struggle we are standing all prepared at last!
> Soon Hitler flags will flutter over every street.
> Our servitude will very soon be past![83]

The song had already gained some currency in the movement, but Goebbels now publicized it far and wide, prophesying that it would soon be sung by schoolchildren, workers, soldiers, everyone. He was right. Before the year was over, it had been published, issued on a gramophone record and turned into the official anthem of the Nazi Party. After 1933 it became in effect the national battle hymn of the Third Reich, alongside the old-established *Deutschland, Deutschland über Alles* ('Germany, Germany before all').[84] Wessel became the object of something like a secular religious cult propagated by the Nazis, celebrated in film, and commemorated in countless ceremonies, memorials and sites of pilgrimage.

That such an open celebration of brutal physical force could become the battle hymn of the Nazi Party speaks volumes for the central role that violence played in its quest for power. Cynically exploited for publicity purposes by manipulative propagandists like Goebbels, it became a way of life for the ordinary young brownshirt like Wessel, as it was for the young unemployed workers of the Red Front-Fighters' League. Other songs were more explicit still, such as the popular 'Song of the Storm Columns', which was chanted by marching brownshirts on the streets of Berlin from 1928 onwards:

> We are the Storm Columns, we put ourselves about,
> We are the foremost ranks, courageous in a fight.
> With sweating brows from work, our stomachs without food!
> Our calloused, sooty hands our rifles firmly hold.
>
> So stand the Storm Columns, for racial fight prepared.
> Only when Jews bleed, are we liberated.
> No more negotiation; it's no help, not even slight:
> Beside our Adolf Hitler we're courageous in a fight.
>
> Long live our Adolf Hitler! We're already marching on.
> We're storming in the name of German revolution.
> Leap onto the barricades! Defeat us only death can.
> We're Storm Columns of Hitler's dictatorship of one man.[85]

This kind of aggression found its outlet in constant clashes with rival paramilitaries on the streets. In the middle period of the Republic, beginning in 1924, all sides did indeed draw back from political violence on the scale of the January uprising of 1919, the Ruhr civil war of 1920 or the multiple conflicts of 1923, but if they put away their machine guns, it was only to replace them with rubber truncheons and knuckledusters. Even in the relatively stable years of 1924–9, it was claimed that 29 Nazi activists had been killed by Communists, while the Communists themselves reported that 92 'workers' had been killed in clashes with 'fascists' from 1924 to 1930. Twenty-six members of the Steel Helmets were said to have fallen in the fight against Communism and 18 members of the Reichsbanner in various incidents of political violence from 1924 to 1928.[86] These were only the most serious consequences of the continual fighting between rival paramilitary groups; the same sources counted injuries sustained in the battles in the thousands, many of them more serious than mere bruises or broken bones.

In 1930 the figures rose dramatically, with the Nazis claiming to have suffered 17 deaths, rising to 42 in 1931 and 84 in 1932. In 1932, too, the Nazis reported that nearly ten thousand of their rank-and-file had been wounded in clashes with their opponents. The Communists reported 44 deaths in fights with the Nazis in 1930, 52 in 1931 and 75 in the first six months of 1932 alone, while over 50 Reichsbanner men died in battles with the Nazis on the streets from 1929 to 1933.[87] Official sources broadly corroborated these claims, with one estimate in the Reichstag, not disputed by anybody, putting the number of dead in the year to March 1931 at no fewer than 300.[88] The Communists played their part with as much vigour as the Nazis. When the sailor Richard Krebs, leader of a detachment of a hundred members of the Red Front-Fighters' League, was instructed to break up a Nazi meeting in Bremen addressed by Hermann Göring, for instance, he made sure that 'each man was armed with a blackjack or brass knuckles'. When he rose to speak, Göring ordered him to be thrown out after he had said only a few words; the brownshirts lining the hall rushed to the centre, and:

A terrifying mêlée followed. Blackjacks, brass knuckles, clubs, heavy buckled belts, glasses and bottles were the weapons used. Pieces of glass and chairs hurtled over the heads of the audience. Men from both sides broke off chair legs and used them as bludgeons. Women fainted in the crash and scream of battle. Already dozens of heads and faces were bleeding, clothes were torn as the fighters dodged about amid masses of terrified but helpless spectators. The troopers fought like lions. Systematically they pressed us towards the main exit. The band struck up a martial tune. Hermann Göring stood calmly on the stage, his fists on his hips.[89]

Scenes like this were being played out all over Germany in the early 1930s. Violence was particularly severe at election-time; of the 155 killed in political clashes in Prussia in the course of 1932, no fewer than 105 died in the election months of June and July, and the police counted 461 political riots with 400 injuries and 82 deaths in the first seven weeks of the campaign.[90] The task of curbing political violence was not helped by the fact that the political parties most heavily implicated got together at intervals and agreed on an amnesty for political prisoners, thus releasing them from prison to engage in a fresh round of beatings and killings. The last such amnesty came into effect on 20 January 1933.[91]

II

Facing this situation of rapidly mounting disorder was a police force that was distinctly shaky in its allegiance to Weimar democracy. Unlike the army, it continued to be decentralized after 1918. The Social Democrat-dominated Prussian government in Berlin, however, failed to seize the opportunity to create a new public-order force which would be the loyal servant of Republican law enforcement. The force was inevitably recruited from the ranks of ex-soldiers, since a high proportion of the relevant age group had been conscripted during the war. The new force found itself run by ex-officers, former professional soldiers and Free Corps fighters. They set a military tone from the outset and were hardly enthusiastic supporters of the new political order.[92] They were backed up by the political police, which had a long tradition in Prussia, as in other German and European states, of concentrating its efforts on the monitoring, detection and at times suppression of socialists and revolutionaries.[93] Its officers, like those of other police departments, considered themselves above party politics. Rather like the army, they were serving an abstract notion of 'the state' or the Reich, rather than the specific democratic institutions of the newly founded Republic. Not surprisingly, therefore, they continued to mount surveillance operations not only over the political extremes but also over the Social Democrats, the party of government in Prussia and, in a sense, their employers. The old tradition of seeking subversives primarily on the left wing of the political spectrum thus lived on.[94]

The bias of the police and the judiciary was particularly apparent in the case of a Social Democrat like the Reichstag deputy Otto Buchwitz in Silesia, who recalled later with considerable bitterness how stormtroopers began to disrupt his speeches from December 1931 onwards. Brownshirts occupied the seats at his meetings, shouted insults at him, and on one occasion fired a shot at him, causing mass panic amongst his listeners and leading to a brawl in which more shots were fired by both stormtroopers and Reichsbanner men. Several Nazis and Social Democrats had to be taken to hospital, and not a single table or chair in the hall was left intact. After this, gangs of eight to ten Nazi stormtroopers harassed Buchwitz outside his house when he left for work in the morning, twenty or more crowded round him when he came back to his office after lunch, and between one and two hundred hassled him on the way home, singing a specially composed song with the words 'When the revolvers are shot, Buchwitz'll cop the lot!' Nazi demonstrations always halted outside his house, chanting 'Death to Buchwitz!' Not only did his complaints to the police and requests for protection go completely unheeded, but when he lost his parliamentary immunity with the dissolution of the Reichstag in 1932, he was hauled before the courts for illegal possession of a weapon at the December 1931 brawl and sentenced to three months in prison. Not one Nazi among those involved in the affair was prosecuted. After his release, Buchwitz was refused permission to carry a gun, but always had one on him anyway, and demonstratively released the safety catch if the brownshirts got too close. His complaint to the Social Democratic Interior Minister of Prussia, Carl Severing, met with the response that he should not have got involved in a shooting-match in the first place. Buchwitz's feeling of betrayal by the Social Democratic leadership was only strengthened when a large contingent of rank-and-file Communist activists came up to him before a speech he was due to give at the funeral of a Reichsbanner man shot by the Nazis, and explained that they were there to protect him from a planned assassination attempt by the brownshirts. Neither the police nor the Reichsbanner were anywhere to be seen.[95]

The police for their part regarded the Red Front-Fighters' League as criminals. This not only followed a long police tradition of conflating crime and revolution, but also reflected the fact that Communist strong-holds tended to be based in poor, slum areas that were the centres of organized crime. As far as the police were concerned, the Red Front-Fighters were thugs, out for material gain. For the Communists, the police were the iron fist of the capitalist order, which had to be smashed, and they frequently targeted policemen in acts of physical aggression all the way up to murder. This meant that in clashes with the Communists, a tired, nervous and apprehensive police force was only too prone to make use of the pistols with which it was customarily armed. Prolonged fighting in Berlin in 1929 achieved fame as 'Blood-May', when 31 people, includ-ing innocent passers-by, were killed, mostly by police gunshots; over two hundred were wounded, and more than a thousand were arrested in the course of Communist demonstrations in the working-class district of

Wedding. Stories that newspaper reporters covering the events were beaten up by the police only made press comment more critical, while the police themselves reacted with barely concealed contempt for a democratic political order that had failed to defend them from injury and insult.[96]

Alienated from the Republic by continual Communist polemics and by Social Democratic attempts to curb their powers, the police were also troubled by the slowness of promotion, and many younger policemen felt their careers blocked.[97] Professionalization had made great strides amongst detective forces in Germany, as in other countries, with fingerprinting, photography and forensic science prized as new and startlingly effective aids to detection. Individual detectives such as the famous Ernst Gennat, head of the Berlin murder squad, became celebrated in their own right, and the force claimed some impressive detection rates of serious crimes in the mid-1920s. Yet the police attracted massively hostile comment in the press and news media for failing to arrest serial killers, like Fritz Haarmann in Hanover, or Peter Kürten in Düsseldorf, before they had claimed a whole series of victims. The police in their turn felt that the rampant political violence and disorder of the era were forcing them to divert precious resources from fighting crimes such as these.[98] Not surprisingly, therefore, policemen began to sympathize with the Nazis' attacks on the Weimar Republic. In 1935, a report claimed that 700 uniformed policemen had been members of the party before 1933, while in Hamburg 27 officers out of 240 had joined by 1932.[99]

Reich Chancellor Brüning decided to use the police, however, to curb political violence on the right as well as the left, because the chaos on the streets was deterring foreign banks from issuing loans to Germany.[100] His resolve was strengthened by two serious incidents that occurred in 1931. In April, the brownshirt leader in north-eastern Germany, Walther Stennes, got into a dispute with Party headquarters and briefly occupied the Nazis' central offices in Berlin, beating up the SS guards stationed there and forcing Goebbels to flee to Munich. Stennes denounced the extravagance of the Party bosses and their betrayal of socialist principles. But, although he undoubtedly articulated the feelings of some stormtroopers, he had little real support. Indeed there is some indication that he was secretly subsidized by Brüning's government in order to create divisions within the movement. Hitler fired the brownshirt leader Franz

Pfeffer von Salomon, who had failed to prevent this debacle, recalled Ernst Röhm from his Bolivian exile to take over the organization, and forced all the brownshirts to swear a personal oath of allegiance to him. Stennes was expelled, with the incidental consequence that many conservative businessmen and military leaders now became convinced that the Nazi movement had lost much of its subversive drive.[101] Nevertheless, there remained very real tensions between the ceaseless activism of the stormtroopers and the political calculation of the Party leaders, which were to surface repeatedly in the future.[102] More seriously, the Stennes revolt indicated that many brownshirts were keen to unleash revolutionary violence on a considerable scale, a lesson that was not lost on the nervous Reich government.

These suspicions were confirmed with the discovery of the so-called Boxheim documents in November 1931. Nazi papers seized by the police in Hesse showed that the SA was planning a violent putsch, to be followed by food rationing, the abolition of money, compulsory labour for all, and the death penalty for disobeying the authorities. The reality fell some way short of the police's claims, since the Boxheim documents were in fact only of regional significance, and had been devised without the knowledge of his superiors by a young Party official in Hesse, Werner Best, to guide Party policy in the event of an attempted Communist uprising in Hesse. Hitler quickly distanced himself from the affair and all SA commanders were ordered to desist from making any more contingency plans of this kind. Criminal proceedings were eventually dropped for lack of clear evidence of treason against Best.[103] But the damage had been done. Brüning obtained a decree on 7 December banning the wearing of political uniforms and backed it with a strongly worded attack on Nazi illegality. Referring to Hitler's constantly reiterated assurances that he intended to come to power legally, Brüning said: 'If one declares that, having come to power by legal means, one will then break the bounds of the law, that is not legality.'[104]

The ban on uniforms had little effect, since the brownshirts carried on marching, only dressed in white shirts instead, and violence continued during the winter. Rumours of an impending Communist insurrection, coupled with pressure from Schleicher, stayed Brüning's hand during this period, but Communist electoral setbacks in Hamburg, Hesse and Oldenburg convinced him in the spring of 1932 that the moment had come to ban the brownshirts altogether. Under heavy pressure from the other political parties, particularly the Social Democrats, and with the support of the worried military, Brüning and General Groener (whom he had appointed Interior Minister in October 1931 in addition to his existing responsibilities as Minister of Defence) persuaded a reluctant Hindenburg to issue a decree outlawing the stormtroopers on 13 April 1932. The police raided brownshirt premises all over Germany, confiscating military equipment and insignia. Hitler was beside himself with rage but impotent to act. Yet despite the ban, clandestine membership of the stormtroopers continued to grow in many areas. In Upper and Lower Silesia, for instance, there were 17,500 stormtroopers in December 1931, and no fewer than 34,500 by the following July. The outlawing of the brownshirts had only a slightly dampening effect on levels of political violence, and the presence of Nazi sympathizers in the lower ranks of the police allowed the Nazi paramilitaries a fair degree of latitude in continuing their operations.[105] Claims that the Nazi Party and their paramilitary wing would have virtually ceased to exist had the ban been continued for a year or more were thus very wide of the mark.[106]

The new situation after the Nazis' electoral breakthrough not only sharply escalated the level of violence on the streets, it also radically altered the nature of proceedings in the Reichstag. Rowdy and chaotic enough even before September 1930, it now became virtually unmanageable, as 107 brown-shirted and uniformed Nazi deputies joined 77 disciplined and well-organized Communists in raising incessant points of order, chanting, shouting, interrupting and demonstrating their total contempt for the legislature at every juncture. Power drained from the Reichstag with frightening rapidity, as almost every session ended in uproar and the idea of calling it together for a meeting came to seem ever more pointless. From September 1930 only negative majorities were possible in the Reichstag. In February 1931, recognizing the impossibility of carrying on, it adjourned itself for six months as the parties of the extreme right and left demonstratively walked out of a debate after amendments to the parliamentary rule book made it more difficult for them to obstruct business. The deputies did not return until October.[107] The Reichstag sat on average a hundred days a year from 1920 to 1930. It was in session for fifty days between October 1930 and March 1931; after that, it only met on twenty-four further days up to the elections of

July 1932. From July 1932 to February 1933 it convened for a mere three days in six months.[108]

By 1931, therefore, decisions were no longer really being made by the Reichstag. Political power had moved elsewhere – to the circle around Hindenburg, with whom the right to sign decrees and the right to appoint governments lay, and to the streets, where violence continued to escalate, and where growing poverty, misery and disorder confronted the state with an increasingly urgent need for action. Both these processes greatly enhanced the influence of the army. Only in such circumstances could someone like its most important political representative, General Kurt von Schleicher, become one of the key players in the drama that followed. Ambitious, quick-witted, talkative and rather too fond of political intrigue for his own good, Schleicher was a relatively unknown figure before he suddenly shot to prominence in 1929, when a new office was created for him, the 'Ministerial Office', which had the function of representing the armed forces in their relations with the government. A close collaborator of Groener for many years, and a disciple of the leading general of the early 1920s, Hans von Seeckt, Schleicher had forged many political connections through running a variety of offices at the interface of military and political affairs, most recently the army section of the Defence Ministry. The dissident Russian Communist Leon Trotsky described him as 'a question mark with the epaulettes of a general'; a contemporary journalist saw him as a 'sphinx in uniform'. But for the most part Schleicher's aims and beliefs were clear enough: like many German conservatives in 1932, he thought that an authoritarian regime could be given legitimacy by harnessing and taming the popular might of the National Socialists. In this way, the German army, for which Schleicher spoke, and with which he continued to have very close contacts, would get what it wanted in the way of rearmament.[109]

Brüning's government ran into increasing difficulties with Schleicher and the circle around President Hindenburg after the elections of September 1930. With the Communists and the Nazis baying for his blood, the Nationalists trying to oust him, and far-right fringe groups divided over whether to support him or not, Brüning had no option but to rely on the Social Democrats. For their part, the leaders of what was still the largest party in the Reichstag were sufficiently shocked by the election results to promise that they would not repeat their earlier rejection of the budget.

Brüning's dependence on the tacit toleration of his policies by the Social Democrats won him no credit at all among the circle around Hindenburg, led by his son Oskar and his State Secretary Meissner, who regarded this as a shameful concession to the left.[110] The Chancellor's main priorities now lay in the field of foreign policy, where he made some headway in securing the end of reparations – abrogated by the Hoover Moratorium on 20 June 1931 and effectively ended by the Lausanne Conference, for which Brüning had laid much of the groundwork, in July 1932. And although he failed to achieve the creation of an Austro-German Customs Union, he did conduct successful negotiations in Geneva for the international recognition of German equality in questions of disarmament, a principle eventually conceded in December 1932. However, none of this did anything to strengthen the Chancellor's political position. After many months in office, he had still failed to win over the Nationalists and was still dependent on the Social Democrats. This meant that any plans either Brüning himself or the circle around Hindenburg might have had to amend the constitution decisively in a more authoritarian direction were effectively stymied, since this was the one thing to which the Social Democrats would never give their assent. To men such as Schleicher, shifting the government's mass support from the Social Democrats to the Nazis seemed increasingly to be the better option.[111]

III

As 1932 dawned, the venerable Paul von Hindenburg's seven-year term of office as President was coming to an end. In view of his advanced years – he was 84 – Hindenburg was reluctant to stand again, but he had let it be known that he would be willing to continue in office if his tenure could simply be prolonged without an election. Negotiations over automatically renewing Hindenburg's Presidency foundered on the refusal of the Nazis to vote in the Reichstag for the necessary constitutional change without the simultaneous dismissal of Brüning and the calling of a fresh general election in which, of course, they expected to make further huge gains.[112] Hindenburg was thus forced to undergo the indignity of presenting himself to the electorate once more. But this time things were very different from the first time round, in 1925. Of course, Thälmann stood

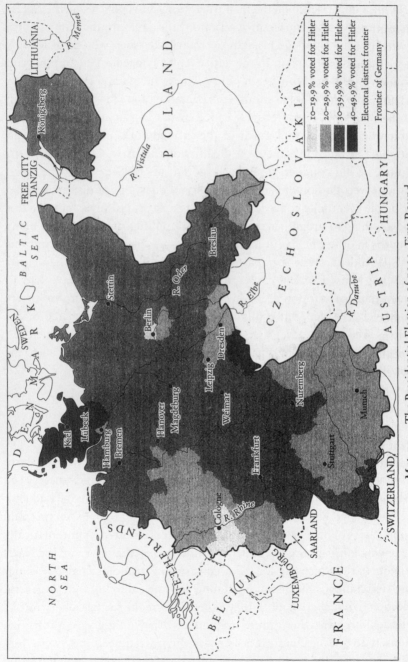

Map 12.   The Presidential Election of 1932. First Round

again for the Communists. But in the meantime Hindenburg had been far outflanked on the right; indeed, the entire political spectrum had shifted rightwards since the Nazi electoral landslide of September 1930. Once the election was announced, Hitler could hardly avoid standing as a candidate himself. Several weeks passed while he dithered, however, fearful of the consequences of running against such a nationalist icon as the hero of Tannenberg. Moreover, technically he was not even allowed to stand since he had not yet acquired German citizenship. Hurried arrangements were made for him to be appointed as a civil servant in Braunschweig, a measure that automatically gave him the status of a German citizen, confirmed when he took the oath of allegiance (to the Weimar constitution, as all civil servants had to) on 26 February 1932.[113] His candidacy transformed the election into a contest between right and left in which Hitler was unarguably the candidate for the right, which made Hindenburg, extraordinarily, incredibly, the candidate for the left.

The Centre and the liberals backed Hindenburg, but what was particularly astonishing was the degree of support he received from the Social Democrats. This was not merely because the party considered him the only man who could stop Hitler – a point the party's propaganda made repeatedly throughout the election campaign – but for positive reasons as well. The party leaders were desperate to re-elect Hindenburg because they thought that he would keep Brüning in office as the last chance of a return to democratic normality.[114] Hindenburg, declared the Social Democratic Prussian Minister-President Otto Braun, was the 'embodiment of calm and constancy, of manly loyalty and devotion to duty for the whole people', a 'man on whose work one can build, as a man of pure desire and serene judgment'.[115] Already at this time, as these astonishing sentences showed, the Social Democrats were beginning to lose touch with political reality. Eighteen months of tolerating Brüning's cuts in the name of preventing something worse had relegated them to the sidelines of politics and robbed them of the power of decision. Despite disillusionment and defections amongst their members, their disciplined party machine duly delivered more than 8 million votes to the man who was to dismantle the Republic from above, in an effort to keep in office a Chancellor whom Hindenburg actually disliked and distrusted, and whose policies had been lowering the living standards and destroying the jobs of the very people the Social Democrats represented.[116]

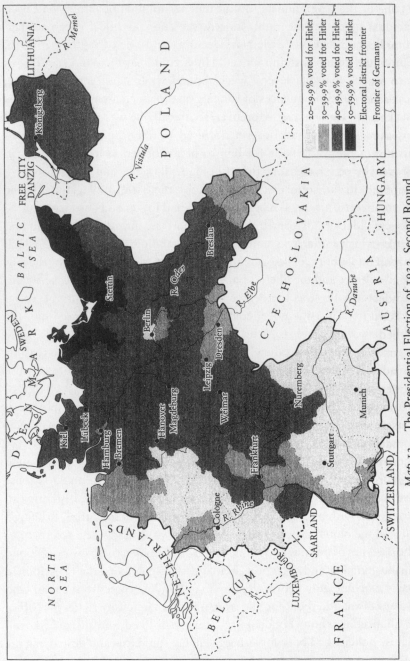

Map 13.   The Presidential Election of 1932. Second Round

The threat of a Nazi victory was real enough. The Goebbels propaganda machine found a way of combating Hindenburg without insulting him: he had done great service to the nation, but now was the time for him finally to step aside in favour of a younger man, otherwise the drift into economic chaos and political anarchy would continue. The Nazis unleashed a massive campaign of rallies, marches, parades and meetings, backed by posters, flysheets and ceaseless exhortations in the press. But it was not enough. In the first ballot, Hitler only managed to win 30 per cent of the vote. Yet despite the efforts of the Social Democrats and the electoral strength of the Centre Party, Hindenburg did not quite manage to obtain the overall majority required. He gained only 49.6 per cent of the vote, tantalizingly short of what he needed. On the left, Thälmann offered another alternative. On the right, Hindenburg had been outflanked not only by Hitler but also by Theodor Duesterberg, the candidate put up by the Steel Helmets, who received 6.8 per cent of the vote in the first ballot, which would have been more than enough to have pushed Hindenburg over the winning margin.[117]

For the run-off, between Hitler, Hindenburg and Thälmann, the Nazis pulled out all the stops. Hitler rented an aeroplane and flew across Germany from town to town, delivering 46 speeches the length and breadth of the land. The effect of this unprecedented move, billed as Hitler's 'flight over Germany', was electrifying. The effort paid off. Thälmann was reduced to a marginal 10 per cent, but Hitler boosted his vote massively to 37 per cent with over 13 million votes cast in his favour. Hindenburg, with the combined might of all the major parties behind him apart from the Communists and the Nazis, only managed to increase his support to 53 per cent. Of course, despite the hiccup of the first ballot, his re-election had been foreseeable from the start. What really mattered was the triumphant forward march of the Nazis. Hitler had not been elected, but his party had won more votes than ever before. It was beginning to look unstoppable.[118] In 1932, better organized and better financed than in 1930, the Nazi Party had run an American-style Presidential campaign focusing on the person of Hitler as the representative of the whole of Germany. It had concentrated its efforts not so much on winning over the workers, where its campaign of 1930 had largely failed, but in garnering the middle-class votes that had previously gone to the splinter-parties and the parties of the liberal and conservative Protestant electorate. Eighteen months of worsening unemployment and economic crisis had further radicalized these voters in their disillusion with the Weimar Republic, over which, after all, Hindenburg had been presiding for the past seven years. Goebbels's propaganda apparatus targeted specific groups of voters with greater precision than ever before, above all women. In the Protestant countryside, rural discontent had deepened to the point where Hitler actually defeated Hindenburg in the second round in Pomerania, Schleswig-Holstein and Eastern Hanover.[119] And the Nazi movement's new status as Germany's most popular political party was underlined by further victories in the state elections held later in the spring – 36.3 per cent in Prussia, 32.5 per cent in Bavaria, 31.2 per cent in Hamburg, 26.4 per cent in Württemberg, and, above all, 40.9 per cent in Saxony-Anhalt, a result that gave them the right to form a state government. Once more, Hitler had taken to the air, delivering 25 speeches in quick succession. Once more, the Nazi propaganda machine had proved its efficiency and its dynamism.

Brüning's attempts to curb the Nazi Party's rise had obviously failed to make any kind of impact. The time seemed to many in President Hindenburg's entourage to be ripe for a different tactic. Despite his election victory, Hindenburg was far from satisfied with the result. The fact that he had run into such serious opposition was highly displeasing to a man who was increasingly treating his position like that of the unelected Kaiser he had once served. Brüning's cardinal sin was to have failed to persuade the Nationalists to support Hindenburg's re-election. When it became clear that they were backing Hitler, Brüning's days were numbered. Despite the Reich Chancellor's tireless campaigning on his behalf, the old Field-Marshal, who embodied for many the Prussian traditions of monarchism and Protestant conservatism, was deeply resentful at his dependence on the votes of the Social Democrats and the Centre Party, which made him look like the candidate of the left and the clericals, as, indeed, in the end, he was. Moreover, the army was becoming impatient with the crippling effects of Brüning's economic policies on the arms industry, and considered that his ban on the brownshirts got in the way of recruiting them as auxiliary troops, a prospect that became more enticing the more members they acquired. Finally, Hindenburg's attention was drawn to a moderate measure of land reform being proposed by the government in the east, in which bankrupt estates would be broken up and provided as smallholdings to the unemployed. As a representative of the landed interest himself, with an estate of his own, Hindenburg was persuaded that this smacked of socialism.[120] In an atmosphere heavy with behind-the-scenes intrigue, with Schleicher undermining Groener's standing with the army and Hitler promising to tolerate a new government if it lifted the ban on the brownshirts and called new elections to the Reichstag, Brüning rapidly became more isolated. When Groener was forced to resign on 11 May 1932, Brüning's position was left completely exposed. Continually undermined by intrigues in Hindenburg's entourage, he saw no alternative but to tender his resignation, which he did on 30 May 1932.[121]

IV

The man whom Hindenburg appointed as the new Reich Chancellor was an old personal friend, Franz von Papen. A landed aristocrat whose position in the Centre Party, for which he had sat as an obscure and not very active deputy in the Prussian Parliament, Papen was even further to the right than Brüning himself. During the First World War he had been expelled from the United States, where he was military attaché at the German Embassy, for spying, or 'activities incompatible with his status', as the conventional diplomatic phrase went, and joined the German General Staff. During the 1920s he used the wealth brought him by a marriage to the daughter of a rich industrialist to buy a majority share in the Centre Party's newspaper, *Germania*. Papen thus had close contacts with some of the key social and political forces in the Weimar Republic, including the landed aristocracy, the Foreign Office, the army, the industrialists, the Catholic Church and the press. Indeed, he had been recommended to Hindenburg by Schleicher as someone who would be sympathetic to the army's interests. Even more than Brüning, he represented a form of Catholic political authoritarianism common throughout Europe in the early 1930s. Papen had long been at odds with his party, and he had openly championed Hindenburg against the Centre candidate Marx in the 1925 Presidential election. The Centre disowned Papen, who in his turn handed in his party membership card, proclaiming that he sought a 'synthesis of all truly nationalistic forces – from whatever

camp they may come – not as a party man, but as a German'.[122] Now the
break was complete.[123]

These events marked, explicitly as well as in retrospect, the end of
parliamentary democracy in Germany. Most members of the new cabinet
were without party affiliation, apart from a couple who were, nominally
at least, members of the Nationalist Party. Papen and his fellow-
ideologues, including Schleicher, saw themselves as creating a 'New
State', above parties, indeed opposed to the very principle of a multi-party
system, with the powers of elected assemblies even more limited than
they had been in Brüning's more modest vision. The kind of state they
were thinking of was indicated by Papen's Interior Minister, Wilhelm
Freiherr von Gayl, who had helped create a racist, authoritarian, military
state in the area ceded to Germany by the Treaty of Brest-Litovsk in
1918.[124] Among Gayl's proposals were the restriction of voting rights to
a minority and the drastic reduction of parliamentary powers.[125] Papen's
self-appointed task was to roll back history, not just Weimar democracy
but everything that had happened in European politics since the French
Revolution, and re-create in the place of modern class conflict the hierarchical basis of *ancien régime* society.[126] As a small but potent symbol
of this intention, he abolished the use of that classic symbol of the French
Revolution, the guillotine, for executions in parts of Prussia where it had
been introduced in the nineteenth century, and replaced it with the
traditional Prussian instrument of the hand-held axe.[127] Meanwhile, in a
more immediately practical way, Papen's government began extending
the curbs imposed by its predecessor on the radical press to democratic
newspapers as well, banning popular left-liberal publications like the
Social Democratic daily paper *Forwards* twice within a few weeks, pro-
scribing popular left-liberal papers like the *Berlin People's Paper* (*Berliner
Volkszeitung*) on two separate occasions, and convincing liberal commentators that press freedom had finally been abolished.[128]

Papen's utopian conservatism did scant justice to the political realities
of 1932. Papen's cabinet was made up of men with relatively little
experience. So many of them were unknown aristocrats that it was
widely known as the 'cabinet of barons'. In the discussions that preceded
Brüning's resignation, Papen and Schleicher had agreed that they needed
to win over the Nazis to provide mass support for the anti-democratic
policies of the new government. They secured Hindenburg's agreement

to dissolve the Reichstag and call fresh elections, which Hitler had been demanding in the expectation that they would lead to a further increase in the Nazi vote. The elections were set for the end of July 1932. In addition, they also conceded Hitler's demand for a lifting of the ban on the brownshirts. This would, thought Schleicher, tame Nazi extremism and among other things persuade the brownshirts to act as an auxiliary army with which the limitations on the strength of the German armed forces imposed by the Treaty of Versailles could be decisively circumvented.[129] But it proved another disastrous miscalculation. Masses of stormtroopers flooded triumphantly back onto the streets, and beatings, pitched battles, woundings and killings, never entirely absent even during the period of the ban since the previous April, quickly reached record new levels. Even so, public opinion was shocked when, on 17 July 1932, a march staged by thousands of Nazi stormtroopers through the Communist stronghold of Altona, a working-class municipality on the Prussian side of the state border of Hamburg, ran into violent resistance from thousands of heavily armed Red Front-Fighters. Richard Krebs, in charge of 800 Communist sailors and dockers ready to drive the Nazis from the waterfront, reported later how the Red Front-Fighters were under orders to attack the stormtroopers in the streets. Stones, rubbish and all kinds of missiles were hurled at the passing marchers. According to some reports, there were Communist sharp-shooters on the roofs, ready to massacre the stormtroopers below. Someone, nobody was sure who, fired a shot. Immediately, the police panicked and opened fire with everything they had, spraying the locality with bullets and causing panic flight in all directions. The Communists were driven away along with the rest. Their attempt to stop the brownshirt march through their territory had been an abject failure.[130] Eighteen people were killed and more than a hundred injured. Most of the deaths were caused, as autopsy reports revealed, by bullets fired from police revolvers. The depths of violence to which German political confrontations had now sunk clearly demanded action by the government.[131]

Far from banning the paramilitaries again, however, Papen seized on the events of 'Bloody Sunday' in Altona to depose the state government of Prussia, which was led by the Social Democrats Otto Braun and Carl Severing, on the grounds that it was no longer capable of maintaining law and order. This was the decisive blow against the Social Democrats which he had been put into office to achieve. Papen had a sort of precedent in Ebert's deposition of the Saxon and Thuringian state governments in 1923, but Prussia, covering more than half the territory of the Reich, with a population greater than that of France, was a far more significant target. The central position of the army in the strife-torn political situation of 1932 was graphically illustrated as heavily armed combat troops took to the streets of Berlin, and a military state of emergency was declared throughout the capital city. The Social Democrat-controlled police force was simply pushed aside; any attempt by the Prussian government to use it as a means of resisting the armed strength of the military would only have led to confusion. Its manpower was too small, and the senior and middle-ranking officers were either disillusioned with the Republic, sympathized with Papen, or had been won over by the Nazis.[132]

If Papen and Schleicher feared a workers' uprising, they were wrong. Many rank-and-file members of the Reichsbanner were ready to take up arms, and machine guns, pistols and carbines had been assembled to defend the party headquarters in the event of a putsch until the police, who, the party assumed – wrongly, as it turned out – would resist any attempt to overthrow the Republic, arrived on the scene. A recent increase in numbers had brought the strength of the Reichsbanner's Republican Defence Units up to more than 200,000. But they were heavily outnumbered by the combined forces of some three-quarters of a million brownshirts and Steel Helmets, who would certainly have mobilized against them had they staged an uprising. They were poorly trained and ill prepared. And they would have been no match for the well-equipped forces of the German army. The Communists, who had better reserves of arms, were certainly not going to take them up to defend the Social Democrats.[133]

In the situation of July 1932, when Hindenburg, the military leadership and the conservatives were all extremely anxious to avoid provoking a civil war in Germany, an armed uprising by the Reichsbanner might have forced a climbdown by Papen, or an intervention by the Reich President. One can never know. The call to resist never came. The law-abiding traditions of the Social Democrats compelled them to put a ban on any armed resistance to an act that was sanctioned by the head of state and the legally constituted government, backed by the armed forces and not opposed by the police.[134] All that remained as an option for Braun and

Severing were rhetorical protests and lawsuits brought against Papen on the ground that he had breached the constitution. On 10 October 1932, the State Court ruled in part at least in favour of the Braun cabinet, which therefore continued to be a thorn in the Reich government's flesh by representing Prussia in the Reich Council, the upper chamber of the national legislature.[135] Meanwhile, Papen secured from the President his own appointment as Reich Commissioner to carry out the business of government in Prussia, while punctilious civil servants dithered and suspended business until the legal position was resolved.[136]

Papen's coup dealt a mortal blow to the Weimar Republic. It destroyed the federal principle and opened the way to the wholesale centralization of the state. Whatever happened now, it was unlikely to be a full restoration of parliamentary democracy. After 20 July 1932 the only realistic alternatives were a Nazi dictatorship or a conservative, authoritarian regime backed by the army. The absence of any serious resistance on the part of the Social Democrats, the principal remaining defenders of democracy, was decisive. It convinced both conservatives and National Socialists that the destruction of democratic institutions could be achieved without any serious opposition. The Social Democrats had received plenty of advance warning of the coup. Yet they had done nothing. They were paralysed not only by the backing given to the coup by the man they had so recently supported in the Presidential election campaign, Paul von Hindenburg, but also by their catastrophic defeat in the Prussian parliamentary elections of April 1932. While the Nazis had increased their representation in the Prussian legislature from 9 seats to 162, and the Communists from 48 to 57, the Social Democrats had lost a third of their mandates, falling from 137 to 94. No party now had a majority, and the existing administration, led by Braun and Severing, carried on as a minority government with a correspondingly weakened political legitimacy. Beyond this, too, a sense of impotence had spread throughout the party leadership during the long months of passive toleration of Brüning's savage policy of cuts. The trade unions were powerless to do anything against the coup because the massive unemployment made a general strike impossible; millions of desperate, jobless people would have had little choice but to take on work as strikebreakers, and they knew it. A repeat of the united labour movement stand that had defeated the Kapp putsch in 1920 was thus out of the question. The Nazis were jubilant. 'You only have to bare your teeth at the reds and they knuckle under', wrote the Nazi propaganda chief Joseph Goebbels in his diary for 20 July: the Social Democrats and trade unions, he observed with satisfaction, 'aren't lifting a finger'. 'The reds', he noted not long after, 'have missed their big chance. It's never going to come again.'[137]

FATEFUL DECISIONS

I

The Papen coup took place in the midst of Germany's most frenetic and most violent election campaign yet, fought in an atmosphere even less rational and more vicious than that of two years before. Hitler once more flew across Germany from venue to venue, speaking before huge crowds at more than fifty major meetings, denouncing the divisions, humiliations and failures of Weimar and offering a vague but potent promise of a better, more united nation in the future. Meanwhile, the Communists preached revolution and announced the imminent collapse of the capitalist order, the Social Democrats called on the electors to rise up against the threat of fascism, and the bourgeois parties advocated a restorative unity they were patently unable to deliver.[138] The decay of parliamentary politics was graphically illustrated by the increasingly emotive propaganda style of the parties, including even the Social Democrats. Surrounded by increasingly violent street clashes and demonstrations, the political struggle became reduced to what the Social Democrats called – without the slightest hint of criticism – a war of symbols. Engaging a psychologist – Sergei Chakhotin, a radical Russian pupil of Pavlov, the discoverer of the conditioned response – to help them fight elections in the course of 1931, the Social Democrats realized that an appeal to reason was not enough. 'We have to work on feelings, souls and emotions so that reason wins the victory.' In practice, reason got left far behind. In the elections of July 1932 the Social Democrats ordered all their local groups to ensure that party members wore a party badge, used the clenched-fist greeting when encountering each other, and shouted the slogan 'Freedom!' at appropriate opportunities. In the same spirit, the Communists had long since been using the symbol of the hammer and sickle and a variety of slogans and greetings. In adopting this style, the parties were placing themselves on the same ground as the Nazis, with whose swastika symbol, 'Hail Hitler!' greeting and simple, powerful slogans they found it very difficult to compete.[139]

Seeking for an image that would be dynamic enough to counter the appeal of the Nazis, the Social Democrats, the Reichsbanner, the trade unions, and a number of other working-class organizations connected with the socialists came together on 16 December 1931 to form the 'Iron Front' to fight the 'fascist' menace. The new movement borrowed heavily from the arsenal of propaganda methods developed by the Communists and the National Socialists. Long, boring speeches were to be replaced by short, sharp slogans. The labour movement's traditional emphasis on education, reason and science was to yield to a new stress on the rousing of mass emotions through street processions, uniformed marches and collective demonstrations of will. The new propaganda style of the Social Democrats even extended to the invention of a symbol to counter that of the swastika and the hammer and sickle: three parallel arrows, express-ing the three major arms of the Iron Front. None of this did much to help the traditional labour movement, many of whose members, not least those who occupied leading positions in the Reichstag, remained scep-tical, or proved unable to adapt to the new way of presenting their policies. The new propaganda style placed the Social Democrats on the same ground as the Nazis; but they lacked the dynamism, the youthful vigour or the extremism to offer them effective competition. The symbols, the marches and the uniforms failed to rally new supporters to the Iron Front, since the entrenched organizational apparatus of the Social Democrats remained in control. On the other hand, it did not allay the fears of middle-class voters about the intentions of the labour movement.[140]

Even more revealing were the election posters used by the parties in the campaigns of the early 1930s. A common feature to almost all of them was their domination by the figure of a giant, half-naked worker who had come by the late 1920s to symbolize the German people, replacing the ironically modest little figure of the 'German Michel' in his sleeping-cap or the more rarified female personification of *Germania* that had previously stood for the nation. Nazi posters showed the giant worker towering above a bank labelled 'International High Finance', destroying it with massive blows from a swastika-bedaubed compressor; the Social Democrats' posters portrayed the giant worker elbowing aside Nazis and Communists; the Centre Party's posters carried a cartoon of the giant worker, less scantily clad perhaps, but still with his sleeves rolled up, forcibly removing tiny Nazis and Communists from the parliament building; the People's Party depicted the giant worker, dressed only in a loincloth, sweeping aside the soberly dressed politicians of all the other warring factions in July 1932, in an almost exact reversal of what was actually to happen in the elections; even the staid Nationalist Party used a giant worker in its posters, though only to wave the black-white-red flag of the old Bismarckian Reich.[141] All over Germany, electors were confronted with violent images of giant workers smashing their opponents to pieces, kicking them aside, yanking them out of parliament, or looming over frock-coated and top-hatted politicians who were almost universally portrayed as insignificant and quarrelsome pygmies. Rampant masculinity was sweeping aside the squabbling, ineffective and feminized political factions. Whatever the intention, the subliminal message was that it was time for parliamentary politics to come to an end: a message made explicit in the daily clashes of paramilitary groups on the streets, the ubiquity of uniforms at the hustings, and the non-stop violence and mayhem at electoral meetings.

None of the other parties could compete with the Nazis on this territory. Goebbels might have complained that 'they are now stealing our methods from us', but the three arrows had no deep symbolic resonance, unlike the familiar swastika. If the Social Democrats were to have stood any chance of beating the Nazis at their own game, they should have started earlier.[142] Goebbels fought the election not on the performance of the Papen cabinet but on the performance of the Weimar Republic. The main objects of Nazi propaganda this time, therefore, were the voters of the Centre Party and the Social Democrats. In apocalyptic terms, a flood of posters, placards, leaflets, films and speeches delivered to vast open-air assemblies, purveyed a drastic picture of the 'red civil war over Germany' in which voters were confronted with a stark choice: either the old forces of betrayal and corruption, or a national rebirth to a glorious future. Goebbels and his propaganda team aimed to overwhelm the electorate with an unremitting barrage of assaults on their senses. Saturation

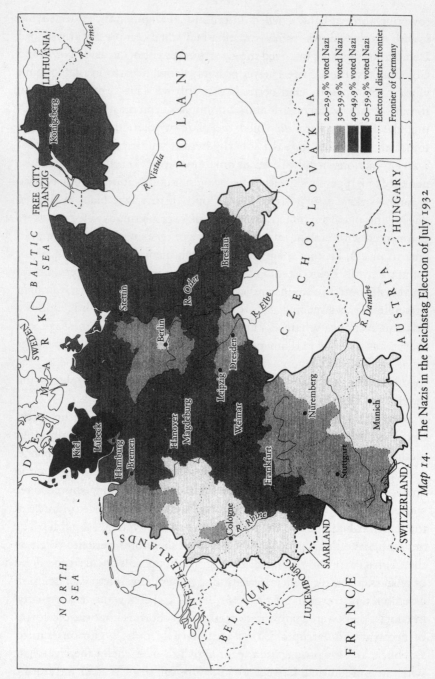

Map 14.   The Nazis in the Reichstag Election of July 1932

20–29.9% voted Nazi
30–39.9% voted Nazi
40–49.9% voted Nazi
50–59.9% voted Nazi
Electoral district frontier
Frontier of Germany

coverage was to be achieved not only by mass publicity but also by a concerted campaign of door-knocking and leafleting. Microphones and loudspeakers blasted out Nazi speeches over every public space that could be found. Visual images, purveyed not only through posters and magazine illustrations but also through mass demonstrations and marches in the streets, drove out rational discourse and verbal argument in favour of easily assimilated stereotypes that mobilized a whole range of feelings, from resentment and aggression to the need for security and redemption. The marching columns of the brownshirts, the stiff salutes and military poses of the Nazi leaders conveyed order and dependability as well as ruthless determination. Banners and flags projected the impression of ceaseless activism and idealism. The aggressive language of Nazi propaganda created endlessly repeated stereotypical images of their opponents – the 'November criminals', the 'red bosses', the 'Jewish wire-pullers', the 'red murder-pack'. Yet, given the Nazis' need to reassure the middle classes, the giant worker was now in some instances portrayed in a benevolent pose, no longer wild and aggressive, but wearing a shirt and handing tools of work to the unemployed instead of wielding them as weapons to destroy his opponents; the Nazis were prepared for responsible government.[143]

This unprecedentedly intense electoral propaganda soon brought its desired results. On 31 July 1932, the Reichstag election revealed the folly of Papen's tactics. Far from rendering Hitler and the Nazis more amenable, the election brought them a further massive boost in power, more than doubling their vote from 6.4 million to 13.1 million and making them by far the largest party in the Reichstag, with 230 seats, nearly a hundred more than the next biggest group, the Social Democrats, who managed to limit their losses to 10 more seats and sent 133 deputies to the new legislature. The 18.3 per cent of the vote the Nazis had obtained in September 1930 was also more than doubled, to 37.4 per cent. The continued polarization of the political scene was marked by another increase for the Communists, who now sent 89 deputies to the Reichstag instead of 77. And while the Centre Party also managed to increase its vote and gain 75 mandates in the new parliament, its highest ever number, the Nationalists registered further losses, going down from 41 seats to 37, reducing them almost to the status of a fringe party. Most striking of all, however, was the almost total annihilation of the parties of the centre. The People's Party lost 24 out of its 31 seats, the Economy Party 21 out of its 23, and the State Party, formerly the Democrats, 16 out of its 20. The congeries of far-right splinter-groups that had attracted such strong middle-class support in 1930 now also collapsed, retaining only 9 out of their previous 55 mandates. Left and right now faced each other in the Reichstag across a centre shrunken to insignificance: a combined Social Democrat/Communist vote of 13.4 million confronted a Nazi vote of 13.8 million, with all the other parties combined picking up a mere 9.8 million of the votes cast.[144]

The reasons for the Nazis' success at the polls in July 1932 were much the same as they had been in September 1930; nearly two more years of sharply deepening crisis in society, politics and the economy had rendered these factors even more powerful than they had been before. The election confirmed the Nazis' status as a rainbow coalition of the discontented, with, this time, a greatly increased appeal to the middle classes, who had evidently overcome the hesitation they had displayed two years earlier, when they had turned to the splinter-groups of the right. Electors from the middle-class parties had by now almost all found their way into the ranks of Nazi Party voters. One in two voters who had supported the splinter-parties in September 1930 now switched to the Nazis, and one in three of those who had voted for the Nationalists, the People's Party and the State Party in the previous Reichstag election. One previous non-voter in five now went to the polls to cast his or (especially) her vote for the Nazis. Even one in seven of those who had previously voted Social Democrat now voted Nazi. Thirty per cent of the Party's gains came from the splinter-parties. These voters included many who had supported the Nationalists in 1924 and 1928. Even a few Communist and Catholic Centre Party voters switched, though this was roughly balanced out by those who switched back the other way. The Nazi Party continued to be attractive mainly to Protestants, with only 14 per cent of Catholic voters supporting it as against 40 per cent of non-Catholics. Sixty per cent of Nazi voters on this occasion were from the middle classes, broadly defined; 40 per cent were wage-earning manual workers and their dependants, though, as before, these were overwhelmingly workers whose connection with the labour movement, for a variety of reasons, had always been weak. The negative correlation between the size of the Nazi vote in any constituency, and the level of unemployment, was as strong as ever.

The Nazis continued to be a catch-all party of social protest, with particularly strong support from the middle classes, and relatively weak support in the traditional industrial working class and the Catholic community, above all where there was a strong economic and institutional underpinning of the labour movement or Catholic voluntary associations.[145]

Yet while July 1932 gave the Nazi Party a massive boost in the Reichstag, it was none the less something of a disappointment to its leaders. For them, the key factor in the result was not that they had improved on the previous Reichstag poll, but that they had not improved on their performance in the second round of the Presidential elections the previous March or the Prussian elections the previous April. There was a feeling, therefore, that the Nazi vote had finally peaked. In particular, despite a massive effort, the Party had only enjoyed limited success in its primary objective of breaking into the Social Democratic and Centre Party vote. So there was no repeat of the jubilation with which the Nazis had greeted their election victory of September 1930. Goebbels confided to his diary his feeling that 'we have won a tiny bit', no more. 'We won't get to an absolute majority this way,' he concluded. The election therefore lent a fresh sense of urgency to the feeling that, as Goebbels put it, 'something must happen. The time for opposition is over. Now deeds!'[146] The moment to grasp for power had arrived, he added the following day, and he noted that Hitler agreed with his view. Otherwise, if they stuck to the parliamentary route to power, the stagnation of their voting strength suggested that the situation might start to slip out of their grasp. Yet Hitler ruled out entering a coalition government led by another party, as indeed he was entitled to do, given the fact that his own Party now held by far the largest number of seats in the national legislature. Immediately after the election, therefore, Hitler insisted that he would only enter a government as Reich Chancellor. This was the only position that would preserve the mystique of his charisma amongst his followers. Unlike a subordinate cabinet position, it would also give him a good chance of turning dominance of the cabinet into a national dictatorship by using the full forces of the state that would then be at his disposal.

II

How those forces might be employed was graphically illustrated by an incident that occurred early in August 1932. In an attempt to master the situation, Papen had imposed a ban on public political meetings on 29 July. This merely had the effect of depriving activists of legitimate political outlets for their inflamed political passions. So it fuelled the violence on the streets still further. On 9 August, therefore, he promulgated another emergency Presidential decree imposing the death penalty on anyone who killed an opponent in the political struggle out of rage or hatred. He intended this to apply above all to the Communists. But in the small hours of the following morning, a group of drunken brownshirts, armed with rubber truncheons, pistols and broken-off billiard cues, broke into a farm in the Upper Silesian village of Potempa and attacked one of the inhabitants, a Communist sympathizer, Konrad Pietzuch. The brownshirts struck him across the face with a billiard cue, beat him senseless, laid into him with their boots as he lay on the ground, and finished him off with a revolver. Pietzuch was Polish, making this into a racial as well as a political incident, and some of the brownshirts had a personal grudge against him. Nevertheless, it was clearly a political murder under the terms of the decree, and five of the brownshirts were arrested, tried and sentenced to death in the nearby town of Beuthen. As soon as the verdict was announced, brownshirted Nazi stormtroopers rampaged through the streets of Beuthen, wrecking Jewish shops and trashing the offices of liberal and left-wing newspapers. Hitler personally and publicly condemned the injustice of 'this monstrous blood-verdict', and Hermann Göring sent an open message of solidarity to the condemned 'in boundless bitterness and outrage at the terror-judgment that has been served on you.'[147]

The murder now became an issue in the negotiations between Hitler, Papen and Hindenburg over Nazi participation in the government. Ironically, President Hindenburg was in any case reluctant to accept Hitler as Chancellor because appointing a government led by the leader of the party that had won the elections would now look too much like going back to a parliamentary system of rule. Now he was dismayed by the Potempa murder, too. 'I have had no doubts about your love for the

Fatherland,' he told Hitler patronizingly on 13 August 1933. 'Against possible acts of terror and violence,' he added, however, 'as have, regrettably, also been committed by members of the SA divisions, I shall intervene with all possible severity.' Papen, too, was unwilling to allow Hitler to lead the cabinet. After negotiations had broken down, Hitler declared:

German racial comrades! Anyone amongst you who possesses any feeling for the struggle for the nation's honour and freedom will understand why I am refusing to enter this government. Herr von Papen's justice will in the end condemn perhaps thousands of National Socialists to death. Did anyone think they could put my name as well to this blindly aggressive action, this challenge to the entire people? The gentlemen are mistaken! Herr von Papen, now I know what your bloodstained 'objectivity' is! I want victory for a nationalistic Germany, and annihilation for its Marxist destroyers and corrupters. I am not suited to be the hangman of nationalist freedom fighters of the German people![148]

Hitler's support for the brutal violence of the stormtroopers could not have been clearer. It was enough to intimidate Papen, who had never intended his decree to apply to the Nazis, into commuting the condemned men's sentences to life imprisonment on 2 September, in the hope of placating the leading Nazis.[149] Shortly after the incident, Hitler had sent the brownshirts on leave for a fortnight, fearing another ban. He need not have bothered.[150]

Nevertheless, the Nazis, who had scented power after the July poll, were bitterly disappointed at the leadership's failure to join the cabinet. The breakdown of negotiations with Hitler also left Papen and Hindenburg with the problem of gaining popular legitimacy. The moment for destroying the parliamentary system seemed to have arrived, but how were they to do it? Papen, with Hindenburg's backing, determined to dissolve the new Reichstag as soon as it met. He would then use – or rather, abuse – the President's power to rule by decree to declare that there would be no more elections. However, when the Reichstag finally met in September, amidst chaotic scenes, Hermann Göring, presiding over the session, according to tradition, as the representative of the largest party, deliberately ignored Papen's attempts to declare a dissolution and allowed a Communist motion of no-confidence in the government to go ahead. The motion won the support of 512 deputies, with only 42 voting against and 5 abstentions. The vote was so humiliating, and demonstrated Papen's lack of support in the country so graphically, that the plan to abolish elections was abandoned. Instead, the government saw little alternative but to follow the constitution and call a fresh Reichstag election for November.[151]

The new election campaign saw Hitler, enraged at Papen's tactics, launch a furious attack on the government. A cabinet of aristocratic reactionaries would never win the collaboration of a man of the people such as himself, he proclaimed. The Nazi press trumpeted yet another triumphant swing by 'the Leader' through the German states; but all its boasts of a massive turnout and wild enthusiasm for Hitler's oratory could not disguise, from the Party leadership at least, the fact that many of the meeting-halls where Hitler spoke were now half-empty, and that the many campaigns of the year had left the Party in no financial condition to sustain its propaganda effort at the level of the previous election. Moreover, Hitler's populist attacks on Papen frightened off middle-class voters, who thought they saw the Nazis' 'socialist' character coming out again. Participation in a bitter transport workers' strike in Berlin alongside the Communists in the run-up to the election did not help the Party's image in the Berlin proletariat, although this had been Goebbels' aim, and it also put off rural voters and repelled some middle-class electors, too. The once-novel propaganda methods of the Party had now become familiar to all. Goebbels had nothing left up his sleeve to startle the electorate with. Nazi leaders gloomily resigned themselves to the prospect of severe losses on polling day.[152]

The mood amongst large parts of the Protestant middle classes was captured in the diary of Louise Solmitz, a former schoolteacher living in Hamburg. Born in 1899, and married to an ex-officer, she had long been an admirer of Hindenburg and Hugenberg, saw Brüning with typical Protestant disdain as a 'petty Jesuit', and complained frequently in her diary about Nazi violence.[153] But in April 1932 she had gone to hear Hitler speak at a mass meeting in a Hamburg suburb and had been filled with enthusiasm by the atmosphere and the public, drawn from all walks of life, as much as by the speech.[154] 'The Hitler spirit carries you away,' she wrote, 'is German, and right.'[155] All her family's middle-class friends were supporting Hitler before long, and there was little doubt that they voted for him in July. But they were repelled both by Göring's cavalier treatment of the Reichstag when it met, and by what they saw as the Nazis' move to the left in the November election campaign. They now inclined more towards Papen, though never with much enthusiasm because he was a Catholic. 'I've voted for Hitler twice,' said an old friend, an ex-soldier, 'but not any more.' 'It's sad about Hitler,' said another acquaintance: 'I can't go along with him any more.' Hitler's backing of the Berlin transport workers' strike, Louise Solmitz thought, cost him thousands of votes. He was not interested in Germany, she concluded pessimistically, only in power. 'Why has Hitler abandoned us, after he showed us a future which one could say yes to?' she asked. In November the Solmitzes voted for the Nationalists.[156]

Faced with this kind of disillusion, it was not surprising that the Nazis did badly. The election, on a much lower turnout than in July, registered a sharp fall in the Party's vote, from 13.7 million to 11.7, reducing its representation in the Reichstag from 230 seats to 196. The Nazis were still by a very long way the largest party. But now they had fewer seats than the combined total of the two 'Marxist' parties.[157] 'Hitler in Decline', the Social Democratic *Forwards* proclaimed.[158] 'We have suffered a set-back,' confided Joseph Goebbels to his diary.[159] By contrast, the election registered some gains for the government. The Nationalists improved their representation from 37 to 51 seats, the People's Party from 7 to 11. Many of their voters had returned from their temporary exile in the Nazi Party. But these were still miserably low figures, little more than a third of what the two parties had scored in their heyday in 1924. The pathetic decline of the former Democrats, the State Party, continued, as their representation went down from 4 seats to 2. The Social Democrats lost another 12 seats, taking them down to 121, their lowest figure since 1924. On the other hand the Communists, still the third largest party, continued to improve their position, gaining another 11 seats, which gave them a total of 100, not far behind the Social Democrats. For many middle-class Germans, this was a terrifyingly effective performance that threatened the prospect of a Communist revolution in the not-too-distant future. The Centre Party also saw a small decline, down from 75 seats to 70, with some of these votes going to the Nazis, as with their Bavarian wing, the Bavarian People's Party.[160]

Overall, the Reichstag was even less manageable than before. One hundred Communists now confronted 196 Nazis across the chamber,

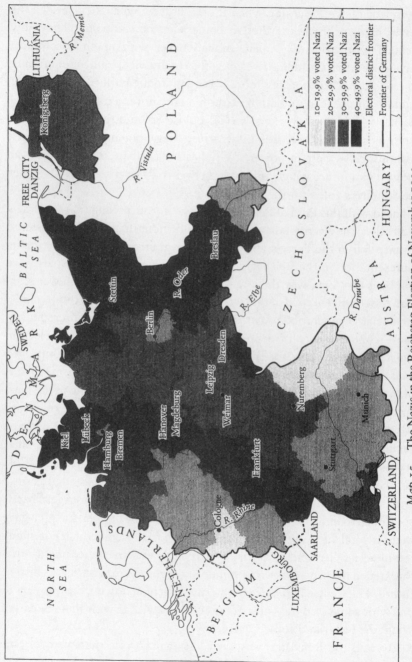

Map 15. The Nazis in the Reichstag Election of November 1932

both intent on destroying a parliamentary system they hated and despised. As a result of the government's rhetorical assault on them during the campaign, the Centre and the Social Democrats were more hostile to Papen than ever. Papen had completely failed to reverse his humiliation in the Reichstag on 12 September. He still faced an overwhelming majority against his cabinet in the new legislature. Papen considered cutting the Gordian knot by banning both Nazis and Communists and using the army to enforce a Presidential regime, bypassing the Reichstag altogether. But this was not a practical possibility, for by this point, fatally, he had lost the confidence of the army and its leading officers, too. Earlier in the year, the army hierarchy had pushed out the Minister of Defence, General Wilhelm Groener, finding his willingness to compromise with the Weimar Republic and its institutions no longer appropriate in the new circumstances. He was replaced by Schleicher, whose views were now more in tune with those of the leading officers. For his part, Schleicher was annoyed that the Chancellor had had the nerve to develop his own ideas and plans for an authoritarian regime instead of following the instructions of the man who had done so much to put him into power in the first place, that is, himself. Papen had also signally failed to deliver the parliamentary majority, made up principally of the Nazis and the Centre Party, that Schleicher and the army had been looking for. It was time for a new initiative. Schleicher quietly informed Papen that the army was unwilling to risk a civil war and would no longer give him its support. The cabinet agreed, and Papen, faced with uncontrollable violence on the streets and lacking any means of preventing its further escalation, was forced to announce his intention to resign.[161]

III

Two weeks of complicated negotiations now followed, led by Hindenburg and his entourage. By this time, the constitution had in effect reverted to what it had been in the Bismarckian Reich, with governments being appointed by the head of state, without reference to parliamentary majorities or legislatures. The Reichstag had been pushed completely to the margins as a political factor. It was, in effect, no longer needed, not even to pass laws. Yet the problem remained that any government which tried to change the constitution in an authoritarian direction without the legitimacy afforded by the backing of a majority in the legislature would run a serious risk of starting a civil war. So the search for parliamentary backing continued. Since the Nazis would not play ball, Schleicher was forced to take on the Chancellorship himself on 3 December. His ministry was doomed from the start. Hindenburg resented his overthrow of Papen, whom he liked and trusted, and many of whose ideas he shared. For a few weeks, Schleicher, less hated by the Centre Party and the Social Democrats than Papen had been, earned a respite by avoiding any repetition of Papen's authoritarian rhetoric. He continued to hope that the Nazis might come round. They had been weakened by the November elections and were divided over what to do next. Moreover, early in December, in local elections held in Thuringia, their vote plummeted by some 40 per cent from the previous July's national high. A year of strenuous electioneering had also left the Party virtually bankrupt. Things seemed to be playing into Schleicher's hands.[162]

Within the Nazi Party, voices now began to be raised criticizing Hitler for his refusal to join a coalition government except at its head. Chief among these was the Party's Organization Leader, Gregor Strasser, who was only too conscious of the parlous state to which, as he increasingly thought, Hitler had reduced the Party organization so painstakingly built up over the previous years. Strasser began to cultivate both big business, with a view to replenishing Party funds, and trade unions, which he sought to win over to the idea of participating in a broad-based national coalition. Aware of his views, however, his enemies in the Nazi leadership, chief among them Joseph Goebbels, started to intrigue behind his back and to accuse him of trying to sabotage the Party's drive for power.[163] Matters came to a head when Schleicher, seeking to put pressure on Hitler to join the cabinet, began separate negotiations with Strasser about a possible post in the government. Hitler, however, was adamant that the Nazis should not join any government of which he was not the head. At a fraught meeting with Hitler, Strasser pleaded in vain for his point of view. Rebuffed once more, he resigned all his Party posts on 8 December in a fit of wounded pride.

Hitler moved swiftly to prevent a Party split, firing known supporters of his former second-in-command and appealing in person to waverers. In a brief, whirlwind tour across the country, Hitler addressed group after group of Party functionaries and convinced them of the rightness of his position, by casting Strasser in the role of traitor, rather as Stalin was casting Trotsky in the role of traitor in the Soviet Union at around the same time. The danger of a split had been real; Hitler and Goebbels certainly took it extremely seriously. But it was based on tactical considerations, not on matters of principle. In no sense did Strasser represent an alternative vision of the future to Hitler's; his ideological position was very similar to his leader's, and he had fully supported the expulsion in 1930 of his brother Otto, whose opinions had indeed been well to the left of the Party mainstream. Nor did Gregor Strasser put up any kind of a fight in December 1932. Had he campaigned for his point of view he might well have taken a substantial portion of the Party with him, leaving it fatally damaged. Instead, he did nothing. He went off on holiday in Italy immediately after his resignation, and although he was not actually expelled from the Party, he played no further role in its affairs and effectively withdrew from political life. Hitler appointed himself Party Organization Leader and dismantled Strasser's centralized structure of Party management just in case someone else should take it over. The crisis in the Party had passed. Hitler and the leadership could breathe again.[164]

Schleicher's failure to win over the Nazis was to prove decisive. Superficially, to be sure, his prospects at the turn of the year did not seem too bad. The Nazi Party was in decline, and even its successful performance in the regional election in the small state of Lippe on 15 January, when it won 39.5 per cent of the vote, failed to convince many, given that the total size of the electorate was only 100,000. A massive propaganda effort and a campaign of unprecedented intensity had still failed to improve on the Nazi vote of July 1932. Hitler and Goebbels were able to revive flagging Nazi spirits and strengthen the Party's resolve by trumpeting the result as a triumph, but most leading figures in the political world knew better.[165] In other respects, too, the Nazis seemed to be on the wane. Their share of the vote in student union elections, for instance, declined from 48 per cent in 1932 to 43 per cent at the beginning of 1933.[166] Meanwhile, the world economic situation was at last beginning to look up, the Depression seemed to be bottoming out, and Schleicher, recognizing the possibilities offered by Germany's departure from the Gold Standard eighteen months before, was preparing a massive job-creation

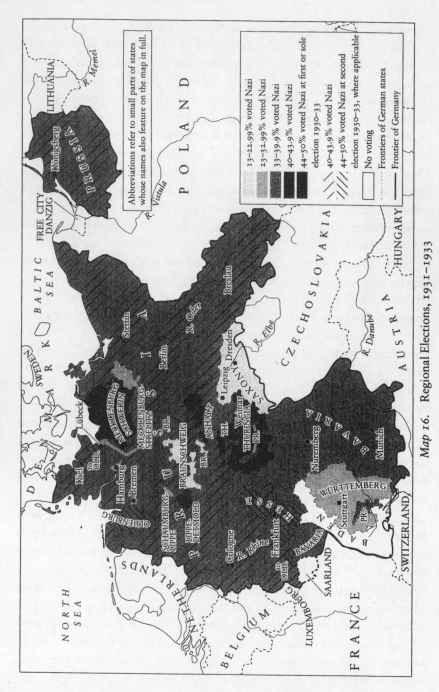

Map 16. Regional Elections, 1931–1933

programme to relieve unemployment through the state provision of public works. This boded ill for the Nazis, whose rise to electoral predominance had been the product above all of the Depression. They had peaked in regional elections, too, and everyone knew it.

But the decline of the Nazis and the revival of the economy were only likely to become important factors over a number of months or even years. Schleicher did not have months or years to play with, only weeks. For Hindenburg and his advisers, above all, his son Oskar, State Secretary Meissner, and ex-Chancellor Franz von Papen, it seemed more urgent than ever at this point to tame the Nazis by bringing them into government. The Nazis' recent losses and divisions seemed to have put them in a position where it would be easier to do this. But if their decline continued, then in the foreseeable future, with an economic upswing on the way, it seemed possible that the old political parties might recover and parliamentary government return, possibly even involving the Social Democrats. Alfred Hugenberg was equally alarmed at such a prospect. Some of Schleicher's economic schemes, which included a possible nationalization of the steel industry and his repeal, carried out in December, of Papen's wage and benefit cuts imposed the previous September, also caused concern among elements in the business world whose interests Papen, Hindenburg and Hugenberg took seriously. As the owner of a landed estate, Hindenburg was further alienated by Schleicher's proposals for land reform in East Elbia, distributing bankrupt Junker estates to the peasantry. A coalition of conservative forces began to form around Hindenburg with the aim of getting rid of Schleicher, whose announcement that he favoured neither capitalism nor socialism they found extremely worrying.[167]

The conspirators secured the backing of the Steel Helmets and their leaders Franz Seldte and Theodor Duesterberg, for a plan to oust Schleicher and replace him with a Reich Chancellor whom they would find more acceptable. Half a million strong, the Steel Helmets were a potentially formidable fighting force. However, they were deeply divided, their leaders Seldte and Duesterberg were at daggers drawn, and they were chronically unable to decide whether or not to throw in their lot with the Nazis or with the conservatives. Their commitment to be 'above parties' was a constant source of internal dispute instead of the unifying slogan it was supposed to be. In this situation, many senior figures in the veterans' organization pressed with some success for its return to welfare activities, military training, the 'protection' of Germany's eastern borders through a strong paramilitary presence, and similar practical tasks. The Steel Helmets thought of themselves above all as a reserve army, to be called upon if necessary to augment the official military forces, whose numbers were little more than a fifth of their own, thanks to the restrictions imposed by the Treaty of Versailles. Duesterberg's disastrous showing in the Presidential elections had convinced many that a withdrawal from the political battlefield was advisable. His background as a Prussian officer caused him to mistrust the Nazis and to consider them too vulgar and disorderly to be worthy partners. But Duesterberg's own position had been weakened by the revelation, shocking to many Steel Helmets, that he had Jewish ancestry. It was Seldte, therefore, who lent the Steel Helmets' name to the conspiracy to oust Schleicher early in 1933.[168]

Papen himself, though in the thick of the conspiracy, was clearly out of the running for the Chancellorship, since he had alienated almost everyone outside Hindenburg's entourage over the previous few months and had no popular backing in the country. Frantic negotiations finally led to a plan to put Hitler in as Chancellor, with a majority of conservative cabinet colleagues to keep him in check. The scheme was lent urgency by rumours that Schleicher, in collaboration with the chief of the army command, General Kurt von Hammerstein, was preparing a counter-coup. He apparently intended to establish an authoritarian corporate state, to eliminate the Reichstag by Presidential decree, to put the army in control, and to suppress the Nazis altogether, as well as the Communists. 'If a new government is not formed by 11 o'clock,' Papen told Hugenberg and the Steel Helmets' leaders on 30 January, 'the army will march. A military dictatorship under Schleicher and Hammerstein is looming.'[169]

The rumour did the rounds because it was known in political circles that Schleicher's failure to secure parliamentary support left him no option but to ask the President for wide-ranging, effectively extra-constitutional powers to overcome the crisis. When he went to Hindenburg with this request, the aged President and his entourage saw this as their chance to rid themselves of this irritating and untrustworthy intriguer, and refused. After he was rebuffed, some expected Schleicher and the army to take matters into their own hands and seize the powers they wanted anyway. But Schleicher and the army only ever considered a putsch for the eventuality of Papen returning to the Reich Chancellery, and this was only because they thought that Papen's appointment might well lead to the outbreak of civil war. Keen to avoid this situation arising, however, Schleicher now saw a Hitler Chancellorship as a welcome solution, as far as the army was concerned. 'If Hitler wants to establish a dictatorship in the Reich,' he said confidently, 'then the army will be the dictatorship within the dictatorship.'[170] Refused permission by the President to govern unconstitutionally, Schleicher had no option but to tender his resignation. Negotiations had already been in progress for some time in the circle around Hindenburg with a view to appointing Hitler in his stead. Finally, at about half past eleven on the morning of 30 January 1933, Hitler was sworn in as Reich Chancellor. The government of which he was head was dominated numerically by Papen and his fellow conservatives. The radical wing of the much-shrunken Nationalist Party entered the government, with Alfred Hugenberg taking over the Economics Ministry and the Ministry of Food. Konstantin Freiherr von Neurath, already Foreign Minister in the Papen and Schleicher governments, continued in office, as did Lutz Graf Schwerin von Krosigk in the Finance Ministry and, a little later, Franz Gürtner, for the Nationalists, in the Ministry of Justice. The army ministry was taken over by Werner von Blomberg. Franz Seldte, representing the Steel Helmets, moved into the Ministry of Labour.

Only two major offices of state went to the Nazis, but both of them were key positions on which Hitler had insisted as a condition of the deal: the Ministry of the Interior, occupied by Wilhelm Frick, and the Reich Chancellery itself, occupied by Hitler. Hermann Göring was appointed Reich Minister Without Portfolio and Acting Prussian Minister of the Interior, which gave him direct control over the police in the greater part of Germany. The Nazis could thus manipulate the whole domestic law-and-order situation to their advantage. If they moved even with only a modicum of skill, the way would soon be free for the brownshirts to unleash a whole new level of violence against their opponents on the streets. Franz von Papen became Vice-Chancellor and continued to rule Prussia as Reich Commissioner, nominally Göring's superior. Surrounded by friends of Papen, who had the all-important ear of Reich President Hindenburg, Hitler and the Nazis – vulgar, uneducated, inexperienced in government – would surely be easy enough to control. 'You are wrong,' Papen haughtily told a sceptical associate who had voiced his alarm: 'We've engaged him for ourselves.'[171] 'Within two months,' Papen confidently told a worried conservative acquaintance, 'we will have pushed Hitler so far into a corner that he'll squeak.'[172]

5

CREATING THE
THIRD REICH

THE TERROR BEGINS

I

That Hitler's appointment as Reich Chancellor was no ordinary change of government became immediately clear, as Goebbels organized a torchlit parade of brownshirts, Steel Helmets and SS men through Berlin, beginning at seven in the evening on 30 January 1933 and going on well past midnight. One pro-Nazi newspaper, carried away with enthusiasm, put the number of marchers at 700,000.[1] More plausible than this quite fantastic figure was the report of another paper, which described the parades sympathetically as 'an unforgettable experience', that 18,000 brownshirts and SS men, 3,000 Steel Helmets and 40,000 non-uniformed civilians, 61,000 in all had taken part; a third estimate from a more hostile source put the number of uniformed marchers at no more than 20,000. Crowds of curious onlookers lined the streets to watch the march. Many cheered as the paramilitaries passed by. The spectacle was typical of the kind of stage-management which Goebbels was to perfect over the coming years. Watching the march in a Berlin street, the young Hans-Joachim Heldenbrand happened to be standing at the spot where the stormtroopers paused to exchange their guttering torches for new, freshly lit ones. Scanning their faces as the evening went on, he began to notice the same men appearing in front of him again and again. 'There,' said his father to him, 'you see the con trick. They're constantly marching round in a circle as if there were a hundred thousand of them.'[2]

As the columns of uniformed paramilitaries marched past, the aged Hindenburg came to the first-floor window of his official residence to take the salute. To symbolize the relative positions of Nationalists and Nazis in the new government, Goebbels had arranged for the SA to head up the parade and the Steel Helmets to follow them. After Hindenburg had been standing stiffly for some hours, his attention began to slip and his mind to wander back to the glorious early days of the First World War. One of his entourage later told the British writer John Wheeler-Bennett:

The brownshirts passed at a shambling pace, to be followed by the field-grey ranks of the Steel Helmets, moving with a precision born of discipline. The old Marshal watched them from his window as in a dream, and those behind him saw him beckon over his shoulder. 'Ludendorff', the old man said, with a return to its harsh barking, 'how well your men are marching, and what a lot of prisoners they've taken!'[3]

Befuddled or not, Hindenburg was presented by the Nationalist press as the central figure in the jubilation, and the parades as a 'tribute to Hindenburg' by 'his people'.[4] The police did their part, accompanying and, in effect, taking part in the general jubilation, and beaming a search-light on the window where the President stood, so that everyone could observe him acknowledging the cheers of the marchers.[5] Black, white and red flags were everywhere. Over the radio, Hermann Göring compared the crowds to those who had gathered to celebrate the outbreak of the First World War. The 'mood', he said, 'could only be compared with that of August 1914, when a nation also rose up to defend everything it possessed.' The 'shame and disgrace of the last fourteen years' had been wiped out. The spirit of 1914 had been revived.[6] These were sentiments with which every Nationalist could agree. Germany, as one Nationalist paper declared, was witnessing a 'second August-miracle'.[7] A few days later, seeing the marchers on the streets amongst the crowds, Louise Solmitz made the same comparison: 'It was like 1914, everyone could have fallen into everyone else's arms in the name of Hitler. Intoxication without wine.'[8] She may not have recalled at that moment that the spirit of 1914 betokened war: the mobilization of an entire people as the basis for waging armed conflict, the suppression of internal dissent as preparation for international aggression. But this was what the Nazis were now aiming for, as Göring's statement implied. From 30 January onwards, German society was to be put as quickly as possible on a permanent war footing.[9]

Goebbels was jubilant at the celebrations. He had already been able to organize a live commentary on the state radio, though as yet he had no official position in the new cabinet. The results more than met his expectations:

Great jubilation. Down there the people are creating an uproar ... The torches come. It starts at 7 o'clock. Endless. Till 10 o'clock. At the Kaiserhof. Then the Reich Chancellery. Till after 12 o'clock. Unending. A million people on the move. The Old Man takes the salute at the march-past. Hitler in the house next door. Awakening! Spontaneous explosion of the people. Indescribable. Always new masses. Hitler is in raptures. His people are cheering him ... Wild frenzy of enthusiasm. Prepare the election campaign. The last. We'll win it hands down.[10]

Choruses of the national anthem alternated with the Horst Wessel Song as the uniformed columns marched on, through the Brandenburg Gate and past the government buildings.[11]

Many people found themselves caught up in the enthusiastic demonstrations. The torchlit parades were repeated in many other towns and cities outside Berlin on the following evenings.[12] In Berlin, on the afternoon of 31 January, the National Socialist German Students' League staged its own parade, which ended up in front of the Stock Exchange ('The "Mecca" of German Jewry', as a right-wing newspaper put it). Emerging stockbrokers were greeted by the students with chants of 'Judah perish!'[13] Watching another torchlit parade in Hamburg on 6 February, Louise Solmitz was 'drunk with enthusiasm, blinded by the light of the torches right in our faces, and always enveloped in their vapour as in a sweet cloud of incense'. Like many respectable bourgeois families, the Solmitzes took their children to witness the extraordinary scenes: 'So far, the impressions they had had of politics', Solmitz remarked, 'had been so deplorable that they should now have a really strong impression of nationhood, as we had once, and keep it as a memory. And so they did.' From ten at night onwards, she reported,

20,000 brownshirts followed one another like waves in the sea, their faces shone with enthusiasm in the light of the torches. 'For our Leader, our Reich Chancellor Adolf Hitler, a threefold Hail!' They sang 'The Republic is shit' ... Next to us a little boy 3 years of age raised his tiny hand again and again: 'Hail Hitler, Hail Hitler-man!' 'Death to the Jews' was also sometimes called out and they sang of the blood of the Jews which would squirt from their knives.

'Who took that seriously then?', she added later to her diary.[14]

The young Melita Maschmann was taken by her conservative parents to watch the torchlight parade on 30 January, and remembered the scene vividly many years later, recalling not just the enthusiasm but also the threatening undertones of violence and aggression that accompanied the parade, including

the crashing tread of the feet, the sombre pomp of the red and black flags, the flickering light from the torches on the faces and the songs with melodies that were at once inflaming and sentimental.

For hours the columns marched by. Again and again amongst them we saw groups of boys and girls scarcely older than ourselves . . . At one point somebody suddenly leaped from the ranks of the marchers and struck a man who had been standing only a few paces away from us. Perhaps he had made a hostile remark. I saw him fall to the ground with blood streaming down his face and I heard him cry out. Our parents hurriedly drew us away from the scuffle, but they had not been able to stop us seeing the man bleeding. The image of him haunted me for days.

The horror it inspired in me was almost imperceptibly spiced with an intoxicat-ing joy. 'We want to die for the flag', the torch-bearers had sung . . . I was overcome with a burning desire to belong to these people for whom it was a matter of death and life . . . I wanted to escape from my childish, narrow life and I wanted to attach myself to something that was great and fundamental.[15]

For such respectable middle-class people, the violence that accompanied the marches seemed incidental and not particularly threatening. But for others, Hitler's appointment already presaged disaster. As the foreign press corps observed the march-past from a window of the Reich Press Office, one journalist was heard to remark that they were witnessing the equivalent of Mussolini's seizure of power in Italy eleven years before – 'the march on Rome in German form'.[16]

Communists, in particular, knew that the Hitler government was likely to crack down hard on their activities. Already on the evening of 30 January, the right-wing press was calling for the party to be banned after shots were fired from a house in Charlottenburg at a marching column of torch-bearing stormtroopers, resulting in the death of a policeman as well as a brownshirt.[17] The *Red Flag* was banned and copies confiscated, and the police made more than sixty arrests as a shooting-match broke out between Nazis and Communists in Spandau.[18] There were similar, though less spectacular clashes in Düsseldorf, Halle, Hamburg and Mannheim, while elsewhere the police immediately proscribed all demonstrations by the Communists. In Altona, Chemnitz, Müncheberg, Munich and Worms, and various working-class districts in Berlin, the Communists staged public demonstrations against the new cabinet. Five thousand workers were reported to have marched against the new cabinet in Weissenfels, and there were similar, though smaller demonstrations elsewhere.[19] In one of the most remarkable of these, in the little Württemberg town of Mössingen, where nearly a third of the votes had been cast for the Communists in the 1932 elections, the men staged a general strike. With up to 800 from a total population of no more than 4,000 marching through the streets against the new government, the inhabitants of the small industrial centre soon learned the realities of the situation, as the police moved in and began to arrest those identified as the ringleaders, eventually apprehending over 80 participants, 71 of whom were subsequently convicted of treason. In charge of the police operation was the conservative Catholic government of the Württemberg State President Eugen Bolz, who evidently feared a general Communist uprising. Looking back on these events many years later, one of the participants said proudly that if everyone else had followed the example of Mössingen, the Nazis would never have succeeded. For another, it was an equal source of pride that, as he said with pardonable exaggeration, 'Nothing happened, not nowhere, except here.'[20]

In a number of towns and cities there was a good deal of preparedness on the part of rank-and-file members of the labour parties to collaborate in the face of the Nazi threat. But neither the Communists nor the Social Democrats did anything to co-ordinate protest measures on a wider scale. Although the Communist Party did immediately urge a general strike, it knew that the prospects of one occurring were zero without the co-operation of the unions and the Social Democrats, who were unwilling to allow themselves to be manipulated in this way. For the Comintern, the appointment of the Hitler cabinet showed that monopoly capital had succeeded in co-opting the Nazis into its plans to break the proletariat's resistance to the creation of a fascist dictatorship. The key figure in the cabinet according to this view was thus Hugenberg, the representative of industry and the big estates. Hitler was nothing more than his tool.[21] A number of left-wing Social Democrats, including Kurt Schumacher, one of the party's most prominent Reichstag deputies, shared this view. The Communists also feared that the 'fascist dictatorship' would mean a violent crack-down on the labour movement, increased exploitation of the workers, a headlong drive towards an 'imperialist war'.[22] By 1 February 1933 the Communist press was already reporting a 'wave of banning orders in the Reich', and a 'storm over Germany' in which 'Nazi terror bands' were murdering workers and smashing up trade union premises and Communist Party offices. More would surely come.[23]

Others were less sure of what the new cabinet meant. So many governments, so many Reich Chancellors, had come and gone over the past few years that a number of people evidently thought the new one would make little difference and be as short-lived as its predecessors. Even the enthusiastic Louise Solmitz noted in her diary:

And what a cabinet!!! As we didn't dare dream of in July. Hitler, Hugenberg, Seldte, Papen!!! On each of them hangs a large part of my German hope. National Socialist élan, German Nationalist reason, the unpolitical Steel Helmets and Papen, whom we have not forgotten. It is so inexpressibly beautiful that I'm writing it down quickly before the first discordant note is struck . . .[24]

To many readers of the newspapers that reported Hitler's appointment, the jubilation of the brownshirts must have appeared exaggerated. The key feature of the new government, symbolized by the participation of the Steel Helmets in the march-past, was surely the heavy numerical domination of the conservatives. 'No nationalistic, no revolutionary government, although it carries Hitler's name', confided a Czech diplomat based in Berlin to his diary: 'No Third Reich, hardly even a 2½.'[25] A more alarmist note was sounded by the French ambassador, André François-Poncet. The perceptive diplomat noted that the conservatives were right to expect Hitler to agree to their programme of 'the crushing of the left, the purging of the bureaucracy, the assimilation of Prussia and the Reich, the reorganization of the army, the re-establishment of military service'. They had put Hitler into the Chancellery in order to discredit him, he observed; 'they have believed themselves to be very ingenious, ridding themselves of the wolf by introducing him into the sheepfold.'[26]

II

The complacent belief of Franz von Papen and his friends that they had Hitler where they wanted him did not last long. The Nazis occupied only three cabinet posts. But the authority that came with Hitler's position as Reich Chancellor was considerable. Just as important was the fact that the Nazis held both the Reich and the Prussian Ministries of the Interior. With these went extensive powers over law and order. Göring's occupancy of the Prussian post in particular gave him control over the police in the majority of the Reich's territory. As Reich Commissioner, Papen might be his nominal superior, but it would not be easy for him to interfere in the day-to-day running of the Ministry in matters such as the maintenance of order. Moreover, the new Minister of Defence, General Werner von Blomberg, appointed at the army's behest the day before Hitler took office, was far more sympathetic to the Nazis than either Papen or Hindenburg realized. An impulsive, energetic man, Blomberg had won a formidable reputation as a staff planner in the First World War and had later become Chief of the General Staff. He was very much the army's man in government. But he was also easily influenced by strong impressions. On visiting the Soviet Union to inspect German military installations there, he had been so impressed by the Red Army that he had seriously considered joining the Communist Party, entirely ignoring the hair-raising political implications of such a decision. Narrowly military in his outlook, and almost entirely ignorant of politics, he was putty in the hands of someone like Hitler.[27]

Blomberg banned officers from joining the Nazi Party, and jealously guarded the independence of the army. His loyalty to Hitler made it seem unnecessary for the Nazis to undermine the army from within. Still, they had to be sure that the army would not interfere in the violence they were now contemplating unleashing on the country. Hitler underlined his respect for the army's neutrality in an address to senior officers on 3 February 1933. He won their approval with his promises to restore conscription, destroy Marxism and fight the Treaty of Versailles. The officers present made no objection as he held out to them the intoxicating long-term prospect of invading Eastern Europe and 'Germanizing' it by expelling scores of millions of native Slav inhabitants. The army's neutrality meant, of course, its non-interference, and Hitler went out of his way to tell the officers that the 'internal struggle' was 'not your business'. He was helped in his efforts to neutralize the army by the appointment, on Blomberg's suggestion, of Colonel Walther von Reichenau, a vigorous, ambitious and much-decorated staff officer, as Blomberg's chief assistant. Reichenau was another admirer of Hitler and was on good personal terms with him. Together with Blomberg he quickly moved to isolate the army's commander-in-chief, General Kurt von Hammerstein, an aristocratic conservative who never tried to disguise his contempt for the Nazis. In February 1933 Hammerstein banned officers from inviting politicians to social events, as a way of trying to minimize relations with leading Nazis such as Göring, to whom he always referred snobbishly by his actual rank from pre-Nazi days, 'captain (retired)', except when he called him by his nickname, the 'pilot who's gone round the bend'. Hammerstein was a real potential threat because he reported directly to the President. Within a short space of time, however, Blomberg had succeeded in restricting Hammerstein's access to Hindenburg to strictly military matters. On 4 April 1933 Blomberg became a member of the newly created Reich Defence Council, a political body which effectively bypassed the army leadership and put military policy in the hands of Hitler, who chaired it, and a small group of leading ministers. Through these moves, Hammerstein and his supporters were effectively neutralized. In any case, Hammerstein was too Olympian, too distant, to engage in serious political intrigue. Now that Schleicher was safely out of the way, neither he nor any of the other army leaders was capable of mobilizing opposition to the Nazis in the first half of 1933.[28]

With Frick and Göring at the helm, and the army relegated to the sidelines, the prospects of curbing Nazi violence were now worse than ever. Almost immediately, the Nazis capitalized on this carefully engineered situation and unleashed a campaign of political violence and terror that dwarfed anything seen so far. On 30 and 31 January the triumphant parades and processions of the SA and SS had already demonstrated their new-found confidence and power over their opponents on the streets. They had also been accompanied by incidences of violence and antisemitism. Now these quickly began to multiply. Bands of storm-troopers began attacking trade union and Communist offices and the homes of prominent left-wingers. They were helped on 4 February by a decree allowing for the detention for up to three months of those engaged in armed breaches of the peace or acts of treason, a decree that self-evidently was not going to be applied to Hitler's stormtroopers.[29]

The intensity of the violence increased considerably when Göring, acting as Prussian Minister of the Interior, ordered the Prussian police on 15–17 February to cease its surveillance of the Nazis and associated paramilitary organizations and to support what they were doing as far as they were able. On 22 February he went a step further and set up an 'auxiliary police' force made up from members of the SA, SS and Steel Helmets, the last-named decidedly the junior partners. This gave the stormtroopers the green light to go on the rampage without any serious interference from the formal state guardians of law and order. While the police, purged of Social Democrats since the Papen coup, pursued Communists and broke up their demonstrations, the new force, with the agreement of the police, broke into party and trade union offices, destroyed documents and expelled the occupants by force. The brunt of this violence was undoubtedly borne by the Communist Party and its members. They had already been under close police surveillance during the Weimar Republic. The Social Democratic government in Prussia claimed in the early 1930s, for instance, that it was presented with confidential reports on secret sessions of the Communist Party's Central Committee within a few hours of the sessions taking place. Police spies were active at every level of the party hierarchy. Frequent clashes with the Red Front-Fighters' League, involving injuries to police officers, sometimes fatal, had led to police investigations including searches of Communist Party premises. Documents confiscated in 1931–2 included address-lists of party officials and active members. The police were extremely well informed about the party, therefore, regarded it as an enemy after the experience of innumerable armed clashes, and from 30 January onwards put their information at the disposal of the new government. It did not hesitate to use it.[30]

The Social Democrats and trade unions were almost as hard hit as the Communists in the mounting Nazi repression of the second half of February 1933. The government was able to build on a wide degree of public consensus among middle-class voters in its suppression of the Communists, who had always been regarded as a threat to public order and private property. The fact that the Communists had continually increased their electoral support to a point where, early in 1933, they had 100 seats in the Reichstag, was extremely alarming to many who feared that they would repeat the violence, murder and torture that had been the hallmark of the 'Red Terror' in Russia in 1918–21, should they ever achieve power in Germany. But matters were very different where the Social Democrats were concerned. They were, after all, the political force that had been the mainstay of the Weimar Republic for many years. They had 121 seats in the Reichstag to the Nazis' 196. They had formed a key element in a number of its governments. They had supplied Reich Chancellors and Prussian Minister-Presidents as well as the Republic's first Head of State, Friedrich Ebert. They had the long-term support of millions of working-class voters, relatively few of whom had deserted them for the Nazis or the Communists, and had enjoyed the support or at least the respect, however grudging and conditional, of many Germans at various times. In 1930 the membership of their party stood at over a million.[31]

Some units of the Social Democrats and their paramilitary affiliate, the Reichsbanner, were prepared to act; a few had managed to gather weapons and munitions, and others staged demonstrations on 30 January and the next day. Leading Social Democrats and trade unionists met in Berlin on 31 January to plan a nationwide general strike. But while local organizations waited, the national leadership dithered, conscious of the difficulties of staging a strike in the middle of the worst unemployment crisis the nation had ever seen. The unions feared that Nazi stormtroopers would occupy the factories in such a situation. And how could the party justify illegal action in defence of legality? 'The Social Democrats and the entire Iron Front', declared the party's daily paper *Forwards* on 30 January 1933, 'are placing themselves, in relation to this government and its threat of a putsch, with both feet firmly on the ground of the constitution and of legality. They will *not* take the first step away from this ground.' In the following weeks there were some isolated actions. Thousands of socialists staged a rally in the Pleasure Gardens in Berlin on 7 February, while on 19 February a rally of 15,000 workers in Lübeck celebrated the release from custody of a leading local Social Democrat, Julius Leber, after a brief general strike in the city. But no general policy of resistance emerged from the centre.[32]

With every day that passed, the state-sponsored terror to which Social

Democrats were subjected grew steadily worse. By the beginning of February 1933 local and regional authorities, acting under pressure from Wilhelm Frick, the Nazi Reich Minister of the Interior in Berlin, and his counterpart in Prussia, Hermann Göring, had already begun to impose bans on particular issues of Social Democratic newspapers. Characteristically, the Social Democrats' reaction was to institute legal actions before the Reich Court in Leipzig to compel Frick and Göring to allow the papers to be published, a tactic that met with some success.[33] As the month progressed, however, gangs of brownshirts began to break up Social Democratic meetings and beat up the speakers and their audiences. On 24 February Albert Grzesinski, the Social Democrat who had formerly been Prussian Minister of the Interior, was complaining that 'several of my meetings have been broken up and a substantial number of those present had to be taken away with serious injuries'. The party's executive committee reacted by cutting back sharply on meetings in order to avoid further casualties. Whatever police protection had been provided for meetings before 30 January had been entirely removed on the orders of the Interior Ministry.[34] Nazi stormtroopers could now beat up and murder Communists and Social Democrats with impunity. On 5 February 1933, in one particularly shocking incident, a young Nazi shot dead the Social Democratic mayor of Stassfurt. A few days later, when the Social Democratic official daily *Forwards* condemned the killing of a Communist by stormtroopers during a street battle in Eisleben, the Police President of Berlin banned the paper for a week.[35]

Within a few months of Papen's coup of 20 July 1932, the prospects for a workers' uprising had dramatically worsened. The failure to resist Papen had deepened the sense of impotence in the labour movement already created by the Social Democrats' passive support for Brüning and active backing for Hindenburg. The police and the army were no longer trying to hold the ring between paramilitaries of the right and the left. Encouraged by the conservatives around Hugenberg and Seldte, they had swung decisively over to the support of the former. In this situation, an armed uprising by the labour movement would have been suicidal. Moreover, despite a whole variety of local initiatives, grass-roots negotiations and formal and informal approaches at every level, the Social Democrats and the Communists were still not prepared to work together in a last-ditch defence of democracy. And even had they done so, their combined forces could never have hoped to match the numbers, the weaponry and the equipment of the army, the brownshirts, the Steel Helmets and the SS. Had an uprising been attempted, it would doubtless have met the same fate as the workers' uprising staged in Vienna a year later against the *coup d'état* that established the 'clerico-fascist' dictatorship of Engelbert Dollfuss, in which the well-equipped and well-armed socialists were crushed by the Austrian army within a few days.[36] The last thing the German Social Democratic leadership wanted to do was to shed the workers' blood, least of all in collaboration with the Communists, who they rightly thought would ruthlessly exploit any violent situation to their own advantage.[37] Throughout the early months of 1933, therefore, they stuck rigidly to a legalistic approach and avoided anything that might provoke the Nazis into even more violent action against them.

III

Once more, in February 1933, Germany was in the grip of election fever. The parties were campaigning furiously for the Reichstag elections that had been one of Hitler's conditions for accepting the office of Reich Chancellor on 30 January. The date had been fixed for 5 March. Hitler proclaimed on many occasions during the election campaign that the Nazi movement's main enemy was 'Marxism'. 'Never, never will I stray from the task of stamping out Marxism . . . There can only be one victor: either Marxism or the German people! And Germany will triumph!' This referred, of course, to the Communists and the Social Democrats. Hitler's belligerent language, in the circumstances of early 1933, was an encouragement to his stormtroopers to take the law into their own hands. But its aggressiveness extended well beyond the left to threaten other supporters, or former supporters, of Weimar democracy as well. The movement, he said on 10 February 1933, would be 'intolerant against anyone who sins against the nation'.[38] 'I repeat', Hitler declared on 15 February, 'that our fight against Marxism will be relentless, and that every movement which allies itself to Marxism will come to grief with it.'[39]

This threat was uttered in Stuttgart in a speech devoted to a furious attack on the Württemberg State President, Eugen Bolz, who had declared the new Reich government to be an enemy of freedom. Bolz, complained Hitler, had not stepped in to defend the Nazi Party's freedom when it had been persecuted in his state during the 1920s. He went on:

Those who made no mention of our freedom for fourteen years have no right to talk about it today. As Chancellor I need only use one law for the protection of the national state, just as they made a law for the protection of the Republic back then, and then they would realize that not everything they called freedom was worthy of the name.[40]

The Centre Party, like the Communists and Social Democrats, had proved relatively immune to the electoral advances of the Nazis, and so was another prime target for intimidation in the election campaign. Before long, it was beginning to feel the impact of state terror just as the Social Democrats were. Already in mid-February, twenty Centre Party newspapers had been banned for criticizing the new government, public meetings were forbidden in a number of localities by the authorities, and a wave of dismissals or suspensions of civil servants and administrators known to be Centre Party members had begun, including the police chief of Oberhausen and a Ministerial Director in the Prussian Interior Ministry. A speech by Heinrich Brüning condemning these dismissals sparked violent attacks by stormtroopers on Centre Party election meetings in Westphalia. The former Reich Minister Adam Stegerwald was beaten up by brownshirts at a Centre Party meeting in Krefeld on 22 February. One local party newspaper after another was banned or had its offices trashed by rampaging gangs of brownshirts. Local party premises were attacked, and supplies of election posters seized, not just by SA men but also by the political police. The bishops prayed for peace, while the party appealed to the constitution and, in a pathetic sign of its political bankruptcy, urged the electorate to vote for a restoration of the long-since discredited Brüning government.[41]

Hitler professed himself alarmed by these incidents, and on 22 February, after the Centre Party had protested vehemently against these events, proclaimed: 'Provocative elements are attempting, under the guise of the Party, to discredit the National Socialist Movement by disrupting and breaking up Centre Party assemblies in particular. I expect', he said severely, 'all National Socialists to distance themselves from these designs with the utmost discipline. The enemy who must be felled on March 5 is Marxism!' Yet this was also coupled with a threat to 'attend to the Centre' if it supported 'Marxism' in the elections, and, taken together with Hitler's savage attack on Bolz less than a fortnight before, it was enough to ensure that the violence continued.[42] And, while the brownshirts unfolded this campaign of violence on the ground, Hitler and the leading Nazis were making it clear in their more unguarded moments that the coming election would be the last, and that, whatever happened, Hitler would not resign as Chancellor. 'If we do one day achieve power,' he had declared in a public address given on 17 October 1932, 'we will hold on to it, so help us God. We will not allow them to take it away from us again.'[43] The results of the election, he said in February 1933, would have no effect on his government's programme. 'It will not deter us should the German people abandon us in this hour. We will adhere to whatever is necessary to keep Germany from degenerating.'[44]

On other occasions, more circumspectly but less plausibly, Hitler announced that he only wanted four years to put his programme into effect, and then, in 1937, when the next Reichstag elections were due, the German people could judge whether or not it had been a good one. He outlined what that programme was in a lengthy speech delivered to a huge audience in the Berlin Sports Palace on 10 February in an atmosphere of ecstatic adulation. With all the resources of the state now at its disposal, the Party arranged for the hall to be decked out with flags bearing the swastika symbol and banners with anti-Marxist slogans. Radio microphones broadcast Hitler's words to the entire nation. Choruses of the national anthem, shouts of 'Hail!' and enthusiastic cheers and shouts preceded the speech and rose in a crescendo as Hitler entered the arena. As so often in his career, Hitler, beginning slowly and quietly so as to secure the rapt attention of his enormous audience, went over the history of the Nazi Party and the alleged crimes of the Weimar Republic since 1919 – the inflation, the impoverishment of the peasantry, the rise of unemployment, the ruin of the nation. What would his government do to change this parlous situation? His answer avoided any specific commitments at all. He said grandly that he was not going to make any 'cheap promises'. Instead, he declared that his programme was to rebuild the German nation without foreign aid, 'according to eternal laws valid for all time', on the basis of the people and the soil, not according to ideas of class. Once more, he held up the intoxicating vision of a Germany united in a new society that would overcome the divisions of class and creed that had racked it over the past fourteen years. The workers, he declared, would be freed from the alien ideology of Marxism and led back to the national community of the entire German race. This was a 'programme of national resurrection in all areas of life'.

He ended with an almost religious appeal to his audience in the Sports Palace and across the nation:

For fourteen years the parties of disintegration, of the November Revolution, have seduced and abused the German people. For fourteen years they wreaked destruction, infiltration, and dissolution. Considering this, it is not presumptuous of me to stand before the nation today, and plead to it: German people, give us four years' time and then pass judgment upon us. German people, give us four years, and I swear to you, just as we, just as I have taken this office, so shall I leave it. I have done it neither for salary nor for wages; I have done it for your sake! . . . For I cannot divest myself of my faith in my people, cannot dissociate myself from the conviction that this nation will one day rise again, cannot divorce myself from my love for this, my people, and I cherish the firm conviction that the hour will come at last in which the millions who despise us today will stand by us and with us will hail the new, hard-won and painfully acquired German Reich we have created together, the new German kingdom of greatness and power and glory and justice. Amen.[45]

What Hitler was promising Germany was, therefore, in the first place the suppression of Communism and, beyond that, of the other Weimar parties, principally the Social Democrats and the Centre Party. Other than that he had nothing much concrete to offer. But many saw this as a virtue. 'I'm delighted at Hitler's lack of a programme,' wrote Louise Solmitz in her diary, 'for a programme is either lies, weakness, or designed to catch silly birds. – The strongman acts from the necessity of a serious situation and can't allow himself to be bound.' One of her acquaintances, previously indifferent to Nazism, told her she was voting for Hitler precisely because he had no programme but Germany.[46] Hitler's dramatic and emotional claim that all he needed was four years was designed to heighten the feeling in his listeners that he was engaged in a Christ-like pilgrimage of self-sacrifice. These sentiments were repeated in further speeches at other venues in the following days, to similarly enthusiastic audiences.

Hitler was backed in his election campaign by a fresh, indeed unprecedented flow of funds from industry. On 11 February he opened an international motor show in Berlin, and announced an ambitious programme of road building and tax breaks to help automobile manufacturers.[47] On 20 February a large group of leading industrialists met at Göring's official residence, and were joined by Hitler, who once more declared that democracy was incompatible with business interests, and Marxism had to be crushed. The forthcoming election was crucial in this struggle. If the government failed to win, it would be compelled to use force to achieve its ends, he threatened. The last thing business wanted was a civil war. The message was clear: they had to do everything in their power to ensure a victory for the coalition – a coalition in which some leading businessmen evidently still thought that Papen and the conservatives were the key players. After Hitler left the meeting, Göring reminded his listeners that the forthcoming election would be the last, not just for the next four years but probably for the next hundred. Hjalmar Schacht, the politically well-connected financier who had been the architect of the post-inflation stabilization programme in 1923–4, then announced that business would be expected to contribute three million Reichsmarks to the government's election fund. Some of those present still insisted that a portion of the money should go to the conservative coalition partners of the Nazis. But they paid up all the same.[48] The new funds made a real difference to the Nazi Party's ability to fight the election, in contrast to the lack of resources that had so hampered it the previous November. They enabled Goebbels to mount a new kind of campaign, portraying Hitler as the man who was reconstructing Germany and destroying the Marxist menace, as everybody could see on the streets. Fresh resources, notably the radio, were brought to bear on the Nazis' behalf, and with a fighting fund vastly bigger than before, Goebbels really could saturate the electorate this time.[49]

Nevertheless, the Nazi campaign was no triumphant procession towards the ratification of power. The party was well aware that its popularity had faded in the second half of 1932, while that of the Communists had been growing. Of all their opponents, the Nazis feared and hated the Communists most. In countless street-battles and meeting-hall clashes the Communists had shown that they could trade punch for punch and exchange shot for shot with their brownshirt counterparts. It was all the more puzzling to the Nazi leadership, therefore, that after the initial Communist demonstrations in the immediate aftermath of 30 January 1933, the Red Front-Fighters' League had shown no inclination to respond in kind to the massive wave of violence that swept over the Communist party, above all after the brownshirts' enrolment as auxiliary police on 22 February, as the Nazi stormtroopers took matters into their own hands and vented their pent-up spleen on their hated enemies. Isolated incidents and brawls continued to occur, and the Red Front-Fighters' League did not take this nationwide assault entirely lying down, but there was no observable escalation of Communist violence, no indication of any kind that a concerted response was being mounted on the orders of the Community Party's politburo.

The relative inaction of the Communists reflected above all the party leadership's belief that the new government – the last, violent, dying gasp of a moribund capitalism – would not last more than a few months before it collapsed. Aware of the risk that the party might be banned, the German Communists had made extensive preparations for a lengthy period of illegal or semi-legal existence, and no doubt stockpiled as substantial a quantity of weapons as they were able. They knew, too, that the Red Front-Fighters' League would get no support from the Social Democrats' paramilitary associate, the Reichsbanner, with which it had clashed repeatedly over the previous years. The party's constantly reiterated demands for a 'unity front' with the Social Democrats stood no chance of becoming reality, since it was only willing to enter into it if the 'social fascists', as it called them, gave up all their political independence and, in effect, put themselves under Communist Party leadership. The party stuck rigidly to the doctrine that the Hitler government signalled the temporary triumph of big business and 'monopoly capitalism', and insisted that it heralded the imminent arrival of the 'German October'. Even on 1 April 1933, an appropriately symbolic date for such a proclamation, the Executive Committee of the Comintern resolved:

Despite the fascist terror, the revolutionary upturn in Germany will inexorably grow. The masses' defence against fascism will inexorably grow. The establishment of an openly fascist dictatorship, which has shattered every democratic illusion in the masses and is liberating the masses from the influence of the Social Democrats, is accelerating the tempo of Germany's development towards a proletarian revolution.[50]

As late as June 1933 the Central Committee of the German Communist Party was proclaiming that the Hitler government would soon collapse under the weight of its internal contradictions, to be followed immediately by the victory of Bolshevism in Germany.[51] Communist inaction, therefore, was the product of Communist over-confidence, and the fatal illusion that the new situation posed no overwhelming threat to the party.

But to the leading Nazis it suggested something more sinister: the Communists were preparing in secret for a nationwide uprising. The fears of civil war that had plagued German politics in late 1932 and early 1933 did not vanish overnight. After all, the Communists were constantly proclaiming that the advent of a fascist government was the prelude to an imminent and unstoppable proletarian revolution that would replace bourgeois democracy with a Soviet Germany. Yet the Communists refused even to react to an obvious provocation such as a massive police raid on their party headquarters at the Karl-Liebknecht-House in Berlin on 23 February and its supposed revelation of plans for a revolutionary uprising. The more they waited, the more nervous the Nazi leaders grew. Surely something must happen soon?[52] The aesthete Harry Graf Kessler reported rumours amongst his well-connected friends that the Nazis were planning a fake assassination attempt on Hitler in order to justify a 'bloodbath' in which they would mow down their enemies. Similar rumours were rife in the last week of February. The tension was becoming unbearable. Soon, it would find spectacular release.[53]

FIRE IN THE REICHSTAG

I

In February 1931, the young Dutch construction worker Marinus van der Lubbe began a lengthy trek across Central Europe, trying to work his way towards the Soviet Union, a state which he greatly admired. Born on 13 January 1909 in Leiden, he had grown up in circumstances of the direst poverty. His drunken father had deserted the family soon after Marinus's birth and, at the age of 12, van der Lubbe had lost his mother, too. After her death he trained as a mason, came into contact with the labour movement and joined the Communist youth movement. But he soon came to dislike the party's strict code of discipline and authoritarian structure, and left it in 1931 to join a radical anarcho-syndicalist organization which elevated 'propaganda by the deed' into its main principle of action. With his eyesight severely impaired by an accident at work, he found it difficult to get a job, and stayed mainly in dosshouses and barns during his journey towards Russia. He only got as far as Poland, however, before he started back, reaching Berlin on 18 February 1933. Here, he found the political situation increasingly desperate, the passivity of the mainstream labour parties incomprehensible. While the Nazis had free rein in everything they did, the left was being ruthlessly suppressed. It was time, he thought, for the unemployed, deserted by all sides, to strike a blow for freedom and bread. A believer in direct action since his anarcho-syndicalist days, he decided to protest against the bourgeois state and its increasing suppression of the labour movement. The unemployed themselves, he discovered in his visits to labour exchanges, were sunk deep in apathy, incapable of mounting their own protest. Somebody had to do it for them.[54]

Arson was the method he chose. By causing spectacular damage to the institutions of the state, or rather, to buildings that housed them, he would, he thought, demonstrate that they were far from invulnerable, and rouse the unemployed to spontaneous mass action themselves. He had already been found guilty by a court in Leiden of damage to property, and was no stranger to impulsive and unplanned acts of protest; indeed, his predilection for them had been the principal cause of his break with the Dutch Communists. Now he was to undertake the same thing in Germany. He began with symbols of the state's oppression of the unemployed, and the predominance, as he believed, of the old order. On 25 February van der Lubbe attempted to burn down a welfare office in the Berlin district of Neukölln, then, more ambitiously, the town hall and the former royal palace. All three attempts were frustrated through immediate discovery and were barely reported in the press. Clearly, something more dramatic and better prepared was required. Seeking out the supreme symbol of the bourgeois political order that, he thought, had made his life and that of so many other unemployed young men a misery, he decided to burn down the Reichstag.[55]

On the morning of 27 February, van der Lubbe spent his last remaining money on matches and firelighters. After checking the building to establish the best way in, he waited until nightfall, then gained entry to the empty and darkened Reichstag building at about nine in the evening. His senses sharpened in the dark by long practice thanks to his impaired vision, he first tried to set light to the furniture in the restaurant, then, on meeting with no success, he found his way into the debating chamber, where the curtains proved easily combustible. Soon, the wooden panelling was blazing and the fire had gained sufficient strength for the dome above the chamber to act as a kind of chimney, fanning the flames by creating an upward draught. Meanwhile, van der Lubbe rushed through the rest of the building attempting to start other fires. Eventually, he was caught and overpowered by Reichstag officials. By the time he was arrested, the building was ablaze, and the fire brigade, despite arriving promptly on the scene, could do nothing but dampen the ruins of the main chamber and do its best to save the rest.

Across the way from the blazing building, Hitler's intimate Putzi Hanfstaengl, lodging temporarily in Göring's official residence, was woken up by the housekeeper, who pointed through the window at the flames. Hanfstaengl immediately telephoned Goebbels, who at first thought that the notoriously frivolous socialite was joking. But Putzi insisted he was not. Goebbels checked the story out – and found it was true. Before long, he had alerted Hitler.[56] The Nazi leaders, Hitler, Goebbels, and Göring met at the scene. Rudolf Diels, the (non-Nazi) head of the Prussian political police, and one of the first senior figures to arrive, found van der Lubbe already under interrogation by his officers:

His upper body naked, sweating, and smeared with dirt, he sat in front of them, breathing heavily. He was gasping for breath as if he had just completed a tremendous task. A wild look of triumph was in the burning eyes of the pale, emaciated young face. I sat opposite him a few times more that night at police headquarters and listened to his confused stories. I read the Communist leaflets that he carried with him in his trouser pocket. They were of the kind that were being publicly distributed everywhere in those days . . .

The frank confessions of Marinus van der Lubbe could in no way lead me to think that such a little fire-raiser, who knew his crazy business so well, needed helpers. Why shouldn't just a single match suffice to set light to the cold, flammable pomp of the plenary chamber, the old upholstered furniture and heavy curtains and the bone-dry wooden splendour of the panelling? But this specialist employed a whole rucksack full of incendiary devices.[57]

Subsequent investigation turned up a mass of documentary evidence confirming his story that he had been acting alone.[58]

Summoned to report to the group of leading Nazis gathered on a balcony above the Chamber, Diels encountered a scene of frightening hysteria. Remembering these dramatic events after the war, he continued:

Hitler had propped himself up on the stone parapet of the balcony with both arms and stared silently into the red sea of flames. The first storms lay behind him. As I entered, Göring walked towards me. In his voice lay the whole ominous emotionalism of that dramatic hour: 'This is the beginning of the Communist uprising! Now they'll strike out! There's not a minute to waste!'

Göring could not continue. Hitler turned to the assembled company. I now saw that his face was flaming red with excitement and from the heat that was gathering in the cupola. He shouted as if he wanted to burst, in an unrestrained way such as I had not previously experienced with him: 'There will be no more mercy now; anyone who stands in our way will be butchered. The German people won't have any understanding for leniency. Every Communist functionary will be shot where he is found. The Communist deputies must be hanged this very night. Everybody in league with the Communists is to be arrested. Against Social Democrats and Reichsbanner too there will be no more mercy!'

I reported the results of the first interrogations of Marinus van der Lubbe – that in my opinion he was a madman. But Hitler was not the right man to tell this to: he mocked my childish credulity: 'It's a really ingenious, long-prepared thing. These criminals have worked it out very nicely, but they've miscalculated, haven't they, my Party Comrades! These subhumans don't suspect at all how much the people is on our side. In their mouseholes, from which they now want to come out, they don't hear anything of the rejoicing of the masses', and so it went on.

I asked Göring to step aside, but he didn't let me speak. Highest emergency footing for the police, ruthless use of firearms, and anything else that follows in such a case from major military alarm orders.'[59]

It was, Diels told a subordinate, a 'mad-house'. But the time for action against the Communists had come none the less.[60]

A few hours after the Reichstag fire, police squads began to dig out lists of Communists prepared some months or even years previously for the eventuality of a ban on the party, and set off in cars and vans to haul them out of bed. The Communists had a hundred deputies in the Reichstag and thousands of representatives in other legislatures, officials, bureaucrats, organizers and activists. Many of the lists were out of date, but the precipitate and unplanned nature of the action netted a good number of prisoners who might otherwise have escaped, as well as missing many who simply could not be found. Four thousand were arrested altogether. Diels and the police quietly ignored Göring's instruction that they should be shot.[61] While this massive operation was under way, Göring's adviser Ludwig Grauert stepped in. Grauert was the former head of the north-west German iron and steel employers' association, and he had just been appointed to head the police department of the Prussian Interior Ministry. A Nationalist by political inclination, he now suggested an emergency decree to provide legal cover for the arrests and to deal with any further acts of violence by the Communists. A law had already been proposed to the cabinet on 27 February, before the fire, by the arch-conservative Minister of Justice, Franz Gürtner, who, like the other conservatives in the cabinet, enthusiastically supported draconian measures for the suppression of public disorder, which they blamed entirely on the Communists and Social Democrats. Gürtner's measure proposed serious restrictions on civil liberties in the interests of preventing the Communists from launching a general strike. The publication of demands for action of this kind was to be treated as high treason, which was punishable by death.[62] But this proposal was now overtaken by the new situation.

The Nazi Reich Minister of the Interior, Wilhelm Frick, saw in Grauert's draft the opportunity to extend his power over the federated states, and introduced a crucial new clause 2, allowing the cabinet, rather than the President, to intervene, much as Papen had done in Prussia in 1932. Beyond this, the draft decree, drawing on internal discussions of emergency legislation from the early 1920s, suspended several sections of the Weimar constitution, particularly those governing freedom of expression, freedom of the press, and freedom of assembly and associ- ation. It allowed the police to detain people in protective custody indefi- nitely and without a court order, in contrast to previous laws and decrees, which had set strict time limits before judicial intervention occurred. Most of these measures had been considered on various occasions before, and had a high degree of support in the higher civil service. But they went much further than anything before. Presenting the decree to the cabinet at 11 o'clock on the morning of 28 February, Hitler reminded his Con- servative colleagues that the coalition had intended from the outset to destroy the Communists: 'The psychologically correct moment for the confrontation has now arrived. There is no purpose in waiting any longer for it.'[63]

Hitler made plain his intention of proceeding ruthlessly and with little regard to the niceties of the law. The struggle against the Communists, he said, 'must not be made dependent on judicial considerations'. And he held out to his cabinet colleagues the enticing prospect of a massive victory in the forthcoming elections on the basis of the banning of the Communists, Germany's third largest party, together with the alarm in the general public caused by the arson attempt.[64] Göring spoke next, claiming that van der Lubbe had been seen with leading Communists such as Ernst Torgler shortly before he entered the Reichstag. The Com- munists, he said, were planning not only the destruction of public buildings but also the 'poisoning of public kitchens' and the kidnapping of the wives and children of government ministers. Before long, he was claiming to have detailed proof that the Communists had been stockpiling explosives in order to carry out a campaign of sabotage against electricity works, the railways, 'as well as all other large concerns important for life support'.[65]

Overriding Papen's objections to clause 2, the cabinet agreed to present the decree to Hindenburg, who signed it despite the fact that it ceded a significant part of his powers to the Hitler government. It came into effect immediately. Paragraph 1 suspended key articles of the Weimar constitution and declared:

Thus restrictions on personal liberty, on the right of free expression of opinion, including freedom of the press, on the right of assembly and association, and violations of the privacy of postal, telegraphic and telephonic communications, and warrants for house-searches, orders for confiscations as well as restrictions on property rights are permissible beyond the legal limits otherwise prescribed.

Paragraph 2 allowed the government to take over the federated states if public order was endangered. These two paragraphs, valid 'until further notice', provided the legal pretext for everything that was to follow in the next few months.[66] The Nazi seizure of power could now begin in earnest.

II

The Reichstag fire decree was launched amidst a barrage of propaganda in which Göring and the Nazi leadership painted a drastic picture of an imminent 'German Bolshevik Revolution' accompanied by outrages and atrocities of every kind. The propaganda had its effect. Ordinary middle-class citizens like Louise Solmitz shuddered to think of the fate that Germany had so narrowly escaped, and were impressed by the proofs of the dastardly Communist plot that Göring provided 'by the hundred-weight'.[67] Over two hundred telegrams poured into the Ministry of Justice from local Nazi groups all over the country, demanding that the 'sub-humans' whose 'demonic annihilation plans' threatened to turn 'our Fatherland into a blood-soaked expanse of rubble' should be shot out of hand, or publicly strangled in front of the Reichstag building. 'Annihilation of the red pack of criminals down to the last man' was the demand that came from many quarters, and some local Nazi authorities expressed their fear that public disorder would occur if the culprits were not immediately executed.[68] Goebbels's propaganda now set loose the pent-up fury of the brownshirts against their Communist opponents. The stormtroopers, who believed themselves to be virtually immune from prosecution by their previous enrolment as auxiliary police, had already released some of their tension in widespread acts of violence, but this was the moment they had really been waiting for. One stormtrooper wrote later of the aftermath of 28 February 1933:

We were prepared; we knew the intentions of our enemies. I had put together a small 'mobile squad' of my storm from the most daring of the daring. We lay in wait night after night. Who was going to strike the first blow? And then it came. The beacon in Berlin, signs of fire all over the country. Finally the relief of the order: 'Go to it!' And we went to it! It was not just about the purely human 'you or me', 'you or us', it was about wiping the lecherous grin off the hideous, murderous faces of the Bolsheviks for all time, and protecting Germany from the bloody terror of unrestrained hordes.[69]

All over Germany, however, it was now the brownshirts who visited 'the bloody terror of unrestrained hordes' upon their enemies. Their violence was the expression of long-nurtured hatred, their actions directed against individual 'Marxists' and Communists often known to them personally. There was no coordinated plan, no further ambition on their part than the wreaking of terrible physical aggression on men and women they feared and hated.[70]

The brownshirts and the police might have been prepared; but in crucial respects their Communist opponents were not. The Communist Party leadership was taken unawares by the events of 27–8 February. It thought that it would be entering another period of relatively mild repression such as it had successfully survived in 1923 and 1924. This time, however, things were very different. The police were backed by the full ferocity of the brownshirts. The party leader and former candidate for the Reich Presidency Ernst Thälmann and his aides were arrested on 3 March in his secret headquarters in Berlin-Charlottenburg. Ernst Torgler, the party's floor leader in the Reichstag, gave himself up to the police on 28 February in order to refute the government's accusation that he and the party leadership had ordered the burning of the Reichstag building. Of the leading party figures, Wilhelm Pieck left Germany in the spring, Walter Ulbricht, head of the party in Berlin, in the autumn. Strenuous efforts were made to smuggle out other politburo members, but many of them were arrested before they could escape. All over the country, Communist Party organizations were smashed, offices occupied, activists taken into custody. Often the stormtroopers carried off any funds they could lay their hands on, and looted the homes of Communist Party members for cash and valuables while the police looked on. Soon the wave of arrests swelled to many times the number originally envisaged. Ten thousand Communists had been put into custody by 15 March. Official records indicated that 8,000 Communists were arrested in the Rhine and Ruhr district in March and April 1933 alone. Party functionaries were obliged to admit that they had been compelled to carry out a 'retreat', but insisted that it was an 'orderly retreat'. In fact, as Pieck conceded, within a few months most of the local functionaries were no longer active, and many rank-and-file members had been terrorized into silence.[71]

Hitler evidently feared that there would be a violent reaction if he obtained a decree outlawing the Communist Party altogether. He preferred instead to treat individual Communists as criminals who had planned illegal acts and were now going to pay the consequences. That way, the majority of Germans might be won over to tolerate or even support the wave of arrests that followed the Reichstag fire and would not fear that this would be followed by the outlawing of other political parties. It was for this reason that the Communist Party was able to contest the elections of 5 March 1933, despite the fact that a large number of its candidates were under arrest or had fled the country, and there was never any chance that the 81 deputies who were elected would be able to take up their seats; indeed, they were arrested as soon as the police were able to locate them. By allowing the party to put up candidates in the election, Hitler and his fellow ministers also hoped to weaken the Social Democrats. If Communist candidates had not been allowed to stand, then many of the electors who would have voted for them might have cast their ballot for the Social Democrats instead. As it was, the Social Democrats were deprived of this potential source of support. Even towards the end of March the cabinet still felt unable to issue a formal prohibition of the Communist Party. Nevertheless, as well as being murdered, beaten up or thrown into makeshift torture centres and prisons set up by the brownshirts, Communist functionaries, particularly if they had been arrested by the police, were prosecuted in large numbers through the regular criminal courts.

Mere membership of the party was not in itself illegal. But police officials, state prosecutors and judges were overwhelmingly conservative men. They had long regarded the Communist Party as a dangerous, treasonable and revolutionary organization, particularly in the light of the events of the early Weimar years, from the Spartacist uprising in Berlin to the 'red terror' and the hostage shootings in Munich. Their view had been amply confirmed by the street violence of the Red Front-Fighters' League and now, many thought, by the Reichstag fire. The Communists had burned down the Reichstag, so all Communists must be guilty of treason. Even more tortuous reasoning was sometimes employed. In some cases, for instance, the courts argued that since the Communist Party was no longer able to pursue its policies of changing the German constitution by parliamentary means, it must be trying to change it by force, which was now a treasonable offence, so anyone who belonged to it must be doing the same. Increasingly, therefore, the courts treated membership of the party after 30 January 1933, occasionally even before that, as a treasonable activity. In all but name, the Communist Party was effectively outlawed from 28 February 1933, and completely banned from 6 March onwards, the day after the election.[72]

Having driven the Communists from the streets in a matter of days after 28 February, Hitler's stormtroopers now ruled the cities, parading their newly won supremacy in the most obvious and intimidatory manner. As the Prussian political police chief Rudolf Diels later reported, the SA, in contrast to the Party, was prepared to seize power.

It did not need a unified leadership; the 'Group Staff' set an example but gave no orders. The SA storm-squads, however, had firm plans for operations in the Communist quarters of the city. In those March days every SA man was 'on the heels of the enemy', each knew what he had to do. The storm-squads cleaned up the districts. They knew not only where their enemies lived, they had also long ago discovered their hideouts and meeting places . . . Not only the Communists, but anybody who had ever spoken out against Hitler's movement, was in danger.[73]

Brownshirt squads stole cars and pick-up trucks from Jews, Social Democrats and trade unions, or were presented with them by nervous businessmen hoping for protection. They roared along Berlin's main streets, weapons on show and banners flying, advertising to everyone who was the boss now. Similar scenes could be observed in towns and cities across the land. Hitler, Goebbels, Göring and the other Nazi leaders had no direct control over these events. But they had both unleashed them, by enrolling the Nazi stormtroopers along with the SS and Steel Helmets as auxiliary police on 22 February, and given them general, more than implicit approval, by the constant, repeated violence of their rhetorical attacks on 'Marxists' of all kinds.

Once more, a dialectical process was at work, forged in the days when the Nazis often faced police hostility and criminal prosecution for their violence: the leadership announced in extreme but unspecific terms that action was to be taken, and the lower echelons of the Party and its paramilitary organizations translated this in their own terms into specific, violent action. As a Nazi Party internal document later noted, action of this kind, by a nod-and-a-wink, had become already the custom in the 1920s. At this time, the rank-and-file had become used to reading into their leaders' orders rather more than the actual words that their leaders uttered. 'In the interest of the Party,' the document continued, 'it is also in many cases the custom of the person issuing the command – precisely in cases of illegal political demonstrations – not to say everything and just to hint at what he wants to achieve with the order.'[74] The difference now was that the leadership had the resources of the state at its disposal. It was able by and large to convince civil servants, police, prison administrators and legal officials – conservative nationalists almost to a man – that the forcible suppression of the labour movement was justified. So it persuaded them that they should not merely stand aside when the stormtroopers moved in, but should actively help them in their work of destruction. This pattern of decision-making and its implementation was to be repeated on many occasions subsequently, most notably in the Nazis' policy towards the Jews.

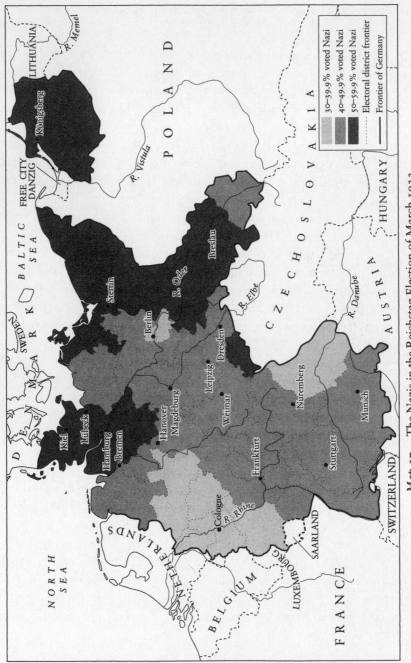

Map 17.   The Nazis in the Reichstag Election of March 1933

III

The Nazis' campaign for the Reichstag elections of 5 March 1933 achieved saturation coverage all over Germany.[75] Now the resources of big business and the state were thrown behind their efforts, and, as a result, the whole nature of the election was transformed. In the small north German town of Northeim, for instance, as in virtually every other locality, the elections were held in an atmosphere of palpable terror. The local police were positioned by the railway station, bridges and other key installations, advertising the regime's claim that such places were vulnerable to terrorist attacks by the Communists. The local stormtroopers were authorized to carry loaded firearms on 28 February and enrolled as auxiliary police on 1 March, whereupon they ostentatiously began to mount patrols in the streets, and raided the houses of local Social Democrats and Communists, accusing them both of preparing a bloodbath of honest citizens. The Nazi newspaper reported that a worker had been arrested for distributing a Social Democratic election leaflet; such activities on behalf of the Social Democrats and the Communists were forbidden, it announced. Having silenced the main opposition, the Nazis set up radio loudspeakers in the Market Square and on the main street, and every evening from 1 to 4 March Hitler's speeches were amplified across the whole town centre. On election eve, six hundred stormtroopers, SS men, Steel Helmets and Hitler Youth held a torchlight parade through the town, ending in the city park to listen to loudspeakers booming out a radio relay of a speech by Hitler that was simultaneously blared out to the public in four other major public locations in the town centre. Black-white-red flags and swastika banners bedecked the main streets, and were displayed in shops and stores. Opposition propaganda was nowhere to be seen. On election day – a Sunday – the brownshirts and SS patrolled and marched menacingly through the streets, while the Party and the Steel Helmets organized motor transport to get people to the polling stations. The same combination of terror, repression and propaganda was mobilized in every other community, large and small, across the land.[76]

When the results of the Reichstag elections came in, it seemed that these tactics had paid off. The coalition parties, Nazis and Nationalists, won 51.9 per cent of the vote. 'Unbelievable figures,' wrote Goebbels triumphantly in his private diary for 5 March 1933: 'it's like we're on a high.'[77] Some constituencies in central Franconia saw the Nazi vote at over 80 per cent, and in a few districts in Schleswig-Holstein the Party gathered nearly all the votes cast. Yet the jubilation of the Party bosses was ill-placed. Despite massive violence and intimidation, the Nazis themselves had still managed to secure only 43.9 per cent of the vote. The Communists, unable to campaign, with their candidates in hiding or under arrest, still managed 12.3 per cent, a smaller drop from their previous vote than might have been expected, while the Social Democrats, also suffering from widespread intimidation and interference with their campaigning, did only marginally worse than in November 1932, with 18.3 per cent. The Centre Party more or less held its own at 11.2 per cent, despite losses to the Nazis in some parts of the south, and the other, now minor, parties repeated their performance of the previous November with only slight variations.[78]

Seventeen million people voted Nazi, and another 3 million National-ist. But the electorate numbered almost 45 million. Nearly 5 million Communist votes, over 7 million Social Democrats, and a Centre Party vote of 5.5 million, testified to the complete failure of the Nazis, even under conditions of semi-dictatorship, to win over a majority of the electorate.[79] Indeed, at no time since their rise to electoral prominence at the end of the 1920s had they managed to win an absolute majority on their own at the Reich level or within any of the federated states. More-over, the majority they obtained together with their coalition partners the Nationalists in March 1933 fell far short of the two-thirds needed to secure an amendment of the constitution in the Reichstag. What the elections did make clear, however, was that nearly two-thirds of the voters had lent their support to parties – the Nazis, the Nationalists, and the Communists – who were open enemies of Weimar democracy. Many more had voted for parties, principally the Centre Party and its southern associate the Bavarian People's Party, whose allegiance to the Republic had all but vanished and whose power over their constituencies was now being seriously eroded. In 1919, three-quarters of the voters had backed the Weimar coalition parties. It had taken only fourteen short years for this situation to be effectively reversed.[80]

The violence rose to new heights after the elections on 5 March. In Königsberg, in East Prussia, for example, the SA invaded the local Social

Democrat headquarters on election night, destroyed the contents and turned the premises into a makeshift torture centre, where they administered beatings so severe that the Communist Reichstag deputy Walter Schütz died from the injuries he received there. Trade union offices were ransacked, typewriters stolen, furniture broken up, cash stolen and documents burned.[81] In Wuppertal, a brownshirt detachment hauled the worker Heinrich B., an ex-Communist, out of his home; his corpse was found on an allotment the next day. On 1 April in the same district, eight stormtroopers ambushed the 62-year-old worker August K., a former bandleader for the local Communist music group, on his way home and shot him down, causing fatal injuries.[82] Social Democrats were hard hit, too. On 9 March Wilhelm Sollmann, a Social Democratic Reichstag deputy and a leading figure in the party in Cologne, was attacked by brownshirts and SS men in his home, beaten up, taken off to the local Nazi Party headquarters, tortured for two hours and made to drink castor oil and urine, before the police arrived and took him to a prison hospital to patch up his wounds. On 13 March the brownshirts in Braunschweig started to force Social Democratic town councillors and deputies in the state parliament to 'volunteer' to resign their seats, beating one of them to death when he refused. At this point, too, the Nazis were beginning to raid Social Democratic party offices in the search for cash and other loot. The head of the Social Democratic press in Chemnitz, Georg Landgraf, was shot dead on 13 March after refusing to reveal to a gang of brownshirts the whereabouts of the party funds. Protest at such actions was difficult if not impossible, because all Social Democratic newspapers had been banned for fourteen days since the beginning of March, an order that was renewed for another fourteen days on its expiry, and so on, until it became permanent.[83]

The looting did not escape the attention of the more honest officers amongst the police. On 19 April 1933, for instance, the police commissioner in Hesse circulated police stations and local administrators condemning the illegal confiscation of the property of Marxist organizations during the raids, including the removal of musical instruments, gym equipment and even beds, all clearly intended for the private use of the looters.[84] Efforts were subsequently made to regularize the position and set up proper institutions to manage the assets of the banned parties and unions, not least because these included funds used to support unemployed former members; but by the time this had been done, a lot of money and property had disappeared into the hands of individual brownshirts. A law was eventually passed on 26 May 1933 assigning the property of the (still technically legal) Communist Party to the federated states.[85] In the midst of all this mayhem, many stormtroopers took the opportunity to settle old personal scores. In Wuppertal, for example, Friedrich D. was hauled out of his bedroom at four in the morning by a group of stormtroopers under the command of storm leader Puppe. His body was found two days later. He was murdered because he had been conducting a relationship with Puppe's sister which Puppe had for some time been trying to stop. Puppe was not prosecuted for this murderous act of spite. Even brownshirts themselves were not immune: one long-term Nazi, Karl W., was arrested, beaten up and imprisoned after accusing the brownshirt leader in Wuppertal of embezzlement and corruption, not the only incident of its kind to be reported at this time. What went on in Wuppertal must have been repeated many hundreds of times over in other parts of the country.[86]

This campaign of violence, unleashed by a brownshirt organization whose numbers were growing daily until they reached over two million by the summer of 1933, provided the essential context for the co-ordination of the federated states along the lines already put into practice by Papen in his takeover of Prussia the previous summer.[87] The State Court had ruled that takeover partially illegal, and the Social Democratic government displaced by Papen had had some success in using the Federal Council, representing the states, to block measures of the Reich government. Hitler's cabinet had secured an emergency decree on 6 February 1933 putting an end to this situation, but the new Nazi representatives of Prussia on the Federal Council saw their legitimacy denied by the council when it met on 16 February pending a decision by the State Court. Meanwhile, however, the council resolved to cease meeting until the legal situation was clarified, and in the resulting hiatus, regional organizations of the brownshirts and the Nazi Party moved in to co-ordinate the state governments from below. Most of the federated states were ruled by minority governments, reflecting the almost total blockage of legislative bodies by this time, and they lacked the legitimacy to offer any more than token resistance. In the period between 6 and 15 March 1933 Nazi police officers and 'auxiliary police' units of the SA and

SS raised the swastika on official buildings everywhere. This heavily symbolic gesture was tolerated or approved by the majority of state government ministers, who were intimidated by simultaneous demonstrations of massed columns of stormtroopers in front of government buildings. Ministers who objected either resigned or were put under house arrest by detachments of brownshirts. Reich Interior Minister Frick then installed state commissioners who proceeded to dismiss existing police chiefs and appoint Nazis in their stead, and to replace elected government ministers with their own nominees. Only in Hamburg, Württemberg and Hesse did the state parliaments, in the absence of the Communist deputies and through the abstention of the Social Democrats, appoint new coalition governments in which all the ministries were held by Nazis and Nationalists. Under these circumstances, state elections held in early March (the most important being the elections of 12 March in Prussia) were largely meaningless.[88]

The paramilitary affiliate of the Social Democratic 'Iron Front', the Reichsbanner, had already been crippled by the police occupation of many of its offices in February; in early March, immediately after the election, the state governments began to issue banning orders and arrest leading officials, so that one branch after another began to dissolve itself to avoid further persecution. In this atmosphere, a number of leading Social Democrats such as Otto Braun and Albert Grzesinski fled the country to avoid arrest or worse.[89] The leader of the Reichsbanner, Karl Höltermann, had already left on 2 May. An attempt by Social Democratic leaders to persuade Göring to lift the ban on their party's newspapers met with the response that it would continue until foreign socialist newspapers ceased their 'campaign' against the Reich government. It was an indication of how little they still understood the Nazis' methods that leading Social Democrats actually travelled to other European countries to try and explain the situation. The Socialist International reacted with a strong public condemnation of the Nazi terror ('the unspeakable and abominable misdeeds which the despots of Germany are committing day by day'). They added an appeal for joint action with the Communists. In a futile attempt to placate Göring, the German Social Democrats' leader Otto Wels immediately resigned his seat on the International's executive.[90] Such tactical concessions predictably did nothing to slow down the regime's drive to suppress the left.[91]

The Communists and Social Democrats, taken together, represented nearly a third of the electorate. Yet they crumbled virtually without resistance. The government was able to move against them on a nation-wide basis because the Reichstag fire decree permitted it to override the sovereignty of the federated states in order to carry out the operation, using the precedent of Papen's removal of the Social Democratic minority government in Prussia the previous summer. Further back still, Reich President Ebert had done the same thing with the left-wing state govern-ments in Saxony and Thuringia in 1923. The supposed Communist threat that justified the move was not particularly serious either in 1923 or ten years later. In 1933, the public disorder that supplied the reason for declaring a state of emergency was overwhelmingly the creation of the Nazis themselves. The purpose of this rapid co-ordination of the federated states was, not least, to overcome the hesitations of previous state govern-ments in using emergency powers to crush the parties of the left with the thoroughness that the Nazi leadership in Berlin required.

IV

This sequence of events had particularly sinister consequences in Bavaria. Here, the conservative state government in office on 28 February went along with the Reich government in banning Communist meet-ings and closing down the Communist press. It also arrested those it regarded as the leading figures in the regional Communist Party. But this was not enough for the Nazis, and on 9 March 1933, therefore, Frick appointed Adolf Wagner, the Nazi Regional Leader of Upper Bavaria, as State Commissioner in the Bavarian Ministry of the Interior. More ominously still, Heinrich Himmler, the Munich-based leader of the SS, was also immediately appointed Provisional Police President. He ordered a large-scale round-up of oppositional figures that soon began to encompass non-Communist enemies of the regime as well. Such was the scale of repression that state prisons and police cells proved completely inadequate. A new means of housing the Nazis' political opponents in Bavaria had to be found. On 20 March, therefore, Himmler announced to the press that 'a concentration camp for political prisoners' would be opened at Dachau, just outside Munich. It was to be Germany's first concentration camp, and it set an ominous precedent for the future.

The camp was intended for the imprisonment in 'protective custody' of 'all Communist and, where necessary, Reichsbanner and Social Democrat officials', as the Nazi press reported the next day. On 22 March 1933 four police trucks ferried some two hundred prisoners from the state gaols at Stadelheim and Landsberg to the camp site, built around a disused factory on the outskirts of town. Citizens of Dachau gathered in the streets and outside the factory gates to watch them pass by. Initially run by a police detachment, the camp was put into the hands of the SS early in April, with the notoriously rough SS leader Hilmar Wäckerle as its commandant. Wäckerle introduced a regime of violence and terror at Himmler's behest. On 11 April the new SS guards took four Jewish inmates out of the gates and shot them in the open, claiming that they were trying to escape; one of them managed to survive and was hospitalized in Munich, where he died; but not before providing the medical staff with such appalling details of the brutality that now reigned in the camp that they called in the public prosecutor. By the end of May, twelve of the inmates had been murdered or tortured to death. Corruption, extortion and embezzlement were rife among the guards, and the prisoners were exposed to arbitrary acts of cruelty and sadism in a world without regulations or rules.[92]

Himmler's act set a widely imitated precedent. Soon, concentration camps were opening up all over the country, augmenting the makeshift gaols and torture centres set up by the brownshirts in the cellars of recently captured trade union offices. Their foundation was given wide publicity, ensuring that everyone knew what would happen to those who dared oppose the 'national revolution'. The idea of setting up camps to house real or supposed enemies of the state was not in itself, of course, new. The British had used such camps for civilians on the opposing side in the Boer War, in which conditions were often very poor and death rates of inmates high. Shortly afterwards, the German army had 'concentrated' 14,000 Herero rebels in camps in South-West Africa during the war of 1904–7, treating them so harshly that 500 were said to be dying every month at the camps in Swakopmund and Lüderitz Bay. The camps had an eventual death rate of 45 per cent, justified by the German administration in terms of the elimination of 'unproductive elements' in the native population.[93] These precedents were familiar to the Nazis; in

1921, Hitler had already declared that they would imprison German Jews in 'concentration camps' along the lines of those used by the British. Paragraph 16 of the constitution that the Nazis had intended to put into effect if they had succeeded in seizing power in November 1923 had stated that 'security risks and useless eaters' would be put in 'collection camps' and made to work; anyone who resisted would be killed. More recently, the Nazi press had carried an article in August 1932 proclaiming that, on assuming power, the Nazis would 'immediately arrest and condemn all Communist and Social Democratic functionaries ... [and] quarter all suspects and spiritual instigators in concentration camps'. This warning was repeated openly by Reich Interior Minister Frick on 8 March 1933.[94] Dachau was not, therefore, an improvised solution to an unexpected problem of overcrowding in the gaols, but a long-planned measure that the Nazis had envisaged virtually from the very beginning. It was widely publicized and reported in the local, regional and national press, and served as a stark warning to anyone contemplating offering resistance to the Nazi regime.[95]

Conditions in the concentration camps and detention centres of the SA and SS in March and April have been aptly described as 'a makeshift sadistic anarchy'.[96] SA and SS violence seldom involved the refined, inventive kind of torture later practised by secret policemen in regimes like the military dictatorships in Argentina, Chile or Greece in the 1970s. What they vented on their prisoners was often barely controlled anger. Nothing much more sophisticated was involved in the torture than fists, jackboots, and rubber truncheons. On some occasions the police, now freed from any constraints they might have felt applied under the Weimar Republic, joined in, looked on, or employed their brownshirt auxiliaries to beat confessions out of their prisoners. The Communist worker Friedrich Schlotterbeck, arrested in 1933, reported later how he was interrogated at police headquarters by a group of SS men. They punched him in the face, beat him with rubber truncheons, tied him up, hit him over the head with a wooden bar, kicked him when he fell to the floor, and threw water over him when he lost consciousness. A police officer fired questions at him in the quieter moments, and intervened only when one of the SS men, enraged at Schlotterbeck's vigorous physical resistance, pulled a revolver and threatened to shoot the prisoner. Having failed to confess, he was taken back to his cell, sore, covered in cuts and bruises, blood streaming down his face, and barely able to walk. Schlotterbeck was treated kindly by the warders, who none the less had to inform him that they had to keep the light on in his cell and check on him regularly in case he tried to kill himself. He was to spend the next decade and more in penitentiaries and concentration camps.[97] His experience was not untypical of that of the committed Communist who refused to give in.

Social Democrats fared no better at the hands of the stormtroopers, who made no distinction of sex in their violent assaults on representatives of the left. One of many Social Democratic women who were attacked was Marie Jankowski, a city councillor for the Köpenick district in Berlin, who was arrested, beaten with rubber truncheons, hit in the face, and made to sign a document promising not to take part in politics again.[98] The lack of any detailed central co-ordination of such activities, which were spread unevenly all across Germany, makes any precise estimation of their extent impossible. But available figures for formally registered arrests demonstrated beyond doubt that this was violence on a vast and unprecedented scale. Official reports indicated at least 25,000 arrests in Prussia alone in the course of March and April, though this figure omitted Berlin and did not count 'wild' arrests by brownshirts that were not reported to the authorities. Arrests carried out in Bavaria already numbered around 10,000 by the end of April, and twice as many by the end of June. Moreover, many of those arrested were imprisoned for only a few days or weeks before being released: in the Oranienburg camp, for instance, 35 per cent of the inmates were kept inside for between one and four weeks, and less than 0.4 per cent stayed for over a year.[99] The 27,000 persons registered as being in protective custody across Germany at the end of July 1933 were thus, by and large, not the same people who had been in protective custody three or four months before, so that the total number of people who passed through the camps was far higher than this.[100] In addition, by no means all the Nazis' Social Democratic and, especially, Communist opponents had been taken off to the camps; many thousands more had been put in state prisons and police cells across the Reich.

The sheer scale of the repression can be gauged by the fact that the Communist Party leadership reported that 130,000 party members had been arrested and imprisoned by the end of 1933, and 2,500 had been murdered. These figures were probably something of an exaggeration, but they did not deceive when it came to estimating the impact of the repression on the party's organization. In the Ruhr area, for example, almost half the entire party membership was taken into custody. As early as the end of March, the Prussian police reported that some 20,000 Communists had been seized and put into gaol.[101] Even the most conservative, quasi-official reckoning put the total number of political arrests in Germany in 1933 at over 100,000, and the number of deaths in custody at nearly 600.[102] This was violence and murder on a staggering level, not seen in Germany since the early days of the Weimar Republic.

This massive, brutal and murderous assault on the Nazis' opponents was formally sanctioned by the Reichstag fire decree, which, however, was based on the idea that the Communists had been attempting a revolutionary uprising, and had nothing to say about the Social Democrats. The idea that the Social Democrats sympathized with or supported the Communists' preparations for an uprising was even more absurd than the claim that the Communists had been about to stage one. Yet many middle-class Germans appear to have accepted that the regime was justified in its violent repression of 'Marxism', of whatever variety. Years of beatings and killings and clashes on the streets had inured people to political violence and blunted their sensibilities. Those who had their doubts could not have failed to notice what the police and their Nazi stormtrooper auxiliaries were doing to the Nazis' opponents in these weeks. Many of them must have paused for thought before voicing their disquiet. Anyone who was alarmed by the extent of the disorder may well have been reassured by Hitler's public denunciation on 10 March 1933 of acts of violence against foreigners, which he blamed on Communist infiltrators in the SA, and his exhortation to the stormtroopers to stop 'harassment of individuals, the obstruction of cars, and disruptions to business'.

However, Hitler went on to tell the brownshirts, they must 'never let yourselves be distracted for one second from our watchword, which is the destruction of Marxism'. 'The national uprising will continue to be carried out methodically and under control from above,' he said, and only 'when these orders meet with resistance' should they act to ensure that 'this resistance be immediately and thoroughly broken'. This last qualification was of course licence enough to continue the violence unabated and, indeed, escalate it still further.[103] When a leading Nationalist protested to Hitler on 10 March about the destruction of the legal order, followed by a phone call to the same effect by Papen on 19 March, Hitler angrily accused them of trying 'to put a stop to the nationalist revolution'. The 'November criminals' of 1918 and those who had tried to suppress the Nazi Party during the Weimar period had been far worse, he said. Praising the 'phenomenal discipline' of the stormtroopers, he condemned at the same time the 'weakness and cowardice of our bourgeois world in proceeding with kid gloves instead of the iron fist' and warned that he would not let anyone stop him from the 'annihilation and extirpation of Marxism'.[104]

Germany was well on the way to becoming a dictatorship even before the Reichstag fire decree and the elections of 5 March 1933. But these two events undoubtedly speeded it up and provided it with the appearance, however threadbare, of legal and political legitimation. After his election victory, Hitler told the cabinet on 7 March that he would seek a further legal sanction in the form of an amendment to the constitution that would allow the cabinet to bypass both the Reichstag and the President and promulgate laws on its own. Such a measure had precedents in aspects of emergency legislation under the Weimar Republic. Nevertheless, it would clearly go much further than anything seen before. Hitler had long dreamed of introducing it.[105] This Enabling Act would set the seal on the hated democracy of the Weimar Republic and complete the work of what the Nazis had begun on 30 January 1933 by calling into being a 'government of nationalist concentration'. It was not long before Goebbels and the other leading Nazis had renamed it a 'government of the nationalist uprising'. By early March it had become simply a 'nationalist revolution', emphasizing that far more than the actions of mere cabinet government was involved. Soon it was to be the 'National Socialist Revolution', finally consigning Hitler's non-Nazi coalition partners to political oblivion.[106]

DEMOCRACY DESTROYED

I

Revolutionary rhetoric and unbridled violence on the streets were not exactly what Papen and Hitler's other cabinet allies had been expecting when they had agreed to Hitler's becoming Reich Chancellor two months before, for all their approval of the police crackdown on the left. They had rather expected that bringing the Nazis into government would put a stop to all this. For worried conservatives and traditionalists, including Reich President Hindenburg, who after all still possessed at least the formal power to sack Hitler and replace him with someone else, the Nazis therefore staged a reassuring ceremony to mark the state opening of the newly elected Reichstag. Given the unavailability of the gutted and ruined Reichstag building, the ceremony had to take place elsewhere. Hitler and his conservative allies agreed to hold it in the garrison church at Potsdam, the symbolic locus of the Prussian monarchy, on 21 March 1933, the exact anniversary of the day on which the inaugural Reichstag had met after Bismarck's founding of the Second Reich. The elaborate ceremony was planned down to the last detail by Goebbels as a propaganda demonstration of the unity of the old Reich and the new. Hindenburg stood next to the Kaiser's vacant throne, dressed in the uniform of a Prussian Field-Marshal, to receive the obeisance of the frock-coated Hitler, who bowed and shook his hand. The Reich Chancellor gave a speech notable for its studied moderation, praising Hindenburg for his historical role in entrusting the fate of Germany to a new generation. Wreaths were laid on the tombs of the Prussian kings, and Hindenburg then reviewed a massive parade of the paramilitaries and the army.

The ritual was more important for the visual images it conveyed than for the speeches that were delivered. Here was Hitler appearing as a soberly dressed civilian statesman, humbly acknowledging the supremacy of the Prussian military tradition. Here were flags in the imperial colours of black, white and red, that had already officially replaced the black, red and gold of the Weimar Republic on 12 March. Here were the Prussian military grandees in their sometimes outlandish uniforms redolent of monarchist tradition. Here was the Protestant church, implicitly re-asserting its supremacy alongside that of the army and the throne. Here was the restoration of the old Germany, wiping history clean of the tainted memory of Weimar democracy.[107] Not surprisingly, the Social Democrats declined the invitation to attend. In a further piece of symbol-ism, Hitler for his part refused to go to a service at the Catholic parish church in Potsdam on the grounds that Catholic priests, still loyal to the Centre Party and critical of what they regarded as the Nazis' godless ways, had barred some leading Nazis from receiving the sacraments. This was a clear warning to the Church that it was time to fall into line.[108]

Two days later, in the Kroll Opera House, designated as the temporary home of the Reichstag, Hitler, now dressed, like the other Nazi deputies, in a brownshirt paramilitary uniform, spoke to the Reichstag in a very different atmosphere. Standing beneath a huge swastika banner, he intro-duced the long-planned measure that would enable the Reich Chancellor to prepare laws that deviated from the constitution without the approval of the Reichstag and without reference to the President. This 'Enabling Act' would have to be renewed after four years, and the existence of the Reichstag itself, the upper legislative chamber representing the federated states, and the position of the Reich President, was not to be affected. What it meant, however, was that the Weimar constitution would be a dead letter, and the Reichstag would be shut out of the legislative process altogether. The passage of the Enabling Act was by no means assured: 94 out of the 120 elected Social Democrats were still able to vote – of those absent, some were in prison, some were ill, and some stayed away because they feared for their lives. Hitler knew in any case that he would not get the Social Democrats' support. An amendment of the Weimar constitution required both a two-thirds quorum and a two-thirds majority of those present. Hermann Göring, as the Reichstag's presiding officer, reduced the quorum from 432 to 378 by not counting the Commun-ist deputies, even though they had all been legally elected. This was a high-handed decision that had no legitimacy in law whatsoever.[109] Yet even after this illegal manoeuvre, the Nazis still needed the votes of the Centre Party to push the measure through.

By this point in its history, the party had long since ceased to be a supporter of democracy. Following the general trend of political Catholicism in interwar Europe, it had come to support the principles of authoritarianism and dictatorship out of fear of Bolshevism and revolution. True, what seemed to be shaping up in Germany was not quite the kind of 'clerico-fascist' regime to which Catholic politicians were soon to lend their support in Austria and Spain. But in 1929 the Catholic Church had safeguarded its position in Italy through a Concordat with Mussolini, and the prospect of a similar arrangement was now held out to it in Germany as well. The escalating terror to which Catholics and their political representatives, newspapers, speakers and local officials had been subjected since the middle of February made the Centre Party look anxiously for guarantees that the Church would survive. Now, under stronger clerical influence than ever before, and led by a Catholic priest, Prelate Ludwig Kaas, the party was reassured in two days of discussions with Hitler that the rights of the Church would not be affected by the Enabling Act. The doubts of Heinrich Brüning and his close advisers were assuaged. The federated states, bastions of Catholicism in the south, would remain intact, despite their takeover by Reich Commissioners appointed from Berlin, and the judiciary would stay independent. These promises, combined with heavy pressure from the Vatican, proved sufficient to win the Centre Party deputies over to supporting the measure that in the long run was bound to mean their own political demise.[110]

The deputies arrived at the Kroll Opera House in an atmosphere heavy with violence and intimidation. The Social Democrat Wilhelm Hoegner remembered:

Wild chants greeted us: 'We want the Enabling Law!' Young lads with the swastika on their chests looked us cheekily up and down, virtually barring the way for us. They quite made us run the gauntlet, and shouted insults at us like 'Centrist pig', 'Marxist sow'. In the Kroll Opera it was swarming with armed SA and SS ... The debating chamber was decorated with swastikas and similar ornaments ... When we Social Democrats had taken our places on the far left,

SA and SS men placed themselves by the exits and along the walls behind us in a half-circle. Their attitude did not bode well for us.[111]

Hitler began his speech with his usual diatribes against the 'November criminals' of 1918 and boasted of his removal of the threat of Communism. He repeated his promise to protect the interests of the Churches, particularly in the schools, a major bone of contention under the Weimar Republic. He ended, however, with an unmistakeable threat of violent repression should the measure be rejected. The 'government of the nationalist uprising', he declared, was 'determined and ready to deal with the announcement that the Act has been rejected and with it that resistance has been declared. May you, gentlemen, now take the decision yourselves as to whether it is to be peace or war.' This did not fail to have an effect on wavering Centre Party deputies such as Heinrich Brüning, who now decided to vote for the Act. 'They fear', as Joseph Wirth, one of the party's leading figures and a former Reich Chancellor himself, told the Social Democrats in private, 'that if the Act is rejected, the Nazi revolution will break out and there will be bloody anarchy'.[112]

In the face of such threats, the Social Democrats had decided that their chairman, Otto Wels, should adopt a moderate, even conciliatory tone in his speech for the opposition, fearing that otherwise he might be shot down or beaten up by the brownshirts who were standing threateningly round the edge of the chamber, or arrested as he went out. What he had to say, however, was dramatic enough. He defended the achievements of the Weimar Republic in bringing about equality of opportunity, social welfare and the return of Germany to the international community. 'Freedom and life can be taken from us, but not honour.' Wels was not exaggerating: several prominent Social Democrats had already been killed by the Nazis, and he himself was carrying a cyanide capsule in his waist pocket as he spoke, ready to swallow should he be arrested and tortured by the brownshirts after delivering his speech. His voice choking with emotion, he ended with an appeal to the future:

In this historic hour, we German Social Democrats solemnly profess our allegiance to the basic principles of humanity and justice, freedom and socialism. No Enabling Law gives you the right to annihilate ideas that are eternal and indestructible. The Anti-Socialist Law did not annihilate the Social Democrats. Social Democracy can also draw new strength from fresh persecutions. We greet the persecuted and the hard-pressed. Their steadfastness and loyalty deserve admiration. The courage of their convictions, their unbroken confidence, vouch for a brighter future.

Wels's peroration was greeted with uproar in the chamber, the mocking, raucous laughter of the Nazi deputies drowning out the applause from his own benches.

Hitler's response was contemptuous. The Social Democrats had sent the speech to the press in advance of the session, and Hitler's staff had obtained a copy on which to base the Chancellor's reply. He knew that he did not need their votes. 'You think', he said, to thunderous applause from the uniformed ranks of Nazi deputies, 'that your star could rise again! Gentlemen, Germany's star will rise and yours will sink . . . Germany shall be free, but not through you!' After brief speeches by the leaders of the other parties, the deputies voted 444 in favour and 94 against. The once proud German liberals, now represented through the German State Party, were amongst the bill's supporters. Only the Social Democrats voted against. So great was the majority that the bill would have passed even had all 120 Social Democratic and all 81 Communist deputies been present, making the total number of seats 647 instead of 566, and all of them had voted 'no'.[113]

With the Enabling Act now in force, the Reichstag could be effectively dispensed with. From this point on, Hitler and his cabinet ruled by decree, either using President Hindenburg as a rubber stamp, or bypassing him entirely, as the Act allowed them to. Nobody believed that when the four years of the Act's duration had elapsed, the Reichstag would be in a position to object to its renewal, nor was it. As with the Reichstag fire decree, a temporary piece of emergency legislation with some limited precedents in the Weimar period now became the legal, or pseudo-legal basis for the permanent removal of civil rights and democratic liberties. Renewed in 1937 and again in 1939, it was made permanent by decree in 1943. The brownshirt terror on the streets was already comprehensive enough to make it quite clear what was now about to happen. Wels was right to predict that Germany would soon become a one-party state.[114]

II

With the Communists already effectively out of the way since 28 February, and the Enabling Act in force, the regime now turned its attention to the Social Democrats and the trade unions. They had already been subjected to widespread arrests, beatings, intimidation, even murder, and to the occupation of their premises and the banning of their newspapers. Now the full fury of the Nazis was turned upon them. They were in no condition to resist. The ability to work together with the unions had been crucial to the Social Democrats in defeating the Kapp putsch in 1920. But it was no longer present in the spring of 1933. Both wings of the labour movement had been united in their disapproval of the appointment of Hitler as Chancellor in January 1933. And both had suffered similar acts of violence and repression in the following two months, with trade union premises being occupied and trashed by gangs of stormtroopers in growing numbers. Up to 25 March, according to the unions themselves, union offices had been occupied by brownshirts, SS or police units in 45 separate towns throughout the Reich. Such pressure was the most direct possible threat to the continued existence of the unions as the functional representatives of the workers in negotiating pay and conditions with their employers. It also drove a rapidly deepening cleft between the trade unions on the one hand and the Social Democrats on the other.

As the political repression and marginalization of the Social Democrats rapidly became more obvious, so the trade unions under Theodor Leipart began to try to preserve their existence by distancing themselves from the Social Democratic Party and seeking an accommodation with the new regime. On 21 March the leadership denied any intention of playing a role in politics and declared that it was prepared to carry out the social function of the trade unions 'whatever the kind of state regime' in power.[115] The Nazis were aware, of course, that they had little support among trade unionists; the Nazi factory cell organization[116] was not popular, and only managed single-figure percentages in the great majority of the elections to works councils held in the first months of 1933. Only in a very few areas, like the Krupp works, the chemical industry, some steelworks, or the Ruhr coal mines, did it do significantly better, showing that some workers in some major branches of industry were beginning to accommodate themselves to the new regime.[117] Alarmed at the general result, however, the Nazis enforced an indefinite postponement of the remaining works council elections.

Despite their annoyance at this arbitrary interference in their democratic rights, the trade union leader Theodor Leipart and his designated successor Wilhelm Leuschner intensified their efforts to secure the institutional survival of their movement. They were encouraged in their efforts at a compromise by their belief that the Nazis were serious about setting up the job-creation schemes they had been demanding for many years. On 28 April they concluded an agreement with the Christian and Liberal Trade Unions that was intended to form the first step towards a complete unification of all trade unions in a single national organization. 'The nationalist revolution', began the unification document, 'has created a new state. This state wants to bring together the whole German nation in unity and asserts its power.' The unions evidently thought that they had a positive part to play in this process, and wanted to play it independently. As a sign that they would do so, they agreed to support Goebbels's public declaration that May Day, traditionally the occasion for massive public demonstrations of the labour movement's strength, would be a public holiday for the first time. This was a long-cherished desire of the labour movement. The unions agreed that it would be known as the 'Day of National Labour'. This act, once more, symbolized the new regime's synthesis of the seemingly divergent traditions of nationalism and socialism.[118]

On the day itself, trade union premises, in a departure from labour movement tradition that many older workers must have found scandalous and depressing, were decked out with the old national colours of black, white and red. Karl Schrader, president of the textile workers' union, marched in the Berlin procession under the sign of the swastika, not the only union official to do so. Few, indeed, took part in the 'flying' counter-demonstrations staged with lightning speed at various locations by the Communists, or the quiet commemorations of the day held behind locked doors by the Social Democrats in their own secret meeting-places. Hundreds of thousands, perhaps even millions of people marched through the streets led by brass bands of stormtroopers playing the Horst Wessel Song and patriotic tunes. They streamed towards vast open-air meeting-places, where they listened to speeches and readings from nationalistic 'worker-poets'. In the evening, Hitler's voice boomed out over the radio, assuring all German workers that unemployment would soon be a thing of the past.[119]

The Tempelhof field in Berlin was packed with a vast assembly of over a million people arranged, military-style, in twelve huge squares, surrounded by a sea of Nazi flags, with three huge Nazi banners illuminated by searchlights. After dark, firework displays culminated in the emergence from the gloom of vast glowing swastikas lighting up the sky. The media blared forth their celebration of the winning over of the workers to the new regime. It was a proletarian counterpart of the ceremony held for the upper classes at Potsdam ten days before.[120] The masses, however, did not appear at the ceremonies entirely of their own accord: and the atmosphere was less than wholly enthusiastic. Many workers, especially in state employment, had been threatened with dismissal for non-attendance, while thousands of industrial employees in Berlin had had their timecards confiscated on arriving at work, with the promise that they would only get them back on the Tempelhof field. The general atmosphere of looming violence and widespread intimidation had also played its part in bringing about the formal agreement of trade union leaders to participate.[121]

If the union leaders had thought they would preserve their organizations by such compromises, however, they were in for a rude awakening. In early April the Nazis had already begun secret preparations for a takeover of the entire trade union movement. On 17 April Goebbels noted in his diary:

On 1 May we shall arrange May Day as a grandiose demonstration of the German people's will. On 2 May the trade union offices will be occupied. Co-ordination in this area too. There might possibly be a row for a few days, but then they will belong to us. We must make no allowances any more. We are only doing the workers a service when we free them from the parasitic leadership that has only made their life hard up to now. Once the trade unions are in our hands the other parties and organizations will not be able to hold out for much longer.[122]

On 2 May 1933 brownshirts and SS men stormed into every Social Democratic-oriented trade union office in the land, took over all the trade union newspapers and periodicals, and occupied all the branches of the trade union bank. Leipart and the other leading union officials were arrested and taken into 'protective custody' in concentration camps, where many of them were beaten up and brutally humiliated before being released a week or two later. In a particularly horrific incident, stormtroopers beat four trade union officials to death in the cellar of the trade union building in Duisburg on 2 May. The entire management of the movement and its assets was placed in the hands of the Nazi factory cell organization. On 4 May the Christian Trade Unions and all other union institutions placed themselves unconditionally under Hitler's leadership. The 'row' predicted by Goebbels never materialized. The once-powerful German trade union movement had disappeared without trace virtually overnight.[123] 'The revolution goes on,' trumpeted Goebbels in his diary on 3 May. With satisfaction he noted the widespread arrests of 'bigwigs'. 'We are the masters of Germany,' he boasted in his diary.[124]

Confident that the Social Democratic Party would no longer be able to call upon the unions to support any last-minute resistance it might decide to mount, the regime now began the endgame of closing the party down. On 10 May the government seized the party's assets and property by court order, justified by the General State Prosecutor in Berlin with reference to the supposed embezzlement of trade union funds by Leipart and others, an accusation that had no basis in fact. Wels had arranged for the party's funds and archive to be shipped out of the country, but the Nazis' haul was still considerable. This measure deprived the party of any basis on which it could resurrect either its organization or its newspapers, periodicals and other publications. As a political movement it was effectively finished.[125] Yet, astonishingly, none of this prevented the Social Democrats from lending their support to the government in the Reichstag on 17 May, when Hitler put before the legislature a neutrally worded resolution in favour of German equality in international disarmament negotiations. The declaration had no real meaning except the assertion of German rights and no purpose apart from winning some credit for the regime abroad after months in which it had been heavily criticized all over the world; the government had no intention of taking part in any kind of disarmament process in reality. Nevertheless, the Social Democratic deputies, led by Paul Löbe, thought they would be portrayed as unpatriotic if they boycotted the session, so those who were able to do so turned up and joined in the Reichstag's unanimous approval of the resolution, following a hypocritically moderate and neutrally worded speech by Hitler, to the strains of the national anthem, cries of 'Hail!' from the Nazis, and overt satisfaction from Hermann Göring, who declared in his capacity as presiding officer of the Reichstag that the world had now witnessed the unity of the German people when its international fate was at stake. The deputies' action caused outrage in the party, above all among the leaders now in exile: they condemned the action as the negation of the proud vote against the Enabling Act on 23 March. Otto Wels, who had led the opposition to the vote, withdrew his resignation from the Socialist International. The exiled leadership relocated the party headquarters to Prague. In shame and despair at the failure of the Reichstag deputies to realize that they were being used as part of a Nazi propaganda operation, the most passionate opponent of the decision, Toni Pfülf, one of the leading Socal Democratic women in the Reichstag, boycotted the session and committed suicide on 10 June 1933. Löbe himself was arrested; Wels fled the country.[126]

The gulf between the new party leadership in Prague and those officials and deputies who remained in Germany rapidly deepened. But the regime declared that it could not see any difference between the two wings of the party; those who had decamped to Prague were traitors defaming Germany from a foreign land and those who had not were traitors for aiding and abetting them. On 21 June 1933 Interior Minister Wilhelm Frick ordered the state governments throughout Germany to ban the Social Democratic Party on the basis of the Reichstag fire decree. No Social Democratic deputies in any legislature were to be allowed to take up their seats any more. All Social Democratic meetings, all Social Democratic publications, were prohibited. Membership in the party was declared incompatible with holding any public office or any position in the civil service. On 23 June 1933 Goebbels wrote triumphantly in his diary that the Social Democratic Party had been 'dissolved. Bravo! The total state won't have to wait for long now.'[127]

Social Democrats did not have to wait long either to discover what the total state would mean. As Frick's decree of 21 June was being published, over three thousand Social Democratic functionaries were arrested all over Germany, severely manhandled, tortured, and thrown into prisons or concentration camps. In the Berlin suburb of Köpenick, when they encountered armed resistance from one house, the stormtroopers rounded up 500 Social Democrats, and beat and tortured them over a period of several days, killing 91; this concerted assault, savage even by the standards of the brownshirts, quickly became known as the 'Köpenick Blood-Week'. Particular vengeance was wreaked on anyone associated with the left in Munich in the revolutionary days of 1918–19. Kurt Eisner's former secretary Felix Fechenbach, now editor of the local Social Democratic newspaper in Detmold, had been arrested on 11 March and put into custody along with most of the leading Social Democrats in the province of Lippe. On 8 August a detachment of stormtroopers took him by car out of the state prison, ostensibly to be transferred to Dachau. But on the way, they forced the accompanying policeman out of the vehicle. Then they drove into a wood, where they took Fechenbach a few paces and shot him dead. The Nazi press reported later that he had been 'shot while trying to escape'.[128] Less controversial figures were targeted, too. The former Minister-President of Mecklenburg-Schwerin, Johannes Stelling, a Social Democrat, was taken to a brownshirt barracks, beaten up, and thrown semi-conscious out onto the street, where he was picked up by another gang of stormtroopers, taken off in a car, and tortured to death. His body was sewn into a sack weighted down with stones and thrown into a river. It was later fished out with the bodies of twelve other Social Democratic and Reichsbanner functionaries who had been murdered the same night.[129]

Similar brutal acts of repression against Social Democrats were carried out all over Germany. Particularly notorious was the makeshift concentration camp opened on 28 April at Dürrgoy, on the southern outskirts of Breslau, by the local brownshirt, Edmund Heines. The camp commandant was a former Free Corps leader and member of a far-right assassination squad, who had been convicted of murder under the Weimar Republic. His prisoners included Hermann Lüdemann, former Social Democratic chief administrator of the Breslau district, the former Social Democratic mayor of the city; and the ex-editor of the Social Democrats' daily paper in Breslau. Inmates were subjected to repeated beatings and torture. The camp commandant held regular fire drills throughout the night, and had the prisoners beaten as they returned to their barracks. Heines paraded Lüdemann through the streets of Breslau, dressed as a harlequin, to the accompaniment of jeers and insults from watching stormtroopers. He also kidnapped the former Social Democratic President of the Reichstag, Paul Löbe, against whom he had a personal grudge, from his prison in Spandau; pressure from Löbe's wife and friends quickly secured an order for his release, but he refused to leave, declaring his solidarity with the other Social Democratic prisoners.[130]

With repression such as this, the party was effectively hounded out of existence well before it fell under the same ban as the Communists on 14 July. In retrospect, its chances of survival had been diminishing rapidly for nearly a year. Decisive in this context was its failure to mount any effective opposition to the Papen coup of 20 July 1932; if there had been any moment when it might have stood up for democracy, that was it. But it is easy to condemn its inaction with hindsight; few in the summer of 1932 could have realized that the amateurish and in many ways rather ludicrous government of Franz von Papen would give way little more than six months later to a regime whose extreme ruthlessness and total disregard for the law were difficult for decent, law-abiding democrats to grasp. In many ways, the labour movement leaders' desire to avoid violence in July 1932 was thoroughly to their credit; they were not to know that their decision was to play a key role in opening the way to much greater violence later on.

With the crushing of the labour movement, the Nazis, assisted by the state's law enforcement agencies and the sympathetic inaction of the armed forces, had removed the most serious obstacle to their establishment of a one-party state. The labour movement had been brought to heel, the trade unions smashed, the Social Democratic and Communist Parties, whose combined vote considerably exceeded that of the Nazis in the last fully free elections to the Reichstag in November 1932, had been destroyed in an orgy of violence. There remained, however, another major political force whose members and voters had stayed largely loyal to their principles and representatives throughout the Weimar years: the Centre Party. It derived its strength not simply from political tradition and cultural inheritance, but above all from its identification with the Catholic Church and its adherents. It could not be subjected to the kind of indiscriminate and unbridled brutality that had swept the Communists and the Social Democrats off the political stage. More subtle tactics were required. In May 1933 Hitler and the Nazi leadership set about putting them into action.

III

Clemens August Count von Galen was a Catholic priest of the traditional kind. Born in 1878 into a noble family in Westphalia, he grew up in an atmosphere of aristocratic piety, encouraged by relations such as his great-uncle, Bishop von Ketteler, one of the founders of social Catholicism. The eleventh of thirteen children, Clemens August seemed almost predestined for the priesthood. His parents, their political consciousness awakened by Bismarck's attempt to repress the Catholic Church in the 1870s, taught him that conscience, especially religious conscience, came before obedience to authority. But they also taught him modesty and simplicity, for they were short of money and lived in Spartan circumstances in a castle that lacked running water, indoor toilets and heating in most of the rooms. Educated partly at home, partly at a Jesuit academy, Galen went on to qualify for university at a state school. In 1904 he entered the priesthood after graduating in theology from Innsbruck. From 1906 to 1929 he served as a parish priest in Berlin, an overwhelmingly Protestant city with a strong, mostly atheistic working class. Six feet seven inches tall, Galen was a commanding presence in more ways than one, winning a reputation for personal asceticism as well as an ability to communicate with the poor. There was a large dose of *noblesse oblige* in his attitude to life.[131]

With such a background, it is not surprising that Galen's political views were on the right. He supported the German war effort in 1914–18 and tried (unsuccessfully) to volunteer for military service at the front. He abhorred the 1918 Revolution because it overthrew a divinely ordained state order. He firmly believed in the 'stab-in-the-back' myth of Germany's defeat in the war, opposed the Centre Party's initial commitment to Weimar democracy, and took part, though as a moderating influence, in abortive discussions intended to lead to the foundation of a new Catholic political movement further to the right. Galen excoriated the Weimar constitution as 'godless', echoing Cardinal Michael Faulhaber's condemnation of its secular foundations as 'blasphemy'. Faulhaber, along with many other priests, welcomed the promise of the Nazi leadership to restore strong Christian foundations to the state in 1933. And indeed, Hitler and most of his leading associates were aware of the breadth and depth of Christian allegiance in the majority of the population, and did not want to antagonize it in the course of suppressing parties such as the Centre. They were thus careful in the early months of 1933 to insist repeatedly on the adherence of the new government to the Christian faith. They declared that the 'nationalist revolution' intended to put an end to the materialist atheism of the Weimar left and to propagate a 'positive Christianity' instead, above confession and attuned to the Germanic spirit.[132]

Catholic priests like Galen were generally worried about the position of the Catholic Church in a country where atheistic Communism seemed a major threat. But they also had more secular concerns. The Weimar Republic had seen the Catholic community achieve unprecedented participation in the state, in government and in senior posts in the civil service. In pursuit of the promised Concordat which, they were assured, would preserve these gains, the German bishops withdrew their opposition to Nazism and issued a collective declaration of support for the regime in May. They began to clamp down on local priests who insisted on continuing to voice criticisms of the Nazi movement. Catholic brownshirts and Nazi Party members, unable to attend Mass because the bishops had forbidden the wearing of uniforms in church, began to be seen at Protestant services, where there was no such prohibition, raising the alarming spectacle of a mass defection to the religious opposition. Cardinal Bertram persuaded the bishops to lift the ban.[133] Soon, passive toleration had turned to active support. Many priests took part in the public ceremonies held to mark the 'Day of National Labour' on 1 May. The Fulda Bishops' Conference on 1 June 1933 issued a pastoral letter welcoming the 'national awakening' and the new stress on a strong state authority, though it also expressed concerns about the Nazis' emphasis on race and the looming threat to Catholic lay institutions. Vicar-General Steinmann was photographed raising his arm in the Nazi salute. He declared that Hitler had been given to the German people by God in order to lead them.[134] Catholic student organizations published a declaration of loyalty to the new regime ('the only way to restore Christianity to our culture . . . Hail to our Leader Adolf Hitler'). Catholic newspapers ceased publication or turned themselves into something like Nazi propaganda organs.[135]

While this situation was developing, the Centre Party leader, Prelate

Kaas, went on an extended visit to the Vatican to help draft the Concordat. It soon became clear that he was willing to sacrifice the party as a condition of the regime's signature. In early May he resigned as party leader, pleading ill-health. He was succeeded by the former Reich Chancellor Heinrich Brüning, who immediately became the object of a pale imitation of the leadership cult that surrounded the person of Hitler. Centre Party newspapers now referred to Brüning as the 'Leader' and declared that his Catholic 'retinue' would 'submit' itself to his decisions.[136] All the party's deputies and officials tendered their resignations and gave Brüning full power to reappoint them or find replacements. This included the Reichstag deputies, who owed their election to their place on the party's list of candidates and thus could indeed be replaced at Brüning's whim by others lower down the list. So the Centre Party now, de facto, replaced the idea of an elected Reichstag by an appointed one. Brüning announced a thorough reform of the party's structure, and in the meantime moved closer still to the Nazi regime, persuading his deputies to vote for the government's foreign policy declaration on 17 May 1933 and personally helping Hitler draft the remarkably moderate-sounding speech with which he presented it to the legislature. Brüning's willingness to compromise did not stop the political police from tapping his telephone and opening his mail, as he told the British Ambassador Sir Horace Rumbold in mid-June. According to Rumbold, Brüning now took the view that only the restoration of the monarchy could rescue the situation, an opinion he had in fact held for several years.

The former Chancellor seemed to have little idea of the extent of the repression now bearing down upon his party's members. Its newspapers were being banned or taken away from it. Its local and regional organizations were being closed down one by one. Its ministers in every state had been removed from office. Its civil servants, despite constant reassurances from Hermann Göring, were under continual threat of dismissal. Its 200,000 members were resigning from the party in ever-growing numbers. From May onwards, leading Catholic politicians, lawyers, activists in lay organizations, journalists and writers, were arrested as well, particularly if they had published critical articles about the Nazis or the government. On 26 June 1933, Himmler, as police chief of Bavaria, ordered that not only the entire body of Reichstag and state legislature deputies of the Bavarian People's Party, closely allied to the

Centre, should be taken into 'protective custody' but also all 'those persons who have been particularly active in party politics'.[137] On 19 June the Württemberg State President Eugen Bolz, one of the Centre's leading conservatives, was arrested and severely beaten; senior civil servants such as Helene Weber, who was also a Centre Party Reichstag deputy, were suspended from office; and the organization of the Catholic trade unions was forced to dissolve itself. These were only the most prominent and widely publicized cases in a whole new round of arrests, beatings and dismissals. At a local level, one Catholic lay organization after another came under pressure to close down or join the Nazi Party, arousing widespread concern amongst the Church hierarchy. While Papen and Goebbels demanded the Centre Party's dissolution with increasing vehemence in public, negotiations in Rome, joined towards the end of the month by Papen himself, produced an agreement that the party should cease to exist once the Concordat had been concluded.[138]

The final text of the Concordat, agreed on 1 July with the approval of Papen and Kaas and signed a week later, included a ban on priests engaging in political activity. Centre Party national and state legislators began resigning their seats or transferring to the Nazis, as did a number of councillors in Berlin, Frankfurt and other cities. Even Brüning now finally understood the writing on the wall. The party formally dissolved itself on 5 July, telling its Reichstag deputies, state legislators and local elected representatives to approach their Nazi colleagues with a view to transferring their allegiance to them. The party's members, declared the leadership, now had the opportunity to place themselves 'without reservation' behind the national front led by Hitler. What was left of the party press portrayed the end as the outcome not of external pressure but of an inevitable inner development which placed the Catholic community behind the new Germany in a historic transformation of the national polity. The party administration not only instructed all the party organizations to dissolve themselves but also warned that it was co-operating with the political police in implementing the dissolution procedure. Predictably enough, the Nazis preferred to persuade the party's legislators to resign their seats rather than find a new home in the Nazi Party delegations as they had envisaged.[139]

Together with the labour movement, the Centre Party had offered the only effective resistance to the electoral inroads of the Nazis in the early

1930s. The cohesion and discipline of the two political milieux had been the product, among other things, of the persecution they had both suffered under Bismarck. But while the Social Democrats and, later, the Communists, had been driven into a state of permanent opposition and isolation by the experience of repression, the reaction of the Catholics had been to put reintegration into the national community above almost any other aim. Leading Catholic politicians such as Papen and, to a lesser extent, Brüning and Bolz, lacked the commitment to democracy that had characterized figures such as Wilhelm Marx or Matthias Erzberger in the Republic's early days. The Church as a whole was turning against parliamentary democracy all over Europe in the face of the Bolshevik threat. In this situation, the dissolution of the party seemed a small sacrifice to make in the interests of what almost every leading figure involved saw as the securing of binding guarantees from the new regime for the continued autonomy of the Catholic Church and the full participation of Catholics in the new German order. Just how binding these guarantees were, the Catholics would soon find out.

Meanwhile, on 28 October 1933, Clemens August Count von Galen was consecrated Catholic Bishop of Münster, the first such elevation to take place after the signing of the Concordat. In his address to the congregation, Galen declared that his duty as he saw it was to tell the truth, to pronounce on 'the difference between justice and injustice, on good and bad actions'. Before his installation, he had called on Hermann Göring, the Prussian Minister-President, to whom, in accordance with the terms of the Concordat, he swore an oath of loyalty to the state. In a symbolic act of reciprocity, local Nazi and brownshirt officials from the District Leader downwards filed past him during the consecration ceremony in Münster, saluting him with the outstretched arm of the 'German greeting'. Swastika-bearing columns of stormtroopers and SS men lined the roads for the episcopal procession. They paraded past Galen's palace in a torchlit procession the same evening. The reconciliation of Nazism and Catholicism seemed, at least for the time being, complete.[140]

IV

The destruction of the Communists, the Social Democrats and the Centre Party was the most difficult part of the Nazis' drive to create a one-party state. Together, these three parties represented far more voters than the Nazi Party itself ever won in a free election. In comparison to the problems they posed, getting rid of the other parties was easy. Most of them had lost virtually every vote and seat in the Reichstag they had ever possessed. They were ripe for picking off one by one. By early 1933 the only one among them which had belonged to the coalition of parties that had supported the Weimar Republic from the beginning, the State Party (formerly the Democrats) was drifting helplessly at the mercy of events, reduced to two seats in the Reichstag and issuing pathetic appeals to other parties to take its deputies under their wing. It continued to advertise its opposition to the Nazis, but at the same time it was also advocating the revision of the constitution in an unmistakeably authoritarian direction. It failed to improve its support in the elections of March 1933, though by tagging its candidates onto the much better supported Social Democratic Party list, it increased its representation in the Reichstag from 2 seats to 5. With strong reservations, but unanimously, the party's deputies, including the later Federal German President Theodor Heuss, voted for the Enabling Law on 23 March 1933, cowed by Hitler's threat of a bloodbath should the vote go against him. In practice their votes made no difference, as they must have known. The party's parliamentary floor leader Otto Nuschke began signing his official letters with the 'German freedom greeting' and urged recognition of the government's legitimacy. Meanwhile, civil servants, who had been a major element in the party, were leaving it en masse to join the Nazis in a bid to keep their jobs. Ever since the party had been pushed to the fringe in the elections of 1930 there had been repeated discussions over the question of whether it was worth going on. The brownshirts unleashed a fresh campaign of terror on the few remaining deputies, officials and local councillors who openly declared their allegiance to the party. The government then stripped its Reichstag deputies of their seats, on the grounds that they had stood on the Social Democratic list in the March election and were therefore Social Democrats. After this, the party leadership finally gave up and declared the State Party formally dissolved on 28 June 1933.[141]

The People's Party, which had moved sharply to the right after the death of its leading figure for most of the Weimar years, Gustav Stresemann, in 1929, began to shed its liberal wing in 1931 – 'liberal' being defined by this time as support for the Brüning government, yet another measure of how far the political spectrum had shifted to the right – and agitate for a general coalition of all nationalist forces, including the Nazis. The more the party lost electoral support, however, the more it disintegrated into a chaos of warring factions. With only 7 seats left in the Reichstag after July 1932, the People's Party had been pushed far out onto the political fringe. Its leader by this time, the lawyer Eduard Dingeldey, thought it a good idea to join forces with the Nationalists in a common electoral list in November 1932. This drove out the remaining liberals from the party but failed to bring it any real gains. Alarmed at this sign of further dissolution, Dingeldey abandoned the pact with the Nationalists for the next election, with the result that the People's Party was able to win only 2 seats in March 1933. This was all that was left of the proud tradition of Germany's National Liberal Party, which had dominated the Reichstag in the 1870s and done so much to soften the harsh contours of Bismarck's creation with a broad palette of liberal legislation. While Dingeldey withdrew from politics for two months as a result of a serious illness, the party's remaining members, and in particular civil servants frightened for their jobs, began to leave in large numbers, while others, led by the deputy leader, urged the party to dissolve itself and formally merge with the Nazis. When Dingeldey succeeded in preventing this, the party's right wing resigned. His efforts to obtain an audience with Hitler or Göring were rebuffed. Fearing for the safety of the party's remaining officials and deputies in the general atmosphere of intimidation, Dingeldey announced the dissolution of the People's Party on 4 July. As a reward, he obtained an audience with Hitler three days later, and the Nazi Leader's assurance that former party members would not suffer any discrimination because of their political past. Needless to say, this did not prevent the Nazis from enforcing the resignation of former People's Party deputies from legislatures all over Germany, nor the dismissal of civil servants on grounds of opposition to the National Socialist movement. Dingeldey's protests at such actions were contemptuously brushed aside.[142]

The Nationalist Party under Alfred Hugenberg had hardly been any more successful than the two liberal parties in electoral terms. It had lost almost all its votes to the Nazis in the early 1930s. Yet it regarded itself as the main coalition partner of the Nazis, whom it had always treated with a certain degree of condescension. Leading Nationalists welcomed the fact that the Hitler cabinet marked the definitive end of the parliamentary system and the beginning of a dictatorship. Hugenberg campaigned vigorously in the elections of 5 March 1933 for an overall majority with the Nazis that would provide popular legitimacy for this transformation. Yet the leading Nationalists were uncomfortably aware that this left them extremely vulnerable. They warned against the 'socialism' of the Nazis and pleaded for a 'non-party' government. Certainly, the Nazis were careful to maintain the illusion of a genuine coalition during the campaign. No Nationalist newspapers were banned, no Nationalist meetings broken up and no Nationalist politicians arrested. But the massive repression and violence of the campaign were wholly exerted in favour of the Nazis. On 5 March the Nazis got their reward, increasing their representation in the Reichstag from 196 seats to 288. The Nationalists, by contrast, did not manage to improve their situation significantly, winning 52 seats instead of 51. These seats, and the 8 per cent of the vote they represented, were enough to push the coalition over the 50 per cent mark. But the electoral results demonstrated graphically how unequal the coalition partners were. On the streets, the paramilitary 'fighting leagues' associated with the Nationalists could in no way compete with the might of the brownshirts and the SS. And the Nationalists had failed to win the unconditional allegiance of the Steel Helmets, the one major paramilitary group that seemed to share their political views.

The March election result changed the relationship between the two parties fundamentally. With the Communists now out of the legislature, the Nazis no longer needed the Nationalists to form an overall majority, though they still fell some way short of possessing the two-thirds needed to alter the constitution. Hitler and Göring now began to make it brutally clear to Hugenberg that they were calling the shots. The passage of the Enabling Act with the support of the Nationalists was made palatable for the more conservative party members by the preceding formal opening of the parliament in Potsdam, with its clear reference to the Bismarckian traditions they were dedicated to renewing. But as soon as the Enabling

Act had gone through, Hitler lost no time in declaring that there could be no question of restoring what he regarded as the failed institution of the monarchy. It was at this point, finally, that the Nazis began to apply to the Nationalists the same pressures under which the other parties had already been suffering since the middle of February. On 29 March the office of the party's floor leader in the Reichstag, Ernst Oberfohren, was searched, and on the following day his house was raided. The Nazis revealed that documents found there showed Oberfohren to be the author of anonymous letters attacking Hugenberg. This was enough to persuade the party leader to drop his intention of complaining. Oberfohren had also been taking a suspiciously close interest in the circumstances in which the Reichstag had burned down, suggesting that he shared the Communist view that the arson had been organized by the Nazis. Warned by the raid on his home, Oberfohren immediately resigned his seat. Meanwhile, other senior Nationalists also began to come under pressure. Gunther Gerecke, Reich Commissioner for Work Creation, was accused of embezzlement. The head of the Reich Land League, an organization traditionally close to the Nationalists, was dismissed for illicitly speculating on the corn market. And reports began to come in of the dismissal of civil servants who openly acknowledged their membership of the Nationalist Party.[143]

The Nationalists had entered the coalition on 30 January feeling that they were the senior partners in an alliance with an immature and inexperienced political movement that they would easily be able to control. Two months later, all this had changed. Amid privately expressed fears of the destructive consequences of a full-blown Nazi revolution, they now acknowledged helplessly the impossibility of preventing illegal actions against their own members by a government in which they were still a formal partner. In this situation, it seemed wise to them to adapt to the new, post-democratic order. Hugenberg obtained a restructuring of the party organization that made the 'Leadership Principle' fundamental at every level. Following this, the Nationalists changed their formal designation from the German-Nationalist People's Party to the German-Nationalist Front, to make clear their view that political parties were a thing of the past. But these changes only deprived Hugenberg of the last vestiges of democratic legitimacy and so left his position even more exposed than before. One after another, Nazis in Berlin and in the country at large publicly criticized and pressurized institutions and organizations which Hugenberg considered to be under his aegis, amid a whispering campaign that he was slowing down the 'national revolution'.

Regional organs of the Nazi Party now began to declare that Hugenberg, as Prussian Minister of Agriculture, no longer enjoyed the confidence of the peasantry. There were rumours that he was about to resign from his Prussian posts. Hugenberg's response to these attempts to undermine him was to threaten to quit the cabinet. He believed that by doing so he would invalidate the Enabling Act, since it applied only to what it called the 'present government'. Already, however, the constitutional theorist Carl Schmitt, an influential supporter of the Nazis, had declared that by 'present government' the Act did not mean the particular group of ministers in office when it was passed, but the 'completely different kind of government' which had come into being with the end of the party-political system. Thus the 'present government', and with it the validity of the Enabling Act, would not be affected by the resignation of this minister or that; its nature was, rather, determined by its Leader.[144] Hugenberg's threat was an empty one, another example of the futility of legalistic reasoning in the face of Nazi pressure. Meanwhile, the threat of Nazi violence against his supporters became increasingly explicit. On 7 May Ernst Oberfohren, already hounded out of office by the Nazis, was found dead; in the prevailing atmosphere of ruthless intimidation by the Nazis, many rightly refused to believe the official story that he had shot himself. There were reports of arrests of local Nationalist officials and the banning of some Nationalist meetings. The Nationalists came under increasing pressure to dissolve their paramilitary 'fighting groups'. By this time these groups, mostly student and youth organizations, had increased in strength to 100,000 in the wake of the 'national uprising' and so they were strong enough to cause some concern to the Nazis.

On 30 May 1933 some of the Nationalist leaders met with Hitler to complain about the growing pressure on them to surrender their autonomy. They were met with a 'hysterical outburst of rage' in which the Nazi leader shouted that he would let his 'SA open fire and arrange a bloodbath lasting three days long ... until there's nothing left', if the Nationalist paramilitaries did not wind themselves up of their own accord. This was enough to shake the Nationalists' already weak resolve to resist. In mid-June, therefore, Hitler personally ordered the dissolution of the Nationalist student and youth organizations and the confiscation of their assets. Leading Nationalists associated with these groups, including Herbert von Bismarck, who was also State Secretary in the Prussian administration, were arrested and interrogated; faced with alleged evidence of the groups' infiltration by supposed Marxist elements, Bismarck confessed he had had no idea how bad things had become.

By this time, leading Nationalists such as the ultra-right Catholic historian Martin Spahn had declared that they could not serve two leaders, and had begun defecting to the Nazis. The daily humiliations that the Nationalist 'Leader' Hugenberg had to suffer in the cabinet were becoming more and more pronounced. When he publicly demanded, at an international economic conference, the return of Germany's African colonies, without consulting the cabinet beforehand, the government equally publicly disowned him, embarrassing him before the whole world. On 23 June his non-Nazi conservative cabinet colleagues Papen, Neurath, Schwerin von Krosigk and Schacht joined Hitler in condemning his behaviour. Hugenberg's planned speech to a Nationalist political meeting on 26 June was banned by the police. Complaining bitterly that he was constantly blocked in his ministerial duties and publicly attacked by the Nazi press, he demonstratively tendered his resignation to Hindenburg the same day.

Hugenberg of course did not really intend to leave the government. But the aged President failed completely to meet his expectations; instead of rejecting his letter and intervening with Hitler as he was supposed to, Hindenburg did nothing. A meeting with Hitler to try and resolve the situation amicably only provoked Hitler into demanding that the German-Nationalist Front must be dissolved if Hugenberg's resignation were to be rejected. If this did not happen, 'thousands' of Nationalist civil servants and state employees would be dismissed, he said. But the alternative was a false one; Hitler never had any intention of allowing Hugenberg, the last remaining independent cabinet member of any political stature, to withdraw his resignation. As Hitler was triumphantly reporting Hugenberg's departure to the cabinet, the other leading figures in the German-Nationalist Front met Hitler to conclude a 'Friendship Agreement' in which they agreed the party's 'self-dissolution'.[145] The conditions agreed by the Nationalists – Hitler's formal coalition partner – were superficially less oppressive than those agreed by other parties;

but in practice the Nazis forced any deputies or elected legislators whose views they did not like, such as Herbert von Bismarck, to resign their seats, and only accepted those who they could be confident would follow orders without question. Guarantees that Nationalist civil servants would not suffer because of their party-political past were not treated as binding by the regime. The 'Friendship Agreement' was little more than abject surrender.

With the parties dissolved, the Churches brought to heel, the trade unions abolished and the army neutralized, there was one major political player still to be dealt with: the Steel Helmets, the ultra-nationalist paramilitary veterans' organization. On 26 April 1933, after lengthy negotiations, Franz Seldte, the Steel Helmets' leader, joined the Nazi Party and placed the Steel Helmets under Hitler's political leadership with the guarantee that they would continue to exist as an autonomous organization of war veterans. Those who opposed this move, such as the joint leader of the organization, Theodor Duesterberg, were summarily dismissed. A rapid expansion in numbers to perhaps as many as a million, comprising war veterans drawn from a variety of recently banned organizations including the Reichsbanner, diluted the political commitment of the Steel Helmets still further and opened them up to criticism from the Nazis. As auxiliary police, the Steel Helmets had lent support to the actions of Nazi stormtroopers during the previous months without either fully participating on the one hand, or attempting to restrain them on the other. Their position was rather like that of the army, for whom they regarded themselves indeed as an armed, experienced and fully trained reserve. Their leader Franz Seldte was a member of the cabinet and proved completely incapable of standing up to the bullying of Hitler and Göring. By May, they had been completely neutralized as a political force.[146]

At the end of May, therefore, Hitler took the next step, accusing the Steel Helmets with some plausibility of being infiltrated by substantial numbers of ex-Communists and Social Democrats looking for a substitute for their own, now-banned paramilitary organizations. They were forcibly incorporated into the SA, while still retaining enough of a vestige of their previous autonomy to dissuade them from resisting. The presence of the Steel Helmets' leader Franz Seldte in the cabinet seemed to most of them to guarantee their continued influence where it mattered. Their functions as a reserve army and a veterans' welfare association carried on. Even as late as 1935, renamed the National Socialist German Front-Fighters' League, they still claimed a membership of half a million. The Steel Helmets' aim of the destruction of Weimar democracy and the return of an authoritarian, nationalist regime had self-evidently been achieved: what possible grounds could they have to object to their incorporation into the ranks of Ernst Röhm's brownshirts? The merger caused organizational chaos for a time, but it effectively deprived the Nationalists of any last, lingering chance of being able to mobilize opposition on the streets to the rampaging stormtroopers of the SA.[147]

The paramilitary groups had thus been shut down as effectively as the political parties. By the summer of 1933 the creation of a one-party state was virtually complete. Only Hindenburg remained as a potential obstacle to the achievement of total power, a senile cypher seemingly without any remaining will of his own, whose office had been neutralized by the provisions of the Enabling Act. The army had agreed to stand on the sidelines. Business had fallen into line. On 28 June 1933 Joseph Goebbels had already celebrated the destruction of the parties, the trade unions and the paramilitaries and their replacement by the monopoly of power on the part of the Nazi Party and its affiliated organizations: 'The road to the total state. Our revolution has an uncanny dynamism.'[148]

BRINGING GERMANY INTO LINE

I

On the morning of 6 May 1933, a group of vans pulled up outside Dr Magnus Hirschfeld's Institute for Sexual Science in the smart Tiergarten district of Berlin. Out of them leapt students from the Berlin School for Physical Education, members of the National Socialist German Students' League. They drew up in military formation, then, while some of them took out their trumpets and tubas and started to play patriotic music, the others marched into the building. Their intentions were clearly un-friendly. Hirschfeld's Institute was well known in Berlin, not only for its championing of causes such as the legalization of homosexuality and abortion, and for its popular evening classes in sexual education, but also for its comprehensive collection of books and manuscripts on sexual topics, built up by the director since before the turn of the century. By 1933 it housed between 12,000 and 20,000 books – estimates vary – and an even larger collection of photographs on sexual subjects.[149] The Nazi students who stormed into the Institute on 6 May 1933 proceeded to pour red ink over books and manuscripts, played football with framed photographs, leaving the floor covered in shards of broken glass, and ransacked the cupboards and drawers, throwing their contents onto the floor. Four days later, more vans arrived, this time with stormtroopers carrying baskets, into which they piled as many books and manuscripts as they could and took them out onto the Opera Square. Here they stacked them up in a gigantic heap and set light to them. About 10,000 books are said to have been consumed in the conflagration. As the fire burned on into the evening, the students carried a bust of the Institute's director into the Square and threw it into the flames. Told that the

65-year-old Hirschfeld was abroad recovering from an illness, the storm-troopers said: 'Then hopefully he'll snuff it without us; then we won't need to string him up or beat him to death.'[150]

Wisely, Hirschfeld did not return to Germany. While the Nazi press reported triumphantly on the 'Energetic Action against a Poison Shop' and announced that 'German students fumigate the Sexual Science Insti-tute' run by 'the Jew Magnus Hirschfeld', the venerable sex reformer and champion of homosexual rights remained in France, where he died suddenly on his sixty-seventh birthday, on 14 May 1935.[151] The destruc-tion of his Institute was only one part, if the most spectacular, of a far more wide-ranging assault on what the Nazis portrayed as the Jewish movement to subvert the German family. Sex and procreation were to be indissolubly linked, at least for the racially approved. The Nazis moved with the approval of conservatives and Catholics alike to destroy every branch of Weimar Germany's lively and intricately interconnected con-geries of pressure-groups for sexual freedom, the reform of the abortion law, the decriminalization of homosexuality, the public dispensing of contraceptive advice and anything else that they thought was contributing to the continued decline of the German birth rate. Sex reformers like the Freudian Wilhelm Reich or the long-time campaigner for abortion reform Helene Stöcker were forced into exile, their organizations and clinics closed down or taken over by the Nazis. The police, meanwhile, raided well-known homosexual meeting-places they had previously tacitly toler-ated, while in Hamburg they arrested hundreds of female prostitutes in the harbour district, acting, somewhat bizarrely, on the basis of the Reichstag fire decree 'for the protection of people and state'. If nothing else, the raids illustrated how the decree could be used as legitimation for almost any kind of repressive action by the authorities. The dubious legality of this action was resolved on 26 May 1933, when the cabinet amended the liberal Law against Sexually Transmitted Diseases passed in 1927. The amendments not only recriminalized prostitution, effectively legalized in 1927, but also reintroduced the legal ban on publicity and education relating to abortion and abortifacients.[152] Within a short space of time, the Nazis had dismantled the entire sexual reform movement and extended legal restrictions on sexuality from the existing punitive laws against same-sex relations to many other kinds of sexual activity that were not directed towards the goal of increasing the birth rate.

The attack on sexual liberation had already been foreshadowed in the last years of the Weimar Republic. The years 1929–32 had seen a massive public controversy on abortion law reform, stirred up by the Communists, and reflecting the need of many couples to avoid having children in circumstances of dire poverty and unemployment. Huge demonstrations, rallies, petitions, films, newspaper campaigns and the like had all drawn attention to the issues of illegal abortion and ignorance about contraception, and the police had banned a number of meetings held by sex reformers. On 1 March 1933 a new decree on health insurance had legitimated the closure of state-funded health advice clinics across the land, enforced during the following weeks by gangs of brownshirts. Doctors and staff were thrown out onto the streets; many, particularly if they were Jewish, went into exile. The Nazis argued that the entire system of social medicine developed by the Weimar state was geared towards preventing the reproduction of the strong on the one hand, and shoring up the families of the weak on the other. Social hygiene was to be swept away; racial hygiene was to be introduced in its stead.[153] That meant, as some eugenicists had been arguing since the end of the nineteenth century, drastically reducing the burden of the weak on society by introducing a programme of preventing them from having children.

These ideas had rapidly gained wider currency among doctors, social workers and welfare administrators during the Depression. Well before the end of the Weimar Republic, experts had seized the opportunity afforded by the financial crisis to argue that the best way to reduce the impossible burden of welfare on the economy was to prevent the underclass from reproducing, by subjecting them to forcible sterilization. Before many years had passed, there would thus be fewer indigent families to support. Before long, too, the numbers of alcoholics, 'work-shy', mentally handicapped, criminally inclined and physically disabled people in Germany would be drastically reduced – on the dubious assumption, of course, that all these conditions were overwhelmingly hereditary in nature – and the welfare state would be able to direct its dwindling resources on the deserving poor. Protestant charities, influenced by doctrines of predestination and original sin, broadly welcomed such ideas; the Catholics, bolstered by a stern warning from the Pope in a 1930 encyclical that marriage and sexual intercourse were solely for the purposes of procreation, and that all human beings were endowed with an immortal soul, were strongly against. The appeal of a eugenic approach, even for liberal-minded reformers, was increased by the fact that mental asylums began to fill up rapidly from 1930 as families could no longer afford to care for ill or disabled members, while at the same time mental asylum budgets were drastically cut by local and regional authorities. In 1932 the Prussian Health Council met to discuss a new law allowing voluntary eugenic sterilization. Drafted by the eugenicist Fritz Lenz, who had been contemplating such policies since well before the First World War, it placed the power of advice and application on welfare and medical officials whose word the poor, the confined and the handicapped would have been hard put to gainsay.[154]

This was only part of a much wider crackdown on what the respectable saw as various forms of social deviance. At the height of the economic crisis, no fewer than 10 million people were in receipt of some form of public assistance. As the democratic parties were closed down, municipal and state legislatures taken over and turned into assemblies of cheer-leaders for the local Nazi bosses, and newspapers deprived of their ability to investigate freely matters of social and political concern, welfare agencies, like the police, were freed from any kind of public scrutiny or control. Social workers and welfare administrators had already long been prone to regard claimants as scroungers and layabouts. Now, encouraged by new senior officials put in place by Nazi local and regional adminis-trations, they could give free rein to their prejudices. Regulations passed in 1924 had allowed authorities to make benefits dependent on the recipient agreeing to work 'in suitable cases' on communal job schemes. These had already been introduced on a limited scale before 1933. Three and a half thousand people were working on compulsory labour schemes in Duisburg in 1930, and Bremen had been making such employment a condition of benefit receipt since the previous year. But in the dire eco-nomic situation of the early 1930s only a small proportion of the un-employed were covered – 6,000 out of 200,000 people on benefit in Hamburg in 1932, for example. From the early months of 1933 onwards, however, the number rapidly increased. Such work was not employment in the full sense of the word: it did not involve health insurance or pension contributions, for example, indeed it was not even paid: all that those who were engaged in it got was their welfare support plus, sometimes, pocket-money for travel or a free lunch.[155]

The work was supposedly voluntary, and the schemes were run by the private initiative of charitable institutions such as the Church welfare associations, but the voluntary element became rapidly less visible after March 1933. The urgent problem of mass unemployment was being tackled in the first place by coercion. A typical scheme was the 'Farm Aid' programme of March 1933, which took up initiatives already launched under the Weimar Republic to help the rural economy by drafting in young unemployed people from the towns to work on the land for board and lodging and nominal pay. Again, this was not employment in the proper sense of the word, but by August 1933 it had taken 145,000 people off the unemployment register, 33,000 of them women. Local administrators responsible for the homeless in Hamburg had been claiming since 1931 that they were making life unpleasant for the destitute and forcing them to seek support elsewhere. Such attitudes rapidly became more widespread in 1933. The number of overnight stays in the Hamburg Police Shelter fell from 403,000 in 1930 to 299,000 in 1933, largely as a result of this policy of deterrence. Officials began to argue that vagrants and the 'work-shy' should be sent to concentration camps. On 1 June 1933 the Prussian Interior Ministry issued a decree for the suppression of public begging. Poverty and destitution, already stigmatized before 1933, were now beginning to be criminalized as well.[156]

The police themselves, freed from the constraints of democratic scrutiny, launched a series of large-scale raids on the clubs and meeting-places of Berlin's ring associations, networks of organized crime, in May and June 1933, as part of a campaign against professional criminals. Precincts they regarded as the haunts of criminal gangs were also centres of support for the Communists and their supporters. Such a crackdown was only possible after the Red Front-Fighters' League had been smashed; it also constituted a further intimidation of the local population. Since the Nazis regarded crime, and particularly organized crime, as heavily dominated by Jews, it was not surprising that the police also raided fifty premises in Berlin's 'Barn District' (*Scheunenviertel*) on 9 June 1933, a quarter known not only for its poverty but also for its high Jewish population. Needless to say, the association existed almost wholly in the minds of the Nazis themselves.[157] The ring associations were ruthlessly smashed, their members taken into preventive custody without trial, and their clubs and bars closed down.[158]

In the penal system, where many of these people would eventually end up, the rapidly growing problem of petty crime had already led to pressure for harsher, more deterrent policies in the state prisons. Administrators and penal experts had argued in the last years of the Weimar Republic for the indefinite imprisonment or security confinement of habitual criminals whose hereditary degeneracy, it was assumed, rendered them incapable of improvement. Security confinement was increasingly thought to be the long-term answer to the burden these offenders supposedly imposed on the community. According to which criminologist or prison governor was making the estimate, anything between one in thirteen and one in two of all state prison inmates fell into this category at the end of the 1920s. Security confinement was included in the final drafts of the proposed new Criminal Code under preparation in the second half of the 1920s. Although the draft Code fell foul of the interminable wrangling of Weimar's political parties, these proposals had a wide measure of assent in the penal and judicial establishments and clearly were not going to go away.[159] There was no lack of specialist opinion that thought that the sterilization of genetically defective people should be compulsory.[160] The Weimar welfare state had begun to turn to authoritarian solutions to this crisis that contemplated a serious assault on the bodily rights and integrity of the citizen. These would soon be taken up by the Third Reich and applied with a draconian severity that few under Weimar had even dreamed of. More immediately, state financial cutbacks were in any case forcing penal and welfare administrators to make ever harsher distinctions between the deserving and the undeserving, as conditions in state institutions of one kind and another worsened to the point where it was becoming increasingly difficult to keep everybody in them healthy and alive.[161]

II

The crackdown did not just affect the politically suspect, the deviant and the marginal. It affected every part of German society. Driving the whole process forward was the massive outburst of violence unleashed by the stormtroopers, the SS and the police in the first half of 1933. Reports continually appeared in the press, in suitably bowdlerized form, of brutal beatings, torture and ritual humiliation of prisoners from all walks of life and all shades of political opinion apart from the Nazis. Far from being directed against particular, widely unpopular minorities, the terror was comprehensive in scope, affecting anyone who expressed dissent in public, from whatever direction, against deviants, vagrants, nonconformists of every kind.[162] The widespread intimidation of the population provided the essential precondition for a process that was in train all over Germany in the period from February to July 1933: the process, as the Nazis called it, of 'co-ordination', or to use the more evocative German term, *Gleichschaltung*, a metaphor drawn from the world of electricity, meaning that all the switches were being put onto the same circuit, as it were, so that they could all be activated by throwing a single master switch at the centre. Almost every aspect of political, social and associational life was affected, at every level from the nation to the village.

The Nazi takeover of the federated states provided a key component in this process. Just as important was the 'co-ordination' of the civil service, whose implementation from February 1933 onwards had put such powerful pressure on the Centre Party to knuckle under. Within a couple of weeks of Hitler's appointment, new State Secretaries – the top civil service post – had been appointed in a number of ministries, including Hans-Heinrich Lammers at the Reich Chancellery. In Prussia, adding to the effects of the previous purge carried out by Papen after July 1932, Hermann Göring replaced twelve Police Presidents by mid-February. From March onwards, the violence of the stormtroopers was rapidly forcing politically unacceptable city officials and local mayors out of office – 500 leading municipal civil servants and seventy Lord Mayors by the end of May. Laws eliminating the autonomy of the federated states and providing for each one to be run by a Reich Commissioner appointed in Berlin – all except one were Nazi Party Regional Leaders – meant that there were few obstacles left after the first week of April to the 'co-ordination', or, in other words, Nazification of the civil service at every level. At the same time as the state governments were being overthrown, local Nazis, backed by squads of armed stormtroopers and SS men, were occupying town halls, terrorizing mayors and councils into resigning, and replacing them with their own nominees. Health insurance offices, employment centres, village councils, hospitals, law courts and all other state and public institutions were treated in the same way.

Officials were forced to resign their posts or to join the Nazi Party, and were beaten up and dragged off to prison if they refused.[163]

This massive purge was given legal form by the promulgation on 7 April of one of the new regime's most fundamental decrees, the so-called Law for the Restoration of a Professional Civil Service. Its title appealed to the corporate spirit of conservative civil servants and contained more than an implied criticism of the attempts of Weimar governments, especially in Prussia, to bring committed democrats in from outside the civil service to serve in senior posts. The first aim of the new decree was to regularize and impose centralized order on the widespread forcible ejection of civil servants and officials from their offices by local and regional brownshirt and Party actions. The law provided for the dismissal of untrained officials appointed after 9 November 1918, of 'non-Aryan' civil servants (defined on 11 April as having one or more 'non-Aryan', in other words, Jewish grandparent, and on 30 June as including any civil servant married to a non-Aryan), and of anyone whose previous political activity did not guarantee political reliability, or acting in the interests of the nationalist state, as the law put it. Only those with war service in 1914–18 were exempt.[164]

Justifying the Law on 25 April 1933, Hermann Göring criticized 'time-servers' in the civil service:

It had repelled and disgusted him to see how in his Ministry, whose body of civil servants notoriously consisted of up to 60 per cent of Severing-adherents, swastika badges were already sprouting from the earth like mushrooms after a few days, and how already after four days the clicking of heels and the raising high of hands were already a general sight on the corridors.[165]

Many civil servants did indeed rush to preserve their jobs by becoming members of the Nazi Party, joining the army of those who quickly became known mockingly as the 'March Fallen', after the democrats who lost their lives in the March disturbances of the 1848 Revolution. Between 30 January and 1 May 1933, 1.6 million people joined the Nazi Party, dwarfing the existing Party membership, a Gadarene rush that illustrated as few other things did the degree of the opportunism and *sauve qui peut* that were gripping the German population. Up to 80 per cent of Party members in Catholic areas such as Koblenz-Trier and Cologne-Aachen in the summer of 1933 had only joined within the previous few months.

Indeed, Hitler became worried that this massive influx was changing the character of the Party by making it too bourgeois. But within the short term, at least, it meant the allegiance of the overwhelming majority of civil servants to the new regime.[166] In fact, about 12.5 per cent of senior civil servants in Prussia and around 4.5 per cent elsewhere were dismissed as a result of the law. Further clauses allowed the demotion of civil servants or their compulsory retirement in the interests of administrative simplification; the numbers affected here were roughly similar. Altogether the Law affected between 1 and 2 per cent of the entire professional civil service. The dismissals and demotions had the incidental, and far from unintended effect, of reducing government expenditure as well as imposing racial and political conformity. Meanwhile, on 17 July 1933 Göring issued a decree reserving the right to appoint senior civil servants, university professors and judicial officials in Prussia to himself.[167]

Particularly important within the vast and diverse world of state employees were the judiciary and the prosecution service. There was a distinct threat that Nazi violence, intimidation and murder would run foul of the law. A large number of prosecutions, indeed, were begun by lawyers who did not share the new regime's politically instrumental view of justice. But it was already clear that the majority of judges and lawyers were not going to make any trouble. Out of around 45,000 judges, state prosecutors and judicial officials in Prussia in 1933, only some 300 were dismissed or transferred to other duties on political grounds, despite the fact that very few state lawyers belonged to the Nazi Party at the time of Hitler's appointment as Reich Chancellor on 30 January. Adding on Jewish lawyers and judges dismissed (whatever their political position) on grounds of race made a total of 586. A similarly tiny proportion of the legal profession was dismissed in other German states. No serious objections were raised from the legal profession to these actions. Collective protest became in any case well-nigh impossible when the professional associations of judges, lawyers and notaries were forcibly merged with the League of National Socialist Lawyers into the Front of German Law, headed by Hans Frank, who was appointed Reich Commissioner for the 'Co-ordination of the Judicial System in the States and for the Renewal of the Legal Order' on 22 April. The reservations of the German Judges' League had already been disposed of, as Hitler mentioned the 'irremovability of judges' in a speech on 23 March, and promises were made by the Justice Ministry to improve judges' pay and prestige. Soon, lawyers were falling over themselves to join the Nazi Party, as the state Justice Ministers began to make it clear that promotion and career prospects would be harmed if they did not.[168] Between this point and early 1934, 2,250 prosecutions against SA members and 420 against SS men were suspended or abandoned, not least under pressure from local storm-trooper bands themselves.[169]

These measures were part of a massive and wide-ranging purge of German social institutions in the spring and early summer of 1933. Economic pressure-groups and associations of all kinds were quickly brought into line. Despite the fact that agriculture was nominally in the hands of Hitler's coalition partner Alfred Hugenberg, it was the leader of the Nazi Party's farmers' organization, Walther Darré, who made the running here, forcing a merger of agricultural interest groups into a single Nazi organization well before Hugenberg was eventually obliged to resign his post in the cabinet. Many groups and institutions reacted by trying to pre-empt such forcible co-ordination. In the business sector, employers' associations and pressure-groups such as the Reich Association of German Industry incorporated Nazis onto their boards, declared their loyalty to the regime, and merged with other industrial pressure-groups to form the unitary Reich Corporation of German Industry. By making such a move unprompted, the industrialists sought to ensure that they could ward off the most intrusive attentions of the new regime. At one point, the Nazi functionary Otto Wagener had forcibly occupied the head-quarters of the Reich Association of German Industry, with the clear intention of closing it down. Following the voluntary co-ordination of the Association by itself, he was displaced as Hitler's Commissioner for Economic Questions by Wilhelm Keppler, a long-term intermediary between the Nazis and big business who, unlike Wagener, was trusted by both sides.

On 1 June 1933 business took another step to try and secure its position. Leading businessmen and corporations founded the Adolf Hitler Donation of the German Economy. This was supposed to bring an end to the frequent, sometimes intimidatory extortions exacted from businesses by local SA and Party groups by instituting a regular and proportional system of payments by industrialists to Nazi Party funds. It steered 30 million Reichsmarks into the Party's coffers in the following twelve months. But it failed to secure its primary objective, for its foundation did nothing all the same to prevent lesser Party and SA bosses from continuing to extort smaller sums from businesses at a local level. However, big business was not too worried. Hitler had gone out of his way to reassure its representatives on 23 March that he was not going to interfere with their property and their profits, or indulge in any of the eccentric currency experiments with which the Party had toyed under the influence of Gottfried Feder in the early 1920s.[170] With the trade unions smashed, socialism off the agenda in any form, and new arms and munitions contracts already looming over the horizon, big business could feel satisfied that the concessions it had made to the new regime had largely been worth it.

Voluntary co-ordination was an option open to a whole variety of associations and institutions provided they could get their act together quickly enough. As often as not, however, organizations that had been living a relatively secure and undisturbed existence for decades were confused, divided and overtaken by events. A characteristic example was the Federation of German Women's Associations, the umbrella organization of the moderate German feminists and the German equivalent of the National Councils of Women familiar for many years in other countries. Founded nearly forty years previously, it was a vast and elaborate confederation of many kinds of women's societies, including professional associations like that of the women teachers. Overwhelmingly middle-class in composition, the Federation was deeply divided by the rise of the Nazis, a party for which most of its members were probably voting by 1932. Some senior figures wanted to fight the 'masculinity drunk with victory' that they saw triumphing in the Nazi movement, while others insisted on maintaining the Federation's traditional party-political neutrality. As discussions dragged on, the Nazis resolved the issue for them.

On 27 April 1933 the Baden provincial chapter of the Federation was sent a curt note by the leader of the Nazi women's organization in the province, Gertrud Scholtz-Klink, informing it that it was dissolved. The central leadership of the Federation wrote to the Reich Interior Minister asking in some puzzlement what the legal grounds were for such a peremptory act, and assuring him that the Baden chapter was far from being a danger to public safety. The national leader of the Nazi Women's Front, Lydia Gottschewski, declared somewhat airily that the Baden chapter had been dissolved on the basis of the law of the revolution, and enclosed a form for signature by the Federation's President, in which she was invited to submit the Federation unconditionally to the direction of Adolf Hitler, to expel all its Jewish members, to elect Nazi women to top positions and to join the Nazi Women's Front by 16 May. In vain the Federation pointed out to Gottschewski that it supported the 'national revolution', welcomed the eugenic measures being proposed by the regime and wanted to play its part in the Third Reich. On 15 May, faced with the fact that many of its member associations had already been co-ordinated into one Nazi institution or another, it voted formally to dissolve itself altogether, since its constitution made it impossible for it to belong to another organization.[171]

III

The Nazi 'co-ordination' of German society did not stop at political parties, state institutions, local and regional authorities, professions, and economic pressure-groups. Just how far it went is perhaps best illustrated by returning to the example of the small north German town of Northeim, long dominated by a coalition of liberals and conservatives with a strong Social Democratic movement and a much smaller branch of the Communist Party in opposition. The local Nazis had already managed to manipulate the municipal elections held on 12 March by running as the 'National Unity List' and freezing the other parties out. The Nazi leader in the town, Ernst Girmann, promised the end of Social Democratic corruption, and the end of parliamentarism. Despite all this, the Social Democrats held their own in the local and regional elections, and the Nazis, though they took over the town council, failed to do better than they had in July 1932. The new council met in public, with uniformed brownshirts lining the walls, SS men assisting the police, and chants of 'Hail Hitler!' punctuating the proceedings, in a local version of the intimidation that accompanied the passage of the Enabling Act through the Reichstag. The four Social Democratic councillors were refused permission to sit on any of the committees and not allowed to speak. As they walked out of the meeting, stormtroopers lined up to spit on them as they passed. Two of them resigned shortly afterwards, the other two went in June.

After the last Social Democrat had resigned, Northeim's town council was used purely for announcing measures taken by Girmann; there was no discussion, and the members listened in absolute silence. By this time, some 45 council employees, mostly Social Democrats, had been dismissed from the gas works, the brewery, the swimming pool, the health insurance office and other local institutions under the civil service law of 7 April 1933. Including accountants and administrators, they made up about a quarter of the council's employees. Easing out the town's mayor, a conservative who had held the office since 1903, proved more difficult, since he resisted all attempts to persuade him to go, and stood up to a considerable degree of harassment. In the end, when he went on vacation, the Nazified town council passed a vote of no confidence in him and declared the local Nazi leader Ernst Girmann mayor instead.

By this time, the leading local Communists in Northeim had been arrested, together with a number of Social Democrats, and the main regional newspaper read in the town had started to run stories not only on the concentration camp at Dachau but also on one much closer to Northeim, at Moringen, which had over 300 prisoners by the end of April, many of them from other political groupings besides the main body of inmates, the Communists. At least two dozen of the SS camp guards were local men from around Northeim, and many prisoners were released after a short period in the camp, so that what went on there must have been well known to the townspeople. The local town newspaper, formely liberal in its allegiance, now frequently reported the arrest and imprisonment of citizens for trivial offences such as spreading rumours and making abusive statements about National Socialism. People knew that more serious opposition would meet with more serious repression. Opponents of the regime were dealt with in other ways, too; active Social Democrats were dismissed from their jobs, subjected to house searches, or beaten up if they refused to give the Hitler salute. Pressure was put on their landlords to evict them from their homes. The brownshirts subjected the local Social Democratic party leader's shop to a boycott. Constant petty harassment was henceforth his lot, and that of other former prominent figures in the local labour movement, even if they abstained from all political activity.

Such were the implicit and sometimes explicit threats that lay behind the process of 'co-ordination' in a small town like Northeim, and in thousands of other small towns, villages and cities. The process began in March and rapidly gathered pace during April and May 1933. Like virtually all small towns, Northeim had a rich associational life, much of it more or less unpolitical, some of it not. The local Nazi Party brought all this under control by one means or another. Some clubs and societies were closed down or merged, others taken over. The railway workers in Northeim, an important centre in the national rail network, had already been pressurized by Nazis in senior positions in the local railway yards to enrol in the Nazi factory cell organization even before Hitler became Chancellor, but the Nazis made less progress in dealing with other workers until 4 May, when brownshirts took over the trade union offices and abolished the unions altogether. By this time, Girmann was insisting that every club and association had to have a majority of Nazis or Steel Helmets on its executive committee. Professional associations were merged into the newly founded National Socialist Physicians' League, the National Socialist Teachers' League and similar bodies, which all those concerned knew they had to join if they were to keep their jobs. The popular and well-funded local consumer co-operative was put under Nazi control but was too important to the local economy to close down, despite the fact that the Nazis had previously attacked it as a 'red' institution that undermined independent local businesses. Clubs for the war disabled were merged into the National Socialist War Victims' Association, the Boy Scouts and the Young German Order into the Hitler Youth.

The inexorable pressure for Nazification of voluntary associations in the town met with a variety of responses. The Northeim singing clubs mostly dissolved themselves, though the workers' choir attempted to adjust beforehand by cutting its links with the German Workers' Singing League. The upper-class singing club ('Song Stave') survived by altering its executive committee and consulting the local Nazi Party before changing its membership. The shooting societies, an important part of local life in many parts of Germany, elected Girmann as Chief Captain and were told by him that they had to promote the military spirit rather than existing just for recreational purposes as they had done so far. They survived by flying the swastika, singing the Horst Wessel Song, and opening up some of their shooting competitions to the general public to counter Girmann's charge of social exclusivity. All the local sports clubs, from the swimming association to the football club and the gymnastic societies, were forced to join in a single Northeim Sports Club under Nazi leadership, amid considerable recrimination. Some local social leaders took pre-emptive action to stop the Nazis confiscating their funds. The 'Beautification Club', a well-off association dedicated to improving the town's parks and woods, put all its funds into building a hunting lodge just beyond the town boundary before dissolving itself. And several of the local guilds, informed that they had to elect new committees by 2 May, arranged huge drinking sessions and lavish banquets in order to use up the funds which, they were convinced, would soon fall into the hands of the Nazis.[172]

This process of 'co-ordination' took place in the spring and summer of 1933 at every level, in every city, town and village throughout Germany. What social life remained was at the local inn, or took place in the privacy of people's homes. Individuals had become isolated except when they gathered in one Nazi organization or another. Society had been reduced to an anonymous and undifferentiated mass and then reconstituted in a new form in which everything was done in the name of Nazism. Open dissent and resistance had become impossible; even discussing or planning it was no longer practicable except in secret. Of course, in practice, such a situation remained an aim rather than a reality. The process of co-ordination was less than perfectly carried out, and a formal adherence to the new order through, for example, attaching the name 'National Socialist' to a club, a society or a professional organization, by no means implied a genuine ideological commitment on the part of those involved. Nevertheless, the scale and scope of the co-ordination of German society were breathtaking. And their purpose was not simply to eliminate any space in which opposition could develop. By bringing Germany into line, the new regime wanted to make it amenable to indoctrination and re-education according to the principles of National Socialism.

Reflecting on this process a few years later, the lawyer Raimund Pretzel asked himself what had happened to the 56 per cent of Germans who had voted against the Nazis in the elections of 5 March 1933. How was it, he wondered, that this majority had caved in so rapidly? Why had virtually every social, political and economic institution in Germany fallen into the hands of the Nazis with such apparent ease? 'The simplest, and, if you looked deeper, nearly always the most basic reason', he concluded, 'was fear. Join the thugs to avoid being beaten up. Less clear was a kind of exhilaration, the intoxication of unity, the magnetism of the masses.' Many, he also thought, had felt betrayed by the weakness of their political leaders, from Braun and Severing to Hugenberg and Hindenburg, and they joined the Nazis in a perverse act of revenge. Some were impressed by the fact that everything the Nazis had predicted seemed to be coming true. 'There was also (particularly among intellectuals) the belief that they could change the face of the Nazi Party by becoming a member, even now shift its direction. Then of course many jumped on the bandwagon, wanted to be part of a perceived success.' In the circumstances of the Depression, when times were hard and jobs were scarce, people clung to the mechanical routine of daily life as the only form of security: not to have gone along with the Nazis would have meant risking one's livelihood and prospects, to have resisted could mean risking one's life.[173]

6

HITLER'S CULTURAL
REVOLUTION

DISCORDANT NOTES

I

On 7 March 1933, two days after the Reichstag election, a gang of sixty brownshirts broke into a rehearsal of Verdi's opera *Rigoletto* at the Dresden State Opera led by the famous conductor Fritz Busch. They shouted and heckled the conductor and disrupted the proceedings until he was forced to stop. This was not the first time that such an incident had occurred. On a previous occasion, a large contingent of storm-troopers had bought up almost all the tickets for one of his concerts, and, as he had mounted the rostrum, they had greeted him with raucous chants of 'Down with Busch!' until he had been forced to withdraw. But it was the incident at the rehearsal that prompted the newly Nazified government of Saxony to dismiss him from his post. His musical repu-tation was considerable, but as far as the administrators in Dresden were concerned, he was a nuisance. Busch was not Jewish, nor was he particularly identified with modernism, atonality or any of the other things the Nazis abhorred in the music of the early twentieth century. Nor was he a Social Democrat, indeed, politically he was on the right. Busch had got into bad odour with the Nazis in Saxony because he had strenuously objected to their plans to cut the state cultural budget as part of economy measures during the Depression. On coming to power in Dresden, they accused him of employing too many Jewish singers, of spending too much time away from Dresden, and of demanding too much pay.[1] Busch left for Argentina and never returned, becoming an Argentinian citizen in 1936.[2]

The disruption of Busch's concert and rehearsal gave regional state commissioners the pretext for banning concerts and operas on the grounds that they might give rise to public disorder. The disorder was fomented, of course, by the Nazis themselves, a neat illustration of the dialectic that drove the seizure of power onward from both above and below. Music was a particularly important target for co-ordination. For centuries the Central European classical and Romantic composers had delivered to the world the backbone of the musical repertory. Great orchestras like the Berlin Philharmonic possessed a worldwide reputation. The Wagner music dramas played at Bayreuth held a unique place in world musical culture. Every city precinct, every small town or larger village had its musical clubs, its choirs, its tradition of amateur music-making that was central not just to middle-class life but also to the cultural practice of the working classes as well. The Nazis had not been the only party on the right to feel that this great tradition was being undermined by the musical modernism of the Weimar Republic, which they attributed in their usual crude way to 'Jewish subversion'. Now was their chance to put the situation to rights.

On 16 March, when the principal conductor of the Leipzig Gewandhaus orchestra, Bruno Walter, who was Jewish but, like Busch, in no way a proponent of modernist music, arrived for a rehearsal, he found the doors locked by the Reich Commissioner for Saxony, on the grounds that the safety of the musicians could not be guaranteed. Due to give a concert four days later in Berlin, Walter applied for police protection, but this was turned down on the orders of Goebbels, who made it clear that the concert could only go ahead under the baton of a non-Jewish conductor. After the Berlin Philharmonic's principal conductor, Wilhelm Furtwängler, had refused to conduct in his stead, the composer Richard Strauss agreed to take the rostrum, amidst a blare of triumphant celebrations in the Nazi press. Shortly afterwards, Walter resigned his post in Leipzig and emigrated to Austria. Attempts in the Nazi press to demonstrate that he had Communist sympathies were unlikely to have disguised from many the true reasons for the campaign against him, which were exclusively racial.[3]

Among Germany's leading conductors, Otto Klemperer was the one who most nearly fitted the Nazi caricature of a Jewish musician. A cousin of the literature professor and diarist Victor Klemperer, he was not only Jewish but had also, as director of the avant-garde Kroll Opera House from 1927 to 1930 (in whose building, ironically, the Reichstag convened after the fire of 27–28 February 1933), pioneered radical productions, and made a name for himself as a champion of modernist composers such as Stravinsky. On 12 February Klemperer conducted a controversial production of Wagner's opera *Tannhäuser* in Berlin, which was condemned by the Nazi music press as a 'bastardization of Wagner' and an affront to the composer's memory. By the beginning of March the furore had forced the withdrawal of the production; soon, Klemperer's concerts were being cancelled on the usual specious grounds that public safety could not be guaranteed if he appeared on the rostrum. Klemperer attempted to save himself by insisting that 'he was in complete agreement with the course of events in Germany', but he soon realized the inevitable. On 4 April he, too, left the country.[4] Shortly afterwards, the Reich Law for the Restoration of a Professional Civil Service led to the dismissal not only of Jewish conductors such as Jascha Horenstein in Düsseldorf, but also of singers, and opera and orchestra administrators. Jewish professors in state music academies (most notably, the composers Arnold Schoenberg and Franz Schreker, both teachers at the Prussian Academy of Arts in Berlin) were also dismissed. Music critics and musicologists were sacked from their official posts and ousted from the German press; the best known was Alfred Einstein, probably the most distinguished music critic of his time.[5]

Jewish musicians now had their contracts cancelled all over the land. On 6 April 1933, for example, the Hamburg Philharmonic Society announced: 'The choice of soloists, which had to be made in December last year, will of course be amended so that no Jewish artistes are participating. Frau Sabine Kalter and Herr Rudolf Serkin will be replaced by artistes who are racially German.'[6] In June 1933 Jewish concert agents were banned from working. Musical associations of all kinds, right down to male voice choirs in working-class mining villages and music appreciation societies in the quiet suburbs of the great cities, were taken over by the Nazis and purged of their Jewish members. Such measures were accompanied by a barrage of propaganda in the musical press, attacking composers such as Mahler and Mendelssohn for being supposedly 'un-German' and boasting of the restoration of a true German musical culture. More immediately, the regime focused on expunging obviously avant-garde composers and their works from the repertoire. Demonstrations forced the withdrawal of Kurt Weill's *The Silver Sea* in

Hamburg on 22 February, and his music, long associated with the plays of the Communist writer Bertolt Brecht, was shortly thereafter banned altogether. That Weill was Jewish only made him a more obvious target as far as the Nazis were concerned. He, too, emigrated, along with other left-wing composers such as Hanns Eisler, another of Brecht's musical collaborators and also a pupil of the atonal composer Arnold Schoenberg.[7]

A Jewish musician who managed to stay on was an extreme rarity. One such was the conductor Leo Blech, a popular and pivotal figure in the Berlin State Opera, whose performance of Wagner's *Twilight of the Gods* received a standing ovation in June 1933; Heinz Tietjen, the Intendant of the Opera, managed to persuade Göring to keep him on until he left for Sweden in 1938. Other prominent Jewish musicians like the violinist Fritz Kreisler and the pianist Artur Schnabel, who had both lived in Germany for many years, found it relatively easy to leave because they were not German citizens and in any case were famous enough to make a living anywhere in the world. The opera diva Lotte Lehmann, a sharp critic of Göring's interference in the business of the Berlin State Opera, was by contrast a non-Jewish German citizen, but she was married to a Jew, and she left for New York in protest against the regime's policies. Others, humble orchestra players, teachers, administrators and the like, had no such option available to them.[8]

II

The policy of co-ordination that was affecting musical life as it was almost every other area of German society and culture was not just designed to eliminate alternatives to Nazism and impose surveillance and control on every aspect of German society. At the same time as the stormtroopers were pulverizing Nazism's opponents, Hitler and Goebbels were putting in place the means by which passive supporters would be won over to become active participants in the 'National Socialist revolution', and waverers and the sceptical would be brought round to a more co-operative frame of mind. The new government, declared Goebbels at a press conference on 15 March 1933, will not be satisfied for long with the knowledge that it has 52 per cent behind it while terrorising the other 48 per cent but will, by contrast, see its next task as winning over that other 48 per cent for itself . . . It is not enough to reconcile people more or less to our regime, to move them towards a position of neutrality towards us, we want rather to work on people until they have become addicted to us . . .[9]

Goebbels's statement was as interesting for its admission that nearly half the population was being terrorized as it was for its declared ambition of winning the hearts and minds of those people who had not voted for the coalition in the election of 5 March. There would be a 'spiritual mobilization' comparable to the massive military mobilization of 1914. And in order to bring this mobilization about, Hitler's government put into effect its most original institutional creation, the Reich Ministry for Popular Enlightenment and Propaganda, established by a special decree on 13 March. The post of Minister, with a seat in the cabinet, was given to Joseph Goebbels. His unscrupulous and inventive propaganda campaigns in Berlin, where he was Regional Leader of the Nazi Party, had won the admiration of Hitler, above all during the election campaign that had culminated in the coalition's victory on 5 March.[10]

The new Ministry was set up in the teeth of opposition from cabinet conservatives like Alfred Hugenberg, who distrusted Goebbels's 'social- ist' radicalism.[11] The new Minister's propaganda campaigns over the previous few years had lacked nothing in invective against 'reactionaries' and Nationalists such as himself. Moreover, 'propaganda', as Goebbels himself admitted, was a 'much-maligned' word that 'always has a bitter after-taste'. It was often employed as a term of abuse. Using the word in the title of the new Ministry was, therefore, a bold step. Goebbels justified it by defining propaganda as the art, not of lying or distorting, but of listening to 'the soul of the people' and 'speaking to a person a language that this person understands'.[12] It was not necessarily clear, however, what areas of competence would be covered by 'popular enlightenment and propaganda'. Originally, when the creation of such a ministry had first been discussed early in 1932, Hitler had intended it to cover edu- cation and culture, but by the time it came into being, education had been reserved, more traditionally, for a separate ministry, held by Bern- hard Rust since 30 January 1933.[13] Nevertheless, the primary purpose of

Goebbels's new Ministry, as Hitler declared on 23 March 1933, was to centralize control of all aspects of cultural and intellectual life. 'The government', he declared, 'will embark upon a systematic campaign to restore the nation's moral and material health. The whole educational system, theatre, film, literature, the press, and broadcasting – all these will be used as a means to this end. They will be harnessed to help preserve the eternal values which are part of the integral nature of our people.'[14]

What those values were, of course, would be defined by the regime. The Nazis acted on the premise that they, and they alone, through Hitler, had an inner knowledge and understanding of the German soul. The millions of Germans who had refused to support the Nazi Party – a majority, as we have seen, even in the semi-democratic elections of 5 March 1933 – had been seduced, they believed, by 'Jewish' Bolshevism and Marxism, the 'Jewish'-dominated press and media, the 'Jewish' art and entertainment of Weimar culture, and other similar, un-German forces which had alienated them from their inner German soul. The Ministry's task was thus to return the German people to its true nature. The people, declared Goebbels, had to start 'to think as one, to react as one, and to place itself in the service of the government with all its heart'.[15] The end justified the means, a principle that Goebbels was far from being the only Nazi leader to espouse:

We are not setting up here a Propaganda Ministry that somehow stands on its own and represents an end in itself, but this Propaganda Ministry is a means to an end. If now the end is attained by this means, then the means is good . . . The new Ministry has no other aim than placing the nation unanimously behind the idea of the national revolution. If the aim is achieved, then one may condemn my methods out of hand; that would be a matter of complete indifference since by its labours the Ministry would by then have achieved its aims.[16]

These methods, Goebbels went on, had to be the most modern ones available. 'Technology must not be allowed to run ahead of the Reich: the Reich must keep up with technology. Only the latest thing is good enough.'[17]

In order to fulfil these ambitions, Goebbels staffed his Ministry with young, highly educated Nazis who did not have to contend with the entrenched civil service conservatism that held sway in so many top-level organs of the state. The great majority were pre-1933 members of the Party; almost 100 of the Ministry's 350 officials wore the Party's golden

badge of honour. Their average age was scarcely over 30. Many of them
held the same, or similar positions in the Party Propaganda office, also
run by Goebbels. By 22 March they were ensconced in a grandiose
headquarters, the Leopold Palace on the Wilhelmsplatz. Built in 1737, it
had been refurbished by the famous Prussian state architect Karl Friedrich
Schinkel early in the nineteenth century. The elaborate stucco and plasterwork decorations were not modern enough for Goebbels's taste, however,
and he requested that they be removed. Getting permission to do this
proved too time-consuming for the new Minister, so he took a short cut,
as he wrote in his diary on 13 March 1933:

Since everyone is placing obstacles in the way of the reconstruction and the
furnishing even of my own room, without more ado I take some construction
workers from the SA and during the night I get them to smash down the
plasterwork and wooden facia work, and files that have been vegetating about
on the shelves since the year dot are thrown down the stairs with a thunderous
noise. Only murky dustclouds are left as witnesses to vanished bureaucratic
pomp.

Soon after moving in, the Ministry established separate departments for
propaganda, radio, the press, film, theatre, and 'popular enlightenment'
and secured a blanket authority from Hitler, issued on 30 June 1933,
declaring it responsible not only for all these spheres of activity but also
for the general public relations representation of the regime as a whole,
including to the foreign press. This gave Goebbels the power to override
the objections of other departments of state which considered that the
Propaganda Ministry was infringing on their own sphere of interest. This
was a power that Goebbels was to need on more than one occasion in
the coming months and years as he undertook what he grandly called
the 'spiritual mobilization of the nation'.[18]

The most immediate aim of Nazi cultural politics was to dispose of the
'cultural Bolshevism' which various organs and representatives of the
Nazi Party had declared was infesting the artistic, musical and literary
world of the Weimar Republic. The way the Nazi authorities did this
provided yet more examples, if any were needed, of the sheer breadth
and depth of the process of co-ordination taking place in Germany as the
fundamental basis of social, intellectual and cultural conformity on which
the Third Reich was going to be created. As in other spheres of life, the

process of co-ordination in the cultural sphere involved a general purging of Jews from cultural institutions, and a rapidly escalating offensive against Communists, Social Democrats, leftists, liberals, and anyone of an independent cast of mind. The removal of Jews from cultural life was a particular priority, since the Nazis asserted that they had been responsible for undermining German cultural values through such modernist inventions as atonal music and abstract painting. In practice, of course, these equations did not even remotely correspond to the truth. Modernist German culture was not sustained by the Jews, many of whom in practice were as culturally conservative as other middle-class Germans. But in the brutal power-politics of the first half of 1933, this hardly mattered. For the new Nazi government, backed by the Nationalists, 'cultural Bolshevism' was one of the most dangerous creations of Weimar Germany, and one of the most prominent. As Hitler had written in *My Struggle*, 'artistic Bolshevism is the only possible cultural form and spiritual expression of Bolshevism as a whole'. Chief amongst these cultural expressions were Cubism and Dadaism, which Hitler equated among other things with abstraction. The sooner these horrors were replaced by a truly German culture, the better. The Nazi revolution was not just about eliminating opposition, therefore; it was also about transforming German culture.[19]

III

Purges and departures such as those that could be observed in the German musical scene in the early weeks of the Nazi seizure of power did not go without comment. On 1 April 1933 a group of musicians based in the United States cabled Hitler personally in protest. The Nazi regime responded in characteristic style. German state radio promptly banned the broadcasting of compositions, concerts and recordings involving the signatories, who included the conductors Serge Koussevitsky, Fritz Reiner and Arturo Toscanini.[20] The most notable domestic critic of the purge was Wilhelm Furtwängler. In many respects, Furtwängler was a conservative. He thought, for instance, that Jews should not be given responsibilities in the cultural sphere, that most Jewish musicians lacked a genuine inner affinity with German music, and that Jewish journalists should be removed from their posts. No non-German, he once wrote, had ever written a genuine symphony. He distrusted democracy and what he called 'Jewish-Bolshevist success' under the Weimar Republic.[21] He had no principled objections to the coming to power of the Nazis, therefore, nor did he feel in any way threatened by it. His international fame was enormous. He had been conductor of the Vienna Philharmonic in the 1920s and had enjoyed two successful spells as guest conductor of the New York Philharmonic. His personal charisma was so overwhelming that he is recorded as having fathered no fewer than thirteen illegitimate children in the course of his career. Arrogant and self-confident, he was yet another conservative whose estimation of the Nazis turned out to be woefully inadequate.[22]

Unlike other orchestras, Furtwängler's Berlin Philharmonic was not a state-owned corporation and so was not subject to the law of 7 April that forced the dismissal of Jewish state employees. On 11 April 1933 Furtwängler published an open letter to Goebbels in a liberal daily newspaper, declaring that he was not prepared to terminate the contracts of the Jewish players in his orchestra. The terms in which he wrote indicated not only his self-confidence and his courage but also the extent to which his views overlapped with those of the Nazis to whose policies he was now objecting:

If the struggle against Jewry is directed in the main against those artists who are rootless and destructive themselves, and seek to achieve an effect by kitsch, dry virtuosity and the like, then that's just fine. The struggle against them and the spirit they embody, a spirit that incidentally also has its Germanic representatives, cannot be conducted emphatically or consistently enough. But if this struggle is directed against true artists, that is not in the interest of cultural life . . . It must therefore be said clearly that men like Walter, Klemperer, Reinhardt etc. must be able to say their piece in Germany in future as well.

The dismissal of so many good Jewish musicians, he told Goebbels, was incompatible 'with the restoration of our national dignity that all now welcome with such gratitude and joy'.[23] With Olympian disdain, Furt-wängler went on to ignore in practice a vociferous campaign in the Nazi press for the dismissal of Jewish musicians from his own orchestra, the Berlin Philharmonic, including Szymon Goldberg, its leader, and Joseph Schuster, its principal cellist.[24]

Goebbels was too subtle a politician to react to Furtwängler's public protest with open anger. His lengthy public reply to the great conductor began by welcoming Furtwängler's positive stance towards the 'restoration of national dignity' by the Hitler government. But he warned him that German music should form part of this process, and that art for art's sake was not on the agenda any more. Certainly, Goebbels admitted, art and music had to be of the highest quality, but they also had to be 'aware of their responsibility, accomplished, close to the people, and full of fighting spirit'. Twisting Furtwängler's statement to his own purposes, Goebbels agreed that there should be no more 'experiments' in music – something the conductor had not said at all – then went on to warn him:

It would also, however, be appropriate to protest against artistic experiments at a time when German artistic life is almost entirely determined by the mania for experiment of elements who are distant from the people and of alien race and thereby pollute the artistic reputation of Germany and compromise it before the whole world.

That 'Germanic' musicians had contributed to this deformation of art showed, in Goebbels's view, how far Jewish influence had penetrated. He welcomed Furtwängler as an ally in the struggle to remove it. Genuine artists like him would always have a voice in the Third Reich. As for the men whose silencing had so offended the conductor, the Reich Propaganda Minister brushed their dismissal aside as a triviality while at the same time disingenuously disclaiming responsibility for it:

To complain against the fact that here and there men like Walter, Klemperer, Reinhardt etc. have had to cancel concerts seems all the more inappropriate to me at the moment in the light of the fact that over the past 14 years, genuine German artists have been completely condemned to silence, and the events of the last weeks, which do not meet with our approval, only represent a natural reaction to this fact.[25]

Who these 'genuine German artists' were, he did not say, and indeed he could not, for his claim was a complete invention. Conscious of the damage that would be done to Germany's international musical reputation if he acted rashly, however, Goebbels brought the great conductor and his orchestra to heel not by open confrontation, but by more underhand means. The Depression had deprived the Berlin Philharmonic of most of its state and municipal subsidies. The Reich government made sure that no more were forthcoming until the orchestra was on the verge of bankruptcy. At this point, Furtwängler appealed directly to Hitler himself, who, scandalized that the country's greatest orchestra was in danger of having to wind up its affairs, ordered it to be taken over by the Reich. From 26 October 1933 the Berlin Philharmonic was no longer independent, therefore, and Goebbels and his Ministry were now in a good position to bring it to heel, which eventually they proceeded to do.[26]

IV

The creation of what the Nazis regarded as a truly German musical culture also involved the elimination of foreign cultural influences such as jazz, which they considered to be the offspring of a racially inferior culture, that of the African-Americans. The racist language that was second nature to Nazism was particularly offensive and aggressive in this context. Nazi musical writers condemned 'nigger-music' as sexually provocative, immoral, primitive, barbaric, un-German and thoroughly subversive. It confirmed the widespread Nazi view of American degeneracy, even if some writers diplomatically preferred to emphasize its origins in Africa. The swooning tones of the newly popular saxophone also came in for criticism, though, when saxophone sales began to slump as a consequence, German manufacturers of the instrument riposted by trying to claim that its inventor Adolphe Sax was German (in fact, he was Belgian) and by pointing out that the venerated German composer Richard Strauss had used it in some of his compositions. The prominence of Jewish composers such as Irving Berlin and George Gershwin in the jazz world added another layer of racial opprobrium as far as the Nazis were concerned.[27]

Many jazz, swing and dance-band musicians in Germany were of course foreign, and left the country in the hostile climate of 1933. Yet for all the violence of Nazi polemics, jazz proved almost impossibly difficult to define, and with a few deft rhythmic tweaks, and a suitably conformist demeanour on the part of the players, it proved quite possible for jazz and swing musicians to continue playing in the innumerable clubs, bars, dance-halls and hotels of Germany throughout the 1930s. Bouncers at swanky Berlin nightclubs like the Roxy, Uhu, Kakadu or Ciro turned away the invariably shabbily dressed spies sent by the Nazis, ensuring that their chic clientele could continue to swing to the latest jazz and pseudo-jazz music inside. If a spy should gain entry, the doorman simply rang a secret bell and the musicians rapidly changed the music on their stands before he reached the dance-floor.

The social scene of Weimar days thus carried on through 1933, with few changes except those already forced on it by the economic stringencies of the Depression. Even Jewish musicians were mostly able to continue playing in the clubs up to the autumn of 1933, and some managed to continue for a while thereafter. In Berlin's famous Femina bar, swing bands continued to play to over a thousand dancers through the night, while a system of 225 table telephones with instructions for use in German and English enabled singles to ring up potential partners seated elsewhere in the hall. The standard of the music may not have been very high, but stamping down on everyday – or everynight – pleasures would have been counter-productive, even if the Nazis had been able to do it.[28] Only where singers were overtly political, as in Berlin's famous cabaret venues, did the stormtroopers move in seriously, forcing a mass exodus of Jewish performers and silencing or removing singers and comedians of Communist, Social Democratic, liberal or generally leftist persuasion. Others cleaned up their acts by removing the politics. The Nazis for their part, realizing the popularity of cabaret and the need not to deprive people of all their pleasures, tried to encourage 'positive cabaret', where the jokes were all at the expense of their enemies. There was a story that the celebrated cabarettist Claire Waldoff was daring enough to sing a song satirizing Göring, based on her signature tune, 'Hermann': 'Medals to the left, medals to the right/And his stomach gets fatter and fatter/He is master in Prussia – /Hermann's his name!' Soon, whenever she sang the original version of 'Hermann', her listeners grinned appreciatively as they thought of the satirical lines. But Waldoff did not compose the verses: the joke was wishful thinking and so untrue. It could not disguise the fact that the Nazis had taken the guts out of cabaret by the middle of 1933.[29] For some it was too much. Paul Nikolaus, political conferencier of Berlin's famous Kadeko club – 'The Cabaret of the Comedians' – fled to Lucerne, where he killed himself on 30 March 1933. 'For once, no joke,' he wrote: 'I am taking my own life. Why? I could not return to Germany without taking it there. I cannot work there now, I do not want to work there now, and yet unfortunately I have fallen in love with my Fatherland. I cannot live in these times.'[30]

THE PURGE OF THE ARTS

I

The chill winds of antisemitism, anti-liberalism and anti-Marxism, combined with a degree of stuffy moral disapproval of 'decadence', also howled through other areas of German culture in the first six months of 1933. The film industry proved relatively easy to control because, unlike the cabaret or club scene, it consisted of a small number of large businesses, inevitably perhaps in view of the substantial cost of making and distributing a movie. As in other sectors, those who saw which way the wind was blowing soon began to bend to its pressure without being told explicitly what to do. As early as March 1933 the giant UFA studios, owned by Alfred Hugenberg, still a member of Hitler's cabinet at this time, began a comprehensive policy of dismissing Jewish staff and cutting contacts with Jewish actors. The Nazis soon co-ordinated the German Cinema Owners' Association. Unionized film workers were Nazified, and on 14 July Goebbels established the Reich Film Chamber to oversee the entire movie industry. Through these institutions leading Nazis, and particularly Goebbels, an enthusiastic connoisseur of the movies himself, were able to regulate the employment of actors, directors, cameramen and backroom staff. Jews were gradually removed from every branch of the industry despite the fact that it was not covered by the Law of 7 April. Actors and directors whose politics were unacceptable to the regime were frozen out.[31]

Under the new conditions of censorship and control, a minority of people in the motion picture industry preferred to seek their fortune in the freer atmosphere of Hollywood. Those who found it included the director Fritz Lang, who had scored a series of successes with films such as M: *Murderer Amongst Us, Metropolis* and *The Nibelungen*, an epic that remained favourite viewing for Hitler. Lang's film *The Testament of Dr Mabuse*, an indirect satire on the Nazis, was banned shortly before its scheduled premiere in the spring of 1933. He was followed into exile by Billy Wilder, whose popular romantic films had so far betrayed few hints of the boldness he was to show in his Hollywood films such as *Double Indemnity* and *The Lost Weekend*. Both men created some of Hollywood's most successful movies in the following decades. Other movie directors migrated to Paris, including the Czech-born G. W. Pabst, director of the classic Weimar film *Pandora's Box* and a cinema version of Bertolt Brecht and Kurt Weill's *Threepenny Opera*, and Max Ophüls, born in 1902 in Germany as Max Oppenheimer. Some German directors and film stars, however, had been lured by the pulling power of Hollywood well before the Nazis came to power. The departure of Marlene Dietrich in 1930, for instance, had more to do with money than with politics. One of the few who left as a direct result of the coming of the Third Reich was the Hungarian-born Peter Lorre, who had played the shifty, compulsive child-murderer in Fritz Lang's M; Nazi propaganda later attempted to suggest that the murderer was Jewish, an insinuation entirely absent from Lang's film.[32] But while these emigrés attracted deserved attention, the great majority of the people employed in Germany's thriving film industry stayed. Of the 75 film stars listed in the magazine *Film Week* in 1932 as the most popular in Germany (on the basis of fan-mail received), only 13 emigrated, though these included three of the top five – Lilian Harvey and Kaethe von Nagy, both of whom left in 1939, and Gitta Alpar, who left in 1933. Lower down the list, Brigitte Helm left in 1936, and Conrad Veidt in 1934. Apart from Alpar, only one other star, Elisabeth Bergner, who was Jewish, left in 1933; 35 out of the 75 were still working in German films in 1944–5.[33]

Cinema had become increasingly popular in the course of the late 1920s and early 1930s, above all with the advent of the talkies. But in an age before television, the most popular, and fastest-growing modern means of mass communication was the radio. Unlike the film industry, the radio network was publicly owned, with a 51 per cent stake belonging to the nationwide Reich Radio Company and the other 49 per cent to nine regional stations. Control was exercised by two Reich radio commissioners, one in the Ministry of Posts and Communications and the other in the Interior Ministry, together with a series of regional commissioners. Goebbels was very conscious of the power of radio. During the election campaign of February–March 1933, he had succeeded in blocking all attempts by parties other than the Nazis and the Nationalists to get party-political broadcasts transmitted. Soon, he had secured the replacement of the two existing Reich radio commissioners by his own appointments, and obtained a decree from Hitler on 30 June 1933 vesting control of all broadcasting in the hands of the Propaganda Ministry.

Goebbels immediately enforced a massive purge of broadcasting institutions, with 270 sackings at all levels in the first six months of 1933. This represented 13 per cent of all employees. Jews, liberals, Social Democrats and others not wanted by the new regime were all dismissed, a process made easier by the fact that many of them were on short-term contracts. Radio managers and reporters identified with the previous liberal broadcasting regime, including the founder of German radio, Hans Bredow, were arrested on corruption charges, taken to Oranienburg concentration camp, and condemned in a massive show trial held, after months of preparation, in 1934–5. The majority, however, were willing to carry on under the new regime. Continuity was ensured by the presence of men like Hans Fritsche, a former director of Hugenberg's radio news department in the 1920s and head of the German Wireless Service, who was in charge of news broadcasts under the new regime. Like many others, Fritsche took steps to secure his position by joining the Party, in his case on 1 May 1933. By this time most radio stations had been effectively co-ordinated, and were broadcasting increasing quantities of Nazi propaganda. On 30 March one Social Democratic broadcaster, Jochen Klepper, whose wife was Jewish, was already complaining that 'what is left of the station is almost like a Nazi barracks: uniforms, uniforms of the Party formations'. Just over two months later he too was dismissed.[34]

II

Radio, Goebbels declared in a speech of 25 March 1933, was 'the most modern and the most important instrument of mass influence that exists anywhere'. In the long term, he said, radio would even replace news-papers. But in the meantime, newspapers remained of central importance for the dissemination of news and opinion. They presented an obstacle to the Nazi policy of co-ordination and control more formidable by far than that posed by the film and radio industries. Germany had more daily newspapers than Britain, France and Italy combined, and many more magazines and periodicals of every conceivable type. There were indepen-dent papers and periodicals at national, regional and local level, rep-resenting the whole range of political views from far left to far right. The Nazi Party's attempt to build a successful press empire of its own had not met with much success. Political papers were in decline in the late Weimar Republic and the printed word seemed to take second place to the spoken in winning adherents to the Nazi cause.[35]

In this situation, Goebbels had no option but to move gradually. It was easy enough to close down the official Communist and Social Democratic press, as repeated bannings in the early months of 1933 were followed by total closure once the parties had been swept from the scene. But the rest had to be tackled on a variety of fronts. Direct force and police measures were one way of bringing the press to heel. Conservative dailies such as the *Munich Latest News* (*Münchner Neueste Nachrichten*) were as liable to periodic bannings as centrist and liberal publications. The Catholic *Franconian Press* (*Fränkische Presse*), an organ of the Bavarian People's Party, was forced to carry a front-page declaration on 27 March 1933 apologizing for having printed lies about Hitler and the Nazis for years. Such pressure easily convinced the major press organizations that they would have to adjust to the new climate. On 30 April 1933 the Reich Association of the German Press, the journalists' union, co-ordinated itself, as did so many other similar bodies. It elected Goebbels's colleague Otto Dietrich as its chairman and promised that future member-ship would be compulsory for all journalists and at the same time only open to the racially and politically reliable.[36] On 28 June 1933 the German Newspaper Publishers' Association followed suit by appointing the Nazi Party publisher Max Amann as its chairman and voting Nazis onto its council instead of members who had now become politically undesirable.[37] By this time the press had already been cowed into submission. Non-Nazi journalists could only make their views known by subtle hints and allusions; readers could only glean their meaning by reading between the lines. Goebbels turned the regular open government press conferences that had been held under the Weimar Republic into secret meetings where the Propaganda Ministry passed on detailed instructions to selected journalists on items in the news, sometimes actually supplying articles to be printed verbatim or used as the basis for reports. 'You are to know not only what is happening,' Goebbels told the newspapermen attending his first official press conference on 15 March 1933, 'but also the government's view of it and how you can convey that to the people most effectively.'[38] That they were not to convey any other view did not need to be said.

In the meantime, the Nazis were busily arresting Communist and pacifist journalists as fast as they could. The arrests had begun in the early hours of 28 February 1933. One of the first to be taken into custody was Carl von Ossietzky, editor of *The World Stage*, a high-profile intellectual organ of generally left-wing, pacifist journalism. Ossietzky had earned notoriety not only as a biting critic of the Nazis before 1933 but also for publishing an exposé of a secret and illegal programme of rearmament in the aircraft industry, an act for which he had been put in prison at the end of a sensational trial in May 1932. A massive campaign by writers outside Germany failed to secure his release after his rearrest in 1933. Imprisoned in a makeshift penal camp run by the brownshirts at Sonnenburg, the frail Ossietzky was forced to undertake hard manual labour, including digging what the guards told him was his own grave. Born in Hamburg in 1889, he was not Jewish or Polish or Russian, despite his name, but German in the full sense of the term as employed by the Nazis. Disregarding these facts, the stormtroopers accompanied their regular beatings and kickings of their prisoner with cries of 'Jewish pig' and 'Polish pig'. Never physically strong, Ossietzky only narrowly survived a heart attack on 12 April 1933. Released prisoners who talked discreetly to his friends described him as a broken man after this point.[39]

Ossietzky fared only marginally better than another radical writer of the 1920s, the anarchist poet and playwright Erich Mühsam, whose involvement in Munich's 'regime of the Coffee House Anarchists' in 1919 had already earned him a period in gaol under the Weimar Republic. Arrested after the Reichstag fire, Mühsam was a particular object of hatred for the brownshirts because he was not only a radical writer but also a revolutionary and a Jew. Subjected to endless humiliations and brutalities, he was beaten to a pulp by SS guards in the Oranienburg concentration camp when he refused to sing the Horst Wessel Song, and was soon afterwards found hanged in the camp latrine.[40] His former colleague in the short-lived revolutionary government in Munich, the anarchist and pacifist Ernst Toller (another Jewish writer) had also been in prison for his part in the Revolution. A series of realistic plays attacking the injustices and inequities of German society in the 1920s kept him in the public eye, including a satire on Hitler performed under the ironic title of *Wotan Unbound*. At the end of February 1933 Toller happened to be in Switzerland, and the mass arrests that followed the Reichstag fire persuaded him not to return to Germany. He undertook lengthy lecture tours denouncing the Nazi regime, but the hardships of exile made it impossible for him to continue his life as a writer, and he committed suicide in New York in 1939, driven to despair by the imminent prospect of a new world war.[41]

There were some who were better able to adapt to the literary world outside Germany, most notably the Communist poet and playwright Bertolt Brecht, who left Germany for Switzerland, then Denmark, in 1933, before finding work eventually in Hollywood. One of the most successful exiles was the novelist Erich Maria Remarque, author of *All Quiet on the Western Front*, who despite his name and the heavy hints of the Nazis was not French but German (they also alleged he was Jewish, and had reversed the order of the letters in his original name, Remark, which they claimed, without any evidence to back up their assertion, had been Kramer). He continued to write in exile, and made a good enough living from the sale of film rights to a number of his works to acquire the image of a wealthy playboy in Hollywood and elsewhere in the later 1930s, enjoying much-publicized liaisons with a string of Hollywood actresses.[42] More famous still was the novelist Thomas Mann, whose novels *Buddenbrooks* and *The Magic Mountain*, along with novellas such as *Death in Venice*, had established him as one of the world's literary giants and won him the Nobel Prize for Literature in 1929. Mann had become one of the principal literary supporters of Weimar democracy, and toured Germany and the world ceaselessly lecturing on the need to sustain it. He was under no direct threat of violence or imprisonment from the Nazis, but from February 1933 onwards he remained in Switzerland, despite overtures from the regime for his return. 'I cannot imagine life in Germany as it is today,' he wrote in June 1933, and a few months later, after he had been ousted amid a flurry of hostile rhetoric from the Prussian Academy of Arts along with other democratic authors such as the poet and novelist Ricarda Huch, he made his commitment even firmer, telling a friend: 'As far as I personally am concerned, the accusation that I left Germany does not apply. I was expelled. Abused, pilloried and pillaged by the foreign conquerors of *my* country, for I am an older and better German than they are.'[43]

Thomas Mann's brother Heinrich, author of biting satires on the mores of the German bourgeoisie such as *Man of Straw* and *The Blue Angel*, was dealt with more harshly by the regime, which he had offended by his open criticism of the Nazis in numerous speeches and essays. In 1933 he was deprived of his post as President of the literary section of the Prussian Academy of Arts and went to live in France. There he was joined in August 1933 by the novelist Alfred Döblin, who had been a leading exponent of literary modernism in novels such as *Berlin Alexanderplatz*, set in the low-life and criminal world of the German capital in the postwar years. A Jew and a former Social Democrat, he was effectively proscribed by the Nazis. The same fate overcame another well-known novelist, Lion Feuchtwanger, also Jewish, whose novels *Success* and *The Oppenheims*, published in 1930 and 1933 respectively, were sharply critical of conservative and antisemitic currents in German society and politics; Feuchtwanger was visiting California when he learned that his works had been suppressed, and he did not return to Germany. The novelist Arnold Zweig fled to Czechoslovakia in 1933 and thence to Palestine; he, too, had been proscribed by the regime as a Jew, and was unable to get his works published in Germany any longer.[44]

Under the circumstances of rapidly growing Nazi censorship and control, few writers were able to continue producing work of any quality in Germany after 1933. Even conservative writers distanced themselves from the regime in one way or another. The poet Stefan George, who had gathered round himself a circle of acolytes devoted to the revival of a 'secret Germany' that would sweep aside the materialism of Weimar, offered his 'spiritual collaboration' to the 'new national movement' in 1933, but refused to join any Nazified literary or cultural organizations; several of his disciples were Jews. George died in December 1933, but another prominent radical-conservative writer, Ernst Jünger, who had been close to the Nazis in the 1920s, lived on, indeed, until the very end of the twentieth century, when he was over 100. Jünger, much admired by Hitler for his glorification of the soldier's life in *Storm of Steel*, his novel of the First World War, found that the terrorism of the Third Reich was not at all to his liking, and retreated into what many subsequently called 'inner emigration'. Like others who took this course, he wrote novels without a clear contemporary setting – a good number of writers favoured the Middle Ages – and even if these sometimes cautiously expressed some criticism of terror or dictatorship in a general sense, they were still published, distributed and reviewed so long as they did not attack the regime in an explicit way.[45]

Prominent figures, like the previously unpolitical Expressionist writer Gottfried Benn, who became enthusiastic champions of the new regime, were relatively rare. By the end of 1933 there was scarcely a writer of any talent or reputation left in Germany. The playwright Gerhart Hauptmann, winner of the Nobel Prize for Literature in 1912, was one exception, perhaps. But he was over 70 when Hitler became Chancellor, and well past the peak of his creative powers, when he had been famous for his moving dramas of poverty and exploitation. He continued to write, and tried to show outward conformity by giving the Nazi salute and joining in the singing of the Horst Wessel Song. But he did not become a National Socialist, and his naturalistic plays were frequently attacked by the Nazis for their supposedly negative attitudes. A Hungarian writer who met Hauptmann in Rapallo in 1938 was treated by him to a long catalogue of complaints about Hitler. Hauptmann said bitterly that Hitler had ruined Germany and would soon ruin the world. Why, then, had he not left the country, the Hungarian asked. 'Because I am a coward, do you understand?', Hauptmann shouted angrily, 'I'm a coward, do you understand? I'm a coward.'[46]

III

The loss of so many prominent writers of one kind and another was accompanied by a similar exodus among artists and painters. There was also a parallel here to the wave of persecution that swept the German musical world at the same time. In the art world, however, it was fuelled in addition by the strong personal antipathy shown towards modernism by Hitler, who considered himself an artist at heart. He had declared in *My Struggle* that modernist art was the product of Jewish subversives and 'the morbid excrescences of insane and degenerate men'. His views were shared by Alfred Rosenberg, who took a resolutely traditionalist view of the nature and function of painting and sculpture. While German music in the 1920s was no longer the dominant force it had been in the eighteenth and nineteenth centuries German painting, liberated by Expressionism, abstraction and other modernist movements, had undergone a remarkable renaissance in the first three decades of the twentieth century, outstripping even literature as the most prominent and internationally successful of all the arts. This was what the Nazis, with Alfred Rosenberg in the vanguard, now undertook to destroy, following the precept of Point 25 of the Nazi Party Programme of 1920, which stated: 'we demand the legal prosecution of all tendencies in art and literature of a kind likely to disintegrate our life as a nation.'[47]

Controversy had long raged over the work of painters such as George Grosz, Emil Nolde, Max Beckmann, Paul Klee, Ernst Ludwig Kirchner, Otto Dix and many others. Conservatives as well as Nazis detested their paintings. A major furore had been caused by Grosz's use of religious motifs for the purposes of political caricature, which had already led to Grosz undergoing two (unsuccessful) prosecutions for blasphemy before the Nazis came to power.[48] In July, Alfred Rosenberg excoriated the paintings of Emil Nolde as 'negroid, blasphemous and crude' and the Magdeburg war memorial of Ernst Barlach as an insult to the memory of the dead, whom the artist portrayed, according to Rosenberg, as 'half-idiotic'. Otto Dix's uncompromising representations of the horrors of the trenches in the First World War came in for equally sharp criticism from super-patriotic Nazis. Anything that was not obviously, slavishly representational was liable to arouse hostile comment. Art, according to the Nazis, had to spring, like everything else, from the soul of the people, so 'every healthy SA-man' was as capable of reaching a just conclusion on its value as any art critic was.[49] Not only German, but also foreign artists came in for strongly worded attacks. German galleries and museums had purchased many paintings by French Impressionists and post-Impressionists over the years, and nationalists considered that the money would have been better spent on furthering German art, particularly given the behaviour of the French in the Rhineland and the Ruhr during the Weimar Republic.[50]

Some figures, like Grosz, a member of the Communist Party, saw the writing on the wall even before 30 January 1933 and left the country.[51] The policies of the Nazi state government in Thuringia since 1930 had carried a clear warning of what was to come. It had removed works of painters like Klee, Nolde and Oskar Kokoschka from the state museum in Weimar and ordered the destruction of frescoes by Oskar Schlemmer in the stairwell of the Bauhaus in Dessau, shortly before the Bauhaus itself was closed. All this should have made it clear that Nazi activists were likely to mount a serious assault on artistic modernism. But room for manoeuvre seemed to be supplied by the fact that Expressionism was well regarded by some within the Party, including the Nazi Students' Union in Berlin, which actually mounted an exhibition of German art in July 1933 that included work by Barlach, Macke, Franz Marc, Nolde, Christian Rohlfs and Karl Schmidt-Rottluff. The local Party bosses forced the exhibition's closure after three days. Hitler especially detested Nolde's work, which Goebbels, whose taste was more catholic, rather admired; when the Nazi leader inspected the Propaganda Minister's new house in Berlin in the summer of 1933, he was horrified to see 'impossible' pictures by Nolde hanging on the walls and ordered them to be removed immediately. Nolde was expelled from the Prussian Academy of Arts, to his considerable chagrin, since he had been a member of the Nazi Party virtually since its foundation in 1920. In the course of 1933, local and regional Party bosses sacked twenty-seven art gallery and museum curators, replacing them with Party loyalists who immediately had modernist works removed from exhibition and even in some cases exhibited separately as 'Images of Cultural Bolshevism' in a 'Chamber of Art Horrors'.[52] Other directors and their staff bent with the prevailing wind, joined the Nazi Party, or went along with its policies.[53]

As in other spheres of cultural life, the purging of Jewish artists, whether modernist or traditional, rapidly gathered pace in the spring of 1933. The 'co-ordination' of the Prussian Academy of Arts began with the enforced resignation of the 86-year-old Max Liebermann, Germany's leading Impressionist painter and a past President of the Academy, from his membership as well as his position as Honorary President. Liebermann declared that he had always believed that art had nothing to do with politics, a view for which he was roundly condemned in the Nazi press. Asked how he felt at such an advanced age, the artist replied: 'One can't gobble as much up as one would like to puke.' When he died two years later, only three non-Jewish artists attended the funeral of a once nationally fêted painter. One of them, Käthe Kollwitz, celebrated for her drastic but not overtly political portrayals of poverty, had been forced to resign from the Prussian Academy; the sculptor Ernst Barlach resigned in protest against her expulsion and that of other artists, but stayed in Germany, even though his work was banned, like that of Schmidt-Rottluff.[54]

Paul Klee, a favourite target of Nazi cultural polemics for his supposedly 'negroid' art, was sacked from his professorship in Düsseldorf and left almost immediately for his home country of Switzerland. But other non-Jewish modernist artists decided to see how things would turn out, hoping that Hitler and Rosenberg's anti-modernism would be defeated by more sympathetic figures in the regime, such as Goebbels. Max Beckmann, previously based in Frankfurt, actually moved to Berlin in 1933 in the hope of being able to influence policy to his advantage. Like many of these other artists he was internationally famous, but unlike Grosz or Dix he never produced directly political work, and unlike Kandinsky or Klee he never even tended towards abstraction. Nevertheless, Beckmann's paintings were taken off the walls at the Berlin National Gallery and the artist was dismissed from his teaching post in Frankfurt on 15 April 1933. Sympathetic dealers managed to ensure that he could continue to make a living privately while he waited to see what his eventual fate would be. In contrast, Kirchner agreed to resign from the Academy, but pointed out that he was not Jewish and had never been politically active. Not only Oskar Schlemmer but even the Russian inventor of abstract painting, Wassily Kandinsky, who had been resident in Germany for decades, also thought the assault on modernist art would not last very long and decided to sit it out in Germany.[55]

The Prussian purge was accompanied by similar purges in other parts of Germany. Otto Dix was expelled from the Dresden Academy but continued to work in private even though his paintings were being removed from galleries and museums. The architect Mies van der Rohe refused to resign his membership of the Academy and was expelled. Mies van der Rohe had briefly tried to re-create the Bauhaus in a disused factory in Berlin before it was raided by the police and closed down in April 1933. He protested in vain that it was an entirely unpolitical institution. The founder of the Bauhaus, Walter Gropius, complained that as a war veteran and patriot he had aimed only to re-create a true, living German culture of architecture and design. It was not intended to be political, still less a statement of opposition to the Nazis. But art was anything but unpolitical in Germany at this time, for the radical modernist movements of the Weimar years, from Dadaism to the Bauhaus itself, had propagated the view that art was a means of transforming the world; the Nazis were only adapting this cultural-political imperative to their own purposes. Besides, pinning one's hopes on Joseph Goebbels was always a risky enterprise. The expectation of these artists that he would in time vindicate them would eventually be dashed in the most spectacular manner possible.[56]

IV

It has been estimated that around 2,000 people active in the arts emigrated from Germany after 1933.[57] They included many of the most brilliant, internationally famous artists and writers of their day. Their situation was not made any easier by Goebbels's subsequent decision to deprive them of their German citizenship. For many such exiles, statelessness could mean considerable hardship, difficulty in moving from one country to another, problems in finding work. Without papers, officialdom often refused to recognize their existence. The regime published a series of lists of those whose German citizenship, passports and papers were officially withdrawn, beginning on 23 August 1933 with writers such as Lion Feuchtwanger, Heinrich Mann, Ernst Toller and Kurt Tucholsky; three further lists were issued shortly afterwards, including most of the other prominent emigrés. Thomas Mann was not only deprived of his citizenship but also stripped of the honorary degree he had been awarded by Bonn University; his open letter of protest to the Rector quickly gained cult status among the emigrés.[58] The damage done to German cultural life was enormous. Scarcely a writer of international stature remained, hardly an artist or painter. A whole galaxy of leading conductors and musicians had been forced to leave, and some of Germany's most talented film directors had gone. Some flourished in exile, others did not; all knew that the difficulties culture and the arts faced under the Third Reich were going to be greater than anything most of them encountered abroad.

What was in store for those art and culture lovers who remained in Germany from 1933 was graphically demonstrated by a new play, dedicated to Hitler at his own request, and premiered in the State Theatre in Berlin on 20 April 1933, Hitler's birthday. Present in the audience were Hitler and other leading Nazis, including Goebbels. On the stage, the principal roles were played by Veit Harlan, soon to become one of the mainstays of German cinema in the Third Reich, by the popular actor Albert Bassermann, who had taken on his part only after a personal request from Goebbels that he felt unable to refuse, and by Emmy Sonnemann, a young actress in whom Hermann Göring had more than a passing interest, since he took her as his second wife not long afterwards. At the end of the patriotic drama, there was no applause; instead, the whole audience rose in unison and sang the Horst Wessel Song. Only then did the clapping begin, with the entire cast repeatedly giving the Nazi salute, with the exception of Bassermann, who crossed his arms over his chest and bowed in the traditional theatrical fashion; married to the Jewish actress Else Schiff, and scion of a famous family of liberal politicians, he was ill at ease with the new regime, and emigrated with his wife to the United States the following year. The play was *Schlageter*, and it dramatized the story of the nationalist uprising against the French in the Lower Rhine in the early 1920s. The writer was Hanns Johst, a war veteran who had made his name as an Expressionist dramatist. Johst had gravitated towards the Nazi Party in the late 1920s. His Expressionist method was given a new twist in the final scene, when the firing squad was directed to shoot at the bound figure of Schlageter from the back of the stage, the flashes of its guns passing through his heart right into the auditorium, inviting the audience to identify with his incorporation of the Nazi themes of blood and sacrifice and to become victims of French oppression with him.[59]

But the play quickly became famous for a reason that had nothing to do with the Nazi glitz and razzmatazz of its premiere. Thanks to all the publicity it gained, it was widely felt to symbolize the Nazi attitude to culture. People noted, either from going to see the play or from reading about it in the press, that one of the main characters, Friedrich Thiemann, played by Veit Harlan, rejected all intellectual and cultural ideas and concepts, arguing in a number of scenes with the student Schlageter that they should be replaced by blood, race and sacrifice for the good of the nation. In the course of one such argument, Thiemann declared: 'When I hear "culture", I release the safety catch of my Browning!'[60] To many cultured Germans, this seemed to sum up the Nazis' attitude to the arts, and the phrase quickly went the rounds, becoming wholly detached from its original context. It was soon attributed to various leading Nazis, but above all to Hermann Göring, and simplified in the process to the catchier, wholly apocryphal, but oft-repeated statement: 'When I hear the word culture, I reach for my gun!'[61]

'AGAINST THE UN-GERMAN SPIRIT'

I

Germany's best-known philosopher in the last years of the Weimar Republic, Martin Heidegger, had acquired his formidable reputation as a thinker above all through the publication in 1927 of his massive work on *Being and Time*, a treatise on fundamental philosophical questions such as the meaning of existence and the nature of humanity. Difficult to understand, and often expressed in rebarbatively abstract language, it applied the 'phenomenological' method of his teacher and predecessor in the Chair of Philosophy at Freiburg University, Edmund Husserl, to issues that had troubled philosophers since the Ancient Greeks. It was immediately greeted as a classic. In future years, Heidegger's thought was to have a significant influence on the French existentialists and their followers. More immediately, however, its pessimistic cast of mind reflected the philosopher's gradual emancipation from the Catholicism into which he had been born in 1889 and his turn to a mode of thought more influenced by Protestant ways of thinking. In particular, Heidegger, by the late Weimar years, had come to believe in the need for a renewal of German life and thought, the advent of a new age of spiritual unity and national redemption. By the early 1930s he was beginning to think he had found the answer to what he was looking for in National Socialism.[62]

Heidegger already established contacts behind the scenes with leading figures in Freiburg's National Socialist German Students' League in 1932. He was totally inexperienced in university administration, but, as far as the small group of Nazis amongst the professors were concerned, Heidegger was the man for the job of Rector when the Nazis came into power. He carried both the academic prestige and the political convictions to make him acceptable as a replacement for the liberal professor Wilhelm von Möllendorff, who was due to take office in April 1933. Keen to do the job, Heidegger began talking to the newly Nazified Ministry of Education in Baden, while Möllendorff was persuaded by personal vilification in the local and regional press to stand aside. The Nazi professors put Heidegger forward, and under pressure from within the university and without, he was duly elected as Rector on 21 April 1933 by an almost unanimous vote of the professoriate. Indeed, the only substantial body of professorial opinion that did not support him consisted of the 12 out of 93 holders of chairs in Freiburg who were Jewish. They were not allowed to cast their votes, however, since they had been suspended from their posts under the law of 7 April by the Nazi Reich Commissioner for Baden, Regional Leader Robert Wagner, as 'Non-Aryans'.[63]

On 27 May Heidegger delivered his inaugural address as Rector. Speaking to the assembled professors and brown-shirted Nazi dignitaries, he declared that ' "academic freedom" would no longer be the basis of life in the German university; for this freedom was not genuine, because it is only negative. It means a lack of concern, arbitrariness of views and inclinations, a lack of anchorage in doing things or not doing them.' It was time, he said, for the universities to find their anchor in the German nation and to play their part in the historic mission it was now fulfilling. German students were showing the way. Heidegger's speech was replete with the new language of the leadership principle. In the very first sentence he told his audience that he had taken over the 'spiritual leadership of this university' and he used the pseudo-feudal term 'retinue' to refer to the students and staff, much as leading Nazis were doing in the general sphere of employment and labour relations at this time. With concepts such as these being used by the university's new Rector, it was clear that academic freedom, however it was defined, was definitely a thing of the past.[64] To give symbolic emphasis to this, at the end of the ceremony the attending professors and guests sang the Horst Wessel Song, the text of which was helpfully printed on the back of the programme, together with the instruction that right hands should be raised in the fourth verse and the whole proceeding should end with a shout of 'Hail Victory!' ('*Sieg Heil!*').[65]

Heidegger soon set about bringing his university into line. Formally joining the Nazi Party amid a blaze of publicity on 1 May, the 'Day of National Labour', he now introduced the leadership principle into university administration, bypassing or silencing democratic and representative collegial bodies, and taking a hand in the drafting of a new Baden law that made the Rector into the unelected 'leader' of the university for an unlimited period of time. He soon informed the Baden Ministry of Education that 'we must now commit all our strength to conquering the world of educated men and scholars for the new national political spirit. It will be no easy passage of arms. Hail Victory!'[66] Heidegger denounced a colleague, the chemist Hermann Staudinger, to the state authorities, on false charges, and helped the political police with their enquiries about him, although in the end the police were unconvinced, and Staudinger, pleading the national importance of his work, remained in post. Heidegger was also happy to enforce the dismissal of Jews from the university staff, requesting an exception only for the internationally renowned phililogist Eduard Fraenkel, who was dismissed anyway, and the chemistry professor Georg von Hevesy, a man with powerful international connections and the recipient of large research funds from the Rockefeller Foundation, who was retained until his departure for Denmark the following year. Those Jews forced to sever their connection with the university included Heidegger's own assistant Werner Brock and his mentor Edmund Husserl, although there is no foundation in the oft-repeated story that he personally issued an order banning Husserl from the university library. A patriotic nationalist who had lost his son on the battlefield in the First World War, Husserl had considered himself a personal friend of Heidegger, and was deeply upset at his treatment. 'The future alone will judge which was the true Germany in 1933,' he wrote on 4 May, 'and who were the true Germans – those who subscribe to the more or less materialistic-mythical racial prejudices of the day, or those Germans pure in heart and mind, heirs to the great Germans of the past whose tradition they revere and perpetuate.'[67] When Husserl died in 1938, Heidegger did not attend his funeral.[68]

Joining in the widespread and rapidly growing Hitler cult, Heidegger told students: 'The Führer himself and he alone *is* the German reality, present and future, and its law. Study to know: from now on, all things demand decision, and all action responsibility. Hail Hitler!'[69] His ambition even extended to trying, in collaboration with other, like-minded university rectors, to take a leading role in the entire national university system. In a speech delivered on 30 June 1933, he complained that the 'national revolution' had not yet reached most universities, prompting Nazi students at Heidelberg to launch an impassioned campaign to oust the Rector, the conservative historian Willy Andreas, who was replaced by the Nazi candidate Wilhelm Groh a week later, on 8 July.[70] But Heidegger was completely inexperienced in politics, and he soon got bogged down in the usual university in-fighting about appointments, where he was outmanoeuvred by the bureaucrats in the Baden Ministry of Education and ridiculed by the brown-uniformed students, who considered him little better than a dreamer.

By the beginning of 1934, there were reports in Berlin that Heidegger had established himself as 'the philosopher of National Socialism'. But to other Nazi thinkers, Heidegger's philosophy appeared too abstract, too difficult, to be of much use. He had achieved widespread influence amongst his colleagues by advocating the voluntary reconnection of German university life to the life of the nation through a renewed concentration on fundamental values of knowledge and truth. This all sounded very grand. But though his intervention was welcomed by many Nazis, on closer inspection such ideas did not really seem to be in tune with the Party's. It is not surprising that his enemies were able to enlist the support of Alfred Rosenberg, whose own ambition it was to be the philosopher of Nazism himself. Denied a role at the national level, and increasingly frustrated with the minutiae of academic politics – which seemed to him to betray a sad absence of the new spirit he had hoped would permeate the universities – Heidegger resigned his post in April 1934, though he continued to be a supporter of the Third Reich and consistently refused to reconsider or apologize for his actions in 1933–4 right up to his death in 1976.[71]

II

The Nazi leadership had a relatively easy time with the universities, because, unlike in some other countries, these were all state-funded institutions and university staff were all civil servants. They were thus directly affected by the law of 7 April 1933, which provided for the dismissal of politically unreliable state employees. By the beginning of the academic year 1933–34, 313 full professors had been dismissed, part of a total of 1,145 out of 7,758 established university teachers, or 15 per cent of the whole. In Berlin and Frankfurt the proportion reached nearly a third. By 1934, some 1,600 out of 5,000 university teachers had been forced out of their jobs. Most of the university teachers who were dismissed lost their posts for political reasons; about a third were sacked because they were classified as Jewish.[72] A mass exodus of academics took place; 15.5 per cent of university physics teachers emigrated, and at Göttingen University so many physicists and mathematicians left or were expelled that teaching was seriously disrupted.[73] Those who went were generally better than those who stayed, too; a study of university biologists has shown that the 45 who left their posts and survived the war had an average of 130 citations per person on the standard index of citations of scientific papers between 1945 and 1954, while the comparable score for the survivors of the 292 who stayed was only 42.[74]

World-famous scientists were dismissed from their posts in Germany's universities and research institutes if they were Jewish or had Jewish wives or were known critics of the Nazis. They included twenty past or future Nobel laureates, among them Albert Einstein, Gustav Hertz, Erwin Schrödinger, Max Born, Fritz Haber and Hans Krebs. Einstein, whose theory of relativity had revolutionized modern physics, had been based in Berlin for twenty years. On a visit to America in January and February 1933, he denounced from afar the brutal violence of the Nazis after the Reichstag fire. In retaliation, the government seized his property, while the Education Minister told the Prussian Academy of Science to expel him. Einstein pre-empted this by resigning first, generating a public row in which the Academy accused him of having peddled atrocity stories abroad. He left for the United States again, and spent the rest of his life at Princeton.[75] 'You know, I think,' he wrote on 30 May to his colleague Max Born, who also went into exile, 'that I have never had a particularly favourable opinion of the Germans (morally and politically speaking). But I must confess that the degree of their brutality and cowardice came as something of a surprise to me.'[76]

The chemist Fritz Haber did not share Einstein's pacifist and internationalist instincts; indeed, he had been largely responsible for the development of poison gas as an instrument of warfare in 1914–18, and, though Jewish, was exempt from dismissal because of his war service; but the sacking of numerous Jewish colleagues from his institute caused him to resign on 30 April 1933, declaring openly that he would not be told whom to choose as his collaborators and whom not. He left for Cambridge University, where he was not happy, and died the following year.[77] The loss of famous figures such as these was deeply alarming to many in the German scientific community. In May, the non-Jewish Max Planck, who was equally celebrated as a scientist and by this time had become President of Germany's premier scientific research institution, the Kaiser Wilhelm Society, went to see Hitler in person to protest. He met with a blanket declaration, so he later recalled, that it was impossible to make distinctions between Jews: 'The Jews are all Communists and these are my enemies . . . All Jews cling together like burrs. Wherever one Jew is, other Jews of all types immediately gather.'[78]

Like Haber, some Jewish scientists, including the Nobel laureate James Franck, an experimental physicist at Göttingen University, protested publicly against the treatment of other Jewish scientists and resigned even though they could have stayed in post under the exemption granted to Jewish war veterans. Accused of sabotage in a collective letter signed by forty-two colleagues at the University – only one of them from the field of physics and mathematics – Franck reluctantly left for a post in the United States. The reaction of the Medical Faculty at Heidelberg to the dismissal of Jewish colleagues was remarkable precisely because it was so unusual: in an official statement issued to Baden's Education Ministry on 5 April 1933, the chairman, Richard Siebeck, pointed out the contributions Jews had made to medical science, and criticized the 'impulsive violence' that was pushing aside autonomy and responsibility in the University.[79] His example, and that of his Faculty, found few imitators elsewhere. Most of those non-Jewish scientists who remained, with Max Planck at their head, attempted to preserve the integrity and political neutrality of scientific research by paying lip-service to the regime. Planck began to address meetings of the Kaiser Wilhelm Society with the Nazi salute and the Hitler greeting, in an attempt to avoid further purges. Werner Heisenberg, a physicist awarded the Nobel Prize for his development of quantum mechanics, argued that it was important to remain in Germany to keep scientific values intact. But in time it was to become clear that they were fighting a losing battle.[80]

The vast majority of German professors remained in post. Overwhelmingly conservative in political orientation, they broadly shared the view of Hitler's Nationalist coalition partners that Weimar democracy had been a disaster and that a restoration of old hierarchies and structures was long overdue. Many, however, went beyond this and positively welcomed the National Socialist state, particularly if they taught in the humanities and social sciences. On 3 March, some three hundred university teachers issued an appeal to voters to support the Nazis, and in May no fewer than seven hundred signed an appeal on behalf of Hitler and the National Socialist State. At the University of Heidelberg, the sociologist Arnold Bergsträsser justified the regime's creation of unity between state and society as a way of overcoming the patent failure of democracy; while the lawyer Walter Jellinek defended the 'revolution' of 1933 as anti-liberal but not anti-democratic, and declared that citizens gained the dignity of being fully human only through their subordination to the state. A member of the German People's Party and a strongly right-wing opponent of the Weimar Republic, Jellinek agreed that the regime's anti-Jewish measures were necessary because of the over-crowding of the academic profession. He also thought – presaging the view of later historians – that Hitler's power would be limited by the existence of other power-centres in the Reich. But wherever else this might have been true, it was not the case with the regime's policy towards the Jews, of whom Jellinek was indeed himself one, and he was duly removed from his chair in the course of the nationalist revolution that he so warmly welcomed. Other professors in the same faculty demanded that the law should be the expression of the people's soul, and judges should deliver their verdicts in accordance with Nazi ideology. The Professor of German declared that the Nazi revolution had given new, patriotic meaning to the study of the German language. He condemned 'Jewish thinking' and 'Jewish literature' for undermining Germany's 'will to live'.[81]

Very quickly, newly Nazified Education Ministries made political criteria central not only for appointments but also for teaching and research. Reich Education Minister Bernhard Rust reserved sweeping powers for himself in this area. The Bavarian Minister of Culture told a gathering of professors in Munich in 1933: 'From now on it is not up to you to decide whether or not something is true, but whether it is in the interests of the National Socialist Revolution.'[82] The Nazi leaders cared little for the traditional freedom of teaching and research, or for the values of the traditional university. They cared little, indeed, for science itself. When the Chairman of the Board of Directors of I.G. Farben, the Nobel Prize-winning chemist Carl Bosch, met Hitler in the summer of 1933 to complain about the damage to Germany's scientific interests done by the dismissal of Jewish professors, he got a rough reception. The proportion of sackings was particularly high in physics, he said, where 26 per cent of university staff had been dismissed, including 11 Nobel Prizewinners, and chemistry, where the figure was 13 per cent. This was gravely undermining German science. Brusquely interrupting the elderly scientist, Hitler said he knew nothing about any of this, and Germany could get on for another hundred years without any physics or chemistry at all; then he rang for his adjutant and told him that Bosch wanted to leave.[83]

III

It was above all the students who drove forward the co-ordination process in the universities. They organized campaigns against unwanted professors in the local newspapers, staged mass disruptions of their lectures and led detachments of stormtroopers in house-searches and raids. Another tactic was to underline the political unreliability of some professors by arranging visiting lectures by politically correct figures such as Heidegger, who could be relied upon to give the regime the enthusiastic endorsement that others sometimes failed to provide. At Heidelberg University, one Nazi activist disrupted the work of the physicist Walter Bothe by conducting lengthy marching sessions for SS men on the roof of his institute, directly above his office.[84] In one university after another, respected Rectors and senior administrators were elbowed aside to make way for often mediocre figures whose only claim to their new position was that they were Nazis and enjoyed the support of the Nazi students' organization. A typical figure was Ernst Krieck, a convinced Nazi theorist of male supremacy who became Rector of Frankfurt in 1933; until his sudden elevation he had been a lowly professor of pedagogy in the city's teacher training college.[85] At Darmstadt Technical University, the adjunct lecturer Karl Lieser, who joined the Party early in 1933, aroused the wrath of his colleagues in the Architecture Department by denouncing many of his colleagues to the Hessian Ministry of Education in May;

outraged, the University Senate deprived Lieser of his right to teach, asked the Ministry to dismiss him, and temporarily closed the University in protest. The next day, however, the students reopened and occupied the buildings, while the Ministry named the Mayor of Darmstadt provisional Rector. The professors caved in under this pressure. Lieser was reinstated, and became a professor himself in 1934. By 1938 he had become Rector. These events, which had their parallels in all of Germany's universities, marked a sharp fall in the traditional power of the professoriate. 'We lads have got the university in our hands,' declared the Nazi student leader in Leipzig, Eduard Klemt, 'and we can do with it what we will.'[86]

The students' unions did not rest content with pushing forward the Nazification of the professoriate. They also demanded a formal role in professorial appointments and representation on disciplinary committees. However, this proved a step too far. Participation by the student body in these matters crassly contradicted the leadership principle. By the summer of 1933, Nazified education ministries and university authorities were beginning to clamp down on student disorder, banning students from removing and destroying objectionable books from libraries, and scotching a plan by the national students' union to set up a pillory in each university town, where the publications of 'un-German' professors would be nailed up. No student was actually disciplined for disorderly conduct of a political nature in the first six months of 1933, despite the massive disruption and violence that virtually crippled university life during this period. But the message was now clear: as the Prussian Ministry of Education declared, it was the duty of the student unions 'to keep every one of its members orderly and disciplined'.[87] Before this happened, however, the students dealt their most dramatic and most notorious blow to intellectual freedom and academic autonomy, an act that reverberated around the world and is still remembered whenever people think of Nazism today.

On 10 May 1933, German students organized an 'act against the un-German spirit' in nineteen university towns across the land. They compiled a list of 'un-German' books, seized them from all the libraries they could find, piled them up in public squares and set them alight. In Berlin the book-burning event was joined at the students' request by Joseph Goebbels. He told them that they were 'doing the right thing in committing the evil spirit of the past to the flames' in what he called a

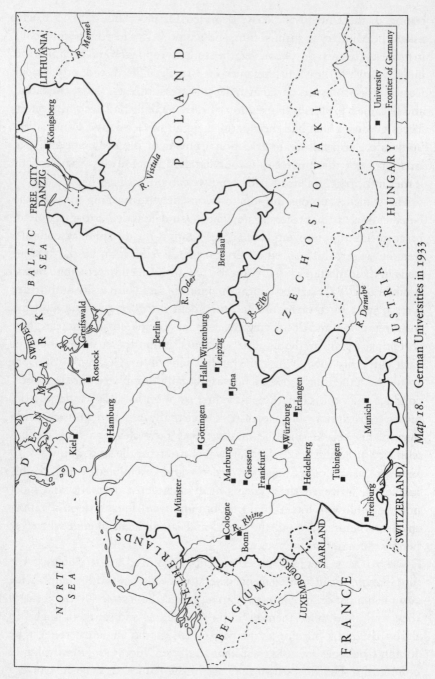

Map 18. German Universities in 1933

'strong, great and symbolic act'.[88] One after another, books were thrown onto the funeral pyre of intellect, to the accompaniment of slogans such as: 'Against class struggle and materialism, for the national community and an idealistic outlook: Marx, Kautsky; Against decadence and moral decay, for discipline and morality in family and state: Heinrich Mann, Ernst Glaeser, Erich Kästner.' The works of Freud were consigned to the flames for their 'debasing exaggeration of man's animal nature', the books of the popular historian and biographer Emil Ludwig were burned for their 'denigration' of the 'great figures' of German history; the writings of the radical pacifist journalists Kurt Tucholsky and Carl von Ossietzky were destroyed for their 'arrogance and presumption'. A particular category in itself was reserved for Erich Maria Remarque, whose critical novel *All Quiet on the Western Front* was thrown onto the fire 'against literary betrayal of the soldiers of the World War, for the education of the nation in the spirit of military preparedness.' Many other books besides those read out in these incantatory slogans were thrown onto the pyres. The national student organization issued 'twelve theses against the un-German spirit' to accompany the action, demanding the introduction of censorship and the purging of libraries and declaring: 'Our opponent is the Jew and anyone who submits to him.'[89]

On 12 March, in a prelude to this action, stormtroopers had already ransacked the library of the trade union centre in Heidelberg, removed books and burned them in a small bonfire outside the door. A similar event had taken place, as we have seen, outside Magnus Hirschfeld's sex research institute in Berlin on 6 May. But the 10 May book-burning was on a much larger scale, and much more thoroughly prepared. Students had been combing libraries and bookshops in readiness for the occasion since the middle of April. Some booksellers courageously refused to hang up posters advertising the event in their shop windows, but many others gave in to the threats with which the students accompanied their action. In Heidelberg, where the book-burning took place on 17 May, the students processed with flaming torches, accompanied by SA, SS and Steel Helmets and members of the duelling corps, and threw Communist and Social Democratic insignia into the flames as well as books. The event was accompanied by the singing of the Horst Wessel Song and the national anthem. Speeches were delivered in which the action was presented as a blow against the 'un-German spirit' represented by writers such as Emil

Julius Gumbel, the statistician of right-wing murders in the Weimar years, hounded out of his chair at the university in the summer of 1932. The Weimar Republic had incorporated this 'Jewish-subversive' spirit; it was now finally consigned to history.[90]

All this marked the culmination of a widespread action 'against the un-German spirit' set in motion weeks before by the Propaganda Ministry.[91] As so often in the history of the Third Reich, the apparently spontaneous action was in fact centrally co-ordinated, though not by Goebbels, but by the national students' union. The Nazi official in charge of purging Berlin's public libraries helpfully provided a list of the books to be burned, and the central office of the national student union wrote and distributed the slogans to be used in the ceremony. In this way, the Nazi students' organization ensured that the book-burning took a roughly similar course in all the university towns where it was carried out.[92] And where the students led, others followed, in localities across the land. At a celebration of the summer solstice of 1933 in the small town of Neu-Isenburg, for instance, a large crowd watched 'Marxist' literature being burned in a huge pile in an open space behind the fire station. As the local women's gymnastics' club danced around the fire, the local Party leader gave a speech, followed by a rendition of the Horst Wessel Song by the assembled multitude. Book-burning was by no means a practice confined to the highly educated.[93]

The Nazi book-burning was a conscious echo of an earlier ritual, performed by radical nationalist students at the celebration of the three-hundredth anniversary of Martin Luther's launching of the Reformation with the publication of his theses attacking the Catholic Church, at the Wartburg in Thuringia on 18 October 1817. At the close of the day's festivities, the students had thrown symbols of authority and 'un-German' books such as the *Code Napoléon* onto a bonfire in a form of symbolic execution. This action may have provided a precedent in Germany's canon of nationalist demonstrations, but in fact it had little in common with its later imitation in 1933, since a principal concern of the Wartburg Festival was to express solidarity with Poland and to demonstrate in favour of the freedom of the German press, constricted by massive censorship from the police regime inspired by Prince Metternich. Still, as the flames rose to the skies in Germany's ancient seats of learning on 10 May 1933, encouraged or tolerated by the newly Nazified university authorities, there must have been more than a few who recalled the poet Heinrich Heine's comment on that earlier event, over a century before: 'Where books are burned, in the end people will be burned too.'[94]

IV

Amid all the violence, intimidation and brutality of the Nazi assault on civil society in the early months of 1933, one particular, small group of Germans came in for a particularly intense degree of hatred and hostility: German Jews. This was not because they were outright opponents of Nazism, like the Communists and the Social Democrats, or because they needed to be intimidated and brought into line like other political and social groups and institutions as part of the rapid Nazi drive to create a dictatorial, one-party state. The Nazi attack on the Jews was of quite a different character. As the expulsion of Jews from key cultural institutions such as the Prussian Academy of Arts, the major orchestras, or the art schools and museums, dramatically illustrated, the Nazis saw the Jews above all as the repositories of an alien, un-German spirit, and their removal as part of a cultural revolution that would restore 'Germanness' to Germany. Antisemitism had always borne a very tenuous and indirect relation to the real role and position of Jews in German society, most of whom lived blameless, conventional and on the whole politically rather conservative lives. But from the very beginning of the Nazi seizure of power, they felt the full force of the stormstroopers' pent-up hatred. Already in the autumn of 1932, indeed, brownshirts had carried out a series of bomb attacks on Jewish shops and businesses, synagogues and other premises. In the weeks following Hitler's appointment as Reich Chancellor, stormtroopers broke into synagogues and desecrated the religious furniture, smashed the windows of Jewish shops, and subjected Jews to random acts of humiliation, shaving off their beards or forcing them, in an imitation of a punishment devised by the Italian Fascists, to drink large quantities of castor oil.[95] The violence reached new levels in the aftermath of the elections of 5 March. The day after the election, gangs of brownshirts rampaged along the Kurfürstendamm, a fashionable shopping street in Berlin, which many Nazis saw as an area where Jews tended to congregate, hunting down Jews and beating them up. In Breslau, a gang of stormtroopers kidnapped the Jewish director of the theatre, beating him to within an inch of his life with rubber truncheons and dog-whips. A synagogue was set on fire in Königsberg in East Prussia, and a Jewish businessman was abducted and beaten so badly that he later died of his injuries. Gangs of stormtroopers daubed and blockaded Jewish shops in several localities.[96]

In Breslau, stormtroopers assaulted Jewish judges and lawyers in the court building on 11 March. The courts suspended business for three days, and when they reconvened, the President of the Court, under pressure from the brownshirts, ruled that henceforth only 17 out of the 364 Jewish lawyers who had hitherto practised in Breslau would be allowed entry into the court building. Other stormtroopers burst into courthouses all over Germany, dragged Jewish judges and lawyers out of the proceedings and beat them up, telling them not to return. The disruption caused by all this was too much even for Hitler, who called on 10 March for a stop to 'individual actions' of this kind if they disrupted official business or harmed the economy (a problem on which he had already received complaints from influential business circles, from the Reichsbank downwards). Hitler also personally forced the Leipzig Party bosses to call off a planned raid on the Reich Court with the object of hauling out Jewish lawyers.[97] Courts lower down the hierarchy were a different matter, however, and here he did not intervene. The Nazi press continued to print rabid incitements to purge the judiciary and the legal profession of Jews, backed by a flood of petitions to the Reich Justice Ministry from 'nationalist' groups of lawyers to the same end. The fact was that while attacks on Jewish shops and businesses were disturbing to Hitler's Nationalist coalition partners, attacks on Jewish lawyers on the whole were not. In the legal profession, the attacks met with little or no resistance even from those who disapproved of them. The trainee judge Raimund Pretzel was sitting in the library of the Berlin courthouse when the brownshirts burst into the building, loudly expelling all the Jews. 'A brownshirt approached me and took up position in front of my work table,' he remembered later. '"Are you Aryan?" Before I had a chance to think, I had said, "Yes." He took a close look at my nose – and retired. The blood shot to my face. A moment too late I felt the shame, the defeat . . . What a disgrace to buy, with a reply, the right to stay with my documents in peace!'[98]

Hitler's intervention only caused a temporary let-up in the sequence of violent incidents, and altogether failed to halt them completely. Little more than a fortnight later, they had begun again. On 25 March 1933, thirty stormtroopers from out of town broke into Jewish homes in Nieder-stetten in the south-west, hauled off the men to the town hall and beat them up with barely controlled savagery; the same morning, in the near-by town of Creglingen, a similar incident led to the deaths of two of the eighteen Jewish men subjected to this treatment. Groups of youths smashed the windows of Jewish shops in Wiesbaden. The regional administrator of Lower Bavaria reported on 30 March:

Early in the morning of the 15th of this month, towards 6 o'clock, a truck with several men dressed in dark uniforms appeared before the house of the Jewish trader Otto Selz, in Straubing. Selz was taken out of his house still dressed in his nightshirt and abducted in the truck. Around 9.30 Selz was discovered in a wood near Weng, Landshut District, shot dead ... Several country people claim to have noticed red armbands with the swastika on some of the men in the truck.[99]

As Hitler's intervention suggested, these incidents were not part of any preconceived plan. Rather, they expressed the antisemitic hatred, fury and violence that lay at the heart of Nazism at every level. The stormtroopers' brutality had hitherto been directed mainly against the Reichsbanner and the Red Front-Fighters' League, but it was now released in all directions by the Nazi election victory. Unchecked by the intervention of the police or by any serious threat of legal prosecution, it vented itself particularly in attacks on Jews. Despite their desire to control the violence, the Nazi leaders in practice continually fuelled it with their rhetoric, and with the constant antisemitic diatribes in the Nazi press, led by Julius Streicher's *The Stormer*.[100] According to one doubtless incomplete estimate, Nazi stormtroopers had murdered 43 Jews by the end of June 1933.[101]

These incidents did not go unnoticed abroad. Foreign newspaper correspondents in Berlin reported seeing Jews with blood streaming down their faces lying in the streets of Berlin after having been beaten senseless. Critical reports began to appear in the British, French and American press.[102] On 26 March the conservative Foreign Minister von Neurath told the American journalist Louis P. Lochner that this 'atrocity propaganda', which he described as reminiscent of Belgian myths about atrocities committed by German troops in 1914, was most likely part of a concerted campaign of misinformation against the German government; revolutions were bound to be accompanied by 'certain excesses'. Unlike Neurath, Hitler himself described the stories openly as 'Jewish atrocity smears'. At a meeting with Goebbels, Himmler and Streicher in Berchtesgaden the same day, Hitler decided to take action, in order to channel the antisemitic energies of the rank-and-file into a concerted action. On 28 March he ordered the Party at every level to prepare a boycott of Jewish shops and businesses to be carried out on 1 April. The action was approved by the cabinet the following day.[103] Far from being a rapid, spur-of-the-moment response to 'atrocity propaganda' abroad, however, the boycott had long been contemplated in Nazi circles, particularly those most hostile to 'Jewish' big businesses such as department stores and finance houses. Neither for the first nor the last time, the leading Nazis assumed an identity of interest, a conspiratorial connection even, between Jews in Europe and Jews in America, that simply was not there. It was necessary to show the Jews, wrote Goebbels in the published version of his diary, 'that one is determined to stop at nothing'.[104]

The unreality of such beliefs was illustrated when the Central Association of German Citizens of Jewish Faith cabled the American Jewish Committee in New York to ask it to call off 'demonstrations hostile to Germany', only to be sharply rebuffed despite divided views in the American Jewish community. Protest meetings in a number of American cities on 27 March were followed by a campaign to boycott German goods that met with an increasing amount of success in the months after 1 April.[105] This only served to confirm Goebbels in his view that the boycott should be carried out 'with the greatest toughness'. 'If the foreign smears come to an end, then it will be stopped,' he added, 'otherwise a fight to the death will begin. Now the German Jews must influence their racial comrades in the world so that they're not in for it over here.' As Goebbels drove through Berlin on 1 April to check the progress of the boycott, he declared himself more than satisfied: 'All Jewish shops are shut. SA sentries are standing in front of the entrances. The public has declared its solidarity. An exemplary discipline obtains. An imposing spectacle!' The spectacle was made more dramatic by a mass demonstration of '150,000 Berlin workers' against 'foreign smears' in the afternoon, and a march-past of 100,000 members of the Hitler Youth in the evening. 'There is', reported Goebbels with satisfaction, 'an indescribable mood of boiling rage ... The boycott is a great moral victory for Germany.' So great was it, indeed, that already the next day he could report triumphantly: 'Foreign countries are gradually coming to their senses.'[106]

Germans reading Goebbels's account when it was published a few months later knew, however, that it put an optimistic construction on the events of 1 April from the Nazi point of view. Certainly there was plenty of activity by the stormtroopers, who posted up garish placards everywhere telling people: 'Don't buy anything in Jewish shops and department stores!', ordering them not to use Jewish lawyers and doctors, and informing them of the supposed reason for all this: 'The Jew is smearing us abroad.' Trucks bedecked with similar posters and full of stormtroopers raced through the streets, and SA and Steel Helmet units stood threateningly outside the doors of Jewish retailers, demanding the identity papers of any shoppers going in. Many non-Jewish shops put up posters advertising the fact that they were 'recognized German-Christian businesses', just to avoid misunderstandings. And as far as the storm-troopers were concerned, the Nazi leadership had made an important point: this action against the Jews was to be centrally co-ordinated, and they were not to commit individual acts of violence. The stormtroopers who enforced the boycott on 1 April did indeed mostly avoid serious breaches of the peace, and kept their behaviour at the level of threats and intimidation. Little actual physical damage seems to have been done to the shops themselves on the day, although in many places the brownshirts daubed slogans on the shop windows, and in a few localities they were unable to resist breaking the glass, looting the contents, arresting objec-tors, or taking the Jewish shop-owners out, driving them through the streets and beating them up when they dropped through exhaustion.[107]

Crowds gathered to see what was going on and stood outside the boycotted shops. Yet, contrary to reports in the Nazi press, they did not demonstrate their anger against the Jews, but remained for the most part passive and silent. In some places, including two department stores in Munich, there were even small counter-demonstrations by citizens, some of them wearing the Party badge, who tried to get past the brownshirt sentries on the door. In Hanover, determined shoppers tried to enter the Jewish shops by force. In most places, however, few went in. To this extent, at least, the boycott was a success. On the other hand, some smaller towns failed to implement the boycott altogether. Everywhere, numerous Jewish shopkeepers shut up shop anyway, to avoid unpleasantness. Warned of the boycott in advance, many people rushed to purchase their goods in the Jewish shops the day before, much to the annoyance of the Nazi press. A young soldier and his girlfriend were overheard in a cinema the evening before the boycott arguing about what they should do. 'Actually one's not supposed to buy anything from the Jews,' he said; 'but it's so terribly cheap,' she replied. 'Then it's poor and doesn't last,' was his answer. 'No, really,' she riposted, 'it's just as good and keeps just as well, really just the same as in Christian shops – and it's so much cheaper.'[108]

Only small shops and businesses were affected by the boycott; the largest Jewish firms, who had borne the brunt of the Nazis' verbal attacks over the years, were exempted because of their importance to the national economy, and because they were major employers who would be forced to lay off workers if the boycott really had a serious impact on their economic position. The Tietz department store chain alone had 14,000 employees. The Nazi employees' organization in the huge Ullstein publishing firm noted that while the company was exempted from the boycott, the banning of many of its publications was leading to the dismissal of many 'good national comrades', thus illustrating the economic dangers of the regime's policies.[109] All this made the boycott a good deal less impressive than Goebbels claimed. The general lack of public opposition to the action was striking, but so too was the general lack of public enthusiasm for it; a combination that was to be repeated more than once in subsequent years when the government launched antisemitic measures of one sort or another. Realizing the problems which the boycott caused, both for the economy and for the regime's reputation abroad, and conceding privately that it had not met with a great deal of success, Hitler and the Party silently dropped the idea of continuing it on a national basis, despite the fact that American newspapers carried on printing 'atrocity stories' about Nazi violence against the Jews in the following weeks and months. But the idea of a boycott took root in the Nazi movement. In the following months, many local newspapers repeatedly called upon their readers not to patronize Jewish shops, while Party activists in a wide variety of localities often placed 'sentries' outside Jewish premises, and organized letter-writing campaigns to rebuke and admonish those customers who dared to enter them.[110]

V

A major purpose of the boycott had been to advertise to the Nazi rank-and-file that antisemitic policy had to be centrally co-ordinated and pursued, as Hitler had written many years before, in a 'rational' manner rather than through spontaneous pogroms and acts of violence. The boycott thus prepared the way for Nazi policy towards the Jews to take on a legal, or quasi-legal, course, in pursuit of the Party Programme's statement that Jews could not be full German citizens and therefore, clearly, could not enjoy full civil rights. A week after the boycott, on 7 April 1933, the Law for the Restoration of a Professional Civil Service added Jews to Communists and other politically unreliable individuals in state employment as targets for dismissal. 'Non-Aryan' civil servants, defined in a supplementary law on 11 April as people with one or more 'non-Aryan, particularly Jewish' grandparent, were to be retired, unless (on Hindenburg's explicit insistence) they were war veterans or had lost a father or son in combat, or had been in the forces before the First World War. Pushed through by Wilhelm Frick, the Nazi Reich Interior Minister, who had already proposed a similar law as a humble Reichstag deputy in 1925, the legislation, in characteristic Nazi style, co-ordinated measures already in progress at the regional and local level, where dismissals of Jewish state employees had been going on for some weeks. Similar provisions were applied to Jewish lawyers, worked out in the Ministry of Justice at the same time and incorporated into a separate law passed on the same day. A decree of 25 April 'Against the Overcrowding of German Schools and Universities' drastically reduced the flow of qualified Jewish Germans into the professions by imposing a quota of 5 per cent Jewish pupils on all schools and universities and 1.5 per cent of new entries each year. The exemptions meant that many Jews were able to continue working – 336 out of a total of 717 Jewish judges and state prosecutors, for example, and 3,167 out of a total of 4,585 Jewish lawyers.[111] Eastern European Jews who had migrated to Germany under the Weimar Republic lost their citizenship by a law of 14 July 1933, in a measure already contemplated by the government of Franz von Papen in 1932. This bundle of different measures meant the end of the civil equality of the Jews that had existed in Germany since 1871.[112]

Those Jews who carried on with their jobs did so in an atmosphere of continuous and steadily mounting suspicion and hostility. The decrees set off a wave of denunciations, personally as well as politically motivated, and many lawyers, civil servants and state employees were obliged to start checking their ancestry, or even to submit themselves to medical examination in an effort to determine their supposed racial character. Ministers and heads of civil service departments were overwhelmingly hostile to any continued Jewish presence in the institutions they ran. Conservatives such as Herbert von Bismarck, State Secretary in the Prussian Interior Ministry, were as enthusiastic supporters of anti-Jewish measures as were their Nazi colleagues. Measures to restrict the civil rights of the Jews had, after all, been part of the Conservative, later Nationalist, Party programme since the early 1890s. Hitler took due account of the feeling of such men that antisemitic policies should not go too far, vetoing a proposal to ban Jewish doctors on 7 April, for example, and trying to ensure that the purge did not have adverse effects on business and the economy. Yet the fact remained that in the basic thrust of his policy of exclusion at this time, his Nationalist colleagues were right behind him.[113]

And where the state led, other institutions followed. A central part of the whole process of co-ordination at every level was the exclusion of Jews from the newly Nazified institutions which resulted from it, from the German Boxing Association, which excluded Jewish boxers on 4 April 1933, to the German Gymnastics League, which 'Aryanized' itself on 24 May. Municipalities began banning Jews from public facilities such as sports fields.[114] In the small north German town of Northeim, where there were only 120 practising Jews in 1932, the boycott of 1 April 1933 seemed half-hearted, only lasting a few hours, and not applying at all to some businesses. Here, as in many other communities, the local Jewish population had been generally accepted, and Nazi antisemitism was regarded as abstract rhetoric without concrete applicability to the Jews everyone knew. Now the boycott suddenly brought home the reality of the situation to all sectors of society. The income of the local Jewish physician in Northeim began to drop as patients left him, while local voluntary associations, including not only the shooting club but even the Veterans' Club, dropped their Jewish members, often for 'non-attendance', since local Jews soon became reluctant to continue participating in the town's associational life; many resigned before being asked to leave. For every old Social Democrat who ostentatiously continued patronizing Jewish shops, there were several local stormtroopers who bought goods there on credit and refused to pay their bills. By the late summer of 1933, amidst a continuous barrage of antisemitic propaganda from the political leaders of the Reich at every level, from newspapers and the media, the Jews of Northeim had effectively been excluded from the town's social life. And what happened in Northeim, happened all over the rest of Germany, too.[115]

Some Jews thought the antisemitic wave would soon pass, rationalized it, or did their best to ignore it. Many, however, were in a state of shock and despair. As widespread as political violence had been before 30 January 1933, the fact that it was now officially sanctioned by the government, and directed so openly against Germany's Jewish population, created a situation that seemed to many to be entirely new. The result was that Jews began to emigrate from Germany, as the Nazis indeed intended. Thirty-seven thousand left in 1933 alone. The Jewish population of Germany fell from 525,000 in January to just under 500,000 by the end of June; and that was merely the fall amongst those who were registered as belonging to the Jewish faith. Many more would follow in subsequent years. But many also decided to stay, particularly if they were elderly.[116] For the older generation, finding a job abroad was difficult if not impossible, especially since most countries were still deep in the throes of the Depression. They preferred to take their chance in the country that had always been their home. Others harboured the illusion that things would get better once the Nazi regime had settled down. The youthful energy of the stormtroopers would surely be tamed, the excesses of the National Socialist Revolution soon be over.

One Jewish citizen who did not have any illusions was Victor Klemperer. He was already complaining in his diary about the 'right-wing terror' before the election of 5 March, when it was relatively limited compared to what was to come. He found himself unable to agree with his friends who spoke up for the Nationalists and supported the banning of the Communist Party. Klemperer was depressed at their failure to recognize the 'true distribution of power' in the Hitler cabinet. The pre-election terror, he wrote on 10 March, was nothing but a 'mild prelude'. The violence and propaganda reminded him of the 1918

Revolution, only this time under the sign of the swastika. He was already wondering how long he would be left in his post at the university. A week later he was writing: 'The defeat of 1918 did not depress me as deeply as the present situation. It's really shocking how day after day naked force, violations of legality, the most terrible hypocrisy, a barbaric frame of mind, express themselves as decrees completely without any concealment.' The atmosphere, he noted despairingly on 30 March, two days before the boycott, was

like the run-up to a pogrom in the depths of the Middle Ages or in innermost Tsarist Russia . . . We are hostages . . . 'We' – the threatened community of Jews. Actually I feel more ashamed than afraid. Ashamed of Germany. I truly have always felt myself to be a German. And I have always imagined that the 20th century and Central Europe are something other than the 14th century and Romania. Wrong!

Like many conservative Jewish Germans, Klemperer, who sympathized with most of what the Nationalists believed in apart from their antisemitism, insisted first and foremost on his German identity. His allegiance was to be severely tested in the months and years to come.

Germany, wrote Klemperer on 20 March 1933, was not going to be rescued by the Hitler government, which seemed to be driving rapidly towards a catastrophe. 'Apart from that,' he added, 'I believe that it will never be able to wash away the ignominy of having fallen prey to it.' One after another he noted the dismissal of Jewish friends and acquaintances from their jobs. He felt guilty when the law of 7 April allowed him to stay in post because he had fought on the front in 1914–18. The egoism, helplessness and cowardice of people dismayed him, still more the open antisemitism and abusive anti-Jewish placards of the students in his university. His wife was ill and suffering from nerves, he was worried about his heart. What kept him going was the business of buying and preparing a plot at Döltzschen, on the outskirts of Dresden, on which to build a new house for himself and his wife, as well as his academic writing; that, and his unquenchable human sympathy and intellectual curiosity. In June he was already beginning to compile a private dictionary of Nazi terminology. His first recorded entry, on 30 June 1933, was *protective custody*.[117]

A 'REVOLUTION OF DESTRUCTION'?

I

The Nazi assault on the Jews in the first months of 1933 was the first step in a longer-term process of removing them from German society. By the summer of 1933 this process was well under way. It was the core of Hitler's cultural revolution, the key, in the Nazi mind, to the wider cultural transformation of Germany that was to purge the German spirit of 'alien' influences such as communism, Marxism, socialism, liberalism, pacifism, conservatism, artistic experimentation, sexual freedom and much more besides. All of these influences were ascribed by the Nazis to the malign influence of the Jews, despite massive evidence to the contrary. Excluding the Jews from the economy, from the media, from state employment and from the professions was thus an essential part of the process of redeeming and purifying the German race, and preparing it to wreak its revenge on those who had humiliated it in 1918. When Hitler and Goebbels talked that summer of the 'National Socialist Revolution', this was in the first place what they meant: a cultural and spiritual revolution in which all things 'un-German' had been ruthlessly suppressed.

Yet the extraordinary speed with which this transformation had been achieved suggested at the same time powerful continuities with the recent past. Between 30 January and 14 July 1933, after all, the Nazis had translated Hitler's Chancellorship in a coalition government dominated by non-Nazi conservatives into a one-party state in which even the conservatives no longer had any separate representation. They had co-ordinated all social institutions, apart from the Churches and the army, into a vast and still inchoate structure run by themselves. They had purged huge swathes of culture and the arts, the universities and the educational system, and almost every other area of German society, of everyone who was opposed to them. They had begun their drive to push out the Jews onto the margins of society, or force them to emigrate. And they were starting to put in place the laws and policies that would determine the fate of Germany and its people, and more besides, over the coming years. Some had imagined that the coalition installed on 30 January 1933 would fall apart like other coalitions before it, within a few months. Others had written off the Nazis as a transient phenomenon that would quickly disappear from the stage of world history together with the capitalist system that had put them in power. All of them had been proved wrong. The Third Reich had come into being by the summer of 1933, and it was clearly there to stay. How, then, did this revolution occur? Why did the Nazis meet with no effective opposition in their seizure of power?

The coming of the Third Reich essentially happened in two phases. The first ended with Hitler's nomination as Reich Chancellor on 30 January 1933. This was no 'seizure of power'. Indeed, the Nazis themselves did not use this term to describe the appointment, since it smacked of an illegal putsch. They were still careful at this stage to refer to an 'assumption of power' and to call the coalition a 'government of national renewal' or, more generally, a government of 'national uprising', depending on whether they wished to stress the legitimacy of the cabinet's appointment by the President or the legitimacy of its supposed backing by the nation.[118] The Nazis knew that Hitler's appointment was the beginning of the process of conquering power, not the end. Nevertheless, had it not happened, the Nazi Party might well have continued to decline as the economy gradually recovered. Had Schleicher been less politically incompetent, he might have established a quasi-military regime, ruling through President Hindenburg's power of decree and then, when Hindenburg, who was in his late eighties, eventually died, ruling in his own right, possibly with a revised constitution still giving a role of sorts to the Reichstag. By the second half of 1932, a military regime of some description was the only viable alternative to a Nazi dictatorship. The slide away from parliamentary democracy into an authoritarian state ruling without the full and equal participation of the parties or the legislatures had already begun under Brüning. It had been massively and deliberately accelerated by Papen. After Papen, there was no going back. A power vacuum had been created in Germany which the Reichstag and the parties had no chance of filling. Political power had seeped away from the legitimate organs of the constitution onto the streets at one end, and into the small cabal of politicians and generals surrounding President Hindenburg at the other, leaving a vacuum in the vast area between, where normal democratic politics take place. Hitler was put into office by a clique around the President; but they would not have felt it necessary to put him there without the violence and disorder generated by the activities of the Nazis and the Communists on the streets.[119]

In such a situation, only force was likely to succeed. Only two institutions possessed it in sufficient measure. Only two institutions could operate it without arousing even more violent reactions on the part of the mass of the population: the army and the Nazi movement. A military dictatorship would most probably have crushed many civil freedoms in the years after 1933, launched a drive for rearmament, repudiated the Treaty of Versailles, annexed Austria and invaded Poland in order to recover Danzig and the Polish Corridor that separated East Prussia from the rest of Germany. It might well have used the recovery of German power to pursue further international aggression leading to a war with Britain and France, or the Soviet Union, or both. It would almost certainly have imposed severe restrictions on the Jews. But it is unlikely on balance that a military dictatorship in Germany would have launched the kind of genocidal programme that found its culmination in the gas chambers of Auschwitz and Treblinka.[120]

A military putsch could, as many feared, have led to violent resistance by the Nazis as well as the Communists. Restoring order would have caused massive bloodshed, leading perhaps to civil war. The army was as anxious to avoid this as the Nazis. Both parties knew that their prospects of success if they tried to seize power alone were dubious, to say the least. The logic of co-operation was therefore virtually inescapable; the only question was what form co-operation would eventually take. All over Europe, conservative elites, armies, and radical, fascist or populist mass movements faced the same dilemma. They solved it in a variety of ways, giving the edge to military force in some countries, like Spain, and to fascist movements in others, like Italy. In many countries in the 1920s and 1930s, democracies were being replaced by dictatorships. What happened in Germany in 1933 did not seem so exceptional in the light of what had already happened in countries such as Italy, Poland, Latvia, Estonia, Lithuania, Hungary, Romania, Bulgaria, Portugal, Yugoslavia or indeed in a rather different way in the Soviet Union. Democracy was soon to be destroyed in other countries, too, such as Austria and Spain. In such countries, political violence, rioting and assassination had been common at various periods since the end of the First World War; in Austria, for instance, serious disturbances in Vienna had culminated in the burning down of the Palace of Justice in 1927; in Yugoslavia, Macedonian assassination squads were causing havoc in the political world; in Poland, a major war with the nascent Soviet Union had crippled the political system and the economy and opened the way to the military dictatorship of General Pilsudski. Everywhere, too, the authoritarian right shared most if not all of the antisemitic beliefs and conspiracy theories that animated the Nazis. The Hungarian government of Admiral Miklós Horthy yielded little to the German far right in its hatred of Jews, fuelled by the experience of the short-lived revolutionary regime led by the Jewish Communist Béla Kun in 1919. The Polish military regime of the 1930s was to impose severe restrictions on the country's large Jewish population. Seen in the European context of the time, neither the political violence of the 1920s and early 1930s, nor the collapse of parliamentary democracy, nor the destruction of civil liberties, would have appeared particularly unusual to a dispassionate observer. Nor was everything that subsequently happened in the history of the Third Reich made inevitable by Hitler's appointment as Chancellor. Chance and contingency were to play their part here, too, as they had before.[121]

Nevertheless, the consequences of the events of 30 January 1933 in Germany were more serious by far than the consequences of the collapse of democracy elsewhere in Europe. The security provisions of the Treaty of Versailles had done nothing to alter the fact that Germany was still Europe's most powerful, most advanced and most populous country. Nationalist dreams of territorial aggrandisement and conquest were present in other authoritarian regimes like Poland and Hungary as well. But these, if realized, were only likely to be of regional significance. What happened in Germany was likely to have a far wider impact than what happened in a small country like Austria, or an impoverished land like Poland. Its significance, given Germany's size and power, had the potential to be worldwide. That is why the events of the first six and a half months of 1933 were so momentous.

How and why did they occur? To begin with, no one would have thought it worth their while shoehorning Hitler into the Reich Chancellery had he not been the leader of Germany's largest political party. The Nazis, of course, never won a majority of the vote in a free election: 37.4 per cent was all they could manage in their best performance, the Reichstag election of July 1932. Still, this was a high vote by any democratic standards, higher than many democratically elected governments in other countries have achieved since. The roots of the Nazis' success lay in the failure of the German political system to produce a viable, nationwide conservative party uniting both Catholics and Protestants on the right; in the historic weakness of German liberalism; in the bitter resentments of almost all Germans over the loss of the war and the harsh terms of the Treaty of Versailles; in the fear and disorientation provoked in many middle-class Germans by the social and cultural modernism of the Weimar years, and the hyperinflation of 1923. The lack of legitimacy of the Weimar Republic, which for most of its existence never enjoyed the support of a majority of the deputies in the Reichstag, added to these influences and encouraged nostalgia for the old Reich and the authoritarian leadership of a figure like Bismarck. The myth of the 'spirit of 1914' and the 'front generation', particularly strong among those too young to have fought in the war, fuelled a strong desire for national unity and an impatience with the multiplicity of parties and the endless compromises of political negotiations. The legacy of the war also included political violence on a massive and destructive scale and helped persuade many non-violent and respectable people to tolerate it to a degree that would be unthinkable in an effectively functioning parliamentary democracy.

A number of key factors, however, stand out from all the rest. The first is the effect of the Depression, which radicalized the electorate, destroyed or deeply damaged the more moderate parties and polarized the political system between the 'Marxist' parties and the 'bourgeois' groups, all of which moved rapidly towards the far right. The ever-growing threat of Communism struck fear into the hearts of bourgeois voters and helped shift political Catholicism towards authoritarian politics and away from democracy, just as it did in other parts of Europe. Business failures and

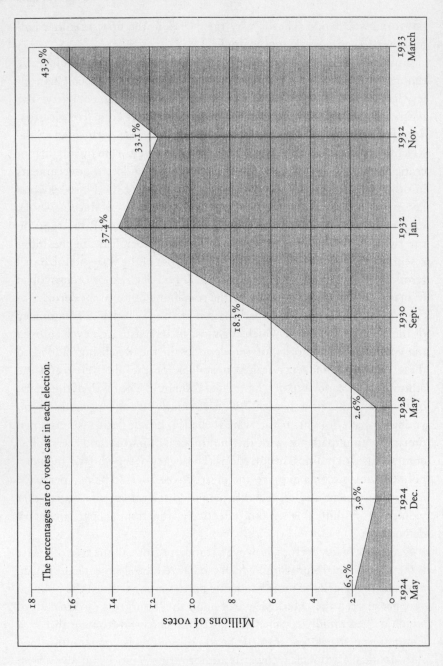

Figure I. The Nazi Vote in Reichstag Elections, 1924–1933

financial disasters helped convince many captains of industry and leaders of agriculture that the power of the trade unions had to be curbed or even destroyed. The political effects of the Depression hugely magnified those of the previous catastrophe of the hyperinflation, and made the Republic seem as if it could deliver nothing but economic disaster. Even without the Depression, Germany's first democracy seemed doomed; but the onset of one of history's worst economic slumps pushed it beyond the point of no return. Moreover, mass unemployment undermined Germany's once-strong labour movement, a solid guarantor of democracy as recently as 1920, when it had managed to defeat the right-wing Kapp putsch despite the toleration of the rebels by the army. Divided and demoralized, and robbed of its key weapon of the political mass strike, the German labour movement was caught between impotent support for the authoritarian regime of Heinrich Brüning on the one hand, and self-destructive hostility to 'bourgeois democracy' on the other.

The second major factor was the Nazi movement itself. Its ideas evidently had a wide appeal to the electorate, or at least were not so outrageous as to put them off. Its dynamism promised a radical cure for the Republic's ills. Its leader Adolf Hitler was a charismatic figure who was able to drum up mass electoral support by the vehemence of his rhetorical denunciations of the unloved Republic, and to convert this into political office, finally, by making the right moves at the right time. Hitler's refusal to enter a coalition government in any other capacity but Reich Chancellor, a refusal that was terminally frustrating to some of his subordinates like Gregor Strasser, was proved right in the end. As deputy to the unpopular Papen or the equally unloved Schleicher, he would have lost heavily in reputation and surrendered a good deal of the charisma that came from being the Leader. The Nazi Party was a party of protest, with not much of a positive programme, and few practical solutions to Germany's problems. But its extremist ideology, adapted and sometimes veiled according to circumstance and the nature of the particular group of people to whom it was appealing, tapped into a sufficient number of pre-existing popular German beliefs and prejudices to make it seem to many well worth supporting at the polls. For such people, desperate times called for desperate measures; for many more, particularly in the middle classes, the vulgar and uneducated character of the Nazis seemed sufficient guarantee that Hitler's coalition partners, well educated and well bred, would be able to hold him in check and curb the street violence that seemed such an unfortunate, but no doubt temporary, accompaniment of the movement's rise to prominence.

The substantial overlap between the Nazis' ideology and that of the conservatives, even, to a considerable extent, that of German liberals, was a third major factor in bringing Hitler into the Reich Chancellery on 30 January 1933. The ideas that were current among almost all German political parties right of the Social Democrats in the early 1930s had a great deal in common with those of the Nazis. These ideas certainly bore enough resemblance to the Nazis' for the bulk of the liberal and conservative parties' supporters in the Protestant electorate to desert them, at least temporarily, for what looked like a more effective alternative. Nor were Catholic voters, and their representative, the Centre Party, any more committed to democracy by this time either. Moreover, even a substantial number of Catholics and workers, or at least those who for whatever reason were not as closely bound into their respective cultural-political milieu as the bulk of their fellows, turned to Nazism too. Only by striking a chord with pre-existing, often deep-seated social and political values could the Nazis rise so rapidly to become the largest party in Germany. At the same time, however, Nazi propaganda, for all its energy and sophistication, did not manage to win round people who were ideologically disinclined to vote for Hitler. Chronically underfunded for most of the time, and so unable to develop its full range of methods, excluded until 1933 from using the radio, and dependent on the voluntary work of often chaotic and disorganized local groups of activists, Goebbels's propaganda offensive from 1930 to 1932 was only one of a number of influences driving people to vote for the Nazis at the polls. Often, indeed, as in the rural Protestant north, they voted without having been reached by the Nazi propaganda machine at all. The Nazi vote was above all a protest vote; and, after 1928, Hitler, Goebbels and the Party leadership recognized this implicitly by removing most of their specific policies, in so far as they had any, from the limelight, and concentrating on a vague, emotional appeal that emphasized little more than the Party's youth and dynamism, its determination to destroy the Weimar Republic, the Communist Party and the Social Democrats, and its belief that only through the unity of all social classes could Germany be reborn. Antisemitism, so prominent in Nazi propaganda in the 1920s, took a back seat, and had little influence in winning the Nazis support in the elections of the early 1930s. More important by far was the image the Party projected on the street, where the marching columns of stormtroopers added to the general image of disciplined vigour and determination that Goebbels sought to project.[122]

The Nazi propaganda effort, therefore, mainly won over people who were already inclined to identify with the values the Party claimed to represent, and who simply saw the Nazis as a more effective and more energetic vehicle than the bourgeois parties for putting them into effect. Many historians have argued that these values were essentially pre-industrial, or pre-modern. Yet this argument rests on a simplistic equation of democracy with modernity. The voters who flocked to the polls in support of Hitler, the stormtroopers who gave up their evenings to beat up Communists, Social Democrats, and Jews, the Party activists who spent their free time at rallies and demonstrations – none of these were sacrificing themselves to restore a lost past. On the contrary, they were inspired by a vague yet powerful vision of the future, a future in which class antagonisms and party-political squabbles would be overcome, aristocratic privilege of the kind represented by the hated figure of Papen removed, technology, communications media and every modern invention harnessed in the cause of the 'people', and a resurgent national will expressed through the sovereignty not of a traditional hereditary monarch or an entrenched social elite but of a charismatic leader who had come from nowhere, served as a lowly corporal in the First World War and constantly harped upon his populist credentials as a man of the people. The Nazis declared that they would scrape away foreign and alien encrustations on the German body politic, ridding the country of Communism, Marxism, 'Jewish' liberalism, cultural Bolshevism, feminism, sexual libertinism, cosmopolitanism, the economic and power-political burdens imposed by Britain and France in 1919, 'Western' democracy and much else. They would lay bare the true Germany. This was not a specific historical Germany of any particular date or constitution, but a mythical Germany that would recover its timeless racial soul from the alienation it had suffered under the Weimar Republic. Such a vision did not involve just looking back, or forward, but both.

The conservatives who levered Hitler into power shared a good deal of this vision. They really did look back with nostalgia to the past, and yearn for the restoration of the Hohenzollern monarchy and the Bismarckian Reich. But these were to be restored in a form purged of what they saw as the unwise concessions that had been made to democracy. In their vision of the future, everyone was to know their place, and the working classes especially were to be kept where they belonged, out of the political decision-making process altogether. But this vision cannot really be seen as pre-industrial or pre-modern, either. It was shared in large measure, for one thing, by many of the big industrialists who did so much to undermine Weimar democracy, and by many modern, technocratic military officers whose ambition was to launch a modern war with the kind of advanced military equipment that the Treaty of Versailles forbade them to deploy. Like other people at other times and in other places, the conservatives, as much as Hitler, manipulated and rearranged the past to suit their own present purposes. They cannot be reduced to expressions of 'pre-industrial' social groups. Many of them, from capitalist Junker landlords looking for new markets, to small retailers and white-collar workers whose means of support had not even existed before industrialization, were as much modern as they were traditional.[123] It was these congruities in vision that persuaded men like Papen, Schleicher and Hindenburg that it would be worth legitimizing their rule by co-opting the mass movement of the Nazi Party into a coalition government whose aim was to erect an authoritarian state on the ruins of the Weimar Republic.

The death of democracy in Germany was part of a much broader European pattern in the interwar years; but it also had very specific roots in German history and drew on ideas that were part of a very specific German tradition. German nationalism, the Pan-German vision of the completion through conquest in war of Bismarck's unfinished work of bringing all Germans together in a single state, the conviction of the superiority of the Aryan race and the threat posed to it by the Jews, the belief in eugenic planning and racial hygiene, the military ideal of a society clad in uniform, regimented, obedient and ready for battle – all this and much more that came to fruition in 1933 drew on ideas that had been circulating in Germany since the last quarter of the nineteenth century. Some of these ideas, in turn, had their roots in other countries or were shared by significant thinkers within them – the racism of Gobineau, the anticlericalism of Schönerer, the paganist fantasies of Lanz von

Liebenfels, the pseudo-scientific population policies of Darwin's disciples in many countries, and much more. But they came together in Germany in a uniquely poisonous mixture, rendered all the more potent by Germany's pre-eminent position as the most advanced and most powerful state on the European Continent. In the years following the appointment of Hitler as Reich Chancellor, the rest of Europe, and the world, would learn just how poisonous that mixture could be.

II

For all his electoral successes, there has never been any doubt that Hitler came into office as the result of a backstairs political intrigue. 'The Germans' did not elect Hitler Reich Chancellor. Nor did they give their free and democratic approval to his creation of a one-party state. Yet some have argued that the Weimar Republic destroyed itself rather than being destroyed by its enemies: a case of political suicide rather than political murder.[124] Of the weakness of the Republic's polity in the supreme crisis of 1930–33 there can be little doubt. The Republic's fatal lack of legitimacy caused people to look all too readily to other political solutions for Germany's ills. But these ills were not just of the Republic's own making. Crucial to the whole process was the way in which democracy's enemies exploited the democratic constitution and democratic political culture for their own ends. Joseph Goebbels was quite explicit about this when he publicly ridiculed:

The stupidity of democracy. It will always remain one of democracy's best jokes that it provided its deadly enemies with the means by which it was destroyed. The persecuted leaders of the NSDAP became parliamentary deputies and so acquired the use of parliamentary immunity, allowances and free travel tickets. They were thus protected from police interference, could allow themselves to say more than the ordinary citizen, and apart from that they also had the costs of their activity paid by their enemy. One can make superb capital from democratic stupidity. The members of the NSDAP grasped that right away and took enormous pleasure in it.[125]

There was no denying the Nazis' supreme contempt for democratic institutions. But it is in the nature of democratic institutions that they presuppose at least a minimal willingness to abide by the rules of democratic politics. Democracies that are under threat of destruction face the impossible dilemma of either yielding to that threat by insisting on preserving the democratic niceties, or violating their own principles by curtailing democratic rights. The Nazis knew this, and exploited the dilemma to the full in the second phase of the coming of the Third Reich, from February to July 1933.

Since the failure of his beer-hall putsch in November 1923, Hitler had always claimed that he was going to come to power by legal means. Indeed, he had said as much on oath in court. After 1923, he knew that a violent *coup d'état* along the lines of the October Revolution in Russia in 1917, or even the threatened 'march on Rome' which had propelled Mussolini into Prime Ministerial office in Italy in 1922, would not work. At every point, therefore, Hitler and his associates sought a legalistic fig-leaf for their actions. All along, they avoided as far as possible giving their opponents the kind of opportunity that the Social Democrats had taken up in fighting Papen's Prussian coup of July 1932 through the courts. The Social Democrats had done this with a certain degree of legal success, though politically their court action had proved completely futile. Avoiding this precedent was why, for instance, Hitler placed so much importance on the Reichstag Fire Decree and the Enabling Act. It was why Göring enrolled the brownshirts and SS as auxiliary police in Prussia rather than simply letting them go on the rampage without so much as a pretence of legal cover for their actions. It was why the Nazi leadership insisted on implementing its initial wave of policies through laws approved by the Reichstag or sanctioned by Presidential decrees. And the strategy of the 'legal revolution' worked. Hitler's constant reassurances that he would act legally helped persuade his coalition partners and his opponents alike that the Nazis could be dealt with by legal means. Legal cover for the Nazis' actions allowed civil servants to draft the decrees and laws they demanded, even where, as with the Civil Service Act of 7 April 1933, they attacked the very principles of neutrality on which the civil service was based by requiring the dismissal of Jewish and politically unreliable bureaucrats from their positions. For civil servants, state employees and many others, the measures by which the Nazis seized power between the end of January and the end of July 1933 seemed irresistible because they appeared to carry the full force of the law.

Yet they did not. At every point in the process, the Nazis violated the law. In the first place, they contradicted the spirit in which the laws had been passed. Article 48 of the Weimar constitution, in particular, which gave the President the power to rule by decree in time of emergency, had never been intended to be the basis for any more than purely interim measures; the Nazis made it into the basis for a permanent state of emergency that was more fictive than real and lasted in a technical sense all the way up to 1945. Nor had Article 48 been intended to introduce measures as far-reaching as those passed on 28 February 1933. It was indeed unfortunate that President Ebert had made such liberal use and broad application of Article 48 earlier in the Republic's history, and doubly so that Reich Chancellors Brüning, Papen and Schleicher had relied on it so heavily in the crisis of the early 1930s. But even that paled into insignificance beside the drastic curtailment of civil liberties ordered on 28 February. Nor was the decree meant to be used by a Chancellor applying the President's rubber stamp. Hitler ensured in his negotiations with Hindenburg in January 1933 that it would be.[126] The Enabling Act was even more clearly a violation of the spirit of the constitution, as was the abolition of free elections that followed. Yet the likelihood of this happening was scarcely a secret, since the leading Nazis clearly proclaimed during the election campaign that the election of 5 March would be the last for many years to come.

The Nazis did not just violate the spirit of the Weimar constitution, they also transgressed against it in a technical, legal sense too. The decree of 6 February 1933 that gave Göring control over Prussia clearly broke the findings of the State Court in the lawsuit brought against Papen by the deposed Social Democratic minority government in Prussia. The Enabling Act was legally invalid because Göring, as President of the Reichstag, did not count the elected Communist deputies. Though the two-thirds majority did not require them to be counted, refusing to recognize their existence was an illegal act. Moreover, the Act's ratification by the Federal Council, the upper chamber of the legislature, representing the federated states, was irregular since the state governments had been overthrown by force and were therefore not properly constituted or represented.[127] These were more than mere technicalities. But they were far outdone by the massive, sustained, and wholly illegal violence perpetrated by Nazi stormtroopers on the streets that already began in mid-February, reached new levels of intensity after the Reichstag fire, and swept across the country in March, April, May and June. The status of many of the perpetrators as auxiliary police in no way legalized the acts they committed. After all, putting someone into a policeman's uniform does not give him a licence to commit murder, to ransack offices, to confiscate funds, or to arrest people, beat them up, torture them and imprison them in hastily erected concentration camps without trial.[128]

German judicial authorities were, in fact, fully aware of the illegal nature of Nazi violence even after the seizure of power. The Reich Ministry of Justice made strenuous efforts to have the mass arrests of the first half of 1933 subjected to a formal legal process; its intervention was simply disregarded. Throughout 1933 there were cases of state prosecutors bringing charges against brownshirts and SS men who had committed acts of violence and murder against their opponents. In August 1933 a special prosecution office was set up to co-ordinate these efforts. In December 1933 the Bavarian state prosecutor attempted to investigate the torturing to death of three prisoners in Dachau concentration camp, and when he was rebuffed, the Bavarian Minister of Justice announced his determination to pursue the matter with all possible vigour. The Reich Minister of the Interior complained in January 1934 that protective custody had been misused in many cases. It was only in April 1934 that a set of regulations was passed detailing who was entitled to arrest people and put them into 'protective custody' and what should happen to them when they got there. In the same year, however, the state prosecutor brought charges against twenty-three stormtroopers and political police officials at Hohnstein concentration camp in Saxony, including the camp commandant, for the torture of inmates, which, Reich Minister of Justice Gürtner emphasized, 'reveals a brutality and cruelty in the perpetrators which are totally alien to German sentiment and feeling'.[129]

Many of those who attempted to prosecute acts of torture and violence committed by Nazi stormtroopers were themselves fully paid-up Nazis. The Bavarian Justice Minister who tried to prosecute acts of torture in Dachau in 1933, for example, was none other than Hans Frank, later to acquire a brutal reputation as Governor-General of Poland during the Second World War. Nothing came of these legal initiatives, which were all frustrated by intervention from above, by Himmler or ultimately by

Hitler himself.[130] An amnesty for crimes committed in the 'national uprising' was passed as early as 21 March 1933, quashing over 7,000 prosecutions.[131] Everybody, including not least the Nazis, was aware throughout 1933 and 1934 that the brutal beatings, torture, maltreatment, destruction of property and violence of all kinds carried out against the Nazis' opponents, up to and including murder by the brown-shirted stormtroopers of the SA and the black-uniformed squads of the SS, were in flagrant violation of the law of the land. Yet this violence was a central, indispensable part of the Nazi seizure of power from February 1933 onwards, and the widespread, in the end almost universal fear that it engendered among Germans who were not members of the Party or its auxiliary organizations was a crucial factor in intimidating Hitler's opponents and bringing his sometimes rather unwilling allies into line.[132]

There can be no doubt, finally, about the ultimate responsibility of Hitler and the Nazi leadership for these illegal acts. Hitler's contempt for the law and the Weimar constitution had been made clear on many occasions. 'We enter the legal agencies and in that way will make our Party the determining factor,' Hitler told the court at the 1930 army officers' trial in Leipzig. 'However, once we possess the constitutional power, we will mould the state into the shape we hold to be suitable.'[133] It was important, he told the cabinet in the immediate aftermath of the Reichstag fire, not to get too hung up on legal niceties in pursuing the supposed Communist perpetrators. Hitler's whole rhetoric, his whole posture in the first months of 1933 amounted to a continual encouragement of acts of violence against the Nazis' opponents. His appeals for discipline almost invariably went hand-in-hand with more generalized rhetorical attacks on their opponents which rank-and-file stormtroopers took as licence to continue the violence unabated. Massive, co-ordinated actions, like the occupation of the trade union offices on 2 May, persuaded ordinary brownshirts that they would not get into too much trouble if they acted on their own initiative on other occasions in the same spirit. And indeed they did not.[134]

Most crucial of all was the fact that Hitler and the Nazis at every level were very much aware of the fact that they were breaking the law. Their contempt for the law, and for formal processes of justice, was palpable, and made plain on innumerable occasions. Might was right. Law was just the expression of power. What counted, in the words of one Nazi journalist, was not the 'mendacious hypocrisy' of Germany's legal and penal systems, but 'the *law of power*, that incorporates itself in the blood ties and military solidarity of one's own race . . . There is neither law nor justice in itself. What had succeeded in asserting itself as "law" in the struggle for power has to be protected, also for the sake of the victorious power.'[135]

III

The illegal nature of the Nazi seizure of power in the first half of 1933 made it, in effect, into a revolutionary overthrow of the existing political system, and indeed the rhetoric of the 'National Socialist Revolution' was designed not least as an implicit justification of illegal acts. But what kind of revolution was it? The conservative administrator Hermann Rauschning, who began by working with the Nazis but by the late 1930s had become one of their fiercest and most persistent critics, described it as a 'nihilist revolution', a 'directionless revolution, a revolution merely for revolution's sake'. It destroyed all social order, all freedom, all decency; it was, as the title of the English edition of his book claimed, a 'revolution of destruction', nothing more.[136] But in his passionate diatribe, that ended with a clarion call for the restoration of true conservative values, Rauschning was doing little more than using 'revolution' as a rhetorical bludgeon with which to beat the Nazis for their overturning of the order he prized. Other revolutions, whatever Rauschning may have thought, delivered more than mere destruction. How then did the Nazi Revolution compare with them?

On the face of it, the Nazi Revolution was not really a revolution at all. The French Revolution of 1789 and the Russian Revolution of 1917 swept away the existing order by force and replaced it with something that the revolutionaries regarded as entirely new. Typically trying to have it both ways, by contrast the Nazis both used the rhetoric of revolution and claimed that they had come to power legally and in accordance with the existing political constitution. They took few concrete steps to abolish the central institutions of the Weimar Republic or to replace them with something else – the eventual abolition of the Presidential office in 1934 was a rarity in this respect. Instead, they preferred to let them atrophy, like the Reichstag, which barely met after 1933 and then only to hear speeches by Hitler, or the Reich cabinet, which itself also eventually ceased to meet.[137] On the other hand, what the conservative elites wanted – the staging of a genuine counter-revolution with the aid of the National Socialists, culminating in a restoration of the Wilhelmine Reich, or something very much like it, with or without the person of the Kaiser on the throne – failed to materialize as well. Whatever else happened in 1933, it was not a conservative restoration. The violence that was central to the seizure of power gave it a distinctly revolutionary flavour. The Nazi rhetoric of 'revolution' was virtually unchallenged after June 1933. Does it have to be taken at face value, then?[138]

Some authors have argued that a direct historical line can be drawn to Nazism from the French Revolution of 1789, the Jacobin 'Reign of Terror' in 1793–4, and the implicit idea of a popular dictatorship in Rousseau's theory of the 'General Will', decided initially by the people but brooking no opposition once resolved upon.[139] The French Revolution was indeed remarkable for its rehearsal of many of the major ideologies that bestrode the historical stage of Europe in the following two centuries, from communism and anarchism to liberalism and conservatism. But National Socialism was not among them. The Nazis, indeed, thought of themselves as undoing all the work of the French Revolution and rolling back the clock, in a political sense at least, much further: to the early Middle Ages. Their concept of the people was racial rather than civic. All the ideologies to which the French Revolution had given birth were to be destroyed. The Nazi Revolution was to be the world-historical negation of its French predecessor, not its historical fulfilment.[140]

If there was a Nazi Revolution, then what did the Nazis think it would be? Once more, the parallel with the French or the Russian Revolution does not seem to work. The French revolutionaries of 1789 possessed a clear set of doctrines on the basis of which they would introduce the sovereignty of the people through representative institutions, while the Russian revolutionaries of October 1917 aimed to overthrow the bourgeoisie and the traditional elites and usher in the rule of the proletariat. By contrast, the Nazis had no explicit plan to reorder society, indeed no fully worked-out model of the society they said they wanted to revolutionize. Hitler himself seems to have thought of the Revolution as a changeover of personnel in positions of power and authority. In a speech to senior Nazi officials on 6 July 1933, he implied that the core of the Revolution lay in the elimination of political parties, democratic institutions and independent organizations. He seems to have regarded the conquest of power as the essence of the Nazi Revolution, and to have used the two terms virtually interchangeably:

The conquest of power requires insight. The conquest of power itself is easy, the conquest is only secure when the renewal of human beings is fitted to the new form . . . The great task is now to regain control of the revolution. History shows more revolutions that have succeeded in the first run-up than those that have also been able to continue afterwards. Revolution must not become a permanent condition, as if the first revolution now had to be followed by a second, the second by a third. We have conquered so much that we will need a very long time to digest it . . . Further development must take place as evolution, existing circumstances must be improved . . .[141]

Fundamentally, therefore, while calling for a cultural and spiritual remaking of Germans in order to fit them to the new form of the Reich, he thought that this had to be done in an evolutionary rather than a revolutionary manner. He went on:

The present structure of the Reich is something unnatural. It is neither conditioned by the needs of the economy nor by the necessities of life of our people . . . We have taken over a given state of affairs. The question is whether we want to retain it . . . The task lies in keeping and reshaping the given construction in so far as it is useable, so that what is good can be preserved for the future, and what cannot be used is removed.[142]

The cultural transformation of the individual German that formed the most revolutionary aspect of the Nazis' intentions could, by analogy, also be achieved by preserving or resurrecting what the Nazis thought of as the good aspects of the German culture of the past, and removing what they conceived of as alien intrusions.

Even the stormtroopers, whose self-proclaimed drive for a 'second revolution' Hitler was explicitly criticizing here, had no real concept of any kind of systematic revolutionary change. A survey of grass-roots Nazi opinion in 1934 showed that a majority of the rank-and-file activists who had been in the Party under the Weimar Republic expected that the regime would bring about a national renaissance, described by one as a 'total reordering of public life' in which Hitler would 'purge Germany of people alien to our country and race who had sneaked into the highest positions and, together with other criminals, brought my German fatherland close to ruin'. A national renaissance in these men's understanding meant above all the reassertion of Germany's position in the world, the overturning of the Treaty of Versailles and its provisions, and the restoration, by war in all probability, of German hegemony in Europe.[143] These men were not revolutionaries in any wider sense, therefore; they had little or no concept of an inner transformation of Germany beyond purging it of Jews and 'Marxists'. The ceaseless activism of the brownshirts was to cause serious problems for the Third Reich in the months and years to come. In the second half of 1933 and the first half of 1934 it was frequently justified by claims that 'the revolution' had to continue. But the stormtroopers' idea of revolution was in the end little more than the continuation of the brawling and fighting to which they had become accustomed during the seizure of power.

For the upper echelons of the Nazi Party, and, above all, for the leadership, continuity was as important as change. The grand opening of the Reichstag in the garrison church at Potsdam after the March elections in 1933, with its ostentatious display of the symbols of the old social and political order, including the presiding throne reserved for the absent Kaiser, and the ceremonial laying of wreaths on the tombstones of the dead Prussian kings, powerfully suggested that Nazism rejected the fundamentals of revolution and linked itself symbolically to key traditions from the German past. This may not have been the whole story, but it was more than a mere propaganda exercise or a cynical sop to Hitler's conservative allies. Moreover, the fact that so many people went over to Nazism in the weeks and months after Hitler became Chancellor, or at least tolerated it and offered no opposition, cannot just be put down to mere opportunism. This might be an explanation for an ordinary regime, but not for one with such pronounced and radical characteristics as that of the Nazis; and the speed and enthusiasm with which so many people came to identify with the new regime strongly suggests that a large majority of the educated elites in German society, whatever their political allegiance up to that point, were already predisposed to embrace many of the principles upon which Nazism rested.[144] The Nazis not only seized political power, they also seized ideological and cultural power in the opening months of the Third Reich. This was not only a consequence of the vague and protean quality of many of their own ideological statements, which offered all things to all people; it also derived from the way in which Nazi ideas appealed directly to many of the principles and beliefs which had spread through the German educated elite since the late nineteenth century. In the wake of the First World War, these principles and beliefs were held, not by an embattled revolutionary minority, but by major institutions of society and politics. It was those who rejected them, in part or in their totality, the Communists and the Social Democrats, who thought of themselves as revolutionaries, and were widely regarded as such by the majority of Germans.

All the great revolutions in history have rejected the past, even down to the point of beginning a new dating system with 'Year 1', as the French Revolution did in 1789, or of consigning the previous centuries to the 'dustbin of history', to quote a famous phrase used by Trotsky in the Russian Revolution of 1917.[145] Such fundamentalism could also be found on the far right, for example in Schönerer's plan to introduce a German nationalist calendar instead of the Christian one. Yet even Schönerer's dating system began in the distant past. And for the Nazis and their supporters, the very term 'Third Reich' constituted a powerful symbolic link to the imagined greatness of the past, embodied in the First Reich of Charlemagne and the Second of Bismarck. Thus, as Hitler said on 13 July 1934, the Nazi Revolution restored the natural development of German history that had been interrupted by the alien impositions of Weimar:

For us, the revolution which shattered the Second Germany was nothing more than the tremendous act of birth which summoned the Third Reich into being. We wanted once again to create a state to which every German can cling in love; to establish a regime to which everyone can look up with respect; to find laws which are commensurate with the morality of our people; to install an authority to which each and every man submits in joyful obedience.

For us, the revolution is not a permanent state of affairs. When a deathly check is violently imposed upon the natural development of a people, an act of violence may serve to release the artificially interrupted flow of evolution to allow it once again the freedom of natural development.[146]

Once more, revolution appeared here as little more than the conquest of political power and the establishment of an authoritarian state. What was to be done with power, once gained, did not necessarily fall under the definition of a revolution. Most revolutions have ended, even if only temporarily, in the dictatorship of one man; but none apart from the Nazi revolution has actually been launched with this explicitly in mind. Even the Bolshevik Revolution was meant to put in place a collective dictatorship of the proletariat, led by its political vanguard, until Stalin came along.[147]

Nazism offered a synthesis of the revolutionary and the restorative. A complete overthrow of the social system, such as was preached in Paris in 1789 or Petrograd in October 1917, was not what the Nazis had in mind. At the heart of the system that the Nazis created lay something else. For all their aggressively egalitarian rhetoric, the Nazis were relatively indifferent, in the end, to the inequalities of society. What mattered to them above all else was race, culture and ideology. In the coming years, they would create a whole new set of institutions through which they would seek to remould the German psyche and rebuild the German character. After the purges of artistic and cultural life were complete, it was time for those German writers, musicians and intellectuals who remained to lend their talents with enthusiasm to the creation of a new German culture. The Christianity of the established Churches, so far (for reasons of political expediency) relatively immune from the hostile attentions of the Nazis, would not be protected for much longer. Now the Nazis would set about constructing a racial utopia, in which a pure-bred nation of heroes would prepare as rapidly and as thoroughly as possible for the ultimate test of German racial superiority: a war in which they would crush and destroy their enemies, and establish a new European order that would eventually come to dominate the world. By the summer of 1933 the ground had been cleared for the construction of a dictatorship the like of which had never yet been seen. The Third Reich was born: in the next phase of its existence, it was to rush headlong into a dynamic and increasingly intolerant maturity.

Notes

Preface

1. Michael Ruck, *Bibliographie zum Nationalsozialismus* (2 vols., Darmstadt, 2000 [1995]).

2. Norbert Frei, *National Socialist Rule in Germany: The Führer State 1933–1945* (Oxford, 1993 [1987]); Ludolf Herbst, *Das nationalsozialistische Deutschland 1933–1945* (Frankfurt am Main, 1996). Among many other shorter accounts, Hans-Ulrich Thamer, *Verführung und Gewalt: Deutschland 1933–1945* (Berlin, 1986) is a smooth synthesis; Jost Dülffer, *Nazi Germany 1933–1945: Faith and Annihilation* (London, 1996 [1992]), and Bernd-Jürgen Wendt, *Deutschland 1933–1945: Das Dritte Reich. Handbuch zur Geschichte* (Hanover, 1995) are useful, crisp introductions.

3. Detlev J. K. Peukert, *Volksgenossen und Gemeinschaftsfremde – Anpassung, Ausmerze, Aufbegehren unter dem Nationalsozialismus* (Cologne, 1982); English edn., *Inside Nazi Germany: Conformity, Opposition and Racism in Everyday Life* (London, 1989).

4. Jeremy Noakes and Geoffrey Pridham (eds.), *Nazism 1919–1945* (4 vols., Exeter, 1983–98 [1974]).

5. William L. Shirer, *The Rise and Fall of the Third Reich: A History of Nazi Germany* (New York, 1960); Klaus Epstein's review is in *Review of Politics*, 23 (1961), 130–45.

6. Karl Dietrich Bracher, *The German Dictatorship: The Origins, Structure, and Consequences of National Socialism* (New York, 1970 [1969]).

7. Ian Kershaw, *Hitler*, I: *1889–1936: Hubris* (London, 1998); idem, *Hitler*, II: *1936–1945: Nemesis* (London, 2000).

8. Michael Burleigh, *The Third Reich: A New History* (London, 2000).

9. I am thinking here of works like Orlando Figes, *A People's Tragedy: The Russian Revolution 1891–1924* (London, 1996), or Margaret Macmillan, *Peacemakers: The Paris Conference of 1919 and its Attempt to End War* (London, 2001).

10. Starting with Martin Broszat's *Der Staat Hitlers: Grundlegung und Entwicklung seiner inneren Verfassung* (Munich, 1969), another book which bears repeated

rereading, and represented above all by Hans Mommsen's brilliant essays, collected in his *Der Nationalsozialismus und die deutsche Gesellschaft: Ausgewählte Aufsätze* (Reinbek, 1991) and *From Weimar to Auschwitz: Essays in German History* (Princeton, 1991).

11. This follows and carries further the technique already used in my earlier books *Death in Hamburg: Society and Politics in the Cholera Years 1830–1910* (Oxford, 1987) and *Rituals of Retribution: Capital Punishment in Germany 1600–1987* (Oxford, 1996).

12. Karl Marx, *The Eighteenth Brumaire of Louis Bonaparte* (1852), in Lewis Feuer (ed.), *Marx and Engels: Basic Writings on Politics and Philosophy* (New York, 1959), 360.

13. L. P. Hartley, *The Go-Between* (London, 1953), preface.

14. See Richard J. Evans, 'History, Memory, and the Law: The Historian as Expert Witness', *History and Theory*, 41 (2002) 277–96; and Henry Rousso, *The Haunting Past: History, Memory, and Justice in Contemporary France* (Philadelphia, 2002 [1998]).

15. Ian Kershaw, *Popular Opinion and Political Dissent in the Third Reich: Bavaria 1933–1945* (Oxford, 1983), vii.

16. Konrad Heiden, *Geschichte des Nationalsozialismus: Die Karriere einer Idee* (Berlin, 1932); idem, *Adolf Hitler: Das Zeitalter der Verantwortungslosigkeit. Eine Biographie* (Zürich, 1936); Ernst Fraenkel, *The Dual State* (New York, 1941); Franz Neumann, *Behemoth: The Structure and Practice of National Socialism* (New York, 1942).

17. Friedrich Meinecke, *Die deutsche Katastrophe* (Wiesbaden, 1946), available in a comically literal English translation by Sidney B. Fay, *The German Catastrophe: Reflections and Recollections* (Cambridge, Mass., 1950). For a highly critical discussion, see Imanuel Geiss, 'Kritischer Rückblick auf Friedrich Meinecke', in idem, *Studien über Geschichte und Geschichtswissenschaft* (Frankfurt am Main, 1972), 89–107. For a defence, see Wolfgang Wippermann, 'Friedrich Meineckes "Die deutsche Katastrophe": Ein versuch zur deutschen Vergangenheitsbewältigung', in Michael Erbe (ed.), *Friedrich Meinecke heute: Bericht über ein Gedenk-Colloquium zu seinem 25. Todestag am 5. und 6. April 1979* (Berlin, 1981), 101–21.

18. Thus the catalogue of questions posed at the outset of Karl Dietrich Bracher's classic *Stufen der Machtergreifung*, volume I of Karl Dietrich Bracher et al., *Die nationalsozialistische Machtergreifung: Studien zur Errichtung des totalitären Herrschaftssystems in Deutschland 1933/34* (Frankfurt am Main, 1974 [1960]), 17–18.

19. Among many good discussions of the historiography of Nazism and the Third Reich, see especially the brief survey by Jane Caplan, 'The Historiography of National Socialism', in Michael Bentley (ed.), *Companion to Historiography* (London, 1997), 545–90, and the longer study by Ian Kershaw, *The Nazi Dictatorship: Problems and Perspectives of Interpretation* (4th edn., London, 2000 [1985]).

20. Mark Mazower, *Dark Continent: Europe's Twentieth Century* (London, 1998).

21. For a good survey of Marxist interpretations, placed in their contemporary political context, see Pierre Ayçoberry, *The Nazi Question: An Essay on the Interpretations of National Socialism (1922–1975)* (New York, 1981 [1979]).

22. For East German work, see the discussion in Andreas Dorpalen, *German History in Marxist Perspective: The East German Approach* (Detroit, 1988). There is a representative selection, with a judicious commentary, in Georg G. Iggers (ed.), *Marxist Historiography in Transformation: New Orientations in Recent East German History* (Oxford, 1992). One of the finest and subtlest of Marxist historians of the Third Reich was Tim Mason: see in particular his *Nazism, Fascism and the Working Class: Essays by Tim Mason* (ed. Jane Caplan, Cambridge, 1995) and *Social Policy in the Third Reich: The Working Class and the 'National Community'* (ed. Jane Caplan, Providence, RI, 1993 [1977]).

23. Shirer, *The Rise and Fall*; Alan J. P. Taylor, *The Course of German History* (London, 1945); Edmond Vermeil, *Germany in the Twentieth Century* (New York, 1956).

24. Ayçoberry, *The Nazi Question*, 3–15.

25. Rohan d'Olier Butler, *The Roots of National Socialism 1783–1933* (London, 1941), is the classic example of such wartime propaganda; another was Fossey J. C. Hearnshaw, *Germany the Aggressor throughout the Ages* (London, 1940). For an intelligent contemporary response, see Harold Laski, *The Germans – are they Human?* (London, 1941).

26. For a general discussion of these issues, see Richard J. Evans, *Rethinking German History: Nineteenth-Century Germany and the Origins of the Third Reich* (London, 1987), esp. 1–54. There is an excellent brief collection of documents, with commentary, in John C. G. Röhl (ed.), *From Bismarck to Hitler: The Problem of Continuity in German History* (London, 1970). When I was an undergraduate, I was introduced to these controversies by the handy compendium of excerpts in John L. Snell (ed.), *The Nazi Revolution – Germany's Guilt or Germany's Fate?* (Boston, 1959).

27. This applies even to the relatively sophisticated writings of Germans exiled by the Third Reich, such as Hans Kohn, especially *The Mind of Germany: The Education of a Nation* (London, 1961), and Peter Viereck, *Metapolitics: From the Romantics to Hitler* (New York, 1941).

28. Keith Bullivant, 'Thomas Mann and Politics in the Weimar Republic', in idem (ed.), *Culture and Society in the Weimar Republic* (Manchester, 1977), 24–38; Taylor, *The Course*, 92–3.

29. Gerhard Ritter, 'The Historical Foundations of the Rise of National-Socialism', in Maurice Beaumont *et al.*, *The Third Reich: A Study Published under the Auspices of the International Council for Philosophy and Humanistic Studies with the Assistance of UNESCO* (New York, 1955), 381–416; idem, *Europa und die deutsche Frage: Betrachtungen über die geschichtliche Eigenart des deutschen Staatsgedankens* (Munich, 1948); Christoph Cornelissen, *Gerhard Ritter: Geschichtswissenschaft und Politik im 20. Jahrhundert* (Düsseldorf, 2001); Ritter's

arguments can be dated back to 1937, when they were framed in rather less negative terms (ibid., 524–30). For a variety of other views, see Hans Kohn (ed.), *German History: Some New German Views* (Boston, 1954). An early, but only partially successful attempt by a German historian to break the mould was Ludwig Dehio, *Germany and World Politics* (London, 1959 [1955]), which still emphasized the primacy of international factors.

30. See, among many other treatments of the topic, Karl Dietrich Bracher, *Die totalitäre Erfahrung* (Munich, 1987) and Leonard Shapiro, *Totalitarianism* (London, 1972). The classic, much-criticized exposition of the basic theory is by Carl J. Friedrich and Zbigniew K. Brzezinski, *Totalitarian Dictatorship and Autocracy* (New York, 1963), the pioneering philosophical text by Hannah Arendt, *The Origins of Totalitarianism* (New York, 1958).

31. Eckard Jesse (ed.), *Totalitarismus im 20. Jahrhundert* (Baden-Baden, 1996) and Alfons Söllner (ed.), *Totalitarismus: Eine Ideengeschichte des 20. Jahrhunderts* (Berlin, 1997).

32. See in particular the fruitful comparisons in Ian Kershaw and Moshe Lewin (eds.), *Stalinism and Nazism: Dictatorships in Comparison* (Cambridge, 1997), and the useful and well-informed discussion in Kershaw, *The Nazi Dictatorship*, 20–46.

33. Jürgen Steinle, 'Hitler als "Betriebsunfall in der Geschichte"', *Geschichte in Wissenschaft und Unterricht*, 45 (1994), 288–302, for an analysis of this argument.

34. Karl Dietrich Bracher, *Die Auflösung der Weimarer Republik: Eine Studie zum Problem des Machtverfalls in der Demokratie* (3rd edn., Villingen, 1960 [1955]); idem, *et al.*, *Die nationalsozialistische Machtergreifung*.

35. Broszat, *Der Staat Hitlers*; idem, *et al.* (eds.), *Bayern in der NS-Zeit* (6 vols., Munich, 1977–83); Peukert, *Inside Nazi Germany*; see also the useful commentary on the development of research in the latest German edition of Norbert Frei's brief history, *Der Führerstaat: Nationalsozialistische Herrschaft 1933 bis 1945* (Munich, 2001 [1987]), 281–304. Recent attempts to delegitimize Broszat's work on the grounds that, like other German historians of his generation, he had belonged to the Hitler Youth in adolescence, and with many others had been enrolled as a member of the Nazi Party (though without his knowledge), fail to convince not least because they fail to address what he actually wrote as a historian (Nicolas Berg, *Der Holocaust und die westdeutschen Historiker: Erforschung und Erinnerung* (Cologne, 2003), esp. 613–15).

36. Amongst many studies and collections, see, for example, Robert Gellately and Nathan Stoltzfus (eds.), *Social Outsiders in Nazi Germany* (Princeton, 2001); Michael Burleigh and Wolfgang Wippermann, *The Racial State: Germany 1933–1945* (Cambridge, 1991); Henry Friedlander, *The Origins of Nazi Genocide: From Euthanasia to the Final Solution* (Chapel Hill, NC, 1995); Wolfgang Ayass, *'Asoziale' im Nationalsozialismus* (Stuttgart, 1995); Peter Longerich, *Politik der Vernichtung: Eine Gesamtdarstellung der nationalsozialistischen Judenverfolgung* (Munich, 1998); Ulrich Herbert, *Hitler's Foreign Workers: Enforced Foreign Labor in Germany under the Third Reich* (Cambridge, 1997 [1985]).

37. Richard J. Evans, *In Hitler's Shadow: West German Historians and the Attempt to Escape from the Nazi Past* (New York, 1989); idem, *Rituals*.

38. Richard J. Evans, *Telling Lies About Hitler: The Holocaust, History, and the David Irving Trial* (London, 2002).

39. Peter Longerich, *Der ungeschriebene Befehl: Hitler und der Weg zur 'Endlösung'* (Munich, 2001), 9–20.

40. Victor Klemperer, *LTI: Notizbuch eines Philologen* (Leipzig, 1985 [1946]).

Chapter 1 THE LEGACY OF THE PAST

1. Continuities between the Bismarckian Reich and the coming of the Third Reich form the central thesis of Hans-Ulrich Wehler, *Deutsche Gesellschaftsgeschichte*, III: *Von der 'Deutschen Doppelrevolution' bis zum Beginn des Ersten Weltkrieges 1849–1914* (Munich, 1995), and Heinrich August Winkler, *Der lange Weg nach Westen*, I: *Deutsche Geschichte vom Ende des Alten Reiches bis zum Untergang der Weimarer Republik* (Munich, 2000).

2. Friedrich Meinecke, 'Bismarck und das neue Deutschland', in idem, *Preussen und Deutschland im 19. und 20. Jahrhundert* (Munich, 1918), 510–31, quoted and translated in Edgar Feuchtwanger, *Bismarck* (London, 2002), 7.

3. Elizabeth Knowles (ed.), *The Oxford Dictionary of Quotations* (5th edn., Oxford, 1999), 116.

4. Quoted without attribution in Alan J. P. Taylor, *Bismarck: The Man and the Statesman* (London, 1955), 115.

5. For a good brief overview of this and the following period, see David Blackbourn, *The Fontana History of Germany 1780–1918: The Long Nineteenth Century* (London, 1997); more detail in James J. Sheehan, *German History 1770–1866* (Oxford, 1989); more still in Thomas Nipperdey, *Germany from Napoleon to Bismarck* (Princeton, 1986 [1983]), and even more in Hans-Ulrich Wehler, *Deutsche Gesellschaftsgeschichte*, II: *Von der Reformära bis zur industriellen und politischen 'Deutschen Doppelrevolution' 1815–1845/49* (Munich, 1987).

6. Taylor, *The Course*, 69.

7. For the debate on this issue, see in particular Geoff Eley, *From Unification to Nazism: Reinterpreting the German Past* (London, 1986), 254–82; David Blackbourn and Geoff Eley, *The Peculiarities of German History: Bourgeois Society and Politics in Nineteenth-Century Germany* (Oxford, 1984); Evans, *Rethinking German History*, 93–122; Richard J. Evans (ed.), *Society and Politics in Wilhelmine Germany* (London, 1978); Jürgen Kocka, 'German History Before Hitler: The Debate about the German *Sonderweg*', *Journal of Contemporary History*, 23 (1988), 3–16; Robert G. Moeller, 'The Kaiserreich Recast? Continuity and Change in Modern German Historiography', *Journal of Social History*, 17 (1984), 655–83.

8. Bismarck has been well served by his biographers. For the best two in narrative

form, see Ernst Engelberg, *Bismarck* (2 vols., Berlin, 1985 and 1990) and Otto Pflanze, *Bismarck* (3 vols., Princeton, 1990).

9. Heinrich August Winkler, *Der lange Weg nach Westen*, II: *Deutsche Geschichte vom 'Dritten Reich' bis zur Wiedervereinigung* (Munich, 2000), 645–8.

10. Heinrich August Winkler, *The Long Shadow of the Reich: Weighing up German History* (The 2001 Annual Lecture of the German Historical Institute, London; London, 2002). Lothar Kettenacker, 'Der Mythos vom Reich', in Karl H. Bohrer (ed.), *Mythos und Moderne* (Frankfurt am Main, 1983), 262–89.

11. Karl Marx, 'Randglossen zum Programm der deutschen Arbeiterpartei' (Kritik des Gothaer Programms, 1875), in Karl Marx, Friedrich Engels, *Ausgewählte Schriften* (2 vols., East Berlin, 1968), II. 11–28, at 25.

12. Otto Büsch, *Militärsystem und Sozialleben im alten Preussen 1713–1807: Die Anfänge der sozialen Militarisierung der preussisch-deutschen Gesellschaft* (Berlin, 1962).

13. Horst Kohl (ed.), *Die politischen Reden des Fürsten Bismarck* (14 vols., Stuttgart, 1892–1905), II. 29–30.

14. Lothar Gall, *Bismarck: The White Revolutionary* (2 vols., London, 1986 [1980]), the outstanding analytical study of Bismarck.

15. For the history of conscription, see Ute Frevert, *Die kasernierte Nation: Militärdienst und Zivilgesellschaft in Deutschland* (Munich, 2001); German militarism in a wider context is covered by Volker R. Berghahn, *Militarism: The History of an International Debate 1861–1979* (Cambridge, 1984 [1981]), idem (ed.), *Militarismus* (Cologne, 1975), Martin Kitchen, *A Military History of Germany from the Eighteenth Century to the Present Day* (London, 1975) and Gordon A. Craig's classic *The Politics of the Prussian Army 1640–1945* (New York, 1964 [1955]); unconventional reflections in Geoff Eley, 'Army, State and Civil Society: Revisiting the Problem of German Militarism', in idem, *From Unification to Nazism*, 85–109.

16. Martin Kitchen, *The German Officer Corps 1890–1914* (Oxford, 1968); Karl Demeter, *Das deutsche Offizierkorps in Gesellschaft und Staat 1650–1945* (Frankfurt am Main, 1962). For the permanent threat of a *coup d'état*, see Volker R. Berghahn, *Germany and the Approach of War in 1914* (London, 1973), 13–15.

17. See Richard J. Evans, *Rethinking German History*, 248–90; idem, *Rereading German History: From Unification to Reunification 1800–1996* (London, 1997), 65–86.

18. Ute Frevert, 'Bourgeois Honour: Middle-class Duellists in Germany from the Late Eighteenth to the Early Twentieth Century', in David Blackbourn and Richard J. Evans (eds.), *The German Bourgeoisie: Essays on the Social History of the German Middle Class from the Late Eighteenth to the Early Twentieth Century* (London, 1991), 255–92; eadem, *Ehrenmänner: Das Duell in der bürgerlichen Gesellschaft* (Munich, 1991).

19. Eley, *From Unification to Nazism*, 85–109; Wehler, *Deutsche Gesellschaftsgeschichte*, III. 873–85.

20. Michael Geyer, 'Die Geschichte des deutschen Militärs von 1860–1956: Ein Bericht über die Forschungslage (1945–1975)', in Hans-Ulrich Wehler (ed.), *Die moderne deutsche Geschichte in der internationalen Forschung 1945–1975* (Göttingen, 1978), 256–86; Helmut Bley, *Namibia under German Rule* (Hamburg, 1996 [1968]).

21. Gesine Krüger, *Kriegsbewältigung und Geschichtsbewusstsein: Realität, Deutung und Verarbeitung des deutschen Kolonialkrieges in Namibia 1904 bis 1907* (Göttingen, 1999); Tilman Dedering, ' "A Certain Rigorous Treatment of all Parts of the Nation": The Annihilation of the Herero in German Southwest Africa 1904', in Mark Levene and Penny Roberts (eds.), *The Massacre in History* (New York, 1999), 205–22.

22. David Schoenbaum, *Zabern 1913: Consensus Politics in Imperial Germany* (London, 1982); Nicholas Stargardt, *The German Idea of Militarism 1866–1914* (Cambridge, 1994); Wehler, *Deutsche Gesellschaftsgeschichte* III. 1125–9.

23. Ulrich von Hassell, *Die Hassell-Tagebücher 1938–1944* (ed. Friedrich Freiherr Hiller von Gaertringen, Berlin, 1989), 436.

24. Wolfgang J. Mommsen, *Das Ringen um den nationalen Staat: Die Gründung und der innere Ausbau des Deutschen Reiches unter Otto von Bismarck 1850–1890* (Berlin, 1993), 439–40; David Blackbourn, *Marpingen: Apparitions of the Virgin Mary in Bismarckian Germany* (Oxford, 1993).

25. Vernon Lidtke, *The Outlawed Party: Social Democracy in Germany, 1878–1890* (Princeton, 1966); Evans, *Rituals*, 351–72.

26. Among many accounts of the Social Democrats' evolution, see Susanne Miller and Heinrich Potthoff, *A History of German Social Democracy: From 1848 to the Present* (Leamington Spa, 1986 [1983]), a useful introductory text from the point of view of the present-day German Social Democrats; Detlef Lehnert, *Sozialdemokratie zwischen Protestbewegung und Regierungspartei 1848–1983* (Frankfurt am Main, 1983), a good brief account; and Stefan Berger, *Social Democracy and the Working Class in Nineteenth- and Twentieth-century Germany* (London, 2000), a more recent survey.

27. Alex Hall, *Scandal, Sensation and Social Democracy: The SPD Press and Wilhelmine Germany 1890–1914* (Cambridge, 1977); Klaus Saul, 'Der Staat und die "Mächte des Umsturzes": Ein Beitrag zu den Methoden antisozialistischer Repression und Agitation vom Scheitern des Sozialistengesetzes bis zur Jahrhundertwende', *Archiv für Sozialgeschichte*, 12 (1972), 293–350; Alex Hall, 'By Other Means: The Legal Struggle against the SPD in Wilhelmine Germany 1890–1900', *Historical Journal*, 17 (1974), 365–86.

28. A convenient brief summary can be found in Gerhard A. Ritter, *Die deutschen Parteien 1830–1914: Parteien und Gesellschaft im konstitutionellen Regierungssystem* (Göttingen, 1985); the classic article on the subject is by M. Rainer Lepsius, 'Parteisystem und Sozialstruktur: Zum Problem der Demokratisierung der deutschen Gesellschaft', in Gerhard A. Ritter (ed.), *Die deutschen Parteien vor 1918* (Cologne, 1973), 56–80.

29. Gerhard A. Ritter, *Wahlgeschichtliches Arbeitsbuch: Materialien zur Statistik des Kaiserreichs 1871–1918* (Munich, 1980), 42.

30. Stanley Suval, *Electoral Politics in Wilhelmine Germany* (Chapel Hill, NC, 1985); Margaret L. Anderson, *Practicing Democracy: Elections and Political Culture in Imperial Germany* (Princeton, 2000).

31. Kurt Koszyk, *Deutsche Presse im 19. Jahrhundert: Geschichte der deutschen Presse*, II (Berlin, 1966).

32. Richard J. Evans (ed.), *Kneipengespräche im Kaiserreich: Die Stimmungsberichte der Hamburger Politischen Polizei 1892–1914* (Reinbek, 1989).

33. Brief introductory survey in Wehler, *Deutsche Gesellschaftsgeschichte*, III. 961–5; more detail in William W. Hagen, *Germans, Poles, and Jews: The Nationality Conflict in the Prussian East, 1772–1914* (Chicago, 1980).

34. Evans (ed.), *Kneipengespräche*, 361–83.

35. Volker R. Berghahn, *Der Tirpitz-Plan: Genesis und Verfall einer innenpolitischen Krisenstrategie unter Wilhelm II.* (Düsseldorf, 1971).

36. For a recent, judicious assessment of the Kaiser's personality and influence, see Christopher Clark, *Kaiser Wilhelm II* (London, 2000).

37. Geoffrey Hosking, *Russia: People and Empire 1552–1917* (London, 1997).

38. George L. Mosse, *The Nationalization of the Masses: Political Symbolism and Mass Movements in Germany from the Napoleonic Wars through the Third Reich* (New York, 1975).

39. Alan Milward and Samuel B. Saul, *The Development of the Economies of Continental Europe 1850–1914* (London, 1977), 19–20.

40. See, in general, Hubert Kiesewetter, *Industrielle Revolution in Deutschland 1815–1914* (Frankfurt am Main, 1989).

41. Volker Ullrich, *Die nervöse Grossmacht 1871–1918: Aufstieg und Untergang des deutschen Kaiserreichs* (Frankfurt am Main, 1997); Joachim Radkau, *Das Zeitalter der Nervosität: Deutschland zwischen Bismarck und Hitler* (Munich, 1998).

42. August Nitschke *et al.* (eds.), *Jahrhundertwende: Der Aufbruch in die Moderne 1880–1930* (2 vols., Reinbek, 1990).

43. For these arguments, see Blackbourn and Eley, *The Peculiarities*.

44. Peter Pulzer, *The Rise of Political Anti-Semitism in Germany and Austria* (New York, 1964), 112–13; Rosemarie Leuschen-Seppel, *Sozialdemokratie und Antisemitismus im Kaiserreich: Die Auseinandersetzung der Partei mit den konservativen und völkischen Strömungen des Antisemitismus 1871–1914* (Bonn, 1978), 140–42; Richard S. Levy, *The Downfall of the Anti-Semitic Political Parties in Imperial Germany* (New Haven, 1975). See also the pioneering work of Paul W. Massing, *Rehearsal for Destruction* (New York, 1949).

45. I adopt here Marion Kaplan's useful distinction between *assimilation*, involving a complete loss of cultural identity, and *acculturation*, involving the creation of a dual identity of one kind or another in a multicultural milieu: see Marion A. Kaplan, 'The Acculturation, Assimilation, and Integration of Jews in Imperial Germany', *Year Book of the Leo Baeck Institute*, 27 (1982), 3–35.

46. Till van Rahden, *Juden und andere Breslauer: Die Beziehungen zwischen Juden, Protestanten und Katholiken in einer deutschen Grossstadt von 1860 bis 1925* (Göttingen, 2000), 147–9; Peter J.G. Pulzer, *Jews and the German State: The Political History of a Minority, 1848–1933* (Oxford, 1992), 6–7; Shulamit Volkov, *Die Juden in Deutschland 1780–1918* (Munich, 1994); Usiel O. Schmelz, 'Die demographische Entwicklung der Juden in Deutschland von der Mitte des 19. Jahrhunderts bis 1933', *Bulletin des Leo Baeck Instituts*, 83 (1989), 15–62, at 39–41; Jacob Toury, *Soziale und politische Geschichte der Juden in Deutschland 1847–1871: Zwischen Revolution, Reaktion und Emanzipation* (Düsseldorf, 1977), 60; Monika Richarz, *Jüdisches Leben in Deutschland*, II: *Selbstzeugnisse zur Sozialgeschichte im Kaiserreich* (Stuttgart, 1979), 16–17; Anthony Kauders, *German Politics and the Jews: Düsseldorf and Nuremberg 1910–1933* (Oxford, 1996), 26; Kerstin Meiring, *Die christlich–jüdische Mischehe in Deutschland, 1840–1933* (Hamburg, 1998).

47. Pulzer, *Jews*, 106–20.

48. Dietz Bering, *The Stigma of Names: Antisemitism in German Daily Life, 1812–1933* (Cambridge, 1992 [1987]).

49. Pulzer, *Jews*, 5, 11.

50. Niall Ferguson, *The World's Banker: The History of the House of Rothschild* (London, 1998); Fritz Stern, *Gold and Iron: Bismarck, Bleichröder and the Building of the German Empire* (New York, 1977).

51. Robert Gellately, *The Politics of Economic Despair: Shopkeepers and German Politics, 1890–1914* (London, 1974), 42–3; Richarz, *Jüdisches Leben*, II. 17, 23–35.

52. Ibid., 31–4.

53. Peter Pulzer, 'Jews and Nation-Building in Germany 1815–1918', *Year Book of the Leo Baeck Institute*, 41 (1996), 199–214.

54. See, in particular, Werner E. Mosse, *Jews in the German Economy: The German-Jewish Economic Élite 1820–1935* (Oxford, 1987), and idem, *The German-Jewish Economic Élite 1820–1935: A Socio-Cultural Profile* (Oxford, 1989), not only fine works of scholarship but also nostalgic celebrations of the achievements of the social group into which Mosse himself was born.

55. Pulzer, *The Rise*, 94–101, 113; Shulamit Volkov, *Jüdisches Leben und Antisemitismus im 19. und 20. Jahrhundert* (Munich, 1990).

56. For Böckel and the antisemitic movement more generally, see David Peal, 'Antisemitism by Other Means? The Rural Cooperative Movement in Late 19th Century Germany', in Herbert A. Strauss (ed.), *Hostages of Modernization: Studies on Modern Antisemitism 1870–1933/39: Germany – Great Britain – France* (Berlin, 1993), 128–49; James N. Retallack, *Notables of the Right: The Conservative Party and Political Mobilization in Germany, 1876–1918* (London, 1988), esp. 91–9; Hans-Jürgen Puhle, *Agrarische Interessenpolitik und preussischer Konservatismus im wilhelminischen Reich 1893–1914: Ein Beitrag zur Analyse des Nationalismus in Deutschland am Beispiel des Bundes der Landwirte und der Deutsch-Konservativen Partei* (Hanover, 1967) esp. 111–40.

57. Pulzer, *The Rise*, 53–5, 116; Wehler, *Deutsche Gesellschaftsgeschichte*, III. 924–34; Thomas Nipperdey, *Deutsche Geschichte 1866–1918*, II: *Machtstaat vor der Demokratie* (Munich, 1992), 289–311.

58. Jacob Katz, *From Prejudice to Destruction: Anti-Semitism, 1700–1933* (Cambridge, Mass. 1980), is a classic general survey. For Catholic antisemitism in Germany, see Olaf Blaschke, *Katholizismus und Antisemitismus im Deutschen Kaiserreich* (Göttingen, 1997); Helmut Walser Smith, 'The Learned and the Popular Discourse of Anti-Semitism in the Catholic Milieu in the Kaiserreich', *Central European History*, 27 (1994), 315–28. Werner Jochmann, *Gesellschaftskrise und Judenfeindschaft in Deutschland 1870–1945* (Hamburg, 1988), has a good introductory chapter, 30–98. James F. Harris, *The People Speak! Anti-Semitism and Emancipation in Nineteenth-Century Bavaria* (Ann Arbor, 1994), dismisses socioeconomic factors too easily; the history of antisemitism cannot be reduced to the otherwise unexplained influence of a free-floating discourse.

59. Wilhelm Marr, *Vom jüdischen Kriegsschauplatz: Eine Streitschrift* (Berne, 1879), 19, cited in Pulzer, *The Rise*, 50; see also Marr's pamphlet *Der Sieg des Judenthums über das Germanenthum vom nicht konfessionellen Standpunkt aus betrachtet* (Berlin, 1873).

60. Moshe Zimmermann, *Wilhelm Marr: The Patriarch of Anti-Semitism* (New York, 1986), 89, 150–51, 154; Daniela Kasischke-Wurm, *Antisemitismus im Spiegel der Hamburger Presse während des Kaiserreichs (1884–1914)* (Hamburg, 1997), 240–46.

61. Ibid., 77.

62. Wehler, *Deutsche Gesellschaftsgeschichte*, III. 925–9.

63. Evans (ed.), *Kneipengespräche*, 317.

64. Ibid., 313–21.

65. Leuschen-Seppel, *Sozialdemokratie*, esp. 36, 96, 100, 153, 171; Evans (ed.), *Kneipengespräche*, 302–6, 318–19. These points, made in response to the sweeping claims of Daniel J. Goldhagen, *Hitler's Willing Executioners: Ordinary Germans and the Holocaust* (New York, 1996), can be followed at greater length in Evans, *Rereading*, 119–44.

66. Stefan Scheil, *Die Entwicklung des politischen Antisemitismus in Deutschland zwischen 1881 und 1912: Eine wahlgeschichtliche Untersuchung* (Berlin, 1999).

67. See in particular Harris, *The People Speak!*, and Helmut Walser Smith, *The Butcher's Tale: Murder and Anti-Semitism in a German Town* (New York, 2002) (which has excellent detail, but exaggerates the significance of a 'ritual murder' accusation in an obscure small town in the Prussian far east). See also Christoph Nonn, *Eine Stadt sucht einen Mörder: Gerücht, Gewalt und Antisemitismus im Kaiserreich* (Göttingen, 2002). For hostile press reactions to an earlier ritual murder accusation, see Kasischke-Wurm, *Antisemitismus*, 175–82.

68. Evidence in David Kertzer, *Unholy War: The Vatican's Role in the Rise of Modern Anti-Semitism* (London, 2001), though the author's claims for the significance of this material are too sweeping. For social and cultural studies of

Catholic antisemitism in Germany, which leave no doubt about its pervasiveness, see Blaschke, *Katholizismus und Antisemitismus*; Michael Langer, *Zwischen Vorurteil und Aggression: Zum Judenbild in der deutschsprachigen katholischen Volksbildung des 19. Jahrhunderts* (Freiburg, 1994); Walter Zwi Bacharach, *Anti-Jewish Prejudices in German-Catholic Sermons* (Lewiston, Pa., 1993); David Blackbourn, 'Roman Catholics, the Centre Party and Anti-Semitism in Imperial Germany', in Paul Kennedy and Anthony Nicholls (eds.), *Nationalist and Racialist Movements in Britain and Germany before 1914* (London, 1981), 106–29; and, for the international comparative dimension, Olaf Blaschke and Aram Mattioli (eds.), *Katholischer Antisemitismus im 19. Jahrhundert: Ursachen und Traditionen im internationalen Vergleich* (Zurich, 2000). For peasant protest and antisemitism in the Catholic community, see Ian Farr, 'Populism in the Countryside: The Peasant Leagues in Bavaria in the 1890s', in Evans (ed.), *Society and Politics*, 136–59.

69. See, for example, Norbert Kampe, *Studenten und 'Judenfrage' im deutschen Kaiserreich: Die Entstehung einer akademischen Trägerschicht des Antisemitismus* (Göttingen, 1988).

70. Stephen Wilson, *Ideology and Experience: Antisemitism in France at the Time of the Dreyfus Affair* (New York, 1982 [1980]); John D. Klier and Shlomo Lambroza (eds.) *Pogroms: Anti-Jewish Violence in Modern Russian History* (Cambridge, 1992).

71. David Blackbourn, *Populists and Patricians: Essays in Modern German History* (London, 1987), 217–45 ('The Politics of Demagogy in Imperial Germany').

72. Julius Langbehn, *Rembrandt als Erzieher* (38th edn., Leipzig, 1891 [1890]), 292; idem, *Der Rembrandtdeutsche: Von einem Wahrheitsfreund* (Dresden, 1892), 184, both quoted in Pulzer, *The Rise*, 242; see also Fritz Stern, *The Politics of Cultural Despair: A Study in the Rise of the German Ideology* (New York, 1961).

73. Lessing's play, first published in 1779, was a plea for religious toleration, especially of the Jews. For the quote, see Cosima Wagner, *Die Tagebücher* (ed. Martin Gregor-Dellin and Dietrich Mack, Munich, 1977), II. 852 (18 Dec. 1881); also 159, 309; Jacob Katz, *The Darker Side of Genius: Richard Wagner's Anti-Semitism* (Hanover, 1986), is a sane guide through this controversial subject.

74. George L. Mosse, *The Crisis of German Ideology: Intellectual Origins of the Third Reich* (London, 1964), 88–107; Annette Hein, *'Es ist viel "Hitler" in Wagner': Rassismus und antisemitische Deutschtumsideologie in den 'Bayreuther Blätter' (1878–1938)* (Tübingen, 1996).

75. Winfried Schüler, *Der Bayreuther Kreis von seiner Entstehung bis zum Ausgang der wilhelminischen Ära* (Münster, 1971); Andrea Mork, *Richard Wagner als politischer Schriftsteller: Weltanschauung und Wirkungsgeschichte* (Frankfurt am Main, 1990); Houston Stewart Chamberlain, *Die Grundlagen des XIX. Jahrhunderts* (2 vols., Munich, 1899); Geoffrey G. Field, *Evangelist of Race: The Germanic Vision of Houston Stewart Chamberlain* (New York, 1981).

76. Ludwig Woltmann, *Politische Anthropologie* (ed. Otto Reche, Leipzig, 1936 [1900]), 16–17, 267, quoted in Mosse, *The Crisis*, 100–102.

77. Woodruff D. Smith, *The Ideological Origins of Nazi Imperialism* (New York, 1986), 83–111; also Karl Lange, 'Der Terminus "Lebensraum" in Hitlers *Mein Kampf*', *Vierteljahrshefte für Zeitgeschichte* (hereinafter *VfZ*) 13 (1965), 426–37.

78. Paul Crook, *Darwinism, War and History: The Debate Over the Biology of War from the 'Origin of Species' to the First World War* (Cambridge, 1994), esp. 30, 83; Imanuel Geiss (ed.), *July 1914: The Outbreak of the First World War. Selected Documents* (London, 1967), 22; Holger Afflerbach, *Falkenhayn: Politisches Denken und Handeln im Kaiserreich* (Munich, 1994); see Evans, *Rereading*, 119–44, for a general consideration of the history and historiography of German Social Darwinism.

79. See, in general, Paul Weindling, *Health, Race and German Politics between National Unification and Nazism 1870–1945* (Cambridge, 1989), and Peter Weingart *et al.*, *Rasse, Blut und Gene: Geschichte der Eugenik und Rassenhygiene in Deutschland* (Frankfurt am Main, 1992 [1988]).

80. Sheila F. Weiss, *Race Hygiene and National Efficiency: The Eugenics of Wilhelm Schallmayer* (Berkeley, 1987); Evans, *Rituals*, 438; Roger Chickering, *Imperial Germany and a World Without War: The Peace Movement and German Society, 1892–1914* (Princeton, 1975), 125–9.

81. The pioneering article by Jeremy Noakes, 'Nazism and Eugenics: The Background to the Nazi Sterilization Law of 14 July 1933', in Roger Bullen *et al.* (eds.), *Ideas into Politics: Aspects of European History 1880–1950* (London, 1984), 75–94, is still an indispensable guide to these various thinkers.

82. Karl Heinz Roth, 'Schein-Alternativen im Gesundheitswesen: Alfred Grotjahn (1869–1931) – Integrationsfigur etablierter Sozialmedizin und nationalsozialistischer "Rassenhygiene"', in Karl Heinz Roth (ed.), *Erfassung zur Vernichtung: Von der Sozialhygiene zum 'Gesetz über Sterbehilfe'* (Berlin, 1984), 31–56; more generally, Sheila Weiss, 'The Race Hygiene Movement in Germany', in Mark B. Adams (ed.), *The Wellborn Science: Eugenics in Germany, France, Brazil, and Russia* (New York, 1990), 8–68.

83. His actual name was Adolf Lanz, but he called himself Jörg Lanz von Liebenfels for effect. Hans-Walter Schmuhl, *Rassenhygiene, Nationalsozialismus, Euthanasie: Von der Verhütung zur Vernichtung 'lebensunwerten Lebens', 1890–1945* (Göttingen, 1987); Wilfried Daim, *Der Mann, der Hitler die Ideen gab: Die sektiererischen Grundlagen des Nationalsozialismus* (Vienna, 1985 [1958]).

84. Weiss, 'The Race Hygiene Movement', 9–11.

85. Max Weber, 'Der Nationalstaat und die Volkswirtschaftpolitik', in idem, *Gesammelte politische Schriften* (ed. J. Winckelmann, 3rd edn., Tübingen, 1971), 23.

86. Richard Hinton Thomas, *Nietzsche in German Politics and Society 1890–1918* (Manchester, 1983), esp. 80–95. For a recent attempt to assess Nietzsche's work in this general context, see Bernhard H. F. Taureck, *Nietzsche und der Faschismus: Ein Politikum* (Leipzig, 2000).

87. Steven E. Aschheim, *The Nietzsche Legacy in Germany 1890–1990* (Berkeley, 1992).

88. Mosse, *The Crisis*, 204–7; Walter Laqueur, *Young Germany: A History of the German Youth Movement* (London, 1962); Jürgen Reulecke, '*Ich möchte einer werden so wie die . . .*' *Männerbünde im 20. Jahrhundert* (Frankfurt am Main, 2001); Daim, *Der Mann*, 71–2.

89. Alastair Thompson, *Left Liberals, the State, and Popular Politics in Wilhelmine Germany* (Oxford, 2000).

90. Stefan Breuer, *Ordnungen der Ungleichheit – die deutsche Rechte im Widerstreit ihrer Ideen 1871–1945* (Darmstadt, 2001), provides a thematic survey, emphasizing (370–76) the failure of an effective synthesis before the arrival of Nazism.

91. Andrew G. Whiteside, *The Socialism of Fools: Georg von Schönerer and Austrian Pan-Germanism* (Berkeley, 1975), esp. 73.

92. John W. Boyer, *Political Radicalism in Late Imperial Vienna: Origins of the Christian Social Movement, 1848–1897* (Chicago, 1981).

93. Pulzer, *The Rise*, 207.

94. Brigitte Hamann, *Hitler's Vienna: A Dictator's Apprenticeship* (Oxford, 2000), 236–53, provides a comprehensive survey of Schönerer and other Viennese ideologues of the day.

95. Carlile A. Macartney, *The Habsburg Empire 1790–1918* (London, 1968), 632–5, 653–7, 666, 680, 799; Pulzer, *The Rise*, 149–60, 170–74, 206–9; Carl E. Schorske, *Fin-de-Siècle Vienna: Politics and Culture* (New York, 1980), 116–180; Massing, *Rehearsal*, 241; Hellmuth von Gerlach, *Von rechts nach links* (Hildesheim, 1978 [1937]), 112–14; Andrew G. Whiteside, *Austrian National Socialism before 1918* (The Hague, 1962).

96. Woodruff D. Smith, *The German Colonial Empire* (Chapel Hill, NC, 1978); Fritz Ferdinand Müller, *Deutschland-Zanzibar-Ostafrika: Geschichte einer deutschen Kolonialeroberung 1884–1890* (Berlin, 1990 [1959]).

97. Gerhard Weidenfeller, *VDA: Verein für das Deutschtum im Ausland: Allgemeiner Deutscher Schulverein (1881–1918). Ein Beitrag zur Geschichte des deutschen Nationalismus und Imperialismus im Kaiserreich* (Berne, 1976).

98. Geoff Eley, *Reshaping the German Right: Radical Nationalism and Political Change after Bismarck* (London, 1980), 366; Roger Chickering, *We Men Who Feel Most German: A Cultural Study of the Pan-German League 1886–1914* (London, 1984), 24–73; Wilhelm Deist, *Flottenpolitik und Flottenpropaganda: Das Nachrichtenbüro des Reichsmarineamts 1897–1914* (Stuttgart, 1976); Richard Owen, 'Military-Industrial Relations: Krupp and the Imperial Navy Office', in Evans (ed.), *Society and Politics*, 71–89; Marilyn Shevin Coetzee, *The German Army League: Popular Nationalism in Wilhelmine Germany* (New York, 1990); Richard W. Tims, *Germanizing Prussian Poland: The H-K-T Society and the Struggle for the Eastern Marches in the German Empire 1894–1919* (New York, 1941); Adam Galos et al., *Die Hakatisten: Der Deutsche Ostmarkenverein 1894–1934* (Berlin, 1966).

99. Chickering, *We Men*, 128, 268–71; Coetzee, *The German Army League*,

19–23; Ute Planert, *Antifeminismus im Kaiserreich: Diskurs, soziale Formation und politische Mentalität* (Göttingen, 1998), 118–76.

100. Chickering, *We Men*, 102–21.

101. Ibid., 284–6; Wehler, *Deutsche Gesellschaftsgeschichte* III. 1071–81; extracts in English translation in Roderick Stackelberg and Sally A. Winkle (eds.), *The Nazi Germany Sourcebook: An Anthology of Texts* (London, 2002), 20–26.

102. Chickering, *We Men*, 74–97, 284–6.

103. Ibid., 122–32; also Klaus Bergmann, *Agrarromantik und Grossstadtfeindschaft* (Meisenheim, 1970).

104. Chickering, *We Men*, 253–91; Eley, *Reshaping*, 316–34; Dirk Stegmann, *Die Erben Bismarcks: Parteien und Verbände in der Spätphase des Wilhelminischen Deutschlands: Sammlungspolitik 1897–1914* (Cologne, 1970), 352–48; Fritz Fischer, *War of Illusions: German Politics from 1911 to 1914* (London, 1975 [1969]).

105. Iris Hamel, *Völkischer Verband und nationale Gewerkschaft: Der Deutschnationale Handlungsgehilfenverband, 1893–1933* (Frankfurt am Main, 1967); Planert, *Antifeminismus*, 71–9.

106. Extracts from the memorandum, and the Kaiser's response, can be found in Röhl, *From Bismarck to Hitler*, 49–52, and Stackelberg and Winkle (eds.), *The Nazi Germany Sourcebook*, 29–30.

107. Hartmut Pogge-von Strandmann, 'Staatsstreichpläne, Alldeutsche und Bethmann Hollweg', in idem and Imanuel Geiss, *Die Erforderlichkeit des Unmöglichen: Deutschland am Vorabend des ersten Weltkrieges* (Frankfurt am Main, 1965), 7–45; the texts of the replies by Bethmann and the Kaiser are printed on pages 32–9; the Kaiser's relations with Chamberlain are documented in Röhl, *From Bismarck to Hitler*, 41–8.

108. For an excellent discussion of contemporary views on the likely length of the war, see Hew Strachan, *The First World War*, I: *To Arms* (Oxford, 2001), 1005–14.

109. Martin Kitchen, *The Silent Dictatorship: The Politics of the German High Command under Hindenburg and Ludendorff, 1916–1918* (London, 1976). The best recent general survey is Roger Chickering, *Imperial Germany and the Great War, 1914–1918* (Cambridge, 1998).

110. Among a huge literature, Figes, *A People's Tragedy* stands out as the best recent survey.

111. Robert Service, *Lenin: A Political Life* (3 vols., London, 1985–95) is the standard biography; Lenin's attempts to stimulate a revolution in Germany are best approached through the activities of the Soviet emissary Karl Radek; see Marie-Luise Goldbach, *Karl Radek und die deutsch-sowjetischen Beziehungen 1918–1923* (Bonn, 1973), and Warren Lerner, *Karl Radek: The Last Internationalist* (Stanford, Calif., 1970).

112. Heinrich August Winkler, *Von der Revolution zur Stabilisierung: Arbeiter und Arbeiterbewegung in der Weimarer Republik 1918 bis 1924* (Bonn, 1984), esp. 114–34, and 468–552.

113. Arno J. Mayer, *Politics and Diplomacy of Peacemaking: Containment and Counterrevolution at Versailles 1918–1919* (2nd edn., New York, 1969 [1967]) for the general context; Oszkár Jászi, *Revolution and Counter-Revolution in Hungary* (London, 1924), for a contemporary account of events.

114. *Berliner Tageblatt*, 1 August 1918, cited in David Welch, *Germany, Propaganda and Total War, 1914–1918: The Sins of Omission* (London, 2000), 241. See also Aribert Reimann, *Der grosse Krieg der Sprachen: Untersuchungen zur historischen Semantik in Deutschland und England zur Zeit des Ersten Weltkriegs* (Essen, 2000).

115. For the best recent brief account, see Chickering, *Imperial Germany*, 178–91.

116. Welch, *Germany*, 241–2; Wilhelm Deist, 'Censorship and Propaganda in Germany during the First World War', in Jean-Jacques Becker and Stéphane Audoin-Rouzeau (eds.), *Les Sociétés européennes et la guerre de 1914–1918* (Paris, 1990), 199–210; Alice Goldfarb Marquis, 'Words as Weapons: Propaganda in Britain and Germany during the First World War', *Journal of Contemporary History*, 13 (1978), 467–98.

117. Fritz Fischer, *Germany's Aims in the First World War* (London, 1967 [1961]), *passim*.

118. Bullitt Lowry, *Armistice 1918* (Kent, Ohio, 1996); Hugh Cecil and Peter Liddle (eds.), *At the Eleventh Hour: Reflections, Hopes and Anxieties at the Closing of the Great War, 1918* (Barnsley, 1998).

119. *Stenographischer Bericht über die öffentlichen Verhandlungen des 15. Untersuchungsausschusses der verfassungsgebenden Nationalversammlung*, II (Berlin, 1920), 700–701 (18 November 1919). See also Erich Ludendorff, *Kriegführung und Politik* (Berlin, 1922), and Paul von Hindenburg, *Aus meinem Leben* (Leipzig, 1920), 403; more generally, Friedrich Freiherr Hiller von Gaertringen, ' "Dolchstoss-Diskussion" und "Dolchstosslegende" im Wandel von vier Jahrzehnten', in Waldemar Besson and Friedrich Freiherr Hiller von Gaertringen (eds.), *Geschichts- und Gegenwartsbewusstsein* (Göttingen, 1963), 122–60. Also, more recently, Jeffrey Verhey, *The Spirit of 1914: Militarism, Myth and Mobilization in Germany* (Cambridge, 2000), 219–23, and Chickering, *Imperial Germany*, 189–91.

120. William II, *My Memoirs 1878–1918* (London, 1922), 282–3. More generally, see Wilhelm Deist, 'The Military Collapse of the German Empire: The Reality Behind the Stab-in-the-Back Myth', *War in History*, 3 (1996), 186–207.

121. Friedrich Ebert, *Schriften, Aufzeichnungen, Reden* (2 vols., Dresden, 1936), II. 127; Ebert went on to blame the defeat on 'the preponderance of the enemy in men and material' (127).

122. Gerhard A. Ritter and Susanne Miller (eds.), *Die deutsche Revolution 1918–1919 – Dokumente* (Frankfurt am Main, 1968), is an excellent selection of documents; Francis L. Carsten, *Revolution in Central Europe 1918–1919* (London, 1972) is a good narrative.

123. From a large literature, see Harold Temperley (ed.), *A History of the Peace Conference of Paris* (6 vols., London, 1920–24), and Manfred F. Boemeke *et al.*

(eds.), *The Treaty of Versailles: A Reassessment after 75 Years* (Washington, DC, 1998), a collection of scholarly papers issued on the eightieth anniversary of the end of the war.

124. Mayer, *Politics and Diplomacy*.

125. Arthur S. Link (ed.), *The Papers of Woodrow Wilson* (69 vols., Princeton, 1984), XL. 534–9; more generally, Lloyd E. Ambrosius, *Wilsonian Statecraft: Theory and Practice of Liberal Internationalism during World War I* (Wilmington, Del., 1991), Thomas J. Knock, *To End All Wars: Woodrow Wilson and the Quest for a New World Order* (New York, 1992), and Arthur Walworth, *Wilson and his Peacemakers: American Diplomacy at the Paris Peace Conference, 1919* (New York, 1986).

126. Winkler, *Von der Revolution*, 94–5; Carsten, *Revolution*, 271–98.

127. John Horne and Alan Kramer, *German Atrocities 1914: A History of Denial* (London, 2001), 345–55, 446–50; Gerd Hankel, *Die Leipziger Prozesse: Deutsche Kriegsverbrechen und ihre strafrechtliche Verfolgung nach dem Ersten Weltkrieg* (Hamburg, 2003).

128. Bruce Kent, *The Spoils of War: The Politics, Economics and Diplomacy of Reparations 1918–1932* (Oxford, 1989).

129. Alan Sharp, *The Versailles Settlement: Peacekeeping in Paris, 1919* (London, 1991).

130. Fischer, *Germany's Aims, passim*.

131. For a good defence of the treaties, see Macmillan, *Peacemakers*.

132. Abel Testimony (hereinafter AT) 114, in Peter H. Merkl, *Political Violence under the Swastika: 581 Early Nazis* (Princeton, 1975), 191.

133. AT 334, ibid., 192–3.

134. AT 248, ibid., 194–5.

135. See the classic, and still standard, study by Fischer, *Germany's Aims*.

136. Eley, *Reshaping*, 333, 339–42; Dirk Stegmann, 'Zwischen Repression und Manipulation: Konservative Machteliten und Arbeiter- und Angestelltenbewegung 1910–1918: Ein Beitrag zur Vorgeschichte der DAP/NSDAP', *Archiv fur Sozialgeschichte*, 12 (1972), 351–432.

137. Heinz Hagenlücke, *Die deutsche Vaterlandspartei: Die nationale Rechte am Ende des Kaiserreiches* (Düsseldorf, 1997); Verhey, *The Spirit of 1914*, 178–85; Mosse, *The Crisis*, 218–26.

138. Ernst Jünger, *In Stahlgewittern: Aus dem Tagebuch eines Stosstruppführers* (Hanover, 1920). For a new English edition, see idem, *Storm of Steel* (London, 2003).

139. Richard Bessel, *Germany after the First World War* (Oxford, 1993), 256–61.

140. Theodore Abel, *Why Hitler Came to Power* (Cambridge, Mass., 1986 [1938]), 21, quoting *Frankfurter Zeitung*, 27 November 1918.

141. Quoted in Abel, *Why Hitler*, 24, testimony 4.3.4, also 2.3.2.

142. Ibid., 26, quoting testimony 4.1.2.

143. AT 199, in Merkl, *Political Violence*, 167.

144. Testimony 2.8.5, in Abel, *Why Hitler*, 27–8.

145. Christoph Jahr, *Gewöhnliche Soldaten: Desertion und Deserteure im deutschen und britischen Heer 1914–1918* (Göttingen, 1998); Benjamin Ziemann, 'Fahnenflucht im deutschen Heer 1914–1918', *Militärgeschichtliche Mitteilungen*, 55 (1996), 93–130.

146. Wolfgang Kruse, 'Krieg und Klassenheer: Zur Revolutionierung der deutschen Armee im Ersten Weltkrieg', *Geschichte und Gesellschaft*, 22 (1996), 530–61.

147. Merkl, *Political Violence*, 152–72.

148. Robert W. Whalen, *Bitter Wounds: German Victims of the Great War, 1914–1939* (Ithaca, NY, 1984); Deborah Cohen, *The War Come Home: Disabled Veterans in Britain and Germany, 1914–1918* (Berkeley, 2001); Bessel, *Germany*, 274–9.

149. Volker R. Berghahn, *Der Stahlhelm: Bund der Frontsoldaten 1918–1935* (Düsseldorf, 1966), 13–26, 105–6, 286; *Stahlhelm und Staat* (8 May 1927), excerpted and translated in Anton Kaes *et al.* (eds.), *The Weimar Republic Sourcebook* (Berkeley, 1994), 339–40.

150. Bessel, *Germany*, 283–84; also, Ulrich Heinemann, *Die verdrängte Niederlage: Politische Öffentlichkeit und Kriegsschuldfrage in der Weimarer Republik* (Göttingen, 1983).

151. Frevert, *Die kasernierte Nation*; Geoff Eley, 'Army, State and Civil Society' in idem, *From Unification to Nazism*, 85–109; and more generally Berghahn (ed.), *Militarismus*.

152. Evans, *Kneipengespräche*, 31–2, 339.

153. Bessel, *Germany*, 256–70.

154. Sebastian Haffner, *Defying Hitler: A Memoir* (London, 2002), 10–15.

155. Michael Wildt, *Generation des Unbedingten: Das Führungskorps des Reichssicherheitshauptamtes* (Hamburg, 2002), 41–52.

156. Berghahn, *Der Stahlhelm*, esp. 65–6; Karl Rohe, *Das Reichsbanner Schwarz Rot Gold: Ein Beitrag zur Geschichte und Struktur der politischen Kampfverbände zur Zeit der Weimarer Republik* (Düsseldorf, 1966); Kurt G. P. Schuster, *Der Rote Frontkämpferbund 1924–1929: Beiträge zur Geschichte und Organisationsstruktur eines politischen Kampfbundes* (Düsseldorf, 1975).

157. James M. Diehl, *Paramilitary Politics in Weimar Germany* (Bloomington, Ind., 1977), provides a clear guide through the undergrowth of the paramilitaries. See also Martin Sabrow, *Der Rathenaumord: Rekonstruktion einer Verschwörung gegen die Republik von Weimar* (Munich, 1994), for an excellent investigation of the world of the armed conspirators.

158. Erhard Lucas, *Märzrevolution im Ruhrgebiet* (3 vols., Frankfurt am Main, 1970–78), a classic of politically committed history; George Eliasberg, *Der Ruhrkrieg von 1920* (Bonn, 1974), a more sober, less detailed account, sympathetic to the moderate Social Democrats.

159. See the classic study of this literature by Klaus Theweleit, *Male Fantasies* (2 vols., Cambridge, 1987 and 1989 [1978]); for some reservations, Evans, *Rereading*, 115–18.

160. On the Free Corps, Robert G. L. Waite, *Vanguard of Nazism. The Free Corps Movement in Postwar Germany 1918–1923* (Harvard, 1952), is still the best account in English. See also Hagen Schulze, *Freikorps und Republik 1918–1920* (Boppard, 1969), and Emil J. Gumbel, *Verschwörer: Zur Geschichte und Soziologie der deutschen nationalistischen Geheimbünde 1918–1924* (Heidelberg, 1979 [1924]).

161. Volker Ullrich, *Der ruhelose Rebell: Karl Plättner 1893–1945. Eine Biographie* (Munich, 2000); and Manfred Gebhardt, *Max Hoelz: Wege und Irrwege eines Revolutionärs* (Berlin, 1983).

Chapter 2   THE FAILURE OF DEMOCRACY

1. Quoted in Winkler, *Von der Revolution* 39; see also the useful study by Dieter Dowe and Peter-Christian Witt, *Friedrich Ebert 1871–1925: Vom Arbeiterführer zum Reichspräsidenten* (Bonn, 1987), and the exhibition catalogue by Walter Mühlhausen, *Friedrich Ebert: Sein Leben, sein Werk, seine Zeit* (Heidelberg, 1999). The informative biography by Georg Kotowski, *Friedrich Ebert: Eine politische Biographie*, I: *Der Aufstieg eines deutschen Arbeiterführers 1871 bis 1917* (Wiesbaden, 1963) remained unfinished.

2. Anthony J. Nicholls, *Weimar and the Rise of Hitler* (4th edn., London, 2000 [1968]), is a reliable brief guide to these events. Among recent general political histories, Hans Mommsen, *The Rise and Fall of Weimar Democracy* (Chapel Hill, NC, 1996 [1989]), and Heinrich August Winkler, *Weimar 1918–1933: Die Geschichte der ersten deutschen Demokratie* (Munich, 1993) are outstanding.

3. For this argument, see Theodor Eschenburg, *Die improvisierte Demokratie* (Munich, 1963). Other classic studies, still worth reading, include the richly empirical narrative by Erich Eyck, *A History of the Weimar Republic* (2 vols., Cambridge, 1962–4 [1953–6]), written from a liberal perspective, and the two volumes by the socialist Arthur Rosenberg, *The Birth of the German Republic* (Oxford, 1931 [1930]) and *A History of the German Republic* (London, 1936 [1935]), both brimming with stimulating and controversial theses, particularly on continuities from the Wilhelmine period.

4. Heinrich Hannover and Elisabeth Hannover-Drück, *Politische Justiz 1918–1933* (Frankfurt am Main, 1966), 76–7, 89.

5. For differing views on Article 48, see Nicholls, *Weimar*, 36–7; Detlev J. K. Peukert, *The Weimar Republic: The Crisis of Classical Modernity* (London, 1991 [1987]), 37–40; and Harald Boldt, 'Der Artikel 48 der Weimarer Reichsverfassung: Sein historischer Hintergrund und seine politische Funktion', in Michael Stürmer (ed.), *Die Weimarer Republik: Belagerte Civitas* (Königstein in Taunus, 1980), 288–309. The standard general work on the Weimar constitution is Ernst Rudolf Huber, *Deutsche Verfassungsgeschichte seit 1789*, V–VII (Stuttgart, 1978–84); see also Reinhard Rürup, 'Entstehung und Grundlagen der Weimarer Verfassung', in

Eberhard Kolb (ed.), *Vom Kaiserreich zur Weimarer Republik* (Cologne, 1972), 218–43. Ebert's abuse of Article 48 was already criticized by contemporaries; see Gerhard Schulz, 'Artikel 48 in politisch-historischer Sicht', in Ernst Fraenkel (ed.), *Der Staatsnotstand* (Berlin, 1965), 39–71. Ludwig Richter, 'Das präsidiale Notverordnungsrecht in den ersten Jahren der Weimarer Republik: Friedrich Ebert und die Anwendung des Artikels 48 der Weimarer Reichsverfassung', in Eberhard Kolb (ed.) *Friedrich Ebert als Reichspräsident: Amtsführung und Amtsverständnis* (Munich, 1997), 207–58, attempts a defence.

6. Dowe and Witt, *Friedrich Ebert*, 155–7.

7. Werner Birkenfeld, 'Der Rufmord am Reichspräsidenten: Zu Grenzformen des politischen Kampfes gegen die frühe Weimarer Republik 1919–1925', *Archiv für Sozialgeschichte*, 15 (1965), 453–500.

8. Heinrich August Winkler, *Der Schein der Normalität: Arbeiter und Arbeiterbewegung in der Weimarer Republik 1924 bis 1930* (Bonn, 1985), 231–4.

9. Victor Klemperer, *Leben sammeln, nicht fragen wozu und warum*, II: *Tagebücher 1925–1932* (Berlin, 1996), 56 (14 May 1925).

10. John W. Wheeler-Bennett, *Hindenburg: The Wooden Titan* (London, 1936), 250–51. Wheeler-Bennett's remarkably shrewd and well-informed portrait was based on lengthy conversations with members of Hindenburg's entourage and with many leading contemporary conservative German politicians, with whom he was on good personal terms as an upper-class Englishman running a stud farm in northern Germany. See also Walter Hubatsch, *Hindenburg und der Staat: Aus den Papieren des Generalfeldmarschalls und Reichspräsidenten von 1878 bis 1934* (Göttingen, 1966).

11. Andreas Dorpalen, *Hindenburg and the Weimar Republic* (Princeton, 1964), sees Hindenburg as an unpolitical figure, reluctantly dragged into politics by the power of his personal myth.

12. Nicholls, *Weimar*, 39–40; Jürgen Falter, *Hitlers Wähler* (Munich, 1991), 130–35.

13. See the classic article by Gerhard A. Ritter, 'Kontinuität und Umformung des deutschen Parteiensystems 1918–1920', in Eberhard Kolb (ed.), *Vom Kaiserreich zur Weimarer Republic* (Cologne, 1972), 218–43.

14. Vernon L. Lidtke, *The Alternative Culture: Socialist Labor in Imperial Germany* (New York, 1985).

15. Horstwalter Heitzer, *Der Volksverein für das katholische Deutschland im Kaiserreich 1890–1918* (Mainz, 1979); Gotthard Klein, *Der Volksverein für das katholische Deutschland 1890–1933: Geschichte, Bedeutung, Untergang* (Paderborn, 1996); Dirk Müller, *Arbeiter, Katholizismus, Staat: Der Volksverein für das katholische Deutschland und die katholischen Arbeiterorganisationen in der Weimarer Republik* (Bonn, 1996); Doris Kaufmann, *Katholisches Milieu in Münster 1928–1933* (Düsseldorf, 1984).

16. Wilhelm L. Guttsman, *Workers' Culture in Weimar Germany: Between Tradition and Commitment* (Oxford, 1990).

17. Lynn Abrams, *Workers' Culture in Imperial Germany: Leisure and Recreation in the Rhineland and Westphalia* (London, 1992).

18. Bracher *et al.*, *Die nationalsozialistische Machtergreifung*, I. 41, 58–9, quoting Max Weber's prediction to this effect.

19. Bracher, *Die Auflösung*, 21–7, 64–95.

20. See Huber, *Deutsche Verfassungsgeschichte*, VI. 133, and the discussion in Eberhard Kolb, *The Weimar Republic* (London, 1988), 150–51. For criticisms of proportional representation, see especially Eberhard Schanbacher, *Parlamentarische Wahlen und Wahlsystem in der Weimarer Republik: Wahlgesetzgebung und Wahlreform im Reich und in den Ländern* (Düsseldorf, 1982). Falter, *Hitlers Wähler*, 126–35, has some informed speculation that, on balance, sustains the negative view.

21. Christoph Gusy, *Die Weimarer Reichsverfassung* (Tübingen, 1997), 97–8.

22. See the useful lists on the endpapers of Hagen Schulze, *Weimar: Deutschland 1917–1933* (Berlin, 1982).

23. See, for example, Klaus Reimer, *Rheinlandfrage und Rheinlandbewegung (1918–1933): Ein Beitrag zur Geschichte der regionalistischen Bewegung in Deutschland* (Frankfurt am Main, 1979).

24. Nicholls, *Weimar*, 33–6, exaggerates the problems caused. For Prussia, see Hagen Schulze, *Otto Braun oder Preussens demokratische Sendung* (Frankfurt am Main, 1977), Dietrich Orlow, *Weimar Prussia 1918–1925: The Unlikely Rock of Democracy* (Pittsburgh, 1986), and Hans-Peter Ehni, *Bollwerk Preussen? Preussen-Regierung, Reich-Länder-Problem und Sozialdemokratie 1928–1932* (Bonn, 1975).

25. Details in Alfred Milatz, *Wähler und Wahlen in der Weimarer Republik* (Bonn, 1965) and Jürgen Falter *et al.*, *Wahlen und Abstimmungen in der Weimarer Republik: Materialen zum Wahlverhalten 1919–1933* (Munich, 1986).

26. Schulze, *Weimar*, endpapers.

27. Winkler, *Von der Revolution*; idem, *Der Schein*; idem, *Der Weg in die Katastrophe: Arbeiter und Arbeiterbewegung in der Weimarer Republik 1930 bis 1933* (Bonn, 1987), is a comprehensive and exhaustive survey, sympathetic to the Social Democrats. Strong criticism in Bracher *et al.*, *Die nationalsozialistische Machtergreifung*, I. 58–9; emphasis on the growing, 'middle-aged' timidity of the party in Richard N. Hunt, *German Social Democracy 1918–1933* (New Haven, 1964), esp. 241–59.

28. Larry Eugene Jones, *German Liberalism and the Dissolution of the Weimar Party System, 1918–1933* (Chapel Hill, NC, 1988), 67–80.

29. Erich Matthias and Rudolf Morsey, 'Die Deutsche Staatspartei', in Matthias and Morsey (eds.), *Das Ende der Parteien 1933: Darstellungen und Dokumente* (Düsseldorf, 1960), 29–97, at 31–54; Werner Schneider, *Die Deutsche Demokratische Partei in der Weimarer Republik, 1924–1930* (Munich, 1978); Diehl, *Paramilitary Politics*, 269–76; Jones, *German Liberalism*, 369–74; Klaus Hornung, *Der Jungdeutsche Orden* (Düsseldorf, 1958).

30. Detlef Junker, *Die Deutsche Zentrumspartei und Hitler: Ein Beitrag zur Problematik des politischen Katholizismus in Deutschland* (Stuttgart, 1969); Rudolf Morsey, *Der Untergang des politischen Katholizismus: Die Zentrumspartei zwischen christlichem Selbstverständnis und 'Nationaler Erhebung'* 1932/33 (Stuttgart, 1977); Karsten Ruppert, *Im Dienst am Staat von Weimar: Das Zentrum als regierende Partei in der Weimarer Demokratie* 1923–1930 (Düsseldorf, 1992). For the Bavarian People's Party, see Klaus Schönhoven, *Die Bayerische Volkspartei* 1924–1932 (Düsseldorf, 1972). For the general European context, Eric Hobsbawm, *Age of Extremes: The Short Twentieth Century* 1914–1991 (London, 1994), 114–15.

31. Quoted in Rudolf Morsey, 'Die Deutsche Zentrumspartei', in Matthias and Morsey (eds.), *Das Ende*, 279–453, at 290–91.

32. Max Miller, *Eugen Bolz* (Stuttgart, 1951), 357–8, quoted in Morsey, 'Die Deutsche Zentrumspartei', 292; see also Joachim Sailer, *Eugen Bolz und die Krise des politischen Katholizismus in der Weimarer Republik* (Tübingen, 1994).

33. John Cornwell, *Hitler's Pope: The Secret History of Pius XII* (London, 1999), esp. 96–7, 116–17, 120–51; drawing heavily on Klaus Scholder, *The Churches and the Third Reich* (2 vols., London, 1987–8 [1977, 1985]); Morsey, 'Die Deutsche Zentrumspartei', 301, on pressure from the Vatican.

34. Werner Angress, *Stillborn Revolution: The Communist Bid for Power in Germany,* 1921–1923 (Princeton, 1963); Ben Fowkes, *Communism in Germany under the Weimar Republic* (London, 1984), 148, 161; Eric D. Weitz, *Creating German Communism,* 1890–1990: *From Popular Protests to Socialist State* (Princeton, 1997), 100–31; and, above all, Hermann Weber, *Die Wandlung des deutschen Kommunismus: Die Stalinisierung der KPD in der Weimarer Republik* (2 vols., Frankfurt am Main, 1969).

35. Evans, *Rituals*, 507–9, 574, for one example among many.

36. Maximilian Müller-Jabusch (ed.), *Handbuch des öffentlichen Lebens* (Leipzig, 1931), 442–5, excerpted and translated in Kaes *et al.* (eds.), *The Weimar Republic Sourcebook*, 348–52; see more generally Mommsen, *The Rise and Fall*, 253–60.

37. Bracher, *Die Auflösung*, 309–30; Friedrich Freiherr Hiller von Gaertringen, 'Die Deutschnationale Volkspartei', in Matthias and Morsey (eds.), *Das Ende*, 541–652, at 543–9.

38. Henry Ashby Turner, Jr., *Gustav Stresemann and the Politics of the Weimar Republic* (Princeton, 1965 [1963]), 250–51; Jonathan Wright, *Gustav Stresemann: Weimar's Greatest Statesman* (Oxford, 2002).

39. Broszat, *Der Staat Hitlers*, 19–20.

40. Diehl, *Paramilitary Politics*, 209–43; Berghahn, *Der Stahlhelm*, 103–30.

41. Francis L. Carsten, *The Reichswehr and Politics* 1918–1933 (Oxford, 1966), 3–48; Wolfram Wette, *Gustav Noske: Eine politische Biographie* (Düsseldorf, 1987), 399–459.

42. Carsten, *The Reichswehr*, 106–7; Johannes Erger, *Der Kapp-Lüttwitz-Putsch: Ein Beitrag zur deutschen Innenpolitik* 1919/20 (Düsseldorf, 1967); Erwin Könne-

mann *et al.* (eds.), *Arbeiterklasse siegt über Kapp und Lüttwitz* (2 vols., Berlin, 1971).

43. Cited in Carsten, *The Reichswehr*, 401.

44. Thilo Vogelsang (ed.), 'Neue Dokumente zur Geschichte der Reichswehr, 1930–1933', *VfZ* 2 (1954), 397–436.

45. Friedrich von Rabenau, *Seeckt – aus seinem Leben 1918–1936* (Leipzig, 1940), 359–61, and Otto-Ernst Schüddekopf, *Das Heer und die Republik – Quellen zur Politik der Reichswehrführung 1918 bis 1933* (Hanover, 1955), 179–81. See also the older studies of John W. Wheeler-Bennett, *The Nemesis of Power: The German Army in Politics 1918–1945* (London, 1953), now in most respects outdated, for a highly critical view of the army, and Harold J. Gordon, *The Reichswehr and the German Republic 1919–26* (Princeton, 1957), sympathetic to Seeckt. Basic details in Rainer Wohlfeil, 'Heer und Republik', in Hans Meier-Welcker and Wolfgang von Groote (eds.), *Handbuch zur deutschen Militärgeschichte 1648–1939*, VI (Frankfurt am Main, 1970), 11–304.

46. Carsten, *The Reichswehr*, 276; Ernst Willi Hansen, *Reichswehr und Industrie: Rüstungswirtschaftliche Zusammenarbeit und wirtschaftliche Mobilmachungs-vorbereitungen 1923–1932* (Boppard, 1978); Manfred Zeidler, *Reichswehr und Rote Armee 1920–1933: Wege und Stationen einer ungewöhnlichen Zusammen-arbeit* (Munich, 1993); more generally, Michael Geyer, *Aufrüstung oder Sicherheit: Reichswehr in der Krise der Machtpolitik, 1924–1936* (Wiesbaden, 1980), and Karl Nuss, *Militär und Wiederaufrüstung in der Weimarer Republik: Zur pol-itischen Rolle und Entwicklung der Reichswehr* (Berlin, 1977).

47. Carsten, *The Reichswehr*, 159–60, 168–9, 226.

48. Michael Geyer, 'Professionals and Junkers: German Rearmament and Politics in the Weimar Republic', in Richard Bessel and Edgar Feuchtwanger (eds.), *Social Change and Political Development in Weimar Germany* (London, 1981), 77–133.

49. See the classic study by Craig, *The Politics of the Prussian Army*, 382–467.

50. Eberhard Kolb, 'Die Reichsbahn vom Dawes-Plan bis zum Ende der Weimarer Republik', in Lothar Gall and Manfred Pohl (eds.), *Die Eisenbahn in Deutschland: Von den Anfängen bis zur Gegenwart* (Munich, 1999), 109–64, at 149–50.

51. Jane Caplan, *Government without Administration: State and Civil Service in Weimar and Nazi Germany* (Oxford, 1988), 8–18, 60–61.

52. Gerhart Fieberg (ed.), *Im Namen des deutschen Volkes: Justiz und National-sozialismus* (Cologne, 1989), 8.

53. Bracher, *Die Auflösung*, 162–72.

54. Caplan, *Government*, 30–36.

55. Ibid., 33–57; Wolfgang Runge, *Politik und Beamtentum im Parteienstaat: Die Demokratisierung der politischen Beamten in Preussen zwischen 1918 und 1933* (Stuttgart, 1965); Anthony J. Nicholls, 'Die höhere Beamtenschaft in der Weimarer Zeit: Betrachtungen zu Problemen ihrer Haltung und ihrer Fortbildung', in Lothar Albertin and Werner Link (eds.), *Politische Parteien auf dem Weg zur parlamen-tarischen Demokratie in Deutschland: Entwicklungslinien bis zur Gegenwart* (Düsseldorf, 1981), 195–207; Hans Fenske, 'Monarchisches Beamtentum und

demokratischer Rechtsstaat: Zum Problem der Bürokratie in der Weimarer Republik', in *Demokratie und Verwaltung: 25 Jahre Hochschule für Verwaltung Speyer* (Berlin, 1972), 117–36; Rudolf Morsey, 'Beamtenschaft und Verwaltung zwischen Republik und "Neuem Staat"', in Karl Dietrich Erdmann and Hagen Schulze (eds.), *Weimar: Selbstpreisgabe einer Demokratie* (Düsseldorf, 1980), 151–68; Eberhard Pikart, 'Preussische Beamtenpolitik 1918–1933', *VfZ* 6 (1958), 119–37.

56. Broszat, *Der Staat Hitlers*, 27–9.

57. AT 28, in Merkl, *Political Violence*, 513.

58. See Rainer Fattmann, *Bildungsbürger in der Defensive: Die akademische Beamtenschaft und der 'Reichsbund der höheren Beamten' in der Weimarer Republik* (Göttingen, 2001).

59. On the whole subject of Germany's economic, and other, war aims, though no longer on the war's origins (which it in fact treats only briefly), Fischer, *Germany's Aims* remains the standard work.

60. The process of inflation during and immediately after the war is recounted in great detail in the first 150 pages of the monumental history by Gerald D. Feldman, *The Great Disorder: Politics, Economic, and Society in the German Inflation, 1914–1924* (New York, 1993). The exchange rates for the whole period are given in table 1 on page 5. Feldman's work supersedes the classic accounts by Constantino Bresciani-Turroni, *The Economics of Inflation: A Study of Currency Depreciation in Post-war Germany* (London, 1937) and Karsten Laursen and Jürgen Pedersen, *The German Inflation 1918–1923* (Amsterdam, 1964). There is a succinct survey of research in Theo Balderston, *Economics and Politics in the Weimar Republic* (London, 2002), 34–60. Stephen B. Webb, *Hyperinflation and Stabilization in Weimar Germany* (Oxford, 1989) links the inflation process to the reparations issue.

61. Feldman, *The Great Disorder*, 5 (table 1), and more generally, with numerous quotations and examples, in chapters 1–8; also Kent, *The Spoils of War*, 45–6, 142–58.

62. Feldman, *The Great Disorder*, 837–9; more pessimistically, Niall Ferguson, *Paper and Iron: Hamburg Business and German Politics in the Era of Inflation, 1897–1927* (Oxford, 1995), esp. 408–19.

63. Feldman, *The Great Disorder*, 5 (table 1). For the Ruhr occupation, see Conan Fischer, *The Ruhr Crisis 1923–1924* (Oxford, 2003); Hermann J. Rupieper, *The Cuno Government and Reparations 1922–1923: Politics and Economics* (The Hague, 1979); and Klaus Schwabe (ed.), *Die Ruhrkrise 1923: Wendepunkt der internationalen Beziehungen nach dem Ersten Weltkrieg* (Paderborn, 1985).

64. *Berliner Morgenpost* 251 (21 October 1923), 'Zahlen-Wahnsinn, von Bruno H. Bürgel'.

65. Norman Angell, *The Story of Money* (New York, 1930), 332; Haffner, *Defying Hitler*, 49–50.

66. Fritz Blaich, *Der schwarze Freitag: Inflation und Wirtschaftskrise* (Munich, 1985), 14, 31.

67. *Wirtschaftskurve*, 2 (1923), 1, 29 and 4 (1923), 21, citing the expenditure of

a middling salaried employee's family with one child, quoted in Carl-Ludwig Holtfrerich, *The German Inflation 1914–1923: Causes and Effects in International Perspective* (New York, 1986 [1980]), 261.

68. *Berliner Morgenpost*, 220 (15 September 1923), 'Zurückgehaltene Ware: Weil der "morgige Preis" noch nicht bekannt ist'.

69. Feldman, *The Great Disorder*, 704–6.

70. Holtfrerich, *The German Inflation*, 262–3.

71. Klemperer, *Leben sammeln*, I. 239 (26 February 1920).

72. Ibid., 257 (28 March 1920).

73. Ibid., 262 (1 April 1920).

74. Ibid., 697 (27 May 1923), 700–1 (1 and 2 June 1923). For the speculation mania, see also Haffner, *Defying Hitler*, 46–7.

75. Klemperer, *Leben sammeln*, I. 717 (24 July 1923), 729 (3 August 1923).

76. Ibid., 740 (27/28 August 1923).

77. Ibid., 752 (9 October 1923).

78. Ibid., 751 (9 October 1923).

79. Ibid., 757 (2 November 1923).

80. Ibid., 758 (7 and 16 November 1923).

81. *Berliner Morgenpost*, 213 (7 September 1923): 'Nur noch dreissig Strassenbahn-Linien'.

82. Kent, *The Spoils of War*, 245–8.

83. Feldman, *The Great Disorder*, 741–7.

84. Ibid., 778–93.

85. Ibid., 754–835.

86. Derek H. Aldcroft, *From Versailles to Wall Street 1919–1929* (London, 1977), 125–55.

87. Feldman, *The Great Disorder*, 854–88.

88. Klemperer, *Leben sammeln*, I. 761 (4 December 1923), 763 (20 December 1923).

89. Nikolaus Wachsmann, *Hitler's Prisons: Legal Terror in Nazi Germany* (forthcoming, 2004), chapter 2.

90. Michael Grüttner, 'Working-Class Crime and the Labour Movement: Pilfering in the Hamburg Docks, 1888–1923', in Richard J. Evans (ed.), *The German Working Class 1888–1933: The Politics of Everyday Life* (London, 1982), 54–79.

91. Hans Ostwald, *Sittengeschichte der Inflation: Ein Kulturdokument aus den Jahren des Marksturzes* (Berlin, 1931), esp. 30–31.

92. Martin Geyer, *Verkehrte Welt: Revolution, Inflation, und Moderne. München 1914–1924* (Göttingen, 1998), *passim*.

93. Bernd Widdig, *Culture and Inflation in Weimar Germany* (Berkeley, 2001), 113–33.

94. Geyer, *Verkehrte Welt*, 243–318; more generally, the various studies in Gerald D. Feldman (ed.), *Die Nachwirkungen der Inflation auf die deutsche Geschichte 1924–1933* (Munich, 1985).

95. For a fascinating study of one such clash, see Charles Medalen, 'State Monopoly Capitalism in Germany: The Hibernia Affair', *Past and Present*, 78 (February 1978), 82–112.

96. Henry Ashby Turner, Jr., *German Big Business and the Rise of Hitler* (New York, 1985), 3–18; Gerald D. Feldman, *Army, Industry and Labor in Germany, 1914–1918* (Princeton, 1966); idem, 'The Origins of the Stinnes–Legien Agreement: A Documentation', *Internationale Wissenschaftliche Korrespondenz zur Geschichte der deutschen Arbeiterbewegung*, 19/20 (1973), 45–104.

97. For a summary of the debate on the nature and extent of business investment during the inflation, see Harold James, *The German Slump: Politics and Economics, 1924–1936* (Oxford, 1986), 125–30.

98. Peter Hayes, *Industry and Ideology: I.G. Farben in the Nazi Era* (Cambridge, 1987), 16–17; Gerald D. Feldman, *Hugo Stinnes: Biographie eines Industriellen 1870–1924* (Munich, 1998).

99. Mary Nolan, *Visions of Modernity: American Business and the Modernization of Germany* (New York, 1994).

100. Peukert, *The Weimar Republic*, 112–17.

101. Robert Brady, *The Rationalization Movement in Germany: A Study in the Evolution of Economic Planning* (Berkeley, 1933); James, *The German Slump*, 146–61.

102. Feldman, *The Great Disorder*, 343–44; Harold James, 'Economic Reasons for the Collapse of the Weimar Republic', in Ian Kershaw (ed.), *Weimar: Why did German Democracy Fail?* (London, 1990), 30–57, at 33–4; see also Dieter Hertz-Eichenröde, *Wirtschaftskrise und Arbeitsbeschaffung: Konjunkturpolitik 1925/26 und die Grundlagen der Krisenpolitik Brünings* (Frankfurt am Main, 1982); Fritz Blaich, *Die Wirtschaftskrise 1925/26 und die Reichsregierung: Von der Erwerbslosenfürsorge zur Konjunkturpolitik* (Kallmünz, 1977); and Klaus-Dieter Krohn, *Stabilisierung und ökonomische Interessen: Die Finanzpolitik des deutschen Reiches 1923–1927* (Düsseldorf, 1974).

103. Bernd Weisbrod, *Schwerindustie in der Weimarer Republik: Interessenpolitik zwischen Stabilisierung und Krise* (Wuppertal, 1978), 415–56; James, *The German Slump*, 162–223.

104. Richard Bessel, 'Why did the Weimar Republic Collapse?', in Kershaw (ed.), *Weimar*, 120–52, at 136; Bernd Weisbrod, 'The Crisis of German Unemployment Insurance in 1928/29 and its Political Repercussions', in Wolfgang J. Mommsen (ed.), *The Emergence of the Welfare State in Britain and Germany, 1850–1950* (London, 1981), 188–204; Richard J. Evans, 'Introduction: The Experience of Mass Unemployment in the Weimar Republic' in Richard J. Evans and Dick Geary (eds.), *The German Unemployed: Experiences and Consequences of Mass Unemployment from the Weimar Republic to the Third Reich* (London, 1987), 1–22, at 5–6; Merith Niehuss, 'From Welfare Provision to Social Insurance: The Unemployed in Augsburg 1918–27', in Evans and Geary (eds.), *The German Unemployed*, 44–72.

105. Turner, *German Big Business*, 19–46; Weisbrod, *Schwerindustrie*; see also the brief sketch by J. Adam Tooze, 'Big Business and the Continuities of German History, 1900–1945', in Panikos Panayi (ed.), *Weimar and Nazi Germany: Continuities and Discontinuities* (London, 2001), 173–98.

106. For the Barmat scandal, see Bernhard Fulda, 'Press and Politics in Berlin, 1924–1930' (Cambridge Ph.D. dissertation, 2003), 63–71, 87–117.

107. Dick Geary, 'Employers, Workers, and the Collapse of the Weimar Republic', in Kershaw (ed.), *Weimar*, 92–119.

108. Karl Rohe, *Wahlen und Wählertraditionen in Deutschland* (Frankfurt am Main, 1992), 124.

109. Falter, *Hitlers Wähler*, 327–8; Kurt Koszyk, *Deutsche Presse 1914–1945: Geschichte der deutschen Presse*, III (Berlin, 1972).

110. Babette Gross, *Willi Münzenberg: Eine politische Biographie* (Stuttgart, 1967).

111. Erich Schairer, 'Alfred Hugenberg', *Mit anderen Augen: Jahrbuch der deutschen Sonntagszeitung* (1929), 18–21, cited and translated in Kaes *et al.* (eds.), *The Weimar Republic Sourcebook*, 72–4; Dankwart Guratzsch, *Macht durch Organisation: Die Grundlegung des Hugenbergschen Presseimperiums* (Düsseldorf, 1974), 192–3, 244, 248.

112. Fulda, 'Press and Politics', table 1.

113. Modris Eksteins, *The Limits of Reason: The German Democratic Press and the Collapse of Weimar Democracy* (Oxford, 1975), 129–30, 249–50.

114. Fulda, 'Press and Politics', table 1, and chapter 1 more generally.

115. Falter, *Hitlers Wähler*, 325–39.

116. Oswald Spengler, *Der Untergang des Abendlandes: Umrisse einer Morphologie der Weltgeschichte*, I: *Gestalt und Wirklichkeit* (Vienna, 1918), 73–5.

117. Arthur Moeller van den Bruck, *Das Dritte Reich* (3rd edn., Hamburg, 1931 [Berlin, 1923]), esp. 300, 320; Gary D. Stark, *Entrepreneurs of Ideology: Neo-Conservative Publishers in Germany, 1890–1933* (Chapel Hill, NC 1981); Agnes Stansfield, 'Das Dritte Reich: A Contribution to the Study of the "Third Kingdom" in German Literature from Herder to Hegel', *Modern Language Review*, 34 (1934), 156–72. Moeller van den Bruck originally called his conservative-revolutionary utopia 'the Third Way'; see Mosse, *The Crisis*, 281.

118. Edgar Jung, 'Deutschland und die konservative Revolution', in *Deutsche über Deutschland* (Munich, 1932), 369–82, excerpted and translated in Kaes *et al.*, (eds.), *The Weimar Republic Sourcebook*, 352–4.

119. Jünger, *In Stahlgewittern*; see also Nikolaus Wachsmann, 'Marching under the Swastika? Ernst Jünger and National Socialism, 1918–33', *Journal of Contemporary History*, 33 (1998), 573–89.

120. Theweleit, *Male Fantasies*.

121. The classic study of these, and other, similar strands of thought is by Kurt Sontheimer, *Antidemokratisches Denken in der Weimarer Republik* (Munich, 1978 [1962]).

122. James M. Ritchie, *German Literature under National Socialism* (London, 1983), 10–11; see also Peter Zimmermann, 'Literatur im Dritten Reich', in Jan Berg *et al.* (eds.), *Sozialgeschichte der deutschen Literatur von 1918 bis zur Gegenwart* (Frankfurt am Main, 1981), 361–416; and in particular Jost Hermand and Frank Trommler, *Die Kultur der Weimarer Republik* (Munich, 1978), 128–92.

123. For a good general overview, see Nitschke *et al.* (eds.), *Jahrhundertwende*; on 'moral panics' in the Wilhelmine period, see Richard J. Evans, *Tales from the German Underworld: Crime and Punishment in the Nineteenth Century* (London, 1998), 166–212; Gary Stark, 'Pornography, Society and the Law in Imperial Germany', *Central European History*, 14 (1981), 200–20; Bram Dijkstra, *Idols of Perversity: Fantasies of Female Evil in Fin-de-Siècle Culture* (New York, 1986); Robin Lenman, 'Art, Society and the Law in Wilhelmine Germany: The Lex Heinze', *Oxford German Studies*, 8 (1973), 86–113; Matthew Jefferies, *Imperial Culture in Germany, 1871–1918* (London, 2003); on Weimar culture, Peukert, *The Weimar Republic*, 164–77.

124. Hermand and Trommler, *Die Kultur*, 193–260.

125. Karen Koehler, 'The *Bauhaus*, 1919–1928: Gropius in Exile and the Museum of Modern Art, N. Y., 1938', in Richard A. Etlin (ed.), *Art, Culture and Media under the Third Reich* (Chicago, 2002), 287–315, at 288–92; Barbara Miller Lane, *Architecture and Politics in Germany, 1918–1945* (Cambridge, Mass., 1968), 70–78; Shearer West, *The Visual Arts in Germany 1890–1936: Utopia and Despair* (Manchester, 2000), 143–55; Hans Wingler, *The Bauhaus – Weimar, Dessau, Berlin, Chicago 1919–1944* (Cambridge, Mass., 1978); Frank Whitford, *The Bauhaus* (London, 1984).

126. Gerald D. Feldman, 'Right-Wing Politics and the Film Industry: Emil Georg Strauss, Alfred Hugenberg, and the UFA, 1917–1933', in Christian Jansen *et al.* (eds.), *Von der Aufgabe der Freiheit: Politische Verantwortung und bürgerliche Gesellschaft im 19. und 20. Jahrhundert: Festschrift für Hans Mommsen zum 5. November 1995* (Berlin, 1995), 219–30; Siegfried Kracauer, *From Caligari to Hitler: A Psychological History of the German Film* (Princeton, 1947), 214–16.

127. Andrew Kelly, *Filming All Quiet on the Western Front – 'Brutal Cutting, Stupid Censors, Bigoted Politicos'* (London, 1998), reprinted in paperback as *All Quiet on the Western Front: The Story of a Film* (London, 2002). More generally, on Weimar culture, see the classic essay by Peter Gay, *Weimar Culture: The Outsider as Insider* (London, 1969). Walter Laqueur, *Weimar: A Cultural History 1918–1933* (London, 1974), is good on the conservative majority as well as the avant-garde minority; see also Hermand and Trommler, *Die Kultur*, 350–437, on the visual arts.

128. Erik Levi, *Music in the Third Reich* (London, 1994), 1–13; Hermand and Trommler, *Die Kultur*, 279–350.

129. Michael H. Kater, *Different Drummers: Jazz in the Culture of Nazi Germany* (New York, 1992), 3–28; Peter Jelavich, *Berlin Cabaret* (Cambridge, Mass., 1993), 202.

130. Peukert, *The Weimar Republic*, 178–90.
131. AT 43, in Merkl, *Political Violence*, 173.
132. Abrams, *Workers' Culture*, esp. chapter 7.
133. Richard J. Evans, *The Feminist Movement in Germany 1894–1933* (London, 1976), 122, 141; Rudolph Binion, *Frau Lou: Nietzsche's Wayward Disciple* (Princeton, 1968), 447.
134. James D. Steakley, *The Homosexual Emancipation Movement in* Germany (New York, 1975); John C. Fout, 'Sexual Politics in Wilhelmine Germany: The Male Gender Crisis, Moral Purity, and Homophobia', *Journal of the History of Sexuality*, 2 (1992), 388–421.
135. See the pioneering article by Renate Bridenthal and Claudia Koonz, 'Beyond Kinder, Küche, Kirche: Weimar Women in Politics and Work', in Renate Bridenthal *et al.* (eds.), *When Biology Became Destiny: Women in Weimar and Nazi Germany* (New York, 1984), 33–65.
136. Planert, *Antifeminismus*.
137. Evans, *The Feminist Movement*, 145–201; Klaus Höhnig, *Der Bund Deutscher Frauenvereine in der Weimarer Republik 1919–1923* (Egelsbach, 1995).
138. Atina Grossmann, *Reforming Sex: The German Movement for Birth Control and Abortion Reform 1920–1950* (New York, 1995), 16; Steakley, *The Homosexual Emancipation Movement*; Fout, 'Sexual Politics'; Charlotte Wolff, *Magnus Hirschfeld: A Portrait of a Pioneer in Sexology* (London, 1986).
139. James Woycke, *Birth Control in Germany 1871–1933* (London, 1988), 113–16, 121, 147–8; Grossmann, *Reforming Sex*; Cornelie Usborne, *The Politics of the Body in Weimar Germany: Women's Reproductive Rights and Duties* (London, 1991).
140. Clifford Kirkpatrick, *Nazi Germany: Its Women and Family Life* (New York, 1938), 36; Elizabeth Harvey, 'Serving the Volk, Saving the Nation: Women in the Youth Movement and the Public Sphere in Weimar Germany', in Larry Eugene Jones and James Retallack (eds.), *Elections, Mass Politics, and Social Change in Modern Germany: New Perspectives* (New York, 1992), 201–22; Irene Stoehr, 'Neue Frau und alte Bewegung? Zum Generationskonflikt in der Frauenbewegung der Weimarer Republik', in Jutta Dalhoff *et al.* (eds.), *Frauenmacht in der Geschichte* (Düsseldorf, 1986), 390–400; Atina Grossmann, ' "Girlkultur" or Thoroughly Rationalized Female: A New Woman in Weimar Germany', in Judith Friedlander *et al.* (eds.), *Women in Culture and Politics: A Century of Change* (Bloomington, Ind., 1986), 62–80.
141. Raffael Scheck, *Mothers of the Nation: Right-Wing Women in German Politics, 1918–1923* (forthcoming, 2004); Höhnig, *Der Bund*; Ute Planert (ed.), *Nation, Politik und Geschlecht: Frauenbewegungen und Nationalismus in der Moderne* (Frankfurt am Main, 2000).
142. Merkl, *Political Violence*, 230–89, for personal testimonies; also Peter D. Stachura, *The German Youth Movement, 1900–1945: An Interpretative and Documentary History* (London, 1981), countering the emphasis of earlier work

on the proto-fascist aspects of the youth movement, as in the classic studies of Laqueur, *Young Germany*, Howard Becker, *German Youth: Bond or Free?* (New York, 1946), and Mosse, *The Crisis*, 171–89. See more recently, Jürgen Reulecke, ' "Hat die Jugendbewegung den Nationalsozialismus vorbereitet?" Zum Umgang mit einer falschen Frage', in Wolfgang R. Krabbe (ed.), *Politische Jugend in der Weimarer Republik* (Bochum, 1993), 222–43.

143. Klemperer, *Leben sammeln*, II. 56 (14 May 1925).

144. AT 144, 173, in Merkl, *Political Violence*, 290–310, esp. 303–4; also Margret Kraul, *Das deutsche Gymnasium 1780–1980* (Frankfurt am Main, 1984), 127–56, a useful overview; Folkert Meyer, *Schule der Untertanen: Lehrer und Politik in Preussen 1848–1900* (Hamburg, 1976), taking a strongly negative view of the political influence of the schools; Mosse, *The Crisis*, 149–70, emphasizing national-ist influences. For a good corrective to Meyer, see Marjorie Lamberti, 'Elementary School Teachers and the Struggle against Social Democracy in Wilhelmine Ger-many', *History of Education Quarterly*, 12 (1992), 74–97; and eadem, *State, Society and the Elementary School in Imperial Germany* (New York, 1989).

145. Konrad H. Jarausch, *Deutsche Studenten 1800–1970* (Frankfurt am Main, 1984), esp. 117–22; Michael S. Steinberg, *Sabers and Brown Shirts: The German Students' Path to National Socialism, 1918–1935* (Chicago, 1977); Geoffrey J. Giles, *Students and National Socialism in Germany* (Princeton, 1985), a study on Hamburg University. The literal translation of AStA, *Allgemeiner Studenten-Ausschuss*, is 'General Student Committee'; the functions of these bodies were comparable to those of student unions in the English-speaking world.

146. Michael H. Kater, *Studentenschaft und Rechtsradikalismus in Deutschland 1918–1933: Eine sozialgeschichtliche Studie zur Bildungskrise in der Weimarer Republik* (Hamburg, 1975); idem, 'The Work Student: A Socio-Economic Phenom-enon of Early Weimar Germany', *Journal of Contemporary History*, 10 (1975), 71–94; Wildt, *Generation des Unbedingten*, 72–80.

147. Ibid., 81–142.

148. Ulrich Herbert, *Best: Biographische Studien über Radikalismus, Weltan-schauung und Vernunft 1903–1989* (Bonn, 1996), 42–68.

149. AT 96, in Merkl, *Political Violence*, 236 (italics in original).

150. Maria Tatar, *Lustmord: Sexual Murder in Weimar Germany* (Princeton, 1995) (but see my review of this in many ways unconvincing book in *German History*, 14 (1996), 414–15); more conventionally, Birgit Kreutzahler, *Das Bild des Verbrechers in Romanen der Weimarer Republik: Eine Untersuchung vor dem Hintergrund anderer gesellschaftlicher Verbrecherbilder und gesellschaftlicher Grundzüge der Weimarer Republik* (Frankfurt am Main, 1987); Kracauer, *From Caligari*; Evans, *Rituals*, 531–6.

151. Patrick Wagner, *Volksgemeinschaft ohne Verbrecher: Konzeptionen und Praxis der Kriminalpolizei in der Zeit der Weimarer Republik und des Nationalsoz-ialismus* (Hamburg, 1996), 26–76, 153–79.

152. Evans, *Rituals*, 487–610.

153. Fieberg (ed.), *Im Namen*, 10–22.

154. Johannes Leeb, in *Deutsche Richterzeitung*, 1921, col. 1301, cited in Fieberg (ed.), *Im Namen*, 24–7.

155. Hans Hattenhauer, 'Wandlungen des Richterleitbildes im 19. und 20. Jahrhundert', in Ralf Dreier and Wolfgang Sellert (eds.), *Recht und Justiz im 'Dritten Reich'* (Frankfurt am Main, 1989), 9–33, at 13–16; Henning Grunwald, 'Political Lawyers in the Weimar Republic' (Ph.D. dissertation, Cambridge, 2002).

156. Fieberg (ed.), *Im Namen*, 24–7.

157. Emil J. Gumbel, *Vier Jahre politischer Mord* (Berlin, 1924), 73–5, extracted and tabulated in Fieberg (ed.), *Im Namen*, 29–35.

158. Recent, not wholly convincing attempts to view Weimar's judges in a more favourable light include Irmela Nahel, *Fememorde und Fememordprozesse in der Weimarer Republik* (Cologne, 1991) and Marcus Böttger, *Der Hochverrat in der höchstrichterlichen Rechtsprechung der Weimarer Republik: Ein Fall politischer Instrumentalisierung von Strafgesetzen?* (Frankfurt am Main, 1998).

159. Hannover and Hannover-Drück, *Politische Justiz*, 182–91; Kurt R. Grossmann, *Ossietzky: Ein deutscher Patriot* (Munich, 1963), 195–219; Elke Suhr, *Carl von Ossietzky: Eine Biographie* (Cologne, 1988), 162–8.

160. Hermann Schüler, *Auf der Flucht erschossen: Felix Fechenbach 1894–1933. Eine Biographie* (Cologne, 1981), 171–92.

161. Ilse Staff, *Justiz im Dritten Reich: Eine Dokumentation* (2nd edn., Frankfurt am Main, 1978 [1964]), 22–4.

162. Gotthard Jasper, *Der Schutz der Republik* (Tübingen, 1963).

163. Evans, *Rituals*, 503–6.

164. Ingo Müller, *Hitler's Justice: The Courts of the Third Reich* (London, 1991 [1987]), 10–24.

165. Hannover and Hannover-Drück, *Politische Justiz*, 77.

166. Ralph Angermund, *Deutsche Richterschaft 1918–1945: Krisenerfahrung, Illusion, Politische Rechtsprechung* (Frankfurt am Main, 1990), 33–4.

167. Wehler, *Deutsche Gesellschaftsgeschichte*, III. 907–15, 1086–90; Thomas Nipperdey, *Deutsche Geschichte 1866–1918*, I: *Arbeitswelt und Bürgergeist* (Munich, 1990), 335–73; more specialized work includes Volker Hentschel, *Geschichte der deutschen Sozialpolitik (1880–1980)* (Frankfurt am Main, 1983); Gerhard A. Ritter, *Sozialversicherung in Deutschland und England: Entstehung und Grundzuge im Vergleich* (Munich, 1983); and the pioneering study by Karl Erich Born, *Staat und Sozialpolitik seit Bismarcks Sturz 1890–1914: Ein Beitrag zur Geschichte der innenpolitischen Entwicklung des deutschen Reiches 1880–1914* (Wiesbaden, 1957).

168. David F. Crew, *Germans on Welfare: From Weimar to Hitler* (New York, 1998), 16–31.

169. Articles 119–22, 151–65 of the Weimar constitution (in Huber, *Deutsche Verfassungsgeschichte*, V–VII).

170. Ludwig Preller, *Sozialpolitik in der Weimarer Republik* (Düsseldorf, 1978

[1949]) is still the indispensable, classic guide; more recently, there have been important studies by Detlev J. K. Peukert, *Grenzen der Sozialdisziplinierung: Aufstieg und Krise der deutschen Jugendfürsorge 1878 bis 1932* (Cologne, 1986); Young-Sun Hong, *Welfare, Modernity, and the Weimar State, 1919–1933* (Princeton, 1998), and Crew, *Germans on Welfare*.

171. Otto Riebicke, *Was brachte der Weltkrieg? Tatsachen und Zahlen aus dem deutschen Ringen 1914–18* (Berlin, 1936), 97–112.

172. Whalen, *Bitter Wounds*, 156, 168.

173. Caplan, *Government*, 51, 60; Bessel, 'Why did the Weimar Republic Collapse?', 120–34, at 123–5.

174. Current German data protection laws forbid the use of the full names of private individuals.

175. Full details in Crew, *Germans on Welfare*, 107–15.

176. Ibid., esp. 204–8.

177. For the spread of such ideas, see Richard F. Wetzell, *Inventing the Criminal: A History of German Criminology 1880–1945* (Chapel Hill, NC, 2000); esp. 107–78; Wachsmann, *Hitler's Prisons*, part I; Regina Schulte, *Sperrbezirke: Tugendhaftigkeit und Prostitution in der bürgerlichen Welt* (Frankfurt am Main, 1979), 174–204; Schmuhl, *Rassenhygiene*, 31, 94; Evans, *Rituals*, 526–36.

178. Wagner, *Volksgemeinschaft*, 97–101.

179. Quoted in Evans, *Rituals*, 526–7.

180. Nikolaus Wachsmann et al., ' "Die soziale Prognose wird damit sehr trübe . . .": Theodor Viernstein und die Kriminalbiologische Sammelstelle in Bayern', in Michael Farin (ed.), *Polizeireport München 1799–1999* (Munich, 1999), 250–87.

181. Karl Binding and Alfred Hoche, *Die Freigabe der Vernichtung lebensunwerten Lebens: Ihr Mass und ihre Form* (Leipzig, 1920); Michael Burleigh, *Death and Deliverance: 'Euthanasia', in Germany 1900–1945* (Cambridge, 1994), 11–42; Hong, *Welfare*, 29–276.

182. Victor Klemperer, *Curriculum Vitae: Erinnerungen 1881–1918* (2 vols., Berlin, 1996 [1989]).

183. Klemperer, *Leben sammeln*, I. 8 (23 November 1918) and 9 (24 November 1918).

184. Ibid., 97 (12 April 1919), 109–10 (6 May 1919).

185. See the useful biographical sketch by Martin Chalmers, in Victor Klemperer, *I Shall Bear Witness: The Diaries of Victor Klemperer 1933–1941* (London, 1998), ix–xxi.

186. Klemperer, *Leben sammeln*, I. 600 (29 June 1922).

187. Ibid., II. 377 (10 September 1927).

188. Ibid., 571 (3 September 1929).

189. Ibid., 312 (26 December 1926).

190. Ibid., I. 187 (27 September 1919).

191. Ibid., I. 245 (14 March 1920).

192. Ibid., 248 (14 March 1920).

193. Ibid., 433–4 (20 April 1921).

194. Ibid., II. 49 (27 April 1925).

195. Ibid., 758 (7 August 1932).

196. Martin Liepach, *Das Wahlverhalten der jüdischen Bevölkerung: Zur politischen Orientierung der Juden in der Weimarer Republik* (Tübingen, 1996) esp. p. 211–310; more generally, Wolfgang Benz (ed.) *Jüdisches Leben in der Weimarer Republik* (Tübingen, 1998), 271–80; and Donald L. Niewyk, *The Jews in Weimar Germany* (Baton Rouge, La., 1980), 11–43.

197. Klaus Schwabe, 'Die deutsche Politik und die Juden im Ersten Weltkrieg', in Hans Otto Horch (ed.), *Judentum, Antisemitismus und europäische Kultur* (Tübingen, 1988), 255–66; Egmont Zechlin, *Die deutsche Politik und die Juden im Ersten Weltkrieg* (Göttingen, 1969), esp. 527–41; Saul Friedländer, 'Die politischen Veränderungen der Kriegszeit und ihre Auswirkungen auf die Judenfrage', in Werner E. Mosse (ed.), *Deutsches Judentum in Krieg und Revolution 1916–1923* (Tübingen, 1971), 27–65. See, more generally, Jochmann, *Gesellschaftskrise*, 99–170 ('Die Ausbreitung des Antisemitismus in Deutschland 1914–1923'), and 171–94 ('Der Antisemitismus und seine Bedeutung für den Untergang der Weimarer Republik').

198. Stark, *Entrepreneurs*, 141, 208–9.

199. Jack Wertheimer, *Unwelcome Strangers: East European Jews in Imperial Germany* (New York, 1987), table IV; Wolfgang J. Mommsen, *Bürgerstolz und Weltmachtstreben: Deutschland unter Wilhelm II. 1890 bis 1918* (Berlin, 1995), 434–40; Steven Aschheim, *Brothers and Strangers: The East European Jew in German and German Jewish Consciousness 1800–1923* (Madison, 1982).

200. *Vossische Zeitung*, 6 November 1923, excerpted and translated in Peukert, *The Weimar Republic*, 160 (amended); see also David Clay Large, '"Out with the Ostjuden": The Scheunenviertel Riots in Berlin, November 1923', in Werner Bergmann *et al.* (eds.), *Exclusionary Violence: Antisemitic Riots in Modern Germany* (Ann Arbor, 2002), 123–40, and Dirk Walter, *Antisemitische Kriminalität und Gewalt: Judenfeindschaft in der Weimarer Republik* (Bonn, 1999), esp. 151–4.

201. Peter Pulzer, 'Der Anfang vom Ende', in Arnold Paucker (ed.), *Die Juden im nationalsozialistischen Deutschland 1933–1944* (Tübingen, 1986), 3–15; Trude Maurer, *Ostjuden in Deutschland, 1918–1933* (Hamburg, 1986).

202. Kauders, *German Politics*, 182–91; for Protestantism, see Kurt Nowak and Gérard Raulet (eds.), *Protestantismus und Antisemitismus in der Weimarer Republik* (Frankfurt am Main, 1994). More generally, see Heinrich August Winkler, 'Die deutsche Gesellschaft der Weimarer Republik und der Antisemitismus', in Bernd Martin and Ernst Schulin (eds.), *Die Juden als Minderheit in der Geschichte* (Munich, 1981), 271–89, and Jochmann, *Gesellschaftskrise*, 99–170. For a local study, see Stefanie Schüler-Springorum, *Die jüdische Minderheit in Königsberg, Preussen 1871–1945* (Göttingen, 1996).

Chapter 3 THE RISE OF NAZISM

1. Peter Jelavich, *Munich and Theatrical Modernism: Politics, Playwriting, and Performance 1890–1914* (Cambridge, Mass., 1985), gives a good account of theatre in Munich at the time.

2. For a dramatic description of Eisner, based on wide and unconventional reading in contemporary sources, see Richard M. Watt, *The Kings Depart: The German Revolution and the Treaty of Versailles 1918–19* (London, 1973 [1968]), 312–30 and 354–81. See also Franz Schade, *Kurt Eisner und die bayerische Sozialdemokratie* (Hanover, 1961) and Peter Kritzer, *Die bayerische Sozialdemokratie und die bayerische Politik in den Jahren 1918–1923* (Munich, 1969). For a recent biography, see Bernhard Grau, *Kurt Eisner 1867–1919: Eine Biographie* (Munich, 2001).

3. Allan Mitchell, *Revolution in Bavaria 1918/1919: The Eisner Regime and the Soviet Republic* (Princeton, 1965), 171–2; Freya Eisner, *Kurt Eisner: Die Politik der libertären Sozialismus* (Frankfurt am Main, 1979), 175–80.

4. Mitchell, *Revolution*, for these and subsequent events; see also Winkler, *Von der Revolution*, 184–90, and Heinrich Hillmayr, *Roter und weisser Terror in Bayern nach 1918: Erscheinungsformen und Folgen der Gewaltätigkeiten im Verlauf der revolutionären Ereignisse nach dem Ende des Ersten Weltkrieges* (Munich, 1974).

5. Watt, *The Kings Depart*, 312–30, 354–81; David Clay Large, *Where Ghosts Walked: Munich's Road to the Third Reich* (New York, 1997), 76–92, is another colourful account. Friedrich Hitzer, *Anton Graf Arco: Das Attentat auf Kurt Eisner und die Schüsse im Landtag* (Munich, 1988), tells the assassin's story as researched for a film screenplay by the author. For Hoffmann, see Diethard Hennig, *Johannes Hoffmann: Sozialdemokrat und Bayerischer Ministerpräsident: Biographie* (Munich, 1990).

6. Quoted in Watt, *The Kings Depart*, 364; Hans Beyer, *Von der Novemberrevolution zur Räterepublik in München* (Berlin, 1957) (well-documented East German account), esp. 77–8.

7. Watt, *The Kings Depart*, 366–8.

8. Large, *Where Ghosts Walked*, 70.

9. Carsten, *Revolution*, 218–23; Hannover and Hannover-Drück, *Politische Justiz*, 53–75.

10. See Anthony Nicholls, 'Hitler and the Bavarian Background to National Socialism', in idem and Erich Matthias (eds.), *German Democracy and the Triumph of Hitler: Essays on Recent German History* (London, 1971), 129–59.

11. For a detailed account of Hitler's activities in 1918–19, see Kershaw, *Hitler*, I. 116–21, and Anton Joachimsthaler, *Hitlers Weg begann in München 1913–1923* (Munich, 2000 [1989]), 177–319.

12. Kershaw, *Hitler*: I. 3–13, for a judicious sifting of fact from legend, interpretation from speculation, on Hitler's early years.

13. Carl E. Schorske, 'The Ringstrasse, its Critics, and the Birth of Urban Modernism', in idem, *Fin-de-Siècle Vienna*, 24–115.

14. August Kubizek, *Adolf Hitler: Mein Jugendfreund* (Graz, 1953), provides many details; but see the critique by Franz Jetzinger, *Hitler's Youth* (London, 1958 [1956]), 167–74.

15. The paucity of reliable evidence about Hitler before 1919 has led to intense debate over his claim that he became an extreme, political antisemite in pre-war Vienna as a result of encounters with Jews, particularly 'Eastern Jews', immigrants from Galicia. While Hitler's own version seems overdrawn, recent attempts to argue that he was not antisemitic at all are equally unconvincing. See Kershaw, *Hitler*, I, esp. 49–69, and Joachimsthaler, *Hitlers Weg*, 45–9.

16. Adolf Hitler, *Mein Kampf* (trans. Ralph Manheim, introd. D.C. Watt, London, 1969 [1925/6]), 39–41.

17. Ibid., 71, 88, 95.

18. Kershaw, *Hitler*, I. 81–7; Joachimsthaler, *Hitlers Weg*, 77–97. Hitler's own account is in *Mein Kampf*, 116–17. For a racy account of bohemian life in Schwabing, see Large, *Where Ghosts Walked*, 3–42.

19. Hitler, *Mein Kampf*, 148–9.

20. Kershaw, *Hitler*, I. 87–101.

21. Hitler, *Mein Kampf*, 11–169.

22. Geyer, *Verkehrte Welt*, 278–318.

23. Hitler to Adolf Gemlich, 16 September 1919, in Eberhard Jäckel and Axel Kuhn (eds.), *Hitler: Sämtliche Aufzeichnungen 1905–1924* (Stuttgart, 1980), 88–90; Ernst Deuerlein, 'Hitlers Eintritt in die Politik und die Reichswehr', *VfZ* 7 (1959), 203–5.

24. 'Anton Drexlers Politisches Erwachen' (1919), reprinted in Albrecht Tyrell (ed.), *Führer befiehl . . .: Selbstzeugnisse aus der 'Kampfzeit' der NSDAP* (Düsseldorf, 1969), 20–22.

25. Tyrell (ed.), *Führer befiehl*, 22; Kershaw, *Hitler*, I. 126–8, 131–9; Ernst Deuerlein (ed.), *Der Aufstieg der NSDAP in Augenzeugenberichten* (Munich, 1974), 56–61. Joachimsthaler, *Hitlers Weg*, 198–319, sifts fact from legend for Hitler's life at this time and referees later controversies; Albrecht Tyrell, *Vom 'Trommler' zum 'Führer': Der Wandel von Hitlers Selbstverständnis zwischen 1919 und 1924 und die Entwicklung der NSDAP* (Munich, 1975) gives a well-informed account of Hitler's early political career. See also Werner Maser, *Die Frühgeschichte der NSDAP: Hitlers Weg bis 1924* (Frankfurt am Main, 1965). For the Thule Society, see Reginald H. Phelps, ' "Before Hitler Came": Thule Society and Germanen Orden', *Journal of Modern History*, 35 (1963), 245–61.

26. Uwe Lohalm, *Völkischer Radikalismus: Die Geschichte des Deutschvölkischen Schutz- und Trutzbundes, 1919–1923* (Hamburg, 1970).

27. Tyrell, *Vom Trommler*, 72–89; Georg Franz-Willing, *Ursprung der Hitlerbewegung 1919–1922* (Preussisch Oldendorf, 1974 [1962]), 38–109.

28. Broszat, *Der Staat Hitlers*, 43–5.

29. Hitler, *Mein Kampf*, 620–21 (translation amended).

30. Reginald H. Phelps, 'Hitler als Parteiredner im Jahre 1920', *VfZ* 11 (1963), 274–330; similarly, Jäckel and Kuhn (eds.), *Hitler*, 115, 132, 166, 198, 252, 455, 656.

31. The phrase 'socialism of fools' – originally 'socialism of the stupid' – is often attributed to the prewar Social Democratic leader August Bebel but probably originated with the Austrian democrat Ferdinand Kronawetter (Pulzer, *The Rise*, 269 and note). It was in general use among Social Democrats in Germany by the 1890s; see Francis L. Carsten, *August Bebel und die Organisation der Massen* (Berlin, 1991), 165.

32. Franz-Willing, *Ursprung*, 120–27; Broszat, *Der Staat Hitlers*, 39.

33. Ernst Nolte, *Three Faces of Fascism: Action Française, Italian Fascism, National Socialism* (New York, 1969 [1963]), and later, in a different and more controversial form, *Der europäische Bürgerkrieg 1917–1945: Nationalsozialismus und Bolschewismus* (Frankfurt am Main, 1987), argued for the primacy of anti-Bolshevism.

34. Hitler, *Mein Kampf*, 289.

35. All quoted in Longerich, *Der ungeschriebene Befehl*, 32–4.

36. Bruno Thoss, *Der Ludendorff-Kreis: 1919–1923. München als Zentrum der mitteleuropäische Gegenrevolution zwischen Revolution und Hitler-Putsch* (Munich, 1978), provides exhaustive detail.

37. Wolf Rüdiger Hess (ed.), *Rudolf Hess: Briefe 1908–1933* (Munich, 1987), 251 (Hess to his parents, 24 March 1920).

38. Joachim C. Fest, *The Face of the Third Reich* (London, 1979 [1970]), 283–314, for a shrewd character sketch of Hess; Smith, *The Ideological Origins*, 223–40; Lange, 'Der Terminus "Lebensraum"', 426–37; Hans Grimm, *Volk ohne Raum* (Munich, 1926); Dietrich Orlow, 'Rudolf Hess: Deputy Führer', in Ronald Smelser and Rainer Zitelmann (eds.), *The Nazi Elite* (London, 1993 [1989]), 74–84. Hans-Adolf Jacobsen, *Karl Haushofer: Leben und Werk* (2 vols., Boppard, 1979) reprints many of Haushofer's writings; Frank Ebeling, *Geopolitik: Karl Haushofer und seine Raumwissenschaft 1919–1945* (Berlin, 1994) is a study of his ideas.

39. Margarete Plewnia, *Auf dem Weg zu Hitler: Der völkische Publizist Dietrich Eckart* (Bremen, 1970); Tyrell, *Vom Trommler*, 190–94; Alfred Rosenberg (ed.), *Dietrich Eckart. Ein Vermächtnis* (4th edn., Munich, 1937 [1928]), with a selection of Eckart's verse.

40. Alfred Rosenberg, *Selected Writings* (ed. Robert Pois, London, 1970); Fest, *The Face*, 247–58; Walter Laqueur, *Russia and Germany: A Century of Conflict* (London, 1965), 55–61, 116–17, 148–53; Adolf Hitler, *Hitler's Table Talk 1941–1944: His Private Conversations* (London, 1973 [1953]), 422–6; Norman Cohn, *Warrant for Genocide: The Myth of the Jewish World-Conspiracy and the Protocols of the Elders of Zion* (London, 1967), esp. 187–237; Reinhard Bollmus, 'Alfred Rosenberg: National Socialism's "Chief Ideologue"', in Smelser and Zitelman (eds.), *The Nazi Elite*, 183–93; Robert Cecil, *The Myth of the Master Race: Alfred Rosenberg and Nazi Ideology* (London, 1972). See also, more generally,

Thomas Klepsch, *Nationalsozialistische Ideologie: Eine Beschreibung ihrer Struktur vor 1933* (Münster, 1990), and the excellent selection of extracts from a variety of Nazi ideologues in Barbara Miller Lane and Leila J. Rupp (eds.), *Nazi Ideology before 1933: A Documentation* (Manchester, 1978).

41. Hans Frank, *Im Angesicht des Galgens: Deutung Hitlers und seiner Zeit auf Grund eigner Erlebisse und Erkenntnisse* (2nd edn., Neuhaus, 1955 [1953]), no page, cited in Fest, *The Face*, 330, and ibid., 38–42, cited in Kershaw, *Hitler*, I. 148; Christoph Klessmann, 'Hans Frank: Party Jurist and Governor-General in Poland', in Smelser and Zitelmann (eds.), *The Nazi Elite*, 39–47.

42. Citing Deuerlein (ed.), *Der Aufstieg*, 108–12.

43. Dietrich Orlow, *The History of the Nazi Party*, I: 1919–1933 (Newton Abbot, 1971 [1969]), 11–37.

44. Kershaw, *Hitler*, I. 160–65; Deuerlein (ed.), *Der Aufstieg*, 135–41.

45. Kershaw, *Hitler*, I. 175–80; Deuerlein (ed.), *Der Aufstieg*, 142–61.

46. Deuerlein (ed.), *Der Aufstieg*, 145–6.

47. Franz-Willing, *Ursprung*, 127.

48. Hannover and Hannover-Drück, *Politische Justiz*, 105–44.

49. Kershaw, *Hitler*, I. 170–73; Peter Longerich, *Die braunen Bataillone: Geschichte der SA* (Munich, 1989), 9–32.

50. Conan Fischer, 'Ernst Julius Röhm: Chief of Staff of the SA and Indispensable Outsider', in Smelser and Zitelmann (eds.), *The Nazi Elite*, 173–82.

51. Ernst Röhm, *Die Geschichte eines Hochverräters* (Munich, 1928), 9, 365–6; Fest, *The Face*, 206, 518–19 (n. 9).

52. Röhm, *Die Geschichte*, 363.

53. Deuerlein (ed.), *Der Aufstieg*, 142–83, for accounts of the growing violence of the Nazi movement in this period; Fischer, 'Ernst Julius Röhm', for details of Röhm's uneasy relationship with Hitler.

54. Kershaw, *Hitler*, I. 180–85.

55. Adrian Lyttelton, *The Seizure of Power: Fascism in Italy 1919–1929* (London, 1973), remains the classic account; Denis Mack Smith, *Mussolini* (London, 1981) is a scathing biography; Richard J. B. Bosworth, *Mussolini* (London, 2002) is a good recent life; Franz-Willing, *Ursprung*, 126–7 for the origins of the Nazi Party's standards. For contacts and influences, see Klaus-Peter Hoepke, *Die deutsche Rechte und der italienische Faschismus: Ein Beitrag zum Selbstverständnis und zur Politik von Gruppen und Verbänden der deutschen Rechten* (Düsseldorf, 1968), esp. 186–94 and 292–5.

56. Amidst a vast and controversial literature, Stanley G. Payne, *A History of Fascism 1914–1945* (London, 1995), is the best general survey, and Kevin Passmore, *Fascism: A Very Short Introduction* (Oxford, 2002) the most useful brief account. Roger Griffin, *International Fascism – Theories, Causes and the New Consensus* (London, 1998), is an influential theoretical text; Kershaw, *The Nazi Dictatorship*, 26–46, gives, as usual, a sensible and level-headed account of the historiography.

57. AT 567, 199, in Merkl, *Political Violence*, 196–7.
58. AT 206, 379, ibid.; for an unusual angle on the Schlageter case, see Karl Radek, 'Leo Schlageter: The Wanderer in the Void', in Kaes *et al.* (eds.), *The Weimar Republic Sourcebook*, 312–14 (originally 'Leo Schlageter: Der Wanderer ins Nichts', *Die Rote Fahne*, 144 (26 June, 1923). For a detailed account of the 'passive resistance', stressing its popular roots, see Fischer, *The Ruhr Crisis*, 84–181; for Schlageter's background in the Free Corps, Waite, *Vanguard*, 235–8; for the sabotage movement organized behind the scenes by the German army, Gerd Krüger, '"Ein Fanal des Widerstandes im Ruhrgebiet": Das "Unternehmen Wesel" in der Osternacht des Jahres 1923. Hingergründe eines angeblichen "Husarenstreiches"', *Mitteilungsblatt des Instituts für soziale Bewegungen*, 4 (2000), 95–140.
59. Sander L. Gilman, *On Blackness without Blacks: Essays on the Image of the Black in Germany* (Boston, 1982).
60. AT 183, in Merkl, *Political Violence*, 193.
61. Gisela Lebeltzer, 'Der "Schwarze Schmach": Vorurteile – Propaganda – Mythos', *Geschichte und Gesellschaft*, 11 (1985), 37–58; Keith Nelson, '"The Black Horror on the Rhine": Race as a Factor in Post-World War I Diplomacy', *Journal of Modern History*, 42 (1970), 606–27; Sally Marks, 'Black Watch on the Rhine: A Study in Propaganda, Prejudice and Prurience', *European Studies Review*, 13 (1983), 297–334. For their eventual fate, see Reiner Pommerin, *'Sterilisierung der Rheinlandbastarde': Das Schicksal einer farbigen deutschen Minderheit 1918–1937* (Düsseldorf, 1979).
62. Richard J. Evans, 'Hans von Hentig and the Politics of German Criminology', in Angelika Ebbinghaus and Karl Heinz Roth (eds.), *Grenzgänge: Deutsche Geschichte des 20. Jahrhunderts im Spiegel von Publizistik, Rechtsprechung und historischer Forschung* (Lüneburg, 1999), 238–64.
63. Kershaw, *Hitler*, I. 185–91; Georg Franz-Willing, *Krisenjahr der Hitlerbewegung 1923* (Preussisch Oldendorf, 1975); Helmuth Auerbach, 'Hitlers politische Lehrjahre und die Münchner Gesellschaft 1919–1923', *VfZ* 25 (1977), 1–45; Franz-Willing, *Ursprung*, 266–99; Ernst Hanfstaengl, *Zwischen Weissem und Braunem Haus: Memoiren eines politischen Aussenseiters* (Munich, 1970).
64. Hitler's views can be found in Hitler, *Hitler's Table Talk*, 154–6. For an excellent account, see Robin Lenman, 'Julius Streicher and the Origins of the NSDAP in Nuremberg, 1918–1923', in Nicholls and Matthias (eds.), *German Democracy*, 161–74 (the source for the opinion of Streicher's verse). For a study of the town's brownshirts, see Eric G. Reiche, *The Development of the SA in Nürnberg, 1922–34* (Cambridge, 1986).
65. Anthony Nicholls, 'Hitler and the Bavarian Background to National Socialism', in idem and Matthias (eds.), *German Democracy*, 111.
66. Franz-Willing, *Krisenjahr*, 295–318; for Ludendorff's activities, see idem, *Putsch und Verbotszeit der Hitlerbewegung November 1923–Februar 1925* (Preussisch Oldendorf, 1977), 9–65.
67. Fest, *The Face*, 113–29; Richard Overy, *Goering: The 'Iron Man'* (London,

1984); Alfred Kube, 'Hermann Goering: Second Man in the Third Reich', in Smelser and Zitelmann (eds.), *The Nazi Elite*, 62–73, categorizes Göring as a 'late-imperialist' conservative; see also the same author's *Pour le mérite und Hakenkreuz: Hermann Goering im Dritten Reich* (2nd edn., Munich, 1987 [1986]), 4–21; Stefan Martens, *Hermann Goering: 'Erster Paladin des Führers' und 'Zweiter Mann im Reich'* (Paderborn, 1985), 15–19; Werner Maser, *Hermann Göring: Hitlers janusköpfiger Paladin: Die politische Biographie* (Berlin, 2000), 13–55.

68. Franz-Willing, *Krisenjahr*, details the development of the Party in 1923. Harold J. Gordon, *Hitler and the Beer Hall Putsch* (Princeton, 1972), provides an exhaustive account of the political background: see especially 25–184 (part I: 'The Contenders in the Struggle for Power'). For the documentary record, see Ernst Deuerlein (ed.), *Der Hitler-Putsch: Bayerische Dokumente zum 8./9. November 1923* (Stuttgart, 1962), 153–308; more briefly in Deuerlein (ed.), *Der Aufstieg*, 184–202.

69. Karl Alexander von Müller, witness statement at Hitler's trial, quoted in Deuerlein (ed.), *Der Aufstieg*, 192–6.

70. Among many accounts of these events, see Kershaw, *Hitler*, I. 205–12; Gordon, *Hitler and the Beer Hall Putsch*, 270–409; Franz-Willing, *Putsch und Verbotszeit*, 66–141; Deuerlein (ed.), *Der Hitler-Putsch*, esp. 308–417, 487–515; selected documents translated in Noakes and Pridham (ed.), *Nazism*, I. 26–34. For Göring, see Maser, *Hermann Göring*, 58–78.

71. Bernd Steger, 'Der Hitlerprozess und Bayerns Verhältnis zum Reich 1923/24', *VfZ* 23 (1977), 441–66.

72. Deuerlein (ed.), *Der Aufstieg*, 203–230; Lothar Gruchmann and Reinhard Weber (eds.), *Der Hitler-Prozess 1924: Wortlaut der Hauptverhandlung vor dem Volksgericht München I* (2 vols., Munich, 1997, 1999) for the complete transcript and judgment. See also Otto Gritschneider, *Bewährungsfrist für den Terroristen Adolf H.: Der Hitler-Putsch und die bayerische Justiz* (Munich, 1990), and idem, *Der Hitler-Prozess und sein Richter Georg Neithardt: Skandalurteil von 1924 ebnet Hitler den Weg* (Munich, 2001).

73. Quoted in Tyrell, *Führer befiehl*, 67, translation in Noakes and Pridham (eds.), *Nazism*, I. 34–5 (slightly amended); Hitler's complete statements in court in Jäckel and Kuhn (eds.), *Hitler*, 1061–216; also Deuerlein (ed.), *Der Aufstieg*, 203–28.

74. See the account of its genesis and composition in Kershaw, *Hitler*, I. 240–53.

75. Hitler, *Mein Kampf*, 307.

76. Ibid., 597–99. The centrality of these ideas to Hitler's 'world-view' was established by Eberhard Jäckel, *Hitler's Weltanschauung: A Blueprint for Power* (Middletown, Conn., 1972 [1969]).

77. Adolf Hitler, *Hitler's Secret Book* (New York, 1961); Martin Broszat, 'Betrachtungen zu "Hitlers Zweitem Buch"', *VfZ* 9 (1981), 417–29.

78. Werner Maser, *Hitlers Mein Kampf: Geschichte, Auszüge, Kommentare* (Munich, 1966), provides details of the book, its composition and its fate; Hermann Hammer, 'Die deutschen Ausgaben von Hitlers "Mein Kampf"', *VfZ* 4 (1956), 161–78, covers its publishing history. The view that Hitler was a power-hungry

opportunist with no consistent aims was central to Alan Bullock's classic biography, *Hitler: A Study in Tyranny* (London, 1953); the argument for consistency was first put by Hugh Trevor-Roper, 'The Mind of Adolf Hitler', in Hitler, *Hitler's Table Talk*, vii–xxxv. The vagaries of Hitler's foreign policy, and its underlying goals, are analysed in Geoffrey Stoakes, *Hitler and the Quest for World Dominion* (Leamington Spa, 1987).

79. Longerich, *Der ungeschriebene Befehl*, 37–9.
80. Kershaw, *Hitler*, I. 218–19, 223–4, 250–53; Broszat, *Der Staat Hitlers*, 13–16.
81. Kershaw, *Hitler*, I. 224–34. For a detailed account of the Nazi Party in the aftermath of the trial and imprisonment of its leader, see Franz-Willing, *Putsch und Verbotszeit*, 162–285.
82. Donald Cameron Watt, 'Die bayerischen Bemühungen um Ausweisung Hitlers 1924', *VfZ* 6 (1958), 270–80. See, more generally, David Jablonsky, *The Nazi Party in Dissolution: Hitler and the Verbotszeit 1923–1925* (London, 1989), and Deuerlein (ed.), *Der Aufstieg*, 231–54.
83. Deuerlein (ed), *Der Aufstieg*, 245.
84. Fest, *The Face*, 215; Longerich, *Die braunen Battaillone*, 51–2.
85. Kershaw, *Hitler*, I. 257–70.
86. Udo Kissenkoetter, 'Gregor Strasser: Nazi Party Organizer or Weimar Politician?', in Smelser and Zitelmann (eds.), *The Nazi Elite*, 224–34.
87. Gregor Strasser to Oswald Spengler, 8 July 1925, in Oswald Spengler, *Spengler Letters 1913–1936* (ed. Arthur Helps, London, 1966), 184.
88. Orlow, *The History of the Nazi Party*, I. 66–7; see also, more generally, Udo Kissenkoetter, *Gregor Strasser und die NSDAP* (Stuttgart, 1978); Peter D. Stachura, *Gregor Strasser and the Rise of Nazism* (London, 1983); and Klepsch, *Nationalsozialistische Ideologie*, 143–50.
89. Elke Fröhlich, 'Joseph Goebbels: The Propagandist', in Smelser and Zitelmann (eds.), *The Nazi Elite*, 48–61; Ralf Georg Reuth, *Goebbels: Eine Biographie* (Munich, 1995), 11–75; and Michel Kai, *Vom Poeten zum Demagogen: Die schriftstellerischen Versuche Joseph Goebbels'* (Cologne, 1999). Joachim C. Fest, 'Joseph Goebbels: Eine Porträtskizze', *VfZ* 43 (1995), 565–80, is a penetrating reassessment of Goebbels's character in the light of his diary. For Goebbels's diary itself, see Elke Fröhlich, 'Joseph Goebbels und sein Tagebuch: Zu den handschriftlichen Aufzeichnungen von 1924 bis 1941', *VfZ* 35 (1987), 489–522. The critique of Bernd Sösemann, 'Die Tagesaufzeichnungen des Joseph Goebbels und ihre unzulänglichen Veröffentlichungen', *Publizistik*, 37 (1992), 213–44, does not convince; Fröhlich's transcriptions were not intended to be a full scholarly edition but simply a way of making the diaries available to historians.
90. Hugh Trevor-Roper, *The Last Days of Hitler* (London, 1947), 67 (also citing Speer to the same effect); Fröhlich, 'Joseph Goebbels', 48.
91. Elke Fröhlich (ed.), *Die Tagebücher von Joseph Goebbels: Sämtliche Fragmente*, part I: *Aufzeichnungen 1924–1941*, I: 27. 6. 1924–31. 12. 1930 (Munich, 1987), 48 (23 July 1924).

92. Fröhlich (ed.), *Die Tagebücher*, I/I. 134–5 (14 October 1925).

93. Ibid., 140–41 (6 November 1925); see, more generally, Reuth, *Goebbels*, 76–147.

94. Fröhlich (ed.), *Die Tagebücher*, I/I. 161–2 (15 February 1926).

95. Kershaw, *Hitler*, I. 270–77; Reuth, *Goebbels*, 76–107; Helmut Heiber (ed.), *The Early Goebbels Diaries: The Journals of Josef Goebbels from 1925–1926* (London, 1962), 66–7.

96. Fröhlich (ed.), *Die Tagebücher*, I/I. 171–3 (13 April 1926) and 174–5 (19 April 1926).

97. Kershaw, *Hitler*, I. 277–9; Deuerlein (ed.), *Der Aufstieg*, 255–302. The word *Gau* for 'Region' deliberately called to mind tribal divisions of Germany in the early Middle Ages.

98. Kershaw, *Hitler*, I. 278–9; Orlow, *The History of the Nazi Party*, I. 69–75.

99. Noakes and Pridham (eds.), *Nazism*, I. 36–56; also, Erwin Barth, *Joseph Goebbels und die Formierung des Führer-Mythos 1917 bis 1934* (Erlangen, 1999).

100. For Goebbels's activities in Berlin, see Reuth, *Goebbels*, 108–268.

101. Quoted ibid., 114.

102. Hoover Institution, Stanford, California: NSDAP Hauptarchiv microfilm reel 6 Akte 141: letter from Max Amann to Gustav Seifert, 27 October 1925.

103. Noakes and Pridham (eds.), *Nazism*, I. 58.

104. Gerhard Schulz, *Zwischen Demokratie und Diktatur: Verfassungspolitik und Reichsreform in der Weimarer Republik* (3 vols., Berlin, 1963–92), II: *Deutschland am Vorabend der Grossen Krise* (Berlin, 1987), 149–307; Robert G. Moeller, 'Winners as Losers in the German Inflation: Peasant Protest over the Controlled Economy', in Gerald D. Feldman *et al.* (eds.), *The German Inflation: A Preliminary Balance* (Berlin, 1982), 255–88.

105. Shelley Baranowski, *The Sanctity of Rural Life: Nobility, Protestantism and Nazism in Weimar Prussia* (New York, 1995), 120–23.

106. John E. Farquharson, *The Plough and the Swastika: The NSDAP and Agriculture in Germany, 1928–1945* (London, 1976), 3–12, 25–33; Dieter Hertz-Eichenrode, *Politik und Landwirtschaft in Ostpreussen 1919–1930: Untersuchung eines Strukturproblems in der Weimarer Republik* (Opladen, 1969), 88–9, 329–37.

107. Dieter Gessner, *Agrardepression und Präsidialregierungen in Deutschland 1930–1933: Probleme des Agrarkapitalismus am Ende der Weimarer Republik* (Düsseldorf, 1977), 191–4; idem, *Agrarverbände in der Weimarer Republik: Wirtschaftliche und soziale Voraussetzungen agrarkonservativer Politik vor 1933* (Düsseldorf, 1976), 234–63.

108. Rudolf Rietzler, *'Kampf in der Nordmark': Das Aufkommen des Nationalsozialismus in Schleswig-Holstein (1919–1928)* (Neumünster, 1982); Frank Bajohr (ed.), *Norddeutschland im Nationalsozialismus* (Hamburg, 1993); and the classic regional study by Jeremy Noakes, *The Nazi Party in Lower Saxony 1921–1933* (Oxford, 1971), esp. 104–7.

109. Noakes and Pridham (eds.), *Nazism*, I. 15, 61.

110. Ibid., 15, 61, citing Gottfried Feder, *Das Programm der NSDAP und seine weltanschaulichen Grundgedanken* (Munich, 1934), 15–18.

111. Rudolf Heberle, *Landbevölkerung und Nationalsozialismus: Eine soziologische Untersuchung der politischen Willensbildung in Schleswig-Holstein 1918 bis 1932* (Stuttgart, 1963), 160–71; see also idem, *From Democracy to Nazism: A Regional Case Study on Political Parties in Germany* (New York, 1970 [1945]), an early classic of electoral sociology. For the drive to unify farmers of all types as a single pressure-group, see Jens Flemming, *Landwirtschaftliche Interessen und Demokratie: Ländliche Gesellschaft, Agrarverbände und Staat 1890–1925* (Bonn, 1978), 323–7.

112. Claus-Christian W. Szejnmann, *Nazism in Central Germany: The Brownshirts in 'Red' Saxony* (New York, 1999), 50–51; Falter *et al.*, *Wahlen*, 98.

113. Geoffrey Pridham, *Hitler's Rise to Power: The Nazi Movement in Bavaria 1923–1933* (London, 1973), 84–6.

114. Orlow, *The History of the Nazi Party*, I. 173–5 (somewhat overstating the coherence of the Nazis' electoral strategy); Winkler, *Weimar*, 344–56.

115. Tyrell, *Vom Trommler*, 163–73 for quotes; idem (ed.), *Führer befiehl*, 129–30, 163–4; Kershaw, *Hitler*, I. 294.

116. Orlow, *The History of the Nazi Party*, I. 167–71.

117. Ibid., 171–3.

118. Claudia Koonz, *Mothers in the Fatherland: Women, the Family, and Nazi Politics* (London, 1987), 72–80.

119. Jill Stephenson, *The Nazi Organisation of Women* (London, 1981), 23–74.

120. Peter D. Stachura, *Nazi Youth in the Weimar Republic* (Santa Barbara, Calif., 1975); Laqueur, *Young Germany*, 193; Arno Klönne, *Jugend im Dritten Reich: Dokumente und Analysen* (Cologne, 1982); Hans-Christian Brandenburg, *Die Geschichte der HJ. Wege und Irrwege einer Generation* (Cologne, 1968); Stachura, *The German Youth Movement*.

121. Daniel Horn, 'The National Socialist *Schülerbund* and the Hitler Youth, 1929–1933', *Central European History*, 11 (1978), 355–75; Martin Klaus, *Mädchen in der Hitlerjugend: Die Erziehung zur 'deutschen Frau'* (Cologne, 1980).

122. Baldur von Schirach, *Die Feier der neuen Front* (Munich, 1929). See Michael Wortmann, 'Baldur von Schirach: Student Leader, Hitler Youth Leader, *Gauleiter* in Vienna', in Smelser and Zitelmann (eds.), *The Nazi Elite*, 202–11.

123. See Arthur D. Brenner, *Emil J. Gumbel: Weimar German Pacifist and Professor* (Boston, 2001); quote from *Deutsche Republik*, 2 July 1932, in Steven P. Remy, *The Heidelberg Myth: The Nazification and Denazification of a German University* (Cambridge, Mass., 2002), 11.

124. Geoffrey J. Giles, 'The Rise of the National Socialist Students' Association and the Failure of Political Education in the Third Reich', in Peter D. Stachura (ed.), *The Shaping of the Nazi State* (London, 1978), 160–85; Wortmann, 'Baldur von Schirach', 204–5; Kater, *Studentenschaft und Rechtsradikalismus*; Anselm

Faust, *Der Nationalsozialistische Deutsche Studentenbund: Studenten und Nationalsozialismus in der Weimarer Republik* (Düsseldorf, 1973); Giles, *Students;* Steinberg, *Sabers and Brown Shirts;* Michael Grüttner, *Studenten im Dritten Reich* (Paderborn, 1995), 19–42, 60.

125. Hans-Gerhard Schumann, *Nationalsozialismus und Gewerkschaftsbewegung: Die Vernichtung der deutschen Gewerkschaften und der Aufbau der 'Deutschen Arbeitsfront'* (Hanover, 1958).

126. Merkl, *Political Violence*, 120, 208, 217, 220, 239, 244, 306, 372–3, 427, 515–16.

127. Hamel, *Völkischer Verband.*

128. AT 271, in Merkl, *Political Violence*, 516.

129. Orlow, *The History of the Nazi Party*, I. 271–6.

130. Merkl, *Political Violence*, assesses the reliability of these accounts in the introduction, and attempts a quantitative analysis; Abel, *Why Hitler*, assesses the reliability of the 'biograms' in the introduction, pages 4–9. For a similar analysis of autobiographical essays by pre-1933 Nazis written in 1936–7, see Christoph Schmidt, 'Zu den Motiven "alter Kämpfer" in der NSDAP', in Detlev Peukert and Jürgen Reulecke (eds.), *Die Reihen fast geschlossen: Beiträge zur Geschichte des Alltags unterm Nationalsozialismus* (Wuppertal, 1981), 21–44.

131. Merkl, *Political Violence*, 446–7.

132. AT 140, ibid., 551.

133. Ibid., 453, 457, 505–9; for the role of Nazi propaganda in this period, see Richard Bessel, 'The Rise of the NSDAP and the Myth of Nazi Propaganda', *Wiener Library Bulletin*, 33 (1980), Ian Kershaw, 'Ideology, Propaganda, and the Rise of the Nazi Party', in Peter D. Stachura (ed.), *The Nazi Machtergreifung, 1933* (London, 1983), 162–81; and, above all, Gerhard Paul, *Aufstand der Bilder: Die NS-Propaganda vor 1933* (Bonn, 1990).

134. Merkl, *Political Violence*, 313–63, 383–4.

135. Rudolf Höss, *Commandant of Auschwitz* (London, 1959 [1951]), 42–61.

136. Ibid., 61–3.

137. Jochen von Lang, 'Martin Bormann: Hitler's Secretary', in Smelser and Zitelmann (eds.), *The Nazi Elite*, 7–17; Fest, *The Face*, 191–206.

138. Waite, *Vanguard*, coined the phrase; Merkl, *Political Violence*, dismisses it too easily.

139. AT 493, in Merkl, *Political Violence*, 375.

140. AT 382, ibid., 440.

141. AT 434 and 464, ibid., 444–5.

142. AT 31, ibid., 544–5.

143. AT 520, ibid., 420.

144. AT 415, ibid., 400.

145. AT 59, ibid., 654.

146. AT 548, ibid., 416.

147. AT 8, 31, 32, ibid., 486–7.

148. AT 22, ibid., 602; documentation on the train incident in Martin Broszat, 'Die Anfänge der Berliner NSDAP 1926/27', *VfZ* 8 (1960), 85–118, at 115–18.

149. Merkl, *Political Violence*, 617.

150. Giles, 'The Rise', 163.

151. Merkl, *Political Violence*, 699.

152. Max Domarus (ed.), *Hitler: Speeches and Proclamations 1932–1945: The Chronicle of a Dictatorship* (4 vols., London, 1990– [1962–3]), I. 114 (speech to the Industry Club, Düsseldorf).

153. Turner, *German Big Business*, 114–24. For the Communists, see Weber, *Die Wandlung*, I. 294–318.

154. AT 38, in Merkl, *Political Violence*, 539.

155. AT 416 and 326, ibid., 540.

156. AT 4, ibid., 571.

157. Melita Maschmann, *Account Rendered: A Dossier on my Former Self* (London, 1964), 174–5.

158. Thomas Krause, *Hamburg wird braun: Der Aufstieg der NSDAP 1921–1933* (Hamburg, 1987), 102–7, a convincing critique of Michael Kater, *The Nazi Party: A Social Profile of Members and Leaders, 1919–1945* (Oxford, 1983), 32–8. The 1935 census gives date of entry into the Party for each member, so that it is possible to calculate the composition of the Party at any given date.

159. Detlef Mühlberger, 'A Social Profile of the Saxon NSDAP Membership before 1933', in Szejnmann, *Nazism*, 211–19; more generally, Broszat, *Der Staat Hitlers*, 49–53; Detlef Mühlberger, *Hitler's Followers: Studies in the Sociology of the Nazi Movement* (London, 1991); and Peter Manstein, *Die Mitglieder und Wähler der NSDAP 1919–1933: Untersuchungen zu ihrer schichtmässigen Zusammensetzung* (Frankfurt am Main, 1990 [1987]).

160. Josef Ackermann, 'Heinrich Himmler: Reichsführer-SS', in Smelser and Zitelmann (eds.), *The Nazi Elite*, 98–112; Alfred Andersch, *Der Vater eines Mörders: Eine Schulgeschichte* (Zurich, 1980), on Himmler's father; Bradley F. Smith, *Heinrich Himmler 1900–1926: A Nazi in the Making* (Stanford, Calif., 1971), is the basic work on Himmler's early years.

161. Quoted in Ackermann, 'Heinrich Himmler', 103; see also Josef Ackermann, *Himmler als Ideologe* (Göttingen, 1970).

162. Heinz Höhne, *The Order of the Death's Head: The Story of Hitler's SS* (Stanford, Calif., 1971 [1969]), 26–39.

163. Fest, *The Face*, 171–90, though, as with many other writers on Himmler, he takes an excessively condescending view. Whatever else he may have been, Himmler was neither vacillating, nor petty-bourgeois, nor mediocre, as Fest claims. See Höhne, *The Order*, 26–8, for a sample of colourful descriptions of Himmler, mostly imbued by hindsight.

164. Ibid., 40–46; for Darré, see also Gustavo Corni, 'Richard Walther Darré: The Blood and Soil Ideologue', in Smelser and Zitelmann (eds.), *The Nazi Elite*, 18–27;

and Horst Gies, *R. Walther Darré und die nationalsozialistische Bauernpolitik 1930 bis 1933* (Frankfurt am Main, 1966).
165. Höhne, *The Order*, 46–69; Hans Buchheim, 'The SS – Instrument of Domination', in Helmut Krausnick *et al.*, *Anatomy of the SS State* (London, 1968), 127–203, at 140–43.

Chapter 4 TOWARDS THE SEIZURE OF POWER

1. Quoted in Elizabeth Harvey, 'Youth Unemployment and the State: Public Policies towards Unemployed Youth in Hamburg during the World Economic Crisis', in Evans and Geary (eds.), *The German Unemployed*, 142–70, at 161; see also Wolfgang Ayass, 'Vagrants and Beggars in Hitler's Reich', in Richard J. Evans (ed.), *The German Underworld: Deviants and Outcasts in German History* (London, 1988), 210–237, at 210.
2. Gertrud Staewen-Ordermann, *Menschen der Unordnung: Die proletarische Wirklichkeit im Arbeitsschicksal der ungelernten Grossstadtjugend* (Berlin, 1933), 86, cited in Detlev J. K. Peukert, *Jugend zwischen Krieg und Krise: Lebenswelten von Arbeiterjungen in der Weimarer Republik* (Cologne, 1987), 184; English version in idem, 'The Lost Generation: Youth Unemployment at the End of the Weimar Republic', in Evans and Geary (eds.), *The German Unemployed*, 172–93, at 185.
3. Ruth Weiland, *Die Kinder der Arbeitslosen* (Eberswalde-Berlin, 1933), 40–42, cited in Peukert, *Jugend*, 184.
4. Staewen-Ordemann, *Menschen der Unordnung*, 92, cited in Peukert, 'The Lost Generation', 182.
5. Peukert, *Jugend*, 251–84; Eve Rosenhaft, 'The Unemployed in the Neighbourhood: Social Dislocation and Political Mobilisation in Germany 1929–33', in Evans and Geary (eds.), *The German Unemployed*, 194–227, esp. 209–11; eadem, 'Organising the "Lumpenproletariat": Cliques and Communists in Berlin during the Weimar Republic', in Richard J. Evans (ed.), *The German Working Class 1888–1933: The Politics of Everyday Life* (London, 1982), 174–219; eadem, 'Links gleich rechts? Militante Strassengewalt um 1930', in Thomas Lindenberger and Alf Lüdtke (eds.), *Physische Gewalt: Studien zur Geschichte der Neuzeit* (Frankfurt am Main, 1995), 239–75; Hellmut Lessing and Manfred Liebel, *Wilde Cliquen: Szenen einer anderen Arbeiterbewegung* (Bensheim, 1981).
6. James, *The German Slump*, 132–46.
7. See, in general, Patricia Clavin, *The Great Depression in Europe, 1929–1939* (London, 2000), emphasizing the failure of international co-operation.
8. Charles P. Kindleberger, *The World in Depression 1929–1939* (Berkeley, 1987 [1973]), 104–6.
9. See the graphic account in Piers Brendon, *The Dark Valley: A Panorama of the 1930s* (London, 2000), 62–5.

10. Charles H. Feinstein *et al.*, *The European Economy between the Wars* (Oxford, 1997), 95–9; Theo Balderston, *The Origins and Course of the German Economic Crisis, 1923–1932* (Berlin, 1993); Balderston, *Economics*, 77–99, emphasizes lack of international confidence.

11. Feinstein *et al.*, *The European Economy*, 104–9; Brendan Brown, *Monetary Chaos in Europe: The End of an Era* (London, 1988).

12. See, in general, Dieter Gessner, *Agrardepression und Präsidialregierungen*, and Farquharson, *The Plough and the Swastika*, 1–12.

13. Dietmar Petzina, 'The Extent and Causes of Unemployment in the Weimar Republic', in Peter D. Stachura (ed.), *Unemployment and the Great Depression in Weimar Germany* (London, 1986), 29–48, esp. table 2.3, page 35, drawing on the very useful compilation by Dietmar Petzina *et al.*, *Sozialgeschichtliches Arbeitsbuch*, III: *Materialien zur Geschichte des Deutschen Reiches 1914–1945* (Munich, 1978).

14. Details from Preller, *Sozialpolitik*, 440.

15. Helgard Kramer, 'Frankfurt's Working Women: Scapegoats or Winners of the Great Depression?', in Evans and Geary (eds.), *The German Unemployed*, 108–41, esp. 112–14.

16. Preller, *Sozialpolitik*, 374, 420–21.

17. Rosenhaft, 'The Unemployed in the Neighbourhood', a graphic portrait; see more generally the same author's *Beating the Fascists? The German Communists and Political Violence 1929–1933* (Cambridge, 1983), and Klaus-Michael Mallmann, *Kommunisten in der Weimarer Republik: Sozialgeschichte einer revolutionären Bewegung* (Darmstadt, 1996), 252–61. For the controversy over Mallmann's book, see Andreas Wirsching, ' "Stalinisierung" oder entideologisierte "Nischengesellschaft"? Alte Einsichten und neue Thesen zum Charakter der KPD in der Weimarer Republik', *VfZ* 45 (1997), 449–66, and Klaus-Michael Mallmann, 'Gehorsame Parteisoldaten oder eigensinnige Akteure? Die Weimarer Kommunisten in der Kontroverse – eine Erwiderung', *VfZ* 47 (1999), 401–15.

18. Anthony McElligott, 'Mobilising the Unemployed: The KPD and the Unemployed Workers' Movement in Hamburg-Altona during the Weimar Republic', in Evans and Geary (eds.), *The German Unemployed*, 228–60; Michael Schneider, *Unterm Hakenkreuz: Arbeiter und Arbeiterbewegung 1933 bis 1939* (Bonn, 1999), 47–52.

19. More generally, see Anthony McElligott, *Contested City: Municipal Politics and the Rise of Nazism in Altona, 1917–1937* (Ann Arbor, 1998).

20. Mallmann, *Kommunisten*, 261–83, 381–94.

21. Jan Valtin (pseud.; i.e. Richard Krebs), *Out of the Night* (London, 1941), 3–36. For the mixture of truth and fiction in this remarkable and best-selling work, see Michael Rohrwasser, *Der Stalinismus und die Renegaten: Die Literatur der Exkommunisten* (Stuttgart, 1991), and especially Dieter Nelles, 'Jan Valtins "Tagebuch der Hölle" – Legende und Wirklichkeit eines Schlüsselromans der Totalitarismustheorie', *1999: Zeitschrift für Sozialgeschichte des 20. und 21. Jahrhunderts*,

9 (1994) 11–45. The book ('a socialist classic') was republished by a Trotskyite group in London in 1988 with an excellent 'Postscript' by Lynn Walsh and others, containing valuable details on the author's life and work (659–74). See also the recent study by Ernst von Waldenfels, *Der Spion, der aus Deutschland kam: Das geheime Leben des Seemanns Richard Krebs* (Berlin, 2003).

22. Valtin, *Out of the Night* (1941 edn.), 36–7.

23. Ibid., 64–78.

24. Ibid., 79–328.

25. Dick Geary, 'Unemployment and Working-Class Solidarity: The German Experience 1929–33', in Evans and Geary (eds.), *The German Unemployed*, 261–80.

26. Weber, *Die Wandlung*, 243–7; Fowkes, *Communism*, 145–70; Weitz, *Creating German Communism*, 284–6.

27. Hannes Heer, *Ernst Thälmann in Selbstzeugnissen und Bilddokumenten* (Reinbek, 1975); Willi Bredel, *Ernst Thälmann: Beitrag zu einem politischen Lebensbild* (Berlin, 1948); Irma Thälmann, *Erinnerungen an meinen Vater* (Berlin, 1955).

28. Klemperer, *Leben sammeln*, II. 721 (16 July 1931).

29. McElligott, *Contested City*, 163.

30. Caplan, *Government*, 54 (table 2).

31. Ibid., 100–30.

32. Kershaw, *Hitler*, I. 325–9; Günter Bartsch, *Zwischen drei Stühlen: Otto Strasser. Eine Biographie* (Koblenz, 1990); Patrick Moreau, *Nationalsozialismus von 'links': Die 'Kampfgemeinschaft Revolutionärer Nationalsozialisten' und die 'Schwarze Front' Otto Strassers 1930–1935* (Stuttgart, 1984).

33. Domarus, *Hitler*, I. 88–114.

34. Turner, *German Big Business*, 191–219.

35. For a detailed account, see Bracher, *Die Auflösung*, 287–389; Dorpalen, *Hindenburg*, 163–78; Wheeler-Bennett, *Hindenburg*, 336–49; Winkler, *Der Schein*, 726–823.

36. Bracher, *Die Auflösung*, 229–84, for a broad survey of the politics of the Reichswehr in the crisis; see also Bracher *et al.*, *Die nationalsozialistische Machtergreifung*, III. 1–55; Carsten, *The Reichswehr*, 309–63; Groener quote in Thilo Vogelsang, *Reichswehr, Staat und NSDAP: Beiträge zur deutschen Geschichte 1930–1932* (Stuttgart, 1962), 95.

37. Carsten, *The Reichswehr*, 310–11.

38. Ibid., 318–21; Broszat, *Der Staat Hitlers*, 25.

39. Kershaw, *Hitler*, I. 337–8; Peter Bucher, *Der Reichswehrprozess: Der Hochverrat der Ulmer Reichswehroffiziere 1929–30* (Boppard, 1967), esp. 237–80; Deuerlein, *Der Aufstieg*, 328–42; Reuth, *Goebbels*, 176.

40. Bucher, *Der Reichswehrprozess*, provides full details.

41. Carsten, *The Reichswehr*, 323.

42. Heinrich Brüning, *Memoiren 1918–1934* (ed. Claire Nix and Theoderich Kampmann, Stuttgart, 1970); William L. Patch, Jr., *Heinrich Brüning and the*

Dissolution of the Weimar Republic (Cambridge, 1998), esp. 1–13; for differing estimations of the reliability of these memoirs, see Hans Mommsen, 'Betrachtungen zu den Memoiren Heinrich Brünings', *Jahrbuch für die Geschichte Mittel- und Ostdeutschlands*, 22 (1973), 270–80; Ernest Hamburger, 'Betrachtungen über Heinrich Brünings Memoiren', *Internationale Wissenschaftliche Korrespondenz zur Geschichte der deutschen Arbeiterbewegung*, 8 (1972), 18–39; Arnold Brecht, 'Gedanken über Brünings Memoiren', *Politische Vierteljahresschrift*, 12 (1971), 607–40.

43. Patch, *Heinrich Brüning*, is a well-informed, carefully researched defence of Brüning, updating Werner Conze in this respect; see Conze's review of the first edition of Bracher, *Die Auflösung*, in *Historische Zeitschrift*, 183 (1957), 378–82; more critical is Bracher, *Die Auflösung*, 303–528, and idem, 'Brünings unpolitische Politik und die Auflösung der Weimarer Republik', *VfZ* 19 (1971), 113–23. For a balanced assessment of the significance of 1930, see Hans Mommsen, 'Das Jahr 1930 als Zäsur in der deutschen Entwicklung der Zwischenkriegszeit', in Lothar Ehrlich and Jürgen John (eds.), *Weimar 1930: Politik und Kultur im Vorfeld der NS-Diktatur* (Cologne, 1998). Hans Mommsen, *The Rise and Fall*, 291–5, has a critical and perceptive character-sketch. Astrid Luise Mannes, *Heinrich Brüning: Leben, Wirken, Schicksal* (Munich, 1999), is a good recent biography; Herbert Hömig, *Brüning: Kanzler in der Krise der Republik. Eine Weimarer Biographie* (Paderborn, 2000), a major scholarly study of Brüning's political career that attempts an impartial view.

44. Brüning, *Memoiren*, 247–8.

45. See Fulda, 'Press and Politics', 234–42.

46. Bernd Weisbrod, 'Industrial Crisis Strategy in the Great Depression', in Jürgen Freiherr von Krudener (ed.), *Economic Crisis and Political Collapse: The Weimar Republic, 1924–1933* (New York, 1990), 45–62; Peter-Christian Witt, 'Finanzpolitik als Verfassungs- und Gesellschaftspolitik: Überlegungen zur Finanzpolitik des Deutschen Reiches in den Jahren 1930 bis 1932', *Geschichte und Gesellschaft*, 8 (1982), 387–414.

47. Hömig, *Brüning*, 211–24.

48. Aldcroft, *From Versailles*, 156–86.

49. Kent, *The Spoils of War*, 322–72; Hömig, *Brüning*, 235–57, 270–83.

50. Preller, *Sozialpolitik*, 165, 440–48.

51. Kindleberger, *The World in Depression*, 159–76.

52. James, *The German Slump*, 283–323.

53. Hömig, *Brüning*, 345–77.

54. Barry Eichengreen, *Golden Fetters: The Gold Standard and the Great Depression, 1919–1939* (Oxford, 1992), 270–78, 286.

55. On plans for the reform of the constitution, see the massive study by Schulz, *Zwischen Demokratie und Diktatur*.

56. Kent, *The Spoils of War*, 342–3; Patch, *Heinrich Brüning*, 162–4.

57. Werner Jochmann, 'Brünings Deflationspolitik und der Untergang der Weimarer Republik', in Dirk Stegmann *et al.* (eds.), *Industrielle Gesellschaft und politisches System: Beiträge zur politischen Sozialgeschichte. Festschrift für Fritz Fischer zum siebzigsten Geburtstag* (Bonn, 1978), 97–112.

58. Carl-Ludwig Holtfrerich, 'Economic Policy Options and the End of the Weimar Republic', in Kershaw (ed.), *Weimar*, 58–91, esp. 65–72. The classic essay on the topic is the much-debated 'Zwangslagen und Handlungsspielräume in der grossen Wirtschaftskrise der frühen dreissiger Jahre: Zur Revision des überlieferten Geschichtsbildes', by Knut Borchardt, first published in 1979 and reprinted in Knut Borchardt, *Wachstum, Krisen, Handlungsspielräume der Wirtschaftspolitik* (Göttingen, 1982), 165–82, and idem, *Perspectives on Modern German Economic History and Policy* (Cambridge, 1991).

59. Kindleberger, *The World in Depression*, 174; Patch, *Heinrich Brüning*, 111–15, 156–64, 193, 206–13.

60. Deutsches Volkslied-Archiv, Freiburg-im-Breisgau, Gr. II (cited in Evans, *Rituals*, 531 n. 14).

61. For Brüning's emergency decrees and the economic policies of the last phase of his Chancellorship, see Hömig, *Brüning*, 429–68.

62. Patch, *Heinrich Brüning*, 13, 243–4.

63. Nicholls, *Weimar*, 179; Winkler, *Der Weg*, 178–202.

64. Wolfgang Michalka and Gottfried Niedhart, *Die ungeliebte Republik; Dokumente zur Innen- und Aussenpolitik Weimars 1918–1933* (Munich, 1980), 62, 262, 283–4; Noakes and Pridham (eds.), *Nazism*, I. 70–81; Paul, *Aufstand*, 90–95.

65. Hiller von Gaertringen, 'Die Deutschnationale Volkspartei', in Matthias and Morsey (eds.), *Das Ende*, 549–54.

66. Fröhlich (ed.), *Die Tagebücher*, I/I. 603 (15 September 1930).

67. *Deutsche Allgemeine Zeitung* and *Die Rote Fahne*, 16 September 1930, quoted in Falter, *Hitlers Wähler*, 32.

68. Ibid., 33.

69. Paul, *Aufstand*, 90–94; Richard Bessel, *Political Violence and the Rise of Nazism: The Storm Troopers in Eastern Germany 1925–1934* (London, 1984), 22–3.

70. This is the main thesis of Richard F. Hamilton, *Who Voted for Hitler?* (Princeton, 1981). For a penetrating critique of Hamilton's ecological fallacy, see Krause, *Hamburg wird braun*, 176–7; Hamilton notes a high correlation between areas with a high average income and a high Nazi vote without noting that these areas also had a high population of well-off Jews, who were unlikely to have voted for the Party; it is more likely that the Nazi vote in these areas came from small businessmen, shopkeepers, white-collar workers and the like.

71. Falter, *Hitlers Wähler*, 99, 110, 151–4.

72. Ibid., 136–46; Richard J. Evans, 'German Women and the Triumph of Hitler', *Journal of Modern History*, 48 (1976), 123–75; Helen L. Boak, ' "Our Last Hope":

Women's Votes for Hitler – A Reappraisal', *German Studies Review*, 12 (1989), 289–310; Gerhard Schulz (ed.), *Ploetz Weimarer Republik: Eine Nation in Umbruch* (Freiburg, 1987), 166.

73. Falter, *Hitlers Wähler*, 154–93. See also the interesting discussion of the 'loss of legitimacy of conservative and liberal élites' in Rohe, *Wahlen*, 140–63.

74. Paul, *Aufstand*, 93–4.

75. Falter, *Hitlers Wähler*, 194–230; Falter *et al.*, *Wahlen*, 44.

76. Jürgen Falter, 'How Likely were Workers to Vote for the NSDAP?', in Conan Fischer (ed.), *The Rise of National Socialism and the Working Classes in Weimar Germany* (Oxford, 1996), 9–45; Szejnmann, *Nazism*, 219–29.

77. For a good brief guide through the controversial literature, with further references, see Dick Geary, 'Nazis and Workers before 1933', *Australian Journal of Politics and History*, 48 (2002), 40–51.

78. Falter, *Hitlers Wähler*, 230–66; Hans Speier, *German White-Collar Workers and the Rise of Hitler* (New Haven, 1986).

79. Thomas Childers, *The Nazi Voter: The Social Foundations of Fascism in Germany, 1919–1933* (Chapel Hill, NC, 1981), 262–9.

80. Attempts to explain the Nazis' success in terms of the economically rational response of different groups to their programme miss the central point (William Brustein, *The Logic of Evil: The Social Origins of the Nazi Party, 1925–1933* (New Haven, 1996)).

81. Rosenhaft, *Beating the Fascists?*, 60–64.

82. Ibid., 22–3 (based on files from the subsequent prosecution); Reuth, *Goebbels*, 157–62; Thomas Oertel, *Horst Wessel: Untersuchung einer Legende* (Cologne, 1988); Bernhard Fulda, 'Horst Wessel: Media, Myth and Memory' (unpublished paper to be delivered to the Research Seminar in Modern European History, Cambridge University, November 2003); see also 'Ein politischer Totschlag', *Berliner Tageblatt*, 447 (23 September 1930).

83. Tyrell, *Führer befiehl*, 296–7 (based on a police report from Munich on a brownshirt rally in November 1929, which gave a slightly different version of the third line of the third verse. The fourth verse, not quoted here, is a repeat of the first verse).

84. Reuth, *Goebbels*, 162 and 643 n. 109.

85. Tyrell, *Führer befiehl*, 288–9.

86. Rosenhaft, *Beating the Fascists?*, 6, reporting figures in Adolf Ehrt, *Bewaffneter Aufstand! Enthüllungen über den kommunistischen Umsturzversuch am Vorabend der nationalen Revolution* (Berlin, 1933), 166; *Die Rote Fahne*, 21 November 1931; Nationalsozialistischer Deutscher Frontkämpferbund (ed.), *Der NSDFB (Stahlhelm): Geschichte, Wesen und Aufgabe des Frontsoldatenbundes* (Berlin, 1935), 58–61; Rohe, *Das Reichsbanner*, 342; more generally, Diehl, *Paramilitary Politics, passim*.

87. Rosenhaft, *Beating the Fascists?*, 6, using same sources; Rohe, *Das Reichsbanner*, 342.

88. *Stenographische Berichte über die Verhandlungen des deutschen Reichstags*, 445 (1932), 1602–4.

89. Valtin, *Out of the Night*, 218.

90. Rosenhaft, *Beating the Fascists?*, 8; Diehl, *Paramilitary Politics*, 287.

91. For the effects of the amnesty of 20 January 1933 on violence in one German town, see William S. Allen, *The Nazi Seizure of Power: The Experience of a Single German Town, 1922–1945* (New York, 1984 [1965]), 146–7.

92. Peter Lessmann, *Die preussische Schutzpolizei in der Weimarer Republik: Streifendienst und Strassenkampf* (Düsseldorf, 1989); Eric D. Kohler, 'The Crisis in the Prussian Schutzpolizei 1930–32', in George L. Mosse (ed.), *Police Forces in History* (London, 1975), 131–50; Hsi-Huey Liang, *The Berlin Police Force in the Weimar Republic* (Berkeley, 1970); Siegfried Zalka, *Polizeigeschichte: Die Exekutive im Lichte der historischen Konfliktforschung. Untersuchungen über die Theorie und Praxis der preussischen Schutzpolizei in der Weimarer Republik zur Verhinderung und Bekämpfung innerer Unruhen* (Lübeck, 1979); Jürgen Sigge-mann, *Die kasernierte Polizei und das Problem der inneren Sicherheit in der Weimarer Republik: Eine Studie zum Auf- und Ausbau des innerstaatlichen Sicherheitssystems in Deutschland 1918/19–1933* (Frankfurt am Main, 1980); Johannes Buder, *Die Reorganisation der preussischen Polizei 1918/1923* (Frankfurt am Main, 1986); Johannes Schwarz, *Die bayerische Polizei und ihre historische Funktion bei der Aufrechterhaltung der öffentlichen Sicherheit in Bayern von 1919 bis 1933* (Munich, 1977). See also the interesting, though not always reliable account by the former chief of the Hamburg civil order squad, Lothar Danner, *Ordnungspolizei Hamburg: Betrachtungen zu ihrer Geschichte 1918–1933* (Hamburg, 1958).

93. For a useful brief sketch, see Robert Gellately, *The Gestapo and German Society: Enforcing Racial Policy 1933–1945* (Oxford, 1990), 22–6; more wide-ranging is Robert J. Goldstein, *Political Repression in Nineteenth-Century Europe* (London, 1983).

94. Christoph Graf, *Politische Polizei zwischen Demokratie und Diktatur* (Berlin, 1983).

95. Otto Buchwitz, *50 Jahre Funktionär der deutschen Arbeiterbewegung* (Stuttgart, 1949), 129–36.

96. Thomas Kurz, *'Blutmai': Sozialdemokraten und Kommunisten im Brennpunkt der Berliner Ereignisse von 1929* (Bonn, 1988); Chris Bowlby, 'Blutmai 1929: Police, Parties and Proletarians in a Berlin Confrontation', *Historical Journal*, 29 (1986), 137–58; background in Eve Rosenhaft, 'Working-Class Life and Working-Class Politics: Communists, Nazis, and the State in the Battle for the Streets, Berlin, 1928–1932', in Richard Bessel and Edgar J. Feuchtwanger (eds.), *Social Change and Political Development in Weimar Germany* (London, 1981), 207–40.

97. George C. Browder, *Hitler's Enforcers: The Gestapo and the SS Security Service in the Nazi Revolution* (New York, 1996), 23–8.

98. Richard Bessel, 'Militarisierung und Modernisierung: Polizeiliches Handeln in der Weimarer Republik', in Alf Lüdtke (ed.), *'Sicherheit' und 'Wohlfahrt': Polizei,*

Gesellschaft und Herrschaft im 19. und 20. Jahrhundert (Frankfurt am Main, 1992), 323–43; Theodor Lessing, *Haarmann: Die Geschichte eines Werwolfs. Und andere Kriminalreportagen* (ed. Rainer Marwedel, Frankfurt am Main, 1989); Evans, *Rituals*, 530–35, 591–610.

99. Browder, *Hitler's Enforcers*, 28–9; Danner, *Ordnungspolizei*, 223.

100. Eichengreen, *Golden Fetters*, 286; Hömig, *Brüning*, 525–36.

101. Patch, *Heinrich Brüning*, 148–9; Bessel, *Political Violence*, 54–66.

102. Höhne, *The Order*, 51–62.

103. Herbert, *Best*, 111–19; Patch, *Heinrich Brüning*, 225–7.

104. Ibid., 228–9.

105. Ibid., 249–51; Bessel, *Political Violence*, 29–31.

106. Patch, *Heinrich Brüning*, 251.

107. Bracher, *Die Auflösung*, 377–88.

108. Thomas Mergel, *Parlamentarische Kultur in der Weimarer Republik: Politische Kommunikation, symbolische Politik und Öffentlichkeit im Reichstag* (Düsseldorf, 2002), 179–81.

109. Carsten, *The Reichswehr*, 259–63, 296–308. Useful brief characterization of Schleicher in Henry Ashby Turner, Jr., *Hitler's Thirty Days to Power: January 1933* (London, 1996), 7, 19–21. For a shrewd assessment of Schleicher's relationship with Groener, see Theodor Eschenburg, 'Die Rolle der Persönlichkeit in der Krise der Weimarer Republik: Hindenburg Brüning, Groener, Schleicher', *VfZ* 9 (1961), 1–29 esp. 7–13. For the paradoxical view that Schleicher really wanted to preserve democracy through strengthening the executive, rather along the lines argued by some historians for Brüning, see Wolfram Pyta, 'Konstitutionelle Demokratie statt monarchischer Restauration: Die verfassungspolitische Konzeption Schleichers in der Weimarer Staatskrise', *VfZ* 47 (1999), 417–41.

110. Rohe, *Das Reichsbanner*, 360–65.

111. Carsten, *The Reichswehr*, 333.

112. Otto Meissner, *Staatssekretär unter Ebert – Hindenburg – Hitler: Der Schicksalsweg des deutschen Volkes von 1918–1945 wie ich ihn erlebte* (Hamburg, 1950), 215–17.

113. Rudolf Morsey, 'Hitler als Braunschweiger Reigierungsrat', *VfZ* 8 (1960), 419–48.

114. Donna Harsch, *German Social Democracy and the Rise of Nazism* (Chapel Hill, NC, 1993), 179.

115. *Vorwärts*, 10 March 1932, cited in Winkler, *Der Weg*, 514.

116. Harsch, *German Social Democracy*, 180, citing Carlo Mierendorff, 'Der Hindenburgsieg 1932', *Sozialistische Monatshefte*, 4 April 1932, 297; also Erich Matthias, 'Hindenburg zwischen den Fronten 1932', *VfZ* 8 (1960), 75–84.

117. Winkler, *Der Weg*, 519; also Alfred Milatz, 'Das Ende der Parteien im Spiegel der Wahlen 1930 bis 1933', in Matthias and Morsey (eds.), *Das Ende*, 743–93, at 761–6.

118. Falter, *et al.*, *Wahlen*, 46; Broszat, *Der Staat Hitlers*, 44–5.

119. Paul, *Aufstand*, 98.

120. Bracher, *Die Auflösung*, 511–17, judiciously surveys the subsequent controversy over this point.

121. Gordon A. Craig, 'Briefe Schleichers an Groener', *Die Welt als Geschichte*, 11 (1951), 122–30; Reginald H. Phelps, 'Aus den Groener Dokumenten', *Deutsche Rundschau*, 76 (1950), 1019, and 77 (1951), 26–9; Hömig, *Brüning*, 537–89.

122. Papen's letter of resignation from the Centre Party, printed in Georg Schreiber, *Brüning, Hitler, Schleicher: Das Zentrum in der Opposition* (Cologne, 1932), 17–19, cited in Bracher, *Die Auflösung*, 536; see also the comments in Bracher, *Die Auflösung*, 656 and Morsey, 'Die Deutsche Zentrumspartei', in Matthias and Morsey (eds.), *Das Ende*, 306–14. For a critical assessment of Papen, see Joachim Petzold, *Franz von Papen: Ein deutsches Verhängnis* (Munich, 1995), and the critical discussion of his memoirs by Theodor Eschenburg, 'Franz von Papen', *VfZ* 1 (1953), 153–69.

123. Fest, *The Face*, 229–33; Richard W. Rolfs, *The Sorcerer's Apprentice: The Life of Franz von Papen* (Lanham, Md., 1996).

124. Vejas Gabriel Liulevicius, *War Land on the Eastern Front: Culture, National Identity and German Occupation in World War I* (Cambridge, 2000).

125. See the biting characterization of the ideology of Papen's 'New State' in Bracher, *Die Auflösung*, 536–54.

126. Papen, quoted in Walter Schotte, *Der neue Staat* (Berlin, 1932), 110–24.

127. Evans, *Rituals*, 613–44.

128. Fulda, 'Press and Politics', chapter 4.

129. Edward W. Bennett, *German Rearmament and the West, 1932–1933* (Princeton, 1979), 63–4, 69.

130. Valtin, *Out of the Night*, 309–11, as so often, however, exaggerating the murderous intentions and the degree of preparedness of the Red Front-Fighters.

131. McElligott, *Contested City*, 192–5; Leon Schirmann, *Altonaer Blutsonntag 17. Juli 1932: Dichtung und Wahrheit* (Hamburg, 1994).

132. Lessmann, *Die preussische Schutzpolizei*, 349–70.

133. Rohe, *Das Reichsbanner*, 431–5.

134. Matthias, 'Die Sozialdemokratische Partei Deutschlands', in Matthias and Morsey (eds.), *Das Ende*, 141–5.

135. Bracher, *Die Auflösung*, 559–600; Schulze, *Otto Braun*, 745–86; Huber, *Deutsche Verfassungsgeschichte* VII. 1015–25 and 1192–7; Matthias, 'Die Sozialdemokratische Partei Deutschlands', in Matthias and Morsey (eds.), *Das Ende*, 119–50; Schulz, *Zwischen Demokratie und Diktatur*, III. 920–33; Broszat, *Der Staat Hitlers*, 89.

136. Evans, *Rituals*, 614–15, for one example. More generally, see Winkler, *Der Weg*, 646–81, and Rudolf Morsey, 'Zur Geschichte des "Preussenschlags" am 20. Juli 1932', *VfZ* 9 (1961), 436–9.

137. Joseph Goebbels, *Vom Kaiserhof zur Reichskanzlei: Eine historische Darstellung in Tagebuchblättern (vom 1. Januar 1932 bis zum 1. Mai 1933)* (Munich, 1937 [1934]), 131–5; Winkler, *Der Weg*, 542–53, for the Prussian election.

138. Noakes and Pridham (eds.), *Nazism*, I. 102–3; Martin Broszat, *Hitler and the Collapse of Weimar Germany* (Oxford, 1987 [1984]), 82–91; Winkler, *Der Weg*, 681–98.

139. Matthias, 'Die Sozialdemokratische Partei Deutschlands', in Matthias and Morsey (eds.), *Das Ende*, 222–4 (document no. 11: Rundschreiben des Gauvorstandes Hannover des Reichsbanners, 5 July 1932); Winkler, *Der Weg*, 515; Harsch, *German Social Democracy*, 177–80; Richard Albrecht, 'Symbolkampf in Deutschland 1932: Sergej Tschachotin und der "Symbolkrieg" der drei Pfeile gegen den Nationalsozialismus als Episode im Abwehrkampf der Arbeiterbewegung gegen den Faschismus in Deutschland', *Internationale Wissenschaftliche Korrespondenz zur Geschichte der deutschen Arbeiterbewegung*, 22 (1986), 498–533.

140. Winkler, *Der Weg*, 514–16.

141. Simon Taylor, *Germany 1918–1933: Revolution, Counter-Revolution and the Rise of Hitler* (London, 1983), 112–16; and Hans Bohrmann (ed.), *Politische Plakate* (Dortmund, 1984), 247–62.

142. Paul, *Aufstand*, 178 (quoting Goebbels from a speech of 31 July 1933).

143. Ibid., 133–76, 223–47, 253–66.

144. For the July 1932 election, see Winkler, *Der Weg*, 681–92; summary in Jürgen W. Falter, 'Die Wähler der NSDAP 1928–1933: Sozialstruktur und parteipolitische Herkunft', in Wolfgang Michalka (ed.), *Die nationalsozialistische Machtergreifung* (Paderborn, 1984), 47–59.

145. Falter, *Hitlers Wähler*, 110–13, 369–71. For the Nazi appeal to workers, particularly those still in employment, see Szejnmann, *Nazism*, 219–31.

146. Fröhlich (ed.), *Die Tagebücher*, I/II. 211–12 (1 August 1932).

147. Hannover and Hannover-Drück, *Politische Justiz*, 301–10, quotes on 306; Paul Kluke, 'Der Fall Potempa', *VfZ* 5 (1957), 279–97; Richard Bessel, 'The Potempa Murder', *Central European History*, 10 (1977), 241–54. The decree did not create any new capital offences; murder, from whatever motive, was already covered by the relevant section of the Criminal Code. It was thus no more than a propaganda exercise.

148. Hannover and Hannover-Drück, *Politische Justiz*, 308.

149. Ibid., 310; Karl-Heinz Minuth (ed.), *Akten der Reichskanzlei: Weimarer Republik. Das Kabinett von Papen, 1. Juni bis 3. December 1932* (Boppard, 1989), 146, 491–5. Papen's legal right to commute the sentences was extremely dubious, since the right of commutation lay with the legally constituted head of the Prussian state, and his claim to wield these powers was legally disputed. The murderers were released from prison in March 1933 (Evans, *Rituals*, 615–18, 627–8).

150. *Hitler: Reden, Schriften, Anordnungen. Februar 1925 bis Januar 1933* (5 vols., Institut für Zeitgeschichte, Munich, 1992–8), V/I: *Von der Reichspräsidentenwahl bis zur Machtergreifung, April 1932 – Januar 1933* 304–9.

151. Turner, *Hitler's Thirty Days*, 14–15, following Winkler, *Weimar*, 510–24.

152. Christian Striefler, *Kampf um die Macht: Kommunisten und Nationalsozialisten am Ende der Weimarer Republik* (Berlin, 1993), esp. 177–86; Deuerlein (ed.), *Der Aufstieg*, 402–4. See also Paul, *Aufstand*, 104–8.

153. Werner Jochmann (ed.), *Nationalsozialismus und Revolution: Ursprung und Geschichte der NSDAP in Hamburg 1922–1933* (Frankfurt am Main, 1963), 400, 402, 405, 413–14.

154. Ibid., 405.

155. Ibid., 406.

156. Ibid., 414, 416, 417.

157. Falter, *Hitlers Wähler*, 34–8, 103–7.

158. *Vorwärts*, 13 November 1932, cited in Falter, *Hitlers Wähler*, 37.

159. Fröhlich (ed.), *Die Tagebücher*, I/II. 272 (6 November 1932).

160. Falter, *Hitlers Wähler*, 37–8, 106–7.

161. Bracher, *Die Auflösung*, 644–62; Nicholls, *Weimar*, 163–6.

162. For documentation, see Thilo Vogelsang, 'Zur Politik Schleichers gegenüber der NSDAP 1932', *VfZ* 6 (1958), 86–118.

163. Fröhlich (ed.), *Die Tagebücher*, I/II. 276–88 (1 December 1932).

164. Bracher, *Die Auflösung*, 662–85; Stachura, *Gregor Strasser*; Kershaw, *Hitler*, I. 396–403; Noakes and Pridham (eds.), *Nazism*, 110–15; Orlow, *The History of the Nazi Party*, I. 291–6; Turner, *Hitler's Thirty Days*, 23–8, 84–6, correcting previous accounts.

165. Turner, *Hitler's Thirty Days*, 61–6; Paul, *Aufstand*, 109–10.

166. Grüttner, *Studenten*, 53–5.

167. Noakes and Pridham, *Nazism*, I. 109–11.

168. Berghahn, *Der Stahlhelm*, 187–246.

169. Theodor Duesterberg, *Der Stahlhelm und Hitler* (Wolfenbüttel, 1949), 39, quoted in Turner, *Hitler's Thirty Days*, 154; see also Berghahn, *Der Stahlhelm*, 246–50.

170. Meissner, *Staatssekretär*, 247. See also Bracher, *Die Auflösung*, 707–32; Noakes and Pridham (eds.), *Nazism*, I. 116–20.

171. Lutz, Graf Schwerin von Krosigk, *Es geschah in Deutschland: Menschenbilder unseres Jahrhunderts* (Tübingen, 1951), 147.

172. Ewald von Kleist-Schmenzin, 'Die letzte Möglichkeit', *Politische Studien*, 10 (1959), 89–92, at 92.

Chapter 5   CREATING THE THIRD REICH

1. *Deutsche Zeitung*, 27a (morning edition, 1 February 1933, front page, col. 2). For a selection of press reports, see Wieland Eschenhagen (ed.), *Die 'Machtergreifung': Tagebuch einer Wende nach Presseberichten vom 1. Januar bis 6. März 1933* (Darmstadt, 1982).

2. *Berliner Illustrierte Nachtausgabe*, 26 (31 January 1933), 2, col. 4; *B.Z. am Mittag* 26 (Erste Beilage, 31 January 1933), 3, picture caption, col. 3; Peter Fritzsche, *Germans into Nazis* (Cambridge, Mass., 1998), 139–43; Hans-Joachim Hildenbrand, 'Der Betrug mit dem Fackelzug', in Rolf Italiander (ed.), *Wir erlebten das Ende der Weimarer Republik: Zeitgenossen berichten* (Düsseldorf, 1982), 165.

3. Wheeler-Bennett, *Hindenburg*, 435. Needless to say, Ludendorff was not there at all.

4. *Deutsche Allgemeine Zeitung*, 51 (morning edition, 31 January 1933), front page.

5. *Berliner Börsen-Zeitung*, 51 (morning edition, 31 January 1933), front page, col. 2.

6. *Deutsche Allgemeine Zeitung*, 51 (morning edition, 31 January 1933), front page, col. 3.

7. *Deutsche Zeitung*, 27a (morning edition, 1 February 1933), front page headline.

8. Quoted in Jochmann (ed.), *Nationalsozialismus und Revolution*, 429; Fritzsche, *Germans*, 141.

9. Herbst, *Das nationalsozialistische Deutschland*, 59–60.

10. Fröhlich (ed.), *Die Tagebücher* I/II. 357–9 (31 January 1933).

11. *Deutsche Zeitung*, 26a (morning edition, 31 January 1933), title page, cols. 1–2.

12. For two examples, see Bernd Burkhardt, *Eine Stadt wird braun: Die national-sozialistische Machtergreifung in der Provinz. Eine Fallstudie* (Hamburg, 1980), on the small Swabian town of Mühlacker; Allen, *The Nazi Seizure of Power*, 153–4, on the North German town of Northeim.

13. *Deutsche Zeitung*, 26b (evening edition, 31 January 1933), front page, col. 3; *Vossische Zeitung* 52 (evening edition, 31 January 1933), 3, col. 1.

14. Jochmann, *Nationalsozialismus und Revolution*, 423.

15. Maschmann, *Account Rendered*, 11–12, (translation amended).

16. Quoted in *Deutsche Zeitung*, 27a (morning edition, 1 February 1933), front page, col. 1.

17. *Deutsche Zeitung*, 26b (evening edition, 31 January 1933), 3, col. 2: 'Wieder zwei Todesopfer der roten Mordbestien'.

18. *Berliner Börsen-Zeitung*, 52 (evening edition, 31 January 1933), 2, cols. 2–3.

19. *Welt am Abend*, 26 (31 January 1933), 1–2.

20. Hans-Joachim Althaus *et al.*, *'Da ist nirgends nichts gewesen ausser hier': Das 'rote Mössingen' im Generalstreik gegen Hitler. Geschichte eines schwäbischen Arbeiterdorfes* (Berlin, 1982).

21. Allan Merson, *Communist Resistance in Nazi Germany* (London, 1985), 25–8; Winkler, *Der Weg*, 867–75.

22. Josef and Ruth Becker (eds.), *Hitlers Machtergreifung: Dokumente vom Macht-antritt Hitlers 30. Januar 1933 bis zur Besiegelung des Einparteienstaates 14. Juli 1933* (2nd edn., Munich, 1992 [1983]), 45.

23. *Die Welt am Abend*, 27 (1 February 1933), title page headline; *Die Rote Fahne*, 27 (1 February 1933), front page headline.

24. Jochmann, *Nationalsozialismus und Revolution*, 421.

25. Camill Hoffmann, diary entry for 30 January 1933, cited in Johann Wilhelm Brügel and Norbert Frei (eds.), 'Berliner Tagebuch, 1932–1934: Aufzeichnungen des tschechoslowakischen Diplomaten Camill Hoffmann', *VfZ* 36 (1988), 131–83, at 159.

26. Ministère des affaires étrangères (ed.), *Documents Diplomatiques Français, 1932–1939*, ser. 1, vol. II (Paris, 1966), p. 552, François-Poncet to Boncour, 1 February 1933. This is the central theme of the account by Gotthard Jasper, *Die gescheiterte Zähmung: Wege zur Machtergreifung Hitlers 1930–1934* (Frankfurt am Main, 1986), esp. 126–71. The oft-quoted 'prophecy' of General Ludendorff at this time, that Hitler would plunge Germany into the abyss (see e.g. Kershaw, *Hitler* I. 427), was a later invention of Hans Frank: see Fritz Tobias, 'Ludendorff, Hindenburg, Hitler: Das Phantasieprodukt des Ludendorff-Briefes vom 30. Januar 1933', in Uwe Backes *et al.* (eds.), *Die Schatten der Vergangenheit: Impulse zur Historisierung des Nationalsozialismus* (Frankfurt am Main, 1990), 319–43, and Lothar Gruchmann, 'Ludendorffs "prophetischer" Brief an Hindenburg vom Januar/Februar 1933', *VfZ* 47 (1999), 559–62.

27. Robert J. O'Neill, *The German Army and the Nazi Party 1933–1939* (London, 1966), 34–5.

28. Klaus-Jürgen Müller, *The Army, Politics and Society in Germany 1933–1945: Studies in the Army's Relation to Nazism* (Manchester, 1987), 29–44. O'Neill, *The German Army*, 35–45; Wolfgang Sauer, *Die Mobilmachung der Gewalt* (vol. III of Bracher *et al.*, *Die nationalsozialistische Machtergreifung*), 41–84; Andreas Wirsching, '"Man kann nur Boden germanisieren": Eine neue Quelle zu Hitlers Rede vor den Spitzen der Reichswehr am 3. Februar 1933', *VfZ* 49 (2001), 516–50. The full version of Hitler's address to the army officers on 3 February 1933, reproduced in this article, was recently discovered in the former KGB archive in Moscow and had probably been supplied by Hammerstein's daughter, who was a Communist sympathizer. For another, slightly earlier set of promises by Hitler along similar lines, see Thilo Vogelsang, 'Hitlers Brief an Reichenau vom 4. Dezember 1932', *VfZ* 7 (1959), 429–37.

29. Martin Broszat, 'The Concentration Camps 1933–1945', in Helmut Krausnick *et al.*, *Anatomy of the SS State* (London, 1968 [1965]), 397–504, at 400–401; Bessel, *Political Violence*, 98–9.

30. Siegfried Bahne, 'Die Kommunistische Partei Deutschlands', in Matthias and Morsey (eds.), *Das Ende*, 655–739, at 690; Berghahn, *Der Stahlhelm*, 252.

31. Matthias, 'Die Sozialdemokratische Partei Deutschlands', in Matthias and Morsey (eds.), *Das Ende*, 101–278, at 101–50.

32. Winkler, *Der Weg*, 867–875. *Vorwärts* quoted ibid., 867.

33. Broszat, *Der Staat Hitlers*, 94.

34. Grzesinski to Klupsch *et al.*, 24 February 1933, document 25 in Matthias, 'Die Sozialdemokratische Partei Deutschlands', in Matthias and Morsey (eds.), *Das Ende*, 234–5.

35. Winkler, *Der Weg*, 876–8.

36. Martin Kitchen, *The Coming of Austrian Fascism* (London, 1980), 202–81; Francis L. Carsten, *Fascist Movements in Austria: From Schönerer to Hitler* (London, 1977), 249–70.

37. Winkler, *Der Weg*, 868.

38. Domarus, *Hitler*, I. 247.

39. Ibid., 254.

40. Ibid., 253.

41. Morsey, 'Die Deutsche Zentrumspartei', in Matthias and Morsey (eds.), *Das Ende*, 339–54; Broszat, *Der Staat Hitlers*, 95.

42. Domarus, *Hitler*, I. 256; Broszat, *Der Staat Hitlers*, 249.

43. Domarus, *Hitler*, I. 170.

44. Ibid., 249 (10 February 1933).

45. Ibid., 247–50.

46. Jochmann (ed.), *Nationalsozialismus und Revolution*, 431.

47. Domarus, *Hitler*, I. 250–51.

48. Turner, *German Big Business*, 330–32.

49. Paul, *Aufstand*, 111–13.

50. Printed in Bahne, 'Die Kommunistische Partei Deutschlands', in Matthias and Morsey (eds.), *Das Ende*, document 3, 728–31, at 731.

51. Ibid., 686–696.

52. Hans Mommsen, 'Van der Lubbes Weg in den Reichstag – der Ablauf der Ereignisse', in Uwe Backes *et al.*, *Reichstagsbrand: Aufklärung einer historischen Legende* (Munich, 1986), 33–57, at 42–7.

53. Harry Graf Kessler, *Tagebücher 1918–1937* (ed. Wolfgang Pfeiffer-Belli, Frankfurt am Main, 1961), 707–9.

54. Horst Karasek, *Der Brandstifter: Lehr- und Wanderjahre des Maurergesellen Marinus van der Lubbe, der 1933 auszog, den Reichstag anzuzünden* (Berlin, 1980); Martin Schouten, *Marinus van der Lubbe (1909–1934): Eine Biographie* (Frankfurt, 1999 [1986]); and Fritz Tobias, *The Reichstag Fire: Legend and Truth* (London, 1962).

55. Mommsen, 'Van der Lubbes Weg', 33–42.

56. Fröhlich (ed.), *Die Tagebücher*, part I, vol. II, p. 383.

57. Rudolf Diels, *Lucifer ante Portas: Es spricht der erste Chef der Gestapo* (Stuttgart, 1950), 192–3.

58. Mommsen, 'Van der Lubbes Weg'; Karasek, *Der Brandstifter*; Tobias, *The Reichstag Fire*. Subsequently, the Communists attempted to prove that the Nazis had been behind the arson attempt, but the authenticity of van der Lubbe's statements and associated documentation seems beyond doubt. Moreover, numerous forgeries and falsifications have been found among the documentary evidence purporting to prove Nazi involvement. For attempts to prove Nazi responsibility, see World Committee for the Victims of German Fascism (President Einstein) (ed.), *The Brown Book of the Hitler Terror and the Burning of the Reichstag* (London,

1933), 54–142; Walther Hofer and Alexander Bahar (eds.), *Der Reichstagsbrand: Eine wissenschaftliche Dokumentation* (Freiburg im Breisgau, 1992 [1972, 1978]); for the exposure of the inadequacies of this work, see Backes *et al.*, *Reichstagsbrand*; Karl-Heinz Janssen, 'Geschichte aus der Dunkelkammer: Kabalen um dem Reichstagsbrand. Eine unvermeidliche Enthüllung', *Die Zeit*, 38 (14 September 1979), 45–8; 39 (21 September 1979), 20–24; 40 (28 September 1979), 49–52; 41 (5 October 1979), 57–60; Tobias, *The Reichstag Fire*, esp. 59–78, and Hans Mommsen, 'Der Reichstagsbrand und seine politischen Folgen', *VfZ* 12 (1964), 351–413. A recent attempt to suggest that the Nazis planned the fire rests on an exaggeration of similarities between earlier discussion papers on emergency powers, and the Reichstag Fire Decree: see Alexander Bahar and Wilfried Kugel, 'Der Reichstagsbrand: Neue Aktenfunde entlarven die NS-Täter', *Zeitschrift für Geschichtswissenschaft*, 43 (1995), 823–32, and Jürgen Schmädeke *et al.*, 'Der Reichstagsbrand im neuen Licht', *Historische Zeitschrift*, 269 (1999), 603–51. So far, the conclusion of Tobias and Mommsen that van der Lubbe acted alone has not been shaken.

59. Diels, *Lucifer*, 193–5.

60. Ibid., 180–2. Goebbels appears to have destroyed the originals of his diaries for the last days of February, a fact which has aroused the suspicions of proponents of the view that it was the Nazis who started the fire. In the doctored version published as *Vom Kaiserhof zur Reichskanzlei*, he claimed of the events of that night: 'The Leader does not lose his composure for a moment: admirable' (Fröhlich (ed.), *Die Tagebücher*, I/II. 383).

61. Diels, *Lucifer*, 193–5.

62. Karl-Heinz Minuth (ed.), *Akten der Reichskanzlei: Die Regierung Hitler*, I: *1933–1934* (2 vols., Boppard, 1983), I. 123; Ulrich Kolbe, 'Zum Urteil über die "Reichstagsbrand-Notverordnung" vom 28. 2. 1933', *Geschichte in Wissenschaft und Unterricht*, 16 (1965), 359–70; Broszat, *Der Staat Hitlers*, 92. For Gürtner, see Lothar Gruchmann, *Justiz im Dritten Reich 1933–1940: Anpassung und Unterwerfung in der Ära Gürtner* (Munich, 1988), 70–83.

63. Minuth (ed.), *Die Regierung Hitler 1933–1934*, I. 128–31; Kolbe, 'Zum Urteil', 359–70.

64. Minuth (ed.), *Die Regierung Hitler 1933–1934*, I. 128–31; Broszat, 'The Concentration Camps', 400–402.

65. Minuth (ed.), *Die Regierung Hitler 1933–1934*, I. 131.

66. Quoted in Noakes and Pridham (eds.), *Nazism*, I. 142. For a recent analysis, see Thomas Reithel and Irene Strenge, 'Die Reichstagsbrandverordnung: Grundlegung der Diktatur mit den Instrumenten des Weimarer Ausnahmezustandes', *VfZ* 48 (2000), 413–60.

67. Jochmann (ed.), *Nationalsozialismus und Revolution*, 427.

68. Evans, *Rituals*, 618–24.

69. AT 31, in Merkl, *Political Violence*, 545 (retranslated). The 'storm' was the basic organizational unit of the stormtroopers.

70. Mason, *Social Policy*, 73–87.

71. Bahne, 'Die Kommunistische Partei', in Matthias and Morsey (eds.), *Das Ende*, 693–4, 699–700; Winkler, *Der Weg*, 876–89; Weber, *Die Wandlung*, 246; World Committee (ed.), *The Brown Book*, 184; Broszat, *Der Staat Hitlers*, 101–2.

72. Merson, *Communist Resistance*, 57; Detlev J. K. Peukert, *Die KPD im Widerstand: Verfolgung und Untergrundarbeit an Rhein und Ruhr, 1933 bis 1945* (Wuppertal, 1980), 75–8. See also Horst Duhnke, *Die KPD von 1933 bis 1945* (Cologne, 1972), 101–9; idem, *Die KPD und das Ende von Weimar: Das Scheitern einer Politik 1932–1935* (Frankfurt am Main, 1976), 34–42.

73. Diels, *Lucifer*, 222. See also Hans Bernd Gisevius, *To the Bitter End* (London, 1948).

74. 'Bericht des Obersten Parteigerichts an den Ministerpräsidenten Generalfeldmarschall Göring, 13.2.1939', document ND 3063-PS in *Der Prozess gegen die Hauptkriegsverbrecher vor dem Internationalen Militärgerichtshof, Nürnberg* (Nuremberg, 1949), XXIII. 20–29, at 26.

75. Paul, *Aufstand*, 111–13.

76. Allen, *The Nazi Seizure of Power*, 156–61.

77. Fröhlich (ed.), *Die Tagebücher*, I/II. 387 (5 March 1933).

78. Allen, *The Nazi Seizure of Power*, 160, for a characteristic local example.

79. Falter *et al.*, *Wahlen*, 41, 44; Falter, *Hitlers Wähler*, 38–9.

80. Ibid., 40; for the Catholics, see Oded Heilbronner, *Catholicism, Political Culture and the Countryside: A Social History of the Nazi Party in South Germany* (Ann Arbor, 1998), 239.

81. Bessel, *Political Violence*, 101–2.

82. Ulrich Klein, 'SA-Terror und Bevölkerung in Wuppertal 1933/34', in Detlev Peukert and Jürgen Reulecke (eds.), *Die Reihen fast geschlossen: Beiträge zur Geschichte des Alltags unterm Nationalsozialismus* (Wuppertal, 1981), 45–64, at 51.

83. Winkler, *Der Weg*, 890–91; World Committee (ed.), *The Brown Book*, 204–5; Schneider, *Unterm Hakenkreuz*, 56–73.

84. Dieter Rebentisch and Angelika Raab (eds.), *Neu-Isenburg zwischen Anpassung und Widerstand; Dokumente über Lebensbedingungen und politisches Verhalten 1933–1934* (Neu-Isenburg, 1978), 79.

85. Gerlinde Grahn, 'Die Enteignung des Vermögens der Arbeiterbewegung und der politischen Emigration 1933 bis 1945', *1999: Zeitschrift für Sozialgeschichte des 20. und 21. Jahrhunderts*, 12 (1997), 13–38; Broszat, *Der Staat Hitlers*, 118.

86. Klein, 'SA-Terror', 51–3.

87. Broszat, *Der Staat Hitlers*, 256.

88. Ibid., 136–8.

89. Winkler, *Der Weg*, 888–93, 898–900.

90. Ibid., 916–18.

91. Ibid., 929–32; Broszat, *Der Staat Hitlers*, 118–19.

92. Harold Marcuse, *Legacies of Dachau: The Uses and Abuses of a Concentration*

Camp, 1933–2001 (Cambridge, 2001), 21–3; Hans-Günter Richardi, *Schule der Gewalt: Das Konzentrationslager Dachau, 1933–1934* (Munich, 1983), 48–87, and Johannes Tuchel, *Organisationsgeschichte und Funktion der 'Inspektion der Konzentrationslager' 1933–1938* (Boppard, 1991), 121–58.

93. Bley, *Namibia under German Rule*, 151, 198; Krüger, *Kriegsbewältigung*, 138–44; Joachim Zeller, "'Wie Vieh wurden Hunderte zu Getriebenen und wie Vieh begraben'": Fotodokumente aus dem deutschen Konzentrationslager in Swakopmund/Namibia 1904–1908', *Zeitschrift für Geschichtswissenschaft*, 49 (2001), 226–43.

94. Marcuse, *Legacies of Dachau*, 21–2; Tuchel, *Organisationsgeschichte*, 35–7; Andrej Kaminski, *Konzentrationslager 1896 bis heute: Eine Analyse* (Stuttgart, 1982), 34–38. There is no convincing evidence that Hitler or Himmler drew on the model of labour camps in Soviet Russia (see Evans, *In Hitler's Shadow*, 24–46).

95. For the argument that it was improvised, see Broszat, 'The Concentration Camps', 400–406.

96. Bessel, *Political Violence*, 117.

97. Friedrich Schlotterbeck, *The Darker the Night, the Brighter the Stars: A German Worker Remembers (1933–1945)* (London, 1947), 22–36. For further considerations on Nazi violence, see Lindenberger and Lüdtke (eds.), *Physische Gewalt*, and Bernd Weisbrod, 'Gewalt in der Politik: Zur politischen Kultur in Deutschland zwischen den beiden Weltkriegen', *Geschichte in Wissenschaft und Unterricht*, 43 (1992), 391–404.

98. Numerous cases detailed in World Committee (ed.), *The Brown Book*, 216–18; for Jankowski, 210–11. See also Diels, *Lucifer*, 222.

99. Günter Morsch, 'Oranienburg – Sachsenhausen, Sachsenhausen – Oranienburg', in Ulrich Herbert *et al.* (eds.), *Die nationalsozialistischen Konzentrationslager: Entwicklung und Struktur* (2 vols., Göttingen, 1998), 111–34, at 119.

100. Tuchel, *Organisationsgeschichte*, 103; Karin Orth, *Das System der nationalsozialistischen Konzentrationslager* (Hamburg, 1999), 23–6.

101. Bahne, 'Die Kommunistische Partei Deutschlands', in Matthias and Morsey (eds.) *Das Ende*, 693–4, 699–700; Winkler, *Der Weg*, 876–89; Broszat, 'The Concentration Camps', 406–7; Broszat *et al.* (eds.), *Bayern*, I. 240–41.

102. Fieberg (ed.), *Im Namen*, 68; World Committee (ed.), *The Brown Book*, 332, listed 500 murders up to June.

103. Domarus, *Hitler*, I. 263; Mason, *Social Policy*, 76, presents Hitler's concern about the disorder as genuine; he also notes that the Nazi leadership was kept constantly informed about the nature and extent of violent incidents.

104. Broszat, *Der Staat Hitlers*, 111.

105. Rudolf Morsey (ed.), *Das 'Ermächtigungsgesetz' vom 24. März 1933: Quellen zur Geschichte und Interpretation des 'Gesetzes zur Behebung der Not von Volk und Reich'* (Düsseldorf, 1992), and Michael Frehse, *Ermächtigungsgesetzgebung im Deutschen Reich 1914–1933* (Pfaffenweiler, 1985), 145.

106. Matthias and Morsey (eds.), *Das Ende*, xiii.

107. Klaus-Jürgen Müller, 'Der Tag von Potsdam und das Verhältnis der preussisch-deutschen Militär-Elite zum Nationalsozialismus', in Bernhard Kröner (ed.), *Potsdam – Stadt, Armee, Residenz in der preussisch-deutschen Militärgeschichte* (Frankfurt am Main, 1993), 435–49; Fröhlich (ed.), *Die Tagebücher*, II. 395–7 (22 March 1933); Werner Freitag, 'Nationale Mythen und kirchliches Heil: Der "Tag von Potsdam"', *Westfälische Forschungen*, 41 (1991), 379–430. For Hitler's speech, see Domarus, *Hitler*, I. 272–4.

108. Ibid, 270.

109. Bracher, *Stufen*, 213–36; also Hans Schneider, 'Das Ermächtigungsgesetz vom 24. März 1933', *VfZ* 1 (1953), 197–221, esp. 207–8.

110. Junker, *Die Deutsche Zentrumspartei*, 171–89; Morsey, 'Die Deutsche Zentrumspartei', in Matthias and Morsey (eds.), *Das Ende*, 281–453; Josef Becker, 'Zentrum und Ermächtigungsgesetz 1933: Dokumentation' *VfZ* 9 (1961), 195–210; Rudolf Morsey, 'Hitlers Verhandlungen mit der Zentrumsführung am 31. Januar 1933', *VfZ* 9 (1961), 182–94.

111. Wilhelm Hoegner, *Der schwierige Aussenseiter: Erinnerungen eines Abgeordneten, Emigranten und Ministerpräsidenten* (Munich, 1959), 92.

112. Becker, 'Zentrum und Ermächtigungsgesetz 1933'; Konrad Repgen, 'Zur vatikanischen Strategie beim Reichskonkordat', *VfZ* 31 (1983), 506–35; Brüning, *Memoiren*, 655–57; Domarus, *Hitler*, I. 275–85.

113. Winkler, *Der Weg*, 901–6; Hans J. L. Adolph, *Otto Wels und die Politik der deutschen Sozialdemokratie 1934–1939: Eine politische Biographie* (Berlin, 1971), 262–4; Willy Brandt, *Erinnerungen* (Frankfurt am Main, 1989), 96; Hoegner, *Der Schwierige Aussenseiter*, 93.

114. Broszat, *Der Staat Hitlers*, 117 and n. For the Enabling Act in the context of enabling legislation in the Weimar Republic, see Jörg Biesemann, *Das Ermächtigungsgesetz als Grundlage der Gesetzgebung im nationalsozialistischen Deutschland: Ein Beitrag zur Stellung des Gesetzes in der Verfassungsgeschichte 1919–1945* (Münster, 1992 [1985]).

115. Matthias, 'Die Sozialdemokratische Partei Deutschlands', in Matthias and Morsey (eds.) *Das Ende*, 176–80; Winkler, *Der Weg*, 867–98; Schumann, *Nationalsozialismus und Gewerkschaftsbewegung*; Hannes Heer, *Burgfrieden oder Klassenkampf: Zur Politik der sozialdemokratischen Gewerkschaften 1930–1933* (Neuwied, 1971), very critical of the union leaders; Bernd Martin, 'Die deutschen Gewerkschaften und die nationalsozialistische Machtübernahme', *Geschichte in Wissenschaft und Unterricht*, 36 (1985), 605–31; Henryk Skrzypczak, 'Das Ende der Gewerkschaften', in Wolfgang Michalka (ed.), *Die nationalsozialistische Machtergreifung* (Paderborn, 1984), 97–110.

116. *Nationalsozialistische Betriebszellenorganisation*, or National Socialist Workshop Cell Organization.

117. Winkler, *Der Weg*, 898–909; Gunther Mai, 'Die Nationalsozialistische Betriebszellen-Organisation: Zum Verhältnis von Arbeiterschaft und Nationalsozialismus', *VfZ* 31 (1983), 573–613.

118. Schneider, *Unterm Hakenkreuz*, 76–106, 89 for quotation; Winkler, *Der Weg*, 898–909; Herbst, *Das nationalsozialistische Deutschland*, 68–70.

119. Wieland Elfferding, 'Von der proletarischen Masse zum Kriegsvolk: Massenaufmarsch und Öffentlichkeit im deutschen Faschismus am Beispiel des 1. Mai 1933', in Neue Gesellschaft für bildende Kunst (ed.), *Inszenierung der Macht: Ästhetische Faszination im Faschismus* (Berlin, 1987), 17–50.

120. Peter Jahn (ed.), *Die Gewerkschaften in der Endphase der Republik 1930–1933* (Cologne, 1988), 888–92, 897–8, 916.

121. Dieter Fricke, *Kleine Geschichte des Ersten Mai: Die Maifeier in der deutschen und internationalen Arbeiterbewegung* (Berlin, 1980), 224–9; Fritzsche, *Germans*, 215–35.

122. Goebbels, *Vom Kaiserhof*, 299, and Fröhlich (ed.), *Die Tagebücher*, I/II. 408 (17 April 1933).

123. Winkler, *Der Weg*, 909–29; Michael Schneider, *A Brief History of the German Trade Unions* (Bonn, 1991 [1989]), 204–10.

124. Fröhlich (ed.), *Die Tagebücher*, I/II. 416 (3 May 1933).

125. Winkler, *Der Weg*, 929–32; Grahn, 'Die Enteignung'; Beate Dapper and Hans-Peter Rouette, 'Zum Ermittelungsverfahren gegen Leipart und Genossen wegen Untreue vom 9. Mai 1933', *Internationale Wissenschaftliche Korrespondenz zur Geschichte der deutschen Arbeiterbewegung*, 20 (1984), 509–35; Schneider, *Unterm Hakenkreuz*, 107–17.

126. Winkler, *Der Weg*, 932–40; Matthias, 'Die Sozialdemokratische Partei Deutschlands', in Matthias and Morsey (eds.), *Die Ende*, 168–75, 166–75; for Pfülf's suicide, see 254 n. 6; Broszat, *Der Staat Hitlers*, 120.

127. Fröhlich (ed.), *Die Tagebücher* I/II. 437 (23 June 1933).

128. Schüler, *Auf der Flucht erschossen*, 241–8.

129. For details, see Max Klinger (pseud.; i.e. Curt Geyer), *Volk in Ketten* (Karlsbad, 1934), esp. 96–7; Winkler, *Der Weg*, 943–7; Franz Osterroth and Dieter Schuster, *Chronik der deutschen Sozialdemokratie* (Hanover, 1963), 381; documents in Erich Matthias, 'Der Untergang der Sozialdemokratie 1933', *VfZ* 4 (1956), 179–226 and commentary 250–86; for Berlin and its suburbs, see Reinhard Rürup (ed.), *Topographie des Terrors: Gestapo, SS und Reichssicherheitshauptamt auf dem 'Prinz-Albert-Gelände': Eine Dokumentation* (Berlin, 1987), and Hans-Norbert Burkert et al., *'Machtergreifung' Berlin 1933: Stätten der Geschichte Berlins in Zusammenarbeit mit dem Pädagogischen Zentrum Berlin* (Berlin, 1982), 20–94.

130. Bessel, *Political Violence*, 42, 117–18; Paul Löbe, *Der Weg war lang: Lebenserinnerungen von Paul Löbe* (Berlin, 1954 [1950]), 221–9.

131. Beth A. Griech-Polelle, *Bishop von Galen: German Catholicism and National Socialism* (New Haven, 2002), 9–18.

132. Ibid., 31–2; Richard Steigmann-Gall, *The Holy Reich: Nazi Conceptions of Christianity, 1919–1945* (New York, 2003), 51–85.

133. Hans Müller (ed.), *Katholische Kirche und Nationalsozialismus: Dokumente 1930–1935* (Munich, 1963), 79.

134. Thomas Fandel, 'Konfessionalismus und Nationalsozialismus', in Olaf Blaschke (ed.), *Konfessionen im Konflikt: Deutschland zwischen 1800 und 1970: Ein zweites konfessionelles Zeitalter* (Göttingen, 2002), 299–334, at 314–15; Günther Lewy, *The Catholic Church and Nazi Germany* (New York, 1964), 94–112.

135. Müller, *Katholische Kirche*, 168; see, more generally, Scholder, *The Churches*.

136. Morsey, 'Die Deutsche Zentrumspartei', in Matthias and Morsey (eds.), *Das Ende*, 383–6, quoting *Kölnische Volkszeitung* on 12 May 1933.

137. Broszat, 'The Concentration Camps', 409–11.

138. Lewy, *The Catholic Church*, 45–79.

139. Morsey, 'Die Deutsche Zentrumspartei', in Matthias and Morsey (eds.), *Das Ende*, 387–411; Lewy, *The Catholic Church*, 7–93.

140. Griech-Polelle, *Bishop von Galen*, 45–6, 137–9.

141. Morsey, 'Die Deutsche Staatspartei', in Matthias and Morsey (eds.), *Das Ende*, 55–72; Jones, *German Liberalism*, 462–75 (also for the People's Party).

142. Hans Booms, 'Die Deutsche Volkspartei', in Matthias and Morsey (eds.), *Das Ende*, 521–39.

143. Hiller von Gaertringen, 'Die Deutschnationale Volkspartei', in Matthias and Morsey (eds.), *Das Ende*, 576–99; Larry Eugene Jones, ' "The Greatest Stupidity of My Life": Alfred Hugenberg and the Formation of the Hitler Cabinet', *Journal of Contemporary History*, 27 (1992), 63–87; for a copy of Hugenberg's resignation letter, with other documents, see Anton Ritthaler, 'Eine Etappe auf Hitlers Weg zur ungeteilten Macht: Hugenbergs Rücktritt als Reichsminister', *VfZ* 8 (1960), 193–219.

144. Hiller von Gaertringen, 'Die Deutschnationale Volkspartei', in Matthias and Morsey (eds.), *Das Ende*, 599–603.

145. Ibid., 607–15.

146. Berghahn, *Der Stahlhelm*, 253–70; Broszat, *Der Staat Hitlers*, 121.

147. Hiller von Gaertringen, 'Die Deutschnationale Volkspartei', in Matthias and Morsey (eds.), *Das Ende*, 603–7; Bessel, *Political Violence*, 120–21; Berghahn, *Der Stahlhelm*, 268–74, 286.

148. Fröhlich (ed.), *Die Tagebücher* I/II. 440 (28 June 1933).

149. Hans-Georg Stümke, *Homosexuelle in Deutschland: Eine politische Geschichte* (Munich, 1989).

150. Eyewitness account in Hans-Georg Stümke and Rudi Finkler, *Rosa Winkel, Rosa Listen: Homosexuelle und 'Gesundes Volksempfinden' von Auschwitz bis heute* (Hamburg, 1981), 163–66, quoted and translated in Burleigh and Wippermann, *The Racial State*, 189–90. See also Burkhard Jellonek, *Homosexuelle unter dem Hakenkreuz: Verfolgung von Homosexuellen im Dritten Reich* (Paderborn, 1990). Personal testimonies in Richard Plant, *The Pink Triangle: The Nazi War against Homosexuals* (Edinburgh, 1987).

151. Wolff, *Magnus Hirschfeld*, 414.

152. Grossmann, *Reforming Sex*, 149–50; Gaby Zürn, ' "Von der Herbertstrasse

nach Auschwitz" ', in Angelika Ebbinghaus (ed.), *Opfer und Täterinnen: Frauen-biographien des Nationalsozialismus* (Nördlingen, 1987), 91–101, at 93; Annette F. Timm, 'The Ambivalent Outsider: Prostitution, Promiscuity, and VD Control in Nazi Berlin', in Gellately and Stoltzfus (eds.), *Social Outsiders*, 192–211; Christl Wickert, *Helene Stöcker 1869–1943: Frauenrechtlerin, Sexualreformerin und Pazifistin. Eine Biographie* (Bonn, 1991), 135–40; more generally, Gabriele Czarnow-ski, *Das kontrollierte Paar: Ehe- und Sexualpolitik im Nationalsozialismus* (Weinheim, 1991).

153. Grossmann, *Reforming Sex*, 136–61.

154. Hong, *Welfare*, 261–5; Burleigh, *Death and Deliverance*, 11–42; Jochen-Christoph Kaiser *et al.* (eds.), *Eugenik, Sterilisation, 'Euthanasie': Politische Biologie in Deutschland 1893–1945* (Berlin, 1992), 100–102; idem, *Sozialer Prot-estantismus im 20. Jahrhundert: Beiträge zur Geschichte der Inneren Mission 1914–1945* (Munich, 1989).

155. Ayass, *'Asoziale' im Nationalsozialismus*, 57–60.

156. Elizabeth Harvey, *Youth Welfare and the State in Weimar Germany* (Oxford, 1993), 274–8; Ayass, *'Asoziale' in Nazionalsozialismus*, 13–23, idem, 'Vagrants and Beggars', 211–17; see also Marcus Gräser, *Der blockierte Wohlfahrtsstaat: Unterschichtjugend und Jugendfürsorge in der Weimarer Republik* (Göttingen, 1995), 216–30.

157. Wagner, *Volksgemeinschaft*, 193–213.

158. Patrick Wagner, *Hitlers Kriminalisten: Die deutsche Kriminalpolizei und der Nationalsozialismus* (Munich, 2002), 57–8.

159. Nikolaus Wachsmann, 'From Indefinite Confinement to Extermination: "Habitual Criminals" in the Third Reich', in Gellately and Stoltzfus (eds.), *Social Outsiders*, 165–91; Wachsmann, *Hitler's Prisons*, chapter 2.

160. Robert N. Proctor, *Racial Hygiene: Medicine under the Nazis* (Cambridge, Mass., 1988), 101.

161. Crew, *Germans on Welfare*, 208–12.

162. Broszat, 'The Concentration Camps', 409–11.

163. Caplan, *Government*, 139–41.

164. Noakes and Pridham (eds.), *Nazism*, II. 26–31.

165. Quoted in Hans Mommsen, *Beamtentum im Dritten Reich: Mit ausgewählten Quellen zur nationalsozialistischen Beamtenpolitik* (Stuttgart, 1966), 162.

166. Broszat, *Der Staat Hitlers*, 254; Jürgen W. Falter, ' "Die Märzgefallenen" von 1933: Neue Forschungsergebnisse zum sozialen Wandel innerhalb der NSDAP-Mitgliedschaft während der Machtergreifungsphase', *Geschichte und Gesellschaft*, 24 (1998), 595–616, at 616.

167. Caplan, *Government*, 143–7; Bracher, *Stufen*, 244.

168. Bracher, *Stufen*, 245–6; Fieberg (ed.), *Im Namen*, 87–94; Lothar Gruchmann, 'Die Überleitung der Justizverwaltung auf das Reich 1933–1935', in *Vom Reichs-justizamt zum Bundesministerium der Justiz; Festschrift zum hundertjährigen Gründungstag des Reichsjustizamts* (Cologne, 1977) and Horst Göppinger,

Juristen jüdischer Abstammung im 'Dritten Reich': Entrechtung und Verfolgung (Munich, 1990 [1963]), 183–373.

169. Fieberg (ed.), *Im Namen*, 76–9, 272; Lothar Gruchmann, 'Die Überleitung', in *Vom Reichsjustizamt zum Bundesministerium der Justiz*, 119–60.

170. Bracher, *Stufen*, 264–7; Hayes, *Industry and Ideology*, 85–9.

171. Evans, *The Feminist Movement* 255–60.

172. Allen, *The Nazi Seizure of Power*, 218–32.

173. Haffner, *Defying Hitler*, 111, 114.

Chapter 6 HITLER'S CULTURAL REVOLUTION

1. Josef Wulf, *Musik im Dritten Reich: Eine Dokumentation* (Gütersloh, 1963), 31; Fritz Busch, *Aus dem Leben eines Musikers* (Zurich, 1949), 188–209; Levi, *Music*, 42–3; World Committee (ed.), *The Brown Book*, 180.

2. Michael H. Kater, *The Twisted Muse: Musicians and their Music in the Third Reich* (New York, 1997), 120–24, correcting the account in Busch's memoirs. For the seizure of power in Saxony, see Szejnmann, *Nazism*, 33–4.

3. Gerhard Splitt, *Richard Strauss 1933–1935: Aesthetik und Musikpolitik zu Beginn der nationalsozialistischen Herrschaft* (Pfaffenweiler, 1987), 42–59; Bruno Walter, *Theme and Variations: An Autobiography* (New York, 1966), 295–300; Brigitte Hamann, *Winifred Wagner oder Hitlers Bayreuth* (Munich, 2002), 117–56.

4. Peter Heyworth, *Otto Klemperer: His Life and Times*, I: *1885–1933* (Cambridge, 1983), 413, 415.

5. Levi, *Music*, 44–5; Christopher Hailey, *Franz Schreker, 1878–1934: A Cultural Biography* (Cambridge, 1993), 273, 288; Schreker had already resigned as director of the Berlin School of Music in 1932 after persistent antisemitic harassment.

6. Wulf, *Musik*, 28, reprinting Philharmonische Gesellschaft in Hamburg to Kampfbund für deutsche Kultur, Gruppe Berlin, 6 April 1933.

7. Levi, *Music*, 39–41, 86, 107; see more generally Reinhold Brinkmann and Christoph Wolff (eds.), *Driven into Paradise: The Musical Migration from Germany to the United States* (Berkeley, 1999).

8. Kater, *The Twisted Muse*, 89–91, 120; see also Michael Meyer, *The Politics of Music in the Third Reich* (New York, 1991), 19–26.

9. David Welch, *The Third Reich: Politics and Propaganda* (2nd edn., London, 2002 [1993]), 172–82, at 173–4.

10. Minuth (ed.), *Die Regierung Hitler*, I. 193–5. See Wolfram Werner, 'Zur Geschichte des Reichsministeriums für Volksaufklärung und Propaganda und zur Überlieferung', in idem (ed.), *Findbücher zu Beständen des Bundesarchivs*, XV: *Reichsministerium für Volksaufklärung und Propaganda* (Koblenz, 1979).

11. For the widespread view that Goebbels was a 'socialist', see for example Jochmann (ed.), *Nationalsozialismus und Revolution*, 407–8.

12. Speech of 15 March 1933, quoted in Welch, *The Third Reich*, 174–5; for discussions in 1932, see Fröhlich (ed.), *Die Tagebücher*, I/II. 113–14 and 393 (15 March 1933).

13. Fröhlich, 'Joseph Goebbels', in Smelser and Zitelmann (eds.), *The Nazi Elite*, 55.

14. *Völkischer Beobachter*, 23 March 1933, cited and translated in Welch, *The Third Reich*, 22–3.

15. Quoted in Reuth, *Goebbels*, 269.

16. Quoted in Welch, *The Third Reich*, 175.

17. Quoted ibid., 176.

18. Reuth, *Goebbels*, 271; Fröhlich (ed.), *Die Tagebücher*, I/II. 388 (6 March 1933), 393 (13 March 1933) and 395–7 (22 March 1933); Ansgar Diller, *Rundfunkpolitik im Dritten Reich* (Munich, 1980), 89; Zbynek A.B. Zeman, *Nazi Propaganda* (2nd edn., Oxford, 1973 [1964]), 40. For the structure of the Ministry, see Welch, *The Third Reich*, 29–31.

19. West, *The Visual Arts*, 183–4, also for the quotations.

20. Levi, *Music*, 246 n.5.

21. Fred K. Prieberg, *Trial of Strength: Wilhelm Furtwängler and the Third Reich* (London, 1991), 166–9, citing published and unpublished correspondence and memoranda. For Furtwängler's views on a variety of topics, see Michael Tanner (ed.), *Wilhelm Furtwängler, Notebooks 1924–1945* (London, 1989).

22. For Furtwängler's life and opinions in general, see Prieberg, *Trial of Strength*, *passim*; for reservations about this book, see Evans, *Rereading*, 187–93.

23. The exchange is reprinted in Wulf, *Musik*, 81–2. Max Reinhardt was a well-known theatre director.

24. Levi, *Music*, 199–201.

25. *Berliner Lokal-Anzeiger*, 11 April 1933, reprinted in Wulf, *Musik*, 82–3.

26. Levi, *Music*, 198–202; Peter Cossé, 'Die Geschichte', in Paul Badde *et al.* (eds.), *Das Berliner Philharmonische Orchester* (Stuttgart, 1987), 10–17.

27. Kater, *Different Drummers*, 29–33.

28. Ibid., 47–110.

29. Jelavich, *Berlin Cabaret*, 228–258; 'Hermann' is on 229.

30. Volker Kühn (ed.), *Deutschlands Erwachen: Kabarett unterm Hakenkreuz 1933–1945* (Weinheim, 1989), 335; see, more generally, Christian Goeschel, 'Methodische Überlegungen zur Geschichte der Selbsttötung im Nationalsozialismus', in Hans Medick (ed.), *Selbsttötung als kulturelle Praxis* (forthcoming, 2004).

31. Josef Wulf, *Theater und Film im Dritten Reich: Eine Dokumentation* (Gütersloh, 1964), 265–306.

32. David Thomson, *The New Biographical Dictionary of Film* (4th edn., 2002 [1975]). Claims in some accounts of Dietrich's life, including her own, that she left for political reasons, and that Hitler personally intervened to try and persuade her to return, should be treated with considerable scepticism.

33. David Welch, 'Propaganda and the German Cinema 1933–1945' (unpublished Ph.D. dissertation, London University, 1979), appendix I.

34. Birgit Bernard, '"Gleichschaltung" im Westdeutschen Rundfunk 1933/34', in Dieter Breuer and Gertrude Cepl-Kaufmann (eds.), *Moderne und Nationalsozialismus im Rheinland* (Paderborn, 1997), 301–10; Jochen Klepper, *Unter dem Schatten deiner Flügel: Aus den Tagebüchern der Jahre 1932–1942* (Stuttgart, 1956), 46, 65; Josef Wulf, *Presse und Funk im Dritten Reich: Eine Dokumentation* (Gütersloh, 1964), 277–9, 280–84.

35. Fulda, 'Press and Politics', 231–3, 241–2.

36. Welch, *The Third Reich*, 46; text of the law in Wulf, *Presse und Funk*, 72–3.

37. Ibid., 19–38.

38. Welch, *The Third Reich*, 43–8.

39. Grossmann, *Ossietzky*, 224–74.

40. Ibid., 267; Chris Hirte, *Erich Mühsam: 'Ihr seht mich nicht feige'. Biografie* (Berlin, 1985), 431–50. Accounts differ as to whether this was murder or suicide; the former seems more likely.

41. Dieter Distl, *Ernst Toller: Eine politische Biographie* (Schrobenhausen, 1993), 146–78.

42. Kelly, *All Quiet*, 39–56.

43. Inge Jens (ed.), *Thomas Mann an Ernst Bertram: Briefe aus den Jahren 1910–1955* (Pfullingen, 1960), 178 (letter of 18 November 1933) and Robert Faesi (ed.), *Thomas Mann – Robert Faesi: Briefwechsel* (Zurich, 1962), 23 (Mann to Faesi, 28 June 1933); Klaus Harpprecht, *Thomas Mann: Eine Biographie* (Reinbek, 1995), 707–50; Kurt Sontheimer, 'Thomas Mann als politischer Schriftsteller', *VfZ* 6 (1958), 1–44; Josef Wulf, *Literatur und Dichtung im Dritten Reich: Eine Dokumentation* (Gütersloh, 1963), 24.

44. Ritchie, *German Literature*, 187–99; Wulf, *Literatur, passim*.

45. Robert E. Norton, *Secret Germany: Stefan George and his Circle* (Ithaca, NY, 2002) is now the standard biography. For Jünger, see Paul Noack, *Ernst Jünger: Eine Biographie* (Berlin, 1998), 121–51.

46. Quoted in Wulf, *Literatur*, 132; see also Ritchie, *German Literature*, 9–10, 48–9, 111–32.

47. Frederic Spotts, *Hitler and the Power of Aesthetics* (London, 2002), 152; quotations and context in West, *The Visual Arts*, 183–4; Hitler, *Mein Kampf*, 235.

48. Rosamunde Neugebauer, '"Christus mit der Gasmaske" von George Grosz, oder: Wieviel Satire konnten Kirche und Staat in Deutschland um 1930 ertragen?', in Maria Rüger (ed.), *Kunst und Kunstkritik der dreissiger Jahre: Standpunkte zu künstlerischen und ästhetischen Prozessen und Kontroversen* (Dresden, 1990), 156–65.

49. Josef Wulf, *Die Bildenden Künste im Dritten Reich: Eine Dokumentation* (Gütersloh, 1963), 49–51.

50. Peter Adam, *Arts of the Third Reich* (London, 1992), 59.

51. Jonathan Petropoulos, *The Faustian Bargain: The Art World in Nazi Germany*

(London, 2000), 217. See also Brandon Taylor and Wilfried van der Will (eds.), *The Nazification of Art: Art, Design, Music, Architecture and Film in the Third Reich* (Winchester, 1990).

52. Spotts, *Hitler*, 153–5.

53. Petropoulos, *The Faustian Bargain*, 14–16.

54. Adam, *Arts*, 49–50; Wulf, *Die Bildenden Künste*, 36; Günter Busch, *Max Liebermann: Maler, Zeichner, Graphiker* (Frankfurt am Main, 1986), 146; Peter Paret, *An Artist against the Third Reich: Ernst Barlach 1933–1938* (Cambridge, 2003), 77–92. Liebermann's funeral was placed under heavy surveillance by the political police (Petropoulos, *The Faustian Bargain*, 217).

55. Sean Rainbird (ed.), *Max Beckmann* (London, 2003), 157–64, 273–4; Adam, *Arts*, 53; Petropoulos, *The Faustian Bargain*, 216–21.

56. Wulf, *Die Bildenden Künste*, 39–45; Koehler, 'The *Bauhaus*', 292–3; Igor Golomstock, *Totalitarian Art in the Soviet Union, Third Reich, Fascist Italy and the People's Republic of China* (London, 1990), 21; West, *The Visual Arts*, 83–133.

57. Ritchie, *German Literature*, 187.

58. Ibid., 189; Harpprecht, *Thomas Mann*, 722–50.

59. Ritchie, *German Literature* 58–61; Lothar Gall, *Bürgertum in Deutschland* (Berlin, 1989), 466, also more generally for Bassermann and his family. Johst was quickly appointed co-director of the theatre. See Boguslaw Drewniak, *Das Theater im NS-Staat: Szenarium deutscher Zeitgeschichte 1933–1945* (Düsseldorf, 1983), 46–7; more generally, Glen W. Gadberry (ed.), *Theatre in the Third Reich, the Prewar Years: Essays on Theatre in Nazi Germany* (Westport, Conn., 1995) and John London (ed.), *Theatre under the Nazis* (Manchester, 2000).

60. Ritchie, *German Literature*, 58–61; 'Wenn ich Kultur höre, entsichere ich meinen Browning' (Wulf, *Literatur*, 113).

61. Knowles (ed.), *The Oxford Dictionary of Quotations*, 418, quote 17; for a first, detailed account of 'the war of annihilation against culture', see World Committee (ed.), *The Brown Book*, 160–93.

62. Hugo Ott, *Martin Heidegger: A Political Life* (London, 1993), 13–139.

63. Ibid., 140–48.

64. Martin Heidegger, *Die Selbstbehauptung der deutschen Universität: Rede, gehalten bei der feierlichen Übernahme des Rektorats der Universität Freiburg i. Br. am 27.5.1933* (Breslau, 1934), 5, 7, 14–15, 22.

65. Hans Sluga, *Heidegger's Crisis: Philosophy and Politics in Nazi Germany* (Cambridge, Mass., 1993), 1–4; Guido Schneeberger, *Nachlese zu Heidegger: Dokumente zu seinem Leben und Denken* (Berne, 1962), 49–57. See also the biography by Rüdiger Safranski, *Ein Meister aus Deutschland: Heidegger und seine Zeit* (Munich, 1994).

66. Ott, *Martin Heidegger*, 169, 198–9.

67. Quoted ibid., 185.

68. The only professor of any discipline to do so was the historian Gerhard Ritter. See Cornelissen, *Gerhard Ritter*, 239.

69. Quoted in Ott, *Martin Heidegger*, 164, with a discussion on 165–6 of the casuistry employed by Heidegger's modern admirers in trying to explain such sentiments away. For a useful collection of studies, see Bernd Martin (ed.), *Martin Heidegger und das 'Dritte Reich' Ein Kompendium* (Darmstadt, 1989).

70. Remy, *The Heidelberg Myth*, 14.

71. Ott, *Martin Heidegger*, 235–351.

72. Noakes and Pridham (eds.), *Nazism*, II. 249–250; and for two good local studies, Uwe Dietrich Adam, *Hochschule und Nationalsozialismus: Die Universität Tübingen im Dritten Reich* (Tübingen, 1977), and Notker Hammerstein, *Die Johann Wolfgang Goethe-Universität: Von der Stiftungsuniversität zur staatlichen Hochschule* (2 vols., Neuwied, 1989), I. 171–211.

73. Klaus Fischer, 'Der quantitative Beitrag der nach 1933 emigrierten Naturwissenschaftler zur deutschsprachigen physikalischen Forschung', *Berichte zur Wissenschaftsgeschichte*, 11 (1988), 83–104, revising slightly higher figures in Alan D. Beyerchen, *Scientists under Hitler: Politics and the Physics Community in the Third Reich* (New Haven, 1977), 43–7, and Norbert Schnappacher, 'Das Mathematische Institut der Universität Göttingen', and Alf Rosenow, 'Die Göttinger Physik unter dem Nationalsozialismus', both in Heinrich Becker *et al.* (eds.), *Die Universität Göttingen unter dem Nationalsozialismus: Das verdrängte Kapitel ihrer 250 jährigen Geschichte* (Munich, 1987), 345–73 and 374–409.

74. Ute Deichmann, *Biologists under Hitler* (Cambridge, Mass., 1996 [1992]), 26.

75. Beyerchen, *Scientists*, 43.

76. Max Born (ed.), *The Born–Einstein Letters: Correspondence between Albert Einstein and Max and Hedwig Born from 1916 to 1955* (London, 1971), 113–14.

77. Fritz Stern, *Dreams and Delusions: The Drama of German History* (New York, 1987), 51–76 ('Fritz Haber: The Scientist in Power and in Exile'); Margit Szöllösi-Janze, *Fritz Haber 1868–1934: Eine Biographie* (Munich, 1998), 643–91.

78. Max Planck, 'Mein Besuch bei Hitler', *Physikalische Blätter*, 3 (1947), 143; Fritz Stern, *Einstein's German World* (London, 2000 [1999]), 34–58.

79. Remy, *The Heidelberg Myth*, 17–18. More generally, see Fritz Köhler, 'Zur Vertreibung humanistischer Gelehrter 1933/34', *Blätter für deutsche und internationale Politik*, 11 (1966), 696–707.

80. Beyerchen, *Scientists*, 15–17, 63–4, 199–210.

81. Remy, *The Heidelberg Myth*, 24–9; see also Christian Jansen, *Professoren und Politik: Politisches Denken und Handeln der Heidelberger Hochschullehrer 1914–1935* (Göttingen, 1992).

82. Quoted in Noakes and Pridham (eds.), *Nazism*, II. 252.

83. Ibid., II. 250; Turner, *German Big Business*, 337.

84. Remy, *The Heidelberg Myth*, 20.

85. Ibid., 31.

86. Grüttner, *Studenten*, 71–4.

87. Ibid., 81–6.

88. Axel Friedrichs (ed.), *Die nationalsozialistische Revolution 1933* (Dokumente der deutschen Politik, I, Berlin, 1933), 277; Fröhlich (ed.), *Die Tagebücher*, I/II. 419 (11 May 1933).

89. Various versions printed in Gerhard Sauder (ed.), *Die Bücherverbrennung: Zum 10. Mai 1933* (Munich, 1983), 89–95.

90. Clemens Zimmermann, 'Die Bücherverbrennung am 17. Mai 1933 in Heidelberg: Studenten und Politik am Ende der Weimarer Republik', in Joachim-Felix Leonhard (ed.), *Bücherverbrennung: Zensur, Verbot, Vernichtung unter dem Nationalsozialismus in Heidelberg* (Heidelberg, 1983), 55–84.

91. Wolfgang Strätz, 'Die studentische "Aktion wider den undeutschen Geist"', *VfZ* 16 (1968), 347–72 (mistakenly ascribing the initiative to the Propaganda Ministry); Jan-Pieter Barbian, *Literaturpolitik im 'Dritten Reich': Institutionen, Kompetenzen, Betätigungsfelder* (Frankfurt am Main, 1993), 54–60, 128–42; Hildegard Brenner, *Die Kunstpolitik des Nationalsozialismus* (Hamburg, 1963), 186.

92. Leonidas E. Hill, 'The Nazi Attack on "Un-German" Literature, 1933–1945', in Jonathan Rose (ed.), *The Holocaust and the Book* (Amherst, Mass., 2001), 9–46; Sauder (ed.), *Die Bücherverbrennung*, 9–16; see also Anselm Faust, 'Die Hochschulen und der "undeutsche Geist": Die Bücherverbrennung am 10. Mai 1933 und ihr Vorgeschichte', in Horst Denkler and Eberhard Lämmert (eds.), *'Das war ein Vorspiel nur . . .': Berliner Kolloquium zur Literaturpolitik im 'Dritten Reich'* (Berlin, 1985), 31–50; Grüttner, *Studenten*, 75–77, points out that no instructions from the recently founded Propaganda Ministry can be found in the files of the student unions, and Goebbels gives no hint in his diary that the initiative came from him.

93. Rebentisch and Raab (eds.), *Neu-Isenburg*, 86–7.

94. For the Wartburg events, see Wehler, *Deutsche Gesellschaftsgeschichte*, II. 334–6; Heine's subsequently famous statement was made in *Almansor* (1823), 245, cited in (among many other anthologies) Knowles (ed.), *The Oxford Dictionary of Quotations*, 368. Burning to death was still prescribed as a punishment for murder by arson in Prussia at the time, last used in Berlin in 1812 (Evans, *Rituals*, 213–14).

95. Michael Wildt, 'Violence against Jews in Germany, 1933–1939', in David Bankier (ed.), *Probing the Depths of German Antisemitism: German Society and the Persecution of the Jews 1933–1941* (Jerusalem, 2000), 181–209, at 181–2; Saul Friedländer, *Nazi Germany and the Jews: The Years of Persecution 1933–1939* (London, 1997), 107–10; Walter, *Antisemitische Kriminalität*, 236–43. For a contemporary documentation, see Comité des Délégations Juives (ed.), *Das Schwarzbuch: Tatsachen und Dokumente. Die Lage der Juden in Deutschland 1933* (Paris, 1934). More generally, see Shulamit Volkov, 'Antisemitism as a Cultural Code: Reflections on the History and Historiography of Antisemitism in Imperial Germany', *Year Book of the Leo Baeck Institute*, 23 (1978), 25–46.

96. Longerich, *Politik der Vernichtung*, 26–30.

97. Gruchmann, *Justiz*, 126; Longerich, *Der ungeschriebene Befehl*, 43–4.

98. Haffner, *Defying Hitler*, 125.

99. Halbmonatsbericht des Regierungspräsidenten von Niederbayern und der Oberpfalz, 30. 3. 1933, in Broszat *et al.* (eds.), *Bayern*, I. 432.

100. Friedländer, *Nazi Germany and the Jews*, 41–2.

101. World Committee (ed.), *The Brown Book*, 237, generally on the persecution of the Jews, 222–69.

102. Friedländer, *Nazi Germany and the Jews*, 17–18.

103. Minuth (ed.), *Die Regierung Hitler*, I. 270–71; Longerich, *Der ungeschriebene Befehl*, 44–6.

104. Fröhlich (ed.), *Die Tagebücher*, I/II. 398 (27 March 1933).

105. Moshe R. Gottlieb, *American Anti-Nazi Resistance, 1933–1941: An Historical Analysis* (New York, 1982), 15–24; Deborah E. Lipstadt, *Beyond Belief: The American Press and the Coming of the Holocaust, 1933–1945* (New York, 1986).

106. Fröhlich (ed.), *Die Tagebücher*, I/II. 398–401; Reuth, *Goebbels*, 281; Klemperer, *I Shall Bear Witness*, 9–10.

107. Longerich, *Politik der Vernichtung*, 36–9; more generally, Avraham Barkai, *From Boycott to Annihilation: The Economic Struggle of German Jews, 1933–1945* (Hanover, NH, 1989), 17–25; Helmut Genschel, *Die Verdrängung der Juden aus der Wirtschaft im Dritten Reich* (Berlin, 1966), 47–70.

108. Friedländer, *Nazi Germany and the Jews*, 21–2; Broszat *et al.* (eds.), *Bayern*, I. 433–5; Klemperer, *I Shall Bear Witness*, 10.

109. Friedländer, *Nazi Germany and the Jews*, 24–5; Haffner, *Defying Hitler*, 131–3.

110. Longerich, *Politik der Vernichtung*, 39–41.

111. Friedländer, *Nazi Germany and the Jews*, 26–31.

112. Longerich, *Der ungeschriebene Befehl*, 46.

113. Longerich, *Politik der Vernichtung*, 41–5.

114. Friedländer, *Nazi Germany and the Jews*, 35–7.

115. Allen, *The Nazi Seizure of Power*, 218–22.

116. Konrad Kwiet and Helmut Eschwege, *Selbstbehauptung und Widerstand: Deutsche Juden im Kampf um Existenz und Menschenwürde 1933–1945* (Hamburg, 1984), 50–56.

117. Klemperer, *I Shall Bear Witness*, 5–9; idem, *Tagebücher 1933–1934 (Ich will Zeugnis ablegen bis zum Letzten)*, I (Berlin, 1999 [1995]), 6–15. The German paperback edition, used here, also contains material not included in the English translation.

118. Norbert Frei, ' "Machtergreifung": Anmerkungen zu einem historischen Begriff', *VfZ* 31 (1983), 136–45. The term 'seizure of power' was in fact given currency by the magisterial work of Bracher, Schulz and Sauer, *Die nationalsozialistische Machtergreifung*; but the scope of their vast work made it clear that they intended the concept to cover the period *after* 30 January 1933 and up to the late summer of the same year.

119. The concept of the 'power vacuum' is a central aspect of Bracher's classic account in *Die Auflösung*.

120. See the fascinating speculations in Turner, *Hitler's Thirty Days*, 172–6; these, it seems to me, underestimate the racism and antisemitism of the German officer corps, and its desire to renew 'Germany's bid for world power' which it had so strongly supported earlier in the century; but it is in the nature of this kind of 'what-if' history that guesswork in the end is all we have to fall back on, and there is no way of knowing whether my speculations are any more plausible than Turner's. For some general reflections, see Richard J. Evans, 'Telling It Like It Wasn't', *BBC History Magazine*, 3 (2002), no. 12, 22–5.

121. Volker Rittberger (ed.), *1933: Wie die Republik der Diktatur erlag* (Stuttgart, 1983), esp., 217–21; Martin Blinkhorn, *Fascists and Conservatives: The Radical Right and the Establishment in Twentieth-Century Europe* (London, 1990); idem, *Fascism and the Right in Europe 1919–1945* (London, 2000); Payne, *A History of Fascism*, 14–19.

122. Paul, *Aufstand*, 255–63; Richard Bessel, 'Violence as Propaganda: The Role of the Storm Troopers in the Rise of National Socialism', in Thomas Childers (ed.), *The Formation of the Nazi Constituency, 1919–1933* (London, 1986), 131–46.

123. Geoff Eley, 'What Produces Fascism: Pre-Industrial Traditions or a Crisis of the Capitalist State?', in idem, *From Unification to Nazism*, 254–84; Gessner, *Agrarverbände in der Weimarer Republik*; Geyer, 'Professionals and Junkers'; Peukert, *The Weimar Republic*, 275–81. For an emphasis on the role of pre-industrial elites, see Winkler, *Weimar*, 607.

124. Erdmann and Schulze (eds.), *Weimar*; Heinz Höhne, *Die Machtergreifung: Deutschlands Weg in die Hitler-Diktatur* (Reinbek, 1983), chapter 2 ('Selbstmord einer Demokratie').

125. Joseph Goebbels, *Der Angriff: Aufsätze aus der Kampfzeit* (Munich, 1935), 61.

126. Bracher, *The German Dictatorship*, 246.

127. Ibid., 248–50.

128. Thomas Balistier, *Gewalt und Ordnung: Kalkül und Faszination der SA* (Münster, 1989).

129. *Der Prozess*, XXVI. 300–301 (783-PS), and Broszat, 'The Concentration Camps', 406–23.

130. See, for example Lothar Gruchmann, 'Die bayerische Justiz im politischen Machtkampf 1933/34: Ihr Scheitern bei der Strafverfolgung von Mordfällen in Dachau', in Broszat *et al.* (eds.), *Bayern*, II. 415–28.

131. Wachsmann, *Hitler's Prisons*, chapter 2.

132. Haffner, *Defying Hitler*, 103–25. Dirk Schumann, *Politische Gewalt in der Weimarer Republik: Kampf um die Strasse und Furcht vor dem Bürgerkrieg* (Essen, 2001), esp. 271–368.

133. Hitler, *Hitler: Reden, Schriften, Anordnungen*, III. 434–51, at 445.

134. Bessel, *Political Violence*, 123–5.

135. Ludwig Binz, 'Strafe oder Vernichtung?', *Völkischer Beobachter*, 5 January 1929.

136. Hermann Rauschning, *Germany's Revolution of Destruction* (London, 1939 [1938]), 94, 97–9, 127.

137. Bracher, *Stufen*, 21–2.

138. Richard Bessel, '1933: A Failed Counter-Revolution', in Edgar E. Rice (ed.), *Revolution and Counter-Revolution* (Oxford, 1991), 109–227; Horst Möller, 'Die nationalsozialistische Machtergreifung: Konterrevolution oder Revolution?', *VfZ* 31 (1983), 25–51; Jeremy Noakes, 'Nazism and Revolution', in Noel O'Sullivan (ed.), *Revolutionary Theory and Political Reality* (London, 1983), 73–100; Rainer Zitelmann, *Hitler: The Policies of Seduction* (London, 1999 [1987]).

139. Most notably, Jacob L. Talmon, *The Origins of Totalitarian Democracy* (London, 1952).

140. Bracher, *Stufen*, 25–6.

141. Minuth (ed.), *Die Regierung Hitler*, I. 630.

142. Ibid., 634.

143. AT 6 and 99, in Merkl, *Political Violence*, 469.

144. Bracher, *Stufen*, 48.

145. Leon Trotsky, *The History of the Russian Revolution* (3 vols., London, 1967 [1933–4]), III. 289.

146. Domarus, *Hitler*, I. 487.

147. Richard Löwenthal, 'Die nationalsozialistische "Machtergreifung" – eine Revolution? Ihr Platz unter den totalitären Revolutionen unseres Jahrhunderts', in Martin Broszat et al. (eds.), *Deutschlands Weg in die Diktatur* (Berlin, 1983), 42–74.

Bibliography

Abel, Theodore, *Why Hitler Came to Power* (Cambridge, Mass, 1986 [1938]).

Abrams, Lynn, *Workers' Culture in Imperial Germany: Leisure and Recreation in the Rhineland and Westphalia* (London, 1992).

Ackermann, Josef, *Himmler als Ideologe* (Göttingen, 1970).

——, 'Heinrich Himmler: Reichsführer-SS', in Smelser and Zitelmann (eds.), *The Nazi Elite*, 98–112.

Adam, Peter, *Arts of the Third Reich* (London, 1992).

Adam, Uwe Dietrich, *Hochschule und Nationalsozialismus: Die Universität Tübingen im Dritten Reich* (Tübingen, 1977).

Adolph, Hans J. L., *Otto Wels und die Politik der deutschen Sozialdemokratie 1934–1939: Eine politische Biographie* (Berlin, 1971).

Afflerbach, Holger, *Falkenhayn: Politisches Denken und Handeln im Kaiserreich* (Munich, 1994).

Albrecht, Richard, 'Symbolkampf in Deutschland 1932: Sergej Tschachotin und der "Symbolkrieg" der drei Pfeile gegen den Nationalsozialismus als Episode im Abwehrkampf der Arbeiterbewegung gegen den Faschismus in Deutschland', *Internationale Wissenschaftliche Korrespondenz zur Geschichte der deutschen Arbeiterbewegung*, 22 (1986), 498–533.

Aldcroft, Derek H., *From Versailles to Wall Street 1919–1929* (London, 1977).

Allen, William S., *The Nazi Seizure of Power: The Experience of a Single German Town, 1922–1945* (New York, 1984 [1965]).

Althaus, Hans-Joachim, *et al.*, *'Da ist nirgends nichts gewesen ausser hier': Das 'rote Mössingen' im Generalstreik gegen Hitler. Geschichte eines schwäbischen Arbeiterdorfes* (Berlin, 1982).

Ambrosius, Lloyd E., *Wilsonian Statecraft: Theory and Practice of Liberal Internationalism during World War I* (Wilmington, Del., 1991).

Andersch, Alfred, *Der Vater eines Mörders: Eine Schulgeschichte* (Zurich, 1980).

Anderson, Margaret L., *Practicing Democracy: Elections and Political Culture in Imperial Germany* (Princeton, 2000).

Angell, Norman, *The Story of Money* (New York, 1930).

Angermund, Ralph, *Deutsche Richterschaft 1918–1945: Krisenerfahrung, Illusion, Politische Rechtsprechung* (Frankfurt am Main, 1990).

Angress, Werner, *Stillborn Revolution: The Communist Bid for Power in Germany, 1921–1923* (Princeton, 1963).

Arendt, Hannah, *The Origins of Totalitarianism* (New York, 1958).

Aschheim, Steven E., *Brothers and Strangers: The East European Jew in German and German Jewish Consciousness 1800–1923* (Madison, 1982).

——, *The Nietzsche Legacy in Germany 1890–1990* (Berkeley, 1992).

Auerbach, Helmuth, 'Hitlers politische Lehrjahre und die Münchner Gesellschaft 1919–1923,' *VfZ* 25 (1977), 1–45.

Ayass, Wolfgang, 'Vagrants and Beggars in Hitler's Reich', in Evans (ed.), *The German Underworld*, 210–37.

——, *'Asoziale' im Nationalsozialismus* (Stuttgart, 1995).

Ayçoberry, Pierre, *The Nazi Question: An Essay on the Interpretations of National Socialism (1922–1975)* (New York, 1981).

Bacharach, Walter Zwi, *Anti-Jewish Prejudices in German-Catholic Sermons* (Lewiston, Pa., 1993).

Backes, Uwe, *et al.*, *Reichstagsbrand: Aufklärung einer historischen Legende* (Munich, 1986).

Badde, Paul, *et al.* (eds.), *Das Berliner Philharmonische Orchester* (Stuttgart, 1987).

Bahar, Alexander, and Kugel, Wilfried, 'Der Reichstagsbrand: Neue Aktenfunde entlarven die NS-Täter', *Zeitschrift für Geschichtswissenschaft*, 43 (1995), 823–32.

Bahne, Siegfried, 'Die Kommunistische Partei Deutschlands', in Matthias and Morsey (eds.), *Das Ende*, 655–739.

Bajohr, Frank (ed.), *Norddeutschland im Nationalsozialismus* (Hamburg, 1993).

Balderston, Theo, *The Origins and Course of the German Economic Crisis, 1923–1932* (Berlin, 1993).

——, *Economics and Politics in the Weimar Republic* (London, 2002).

Balistier, Thomas, *Gewalt und Ordnung: Kalkül und Faszination der SA* (Münster, 1989).

Baranowski, Shelley, *The Sanctity of Rural Life: Nobility, Protestantism and Nazism in Weimar Prussia* (New York, 1995).

Barbian, Jan-Pieter, *Literaturpolitik im 'Dritten Reich': Institutionen, Kompetenzen, Betätigungsfelder* (Frankfurt am Main, 1993).

Barkai, Avraham, *From Boycott to Annihilation: The Economic Struggle of German Jews, 1933–1945* (Hanover, NH, 1989).

Barth, Erwin, *Joseph Goebbels und die Formierung des Führer-Mythos 1917 bis 1934* (Erlangen, 1999).

Bartsch, Günter, *Zwischen drei Stühlen: Otto Strasser. Eine Biographie* (Koblenz, 1990).

Becker, Heinrich, *et al.* (eds.), *Die Universität Göttingen unter dem Nationalsozialismus: Das verdrängte Kapitel ihrer 250jährigen Geschichte* (Munich, 1987).

Becker, Howard, *German Youth: Bond or Free?* (New York, 1946).

Becker, Josef, 'Zentrum und Ermächtigungsgesetz 1933: Dokumentation' *VfZ* 9 (1961), 195–210.

——, and Becker, Ruth (eds.), *Hitlers Machtergreifung: Dokumente vom Machtantritt Hitlers 30. Januar 1933 bis zur Besiegelung des Einparteienstaates 14. Juli 1933* (2nd edn., Munich, 1992 [1983]).

Bennett, Edward W., *German Rearmament and the West, 1932–1933* (Princeton, 1979).

Benz, Wolfgang (ed.), *Jüdisches Leben in der Weimarer Republik* (Tübingen, 1998).

Berg, Nicolas, *Der Holocaust und die westdeutschen Historiker: Erforschung und Erinnerung* (Cologne, 2003).

Berger, Stefan, *Social Democracy and the Working Class in Nineteenth- and Twentieth-Century Germany* (London, 2000).

Berghahn, Volker R., *Der Stahlhelm: Bund der Frontsoldaten 1918–1935* (Düsseldorf, 1966).

——, *Der Tirpitz-Plan: Genesis und Verfall einer innenpolitischen Krisenstrategie unter Wilhelm II.* (Düsseldorf, 1971).

——, *Germany and the Approach of War in 1914* (London, 1973).

——, (ed.), *Militarismus* (Cologne, 1975).

——, *Militarism: The History of an International Debate 1861–1979* (Cambridge, 1984 [1981]).

Bergmann, Klaus, *Agrarromantik und Grossstadtfeindschaft* (Meisenheim, 1970).

'Bericht des Obersten Parteigerichts an den Ministerpräsidenten Generalfeldmarschall Göring, 13.2.1939', document ND 3063-PS in *Der Prozess*, XXII. 20–29.

Bering, Dietz, *The Stigma of Names: Antisemitism in German Daily Life, 1812–1933* (Cambridge, 1992 [1987]).

Berliner Börsen-Zeitung 1933.

Berliner Illustrierte Nachtausgabe 1933.

Berliner Lokal Anzeiger 1933.

Berliner Morgenpost 1923.

Berliner Tageblatt 1930.

Bernard, Birgit, '"Gleichschaltung" im Westdeutschen Rundfunk 1933/34', in Dieter Breuer and Gertrude Cepl-Kaufmann (eds.), *Moderne und Nationalsozialismus im Rheinland* (Paderborn, 1997), 301–10.

Bessel, Richard, 'The Potempa Murder', *Central European History*, 10 (1977), 241–54.

——, 'The Rise of the NSDAP and the Myth of Nazi Propaganda', *Wiener Library Bulletin*, 33 (1980), 20–29.

——, *Political Violence and the Rise of Nazism: The Storm Troopers in Eastern Germany 1925–1934* (London, 1984).

——, 'Violence as Propaganda: The Role of the Storm Troopers in the Rise of National Socialism', in Thomas Childers (ed.), *The Formation of the Nazi Constituency, 1919–1933* (London, 1986), 131–46.

——, 'Why did the Weimar Republic Collapse?', in Kershaw (ed.), *Weimar*, 120–34.

——, '1933: A Failed Counter-Revolution', in Edgar E. Rice (ed.), *Revolution and Counter-Revolution* (Oxford, 1991), 109–227.

——, 'Militarisierung und Modernisierung: Polizeiliches Handeln in der Weimarer Republik', in Alf Lüdtke (ed.), *'Sicherheit' und 'Wohlfahrt': Polizei, Gesellschaft und Herrschaft im 19. und 20. Jahrhundert* (Frankfurt am Main, 1992), 323–43.

——, *Germany after the First World War* (Oxford, 1993).

Beyer, Hans, *Von der Novemberrevolution zur Räterepublik in München* (Berlin, 1957).

Beyerchen, Alan D., *Scientists under Hitler: Politics and the Physics Community in the Third Reich* (New Haven, 1977).

Biesemann, Jörg, *Das Ermächtigungsgesetz als Grundlage der Gesetzgebung im nationalsozialistischen Deutschland: Ein Beitrag zur Stellung des Gesetzes in der Verfassungsgeschichte 1919–1945* (Münster, 1992 [1985]).

Binding, Karl, and Hoche, Alfred, *Die Freigabe der Vernichtung lebensunwerten Lebens: Ihr Mass und ihre Form* (Leipzig, 1920).

Binion, Rudolph, *Frau Lou: Nietzsche's Wayward Disciple* (Princeton, 1968).

Birkenfeld, Werner, 'Der Rufmord am Reichspräsidenten: Zu Grenzformen des politischen Kampfes gegen die frühe Weimarer Republik 1919–1925', *Archiv für Sozialgeschichte*, 15 (1965), 453–500.

Blackbourn, David, 'Roman Catholics, the Centre Party and Anti-Semitism in Imperial Germany', in Paul Kennedy and Anthony Nicholls (eds.), *Nationalist and Racialist Movements in Britain and Germany before 1914* (London, 1981), 106–29.

——, *Populists and Patricians: Essays in Modern German History* (London, 1987).

——, *Marpingen: Apparitions of the Virgin Mary in Bismarckian Germany* (Oxford, 1993).

——, *The Fontana History of Germany 1780–1918: The Long Nineteenth Century* (London, 1997).

——, and Eley, Geoff, *The Peculiarities of German History: Bourgeois Society and Politics in Nineteenth-Century Germany* (Oxford, 1984).

——, and Evans, Richard J. (eds.), *The German Bourgeoisie: Essays on the Social History of the German Middle Class from the Late Eighteenth to the Early Twentieth Century* (London, 1991).

Blaich, Fritz, *Die Wirtschaftskrise 1925/26 und die Reichsregierung: Von der Erwerbslosenfürsorge zur Konjunkturpolitik* (Kallmünz, 1977).

——, *Der schwarze Freitag: Inflation und Wirtschaftskrise* (Munich, 1985).

Blaschke, Olaf, *Katholizismus und Antisemitismus im Deutschen Kaiserreich* (Göttingen, 1997).

—— (ed.), *Konfessionen im Konflikt: Deutschland zwischen 1800 und 1970: Ein zweites konfessionelles Zeitalter* (Göttingen, 2002).

——, and Mattioli, Aram (eds.), *Katholischer Antisemitismus im 19. Jahrhundert: Ursachen und Traditionen im internationalen Vergleich* (Zurich, 2000).

Bley, Helmut, *Namibia under German Rule* (Hamburg, 1996 [1968]).

Blinkhorn, Martin, *Fascists and Conservatives: The Radical Right and the Establishment in Twentieth-Century Europe* (London, 1990).

——, *Fascism and the Right in Europe 1919–1945* (London, 2000).

Boak, Helen L., ' "Our Last Hope": Women's Votes for Hitler – A Reappraisal', *German Studies Review*, 12 (1989), 289–310.

Boemeke, Manfred F., *et al.* (eds.), *The Treaty of Versailles: A Reassessment after 75 Years* (Washington, DC, 1998).

Bohrmann, Hans (ed.), *Politische Plakate* (Dortmund, 1984).

Boldt, Harald, 'Der Artikel 48 der Weimarer Reichsverfassung: Sein historischer Hintergrund und seine politische Funktion', in Michael Stürmer (ed.), *Die Weimarer Republik: Belagerte Civitas* (Königstein im Taunus, 1980), 288–309.

Bollmus, Reinhard, 'Alfred Rosenberg: National Socialism's "Chief Ideologue" ', in Smelser and Zitelman (eds.), *The Nazi Elite*, 183–93.

Booms, Hans, 'Die Deutsche Volkspartei', in Matthias and Morsey (eds.), *Das Ende*, 521–39.

Borchardt, Knut, 'Zwangslagen und Handlungsspielräume in der grossen Wirtschaftskrise der frühen dreissiger Jahre: Zur Revision des überlieferten Geschichtsbildes', in idem, *Wachstum, Krisen, Handlungsspielräume der Wirtschaftspolitik* (Göttingen, 1982), 165–82.

——, *Perspectives on Modern German Economic History and Policy* (Cambridge, 1991).

Born, Karl Erich, *Staat und Sozialpolitik seit Bismarcks Sturz 1890–1914: Ein Beitrag zur Geschichte der innenpolitischen Entwicklung des deutschen Reiches 1890–1914* (Wiesbaden, 1957).

Born, Max (ed.), *The Born–Einstein Letters: Correspondence between Albert Einstein and Max and Hedwig Born from 1916 to 1955* (London, 1971).

Bosworth, Richard J. B., *Mussolini* (London, 2002).

Böttger, Marcus, *Der Hochverrat in der höchstrichterlichen Rechtsprechung der Weimarer Republik: Ein Fall politischer Instrumentalisierung von Strafgesetzen?* (Frankfurt am Main, 1998).

Bowlby, Chris, 'Blutmai 1929: Police, Parties and Proletarians in a Berlin Confrontation', *Historical Journal*, 29 (1986), 137–58.

Boyer, John W., *Political Radicalism in Late Imperial Vienna: Origins of the Christian Social Movement, 1848–1897* (Chicago, 1981).

Bracher, Karl Dietrich, *Die Auflösung der Weimarer Republik: Eine Studie zum Problem des Machtverfalls in der Demokratie* (3rd edn., Villingen, 1960 [1955]).

——, *The German Dictatorship: The Origins, Structure, and Consequences of National Socialism* (New York, 1970 [1969]).

——, 'Brünings unpolitische Politik und die Auflösung der Weimarer Republik', *VfZ* 19 (1971), 113–23.

——, *Die totalitäre Erfahrung* (Munich, 1987).

——, et al., Die nationalsozialistische Machtergreifung: Studien zur Errichtung des totalitären Herrschaftssystems in Deutschland 1933/34 (Frankfurt am Main, 1974 [1960]), I: Stufen der Machtergreifung (Bracher), II: Die Anfänge des totalitären Massnahmestaates (Schulz); III: Die Mobilmachung der Gewalt (Sauer).

Brady, Robert, The Rationalization Movement in Germany: A Study in the Evolution of Economic Planning (Berkeley, 1933).

Brandenburg, Hans-Christian, Die Geschichte der HJ. Wege und Irrwege einer Generation (Cologne, 1968).

Brandt, Willy, Erinnerungen (Frankfurt am Main, 1989).

Brecht, Arnold, 'Gedanken über Brünings Memoiren', Politische Vierteljahresschrift, 12 (1971), 607–40.

Bredel, Willi, Ernst Thälmann: Beitrag zu einem politischen Lebensbild (Berlin, 1948).

Brendon, Piers, The Dark Valley: A Panorama of the 1930s (London, 2000).

Brenner, Arthur D., Emil J. Gumbel: Weimar German Pacifist and Professor (Boston, 2001).

Brenner, Hildegard, Die Kunstpolitik des Nationalsozialismus (Hamburg, 1963).

Bresciani-Turroni, Constantino, The Economics of Inflation: A Study of Currency Depreciation in Post-War Germany (London, 1937).

Breuer, Stefan, Ordnung der Ungleichheit – die deutsche Rechte im Widerstreit ihrer Ideen 1871–1945 (Darmstadt, 2001).

Bridenthal, Renate, and Koonz, Claudia, 'Beyond Kinder, Küche, Kirche: Weimar Women in Politics and Work', in Renate Bridenthal et al. (eds.), When Biology Became Destiny: Women in Weimar and Nazi Germany (New York, 1984), 33–65.

Brinkmann, Reinhold, and Wolff, Christoph (eds.), Driven into Paradise: The Musical Migration from Germany to the United States (Berkeley, 1999).

Broszat, Martin, 'Die Anfänge der Berliner NSDAP 1926/27', VfZ 8 (1960), 85–118.

——, 'The Concentration Camps 1933–1945', in Helmut Krausnick et al., Anatomy of the SS State (London, 1968 [1965]), 397–496.

——, Der Staat Hitlers: Grundlegung und Entwicklung seiner inneren Verfassung (Munich, 1969).

——, 'Betrachtungen zu "Hitlers Zweitem Buch"', VfZ 9 (1981), 417–29.

——, Hitler and the Collapse of Weimar Germany (Oxford, 1987 [1984]).

——, et al., (eds.), Bayern in der NS-Zeit (6 vols., Munich, 1977–83).

Browder, George C., Hitler's Enforcers: The Gestapo and the SS Security Service in the Nazi Revolution (New York, 1996).

Brown, Brendan, Monetary Chaos in Europe: The End of an Era (London, 1988).

Brügel, Johann Wilhelm, and Frei, Norbert (eds.), 'Berliner Tagebuch, 1932–1934: Aufzeichnungen des tschechoslowakischen Diplomaten Camill Hoffmann', VfZ 36 (1988), 131–83.

Brüning, Heinrich, *Memoiren 1918–1934* (ed. Claire Nix and Theoderich Kampmann, Stuttgart, 1970).

Brustein, William, *The Logic of Evil: The Social Origins of the Nazi Party, 1925–1933* (New Haven, 1996).

Bucher, Peter, *Der Reichswehrprozess: Der Hochverrat der Ulmer Reichswehroffiziere 1929–30* (Boppard, 1967).

Buchheim, Hans, 'The SS – Instrument of Domination', in Helmut Krausnick *et al.*, *Anatomy of the SS State* (London, 1968 [1965]), 127–203.

Buchwitz, Otto, *50 Jahre Funktionär der deutschen Arbeiterbewegung* (Stuttgart, 1949).

Buder, Johannes, *Die Reorganisation der preussischen Polizei 1918/1923* (Frankfurt am Main, 1986).

Bullivant, Keith, 'Thomas Mann and Politics in the Weimar Republic', in idem (ed.), *Culture and Society in the Weimar Republic* (Manchester, 1977), 24–38.

Bullock, Alan, *Hitler: A Study in Tyranny* (London, 1953).

Burkert, Hans-Norbert, *et al.*, *'Machtergreifung' Berlin 1933: Stätten der Geschichte Berlins in Zusammenarbeit mit dem Pädagogischen Zentrum Berlin* (Berlin, 1982).

Burkhardt, Bernd, *Eine Stadt wird braun: Die nationalsozialistische Machtergreifung in der Provinz. Eine Fallstudie* (Hamburg, 1980).

Burleigh, Michael, *Death and Deliverance: 'Euthanasia', in Germany 1900–1945* (Cambridge, 1994).

——, *The Third Reich: A New History* (London, 2000).

——, and Wippermann, Wolfgang, *The Racial State: Germany 1933–1945* (Cambridge, 1991).

Busch, Fritz, *Aus dem Leben eines Musikers* (Zurich, 1949).

Busch, Günter, *Max Liebermann: Maler, Zeichner, Graphiker* (Frankfurt am Main, 1986).

Büsch, Otto, *Militärsystem und Sozialleben im alten Preussen 1713–1807: Die Anfänge der sozialen Militarisierung der preussisch-deutschen Gesellschaft* (Berlin, 1962).

Butler, Rohan d'Olier, *The Roots of National Socialism 1783–1933* (London, 1941).

Caplan, Jane, *Government without Administration: State and Civil Service in Weimar and Nazi Germany* (Oxford, 1988).

——, 'The Historiography of National Socialism', in Michael Bentley (ed.), *Companion to Historiography* (London, 1997), 545–90.

Carsten, Francis L., *The Reichswehr and Politics 1918–1933* (Oxford, 1966).

——, *Revolution in Central Europe 1918–1919* (London, 1972).

——, *Fascist Movements in Austria: From Schönerer to Hitler* (London, 1977).

——, *August Bebel und die Organisation der Massen* (Berlin, 1991).

Cecil, Hugh, and Liddle, Peter (eds.), *At the Eleventh Hour: Reflections, Hopes and Anxieties at the Closing of the Great War, 1918* (Barnsley, 1998).

Cecil, Robert, *The Myth of the Master Race: Alfred Rosenberg and Nazi Ideology* (London, 1972).

Chamberlain, Houston Stewart, *Die Grundlagen des XIX. Jahrhunderts* (2 vols., Munich, 1899).

Chickering, Roger, *Imperial Germany and a World without War: The Peace Movement and German Society, 1892–1914* (Princeton, 1975).

——, *We Men Who Feel Most German: A Cultural Study of the Pan-German League 1886–1914* (London, 1984).

——, *Imperial Germany and the Great War, 1914–1918* (Cambridge, 1998).

Childers, Thomas, *The Nazi Voter: The Social Foundations of Fascism in Germany, 1919–1933* (Chapel Hill, NC, 1981).

Clark, Christopher, *Kaiser Wilhelm II* (London, 2000).

Clavin, Patricia, *The Great Depression in Europe, 1929–1939* (London, 2000).

Coetzee, Marilyn S., *The German Army League: Popular Nationalism in Wilhelmine Germany* (New York, 1990).

Cohen, Deborah, *The War Come Home: Disabled Veterans in Britain and Germany, 1914–1918* (Berkeley, 2001).

Cohn, Norman, *Warrant for Genocide: The Myth of the Jewish World-Conspiracy and the Protocols of the Elders of Zion* (London, 1967).

Comité des Délégations Juives (ed.), *Das Schwarzbuch: Tatsachen und Dokumente. Die Lage der Juden in Deutschland 1933* (Paris, 1934).

Conze, Werner, review of the first edition of Bracher, *Die Auflösung der Weimarer Republik*, in *Historische Zeitschrift*, 183 (1957), 378–82.

Cornelissen, Christoph, *Gerhard Ritter: Geschichtswissenschaft und Politik im 20. Jahrhundert* (Düsseldorf, 2001).

Corni, Gustavo, 'Richard Walther Darré: The Blood and Soil Ideologue', in Smelser and Zitelmann (eds.), *The Nazi Elite*, 18–27.

Cornwell, John, *Hitler's Pope: The Secret History of Pius XII* (London, 1999).

Cossé, Peter, 'Die Geschichte', in Badde *et al.* (eds.), *Das Berliner Philharmonische Orchester*, 10–17.

Craig, Gordon A., 'Briefe Schleichers an Groener', *Die Welt als Geschichte*, 11 (1951), 122–33.

——, *The Politics of the Prussian Army 1640–1945* (New York, 1964 [1955]).

Crew, David F., *Germans on Welfare: From Weimar to Hitler* (New York, 1998).

Crook, Paul, *Darwinism, War and History: The Debate over the Biology of War from the 'Origin of Species' to the First World War* (Cambridge, 1994).

Czarnowski, Gabriele, *Das kontrollierte Paar: Ehe- und Sexualpolitik im Nationalsozialismus* (Weinheim, 1991).

Daim, Wilfried, *Der Mann, der Hitler die Ideen gab: Die sektiererischen Grundlagen des Nationalsozialismus* (Vienna, 1985 [1958]).

Danner, Lothar, *Ordnungspolizei Hamburg: Betrachtungen zu ihrer Geschichte 1918–1933* (Hamburg, 1958).

Dapper, Beate, and Rouette, Hans-Peter, 'Zum Ermittelungsverfahren gegen Leipart und Genossen wegen Untreue vom 9. Mai 1933', *Internationale Wissenschaftliche Korrespondenz zur Geschichte der deutschen Arbeiterbewegung*, 20 (1984), 509–35.

Dedering, Tilman, ' "A Certain Rigorous Treatment of all Parts of the Nation": The Annihilation of the Herero in German Southwest Africa 1904', in Mark Levene and Penny Roberts (eds.), *The Massacre in History* (New York, 1999), 205–22.

Dehio, Ludwig, *Germany and World Politics* (London, 1959 [1955]).

Deichmann, Ute, *Biologists under Hitler* (Cambridge, Mass., 1996 [1992]).

Deist, Wilhelm, *Flottenpolitik und Flottenpropaganda: Das Nachrichtenbüro des Reichsmarineamts 1897–1914* (Stuttgart, 1976).

——, 'Censorship and Propaganda in Germany during the First World War', in Jean-Jacques Becker and Stéphane Audoin-Rouzeau (eds.), *Les Sociétés européennes et la guerre de 1914–1918* (Paris, 1990), 199–210.

——, 'The Military Collapse of the German Empire: The Reality Behind the Stab-in-the-Back Myth', *War in History*, 3 (1996), 186–207.

Demeter, Karl, *Das deutsche Offizierkorps in Gesellschaft und Staat 1650–1945* (Frankfurt am Main, 1962).

Deuerlein, Ernst, 'Hitlers Eintritt in die Politik und die Reichswehr', *VfZ* 7 (1959), 203–5.

—— (ed.), *Der Hitler-Putsch: Bayerische Dokumente zum 8./9. November 1923* (Stuttgart, 1962).

—— (ed.), *Der Aufstieg der NSDAP in Augenzeugenberichten* (Munich, 1974).

Deutsche Allgemeine Zeitung 1933.

Deutsche Zeitung 1933.

Diehl, James M., *Paramilitary Politics in Weimar Germany* (Bloomington, Ind., 1977).

Diels, Rudolf, *Lucifer ante Portas: Es spricht der erste Chef der Gestapo* (Stuttgart, 1950).

Dijkstra, Bram, *Idols of Perversity: Fantasies of Female Evil in Fin-de-Siècle Culture* (New York, 1986).

Diller, Ansgar, *Rundfunkpolitik im Dritten Reich* (Munich, 1980).

Distl, Dieter, *Ernst Toller: Eine politische Biographie* (Schrobenhausen, 1993).

Domarus, Max (ed.), *Hitler: Speeches and Proclamations 1932–1945: The Chronicle of a Dictatorship* (4 vols., London, 1990– [1962–3]).

Dorpalen, Andreas, *Hindenburg and the Weimar Republic* (Princeton, 1964).

——, *German History in Marxist Perspective: The East German Approach* (Detroit, 1988).

Dowe, Dieter, and Witt, Peter-Christian, *Fredrich Ebert 1871–1925: Vom Arbeiterführer zum Reichspräsidenten* (Bonn, 1987).

Drewniak, Boguslav, *Das Theater im NS-Staat: Szenarium deutscher Zeitgeschichte 1933–1945* (Düsseldorf, 1983).

Duhnke, Horst, *Die KPD von 1933 bis 1945* (Cologne, 1972).

——, *Die KPD und das Ende von Weimar: Das Scheitern einer Politik 1932–1935* (Frankfurt am Main, 1976).

Dülffer, Jost, *Nazi Germany 1933–1945: Faith and Annihilation* (London, 1996 [1992]).

Düsterberg, Theodor, *Der Stahlhelm und Hitler* (Wolfenbüttel, 1949).

Ebeling, Frank, *Geopolitik: Karl Haushofer und seine Raumwissenschaft 1919–1945* (Berlin, 1994).

Ebert, Friedrich, *Schriften, Aufzeichnungen, Reden* (2 vols., Dresden, 1936).

Ehni, Hans-Peter, *Bollwerk Preussen? Preussen-Regierung, Reich-Länder-Problem und Sozialdemokratie 1928–1932* (Bonn, 1975).

Ehrt, Adolf, *Bewaffneter Aufstand! Enthüllungen über den kommunistischen Umsturzversuch am Vorabend der nationalen Revolution* (Berlin, 1933).

Eichengreen, Barry, *Golden Fetters: The Gold Standard and the Great Depression, 1919–1939* (Oxford, 1992).

Eisner, Freya, *Kurt Eisner: Die Politik der libertären Sozialismus* (Frankfurt am Main, 1979).

Eksteins, Modris, *The Limits of Reason: The German Democratic Press and the Collapse of Weimar Democracy* (Oxford, 1975).

Eley, Geoff, *Reshaping the German Right: Radical Nationalism and Political Change after Bismarck* (London, 1980).

——, *From Unification to Nazism: Reinterpreting the German Past* (London, 1986).

Elfferding, Wieland, 'Von der proletarischen Masse zum Kriegsvolk: Massenaufmarsch und Öffentlichkeit im deutschen Faschismus am Beispiel des 1. Mai 1933', in Neue Gesellschaft für bildende Kunst (ed.), *Inszenierung der Macht: Ästhetische Faszination im Faschismus* (Berlin, 1987), 17–50.

Eliasberg, George, *Der Ruhrkrieg von 1920* (Bonn, 1974).

Engelberg, Ernst, *Bismarck* (2 vols., Berlin, 1985 and 1990).

Epstein, Klaus, review of William L. Shirer, *The Rise and Fall of the Third Reich*, in *Review of Politics*, 23 (1961), 130–45.

Erdmann, Karl Dietrich, and Schulze, Hagen (eds.), *Weimar: Selbstpreisgabe einer Demokratie. Eine Bilanz heute* (Düsseldorf, 1980).

Erger, Johannes, *Der Kapp-Lüttwitz-Putsch: Ein Beitrag zur deutschen Innenpolitik 1919/20* (Düsseldorf, 1967).

Eschenburg, Theodor, 'Franz von Papen', *VfZ* 1 (1953), 153–69.

——, 'Die Rolle der Persönlichkeit in der Krise der Weimarer Republik: Hindenburg, Brüning, Groener, Schleicher', *VfZ* 9 (1961), 1–29.

——, *Die improvisierte Demokratie* (Munich, 1963).

Eschenhagen, Wieland (ed.), *Die 'Machtergreifung': Tagebuch einer Wende nach Presseberichten vom 1. Januar bis 6. März 1933* (Darmstadt, 1982).

Evans, Richard J., 'German Women and the Triumph of Hitler', *Journal of Modern History*, 48 (1976), 123–75.

——, *The Feminist Movement in Germany 1894–1933* (London, 1976).

—— (ed.), *Society and Politics in Wilhelmine Germany* (London, 1978).

——, *Death in Hamburg: Society and Politics in the Cholera Years 1830–1910* (Oxford, 1987).

——, *Rethinking German History: Nineteenth-Century Germany and the Origins of the Third Reich* (London, 1987).

—— (ed.), *The German Underworld: Deviants and Outcasts in German History* (London, 1988).

——, *In Hitler's Shadow: West German Historians and the Attempt to Escape from the Nazi Past* (New York, 1989).

—— (ed.), *Kneipengespräche im Kaiserreich: Die Stimmungsberichte der Hamburger Politischen Polizei 1892–1914* (Reinbek, 1989).

——, *Rituals of Retribution: Capital Punishment in Germany 1600–1987* (Oxford, 1996).

——, review of Maria Tatar, *Lustmord: Sexual Murder in Weimar Germany* (Princeton, 1995), in *German History*, 14 (1996), 414–15.

——, *Rereading German History: From Unification to Reunification 1800–1996* (London, 1997).

——, *Tales from the German Underworld: Crime and Punishment in the Ninteenth Century* (London, 1998).

——, 'Hans von Hentig and the Politics of German Criminology', in Angelika Ebbinghaus and Karl Heinz Roth (eds.), *Grenzgänge: Deutsche Geschichte des 20. Jahrhunderts im Spiegel von Publizistik, Rechtsprechung und historischer Forschung* (Lüneburg, 1999), 238–64.

——, *Telling Lies About Hitler: The Holocaust, History, and the David Irving Trial* (London, 2002).

——, 'History, Memory, and the Law: The Historian as Expert Witness', *History and Theory*, 41 (2002), 277–96.

——, 'Telling It Like It Wasn't', *BBC History Magazine*, 3 (2002), no. 12, 22–5.

——, and Geary, Dick (eds.), *The German Unemployed: Experiences and Consequences of Mass Unemployment from the Weimar Republic to the Third Reich* (London, 1987).

Eyck, Erich, *A History of the Weimar Republic* (2 vols., Cambridge, 1962–4 [1953–6]).

Faesi, Robert (ed.), *Thomas Mann – Robert Faesi: Briefwechsel* (Zurich, 1962).

Falter, Jürgen W., 'Die Wähler der NSDAP 1928–1933: Sozialstruktur und parteipolitische Herkunft', in Wolfgang Michalka (ed.), *Die nationalsozialistische Machtergreifung* (Paderborn, 1984), 47–59.

——, *et al.*, *Wahlen und Abstimmungen in der Weimarer Republik: Materialien zum Wahlverhalten 1919–1933* (Munich, 1986).

——, *Hitlers Wähler* (Munich, 1991).

——, 'How Likely were Workers to Vote for the NSDAP?', in Conan Fischer (ed.), *The Rise of National Socialism and the Working Classes in Weimar Germany* (Oxford, 1996), 9–45.

——, ' "Die Märzgefallenen" von 1933: Neue Forschungsergebnisse zum sozialen

Wandel innerhalb der NSDAP-Mitgliedschaft während der Machtergreifungs-phase', *Geschichte und Gesellschaft*, 24 (1998), 595–616.

Fandel, Thomas, 'Konfessionalismus und Nationalsozialismus', in Blaschke (ed.), *Konfessionen*, 299–334.

Farquharson, John E., *The Plough and the Swastika: The NSDAP and Agriculture in Germany, 1928–1945* (London, 1976).

Farr, Ian, 'Populism in the Countryside: The Peasant Leagues in Bavaria in the 1890s', in Evans (ed.), *Society and Politics*, 136–59.

Fattmann, Rainer, *Bildungsbürger in der Defensive: Die akademische Beamten-schaft und der 'Reichsbund der höheren Beamten' in der Weimarer Republik* (Göttingen, 2001).

Faust, Anselm, *Der Nationalsozialistische Deutsche Studentenbund: Studenten und Nationalsozialismus in der Weimarer Republik* (Düsseldorf, 1973).

——, 'Die Hochschulen und der "undeutsche Geist": Die Bücherverbrennung am 10. Mai 1933 und ihr Vorgeschichte', in Horst Denkler and Eberhard Lämmert (eds.), *'Das war ein Vorspiel nur . . .': Berliner Kolloquium zur Literaturpolitik im 'Dritten Reich'* (Berlin, 1985), 31–50.

Feder, Gottfried, *Das Programm der NSDAP und seine weltanschaulichen Grundgedanken* (Munich, 1934).

Feinstein, Charles H., *et al.*, *The European Economy between the Wars* (Oxford, 1997).

Feldman, Gerald D., *Army, Industry and Labor in Germany, 1914–1918* (Princeton, 1966).

——, 'The Origins of the Stinnes–Legien Agreement: A Documentation', *Internationale Wissenschaftliche Korrespondenz zur Geschichte der deutschen Arbeiterbewegung*, 19/20 (1973), 45–104.

—— (ed.), *Die Nachwirkungen der Inflation auf die deutsche Geschichte 1924–1933* (Munich, 1985).

——, *The Great Disorder: Politics, Economic, and Society in the German Inflation, 1914–1924* (New York, 1993).

——, 'Right-Wing Politics and the Film Industry: Emil Georg Strauss, Alfred Hugenberg, and the UFA, 1917–1933', in Christian Jansen *et al.* (eds.), *Von der Aufgabe der Freiheit: Politische Verantwortung und bürgerliche Gesellschaft im 19. und 20. Jahrhundert: Festschrift für Hans Mommsen zum 5. November 1995* (Berlin, 1995), 219–30.

——, *Hugo Stinnes: Biographie eines Industriellen 1870–1924* (Munich, 1998).

Fenske, Hans, 'Monarchisches Beamtentum und demokratischer Rechtsstaat: Zum Problem der Bürokratie in der Weimarer Republik', in *Demokratie und Verwaltung: 25 Jahre Hochschule für Verwaltung Speyer* (Berlin, 1972), 117–36.

Ferguson, Niall, *Paper and Iron: Hamburg Business and German Politics in the Era of Inflation, 1897–1927* (Oxford, 1995).

——, *The World's Banker: The History of the House of Rothschild* (London, 1998).

Fest, Joachim C., *The Face of the Third Reich* (London, 1979 [1970]).
——, 'Joseph Goebbels: Eine Porträtskizze', *VfZ* 43 (1995), 565–80.
Feuchtwanger, Edgar, *Bismarck* (London, 2002).
Fieberg, Gerhard (ed.), *Im Namen des deutschen Volkes: Justiz und Nationalsozialismus* (Cologne, 1989).
Field, Geoffrey G., *Evangelist of Race: The Germanic Vision of Houston Stewart Chamberlain* (New York, 1981).
Figes, Orlando, *A People's Tragedy: The Russian Revolution 1891–1924* (London, 1996).
Fischer, Conan, 'Ernst Julius Röhm: Chief of Staff of the SA and Indispensable Outsider', in Smelser and Zitelmann (eds.), *The Nazi Elite*, 173–82.
——, *The Ruhr Crisis 1923–1924* (Oxford, 2003).
Fischer, Fritz, *Germany's Aims in the First World War* (London, 1967 [1961]).
——, *War of Illusions: German Politics from 1911 to 1914* (London, 1975 [1969]).
Fischer, Klaus, 'Der quantitative Beitrag der nach 1933 emigrierten Naturwissenschaftler zur deutschsprachigen physikalischen Forschung', *Berichte zur Wissenschaftsgeschichte*, 11 (1988), 83–104.
Flemming, Jens, *Landwirtschaftliche Interessen und Demokratie: Ländliche Gesellschaft, Agrarverbände und Staat 1890–1925* (Bonn, 1978).
Fout, John C., 'Sexual Politics in Wilhelmine Germany: The Male Gender Crisis, Moral Purity, and Homophobia', *Journal of the History of Sexuality*, 2 (1992), 388–421.
Fowkes, Ben, *Communism in Germany under the Weimar Republic* (London, 1984).
Fraenkel, Ernst, *The Dual State* (New York, 1941).
Frank, Hans, *Im Angesicht des Galgens: Deutung Hitlers und seiner Zeit auf Grund eigener Erlebnisse und Erkenntnisse* (2nd edn., Neuhaus, 1955 [1953]).
Franz-Willing, Georg, *Ursprung der Hitlerbewegung 1919–1922* (Preussisch Olendorf, 1974 [1962]).
——, *Krisenjahr der Hitlerbewegung 1923* (Preussisch Oldendorf, 1975).
——, *Putsch und Verbotszeit der Hitlerbewegung November 1923–Februar 1925* (Preussisch Olendorf, 1977).
Frehse, Michael, *Ermächtigungsgesetzgebung im Deutschen Reich 1914–1933* (Pfaffenweiler, 1985).
Frei, Norbert, '"Machtergreifung": Anmerkungen zu einem historischen Begriff', *VfZ* 31 (1983), 136–45.
——, *National Socialist Rule in Germany: The Führer State 1933–1945* (Oxford, 1993 [1987]).
——, *Der Führerstaat: Nationalsozialistische Herrschaft 1933 bis 1945* (Munich, 2001 [1987]).
Freitag, Werner, 'Nationale Mythen und kirchliches Heil: Der "Tag von Potsdam"', *Westfälische Forschungen*, 41 (1991), 379–430.
Frevert, Ute, 'Bourgeois Honour: Middle-Class Duellists in Germany from the Late

Eighteenth to the Early Twentieth Century', in Blackbourn and Evans (eds.), *The German Bourgeoisie*, 255–92.

——, *Ehrenmänner: Das Duell in der bürgerlichen Gesellschaft* (Munich, 1991).

——, *Die kasernierte Nation: Militärdienst und Zivilgesellschaft in Deutschland* (Munich, 2001).

Fricke, Dieter, *Kleine Geschichte des Ersten Mai: Die Maifeier in der deutschen und internationalen Arbeiterbewegung* (Berlin, 1980).

Friedlander, Henry, *The Origins of Nazi Genocide: From Euthanasia to the Final Solution* (Chapel Hill, NC, 1995).

Friedländer, Saul, 'Die politischen Veränderungen der Kriegszeit und ihre Auswirkungen auf die Judenfrage', in Werner E. Mosse (ed.), *Deutsches Judentum in Krieg und Revolution 1916–1923* (Tübingen, 1971), 27–65.

——, *Nazi Germany and the Jews: The Years of Persecution 1933–1939* (London, 1997).

Friedrich, Carl J., and Brzezinski, Zbigniew K., *Totalitarian Dictatorship and Autocracy* (New York, 1963).

Friedrichs, Axel (ed.), *Die nationalsozialistische Revolution 1933* (Dokumente der deutschen Politik, I, Berlin, 1933).

Fritzsche, Peter, *Germans into Nazis* (Cambridge, Mass., 1998).

Fröhlich, Elke, 'Joseph Goebbels und sein Tagebuch: Zu den handschriftlichen Aufzeichnungen von 1924 bis 1941, *VfZ* 35 (1987), 489–522.

—— (ed.), *Die Tagebücher von Joseph Goebbels: Sämtliche Fragmente.* part I: *Aufzeichnungen 1924–1941* (Munich, 1987).

——, 'Joseph Goebbels: The Propagandist', in Smelser and Zitelmann (eds.), *The Nazi Elite*, 48–61.

Fulda, Bernhard, 'Press and Politics in Berlin, 1924–1930' (Ph.D. dissertation, University of Cambridge, 2003).

——, 'Horst Wessel: Media, Myth and Memory' (unpublished paper to be delivered to the Research Seminar in Modern European History, Cambridge University, November 2003).

Gadberry, Glen W. (ed.), *Theatre in the Third Reich, the Prewar Years: Essays on Theatre in Nazi Germany* (Westport, Conn., 1995).

Gall, Lothar, *Bismarck: The White Revolutionary* (2 vols., London, 1986 [1980]).

——, *Bürgertum in Deutschland* (Berlin, 1989).

Galos, Adam, *et al.*, *Die Hakatisten: Der Deutsche Ostmarkenverein 1894–1934* (Berlin, 1966).

Gay, Peter, *Weimar Culture: The Outsider as Insider* (London, 1969).

Geary, Dick, 'Unemployment and Working-Class Solidarity: The German Experience 1929–33', in Evans and Geary (eds.), *The German Unemployed*, 261–80.

——, 'Employers, Workers, and the Collapse of the Weimar Republic', in Kershaw (ed.), *Weimar*, 92–119.

——, 'Nazis and Workers before 1933', *Australian Journal of Politics and History*, 48 (2002), 40–51.

Gebhardt, Manfred, *Max Hoelz: Wege und Irrwege eines Revolutionärs* (Berlin, 1983).

Geiss, Imanuel (ed.), *July 1914: The Outbreak of the First World War. Selected Documents* (London, 1967 [1965]).

——, 'Kritischer Rückblick auf Friedrich Meinecke', in idem, *Studien über Geschichte und Geschichtswissenschaft* (Frankfurt am Main, 1972), 89–107.

Gellately, Robert, *The Politics of Economic Despair: Shopkeepers and German Politics, 1890–1914* (London, 1974).

——, *The Gestapo and German Society: Enforcing Racial Policy 1933–1945* (Oxford, 1990).

——, and Stoltzfus, Nathan (eds.), *Social Outsiders in Nazi Germany* (Princeton, 2001).

Genschel, Helmut, *Die Verdrängung der Juden aus der Wirtschaft im Dritten Reich* (Berlin, 1966).

Gerlach, Hellmuth von, *Von rechts nach links* (Hildesheim, 1978 [1937]).

Gessner, Dieter, *Agrarverbände in der Weimarer Republik: Wirtschaftliche und soziale Voraussetzungen agrarkonservativer Politik vor 1933* (Düsseldorf, 1976).

——, *Agrardepression und Präsidialregierungen in Deutschland 1930–1933: Probleme des Agrarkapitalismus am Ende der Weimarer Republik* (Düsseldorf, 1977).

Geyer, Martin, *Verkehrte Welt: Revolution, Inflation, und Moderne. München 1914–1924* (Göttingen, 1998).

Geyer, Michael, 'Die Geschichte des deutschen Militärs von 1860–1956: Ein Bericht über die Forschungslage (1945–1975)', in Hans-Ulrich Wehler (ed.), *Die moderne deutsche Geschichte in der internationalen Forschung 1945–1975* (Göttingen, 1978), 256–86.

——, *Aufrüstung oder Sicherheit: Reichswehr in der Krise der Machtpolitik, 1924–1936* (Wiesbaden, 1980),

——, 'Professionals and Junkers: German Rearmament and Politics in the Weimar Republic', in Richard Bessel and Edgar Feuchtwanger (eds.), *Social Change and Political Development in Weimar Germany* (London, 1981), 77–133.

Gies, Horst, R. *Walther Darré und die nationalsozialistische Bauernpolitik 1930 bis 1933* (Frankfurt am Main, 1966).

Giles, Geoffrey J., 'The Rise of the National Socialist Students' Association and the Failure of Political Education in the Third Reich', in Peter Stachura (ed.), *The Shaping of the Nazi State* (London, 1978), 160–85.

——, *Students and National Socialism in Germany* (Princeton, 1985).

Gilman, Sander L., *On Blackness without Blacks: Essays on the Image of the Black in Germany* (Boston, 1982).

Gisevius, Hans Bernd, *To the Bitter End* (London, 1948).

Goebbels, Joseph, *Der Angriff: Aufsätze aus der Kampfzeit* (Munich, 1935).

——, Vom Kaiserhof zur Reichskanzlei: Eine historische Darstellung in Tagebuchblättern (*vom 1. Januar 1932 bis zum 1. Mai 1933*) (Munich, 1937 [1934]).

Goeschel, Christian, 'Methodische Überlegungen zur Geschichte der Selbsttötung im Nationalsozialismus', in Hans Medick (ed.), *Selbsttötung als kulturelle Praxis* (forthcoming, 2004).

Goldbach, Marie-Luise, *Karl Radek und die deutsch-sowjetischen Beziehungen 1918–1923* (Bonn, 1973).

Goldhagen, Daniel J., *Hitler's Willing Executioners: Ordinary Germans and the Holocaust* (New York, 1996).

Goldstein, Robert J., *Political Repression in Nineteenth-Century Europe* (London, 1983).

Golomstock, Igor, *Totalitarian Art in the Soviet Union, Third Reich, Fascist Italy and the People's Republic of China* (London, 1990).

Göppinger, Horst, *Juristen jüdischer Abstammung im 'Dritten Reich': Entrechtung und Verfolgung* (Munich, 1990 [1963]).

Gordon, Harold J., *The Reichswehr and the German Republic 1919–26* (Princeton, 1957).

——, *Hitler and the Beer Hall Putsch* (Princeton, 1972).

Gottlieb, Moshe R., *American Anti-Nazi Resistance, 1933–1941: An Historical Analysis* (New York, 1982).

Graf, Christoph, *Politische Polizei zwischen Demokratie und Diktatur* (Berlin, 1983).

Grahn, Gerlinde, 'Die Enteignung des Vermögens der Arbeiterbewegung und der politischen Emigration 1933 bis 1945', *1999: Zeitschrift für Sozialgeschichte des 20. und 21. Jahrhunderts*, 12 (1997), 13–38.

Gräser, Marcus, *Der blockierte Wohlfahrtsstaat: Unterschichtjugend und Jugendfürsorge in der Weimarer Republik* (Göttingen, 1995).

Grau, Bernhard, *Kurt Eisner 1867–1919: Eine Biographie* (Munich, 2001).

Griech-Polelle, Beth A., *Bishop von Galen: German Catholicism and National Socialism* (New Haven, 2002).

Griffin, Roger, *International Fascism – Theories, Causes and the New Consensus* (London, 1998).

Grimm, Hans, *Volk ohne Raum* (Munich, 1926).

Gritschneider, Otto, *Bewährungsfrist für den Terroristen Adolf H.: Der Hitler-Putsch und die bayerische Justiz* (Munich, 1990).

——, *Der Hitler-Prozess und sein Richter Georg Neithardt: Skandalurteil von 1924 ebnet Hitler den Weg* (Munich, 2001).

Gross, Babette, *Willi Münzenberg: Eine politische Biographie* (Stuttgart, 1967).

Grossmann, Atina, '"Girlkultur" or Thoroughly Rationalized Female: A New Woman in Weimar Germany', in Judith Friedlander *et al.* (eds.), *Women in Culture and Politics: A Century of Change* (Bloomington, Ind., 1986), 62–80.

——, *Reforming Sex: The German Movement for Birth Control and Abortion Reform 1920–1950* (New York, 1995).

Grossmann, Kurt R., *Ossietzky: Ein deutscher Patriot* (Munich, 1963).

Gruchmann, Lothar, 'Die Überleitung der Justizverwaltung auf das Reich 1933–

1935', in *Vom Reichsjustizamt zum Bundesministerium der Justiz: Festschrift zum hundertjährigen Gründungstag des Reichsjustizamts* (Cologne, 1977).

——, 'Die bayerische Justiz im politischen Machtkampf 1933/34: Ihr Scheitern bei der Strafverfolgung von Mordfällen in Dachau,' in Broszat *et al.* (eds.), *Bayern*, II. 415–428.

——, *Justiz im Dritten Reich 1933–1940: Anpassung und Unterwerfung in der Ära Gürtner* (Munich, 1988).

——, 'Ludendorffs "prophetischer" Brief an Hindenburg vom Januar/Februar 1933', *VfZ* 47 (1999), 559–62.

——, and Weber, Reinhard (eds.), *Der Hitler-Prozess 1924: Wortlaut der Hauptverhandlung vor dem Volksgericht München I* (2 vols., Munich, 1997, 1999).

Grunwald, Henning, 'Political Lawyers in the Weimar Republic', (Ph.D. dissertation, Cambridge, 2002).

Grüttner, Michael, 'Working-Class Crime and the Labour Movement: Pilfering in the Hamburg Docks, 1888–1923', in Richard J. Evans (ed.), *The German Working Class 1888–1933: The Politics of Everyday Life* (London, 1982), 54–79.

——, *Studenten im Dritten Reich* (Paderborn, 1995).

Gumbel, Emil J., *Vier Jahre politischer Mord* (Berlin, 1924).

——, *Verschwörer: Zur Geschichte und Soziologie der deutschen nationalistischen Geheimbünde 1918–1924* (Heidelberg, 1979 [1924]).

Guratzsch, Dankwart, *Macht durch Organisation: Die Grundlegung des Hugenbergschen Presseimperiums* (Düsseldorf, 1974).

Gusy, Christoph, *Die Weimarer Reichsverfassung* (Tübingen, 1997).

Guttsman, Wilhelm L., *Workers' Culture in Weimar Germany: Between Tradition and Commitment* (Oxford, 1990).

Haffner, Sebastian, *Defying Hitler: A Memoir* (London, 2002).

Hagen, William W., *Germans, Poles, and Jews: The Nationality Conflict in the Prussian East, 1772–1914* (Chicago, 1980).

Hagenlücke, Heinz, *Die deutsche Vaterlandspartei: Die nationale Rechte am Ende des Kaiserreiches* (Düsseldorf, 1997).

Hailey, Christopher, *Franz Schreker, 1878–1934: A Cultural Biography* (Cambridge, 1993).

Hall, Alex, 'By Other Means: The Legal Struggle against the SPD in Wilhelmine Germany 1890–1900', *Historical Journal*, 17 (1974), 365–86.

——, *Scandal, Sensation and Social Democracy: The SPD Press and Wilhelmine Germany 1890–1914* (Cambridge, 1977).

Hamann, Brigitte, *Hitler's Vienna: A Dictator's Apprenticeship* (Oxford, 2000).

——, *Winifred Wagner oder Hitlers Bayreuth* (Munich, 2002).

Hamburger, Ernest, 'Betrachtungen über Heinrich Brünings Memoiren', *Internationale Wissenschaftliche Korrespondenz zur Geschichte der deutschen Arbeiterbewegung*, 8 (1972), 18–39.

Hamel, Iris, *Völkischer Verband und nationale Gewerkschaft: Der Deutsch-nationale Handlungsgehilfenverband, 1893–1933* (Frankfurt am Main, 1967).

Hamilton, Richard F., *Who Voted for Hitler?* (Princeton, 1981).

Hammer, Hermann, 'Die deutschen Ausgaben von Hitlers "Mein Kampf"', *VfZ* 4 (1956), 161–78.

Hammerstein, Notker, *Die Johann Wolfgang Goethe-Universität: Von der Stiftungsuniversität zur staatlichen Hochschule* (2 vols., Neuwied, 1989).

Hanfstaengl, Ernst, *Zwischen Weissem und Braunem Haus: Memoiren eines politischen Aussenseiters* (Munich, 1970).

Hänisch, Dirk, 'A Social Profile of the Saxon NSDAP Voters', in Szejnmann, *Nazism*, 219–31.

Hankel, Gerd, *Die Leipziger Prozesse: Deutsche Kriegsverbrechen und ihre strafrechtliche Verfolgung nach dem Ersten Weltkrieg* (Hamburg, 2003).

Hannover, Heinrich and Hannover-Drück, Elisabeth, *Politische Justiz 1918–1933* (Frankfurt am Main, 1966).

Hansen, Ernst W., *Reichswehr und Industrie: Rüstungswirtschaftliche Zusammenarbeit und wirtschaftliche Mobilmachungsvorbereitungen 1923–1932* (Boppard, 1978).

Harpprecht, Klaus, *Thomas Mann: Eine Biographie* (Reinbek, 1995).

Harris, James F., *The People Speak! Anti-Semitism and Emancipation in Nineteenth-Century Bavaria* (Ann Arbor, 1994).

Harsch, Donna, *German Social Democracy and the Rise of Nazism* (Chapel Hill, NC, 1993).

Harvey, Elizabeth, 'Youth Unemployment and the State: Public Policies towards Unemployed Youth in Hamburg during the World Economic Crisis', in Evans and Geary (eds.), *The German Unemployed*, 142–70.

——, 'Serving the Volk, Saving the Nation: Women in the Youth Movement and the Public Sphere in Weimar Germany', in Larry Eugene Jones and James Retallack (eds.), *Elections, Mass Politics, and Social Change in Modern Germany: New Perspectives* (New York, 1992), 201–22.

——, *Youth Welfare and the State in Weimar Germany* (Oxford, 1993).

Hassell, Ulrich von, *Die Hassell-Tagebücher 1938–1944* (ed. Friedrich Freiherr Hiller von Gaertringen, Berlin, 1989).

Hattenhauer, Hans, 'Wandlungen des Richterleitbildes im 19. und 20. Jahrhundert', in Ralf Dreier and Wolfgang Sellert (eds.), *Recht und Justiz im 'Dritten Reich'* (Frankfurt am Main, 1989), 9–33.

Hayes, Peter, *Industry and Ideology: I.G. Farben in the Nazi Era* (Cambridge, 1987).

Hearnshaw, Fossey J. C., *Germany the Aggressor throughout the Ages* (London, 1940).

Heberle, Rudolf, *Landbevölkerung und Nationalsozialismus: Eine soziologische Untersuchung der politischen Willensbildung in Schleswig-Holstein 1918 bis 1932* (Stuttgart, 1963).

——, *From Democracy to Nazism: A Regional Case Study on Political Parties in Germany* (New York, 1970 [1945]).

Heer, Hannes, *Burgfrieden oder Klassenkampf: Zur Politik der sozialdemokratischen Gewerkschaften 1930–1933* (Neuwied, 1971).

——, *Ernst Thälmann in Selbstzeugnissen und Bilddokumenten* (Reinbek, 1975).

Heiber, Helmut (ed.), *The Early Goebbels Diaries: The Journal of Josef Goebbels from 1925–1926* (London, 1962).

Heidegger, Martin, *Die Selbstbehauptung der deutschen Universität: Rede, gehalten bei der feierlichen Übernahme des Rektorats der Universität Freiburg i. Br. am 27. 5. 1933* (Breslau, 1934).

Heiden, Konrad, *Geschichte des Nationalsozialismus: Die Karriere einer Idee* (Berlin, 1932).

——, *Adolf Hitler: Das Zeitalter der Verantwortungslosigkeit. Eine Biographie* (Zurich, 1936).

Heilbronner, Oded, *Catholicism, Political Culture and the Countryside: A Social History of the Nazi Party in South Germany* (Ann Arbor, 1998).

Hein, Annette, *'Es ist viel "Hitler" in Wagner': Rassismus und antisemitische Deutschtumsideologie in den 'Bayreuther Blättern' (1878–1938)* (Tübingen, 1996).

Heinemann, Ulrich, *Die verdrängte Niederlage: Politische Öffentlichkeit und Kriegsschuldfrage in der Weimarer Republik* (Göttingen, 1983).

Heitzer, Horstwalter, *Der Volksverein für das katholische Deutschland im Kaiserreich 1890–1918* (Mainz, 1979).

Hennig, Diethard, *Johannes Hoffmann: Sozialdemokrat und Bayerischer Ministerpräsident: Biographie* (Munich, 1990).

Hentschel, Volker, *Geschichte der deutschen Sozialpolitik (1880–1980)* (Frankfurt am Main, 1983).

Herbert, Ulrich, *Hitler's Foreign Workers: Enforced Foreign Labor in Germany under the Third Reich* (Cambridge, 1997 [1985]).

——, *Best: Biographische Studien über Radikalismus, Weltanschauung und Vernunft 1903–1989* (Bonn, 1996).

—— et al. (eds.), *Die nationalsozialischer Konzentrationslager: Entwicklung und Struktur* (2 vols., Göttingen, 1998).

Herbst, Ludolf, *Das nationalsozialistische Deutschland 1933–1945* (Frankfurt am Main, 1996).

Hermand, Jost, and Trommler, Frank, *Die Kultur der Weimarer Republik* (Munich, 1978).

Hertz-Eichenröde, Dieter, *Politik und Landwirtschaft in Ostpreussen 1919–1930: Untersuchung eines Strukturproblems in der Weimarer Republik* (Opladen, 1969).

——, *Wirtschaftskrise und Arbeitsbeschaffung: Konjunkturpolitik 1925/26 und die Grundlagen der Krisenpolitik Brünings* (Frankfurt am Main, 1982).

Hess, Wolf Rudiger (ed.), *Rudolf Hess: Briefe 1908–1933* (Munich, 1987).

Heyworth, Peter, *Otto Klemperer: His Life and Times*, I: *1885–1933* (Cambridge, 1983).

Hildenbrand, Hans-Joachim, 'Der Betrug mit dem Fackelzug', in Rolf Italiander (ed.), *Wir erlebten das Ende der Weimarer Republik: Zeitgenossen berichten* (Düsseldorf, 1982), 165.

Hill, Leonidas E., 'The Nazi Attack on "un-German" Literature, 1933–1945', in Jonathan Rose (ed.), *The Holocaust and the Book* (Amherst, Mass., 2001), 9–46.

Hiller von Gaertringen, Friedrich Freiherr, 'Die Deutschnationale Volkspartei', in Matthias and Morsey (eds.), *Das Ende*, 541–652.

——, ' "Dolchstoss-Diskussion" und "Dolchstosslegende" im Wandel von vier Jahrzehnten', in Waldemar Besson and Friedrich Freiherr Hiller von Gaertringen (eds.), *Geschichts- und Gegenwartsbewusstsein* (Göttingen, 1963), 122–60.

Hillmayr, Heinrich, *Roter und weisser Terror in Bayern nach 1918: Erscheinungs-formen und Folgen der Gewalttätigkeiten im Verlauf der revolutionären Ereig-nisse nach dem Ende des Ersten Weltkrieges* (Munich, 1974).

Hindenburg, Paul von, *Aus meinem Leben* (Leipzig, 1920).

Hirte, Chris, *Erich Mühsam: 'Ihr seht mich nicht feige'. Biografie* (Berlin, 1985).

Hitler, Adolf, *Mein Kampf* (trans. Ralph Manheim, introd. D. C. Watt, London, 1969 [1925/6]).

——, *Hitler's Secret Book* (New York, 1961).

——, *Hitler's Table Talk 1941–1944: His Private Conversations* (London, 1973 [1953]).

——, *Hitler: Reden, Schriften, Anordnungen. Februar 1925 bis Januar 1933* (5 vols., Institut für Zeitgeschichte, Munich, 1992–8).

Hitzer, Friedrich, *Anton Graf Arco: Das Attentat auf Kurt Eisner und die Schüsse im Landtag* (Munich, 1988).

Hobsbawm, Eric J., *Age of Extremes: The Short Twentieth Century 1914–1991* (London, 1994).

Hoegner, Wilhelm, *Der schwierige Aussenseiter: Erinnerungen eines Abgeord-neten, Emigranten und Ministerpräsidenten* (Munich, 1959).

Hoepke, Klaus-Peter, *Die deutsche Rechte und der italienische Faschismus: Ein Beitrag zum Selbstverständnis und zur Politik von Gruppen und Verbänden der deutschen Rechten* (Düsseldorf, 1968).

Hofer, Walther, and Bahar, Alexander (eds.), *Der Reichstagsbrand: Eine wissen-schaftliche Dokumentation* (Freiburg im Breisgau, 1992 [1972, 1978]).

Höhne, Heinz, *The Order of the Death's Head: The Story of Hitler's SS* (Stanford, Calif., 1971 [1969]).

——, *Die Machtergreifung: Deutschlands Weg in die Hitler-Diktatur* (Reinbek, 1983).

Höhnig, Klaus, *Der Bund Deutscher Frauenvereine in der Weimarer Republik 1919–1923* (Egelsbach, 1995).

Holtfrerich, Carl-Ludwig, *The German Inflation, 1914–1923: Causes and Effects in International Perspective* (New York, 1986 [1980]).

——, 'Economic Policy Options and the End of the Weimar Republic', in Kershaw (ed.), *Weimar*, 58–91.

Hömig, Herbert, *Brüning: Kanzler in der Krise der Republik. Eine Weimarer Biographie* (Paderborn, 2000).

Hong, Young-Sun, *Welfare, Modernity, and the Weimar State, 1919–1933* (Princeton, 1998).

Horn, Daniel, 'The National Socialist *Schülerbund* and the Hitler Youth, 1929–1933', *Central European History*, 11 (1978), 355–75.

Horne, John, and Kramer, Alan, *German Atrocities 1914: A History of Denial* (London, 2001).

Hornung, Klaus, *Der Jungdeutsche Orden* (Düsseldorf, 1958).

Hosking, Geoffrey, *Russia: People and Empire 1552–1917* (London, 1997).

Höss, Rudolf, *Commandant of Auschwitz* (London, 1959 [1951]).

Hubatsch, Walter, *Hindenburg und der Staat: Aus den Papieren des Generalfeldmarschalls und Reichspräsidenten von 1878 bis 1934* (Göttingen, 1966).

Huber, Ernst Rudolf, *Deutsche Verfassungsgeschichte seit 1789*, V–VII (Stuttgart, 1978–84).

Hunt, Richard N., *German Social Democracy 1918–1933* (New Haven, 1964).

Iggers, Georg G. (ed.), *Marxist Historiography in Transformation: New Orientations in Recent East German History* (Oxford, 1992).

Jablonsky, David, *The Nazi Party in Dissolution: Hitler and the Verbotszeit 1923–1925* (London, 1989).

Jäckel, Eberhard, *Hitler's Weltanschauung: A Blueprint for Power* (Middletown, Conn., 1972 [1969]).

——, and Kuhn, Axel (eds.), *Hitler: Sämtliche Aufzeichnungen 1905–1924* (Stuttgart, 1980).

Jacobsen, Hans-Adolf, *Karl Haushofer: Leben und Werk* (2 vols., Boppard, 1979).

Jahn, Peter (ed.), *Die Gewerkschaften in der Endphase der Republik 1930–1933* (Cologne, 1988).

Jahr, Christoph, *Gewöhnliche Soldaten: Desertion und Deserteure im deutschen und britischen Heer 1914–1918* (Göttingen, 1998).

James, Harold, *The German Slump: Politics and Economics, 1924–1936* (Oxford, 1986).

——, 'Economic Reasons for the Collapse of the Weimar Republic', in Kershaw (ed.), *Weimar*, 30–57.

Jansen, Christian, *Professoren und Politik: Politisches Denken und Handeln der Heidelberger Hochschullehrer 1914–1935* (Göttingen, 1992).

Janssen, Karl-Heinz, 'Geschichte aus der Dunkelkammer: Kabalen um den Reichstagsbrand. Eine unvermeidliche Enthüllung', *Die Zeit*, 38 (14 September 1979), 45–8; 39 (21 September 1979), 20–24; 40 (28 September 1979), 49–52; 41 (5 October 1979), 57–60.

Jarausch, Konrad H., *Deutsche Studenten 1800–1970* (Frankfurt am Main, 1984).

Jasper, Gotthard, *Der Schutz der Republik* (Tübingen, 1963).

——, *Die gescheiterte Zähmung: Wege zur Machtergreifung Hitlers 1930–1934* (Frankfurt am Main, 1986).

Jászi, Oszkár, *Revolution and Counter-Revolution in Hungary* (London, 1924).

Jefferies, Matthew, *Imperial Culture in Germany, 1871–1918* (London, 2003).

Jelavich, Peter, *Munich and Theatrical Modernism: Politics, Playwriting, and Performance 1890–1914* (Cambridge, Mass., 1985).

——, *Berlin Cabaret* (Cambridge, Mass., 1993).

Jellonek, Burkhard, *Homosexuelle unter dem Hakenkreuz: Verfolgung von Homosexuellen im Dritten Reich* (Paderborn, 1990).

Jens, Inge (ed.), *Thomas Mann an Ernst Bertram: Briefe aus den Jahren 1910–1955* (Pfullingen, 1960).

Jesse, Eckard (ed.), *Totalitarismus im 20. Jahrhundert* (Baden-Baden, 1996).

Jetzinger, Franz, *Hitler's Youth* (London, 1958 [1956]).

Joachimsthaler, Anton, *Hitlers Weg begann in München 1913–1923* (Munich, 2000 [1989]).

Jochmann, Werner (ed.), *Nationalsozialismus und Revolution: Ursprung und Geschichte der NSDAP in Hamburg 1922–1933* (Frankfurt am Main, 1963).

——, 'Brünings Deflationspolitik und der Untergang der Weimarer Republik', in Dirk Stegmann *et al.* (eds.), *Industrielle Gesellschaft und politisches System: Beiträge zur politischen Sozialgeschichte. Festschrift für Fritz Fischer zum siebzigsten Geburtstag* (Bonn, 1978), 97–112.

——, *Gesellschaftskrise und Judenfeindschaft in Deutschland 1870–1945* (Hamburg, 1988).

Jones, Larry Eugene, *German Liberalism and the Dissolution of the Weimar Party System, 1918–1933* (Chapel Hill, NC, 1988).

——, ' "The Greatest Stupidity of My Life": Alfred Hugenberg and the Formation of the Hitler Cabinet', *Journal of Contemporary History*, 27 (1992), 63–87.

Jünger, Ernst, *In Stahlgewittern: Aus dem Tagebuch eines Stosstruppführers* (Hanover, 1920); English edn., *Storm of Steel* (London, 2003).

Junker, Detlef, *Die Deutsche Zentrumspartei und Hitler: Ein Beitrag zur Problematik des politischen Katholizismus in Deutschland* (Stuttgart, 1969).

Kaes, Anton, *et al.* (eds.), *The Weimar Republic Sourcebook* (Berkeley, 1994).

Kai, Michel, *Vom Poeten zum Demagogen: Die schriftstellerischen Versuche Joseph Goebbels'* (Cologne, 1999).

Kaiser, Jochen-Christoph, *Sozialer Protestantismus im 20. Jahrhundert: Beiträge zur Geschichte der Inneren Mission 1914–1945* (Munich, 1989).

——, *et al.* (eds.), *Eugenik, Sterilisation, 'Euthanasie': Politische Biologie in Deutschland 1893–1945* (Berlin, 1992).

Kaminski, Andrej, *Konzentrationslager 1896 bis heute: Eine Analyse* (Stuttgart, 1982).

Kampe, Norbert, *Studenten und 'Judenfrage' im deutschen Kaiserreich: Die Entstehung einer akademischen Trägerschicht des Antisemitismus* (Göttingen, 1988).

Kaplan, Marion A., 'The Acculturation, Assimilation, and Integration of Jews in Imperial Germany', *Year Book of the Leo Baeck Institute*, 27 (1982), 3–35.

Karasek, Horst, *Der Brandstifter: Lehr- und Wanderjahre des Maurergesellen Marinus van der Lubbe, der 1933 auszog, den Reichstag anzuzünden* (Berlin, 1980).

Kasischke-Wurm, Daniela, *Antisemitismus im Spiegel der Hamburger Presse während des Kaiserreichs (1884–1914)* (Hamburg, 1997).

Kater, Michael H., *Studentenschaft und Rechtsradikalismus in Deutschland 1918–1933: Eine sozialgeschichtliche Studie zur Bildungskrise in der Weimarer Republik* (Hamburg, 1975).

——, 'The Work Student: A Socio-Economic Phenomenon of Early Weimar Germany', *Journal of Contemporary History*, 10 (1975), 71–94.

——, *The Nazi Party: A Social Profile of Members and Leaders, 1919–1945* (Oxford, 1983).

——, *Different Drummers: Jazz in the Culture of Nazi Germany* (New York, 1992).

——, *The Twisted Muse: Musicians and their Music in the Third Reich* (New York, 1997).

Katz, Jacob, *The Darker Side of Genius: Richard Wagner's Anti-Semitism* (Hanover, 1986).

——, *From Prejudice to Destruction: Anti-Semitism, 1700–1933* (Cambridge, Mass., 1980).

Kauders, Anthony, *German Politics and the Jews: Düsseldorf and Nuremberg 1910–1933* (Oxford, 1996).

Kaufmann, Doris, *Katholisches Milieu in Münster 1928–1933* (Düsseldorf, 1984).

Kelly, Andrew, *Filming All Quiet on the Western Front – 'Brutal Cutting, Stupid Censors, Bigoted Politicos'* (London, 1998), reprinted in paperback as *All Quiet on the Western Front: The Story of a Film* (London, 2002).

Kent, Bruce, *The Spoils of War: The Politics, Economics and Diplomacy of Reparations 1918–1932* (Oxford, 1989).

Kershaw, Ian, *Popular Opinion and Political Dissent in the Third Reich: Bavaria 1933–1945* (Oxford, 1983).

——, 'Ideology, Propaganda, and the Rise of the Nazi Party', in Peter D. Stachura (ed.), *The Nazi Machtergreifung, 1933* (London, 1983), 162–81.

—— (ed.), *Weimar: Why did German Democracy Fail?* (London, 1990).

——, *Hitler*, I: *1889–1936: Hubris* (London, 1998).

——, *Hitler*, II: *1936–1945: Nemesis* (London, 2000).

——, *The Nazi Dictatorship: Problems and Perspectives of Interpretation* (4th edn., London, 2000 [1985]).

——, and Lewin, Moshe (eds.), *Stalinism and Nazism: Dictatorships in Comparison* (Cambridge, 1997).

Kertzer, David, *Unholy War: The Vatican's Role in the Rise of Modern Anti-Semitism* (London, 2001).

Kessler, Harry Graf, *Tagebücher 1918–1937* (ed. Wolfgang Pfeiffer-Belli, Frankfurt am Main, 1961).

Kettenacker, Lothar, 'Der Mythos vom Reich', in Karl H. Bohrer (ed.), *Mythos und Moderne* (Frankfurt am Main, 1983), 262–89.

Kiesewetter, Hubert, *Industrielle Revolution in Deutschland 1815–1914* (Frankfurt am Main, 1989).

Kindleberger, Charles P., *The World in Depression 1929–1939* (Berkeley, 1987 [1973]).

Kirkpatrick, Clifford, *Nazi Germany: Its Women and Family Life* (New York, 1938).

Kissenkoetter, Udo, *Gregor Strasser und die NSDAP* (Stuttgart, 1978).

——, 'Gregor Strasser: Nazi Party Organizer or Weimar Politician?', in Smelser and Zitelmann (eds.), *The Nazi Elite*, 224–34.

Kitchen, Martin, *The German Officer Corps 1890–1914* (Oxford, 1968).

——, *A Military History of Germany from the Eighteenth Century to the Present Day* (London, 1975).

——, *The Silent Dictatorship: The Politics of the German High Command under Hindenburg and Ludendorff, 1916–1918* (London, 1976).

——, *The Coming of Austrian Fascism* (London, 1980).

Klaus, Martin, *Mädchen in der Hitlerjugend: Die Erziehung zur 'deutschen Frau'* (Cologne, 1980).

Klein, Gotthard, *Der Volksverein für das katholische Deutschland 1890–1933: Geschichte, Bedeutung, Untergang* (Paderborn, 1996).

Klein, Ulrich, 'SA-Terror und Bevölkerung in Wuppertal 1933/34', in Detlev Peukert and Jürgen Reulecke (eds.), *Die Reihen fast geschlossen: Beiträge zur Geschichte des Alltags unterm Nationalsozialismus* (Wuppertal, 1981) 45–64.

Kleist-Schmenzin, Ewald von, 'Die letzte Möglichkeit: Zur Ernennung Hitlers zur Reichskanzler an 30. Januar 1933', *Politische Studien*, 10 (1959), 89–92.

Klemperer, Victor, *LTI: Notizbuch eines Philologen* (Leipzig, 1985 [1946]).

——, *Leben sammeln, nicht fragen wozu und warum*, I: *Tagebücher 1919–1925*; II: *Tagebücher 1925–1932* (Berlin, 1996).

——, *Curriculum Vitae: Erinnerungen 1881–1918* (2 vols., Berlin, 1996 [1989]).

——, *I Shall Bear Witness: The Diaries of Victor Klemperer 1933–1941* (London, 1998).

——, *Tagebücher 1933–1934 (Ich will Zeugnis ablegen bis zum Letzten, I)*; Berlin, 1999 [1995]).

Klepper, Jochen, *Unter dem Schatten deiner Flügel: Aus den Tagebüchern der Jahre 1932–1942* (Stuttgart, 1956).

Klepsch, Thomas, *Nationalsozialistische Ideologie: Eine Beschreibung ihrer Struktur vor 1933* (Münster, 1990).

Klessmann, Christoph, 'Hans Frank: Party Jurist and Governor-General in Poland', in Smelser and Zitelmann (eds.), *The Nazi Elite*, 39–47.

Klier, John D., and Lambroza, Shlomo (eds.), *Pogroms: Anti-Jewish Violence in Modern Russian History* (Cambridge, 1992).

Klinger, Max (pseud.; i.e. Curt Geyer), *Volk in Ketten* (Karlsbad, 1934).

Klönne, Arno, *Jugend im Dritten Reich: Dokumente und Analysen* (Cologne, 1982).

Kluke, Paul, 'Der Fall Potempa', *VfZ* 5 (1957), 279–97.

Knock, Thomas J., *To End All Wars: Woodrow Wilson and the Quest for a New World Order* (New York, 1992).

Knowles, Elizabeth (ed.), *The Oxford Dictionary of Quotations* (5th edn., Oxford, 1999).

Kocka, Jürgen, 'German History Before Hitler: The Debate about the German *Sonderweg*', *Journal of Contemporary History*, 23 (1988), 3–16.

Koehler, Karen, 'The Bauhaus, 1919–1928: Gropius in Exile and the Museum of Modern Art, N. Y., 1938', in Richard A. Etlin (ed.), *Art, Culture and Media under the Third Reich* (Chicago, 2002), 287–315.

Kohl, Horst (ed.), *Die politischen Reden des Fürsten Bismarck* (14 vols., Stuttgart, 1892–1905).

Kohler, Eric D., 'The Crisis in the Prussian Schutzpolizei 1930–32', in George L. Mosse (ed.), *Police Forces in History* (London, 1975), 131–50.

Köhler, Fritz, 'Zur Vertreibung humanistischer Gelehrter 1933/34', *Blätter für deutsche und internationale Politik*, 11 (1966), 696–707.

Kohn, Hans, *The Mind of Germany: The Education of a Nation* (London, 1961).

—— (ed.), *German History: Some New German Views* (Boston, 1954).

Kolb, Eberhard, *The Weimar Republic* (London, 1988).

——, 'Die Reichsbahn vom Dawes-Plan bis zum Ende der Weimarer Republik', in Lothar Gall and Manfred Pohl (eds.), *Die Eisenbahn in Deutschland: Von den Anfängen bis zur Gegenwart* (Munich, 1999), 109–64.

Kolbe, Ulrich, 'Zum Urteil über die "Reichstagsbrand-Notverordnung" vom 28. 2. 1933', *Geschichte in Wissenschaft und Unterricht*, 16 (1965), 359–70.

Könnemann, Erwin, *et al.* (eds.), *Arbeiterklasse siegt über Kapp und Lüttwitz* (2 vols., Berlin, 1971).

Koonz, Claudia, *Mothers in the Fatherland: Women, the Family, and Nazi Politics* (London, 1987).

Koszyk, Kurt, *Deutsche Presse im 19. Jahrhundert: Geschichte der deutschen Presse*, II (Berlin, 1966).

——, *Deutsche Presse 1914–1945: Geschichte der deutschen Presse*, III (Berlin, 1972).

Kotowski, Georg, *Friedrich Ebert: Eine politische Biographie*, I: *Der Aufstieg eines deutschen Arbeiterführers 1871 bis 1917* (Wiesbaden, 1963).

Kracauer, Siegfried, *From Caligari to Hitler: A Psychological History of the German Film* (Princeton, 1947).

Kramer, Helgard, 'Frankfurt's Working Women: Scapegoats or Winners of the

Great Depression?', in Evans and Geary (eds.), *The German Unemployed*, 108–41.

Kraul, Margret, *Das deutsche Gymnasium 1780–1980* (Frankfurt am Main, 1984).

Krause, Thomas, *Hamburg wird braun: Der Aufstieg der NSDAP 1921–1933* (Hamburg, 1987).

Kreutzahler, Birgit, *Das Bild des Verbrechers in Romanen der Weimarer Republik: Eine Untersuchung vor dem Hintergrund anderer gesellschaftlicher Verbrecherbilder und gesellschaftlicher Grundzüge der Weimarer Republik* (Frankfurt am Main, 1987).

Kritzer, Peter, *Die bayerische Sozialdemokratie und die bayerische Politik in den Jahren 1918–1923* (Munich, 1969).

Krohn, Klaus-Dieter, *Stabilisierung und ökonomische Interessen: Die Finanzpolitik des deutschen Reiches 1923–1927* (Düsseldorf, 1974).

Krüger, Gerd, ' "Ein Fanal des Widerstandes im Ruhrgebiet": Das "Unternehmen Wesel" in der Osternacht des Jahres 1923. Hintergründe eines angeblichen "Husarenstreiches" ', *Mitteilungsblatt des Instituts fur soziale Bewegungen*, 4 (2000), 95–140.

Krüger, Gesine, *Kriegsbewältigung und Geschichtsbewusstsein: Realität, Deutung und Verarbeitung des deutschen Kolonialkrieges in Namibia 1904 bis 1907* (Göttingen, 1999).

Kruse, Wolfgang, 'Krieg und Klassenheer: Zur Revolutionierung der deutschen Armee im Ersten Weltkrieg', *Geschichte und Gesellschaft*, 22 (1996), 530–61.

Kube, Alfred, *Pour le mérite und Hakenkreuz: Hermann Goering im Dritten Reich* (2nd edn., Munich, 1987 [1986]).

——, 'Hermann Goering: Second Man in the Third Reich', in Smelser and Zitelmann (eds.), *The Nazi Elite*, 62–73.

Kubizek, August, *Adolf Hitler: Mein Jugendfreund* (Graz, 1953).

Kühn, Volker (ed.), *Deutschlands Erwachen: Kabarett unterm Hakenkreuz 1933–1945* (Weinheim, 1989).

Kurz, Thomas, *'Blutmai': Sozialdemokraten und Kommunisten im Brennpunkt der Berliner Ereignisse von 1929* (Bonn, 1988).

Kwiet, Konrad, and Eschwege, Helmut, *Selbstbehauptung und Widerstand: Deutsche Juden im Kampf um Existenz und Menschenwürde 1933–1945* (Hamburg, 1984).

Lamberti, Marjorie, *State, Society and the Elementary School in Imperial Germany* (New York, 1989).

——, 'Elementary School Teachers and the Struggle against Social Democracy in Wilhelmine Germany', *History of Education Quarterly*, 12 (1992), 74–97.

Lane, Barbara Miller, *Architecture and Politics in Germany, 1918–1945* (Cambridge, Mass., 1968).

——, and Rupp, Leila J. (eds.), *Nazi Ideology before 1933: A Documentation* (Manchester, 1978).

Lang, Jochen von, 'Martin Bormann: Hitler's Secretary', in Smelser and Zitelmann (eds.), *The Nazi Elite*, 7–17.

Langbehn, Julius, *Rembrandt als Erzieher* (38th edn., Leipzig, 1891 [1890]), 292.

——, *Der Rembrandtdeutsche: Von einem Wahrheitsfreund* (Dresden, 1892).

Lange, Karl, 'Der Terminus "Lebensraum" in Hitlers *Mein Kampf*', *VfZ* 13 (1965), 426–37.

Langer, Michael, *Zwischen Vorurteil und Aggression: Zum Judenbild in der deutschsprachigen katholischen Volksbildung des 19. Jahrhunderts* (Freiburg, 1994).

Laqueur, Walter, *Young Germany: A History of the German Youth Movement* (London, 1962).

——, *Russia and Germany: A Century of Conflict* (London, 1965).

——, *Weimar: A Cultural History 1918–1933* (London, 1974).

Large, David Clay, *Where Ghosts Walked: Munich's Road to the Third Reich* (New York, 1997).

——, ' "Out with the Ostjuden": The Scheunenviertel Riots in Berlin, November 1923', in Werner Bergmann *et al.* (eds.), *Exclusionary Violence: Antisemitic Riots in Modern Germany* (Ann Arbor, 2002), 123–40.

Laski, Harold, *The Germans – are they Human?* (London, 1941).

Laursen, Karsten, and Pedersen, Jürgen, *The German Inflation 1918–1923* (Amsterdam, 1964).

Lebeltzer, Gisela, 'Der "Schwarze Schmach": Vorurteile – Propaganda – Mythos', *Geschichte und Gesellschaft*, 11 (1985), 37–58.

Lehnert, Detlef, *Sozialdemokratie zwischen Protestbewegung und Regierungspartei 1848–1983* (Frankfurt am Main, 1983).

Lenman, Robin, 'Julius Streicher and the Origins of the NSDAP in Nuremberg, 1918–1923', in Nicholls and Matthias (eds.), *German Democracy*, 161–74.

——, 'Art, Society and the Law in Wilhelmine Germany: The Lex Heinze', *Oxford German Studies*, 8 (1973), 86–113.

Lepsius, M. Rainer, 'Parteisystem und Sozialstruktur: Zum Problem der Demokratisierung der deutschen Gesellschaft', in Gerhard A. Ritter (ed.), *Die deutschen Parteien vor 1918* (Cologne, 1973), 56–80.

Lerner, Warren, *Karl Radek: The Last Internationalist* (Stanford, Calif., 1970).

Lessing, Hellmut, and Liebel, Manfred, *Wilde Cliquen: Szenen einer anderen Arbeiterbewegung* (Bensheim, 1981).

Lessing, Theodor, *Haarmann: Die Geschichte eines Werwolfs. Und andere Kriminalreportagen* (ed. Rainer Marwedel, Frankfurt am Main, 1989).

Lessmann, Peter, *Die preussische Schutzpolizei in der Weimarer Republik: Streifendienst und Strassenkampf* (Düsseldorf, 1989).

Leuschen-Seppel, Rosemarie, *Sozialdemokratie und Antisemitismus im Kaiserreich: Die Auseinandersetzung der Partei mit den konservativen und völkischen Strömungen des Antisemitismus 1871–1914* (Bonn, 1978).

Levi, Erik, *Music in the Third Reich* (London, 1994).

Levy, Richard S., *The Downfall of the Anti-Semitic Political Parties in Imperial Germany* (New Haven, 1975).

Lewy, Günther, *The Catholic Church and Nazi Germany* (New York, 1964).

Liang, Hsi-Huey, *The Berlin Police Force in the Weimar Republic* (Berkeley, 1970).

Lidtke, Vernon L., *The Outlawed Party: Social Democracy in Germany, 1878–1890* (Princeton, 1966).

——, *The Alternative Culture: Socialist Labor in Imperial Germany* (New York, 1985).

Liepach, Martin, *Das Wahlverhalten der jüdischen Bevölkerung: Zur politischen Orientierung der Juden in der Weimarer Republik* (Tübingen, 1996).

Lindenberger, Thomas, and Lüdtke, Alf (eds.), *Physische Gewalt: Studien zur Geschichte der Neuzeit* (Frankfurt am Main, 1995).

Link, Arthur S. (ed.), *The Papers of Woodrow Wilson* (69 vols., Princeton, 1966–   ).

Lipstadt, Deborah E., *Beyond Belief: The American Press and the Coming of the Holocaust, 1933–1945* (New York, 1986).

Liulevicius, Vejas Gabriel, *War Land on the Eastern Front: Culture, National Identity and German Occupation in World War I* (Cambridge, 2000).

Löbe, Paul, *Der Weg war lang: Lebenserinnerungen von Paul Löbe* (Berlin, 1954 [1950]).

Lohalm, Uwe, *Völkischer Radikalismus: Die Geschichte des Deutschvölkischen Schutz- und Trutzbundes, 1919–1923* (Hamburg, 1970).

London, John, *Theatre under the Nazis* (Manchester, 2000).

Longerich, Peter, *Die braunen Bataillone: Geschichte der SA* (Munich, 1989).

——, *Politik der Vernichtung: Eine Gesamtdarstellung der nationalsozialistischen Judenverfolgung* (Munich, 1998).

——, *Der ungeschriebene Befehl: Hitler und der Weg zur 'Endlösung'* (Munich, 2001).

Löwenthal, Richard, 'Die nationalsozialistische "Machtergreifung" – eine Revolution? Ihr Platz unter den totalitären Revolutionen unseres Jahrhunderts', in Martin Broszat *et al.* (eds.), *Deutschlands Weg in die Diktatur* (Berlin, 1983), 42–74.

Lowry, Bullitt, *Armistice 1918* (Kent, Ohio, 1996).

Lucas, Erhard, *Märzrevolution im Ruhrgebiet* (3 vols., Frankfurt am Main, 1970–78).

Ludendorff, Erich, *Kriegführung und Politik* (Berlin, 1922).

Lyttelton, Adrian, *The Seizure of Power: Fascism in Italy 1919–1929* (London, 1973).

Macartney, Carlile A., *The Habsburg Empire 1790–1918* (London, 1968).

McElligott, Anthony, 'Mobilising the Unemployed: The KPD and the Unemployed Workers' Movement in Hamburg-Altona during the Weimar Republic', in Evans and Geary (eds.), *The German Unemployed*, 228–60.

——, *Contested City: Municipal Politics and the Rise of Nazism in Altona, 1917–1937* (Ann Arbor, 1998).

Macmillan, Margaret, *Peacemakers: The Paris Conference of 1919 and its Attempt to End War* (London, 2001).

Mai, Gunther, 'Die Nationalsozialistische Betriebszellen-Organisation: Zum Verhältnis von Arbeiterschaft und Nationalsozialismus', *VfZ* 31 (1983), 573–613.

Mallmann, Klaus-Michael, *Kommunisten in der Weimarer Republik: Sozialgeschichte einer revolutionären Bewegung* (Darmstadt, 1996).

——, 'Gehorsame Parteisoldaten oder eigensinnige Akteure? Die Weimarer Kommunisten in der Kontroverse – eine Erwiderung', *VfZ* 47 (1999), 401–15.

Mannes, Astrid Luise, *Heinrich Brüning: Leben, Wirken, Schicksal* (Munich, 1999).

Manstein, Peter, *Die Mitglieder und Wähler der NSDAP 1919–1933: Untersuchungen zu ihrer schichtmässigen Zusammensetzung* (Frankfurt am Main, 1990 [1987]).

Marcuse, Harold, *Legacies of Dachau: The Uses and Abuses of a Concentration Camp, 1933–2001* (Cambridge, 2001).

Marks, Sally, 'Black Watch on the Rhine: A Study in Propaganda, Prejudice and Prurience', *European Studies Review*, 13 (1983), 297–334.

Marquis, Alice Goldfarb, 'Words as Weapons: Propaganda in Britain and Germany during the First World War', *Journal of Contemporary History*, 13 (1978), 467–98.

Marr, Wilhelm, *Der Sieg des Judenthums über das Germanenthum vom nicht konfessionellen Standpunkt aus betrachtet* (Berlin, 1873).

——, *Vom jüdischen Kriegsschauplatz: Eine Streitschrift* (Berne, 1879).

Martens, Stefan, *Hermann Goering: 'Erster Paladin des Führers' und 'Zweiter Mann im Reich'* (Paderborn, 1985).

Martin, Bernd, 'Die deutschen Gewerkschaften und die nationalsozialistische Machtübernahme', *Geschichte in Wissenschaft und Unterricht*, 36 (1985), 605–31.

——(ed.), *Martin Heidegger und das 'Dritte Reich': Ein Kompendium* (Darmstadt, 1989).

Marx, Karl, *The Eighteenth Brumaire of Louis Bonaparte* (1852), in Lewis Feuer (ed.), *Marx and Engels: Basic Writings on Politics and Philosophy* (New York, 1959), 358–88.

——, 'Randglossen zum Programm der deutschen Arbeiterpartei' (Kritik des Gothaer Programms, 1875), in Karl Marx and Friedrich Engels, *Ausgewählte Schriften* (2 vols., East Berlin, 1968), II. 11–28.

Maschmann, Melita, *Account Rendered: A Dossier on my Former Self* (trans. Geoffrey Strachan, London, 1964).

Maser, Werner, *Die Frühgeschichte der NSDAP: Hitlers Weg bis 1924* (Frankfurt am Main, 1965).

——, *Hitlers Mein Kampf: Geschichte, Auszüge, Kommentare* (Munich, 1966).

——, *Hermann Göring: Hitlers janusköpfiger Paladin. Die politische Biographie* (Berlin, 2000).

Mason, Tim W., *Social Policy in the Third Reich: The Working Class and the 'National Community'* (ed. Jane Caplan, Providence, RI, 1993 [1977]).

——, *Nazism, Fascism and the Working Class: Essays by Tim Mason* (ed. Jane Caplan, Cambridge, 1995).

Massing, Paul W., *Rehearsal for Destruction* (New York, 1949).

Matthias, Erich, 'Der Untergang der Sozialdemokratie 1933', *VfZ* 4 (1956), 179–226 and 250–86.

——, 'Hindenburg zwischen den Fronten 1932', *VfZ* 8 (1960), 75–84.

——, and Morsey, Rudolf (eds.), *Das Ende der Parteien 1933: Darstellungen und Dokumente* (Düsseldorf, 1960).

——, 'Die Sozialdemokratische Partei Deutschlands', in Matthias and Morsey (eds.), *Das Ende*, 101–278.

Maurer, Trude, *Ostjuden in Deutschland, 1918–1933* (Hamburg, 1986).

Mayer, Arno J., *Politics and Diplomacy of Peacemaking: Containment and Counterrevolution at Versailles 1918–1919* (2nd edn., New York, 1969 [1967]).

Mazower, Mark, *Dark Continent: Europe's Twentieth Century* (London, 1998).

Medalen, Charles, 'State Monopoly Capitalism in Germany: The Hibernia Affair', *Past and Present*, 78 (February 1978), 82–112.

Meinecke, Friedrich, 'Bismarck und das neue Deutschland', in idem, *Preussen und Deutschland im 19. und 20. Jahrhundert* (Munich, 1918).

——, *Die deutsche Katastrophe* (Wiesbaden, 1946).

——, *The German Catastrophe: Reflections and Recollections* (Cambridge, Mass., 1950).

Meiring, Kerstin, *Die christlich-jüdische Mischehe in Deutschland, 1840–1933* (Hamburg, 1998).

Meissner, Otto, *Staatssekretär unter Ebert – Hindenburg – Hitler: Der Schicksalsweg des deutschen Volkes von 1918–1945, wie ich ihn erlebte* (Hamburg, 1950), 216–17.

Mergel, Thomas, *Parlamentarische Kultur in der Weimarer Republik: Politische Kommunikation, symbolische Politik und Öffentlichkeit im Reichstag* (Düsseldorf, 2002).

Merkl, Peter H., *Political Violence under the Swastika: 581 Early Nazis* (Princeton, 1975).

Merson, Allan, *Communist Resistance in Nazi Germany* (London, 1985).

Meyer, Folkert, *Schule der Untertanen: Lehrer und Politik in Preussen 1848–1900* (Hamburg, 1976).

Meyer, Michael, *The Politics of Music in the Third Reich* (New York, 1991).

Michalka, Wolfgang, and Niedhart, Gottfried, *Die ungeliebte Republik: Dokumente zur Innen- und Aussenpolitik Weimars 1918–1933* (Munich, 1980).

Mierendorff, Carlo, 'Der Hindenburgsieg 1932', *Sozialistische Monatshefte*, 4 April 1932, 297.

Milatz, Alfred, 'Das Ende der Parteien im Spiegel der Wahlen 1930 bis 1933', in Matthias and Morsey (eds.), *Das Ende*, 743–93.

——, *Wähler und Wahlen in der Weimarer Republik* (Bonn, 1965).

Miller, Max, *Eugen Bolz* (Stuttgart, 1951).

Miller, Susanne, and Potthoff, Heinrich, *A History of German Social Democracy: From 1848 to the Present* (Leamington Spa, 1986 [1983]).

Milward, Alan, and Saul, Samuel B., *The Development of the Economies of Continental Europe 1850–1914* (London, 1977).

Ministère des affaires étrangères (ed.), *Documents Diplomatiques Français, 1932–1939*, ser. 1, vol. II (Paris, 1966).

Minuth, Karl-Heinz (ed.), *Akten der Reichskanzlei: Weimarer Republik. Das Kabinett von Papen, 1. Juni bis 3. December 1932* (Boppard, 1989).

—— (ed.), *Akten der Reichskanzlei: Die Regierung Hitler*, I: *1933–1934* (2 vols., Boppard, 1983).

Mitchell, Allan, *Revolution in Bavaria 1918/1919: The Eisner Regime and the Soviet Republic* (Princeton, 1965).

Moeller, Robert G., 'Winners as Losers in the German Inflation: Peasant Protest over the Controlled Economy', in Gerald D. Feldman *et al.* (eds.), *The German Inflation: A Preliminary Balance* (Berlin, 1982), 255–88.

——, 'The Kaiserreich Recast? Continuity and Change in Modern German Historiography', *Journal of Social History*, 17 (1984), 655–83.

Moeller van den Bruck, Arthur, *Das Dritte Reich* (3rd edn., Hamburg, 1931 [Berlin, 1923]).

Möller, Horst, 'Die nationalsozialistische Machtergreifung: Konterrevolution oder Revolution?', *VfZ* 31 (1983), 25–51.

Mommsen, Hans, 'Der Reichstagsbrand und seine politischen Folgen', *VfZ* 12 (1964), 351–413.

——, *Beamtentum im Dritten Reich: Mit ausgewählten Quellen zur nationalsozialistischen Beamtenpolitik* (Stuttgart, 1966).

——, 'Betrachtungen zu den Memoiren Heinrich Brünings', *Jahrbuch für die Geschichte Mittel- und Ostdeutschlands*, 22 (1973), 270–80.

——, 'Van der Lubbes Weg in den Reichstag – der Ablauf der Ereignisse', in Backes *et al.*, *Reichstagsbrand*, 33–57.

——, *Der Nationalsozialismus und die deutsche Gesellschaft: Ausgewählte Aufsätze* (Reinbek, 1991).

——, *From Weimar to Auschwitz: Essays in German History* (Princeton, 1991).

——, *The Rise and Fall of Weimar Democracy* (Chapel Hill, NC, 1996 [1989]).

——, 'Das Jahr 1930 als Zäsur in der deutschen Entwicklung der Zwischenkriegszeit', in Lothar Ehrlich and Jürgen John (eds.), *Weimar 1930: Politik und Kultur im Vorfeld der NS-Diktatur* (Cologne, 1998), 1–13.

Mommsen, Wolfgang J., *Das Ringen um den nationalen Staat: Die Gründung und der innere Ausbau des Deutschen Reiches unter Otto von Bismarck 1850–1890* (Berlin, 1993).

——, *Bürgerstolz und Weltmachtstreben: Deutschland unter Wilhelm II. 1890 bis 1918* (Berlin, 1995).

Moreau, Patrick, *Nationalsozialismus von 'links': Die 'Kampfgemeinschaft Revolutionärer Nationalsozialisten' und die 'Schwarze Front' Otto Strassers 1930–1935* (Stuttgart, 1984).

Mork, Andrea, *Richard Wagner als politischer Schriftsteller: Weltanschauung und Wirkungsgeschichte* (Frankfurt am Main, 1990).

Morsch, Günter, 'Oranienburg – Sachsenhausen, Sachsenhausen – Oranienburg', in Herbert *et al.* (eds.), *Die nationalsozialistischen Konzentrationslager*, 111–34.

Morsey, Rudolf, 'Die Deutsche Zentrumspartei', in Matthias and Morsey (eds.), *Das Ende*, 279–453.

——, 'Hitler als Braunschweiger Reigierungsrat', *VfZ* 8 (1960), 419–48.

——, 'Hitlers Verhandlungen mit der Zentrumsführung am 31. Januar 1933', *VfZ* 9 (1961), 182–94.

——, 'Zur Geschichte des "Preussenschlags" am 20. Juli 1932', *VfZ* 9 (1961), 436–9.

——, *Der Untergang des politischen Katholizismus: Die Zentrumspartei zwischen christlichem Selbstverständnis und 'Nationaler Erhebung' 1932/33* (Stuttgart, 1977).

——, 'Beamtenschaft und Verwaltung zwischen Republik und "Neuem Staat"', in Erdmann and Schulze (eds.), *Weimar*, 151–68.

—— (ed.), *Das 'Ermächtigungsgesetz' vom 24. März 1933: Quellen zur Geschichte und Interpretation des 'Gesetzes zur Behebung der Not von Volk und Reich'* (Düsseldorf, 1992).

Mosse, George L., *The Crisis of German Ideology: Intellectual Origins of the Third Reich* (London, 1964).

——, *The Nationalization of the Masses: Political Symbolism and Mass Movements in Germany from the Napoleonic Wars through the Third Reich* (New York, 1975).

Mosse, Werner E., *Jews in the German Economy: The German-Jewish Economic Élite 1820–1935* (Oxford, 1987).

——, *The German-Jewish Economic Élite 1820–1935: A Socio-Cultural Profile* (Oxford, 1989).

Mühlberger, Detlef, 'A Social Profile of the Saxon NSDAP Membership before 1933', in Szejnmann, *Nazism*, 211–19.

——, *Hitler's Followers: Studies in the Sociology of the Nazi Movement* (London, 1991).

Mühlhausen, Walter, *Friedrich Ebert: Sein Leben, sein Werk, seine Zeit* (Heidelberg, 1999).

Müller, Dirk, *Arbeiter, Katholizismus, Staat: Der Volksverein für das katholische*

Deutschland und die katholischen Arbeiterorganisationen in der Weimarer Republik (Bonn, 1996).

Müller, Fritz Ferdinand, *Deutschland-Zanzibar-Ostafrika: Geschichte einer deutschen Kolonialeroberung 1884–1890* (Berlin, 1990 [1959]).

Müller, Hans (ed.), *Katholische Kirche und Nationalsozialismus: Dokumente 1930–1935* (Munich, 1963).

Müller, Ingo, *Hitler's Justice: The Courts of the Third Reich* (London, 1991 [1987]).

Müller, Klaus-Jürgen, *The Army, Politics and Society in Germany 1933–1945: Studies in the Army's Relation to Nazism* (Manchester, 1987).

——, 'Der Tag von Potsdam und das Verhältnis der preussisch-deutschen Militär-Elite zum Nationalsozialismus', in Bernhard Kröner (ed.), *Potsdam – Stadt, Armee, Residenz in der preussisch-deutschen Militärgeschichte* (Frankfurt am Main, 1993), 435–49.

Müller-Jabusch, Maximilian (ed.), *Handbuch des öffentlichen Lebens* (Leipzig, 1931).

Nahel, Irmela, *Fememorde und Fememordprozesse in der Weimarer Republik* (Cologne, 1991).

Nationalsozialistischer Deutscher Frontkämpferbund (ed.), *Der NSDFB (Stahlhelm): Geschichte, Wesen und Aufgabe des Frontsoldatenbundes* (Berlin, 1935).

Nelles, Dieter, 'Jan Valtins "Tagebuch der Hölle" – Legende und Wirklichkeit eines Schlüsselromans der Totalitarismustheorie', *1999: Zeitschrift für Sozialgeschichte des 20. und 21. Jahrhunderts*, 9 (1994), 11–45.

Nelson, Keith, ' "The Black Horror on the Rhine": Race as a Factor in Post-World War I Diplomacy', *Journal of Modern History*, 42 (1970), 606–27.

Neugebauer, Rosamunde, ' "Christus mit der Gasmaske" von George Grosz, oder: Wieviel Satire konnten Kirche und Staat in Deutschland um 1930 ertragen?', in Maria Rüger (ed.), *Kunst und Kunstkritik der dreissiger Jahre: 29 Standpunkte zu künstlerischen und ästhetischen Prozessen und Kontroversen* (Dresden, 1990), 156–65.

Neumann, Franz, *Behemoth: The Structure and Practice of National Socialism* (New York, 1942).

Nicholls, Anthony J., 'Die höhere Beamtenschaft in der Weimarer Zeit: Betrachtungen zu Problemen ihrer Haltung und ihrer Fortbildung', in Lothar Albertin and Werner Link (eds.), *Politische Parteien auf dem Weg zur parlamentarischen Demokratie in Deutschland: Entwicklungslinien bis zur Gegenwart* (Düsseldorf, 1981), 195–207.

——, *Weimar and the Rise of Hitler* (4th edn., London, 2000 [1968]).

——, and Matthias, Erich (eds.), *German Democracy and the Triumph of Hitler: Essays in Recent German History* (London, 1971).

Niehuss, Merith, 'From Welfare Provision to Social Insurance: The Unemployed in Augsburg 1918–27', in Evans and Geary (eds.), *The German Unemployed*, 44–72.

Niewyk, Donald L., *The Jews in Weimar Germany* (Baton Rouge, La., 1980).

Nipperdey, Thomas, *Germany from Napoleon to Bismarck* (Princeton, 1986 [1983]).

——, *Deutsche Geschichte 1866–1918*, I: *Arbeitswelt und Bürgergeist* (Munich, 1990).

——, *Deutsche Geschichte 1866–1918*, II: *Machtstaat vor der Demokratie* (Munich, 1992).

Nitschke, August, *et al.* (eds.), *Jahrhundertwende: Der Aufbruch in die Moderne 1880–1930* (2 vols., Reinbek, 1990).

Noack, Paul, *Ernst Jünger: Eine Biographie* (Berlin, 1998).

Noakes, Jeremy, *The Nazi Party in Lower Saxony 1921–1933* (Oxford, 1971).

——, 'Nazism and Revolution', in Noel O'Sullivan (ed.), *Revolutionary Theory and Political Reality* (London, 1983), 73–100.

——, 'Nazism and Eugenics: The Background to the Nazi Sterilization Law of 14 July 1933', in Roger Bullen *et al.* (eds.), *Ideas into Politics: Aspects of European History 1880–1950* (London, 1984), 75–94.

——, and Pridham, Geoffrey (eds.), *Nazism 1919–1945* (4 vols., Exeter 1983–98 [1974]).

Nolan, Mary, *Visions of Modernity: American Business and the Modernization of Germany* (New York, 1994).

Nolte, Ernst, *Three Faces of Fascism: Action Française, Italian Fascism, National Socialism* (New York, 1969 [1963]).

——, *Der europäische Bürgerkrieg 1917–1945: Nationalsozialismus und Bolschewismus* (Frankfurt am Main, 1987).

Nonn, Christoph, *Eine Stadt sucht einen Mörder: Gerücht, Gewalt und Antisemitismus im Kaiserreich* (Göttingen, 2002).

Norton, Robert E., *Secret Germany: Stefan George and his Circle* (Ithaca, NY, 2002).

Nowak, Kurt, and Raulet, Gérard (eds.), *Protestantismus und Antisemitismus in der Weimarer Republik* (Frankfurt am Main, 1994).

Nuss, Karl, *Militär und Wiederaufrüstung in der Weimarer Republik: Zur politischen Rolle und Entwicklung der Reichswehr* (Berlin, 1977).

Oertel, Thomas, *Horst Wessel. Untersuchung einer Legende* (Cologne, 1988).

O'Neill, Robert J., *The German Army and the Nazi Party 1933–1939* (London, 1966).

Orlow, Dietrich, *The History of the Nazi Party*, I: *1919–1933* (Newton Abbot, 1971 [1969]).

——, *Weimar Prussia 1918–1925: The Unlikely Rock of Democracy* (Pittsburgh, 1986).

——, 'Rudolf Hess: Deputy Führer', in Smelser and Zitelmann (eds.), *The Nazi Elite*, 74–84.

Orth, Karin, *Das System der nationalsozialistischen Konzentrationslager* (Hamburg, 1999).

Osterroth, Franz, and Schuster, Dieter, *Chronik der deutschen Sozialdemokratie* (Hanover, 1963).

Ostwald, Hans, *Sittengeschichte der Inflation: Ein Kulturdokument aus den Jahren des Marksturzes* (Berlin, 1931).

Ott, Hugo, *Martin Heidegger: A Political Life* (London, 1993).

Overy, Richard, *Goering: The 'Iron Man'* (London, 1984).

Owen, Richard, 'Military-Industrial Relations: Krupp and the Imperial Navy Office', in Evans (ed.), *Society and Politics*, 71–89.

Paret, Peter, *An Artist against the Third Reich: Ernst Barlach 1933–1938* (Cambridge, 2003).

Passmore, Kevin, *Fascism: A Very Short Introduction* (Oxford, 2002).

Patch, William L., Jr., *Heinrich Brüning and the Dissolution of the Weimar Republic* (Cambridge, 1998).

Paul, Gerhard, *Aufstand der Bilder: Die NS-Propaganda vor 1933* (Bonn, 1990).

Payne, Stanley G., *A History of Fascism 1914–1945* (London, 1995).

Peal, David, 'Antisemitism by Other Means? The Rural Cooperative Movement in Late 19th Century Germany', in Herbert A. Strauss (ed.), *Hostages of Modernization: Studies on Modern Antisemitism 1870–1933/39: Germany – Great Britain – France* (Berlin, 1993), 128–49.

Petropoulos, Jonathan, *The Faustian Bargain: The Art World in Nazi Germany* (London, 2000).

Petzina, Dietmar, 'The Extent and Causes of Unemployment in the Weimar Republic', in Peter D. Stachura (ed.), *Unemployment and the Great Depression in Weimar Germany* (London, 1986), 29–48.

——, et al., *Sozialgeschichtliches Arbeitsbuch*, III: *Materialien zur Geschichte des Deutschen Reiches 1914–1945* (Munich, 1978).

Petzold, Joachim, *Franz von Papen: Ein deutsches Verhängnis* (Munich, 1995).

Peukert, Detlev J. K., *Die KPD im Widerstand: Verfolgung und Untergrundarbeit an Rhein und Ruhr, 1933 bis 1945* (Wuppertal, 1980).

——, *Grenzen der Sozialdisziplinierung: Aufstieg und Krise der deutschen Jugendfürsorge 1878 bis 1932* (Cologne, 1986).

——, 'The Lost Generation: Youth Unemployment at the End of the Weimar Republic', in Evans and Geary (eds.), *The German Unemployed*, 172–93.

——, *Jugend zwischen Krieg und Krise: Lebenswelten von Arbeiterjungen in der Weimarer Republik* (Cologne, 1987).

——, *Inside Nazi Germany: Conformity, Opposition and Racism in Everyday Life* (London, 1989 [1982]).

——, *The Weimar Republic: The Crisis of Classical Modernity* (London, 1991 [1987]).

Pflanze, Otto, *Bismarck* (3 vols., Princeton, 1990).

Phelps, Reginald H., 'Aus den Groener Dokumenten', *Deutsche Rundschau*, 76 (1950), 1019, and 77 (1951), 26–9.

——, ' "Before Hitler Came": Thule Society and Germanen Orden', *Journal of Modern History*, 35 (1963), 245–61.

——, 'Hitler als Parteiredner im Jahre 1920', *VfZ* 11 (1963), 274–330.

Pikart, Eberhard, 'Preussische Beamtenpolitik 1918–1933', *VfZ* 6 (1958), 119–37.

Planck, Max, 'Mein Besuch bei Hitler', *Physikalische Blätter*, 3 (1947), 143.

Planert, Ute, *Antifeminismus im Kaiserreich: Diskurs, soziale Formation und politische Mentalität* (Göttingen, 1998).

——, *Nation, Politik und Geschlecht: Frauenbewegungen und Nationalismus in der Moderne* (Frankfurt am Main, 2000).

Plant, Richard, *The Pink Triangle: The Nazi War against Homosexuals* (Edinburgh, 1987).

Plewnia, Margarete, *Auf dem Weg zu Hitler: Der völkische Publizist Dietrich Eckart* (Bremen, 1970).

Pogge-von Strandmann, Hartmut, 'Staatsstreichpläne, Alldeutsche und Bethmann Hollweg', in idem and Imanuel Geiss, *Die Erforderlichkeit des Unmöglichen: Deutschland am Vorabend des ersten Weltkrieges* (Frankfurt am Main, 1965), 7–45.

Pommerin, Reiner, *'Sterilisierung der Rheinlandbastarde': Das Schicksal einer farbigen deutschen Minderheit 1918–1937* (Düsseldorf, 1979).

Preller, Ludwig, *Sozialpolitik in der Weimarer Republik* (Düsseldorf, 1978 [1949]).

Pridham, Geoffrey, *Hitler's Rise to Power: The Nazi Movement in Bavaria 1923–1933* (London, 1973).

Prieberg, Fred K., *Trial of Strength: Wilhelm Furtwängler and the Third Reich* (London, 1992).

Proctor, Robert N., *Racial Hygiene: Medicine under the Nazis* (Cambridge, Mass., 1988).

Der Prozess gegen die Hauptkriegsverbrecher vor dem Internationalen Militärgerichtshof (Nuremberg, 1947).

Puhle, Hans-Jürgen, *Agrarische Interessenpolitik und preussischer Konservatismus im wilhelminischen Reich 1893–1914: Ein Beitrag zur Analyse des Nationalismus in Deutschland am Beispiel des Bundes der Landwirte und der Deutsch-Konservativen Partei* (Hanover, 1967).

Pulzer, Peter J. G., *The Rise of Political Anti-Semitism in Germany and Austria* (New York, 1964).

——, 'Der Anfang vom Ende', in Arnold Paucker (ed.), *Die Juden im nationalsozialistischen Deutschland 1933–1944* (Tübingen, 1986), 3–15.

——, *Jews and the German State: The Political History of a Minority, 1848–1933* (Oxford, 1992).

——, 'Jews and Nation-Building in Germany 1815–1918', *Year Book of the Leo Baeck Institute*, 41 (1996), 199–224.

Pyta, Wolfram, 'Konstitutionelle Demokratie statt monarchischer Restauration: Die verfassungspolitische Konzeption Schleichers in der Weimarer Staatskrise', *VfZ* 47 (1999), 417–41.

Rabenau, Friedrich von, *Seeckt – aus seinem Leben 1918–1936* (Leipzig, 1940).

Radkau, Joachim, *Das Zeitalter der Nervosität: Deutschland zwischen Bismarck und Hitler* (Munich, 1998).

Rahden, Till van, *Juden und andere Breslauer: Die Beziehungen zwischen Juden, Protestanten und Katholiken in einer deutschen Grossstadt von 1860 bis 1925* (Göttingen, 2000).

Rainbird, Sean (ed.), *Max Beckmann* (London, 2003).

Rauschning, Hermann, *Germany's Revolution of Destruction* (London, 1939 [1938]).

Rebentisch, Dieter, and Raab, Angelika (eds.), *Neu-Isenburg zwischen Anpassung und Widerstand: Dokumente über Lebensbedingungen und politisches Verhalten 1933–1934* (Neu-Isenburg, 1978).

Reiche, Eric G., *The Development of the SA in Nürnberg, 1922–1934* (Cambridge, 1986).

Reimann, Aribert, *Der grosse Krieg der Sprachen: Untersuchungen zur historischen Semantik in Deutschland und England zur Zeit des Ersten Weltkriegs* (Essen, 2000).

Reimer, Klaus, *Rheinlandfrage und Rheinlandbewegung (1918–1933): Ein Beitrag zur Geschichte der regionalistischen Bewegung in Deutschland* (Frankfurt am Main, 1979).

Reithel, Thomas, and Strenge, Irene, 'Die Reichstagsbrandverordnung: Grundlegung der Diktatur mit den Instrumenten des Weimarer Ausnahmezustandes', *VfZ* 48 (2000), 413–60.

Remy, Steven P., *The Heidelberg Myth: The Nazification and Denazification of a German University* (Cambridge, Mass., 2002).

Repgen, Konrad, 'Zur vatikanischen Strategie beim Reichskonkordat', *VfZ* 31 (1983), 506–35.

Retallack, James N., *Notables of the Right: The Conservative Party and Political Mobilization in Germany, 1876–1918* (London, 1988).

Reulecke, Jürgen, '"Hat die Jugendbewegung den Nationalsozialismus vorbereitet?" Zum Umgang mit einer falschen Frage', in Wolfgang R. Krabbe (ed.), *Politische Jugend in der Weimarer Republik* (Bochum, 1993), 222–43.

——, *'Ich möchte einer werden so wie die . . .' Männerbünde im 20. Jahrhundert* (Frankfurt am Main, 2001).

Reuth, Ralf Georg, *Goebbels: Eine Biographie* (Munich, 1995).

Richardi, Hans-Günter, *Schule der Gewalt: Das Konzentrationslager Dachau, 1933–1934* (Munich, 1983).

Richarz, Monika, *Jüdisches Leben in Deutschland*, II: *Selbstzeugnisse zur Sozialgeschichte im Kaiserreich* (Stuttgart, 1979).

Richter, Ludwig, 'Das präsidiale Notverordnungsrecht in den ersten Jahren der Weimarer Republik. Friedrich Ebert und die Anwendung des Artikels 48 der Weimarer Reichsverfassung', in Eberhard Kolb (ed.), *Friedrich Ebert als Reichspräsident: Amtsführung und Amtsverständnis* (Munich, 1997), 207–58.

Riebicke, Otto, *Was brauchte der Weltkrieg? Tatsachen und Zahlen aus dem deutschen Ringen 1914–18* (Berlin, 1936).

Rietzler, Rudolf, *'Kampf in der Nordmark': Das Aufkommen des Nationalsozialismus in Schleswig-Holstein (1919–1928)* (Neumünster, 1982).

Ritchie, James M., *German Literature under National Socialism* (London, 1983).

Rittberger, Volker (ed.), *1933: Wie die Republik der Diktatur erlag* (Stuttgart, 1983).

Ritter, Gerhard, *Europa und die deutsche Frage: Betrachtungen über die geschichtliche Eigenart des deutschen Staatsgedankens* (Munich, 1948).

——, 'The Historical Foundations of the Rise of National-Socialism', in Maurice Beaumont *et al.*, *The Third Reich: A Study Published under the Auspices of the International Council for Philosophy and Humanistic Studies with the Assistance of UNESCO* (New York, 1955), 381–416.

Ritter, Gerhard A., 'Kontinuität und Umformung des deutschen Parteiensystems 1918–1920', in Eberhard Kolb (ed.), *Vom Kaiserreich zur Weimarer Republik* (Cologne, 1972), 218–43.

——, *Wahlgeschichtliches Arbeitsbuch: Materialien zur Statistik des Kaiserreichs 1871–1918* (Munich, 1980).

——, *Sozialversicherung in Deutschland und England: Entstehung und Grundzüge im Vergleich* (Munich, 1983).

——, *Die deutschen Parteien 1830–1914: Parteien und Gesellschaft im konstitutionellen Regierungssystem* (Göttingen, 1985).

—— and Miller, Susanne (eds.), *Die deutsche Revolution 1918–1919: Dokumente* (Frankfurt am Main, 1968).

Ritthaler, Anton, 'Eine Etappe auf Hitlers Weg zur ungeteilten Macht: Hugenbergs Rücktritt als Reichsminister', *VfZ* 8 (1960), 193–219.

Rohe, Karl, *Das Reichsbanner Schwarz Rot Gold: Ein Beitrag zur Geschichte und Struktur der politischen Kampfverbände zur Zeit der Weimarer Republik* (Düsseldorf, 1966).

——, *Wahlen und Wählertraditionen in Deutschland* (Frankfurt am Main, 1992).

Röhl, John C. G. (ed.), *From Bismarck to Hitler: The Problem of Continuity in German History* (London, 1970).

Röhm, Ernst, *Die Geschichte eines Hochverräters* (Munich, 1928).

Rohrwasser, Michael, *Der Stalinismus und die Renegaten: Die Literatur der Exkommunisten* (Stuttgart, 1991).

Rolfs, Richard W., *The Sorcerer's Apprentice: The Life of Franz von Papen* (Lanham, Md., 1996).

Rosenberg, Alfred (ed.), *Dietrich Eckart: Ein Vermächtnis* (4th edn., Munich, 1937 [1928]).

——, *Selected Writings* (ed. Robert Pois, London, 1970).

Rosenberg, Arthur, *The Birth of the German Republic* (Oxford, 1931 [1930]).

——, *A History of the German Republic* (London, 1936 [1935]).

Rosenhaft, Eve, 'Working-Class Life and Working-Class Politics: Communists,

Nazis, and the State in the Battle for the Streets, Berlin, 1928–1932', in Richard Bessel and Edgar J. Feuchtwanger (eds.), *Social Change and Political Development in Weimar Germany* (London, 1981), 207–40.

——, 'Organising the "Lumpenproletariat": Cliques and Communists in Berlin during the Weimar Republic', in Richard J. Evans (ed.), *The German Working Class 1888–1933: The Politics of Everyday Life* (London, 1982), 174–219.

——, *Beating the Fascists? The German Communists and Political Violence 1929–1933* (Cambridge, 1983).

——, 'The Unemployed in the Neighbourhood: Social Dislocation and Political Mobilisation in Germany 1929–33', in Evans and Geary (eds.), *The German Unemployed*, 194–227.

——, 'Links gleich rechts? Militante Strassengewalt um 1930', in Lindenberger and Lüdtke (eds.), *Physische Gewalt*, 239–75.

Rosenow, Ulf, 'Die Göttinger Physik unter dem Nationalsozialismus', in Becker *et al.* (eds.), *Die Universität Göttingen*, 345–409.

Rote Fahne, Die, 1933.

Roth, Karl Heinz, 'Schein-Alternativen im Gesundheitswesen: Alfred Grotjahn (1869–1931) – Integrationsfigur etablierter Sozialmedizin und nationalsozialistischer "Rassenhygiene"', in Karl Heinz Roth (ed.), *Erfassung zur Vernichtung: Von der Sozialhygiene zum 'Gesetz über Sterbehilfe'* (Berlin, 1984), 31–56.

Rousso, Henry, *The Haunting Past: History, Memory, and Justice in Contemporary France* (Philadelphia, 2002 [1998]).

Ruck, Michael, *Bibliographie zum Nationalsozialismus* (2 vols., Darmstadt, 2000 [1995]).

Runge, Wolfgang, *Politik und Beamtentum in Parteienstaat: Die Demokratisierung der politischen Beamten in Preussen zwischen 1918 und 1933* (Stuttgart, 1965).

Rupieper, Hermann J., *The Cuno Government and Reparations 1922–1923: Politics and Economics* (The Hague, 1979).

Ruppert, Karsten, *Im Dienst am Staat von Weimar: Das Zentrum als regierende Partei in der Weimarer Demokratie 1923–1930* (Düsseldorf, 1992).

Rürup, Reinhard, 'Entstehung und Grundlagen der Weimarer Verfassung', in Eberhard Kolb (ed.), *Vom Kaiserreich zur Weimarer Republik* (Cologne, 1972), 218–43.

——, (ed.), *Topographie des Terrors: Gestapo, SS und Reichssicherheitshauptamt auf dem 'Prinz-Albrecht-Gelände': Eine Dokumentation* (Berlin, 1987).

Sabrow, Martin, *Der Rathenaumord: Rekonstruktion einer Verschwörung gegen die Republik von Weimar* (Munich, 1994).

Safranski, Rüdiger, *Ein Meister aus Deutschland: Heidegger und seine Zeit* (Munich, 1994).

Sailer, Joachim, *Eugen Bolz und die Krise des politischen Katholizismus in der Weimarer Republik* (Tübingen, 1994).

Sauder, Gerhard (ed.), *Die Bücherverbrennung: Zum 10. Mai 1933* (Munich, 1983).

Saul, Klaus, 'Der Staat und die "Mächte des Umsturzes": Ein Beitrag zu den Methoden antisozialistischer Repression und Agitation vom Scheitern des Sozialistengesetzes bis zur Jahrhundertwende', *Archiv für Sozialgeschichte*, 12 (1972), 293–350.

Schade, Franz, *Kurt Eisner und die bayerische Sozialdemokratie* (Hanover, 1961).

Schairer, Erich, 'Alfred Hugenberg', *Mit anderen Augen: Jahrbuch der deutschen Sonntagszeitung* (1929), 18–21.

Schanbacher, Eberhard, *Parlamentarische Wahlen und Wahlsystem in der Weimarer Republik: Wahlgesetzgebung und Wahlreform im Reich und in den Ländern* (Düsseldorf, 1982).

Schappacher, Norbert, 'Das Mathematische Institut der Universität Göttingen', in Becker *et al.* (eds.), *Die Universität Göttingen*, 345–73.

Scheck, Raffael, *Mothers of the Nation: Right-Wing Women in German Politics, 1918–1923* (forthcoming, 2004).

Scheil, Stefan, *Die Entwicklung des politischen Antisemitismus in Deutschland zwischen 1881 und 1912: Eine wahlgeschichtliche Untersuchung* (Berlin, 1999).

Schirach, Baldur von, *Die Feier der neuen Front* (Munich, 1929).

Schirmann, Leon, *Altonaer Blutsonntag 17. Juli 1932: Dichtung und Wahrheit* (Hamburg, 1994).

Schlotterbeck, Friedrich, *The Darker the Night, the Brighter the Stars: A German Worker Remembers (1933–1945)* (London, 1947).

Schmädeke, Jürgen, *et al.*, 'Der Reichstagsbrand im neuen Licht', *Historische Zeitschrift*, 269 (1999), 603–51.

Schmelz, Usiel O., 'Die demographische Entwicklung der Juden in Deutschland von der Mitte des 19. Jahrhunderts bis 1933', *Bulletin des Leo Baeck Instituts*, 83 (1989), 15–62.

Schmidt, Christoph, 'Zu den Motiven "alter Kämpfer" in der NSDAP', in Detlev J. K. Peukert and Jürgen Reulecke (eds.), *Die Reihen fast geschlossen: Beiträge zur Geschichte des Alltags unterm Nationalsozialismus* (Wuppertal, 1981), 21–44.

Schmuhl, Hans-Walter, *Rassenhygiene, Nationalsozialismus, Euthanasie: Von der Verhütung zur Vernichtung 'lebensunwerten Lebens', 1890–1945* (Göttingen, 1987).

Schneeberger, Guido, *Nachlese zu Heidegger: Dokumente zu seinem Leben und Denken* (Berne, 1962).

Schneider, Hans, 'Das Ermächtigungsgesetz vom 24. März 1933', *VfZ* 1 (1953), 197–221.

Schneider, Michael, *A Brief History of the German Trade Unions* (Bonn, 1991 [1989]).

——, *Unterm Hakenkreuz: Arbeiter und Arbeiterbewegung 1933 bis 1939* (Bonn, 1999).

Schneider, Werner, *Die Deutsche Demokratische Partei in der Weimarer Republik, 1924–1930* (Munich, 1978).

Schoenbaum, David, *Zabern 1913: Consensus Politics in Imperial Germany* (London, 1982).

Scholder, Klaus, *The Churches and the Third Reich* (2 vols., London, 1987–8 [1977, 1985]).

Schönhoven, Klaus, *Die Bayerische Volkspartei 1924–1932* (Düsseldorf, 1972).

Schorske, Carl E., *Fin-de-Siècle Vienna: Politics and Culture* (New York, 1980).

Schotte, Walter, *Der neue Staat* (Berlin, 1932).

Schouten, Martin, *Marinus van der Lubbe (1909–1934): Eine Biographie* (Frankfurt, 1999 [1986]).

Schreiber, Georg, *Brüning, Hitler, Schleicher: Das Zentrum in der Opposition* (Cologne, 1932).

Schüddekopf, Otto-Ernst, *Das Heer und die Republik – Quellen zur Politik der Reichswehrführung 1918 bis 1933* (Hanover, 1955).

Schüler, Hermann, *Auf der Flucht erschossen: Felix Fechenbach 1894–1933. Eine Biographie* (Cologne, 1981).

Schüler, Winfried, *Der Bayreuther Kreis von seiner Entstehung bis zum Ausgang der wilhelminischen Ära* (Münster, 1971).

Schüler-Springorum, Stefanie, *Die jüdische Minderheit in Königsberg, Preussen 1871–1945* (Göttingen, 1996).

Schulte, Regina, *Sperrbezirke: Tugendhaftigkeit und Prostitution in der bürgerlichen Welt* (Frankfurt am Main, 1979).

Schulz, Gerhard, *Zwischen Demokratie und Diktatur: Verfassungspolitik und Reichsreform in der Weimarer Republik* (3 vols., Berlin, 1963–92).

——, 'Artikel 48 in politisch-historischer Sicht', in Ernst Fraenkel (ed.), *Der Staatsnotstand* (Berlin, 1965), 39–71.

—— (ed.), *Ploetz Weimarer Republik: Eine Nation im Umbruch* (Freiburg, 1987).

Schulze, Hagen, *Freikorps und Republik 1918–1920* (Boppard, 1969).

——, *Otto Braun oder Preussens demokratische Sendung* (Frankfurt am Main, 1977).

——, *Weimar: Deutschland 1917–1933* (Berlin, 1982).

Schumann, Hans-Gerhard, *Nationalsozialismus und Gewerkschaftsbewegung: Die Vernichtung der deutschen Gewerkschaften und der Aufbau der 'Deutschen Arbeitsfront'* (Hanover, 1958).

Schuster, Kurt G. P., *Der Rote Frontkämpferbund 1924–1929: Beiträge zur Geschichte und Organisationsstruktur eines politischen Kampfbundes* (Düsseldorf, 1975).

Schwabe, Klaus (ed.), *Die Ruhrkrise 1923: Wendepunkt der internationalen Beziehungen nach dem Ersten Weltkrieg* (Paderborn, 1985).

——, 'Die deutsche Politik und die Juden im Ersten Weltkrieg', in Hans Otto Horch (ed.), *Judentum, Antisemitismus und europäische Kultur* (Tübingen, 1988), 255–66.

Schwarz, Johannes, *Die bayerische Polizei und ihre historische Funktion bei der*

Aufrechterhaltung der öffentlichen Sicherheit in Bayern von 1919 bis 1933 (Munich, 1977).

Schwerin von Krosigk, Lutz Graf, *Es geschah in Deutschland: Menschenbilder unseres Jahrhunderts* (Tübingen, 1951).

Service, Robert, *Lenin: A Political Life* (3 vols., London, 1985–95).

Shapiro, Leonard, *Totalitarianism* (London, 1972).

Sharp, Alan, *The Versailles Settlement: Peacekeeping in Paris, 1919* (London, 1991).

Sheehan, James J., *German History 1770–1866* (Oxford, 1989).

Shirer, William L., *The Rise and Fall of the Third Reich: A History of Nazi Germany* (New York, 1960).

Siggemann, Jürgen, *Die kasernierte Polizei und das Problem der inneren Sicherheit in der Weimarer Republik: Eine Studie zum Auf- und Ausbau des innerstaatlichen Sicherheitssystems in Deutschland 1918/19–1933* (Frankfurt am Main, 1980).

Skzrypczak, Henryk, 'Das Ende der Gewerkschaften', in Wolfgang Michalka (ed.), *Die nationalsozialistische Machtergreifung* (Paderborn, 1984), 97–110.

Sluga, Hans, *Heidegger's Crisis: Philosophy and Politics in Nazi Germany* (Cambridge, Mass., 1993).

Smelser, Ronald, and Zitelmann, Rainer (eds.), *The Nazi Elite* (London, 1989).

Smith, Bradley F., *Heinrich Himmler 1900–1926: A Nazi in the Making* (Stanford, Calif., 1971).

Smith, Denis Mack, *Mussolini* (London, 1981).

Smith, Helmut Walser, 'The Learned and the Popular Discourse of Anti-Semitism in the Catholic Milieu in the Kaiserreich', *Central European History*, 27 (1994), 315–28.

——, *The Butcher's Tale: Murder and Anti-Semitism in a German Town* (New York, 2002).

Smith, Woodruff D., *The German Colonial Empire* (Chapel Hill, NC, 1978).

——, *The Ideological Origins of Nazi Imperialism* (New York, 1986).

Snell, John L. (ed.), *The Nazi Revolution – Germany's Guilt or Germany's Fate?* (Boston, 1959).

Söllner, Alfons (ed.), *Totalitarismus: Eine Ideengeschichte des 20. Jahrhunderts* (Berlin, 1997).

Sontheimer, Kurt, 'Thomas Mann als politischer Schriftsteller', *VfZ* 6 (1958), 1–44.

——, *Antidemokratisches Denken in der Weimarer Republik* (Munich, 1978 [1962]).

Sösemann, Bernd, 'Die Tagesaufzeichnungen des Joseph Goebbels und ihre unzulänglichen Veröffentlichungen', *Publizistik*, 37 (1992), 213–44,

Speier, Hans, *German White-Collar Workers and the Rise of Hitler* (New Haven, 1986).

Spengler, Oswald, *Der Untergang des Abendlandes: Umrisse einer Morphologie der Weltgeschichte*, I: *Gestalt und Wirklichkeit* (Vienna, 1918).

——, *Spengler Letters 1913–1936* (ed. Arthur Helps, London, 1966).

Splitt, Gerhard, *Richard Strauss 1933–1935: Aesthetik und Musikpolitik zu Beginn der nationalsozialistischen Herrschaft* (Pfaffenweiler, 1987).

Spotts, Frederic, *Hitler and the Power of Aesthetics* (London, 2002).

Stachura, Peter D., *Nazi Youth in the Weimar Republic* (Santa Barbara, Calif., 1975).

——, *The German Youth Movement, 1900–1945: An Interpretative and Documentary History* (London, 1981).

——, *Gregor Strasser and the Rise of Nazism* (London, 1983).

—— (ed.), *Unemployment and the Great Depression in Weimar Germany* (London, 1986).

Stackelberg, Roderick, and Winkle, Sally A. (eds.), *The Nazi Germany Sourcebook: An Anthology of Texts* (London, 2002).

Staewen-Ordermann, Gertrud, *Menschen der Unordnung: Die proletarische Wirklichkeit im Arbeitsschicksal der ungelernten Grossstadtjugend* (Berlin, 1933).

Staff, Ilse, *Justiz im Dritten Reich: Eine Dokumentation* (2nd edn., Frankfurt am Main, 1978 [1964]).

Stansfield, Agnes, 'Das Dritte Reich: A Contribution to the Study of the "Third Kingdom" in German Literature from Herder to Hegel', *Modern Language Review*, 34 (1934), 156–72.

Stargardt, Nicholas, *The German Idea of Militarism 1866–1914* (Cambridge, 1994).

Stark, Gary D., 'Pornography, Society and the Law in Imperial Germany', *Central European History*, 14 (1981), 200–220.

——, *Entrepreneurs of Ideology: Neo-Conservative Publishers in Germany, 1890–1933* (Chapel Hill, NC, 1981).

Steakley, James D., *The Homosexual Emancipation Movement in Germany* (New York, 1975).

Steger, Bernd, 'Der Hitlerprozess und Bayerns Verhältnis zum Reich 1923/24', *VfZ* 23 (1977), 441–66.

Stegmann, Dirk, *Die Erben Bismarcks: Parteien und Verbände in der Spätphase des Wilhelminischen Deutschlands: Sammlungspolitik 1897–1914* (Cologne, 1970).

——, 'Zwischen Repression und Manipulation: Konservative Machteliten und Arbeiter- und Angestelltenbewegung 1910–1918. Ein Beitrag zur Vorgeschichte der DAP/NSDAP', *Archiv für Sozialgeschichte*, 12 (1972), 351–433.

Steigmann-Gall, Richard, *The Holy Reich: Nazi Conceptions of Christianity, 1919–1945* (New York, 2003).

Steinberg, Michael S., *Sabers and Brown Shirts: The German Students' Path to National Socialism, 1918–1935* (Chicago, 1977).

Steinle, Jürgen, 'Hitler als "Betriebsunfall in der Geschichte"', *Geschichte in Wissenschaft und Unterricht*, 45 (1994), 288–302.

Stenographischer Bericht über die öffentlichen Verhandlungen des 15. Untersuchungsausschusses der verfassungsgebenden Nationalversammlung, II (Berlin, 1920).

Stephenson, Jill, *The Nazi Organisation of Women* (London, 1981).

Stern, Fritz, *The Politics of Cultural Despair: A Study in the Rise of the German Ideology* (New York, 1961).

——, *Gold and Iron: Bismarck, Bleichröder and the Building of the German Empire* (New York, 1977).

——, *Dreams and Delusions: The Drama of German History* (New York, 1987).

——, *Einstein's German World* (London, 2000 [1999]).

Stoakes, Geoffrey, *Hitler and the Quest for World Dominion* (Leamington Spa, 1987).

Stoehr, Irene, 'Neue Frau und alte Bewegung? Zum Generationskonflikt in der Frauenbewegung der Weimarer Republik', in Jutta Dalhoff *et al.* (eds.), *Frauenmacht in der Geschichte* (Düsseldorf, 1986), 390–400.

Strachan, Hew, *The First World War*, I: *To Arms* (Oxford, 2001).

Strätz, Wolfgang, 'Die studentische "Aktion wider den undeutschen Geist"', *VfZ* 16 (1968), 347–72.

Striefler, Christian, *Kampf um die Macht: Kommunisten und Nationalsozialisten am Ende der Weimarer Republik* (Berlin, 1993).

Stümke, Hans-Georg, *Homosexuelle in Deutschland: Eine politische Geschichte* (Munich, 1989).

——, and Finkler, Rudi, *Rosa Winkel, Rosa Listen: Homosexuelle und 'Gesundes Volksempfinden' von Auschwitz bis heute* (Hamburg, 1981).

Suhr, Elke, *Carl von Ossietzky: Eine Biographie* (Cologne, 1988).

Suval, Stanley, *Electoral Politics in Wilhelmine Germany* (Chapel Hill, NC, 1985).

Szejnmann, Claus-Christian W., *Nazism in Central Germany: The Brownshirts in 'Red' Saxony* (New York, 1999).

Szöllösi-Janze, Margit, *Fritz Haber 1868–1934: Eine Biographie* (Munich, 1998).

Talmon, Jacob L., *The Origins of Totalitarian Democracy* (London, 1952).

Tanner, Michael (ed.), *Wilhelm Furtwängler, Notebooks 1924–1945* (London, 1989).

Tatar, Maria, *Lustmord: Sexual Murder in Weimar Germany* (Princeton, 1995).

Taureck, Bernhard H. F., *Nietzsche und der Faschismus: Ein Politikum* (Leipzig, 2000).

Taylor, Alan J. P., *The Course of German History* (London, 1945).

——, *Bismarck: The Man and the Statesman* (London, 1955).

Taylor, Brandon, and Will, Wilfried van der (eds.), *The Nazification of Art: Art, Design, Music, Architecture and Film in the Third Reich* (Winchester, 1990).

Taylor, Simon, *Germany 1918–1933: Revolution, Counter-Revolution and the Rise of Hitler* (London, 1983).

Temperley, Harold (ed.), *A History of the Peace Conference of Paris* (6 vols., London, 1920–24).

Thälmann, Irma, *Erinnerungen an meinen Vater* (Berlin, 1955).

Thamer, Hans-Ulrich, *Verführung und Gewalt: Deutschland 1933–1945* (Berlin, 1986).

Theweleit, Klaus, *Male Fantasies* (2 vols., Cambridge, 1987 and 1989 [1978]).

Thomas, Richard Hinton, *Nietzsche in German Politics and Society 1890–1918* (Manchester, 1983).

Thompson, Alastair, *Left Liberals, the State, and Popular Politics in Wilhelmine Germany* (Oxford, 2000).

Thomson, David, *The New Biographical Dictionary of Film* (4th edn., 2002 [1975]).

Thoss, Bruno, *Der Ludendorff-Kreis: 1919–1923. München als Zentrum der mitteleuropäischen Gegenrevolution zwischen Revolution und Hitler-Putsch* (Munich, 1978).

Timm, Annette F., 'The Ambivalent Outsider: Prostitution, Promiscuity, and VD Control in Nazi Berlin', in Gellately and Stoltzus (eds.), *Social Outsiders*, 192–211.

Tims, Richard W., *Germanizing Prussian Poland: The H-K-T Society and the Struggle for the Eastern Marches in the German Empire 1894–1919* (New York, 1941).

Tobias, Fritz, *The Reichstag Fire: Legend and Truth* (London, 1962).

——, 'Ludendorff, Hindenburg, Hitler: Das Phantasieprodukt des Ludendorff-Briefes vom 30. Januar 1933', in Uwe Backes *et al.* (eds.), *Die Schatten der Vergangenheit: Impulse zur Historisierung des Nationalsozialismus* (Frankfurt am Main, 1990), 319–43.

Tooze, J. Adam, 'Big Business and the Continuities of German History, 1900–1945', in Panikos Panayi (ed.), *Weimar and Nazi Germany: Continuities and Discontinuities* (London, 2001), 173–98.

Toury, Jacob, *Soziale und politische Geschichte der Juden in Deutschland 1847–1871: Zwischen Revolution, Reaktion und Emanzipation* (Düsseldorf, 1977).

Trevor-Roper, Hugh R., *The Last Days of Hitler* (London, 1947).

——, 'The Mind of Adolf Hitler', in Hitler, *Hitler's Table-Talk*, vii–xxxv.

Trotsky, Leon, *The History of the Russian Revolution* (3 vols., London, 1967 [1933–4]).

Tuchel, Johannes. *Organisationsgeschichte und Funktion der 'Inspektion der Konzentrationslager' 1933–1938* (Boppard, 1991).

Turner, Henry Ashby, Jr., *Gustav Stresemann and the Politics of the Weimar Republic* (Princeton, 1965 [1963]).

——, *German Big Business and the Rise of Hitler* (New York, 1985).

——, *Hitler's Thirty Days to Power: January 1933* (London, 1996).

Tyrell, Albrecht (ed.), *Führer befiehl . . .: Selbstzeugnisse aus der 'Kampfzeit' der NSDAP* (Düsseldorf, 1969).

——, *Vom 'Trommler' zum 'Führer': Der Wandel von Hitlers Selbstverständnis zwischen 1919 und 1924 und die Entwicklung der NSDAP* (Munich, 1975).

Ullrich, Volker, *Die nervöse Grossmacht 1871–1918: Aufstieg und Untergang des deutschen Kaiserreichs* (Frankfurt am Main, 1997).

——, *Der ruhelose Rebell: Karl Plättner 1893–1945. Eine Biographie* (Munich, 2000).

Usborne, Cornelie, *The Politics of the Body in Weimar Germany: Women's Reproductive Rights and Duties* (London, 1991).

Valtin, Jan (pseud.; i.e. Richard Krebs), *Out of the Night* (London, 1941, reprinted with postscript by Lyn Walsh *et al.*, London, 1988).

Verhey, Jeffrey, *The Spirit of 1914: Militarism, Myth and Mobilization in Germany* (Cambridge, 2000).

Vermeil, Edmond, *Germany in the Twentieth Century* (New York, 1956).

Viereck, Peter, *Metapolitics: From the Romantics to Hitler* (New York, 1941).

Vogelsang, Thilo (ed.), 'Neue Dokumente zur Geschichte der Reichswehr, 1930–1933', *VfZ* 2 (1954), 397–436.

——, 'Zur Politik Schleichers gegenüber der NSDAP 1932', *VfZ* 6 (1958), 86–118.

——, 'Hitlers Brief an Reichenau vom 4. Dezember 1932', *VfZ* 7 (1959), 429–37.

——, *Reichswehr, Staat und NSDAP: Beiträge zur deutschen Geschichte 1932–1933* (Stuttgart, 1962).

Völkischer Beobachter 1933.

Volkov, Shulamit, 'Antisemitism as a Cultural Code: Reflections on the History and Historiography of Antisemitism in Imperial Germany', *Year Book of the Leo Baeck Institute*, 23 (1978), 25–46.

——, *Jüdisches Leben und Antisemitismus im 19. und 20. Jahrhundert* (Munich, 1990).

——, *Die Juden in Deutschland 1780–1918* (Munich, 1994).

Vossische Zeitung 1933.

Wachsmann, Nikolaus, 'Marching under the Swastika? Ernst Jünger and National Socialism, 1918–33', *Journal of Contemporary History*, 33 (1998), 573–89.

——, 'From Indefinite Confinement to Extermination: "Habitual Criminals" in the Third Reich', in Gellately and Stoltzfus (eds.), *Social Outsiders*, 165–91.

——, *Hitler's Prisons: Legal Terror in Nazi Germany* (forthcoming, 2004).

——, *et al.*, ' "Die soziale Prognose wird damit sehr trübe . . .": Theodor Viernstein und die Kriminalbiologische Sammelstelle in Bayern', in Michael Farin (ed.), *Polizeireport München 1799–1999* (Munich, 1999), 250–87.

Wagner, Cosima, *Die Tagebücher* (ed. Martin Gregor-Dellin and Dietrich Mack, Munich, 1977).

Wagner, Patrick, *Volksgemeinschaft ohne Verbrecher: Konzeptionen und Praxis der Kriminalpolizei in der Zeit der Weimarer Republik und des Nationalsozialismus* (Hamburg, 1996).

——, *Hitlers Kriminalisten: Die deutsche Kriminalpolizei und der Nationalsozialismus* (Munich, 2002).

Waite, Robert G. L., *Vanguard of Nazism: The Free Corps Movement in Postwar Germany 1918–1923* (Cambridge, Mass., 1952).

Waldenfels, Ernst von, *Der Spion, der aus Deutschland kam: Das geheime Leben des Seemanns Richard Krebs* (Berlin, 2003).

Walter, Bruno, *Theme and Variations: An Autobiography* (New York, 1966).

Walter, Dirk, *Antisemitische Kriminalität und Gewalt: Judenfeindschaft in der Weimarer Republik* (Bonn, 1999).

Walworth, Arthur, *Wilson and his Peacemakers: American Diplomacy at the Paris Peace Conference, 1919* (New York, 1986).

Watt, Donald Cameron, 'Die bayerischen Bemühungen um Ausweisung Hitlers 1924', *VfZ* 6 (1958), 270–80.

Watt, Richard M., *The Kings Depart: The German Revolution and the Treaty of Versailles 1918–19* (London, 1973 [1968]).

Webb, Steven B., *Hyperinflation and Stabilization in Weimar Germany* (Oxford, 1989).

Weber, Hermann, *Die Wandlung des deutschen Kommunismus: Die Stalinisierung der KPD in der Weimarer Republik* (2 vols., Frankfurt am Main, 1969).

Weber, Max, 'Der Nationalstaat und die Volkswirtschaftspolitik', in idem, *Gesammelte politische Schriften* (3rd edn., Tübingen, 1971).

Wehler, Hans-Ulrich, *Deutsche Gesellschaftsgeschichte*, II: *Von der Reformära bis zur industriellen und politischen 'Deutschen Doppelrevolution' 1815–1845/49* (Munich, 1987).

——, *Deutsche Gesellschaftsgeschichte*, III: *Von der 'Deutschen Doppelrevolution' bis zum Beginn des Ersten Weltkrieges 1849–1914* (Munich, 1995).

Weidenfeller, Gerhard, *VDA: Verein für das Deutschtum im Ausland: Allgemeiner Deutscher Schulverein (1881–1918). Ein Beitrag zur Geschichte des deutschen Nationalismus und Imperialismus im Kaiserreich* (Berne, 1976).

Weiland, Ruth, *Die Kinder der Arbeitslosen* (Eberswalde-Berlin, 1933).

Weindling, Paul, *Health, Race and German Politics between National Unification and Nazism 1870–1945* (Cambridge, 1989).

Weingart, Peter, *et al.*, *Rasse, Blut und Gene: Geschichte der Eugenik und Rassenhygiene in Deutschland* (Frankfurt am Main, 1992 [1988]).

Weisbrod, Bernd, *Schwerindustie in der Weimarer Republik: Interessenpolitik zwischen Stabilisierung und Krise* (Wuppertal, 1978).

——, 'The Crisis of German Unemployment Insurance in 1928/29 and its Political Repercussions', in Wolfgang J. Mommsen (ed.), *The Emergence of the Welfare State in Britain and Germany, 1850–1950* (London, 1981), 188–204.

——, 'Industrial Crisis Strategy in the Great Depression', in Jürgen Freiherr von Krudener (ed.), *Economic Crisis and Political Collapse: The Weimar Republic, 1924–1933* (New York, 1990), 45–62.

——, 'Gewalt in der Politik: Zur politischen Kultur in Deutschland zwischen den beiden Weltkriegen', *Geschichte in Wissenschaft und Unterricht*, 43 (1992), 391–404.

Weiss, Sheila F., *Race Hygiene and National Efficiency: The Eugenics of Wilhelm Schallmayer* (Berkeley, 1987).

——, 'The Race Hygiene Movement in Germany, 1904–1945', in Mark B. Adams (ed.), *The Wellborn Science: Eugenics in Germany, France, Brazil, and Russia* (New York, 1990), 8–68.

Weitz, Eric D., *Creating German Communism, 1890–1990: From Popular Protests to Socialist State* (Princeton, 1997).

Welch, David, 'Propaganda and the German Cinema 1933–1945' (unpublished Ph.D. dissertation, London University, 1979).

——, *Germany, Propaganda and Total War, 1914–1918: The Sins of Omission* (London, 2000).

——, *The Third Reich: Politics and Propaganda* (2nd edn., London, 2002 [1993]).

Welt am Abend, Die, 1933.

Wendt, Bernd-Jürgen, *Deutschland 1933–1945: Das Dritte Reich. Handbuch zur Geschichte* (Hanover, 1995).

Werner, Wolfram, 'Zur Geschichte des Reichsministeriums für Volksaufklärung und Propaganda und zur Überlieferung', in idem (ed.), *Findbücher zu Beständen des Bundesarchivs*, XV: *Reichsministerium für Volksaufklärung und Propaganda* (Koblenz, 1979).

Wertheimer, Jack, *Unwelcome Strangers: East European Jews in Imperial Germany* (New York, 1987).

West, Shearer, *The Visual Arts in Germany 1890–1936: Utopia and Despair* (Manchester, 2000).

Wette, Wolfram, *Gustav Noske: Eine politische Biographie* (Düsseldorf, 1987).

Wetzell, Richard F., *Inventing the Criminal: A History of German Criminology 1880–1945* (Chapel Hill, NC, 2000).

Whalen, Robert W., *Bitter Wounds: German Victims of the Great War, 1914–1939* (Ithaca, NY, 1984).

Wheeler-Bennett, John W., *Hindenburg: The Wooden Titan* (London, 1936).

——, *The Nemesis of Power: The German Army in Politics 1918–1945* (London, 1953).

Whiteside, Andrew G., *Austrian National Socialism before 1918* (The Hague, 1962).

——, *The Socialism of Fools: Georg von Schönerer and Austrian Pan-Germanism* (Berkeley, 1975).

Whitford, Frank, *The Bauhaus* (London, 1984).

Wickert, Christl, *Helene Stöcker 1869–1943: Frauenrechtlerin, Sexualreformerin und Pazifistin. Eine Biographie* (Bonn, 1991).

Widdig, Bernd, *Culture and Inflation in Weimar Germany* (Berkeley, 2001).

Wildt, Michael, 'Violence against Jews in Germany, 1933–1939', in David Bankier (ed.), *Probing the Depths of German Antisemitism: German Society and the Persecution of the Jews 1933–1941* (Jerusalem, 2000), 181–209.

——, *Generation des Unbedingten: Das Führungskorps des Reichssicherheitshauptamtes* (Hamburg, 2002).

William II, *My Memoirs 1878–1918* (London, 1922).

Wilson, Stephen, *Ideology and Experience: Antisemitism in France at the Time of the Dreyfus Affair* (New York, 1982 [1980]).

Wingler, Hans, *The Bauhaus – Weimar, Dessau, Berlin, Chicago 1919–1944* (Cambridge, Mass., 1978).

Winkler, Heinrich August, 'Die deutsche Gesellschaft der Weimarer Republik und der Antisemitismus', in Bernd Martin and Ernst Schulin (eds.), *Die Juden als Minderheit in der Geschichte* (Munich, 1981), 271–89.

——, *Von der Revolution zur Stabilisierung: Arbeiter und Arbeiterbewegung in der Weimarer Republik 1918 bis 1924* (Bonn, 1984).

——, *Der Schein der Normalität: Arbeiter und Arbeiterbewegung in der Weimarer Republik 1924 bis 1930* (Bonn, 1985).

——, *Der Weg in die Katastrophe: Arbeiter und Arbeiterbewegung in der Weimarer Republik 1930 bis 1933* (Bonn, 1987).

——, *Weimar 1918–1933: Die Geschichte der ersten deutschen Demokratie* (Munich, 1999).

——, *Der lange Weg nach Westen*, I: *Deutsche Geschichte vom Ende des Alten Reiches bis zum Untergang der Weimarer Republik*; II: *Deutsche Geschichte vom 'Dritten Reich' bis zur Wiedervereinigung* (Munich, 2000).

——, *The Long Shadow of the Reich: Weighing up German History* (The 2001 Annual Lecture of the German Historical Institute, London; London, 2002).

Wippermann, Wolfgang, 'Friedrich Meineckes "Die deutsche Katastrophe": Ein Versuch zur deutschen Vergangenheitsbewältigung', in Michael Erbe (ed.), *Friedrich Meinecke heute: Bericht über ein Gedenk-Colloquium zu seinem 25. Todestag am 5. und 6. April 1979* (Berlin, 1981), 101–21.

Wirsching, Andreas, ' "Stalinisierung" oder entideologisierte "Nischengesellschaft"? Alte Einsichten und neue Thesen zum Charakter der KPD in der Weimarer Republik', *VfZ* 45 (1997), 449–66.

——, ' "Man kann nur Boden germanisieren": Eine neue Quelle zu Hitlers Rede vor den Spitzen der Reichswehr am 3. Februar 1933', *VfZ* 49 (2001), 516–50.

Witt, Peter-Christian, 'Finanzpolitik als Verfassungs- und Gesellschaftspolitik: Überlegungen zur Finanzpolitik des Deutschen Reiches in den Jahren 1930 bis 1932', *Geschichte und Gesellschaft*, 8 (1982), 387–414.

Wohlfeil, Rainer, 'Heer und Republik', in Hans Meier-Welcker and Wolfgang von Groote (eds.), *Handbuch zur deutschen Militärgeschichte 1648–1939*, VI (Frankfurt am Main, 1970), 11–304.

Wolff, Charlotte, *Magnus Hirschfeld: A Portrait of a Pioneer in Sexology* (London, 1986).

Woltmann, Ludwig, *Politische Anthropologie* (ed. Otto Reche, Leipzig, 1936 [1900]).

World Committee for the Victims of German Fascism (President Einstein) (ed.), *The Brown Book of the Hitler Terror and the Burning of the Reichstag* (London, 1933).

Wortmann, Michael, 'Baldur von Schirach: Student Leader, Hitler Youth Leader, *Gauleiter* in Vienna', in Smelser and Zitelmann (eds.), *The Nazi Elite*, 202–11.

Woycke, James, *Birth Control in Germany 1871–1933* (London, 1988).

Wright, Jonathan, *Gustav Stresemann: Weimar's Greatest Statesman* (Oxford, 2002).

Wulf, Josef, *Musik im Dritten Reich: Eine Dokumentation* (Gütersloh, 1963).

——, *Die Bildenden Künste im Dritten Reich: Eine Dokumentation* (Gütersloh, 1963).

——, *Literatur und Dichtung im Dritten Reich: Eine Dokumentation* (Gütersloh, 1963).

——, *Theater und Film im Dritten Reich: Eine Dokumentation*. (Gütersloh, 1964).

——, *Presse und Funk im Dritten Reich: Eine Dokumentation* (Gütersloh, 1964).

Zalka, Siegfried, *Polizeigeschichte: Die Exekutive im Lichte der historischen Konfliktforschung. Untersuchungen über die Theorie und Praxis der preussischen Schutzpolizei in der Weimarer Republik zur Verhinderung und Bekämpfung innerer Unruhen* (Lübeck, 1979).

Zechlin, Egmont, *Die deutsche Politik und die Juden im Ersten Weltkrieg* (Göttingen, 1969).

Zeidler, Manfred, *Reichswehr und Rote Armee 1920–1933: Wege und Stationen einer ungewöhnlichen Zusammenarbeit* (Munich, 1993).

Zeller, Joachim, ' "Wie Vieh wurden Hunderte zu Getriebenen und wie Vieh begraben": Fotodokumente aus dem deutschen Konzentrationslager in Swakopmund/Namibia 1904–1908', *Zeitschrift für Geschichtswissenschaft*, 49 (2001), 226–43.

Zeman, Zbynek A. B., *Nazi Propaganda* (2nd edn., Oxford, 1973 [1964]).

Ziemann, Benjamin, 'Fahnenflucht im deutschen Heer 1914–1918', *Militärgeschichtliche Mitteilungen*, 55 (1996), 93–130.

Zimmermann, Clemens, 'Die Bücherverbrennung am 17. Mai 1933 in Heidelberg: Studenten und Politik am Ende der Weimarer Republik', in Joachim-Felix Leonhard (ed.), *Bücherverbrennung: Zensur, Verbot, Vernichtung unter dem Nationalsozialismus in Heidelberg* (Heidelberg, 1983), 55–84.

Zimmermann, Moshe, *Wilhelm Marr: The Patriarch of Anti-Semitism* (New York, 1986).

Zimmermann, Peter, 'Literatur im Dritten Reich', in Jan Berg *et al.* (eds.), *Sozialgeschichte der deutschen Literatur von 1918 bis zur Gegenwart* (Frankfurt am Main, 1981), 361–416.

Zitelmann, Rainer, *Hitler: The Policies of Seduction* (London, 1999 [1987]).

Zürn, Gaby, ' "Von der Herbertstrasse nach Auschwitz" ', in Angelika Ebbinghaus (ed.), *Opfer und Täterinnen: Frauenbiographien des Nationalsozialismus* (Nördlingen, 1987), 91–101.

Index

Numbers in bold indicate maps.